Days to mat.	.01% equiv.	Days to mat	.01% equiv.	Days to mat.	.01% equiv.	Days to mat.	.01% equiv.	Days to mat.	.01% equiv.	Days to mat.	.01% equiv.
181	$50.28	212	$58.89	243	$67.50	274	$76.11	305	$84.72	336	$93.33
182	50.56	213	59.17	244	67.78	275	76.39	306	85.00	337	93.61
183	50.83	214	59.44	245	68.06	276	76.67	307	85.28	338	93.89
184	51.11	215	59.72	246	68.33	277	76.94	308	85.56	339	94.17
185	51.39	216	60.00	247	68.61	278	77.22	309	85.83	340	94.44
186	51.67	217	60.28	248	68.89	279	77.50	310	86.11	341	94.72
187	51.94	218	60.56	249	69.17	280	77.78	311	86.39	342	95.00
188	52.22	219	60.83	250	69.44	281	78.06	312	86.67	343	95.28
189	52.50	220	61.11	251	69.72	282	78.33	313	86.94	344	95.56
190	52.78	221	61.39	252	70.00	283	78.61	314	87.22	345	95.83
191	53.06	222	61.67	253	70.28	284	78.89	315	87.50	346	96.11
192	53.33	223	61.94	254	70.56	285	79.17	316	87.78	347	96.39
193	53.61	224	62.22	255	70.83	286	79.44	317	88.06	348	96.67
194	53.89	225	62.50	256	71.11	287	79.72	318	88.33	349	96.94
195	54.17	226	62.78	257	71.39	288	80.00	319	88.61	350	97.22
196	54.44	227	63.06	258	71.67	289	80.28	320	88.89	351	97.50
197	54.72	228	63.33	259	71.94	290	80.56	321	89.17	352	97.78
198	55.00	229	63.61	260	72.22	291	80.83	322	89.44	353	98.06
199	55.28	230	63.89	261	72.50	292	81.11	323	89.72	354	98.33
200	55.56	231	64.17	262	72.78	293	81.39	324	90.00	355	98.61
201	55.83	232	64.44	263	73.06	294	81.67	325	90.28	356	98.89
202	56.11	233	64.72	264	73.33	295	81.94	326	90.56	357	99.17
203	56.39	234	65.00	265	73.61	296	82.22	327	90.83	358	99.44
204	56.67	235	65.28	266	73.89	297	82.50	328	91.11	359	99.72
205	56.94	236	65.56	267	74.17	298	82.78	329	91.39	360	100.00
206	57.22	237	65.83	268	74.44	299	83.06	330	91.67	361	100.28
207	57.50	238	66.11	269	74.72	300	83.33	331	91.94	362	100.56
208	57.78	239	66.39	270	75.00	301	83.61	332	92.22	363	100.83
209	58.06	240	66.67	271	75.28	302	83.89	333	92.50	364	101.11
210	58.33	241	66.94	272	75.56	303	84.17	334	92.78	365	101.39
211	58.61	242	67.22	273	75.83	304	84.44	335	93.06	366	101.67

$$\text{Value of an 01 per \$1 million} = \left(\frac{.01\% \times t}{360} \right) \text{\$1 million}$$

where t = days to maturity

"The man
who fights
for his
ideals
is the man
who
is alive."

CERVANTES
author of
DON QUIXOTE

J. Bergstrand

the money market

REVISED EDITION

the money market

MARCIA STIGUM

DOW JONES-IRWIN
Homewood, Illinois 60430

ISBN 0-87094-385-5

Library of Congress Catalog Card No. 83–70057

Printed in the United States of America

1 2 3 4 5 6 7 8 9 0 K 0 9 8 7 6 5 4 3

*To the many market participants
who gave, with grace and enthusiasm, their time
that I might write this story.*

Preface to the first edition

THIS BOOK IS a comprehensive guide to the U.S. money market. It is intended for managers of short-term, fixed-income portfolios; for other corporate financial officers; for personnel in banks, dealerships, and other financial institutions; for people operating in the Eurodollar market, all of whom need to know about the U.S. money market; and for all others who have an interest in the market.

The book describes in detail the operations of money market banks and of money market dealers and brokers. It also describes the principles according to which a liquidity portfolio should be run and contrasts them with the way in which most such portfolios are in fact managed. With this background established, the book turns to the individual markets that comprise the money market. It describes for each such market the instrument traded, the risks, liquidity and return offered, and how the market is made by dealers, brokers, and investors.

The book presents an extensive description of the operation of the Eurodollar market. This market is really an extension of and thus an integral part of the U.S. money market. Therefore a description of the U.S. market would be incomplete without a thorough consideration of the Euromarket and of the interconnections between the two. Also the Euromarket offers interesting and inadequately understood opportunities to managers of short-term portfolios.

It is expected that many of the readers of this book will be relatively new to the money market. Part One provides all of the background needed by such readers to understand the rest of the book. It describes in simple terms what the instruments traded in the money market are, how yields on them are calculated, and how banks under the control of the Federal Reserve System create our money supply.

Much of the material in this book has never appeared in print before because surprisingly little has been written on the money market in recent times; and most of what has been written was incomplete to begin with and is currently out of date due to the rapidity with which change occurs in this innovative and fast-growing market.

In every area of life, people develop special terms or give common terms special meanings in order to describe and to communicate with each other about their particular interests and activities; hence *jargon*. The money market is no exception, and this book uses money market jargon extensively. To aid the reader, each piece of jargon used is carefully defined the first time it appears in the text. Also, there is a Glossary at the end of the book in which a wide range of money market and bond market terms are defined.

A number of examples of simple money market calculations—such as determining equivalent bond yield on discount securities, "figuring the tail," and calculating profit on an arbitrage—are included in this book. Readers who need descriptions of key money market formulas and examples of how they can be used should refer to my other book, *Money Market Calculations: Yields, Break-Evens, and Arbitrage,* also published by Dow Jones-Irwin.

Part Two of this book begins with two chapters that describe respectively the domestic and Euromarket activities of commercial banks. Readers wanting an in-depth discussion of how banks should manage their assets and liabilities—domestic, Euro and foreign-currency denominated—should read Marcia Stigum and Ray Branch, *Managing Bank Assets and Liabilities: Strategies for Risk Control and Profit,* also published by Dow Jones-Irwin.

The pronoun *he* is used frequently throughout this book. It is my opinion that *he* has for years been used to mean *person* and that any attempt to avoid this use of the term leads to nothing but bad and awkward English.

In conclusion I would like to thank the many typists who have labored on this manuscript and in particular Mike Nagle who hunted up numbers and drew diagrams. I would also like to thank Loyola University of Chicago and Northwestern University for the support they gave me while I was researching and writing this book.

Marcia Stigum

Preface to
the revised edition

DURING THE FIVE YEARS that have passed since *The Money Market* was first published, this market has grown tremendously—in many areas by a factor of three—and it has undergone tremendous, sometimes traumatic, changes.

The single most important and wrenching change for the money market was the October 1979 shift in Fed policy. Prior to this shift, the Fed sought to achieve its goals by tightly controlling the level of the Fed funds rate; post shift, the Fed sought to achieve its then principal goal, lowering the rate of inflation, by controlling the growth of the money supply. In turning to monetarism, the Fed had no choice but to loosen its control over the Fed funds rate and thereby over the general level of interest rates. The upshot was that interest rates, short-term and long-term, reached previously unthinkable highs with respect to both level and volatility.

A second significant change that has marked the money market in recent years is growth in all sectors. Fueled by tax cuts, the impact of recession on federal receipts and expenditures, and other factors, Treasury deficits soared from the $40-odd billion range to the $90-plus billion range. The Treasury was thus forced to sell, often in chaotic markets, over 60% more marketable debt than it had five years previously. The Treasury's pattern of borrowing significantly more in the money market was followed by most other institutions. The big banks in particular borrowed and bought more money on all fronts; they increased their purchases of Fed funds, of repo money, and of Euros—the Euromarket having expanded between 1978 and 1983 from $740 billion to almost $2 trillion. It is impossible to put precise numbers on the size of the increase in bank borrowing in many markets, but two telling numbers are available: over the period the amounts of domestic CDs and Euro CDs issued by the big banks rose, respectively, 78% (from $78 to $139 billion) and 278% (from $21 to $79 billion).

Corporations, many of whom were big, cash-rich investors in the money market in 1977, were by 1983 more typically big, cash-poor borrowers. This shift is indicated by three noticeable changes in the market over the period: BAs outstanding rose from $25 to $73 billion; commercial paper outstanding rose from $65 to $181 billion; and everywhere in the market, it was the cash-rich money funds, whose assets rose from $10 billion in 1977 to a peak of $280 billion in late 1982, who were gobbling up, with seemingly unlimited appetite, all the short paper they could find.

High and volatile rates combined with an expansion of borrowing on all sides called for major players in the money market to alter, often dramatically, their ways of operating in this market. To protect themselves against interest rate risk and to meet the demand of their ever more sophisticated customers, banks significantly altered the terms on which they were willing to lend to their major customers. At the same time banks moved in various ways to control more tightly their overall asset and liability management; some went through the wrenching adjustment of setting up a global (domestic plus Euro) book in an attempt to gain better control over the bank's total interest rate exposure and to ensure that every one of the bank's branches, domestic and foreign, worked to maximize not its profits, but the aftertax profits of the bank as a whole.

Money market dealers, faced with more volatile rates and *much* more paper, both to distribute and in which to make a secondary market, found themselves facing a rate risk that had gone up by a large but unquantifiable factor. In response they sought various ways to change how they did business. All sought to control position taking more tightly and to hedge—often in the explosively growing futures markets—the positions they did take; dealers also sought to find steady, dependable profit sources, ones that would lessen their need to depend on big positions plays for big profits. Despite the well-publicized failures of Drysdale and Lombard-Wall, most dealers managed to adjust successfully to the new market environment—to grow and to prosper in it.

As money market dealers grew in size, the business of money market brokers grew apace and then some. Brokers found they had vastly more business to do in their traditional lines of business: governments, Fed funds, Euros, and foreign exchange. In addition they began or expanded brokering operations in CDs, BAs, commercial paper, and muni notes.

High rates, volatile rates, and expanding volume were the major stimuli for the fast-paced and dramatic changes that have occurred in the money market in recent years. The market has also had to deal with many other changes and problems. The International Banking Act of 1978 altered the ground rules under which foreign banks could operate in the U.S. at the same time that New York was coming to rival London as a Eurocenter. The Banking Act of 1980 contained many important changes for both banks and thrifts, and in particular it set the stage for rate deregulation. The Banking Act of 1982 hastened the demise of Reg Q ceilings and set the stage for the introduction of MMDA and of Super-NOW accounts, accounts that finally gave both banks and thrifts the means to effectively compete with money funds for deposits.

Euromarket changes both paralleled and were part of the money market changes we have already described. In addition the Euromarket in recent years experienced significant changes unique to it. On the plus side the Caribbean books of both U.S. and foreign banks grew tremendously in step with the expansion of New York as a Eurocenter. Also, both U.S. and foreign banks were permitted to open International Banking Facilities (IBFs), and they—particularly the Japanese banks—were quick to do so. On the negative side the Euromarket shuddered through the failure of the Luxembourg-based Banco Ambrosiano Holdings, and far worse, a series of souring country loans created fears that some of the world's top banks—and the Euromarket with them—might fail.

For no market or set of markets could five more eventful years have occurred or been imagined. This second edition of *The Money Market* provides a much needed updating of the picture of the market painted in the first edition. It describes all of the major changes that have occurred—the shift in Fed policy, the new markets, the new legislation and regulations, the growth, the difficulties and failures of prominent institutions and borrowers, and the adjustments major market players have made to the vastly changed environment in which they now must operate.

Final note. Readers who need descriptions of key money market formulas and examples of how they can be used should refer to my other book, *Money Market Calculations: Yields, Break-Evens, and Arbitrage,* also published by Dow Jones-Irwin. Readers wanting an in-depth discussion of how banks should manage their assets and liabilities—domestic, Euro, and foreign-currency-denominated—should read Marcia Stigum and Ray Branch, *Managing Bank Assets and Liabilities: Strategies for Risk Control and Profit,* also published by Dow Jones-Irwin.

In conclusion I would like to thank Frank Salvaterra and Arthur Hazlitt, who have spent countless hours hunting up numbers, drawing diagrams, and providing other help without which this revision could never have been completed.

Marcia Stigum
Stratton Mountain, Vt.

Acknowledgments

THERE WAS ONLY ONE WAY that research for this book could be conducted. That was by interviewing at length participants in *every* area of the market: in New York, London, Chicago, and elsewhere. During the months I spent originally studying the market and more recently reviewing it, everywhere I went I received incredible cooperation. People freely gave me hours of time, discussed their operations frankly and articulately, and then sent me on to others elsewhere in the market.

To all of these people, I would like to express a very heartfelt thanks for the patient and thoughtful answers they proffered to my many questions. A particular thank you goes to those who volunteered to read and criticize those chapters that covered their area of specialty. Needless to say, the author bears full responsibility for any remaining errors of fact, of which I hope there are few.

Some organizations have a policy that precludes acknowledging the assistance of company personnel; therefore, the acknowledgments that follow are incomplete. Of the over 300 people I interviewed for the first edition and for this second edition, those whom I can publicly thank are:

THE UNITED STATES

Richard Adams
Robert P. Anczarki
J. Joseph Anderson
James T. Anderson
Timothy H. Anderson
John Astorina
Irving M. Auerbach
Edward G. Austin
David J. Barry
Kevin D. Barry
Robert Bartell
John F. Baumann
Sandra D. Beckner
Paul M. Belica
William Berkowitz
Robert H. Bethke
Paul J. Bielat
Jean Blin
Irving V Boberski
Frank Boswell

Chuck Bradburn
Milton Brafman
Rene O. Branch, Jr.
Donald G. Brodie
Joseph G. Brown
Ernst W. Brutsche
James Byrne
Donald C. Cacciapaglia
Neil J. Call
Francis X. Cavanaugh
Bronislaw Chrobok
Allen B. Clark
Joel I. Cohen
Thomas Coleman
George E. Collins, Jr.
Wayne Cook
Michael J. Corey
Mark Corti
Leonard F. Crescenzo
Roy L. Dainty

Edward T. Daly
James J. DeCantillon
Nicholas J. De Leonardis
Paul de Rosa
Lawrence Deschere
John Desidero
Stanley Diller
Edward I. Dimon
Jay E. Dittus
William Donoghue
Barry Drayson
William J. Duffy
A. Fraser Dunnett
John F. Eckstein III
Burtt R. Ehrlich
Richard P. Eide, Jr.
Bruce A. English
Kenneth F. Entler
Richard L. Falk
Emanuel J. Falzon
Hilliard Farber
Edward C. Fecht
Chester B. Feldberg
Richard C. Fieldhouse
Alvin Flamenbaum
Dennis G. Flynn
Allen B. Frankel
Peter E. Gall
Thomas E. Gardner
William P. Garry
Leonard Gay
Yoshiyasu Genma
Kenneth L. Gestal
Ronald B. Gray
Peter L. Greene
Eric A. Gronningsater
P. Jordan Hamel
Alan Hanley
Gabriel Hauge
Ralph T. Helfrich
Paul Henderson
N. John Hewitt
Bill Hick
Andrew Hieskel
Russel G. Hiller
George R. Hinman
Neil Hirsch
Alan R. Holmes

Richard A. Hottinger
Donald Howard
Mary Joy Hudecz
Howard G. Hudson
James E. Jack
Dale H. Jenkins
Colin Johnson
Glen Johnson
William J. Jordan
Arthur Kaley
Michael Kamins
Michael M. Karnes
George P. Kegler
Richard F. Kezer
Yukyo Kida
William M. Kidder
James R. Killeen
Dennis S. Kite
Aline Krala
John Krause
Morton Lane
Curt J. Landtroop
Gerald Laurain
David N. Lawrence
Ronald Layard-Liesching
Ralph F. Leach
James F. Leary
John F. Lee
John J. Li Vecchi
Robert M. Lynch
James G. McCormick
John D. McElhinney
James E. McKee
Robert McKnew
Robert Mackin
William T. Maher, Jr.
John Mann
Karin L. Maupin
Donald R. A. Marshall
Michael F. Martin
Bruce B. Maxwell
Stan Meheffey
Roger Mehle
James Mehling
James W. Meighen
William Melton
Robert L. Meyers
Ellen Michelson

Michael Mickett
J. Allen Minteer
Joseph T. Monagle, Jr.
Angelo Monteverde
James C. Morton
Edward J. Murphy
John J. Murray
Tsunehiro Nakayama
Hans U. Neukomm
Talat M. Othman
Bernard Pace
Michael J. Paciorek
Edward L. Palmer
Thomas Panosky
Oscar J. Pearl, Jr.
Frank Pedrick
John D. Perini
John H. Perkins
Ralph F. Peters
William H. Pike
Joseph P. Porino
Howard Potter
Donald Reid
Robert Rice
Christine A. Rich
Donald B. Riefler
David L. Roscoe III
Paul J. Rozewicz
Alfred C. Ryan, Jr.
Lawrence J. Saffer
Richard Sandor
Irwin D. Sandberg
John Santulli
R. Duane Saunders
Hugo J. H. Schielke
Christina Seix
Howard Shallcross
Edward Shannon
Nancy F. Shaw
Donald P. Sheahan
Richard Sheldon
Robert L. Siebel

Vance W. Siler
Ronald S. Simpson
Richard Singer
Dennis Slattery
Frank P. Smeal
Brian E. Smith
Philip Smith
Thomas H. Smith
Thomas S. Smith
John S. Spencer
John A. Staley IV
Mark Stalnecker
John William Stanger
James Stanko
Peter D. Sternlight
Robert W. Stone
Werner A. Strange
Thomas Sullivan
David G. Taylor
Myron R. Taylor
Edward M. Thomas
John Tritz
Sheila Tschinkel
Stephen A. Tyler
George M. Van Cleave
John A. Vernazza
Edward M. Voelker
James R. Wartinbee
Henry S. Wattson
Dennis Weatherstone
Peter Werner
Jerry D. Wetterling
Gary F. Whitman
H. David Willey
Gary V. Williamson
Bryan Wilson
John R. Windeler
Thomas R. York
C. Richard Youngdahl
Edward F. Zimmerman, Jr.
Gene R. Zmuda

THE UNITED KINGDOM
A. T. Bell
William C. Bigelow
Brian G. Brown

John M. Bowcott
Trevor N. Cass
Peter Clayton

John E. Clinch
John A. Cummingham
David O. S. Dobell
James E. Geiger
James L. M. Gill
Kirk R. Hagan
Kenneth Haith
J. G. Hill
E. G. Holloway
Maurice Jacques
David B. Johnson
Colin I. Jones
Peter Lee
R. C. Lewis
Allen C. Marple
Ian McGaw
Richard J. Moreland
Peter Nash
Peter V. Nash

Brian Norman
Alan D. Orsich
Geoffrey Osmint
Francesco Redi
John Robertson
Kenneth G. Robinson
Fabian P. Samengo-Turner
Trevor K. Slade
Thomas Franklin Smith
Tim Summerfield
Harrison F. Tempest
Rodney M. Thomas
C. C. Tucker
John Thorne
Robert A. Utting
Lord Wakehurst
Michael Weeks
Jerald M. Wigdortz

LUXEMBOURG
Roland Scharif

M. S.

Contents

PART TWO: THE MAJOR PLAYERS

PART THREE: THE MARKETS

Abbreviations

THIS BOOK is replete with quotations, many of which contain "street" abbreviations of the names of various institutions. The most common are:

Bankers Trust Co.	Bankers
Bank of America	B of A
Chase Manhattan Bank	Chase
Citibank	Citi
Merrill Lynch	Merrill
Manufacturers Hanover Trust Co.	Manny Hanny
Morgan Guaranty Trust Co.	Morgan
Salomon Brothers	Sali

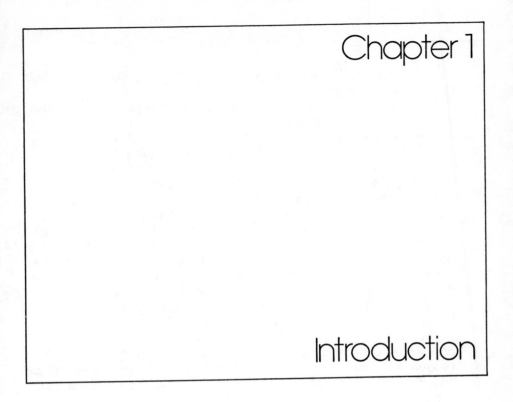

Chapter 1

Introduction

THE U.S. MONEY MARKET is a huge and significant part of the nation's financial system in which banks and other participants trade hundreds of billions of dollars every working day. Where those billions go and the prices at which they are traded affect how the U.S. government finances its debt, how business finances its expansion, and how consumers choose to spend or save. Yet we read and hear little about this market. The conspiratorially minded might consider its existence intentionally obscured. The reason most people are unaware of the money market is that it is a market that few businessmen encounter in their daily activities and in which the general public rarely invests.

The money market is a wholesale market for low-risk, highly-liquid, short-term IOUs. It is a market for various sorts of debt securities rather than equities. The stock in trade of the market includes a large chunk of the U.S. Treasury's debt and billions of dollars worth of federal agency securities, negotiable bank certificates of deposit, bankers' acceptances, municipal notes, and commercial paper. Within the confines of the money market each day, banks—domestic and foreign—actively trade in multimillion-dollar blocks billions of dollars of Federal funds and Eurodollars, and banks and nonbank dealers are each day the recipients of billions of dollars of secured loans through what is called the "repo

1

market." State and municipal governments also finance part of their activities in this market.

The heart of the activity in the money market occurs in the trading rooms of dealers and brokers of money market instruments. During the time the market is open, these rooms are characterized by a frenzy of activity. Each trader or broker sits in front of a battery of direct phone lines linking him to other dealers, brokers, and customers. The phones never ring, they just blink at a pace that makes, especially in the brokers' market, for some of the shortest phone calls ever recorded. Despite the lack of ringing phones, a dealing room is anything but quiet. Dealers and brokers know only one way to hang up on a direct-line phone; they BANG the off button. And the more hectic things get, the harder they bang. Banging phones like drums in a band beat the rhythm of the noise generated in a trading room. Almost drowning that banging out at times is the constant shouting of quotes and tidbits of information.

Unless one spends a lot of time in trading rooms, it's hard to get a feel for what is going on amid all this hectic activity. Even listening in on phones is not very enlightening. One learns quickly that dealers and brokers swear a lot (it's said to lessen the tension), but the rest of their conversations is unintelligible to the uninitiated. Money market people have their own jargon, and until one learns it, it is impossible to understand them.

Once adjusted to their jargon and the speed at which traders converse, one observes that they are making huge trades—$5, $20, $150 million—at the snap of a finger. Moreover nobody seems to be particularly awed or even impressed by the size of the figures. A Fed funds broker asked to obtain $100 million in overnight money for a bank might—nonchalant about the size of the trade—reply, "The buck's yours from the B of A," slam down the phone, and take another call. Fed funds brokers earn only $1 per $1 million on overnight funds, so it takes a lot of trades to pay the overhead and let everyone in the shop make some money.

Despite its frenzied and incoherent appearance to the outsider, the money market efficiently accomplishes vital functions everyday. One is shifting vast sums of money between banks. This shifting is required because the major money market banks, with the exception of the Bank of America, all need a lot more funds than they obtain in deposits, while many smaller banks have more money deposited with them than they can profitably use internally.

The money market also provides a means by which the surplus funds of cash-rich corporations and other institutions can be funneled to banks, corporations, and other institutions that need short-term money. In addition, in the money market the U.S. Treasury can fund huge quantities of debt with ease. And the market provides the Fed with an arena in which to carry out open-market operations destined to influence interest rates and the growth of the money supply. The varied activities of money market participants also determine the structure of short-term interest rates, for example, what the yields on Treasury bills of different maturities are and how much commercial paper issuers have to pay to borrow. The latter rate is an important cost to many corporations, and it influences in particular the interest rate that a consumer who buys a car on time will have to pay on the loan. Finally, one might mention that the U.S. money market is increasingly becoming an international short-term capital market. In it the oil imports of the nationalized French electric company, Electricité de France, as well as the oil imports of Japan and a lot of other non–U.S. trade are financed.

Anyone who observes the money market soon picks out a number of salient features. First and most obvious, it is not one market but a collection of markets for several distinct and different instruments. What makes it possible to talk about *the* money market is the close interrelationships that link all these markets. A second salient feature is the numerous and varied cast of participants. Borrowers in the market include foreign and domestic banks, the Treasury, corporations of all types, the Federal Home Loan Banks and other federal agencies, dealers in money market instruments, and many states and municipalities. The lenders include almost all of the above plus insurance companies, pension funds—public and private—and various other financial institutions. And often standing between borrower and lender is one or more of a varied collection of brokers and dealers.

Another key characteristic of the money market is that it is a wholesale market. Trades are big, and the people who make them are almost always dealing for the account of some substantial institution. Because of the sums involved, skill is of the utmost importance, and money market participants are skilled at what they do. In effect the market is made by extremely talented specialists in very narrow professional areas. A bill trader extraordinaire may have only vague notions as to what the Euromarket is all about, and the Euro specialist may be equally vague on other sectors of the market.

Another principal characteristic of the money market is honor. Every day traders, brokers, investors, and borrowers do hundreds of billions of dollars of business over the phone, and however a trade may appear in retrospect, people do not renege. The motto of the money market is: *My word is my bond.* Of course, because of the pace of the market, mistakes do occur but no one ever assumes that they are intentional, and mistakes are always ironed out in what seems the fairest way for all concerned.

The most appealing characteristic of the money market is innovation. Compared with our other financial markets, the money market is lightly regulated. If someone wants to launch a new instrument or to try brokering or dealing in a new way in existing instruments, he does it. And when the idea is good, which it often is, a new facet of the market is born.

The focus of this book is threefold. First, attention is paid to the major players—who are they, why are they in the market, and what are they attempting to do? A second point of attention is on the individual markets—who is in each market, how and why do they participate in that market, what is the role of brokers and dealers in that market, and how are prices there determined? The final focus is on the relationships that exist among the different sectors of the market, for example, the relationship of Euro rates to U.S. rates, of Treasury bill rates to the Fed funds rate, and of certificate of deposit rates to bill rates.

This book is organized in a manner to enable readers with different backgrounds to read about and understand the money market. Part One contains introductory material for readers who know relatively little about the market. It is preface and prologue to Parts Two and Three, which are the real heart of the book. Thus readers may skim or skip Part One depending on their background and interests. They are, however, warned that they do so at their own peril, since an understanding of its contents is essential for grasping subtleties presented later in the book.

Part one

Some fundamentals

Chapter 2

Funds flows, banks, and money creation

AS PREFACE TO A DISCUSSION OF BANKING, a few words should be said about the U.S. capital market, how banks create money, and the Fed's role in controlling money creation.

Roughly defined, the U.S. capital market is composed of three major parts: *the stock market, the bond market,* and *the money market.* The money market, as opposed to the bond market, is a wholesale market for high-quality, *short-term debt instruments,* or IOUs.

FUNDS FLOWS IN THE U.S. CAPITAL MARKET

Every spending unit in the economy—business firm, household, or government body—is constantly receiving and using funds. In particular, a business firm receives funds from the sale of output and uses funds to cover its costs of production (excluding depreciation) and its current investment in plant, equipment, and inventory. For most firms, *gross saving* from current operations (i.e., *retained earnings plus depreciation allowances*) falls far short of covering current capital expenditures; that is, net funds obtained from current operations are inadequate to pay capital expenditures. As a result, each year most nonfinancial business

7

firms and the nonfinancial business sector as a whole run a large *funds deficit.*

The actual figures rung up by nonfinancial business firms in 1981 are given in column (2) of Table 2–1. They show that during this year business firms retained earnings of $37.9 billion and their capital consumption allowances totaled $263.6 billion, giving them a grand total of $301.5 billion of gross saving with which to finance capital expenditures. The latter, however, totaled $357.6 billion, so the business sector as a whole incurred a $56.1 billion funds deficit.

Running a large funds deficit is a chronic condition for the business sector. It is, moreover, to be expected, since every year the business sector receives a relatively small portion (9 to 13%) of total national income but has to finance a major share of national capital expenditures. In addition, because of the depressed condition of the stock market in recent years, business firms have been able to obtain little financing there. Thus, the bulk of the funds they have obtained to cover their deficits has come through the sale of bonds and money market instruments.

In contrast to the business sector, the consumer sector presents a quite different picture. As Table 2–1 shows, households in 1981 had gross savings of $461.1 billion and made capital expenditures of only $336.0 billion, leaving the sector with a *funds surplus* of $125.1 billion. This funds surplus is, moreover, a persistent phenomenon. Every year consumers as a group save more than they invest in housing and other capital goods.

Most of the consumer sector's annual funds surplus is absorbed by making loans to and equity investments in business firms that must seek outside funds to cover their funds deficits. This flow of funds from the consumer to the business sector is no cause for surprise. In any developed economy in which the bulk of investing is carried on outside the government sector, a substantial amount of funds flow, year in and year out, from consumers, who are the major income recipients, to business firms, which are the major investors.

Consumers and nonfinancial business firms do not make up the whole economy. Two other sectors of major importance are the U.S. government and state and local governments. In neither of these sectors are capital expenditures separated from current expenditures. Thus, for each sector, the recorded funds deficit or funds surplus incurred over the year equals total revenue minus total expenditures, or *net saving.* Both sectors have run funds deficits in most recent years, with the result that they compete with the business sector for the surplus funds generated in the consumer sector. This is what possible "crowding out" of business borrowers by government borrowing is all about.

TABLE 2–1
Funds flows in the U.S. capital market by sector, 1981 annualized rate ($ billions)

Transaction categories	(1) Households	(2) Nonfinancial business	(3) State and local governments*	(4) U.S. government*	(5) Financial business†	(6) Rest of the world
1. Savings (net)	208.6	37.9	4.4	–65.3	14.2	–3.0
2. Depreciation	252.5	263.6	0	0	9.3	0
3. Gross savings (1) + (2)	461.1	301.5	4.4	–65.3	23.5	–3.0
4. Capital expenditures	336.0	357.6	0	0	17.4	0
5. Funds surplus or deficit (3) – (4)	125.1	–56.1	4.4	–65.3	6.1	–3.0
6. Net financial assets acquired	324.5	60.5	23.0	23.0	473.6	33.5
7. Net financial liabilities incurred	125.0	154.0	29.1	100.9	472.2	63.8
8. Net financial investment (6) – (7)	199.5	–93.5	–6.1	–77.9	1.4	–30.3
9. Sector discrepancy (5) + (8)	–74.4	37.4	10.5	12.6	–4.7	27.2

Sectors

* Capital expenditures are included with current expenditures in U.S. and state and local government spending accounts.
† The large size of the entries in lines 6 and 7 for this sector reflects the intersectoral and intrasectoral funds flows that are funneled through financial institutions.
Source: Board of Governors, Federal Reserve System.

For completeness, still another domestic sector has to be added to the picture, *financial* business firms—banks, savings and loan associations, life insurance companies, and others. Most of the funds that these firms lend out to funds-deficit units are not funds of which they are the *ultimate* source. Instead, they are funds that these institutions have "borrowed" from funds-surplus units. If financial institutions only funneled funds from surplus to deficit units, we could omit them from our summary table. However, such activity is profitable, and every year financial firms accumulate gross savings, which exceed their modest capital expenditures, so net, the sector tends to be a *small* supplier of funds.

The final sector in Table 2–1 is the rest of the world. Domestic firms cover some portion of the funds deficits they incur by borrowing abroad, and domestic funds-surplus units occasionally invest abroad. Thus, to get a complete picture of who supplies and demands funds, we must include the rest of the world in our summary table. Also, when the exchange value of the dollar is weak, the central banks of Germany, Japan, and other countries become big buyers of dollars; they typically invest these dollars in U.S. government securities, thereby becoming financers of the U.S. government debt. When the dollar is strong, the converse occurs.

Every funds deficit has to be covered by the receipt of debt or equity capital from outside sources, and every funds surplus must be absorbed by supplying such capital. Thus, if the funds surpluses and deficits incurred by all sectors are totaled, their sum should be zero. Actually, the figures on line 5 of Table 2–1 don't sum horizontally to zero because of inevitable statistical errors. In 1981 recorded sector surpluses exceeded recorded sector deficits by $11.7 billion, indicating that some sectors' deficits had been underestimated and other sectors' surpluses overestimated. The net discrepancy, however, was small relative to the surplus and deficit figures calculated for the major sectors, so the table gives a good overall picture of the direction and magnitude of intersector funds flows within the economy.

Net financial investment by sector

Funds flows between sectors leave a residue of *newly* created financial assets and liabilities. In particular, spending units that borrow incur claims against themselves which appear on their balance sheets as liabilities, while spending units that supply capital acquire financial assets in the form of stocks, bonds, and other securities.

This suggests that, since the consumer sector ran an $125.1 billion funds surplus in 1981, the sector's holdings of financial assets should have increased by a like amount over that year. Things, however, are not so simple. While the consumer sector as a whole ran a funds surplus, many spending units within the sector ran funds deficits. Thus, the appropriate figure to look at is the sector's *net financial investment*, i.e., financial assets acquired minus liabilities incurred. For the household sector, this figure (line 8, Table 2–1) was $199.5 billion in 1981, a number of the right sign but much larger than the sector's funds surplus; the difference between the two figures is due to the statistical errors that inevitably creep into such estimates.

The big funds deficit that the nonfinancial business sector ran up during 1981 indicates that the net rise in its financial liabilities outstanding over the year must have been substantial. The estimated figure ($93.5 billion) confirms this, but again a substantial discrepancy has crept into the picture.

Similar but smaller discrepancies exist between the funds surpluses or deficits run up by the other sectors in Table 2–1 and their net financial investments.

FINANCIAL INTERMEDIARIES

As noted, every year large numbers of business firms and other spending units in the economy incur funds deficits which they cover by obtaining funds from spending units running funds surpluses. Some of this *external financing* involves what is called *direct finance*. In the case of direct finance, the *ultimate funds-deficit unit* (business firm, government body, or other spending unit) either borrows directly from *ultimate funds-surplus units* or sells equity claims against itself directly to such spending units. An example of direct finance would be a corporation covering a funds deficit by issuing new bonds, some of which are sold directly to consumers or nonfinancial business firms that are running funds surpluses.

While examples of direct finance are easy to find, external financing more typically involves *indirect finance*. In that case, the funds flow from the surplus to the deficit unit via a *financial intermediary*. Banks, savings and loan associations, life insurance companies, pension funds, and mutual funds are all examples of financial intermediaries. As this list makes clear, financial intermediaries differ widely in character. Nevertheless, they all perform basically the same function. Every financial intermediary solicits and obtains funds from funds-surplus units by offering in exchange for funds "deposited" with it, claims against itself. The latter, which take many forms, including demand deposits, time deposits, money market and other mutual fund shares, and the cash value of life insurance policies, are known as *indirect securities*. The funds that financial intermediaries receive in exchange for the indirect securities they issue are used by them to invest in stocks, bonds, and other securities issued by ultimate funds-deficit units, that is, in *primary securities*.

All this sounds a touch bloodless, so let's look at a simple example of financial intermediation. Jones, a consumer, runs a $20,000 funds surplus, which he receives in the form of cash. He promptly deposits that cash in a demand deposit at a bank. Simultaneously, some other spending unit, say, the Alpha Company, runs a temporary funds deficit. Jones's bank trades the funds Jones has deposited with it for a loan note (IOU) issued by the Alpha Company. In doing this—accepting Jones's deposit and acquiring the note—the bank is funneling funds from Jones, an ultimate funds-surplus unit, to the Alpha Company, an ultimate funds-deficit unit; in other words, it is acting as a financial intermediary between Jones and this company.

Federal Reserve statistics on the assets and liabilities of different sectors in the economy show the importance of financial intermediation. In particular, at the beginning of 1981 consumers, who are the major suppliers of external financing, held $4,493.6 billion of financial assets. Of this total, $2,241.3 billion represented consumers' deposits at commercial banks, other thrift institutions, and money market funds; $222.5 billion the cash value of their life insurance policies; and $727.1 billion the reserves backing pensions eventually due them. The other $1,820.1 billion represented consumers' holdings of primary securities: corporate stock, U.S. government bonds, state and local bonds, corporate and foreign bonds, and assorted other IOUs. Thus, in early 1981 about 60% of the funds that had flowed out of households running funds surpluses had been channeled to other spending units through financial intermediation.

Financial intermediaries are a varied group. To give some idea of the relative importance of different intermediaries, Table 2–2 lists the assets of all the major intermediaries at the beginning of 1982. As one might expect, commercial banks are by far the most important intermediaries. Following them at a considerable distance are savings and loan associations (S&Ls), life insurance companies, and the fast-growing private pension funds.

The reasons for intermediation

The main reason for all of the intermediation that occurs in our economy is that the mix of primary securities offered by funds-deficit units is unattractive to many funds-surplus units. With the exception of corporate stocks, the minimum denominations on many primary securities are high relative to the size of the funds surpluses that most spending units are likely to run during any short-term period. Also, the amount of debt securities that deficit units want to borrow long term far exceeds the amount that surplus units—consumers and corporations that often desire high

TABLE 2–2
Total financial assets held by major financial institutions,
beginning of 1982 ($ billions)

Institutions	Assets
Commercial banks	$1,531.5
Savings and loans	594.4
Life insurance companies	525.9
Private pension funds	286.7
State and local government retirement funds	332.4
Finance companies	228.4
Federally sponsored credit agencies	212.6
Money market funds*	208.3
Other insurance companies	187.3
Federal Reserve banks	177.7
Mutual savings banks	155.8
Mutual funds	66.5
Credit unions	61.8
Securities brokers and dealers	39.2
Real estate investment trusts	5.5

 * By October 1982, the assets of money market funds, which grew rapidly in recent high-interest-rate years, totaled $230 billion; however by late winter 1983, they had fallen below $200 billion due to competition from newly permitted, federally insured, high-rate deposit accounts at banks and thrifts.
 Source: Board of Governors, Federal Reserve System.

liquidity—choose to lend long term. Finally, some risk is attached to many primary securities, more than most surplus units would like to bear.

The indirect securities offered to savers by financial intermediaries are quite attractive in contrast to primary securities. Many such instruments, e.g., time deposits, have low to zero minimum denominations, are highly liquid, and expose the investor to negligible risk. Financial intermediaries are able to offer such attractive securities for several reasons. First, they pool the funds of many investors in a highly diversified portfolio, thereby reducing risk and overcoming the minimum denominations problem. Second, to the extent that one saver's withdrawal is likely to be met by another's deposit, intermediaries such as banks, and S&Ls can with reasonable safety borrow short term from depositors and lend long term to borrowers. A final reason for intermediation is the tax advantages that some forms of intermediation, e.g., participation in a pension plan, offer individuals.

BANKS, A SPECIAL INTERMEDIARY

Banks in our economy are an intermediary of special importance for several reasons. First, they are by far the largest intermediary; they receive huge quantities of *demand deposits* (i.e., checking account money) and time deposits, which they use to make loans to consumers, corporations, and others. Second, in the course of their lending activity, *banks create money*. The reason is that demand deposits, which are a bank liability, count as part of the money supply—no matter how one defines that supply. And today, thanks to the growing attention paid to the monetarists who argue that the money supply is immensely important in determining economic activity, all eyes tend to focus on growth of the money supply.

Just how banks create money takes a little explaining. We have to introduce a simple device known as a *T-account,* which shows, as the account below illustrates, the changes that occur in the assets and liabilities of a spending unit—consumer, firm, or financial institution—as the result of a specific economic transaction.

**T-Account for a
Spending Unit**

Changes in assets	Changes in liabilities

Consider again Jones, who takes $20,000 in cash and deposits that money in the First National Bank. This transaction will result in the following changes in the balance sheets of Jones and his bank:

Jones		**First National Bank**	
Cash −20,000 Demand deposits +20,000		Reserves (cash) +20,000	Demand deposits Jones +20,000

Clearly, Jones's deposit results in $20,000 of cash being *withdrawn from circulation* and put into bank (cash) reserves, but simultaneously $20,000 of new demand deposits are created. Since every definition of the money supply includes both demand deposits and currency *in circulation,* this deposit has no net effect on the size of the money supply; instead, it simply alters the composition of the money supply.

Now enter the Alpha Company, a funds-deficit unit, which borrows $15,000 from the First National Bank. If the bank makes the loan by crediting $15,000 to Alpha's account, changes will again occur in its balance sheet and in that of the borrower, too.

Alpha Co.		**First National Bank**	
Bank loan +15,000	Demand deposits +15,000	Loan to Alpha Co. +15,000	Demand deposits to Alpha Co. +15,000

As the T-accounts show, the immediate effect of the loan is to *increase* total demand deposits by $15,000, but no offsetting decrease has occurred in the amount of currency in circulation. Thus, by making the loan, the First National Bank has *created* $15,000 of new money (Table 2–3).

The Alpha Company presumably borrows money to make a payment. That in no way alters the money creation aspect of the bank loan. To

TABLE 2–3
Money supply

Step 1:	Jones holds $20,000 in cash.
	Money supply equals:
	$20,000 in cash.
Step 2:	Jones deposits his $20,000 of cash at the First National Bank.
	Money supply equals:
	$20,000 of demand deposits held by Jones.
Step 3:	The First National Bank lends $15,000 to the Alpha Co.
	Money supply equals:
	$20,000 of demand deposits held by Jones.
	+$15,000 of demand deposits held by Alpha Co.
	$35,000 total money supply.

illustrate, suppose Alpha makes a payment for $15,000 to the Beta Company by drawing a check against its new balance and depositing it in another bank, the Second National Bank. Then the following changes will occur in the balance sheets of these two banks.

The Second National Bank		The First National Bank	
Reserves (cash) +15,000	Demand deposits to Beta Co. +15,000	Reserves (cash) −15,000	Demand deposits to the Alpha Co. −15,000

The assumed payment merely switches $15,000 of demand deposits and reserves from one bank to another bank. The payment therefore does not alter the size of the money supply.

Bearing this in mind, let's now examine how the Fed regulates the volume of bank intermediation and what effect its actions have on the money supply and interest rates.

THE FEDERAL RESERVE'S ROLE

The Fed's life has been one of continuing evolution, first in determining what its goals should be and second in learning how to use the tools available to it to promote these goals. When Congress set up the Fed in 1913, it was intended to perform several functions of varying importance. First, the Fed was charged with creating an elastic supply of currency, that is, one that could be expanded and contracted in step with changes in the quantity of currency (as opposed to bank deposits) that the public desired to hold. Creating an elastic currency supply was viewed as important because, under the then existing banking system, when a prominent bank failed and nervous depositors at other banks began demanding currency for deposits, the banks were frequently unable to meet these demands. Consequently, on a number of occasions, the panic of 1907 being a case in point, currency runs on solvent banks forced these banks to temporarily suspend the conversion of deposits into cash. Such suspensions, during which currency traded at a premium relative to bank deposits, inconvenienced depositors and disrupted the economy.

The Fed was to solve this problem by standing ready during panics to extend to the banks at the discount window loans whose proceeds could be paid out in Federal Reserve notes. To the extent that the Fed fulfilled this function, it was acting as a lender of last resort, satiating the public's appetite for cash by monetizing bank assets. Today, acting as a lender of last resort remains an important Fed responsibility, but the Fed fulfills it in a different way.

Congress also intended that the Fed carry out a second and more important function, namely, regulating the overall supply of money and bank credit so that changes in them would promote rather than disrupt economic activity. This function, too, was to be accomplished at the discount window. According to the prevailing doctrine, changes in the money supply and bank credit would be beneficial if they matched the direction and magnitude of changes in the economy's level of productive activity. Such beneficial changes in money and bank credit would, it was envisioned, occur semiautomatically with the Fed in operation. When business activity expanded, so, too, would the demand for bank loans. As growth of the latter put pressure on bank reserves, banks would obtain additional reserves by rediscounting at the Fed (i.e., borrowing against) *eligible paper*—notes, drafts, and bills of exchange arising out of actual commercial transactions. Conversely, when economic activity slackened, bank borrowing at the discount window, bank loans, and the money supply would contract in step.

Events never quite followed this smooth pattern, which in retrospect is not to be regretted. As theorists now realize, expanding money and bank credit without limit during an upswing and permitting them to contract without limit during a downswing, far from encouraging stable growth, tend to amplify fluctuations in income and output. In particular, unlimited money creation during a boom inevitably fuels any inflationary fires and other excesses that develop.

Today, the Fed sees its major policy job as pursuing a *countercyclical monetary policy*. Specifically, it attempts to promote full employment and price stability by limiting the growth of bank intermediation when the economy expands too vigorously and by encouraging it when the economy slips into recession.

Controlling the level
of bank intermediation

The Fed controls the level of bank intermediation—the amount of bank lending and money creating—through several tools. One is *reserve requirements*. Since the 1930s, the Fed has been responsible for setting the limits on the percentage of reserves that member banks are required to hold against deposits made with them. Each member bank must place all of its reserves, except vault cash, on deposit in a non-interest-bearing acount at one of the 12 regional Federal Reserve banks. (All nationally chartered banks must join the Federal Reserve System.) The same requirement does not hold for state-chartered banks, many of which have opted not to join the system because of the high cost of tying up some of the money deposited with them in a non-interest-bearing reserve account at the Fed.[1] Thus, each district Federal Reserve Bank acts in effect as a banker to commercial banks in its district, holding what amounts to checking accounts for them.

The existence at Federal Reserve Banks of member bank reserve accounts explains, by the way, how the Fed can clear checks drawn against one bank and deposited with another so easily. It does so simply by debiting the reserve account of the bank against which the check is drawn and crediting by an equal amount the reserve account of the bank at which the check is deposited.

The member banks' checking accounts also make it easy for the Fed to circulate currency in the form of Federal Reserve notes (a non-interest-bearing *indirect security* issued by the Fed). Currency runs on banks are a thing of the past, but the Fed must still constantly increase the amount of currency in circulation because, as the economy expands, more currency is needed by the public for ordinary transactions. Whenever people demand more currency, they demand it from their commercial banks, which in turn get it from the Fed by trading reserve deposits for currency. Since the Fed, as noted below, creates bank reserves by buying government securities, the currency component of our money supply is in effect created by the Fed through *monetization* of a portion of the federal debt. All of this correctly suggests that the Fed, despite its lofty position at the pinnacle of the financial system, is none other than one more type of financial intermediary.

The second key tool of the Fed is *open-market operations*, that is, purchases and sales of government securities through which it creates

---

[1] As noted below, the 1980 Banking Act calls for the Fed to extend reserve requirements to nonmember banks and nonbank depository institutions, as well, over an 8-year phase-in period.

and destroys member bank reserves. Whenever the Fed, operating through the trading desk of the New York district bank, buys government securities, its purchases inevitably increase bank reserves by an amount equal to the cost of the securities purchased. When the source of the securities purchased is a member bank, this result is obvious. Specifically, a purchase of $10 million of government securities would lead to the following changes in the balance sheets of the Fed and of a member bank.

The Fed		A Member Bank	
Government securities +10 million	Member bank reserves +10 million	Reserves +10 million Government securities −10 million	

Even if the source of the government securities purchased by the Fed is a nonbank spending unit, the result will be essentially the same, since the money received by the seller, say, a nonbank dealer, will inevitably be deposited in a commercial bank, leading to the following balance sheet changes.

The Fed		A Member Bank	
Government securities +10 million	Member bank reserves +10 million	Reserves −10 million	Deposits to nonbank seller +10 million

A Nonbank Seller	
Government securities −10 million Demand deposits +10 million	

In the case of sales of government securities by the Fed, the process described above operates exactly in reverse, and member bank reserves are destroyed.

With the exception of loans extended by the Fed at the discount window (discussed below), the *only* way bank reserves can be created is through Fed purchases of government securities, and the only way they can be destroyed is through sales by the Fed of such securities.[2] Thus,

---

[2] There are some minor exceptions: In particular, movements of Treasury deposit balances between commercial banks and Fed banks affect member bank reserves, but the Fed tracks these movements daily and offsets them through purchases and sales of government securities. Seasonal and long-term changes in the public's demand for currency also affect bank reserves, but these changes too can be and are offset by the Fed through appropriate open-market operations. Finally, under the current system of "dirty" currency

the Fed is in a position to control directly and precisely the quantity of reserves available to the banking system.

The lid on bank intermediation

Taken together, reserve requirements and the Fed's ability to control the level of bank reserves permit the Fed to set a tight limit on the level of intermediation in which banks may engage. Let's use a simple illustration. Suppose the Fed were to require banks to hold reserves equal to 10 percent of total deposits. If the Fed were then to create, say, $90 billion of bank reserves, the maximum deposits banks could create through intermediation would be $900 billion (10 percent of $900 billion being $90 billion).

Naturally, if the Fed were to increase bank reserves through open-market purchases of government securities, that would increase the quantity of deposits banks could create, whereas open-market sales by the Fed would do the reverse. For example, with a 10 percent reserve ratio, every $1 billion of government security purchases by the Fed would permit a $10 billion increase in bank assets and liabilities, whereas $1 billion of sales would do the opposite.

Our example, which points up the potency of *open-market operations* (purchases and sales by the Fed of government securities) as a tool for controlling the level of bank intermediation, is oversimplified. For one thing, the percentage of reserves that must be held by a bank against its deposits varies depending on the type of deposit and the size of the bank accepting the deposit. Currently, required reserve ratios are being phased down to a high of 12 percent against demand deposits at large banks to a low of 0 percent against time deposits maturing in 3½ years or more. Thus, the actual amount of deposits (demand plus time) that a given quantity of reserves will support depends partly on the mix of deposits demanded by the public and partly on the size of the banks receiving those deposits.

This, together with the fact that banks may choose not to fully utilize the reserves available to them, means that some slack exists in the Fed's control over deposit creation. Nevertheless, open-market operations are a powerful tool for controlling the level of bank activity, and they are used daily by the Fed to do so.

The discount window

As noted earlier, the founders of the Fed viewed discounting as its *key* tool. In practice, things have worked out differently. The main reason is

floats, U.S. and foreign central-bank operations in the foreign exchange market may have some effect on domestic bank deposits and reserves.

that over time the Fed switched from controlling bank reserves through discounting to controlling them through open-market operations. This switch makes sense for several reasons. First, it puts the Fed in the position of being able to take the initiative. Second, the size and liquidity of the market for government securities are such that the Fed can make substantial purchases and sales there without disrupting the market or causing more than negligible price changes. The latter is important since the Fed, to fine tune bank reserves, must constantly be in the market buying and selling such securities. Part of this activity results from what is called the Fed's *defensive* operations, open-market purchases and sales designed to counter the effect on bank reserves of outside forces, such as changes in the amount of currency in circulation and movements of Treasury balances between member banks and the Fed. In addition, the Fed undertakes open-market operations to effect whatever overall changes in bank reserves are called for by current monetary policy.

The discount window still exists and banks borrow there. This activity creates some slack in the Fed's control over bank reserves, so the Fed has to limit borrowing at the window. One way it could do this would be charge a high penalty rate on discounts, one that would discourage banks from borrowing except in cases of real and temporary need. The Fed, however, has not followed this course.[3] Instead, it typically sets the discount rate at a level in step with other money market rates, with the result that banks can at times profit by borrowing at the discount window and relending elsewhere. To limit such arbitrage and maintain control over bank reserves, the Fed has made it a policy that borrowing at the discount window is a privilege that a bank may use only sparingly and on a temporary basis.

Today, borrowing at the discount window represents a small but highly variable element in the total reserves available to member banks. In recent years, monthly figures on such borrowings have ranged from $.5 to $1.5 billion. The high numbers all occurred in times of tight money, but even in such periods member bank borrowing represented no more than 2 to 4 percent of total bank reserves.

EXTENDING THE FED'S REACH

Holding non-interest-bearing reserve deposits at the Fed imposes an opportunity cost on a member institution, namely, the interest income foregone by the institution because it cannot use these deposits productively. As interest rates rose secularly over time, so too did the opportunity cost to banks of meeting reserve requirements. As a result, the trend

---

[3] Except for a brief experiment with a modest surcharge in 1980–81.

during the 1960s and 70s was for banks to leave the Federal Reserve System.

The Fed viewed this trend with alarm. It was prepared to live with a situation in which many small state banks were not members. However, the Fed feared that the exit from the system of increasingly more and increasingly larger banks would decrease the effectiveness of its policies and, in particular, limit its ability to control the money supply. As a result, the Fed from 1964 onward urged Congress to amend the Federal Reserve Act to make nonmember banks subject to the same reserve requirements as member banks. A second smaller but growing problem faced by the Fed was that thrift institutions outside its control began to issue *NOW (negotiable order of withdrawal) accounts*. Deposits in such accounts amount, in effect, to interest-bearing demand deposits and as such are *money* by any reasonable definition.

In 1980, Congress passed the landmark *Depository Institutions Deregulation and Monetary Control Act*. One objective of this wide-ranging act was to increase the Fed's control over money creation. To this end, the act, dubbed the *Banking Act of 1980,* calls for the Fed to impose, over an eight-year phase-in period, reserve requirements on nonmember banks and on thrift institutions offering checking accounts, as well. At the same time, reserve requirements on savings and time deposits held by individuals at all depository institutions will be eliminated.

As a quid pro quo for the new reserve requirements, the 1980 act empowers banks and all other depository institutions to issue NOW accounts. It also empowers thrift institutions to make a wider range of investments and grants them access to the discount window. Full implementation of the 1980 act will further blur the once clear line of demarcation between commercial banks and thrifts.

Money supply and Fed control over it

As will be explained in Chapter 3, banks borrow and lend excess reserves to each other in the *Federal funds market*. The rate at which such lending and borrowing occurs is called the *Fed funds rate*. When the Fed cuts back on the growth of bank reserves, this tightens the supply of reserves available to the banking system relative to its demand for them; that, in turn, drives up the Fed funds rate, which, in turn, drives up other short-term interest rates. Thus, any easing or tightening by the Fed necessarily alters not only money supply growth, but also interest rates.

Because of this, the Fed cannot have two independent policies, one to control money supply growth, a second to influence interest rates. If the Fed focuses on pegging interest rates, money supply becomes a residual variable; it is what it is and falls outside the control of the Fed.

Conversely, a Fed decision to strictly control money supply growth implies a loss by the Fed of its ability to independently influence the level of interest rates.

In implementing monetary policy, the Fed in the early 1970s focused primarily on interest rates and more particularly on the Fed funds rate. The Fed viewed money as tight if interest rates were high or rising, as easy if interest rates were low or falling. This policy stance was predicated on the view that high and rising interest rates would discourage spending and the expansion of economic activity, while low or falling rates would do the reverse.

The monetarists, with Milton Friedman at the fore, argued that this analysis was incorrect. According to their theory, giving people more money causes them to increase their spending on goods and services. Therefore, the key to achieving steady economic growth and to controlling inflation is a monetary policy that holds the rate of growth of the money supply strictly in line with the rate of growth of real output achievable by the economy. The clear implication of the monetarist position is that the Fed should seek to peg not the Fed funds rate but the rate of growth of money.

Gradually, grudgingly, and with a prod from Congress in the form of the Humphrey-Hawkins bill passed in 1978, the Fed accepted the monetarist doctrine and shifted the focus of its policy from controlling interest rates to controlling money supply growth, the policy shift being completed under Chairman Paul Volcker.

Pitfalls of monetarism. For monetarists, particularly those residing in the ivory towers of academe, it appeared that the mandate to strictly control the growth of the money supply is one that the Fed could carry out with reasonable ease and a high degree of precision. In practice, however, the policy of controlling money supply growth—whether wise or foolish—has posed serious problems for the Fed.

The first, and hardly trivial, problem facing the Fed has been to determine just what money is. Clearly, the old definition of money, demand deposits plus currency in circulation, is too restrictive since the long-term upward trend in interest rates has spawned not only new types of deposit accounts—NOW accounts and ATS (automatic transfer from savings to demand deposit) accounts—that can be used for transactions purposes, but also a host of other highly liquid investment options, including placements in money market funds. Since liquidity—unlike virginity—is measured in degrees, drawing a line between money and near monies necessarily involves *arbitrary* choices. This being the case, the Fed has for some time found itself struggling simply to define what it is supposed to control.

The Fed's difficulties in defining money are reflected in its decision to publish four different measures of money supply (Table 2–4). Obviously,

TABLE 2–4
The Fed's measures of money stock, February 1983

M1: Currency in circulation plus demand deposits plus other checkable deposits, including NOW accounts and super-NOW accounts.

M2: M1 plus MMDAs plus savings and small (less than $100,000) time deposits at all depository institutions plus balances at money funds (excluding institutions-only funds), plus overnight RPs at banks plus overnight Euros held by nonbank U.S. depositors in the Caribbean branches of U.S. banks minus balances on Keogh and IRA accounts at bank, thrifts, and money funds.

M3: M2 plus large (over $100,000) time deposits at all depository institutions plus term RPs at banks and S&Ls plus balances at institutions-only money funds.

L: M3 plus other liquid assets such as term Eurodollars held by nonbank U.S. residents, bankers' acceptances, commercial paper, Treasury bills, and other liquid governments, and U.S. savings bonds.

the Fed cannot independently control the growth of each of these aggregates. It currently focuses its attention primarily on M1 and M2.

In late 1982 and early 1983, the Fed found that the problem of defining money supply went from being difficult to nigh impossible. In the inelegant but apt words of one street observer, "It's a can of worms." The immediate cause of the problems faced by the Fed, as 1982 became 1983, lay in the Banking Act of 1982. One of its provisions was a mandate to the Depository Institutions Deregulation Committee (DIDC) that this committee design within 60 days an interest-rate-lid-free account to be offered by banks and thrifts that would permit these institutions to compete on equal terms for deposits with money funds.

The DIDC came up, to the surprise of many observers, with not one but two new accounts (Table 2–5). The first, called the *money market deposit account* (*MMDA*), required the depositor, private or corporate, to maintain a minimum balance of $2,500; in exchange the depositor obtained a federally insured account on which he could write three checks and make three preauthorized withdrawals per month and on which the deposit-accepting institution could pay any rate it wished. The Fed chose to view this account as more akin to a savings than a demand deposit account and included it in M2.

The introduction of MMDAs on December 14, 1982, was followed by the introduction of *super-NOW accounts* on January 5, 1983. These accounts, which initially at least were available only to individuals, also required the depositor to maintain a minimum balance of $2,500; in exchange the depositor obtained a federally insured checking account on which he could make unlimited withdrawals and on which the deposit-accepting institution could pay any rate and impose any service charges it wished. The Fed chose to include super-NOW accounts in M1.

The introduction of MMDAs and super-NOW accounts made measur-

TABLE 2–5
The new money market accounts

Name of account	Date of introduction	Minimum balance	Permitted withdrawals	Rate ceiling	Federal insurance	Included in	Reserve requirements‡
MMDA*	12/14/82	$2,500	3 checks +3 other	none	yes	M2	as time deposits
Super NOW†	1/5/83	$2,500	unlimited	none	yes	M1	as transactions accounts

* Available to all depositors.
† Available initially only to individuals.
‡ See Table 5–3.

ing money supply more difficult than ever for the Fed because it blurred even further, if possible, the distinction between instruments in which people hold spending money and instruments in which they hold savings. MMDAs were an immediate success and, in the early weeks of their existence, were drawing several billions of dollars per week from money funds, whose deposits are counted in M2. The new MMDA accounts were also drawing billions of dollars of deposits out of old lower-yielding accounts at banks and thrifts. All this shifting of balances from place to place combined with the introduction of the new accounts made it impossible for the Fed—for a period at least—to interpret the meaning of the growth rates of M1 and M2. Responding to this, the Fed suspended its use of M1 as a guide in policy making and, declared that henceforth it would be guided by M2; in fact, however, it permitted M2 to grow at out-of-bounds rates without responding by tightening. Whatever the Fed said it said it was doing, it appeared in early 1983 as if the Fed were backsliding from a monetarist policy of controlling money supply to its former policy of controlling interest rates.

Defining money, while a tough nut to crack, is only the beginning of the Fed's problems in controlling money supply. A second, equally in-

FIGURE 2–1
Weekly figures for M1 (dubbed by the Fed until January 1981, M1B) change in a highly erratic way from week to week and are rarely on target

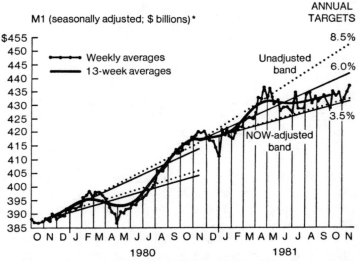

* Data on money supply include NOW accounts. Unadjusted bands refer to money supply including NOW accounts, NOW-adjusted bands to money supply excluding NOW accounts.
Source: The Morgan Bank.

tractable and, from a policy point of view, more serious problem is that a large erratic element appears to be intrinsic in money supply behavior with the result that week-to-week money supply figures fluctuate sharply (Figure 2–1); the Fed also has difficulty in seasonally adjusting these figures. The upshot is that underlying trends in money supply growth are hard to perceive both for the Fed and for outside observers reacting to actual and potential Fed moves.

In accepting and seeking to implement a strictly monetarist policy, the Fed—as had to be the case—has lost control over interest rates (see Figure 2–2). This permitted rates, beginning in 1980, to take off on a

FIGURE 2–2
By becoming monetarist, the Fed has lost control over the Fed funds rate: Federal funds rate (weekly averages as of Wednesday; data through September 1982)

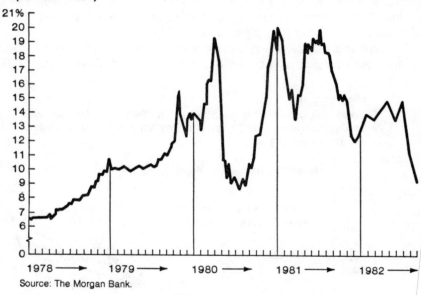

Source: The Morgan Bank.

roller coaster ride. It also created a situation in which strong reactions by money and bond market traders to weekly money supply figures made interest rates highly volatile and unpredictable even on a week-to-week basis.

The price of a monetarist policy in a highly inflationary economy appears to be an extremely high degree of uncertainty with respect to rates in the capital market. This untoward consequence of monetarism can hardly be viewed as contributing to economic stability. The Fed knows this and would like to feed to credit market participants money supply numbers that delineate longer-term trends in money growth. Unfortunately, it can find no way to do so. Consequently, interest rates are likely to remain highly volatile until inflation is cured or the Fed gives up on monetarism and reverts to attempting to influence economic activity and the rate of inflation by adjusting interest rates.

The primary purpose of this brief description of Fed policy is to provide necessary background for Chapters 5 and 6 which cover fundamentals of domestic and Eurobanking. In Chapter 8, we will return to the Fed and examine in greater detail current Fed policy and the constraints it places on banks.

Chapter 3

The instruments in brief

HERE'S A QUICK RUNDOWN of the major money market instruments. Don't look for subtleties; just enough is said to lay the groundwork for later chapters.

DEALERS AND BROKERS

The markets for all money market instruments are made in part by brokers and dealers. *Brokers* bring buyers and sellers together for a commission. By definition, brokers never position securities. Their function is to provide a communications network that links market participants who are often numerous and geographically dispersed. Most brokering in the money market occurs between banks that are buying funds from or selling funds to each other and between dealers in money market instruments.

Dealers make markets in money market instruments by quoting bid and asked prices to each other, to issuers, and to investors. Dealers buy and sell for their own accounts, so assuming positions—long and short—is an essential part of a dealer's operation.

U.S. TREASURY SECURITIES

To finance the U.S. national debt, the Treasury issues several types of securities. Some are nonnegotiable, for example, savings bonds sold to consumers and special issues sold to government trust funds. The bulk of the securities sold by the U.S. Treasury are, however, negotiable.

What form these securities take depends on their maturity. Those with a maturity at issue of a year or less are known as *Treasury bills, T bills* for short or just plain *bills*. T bills bear no interest. An investor in bills earns a return because bills are issued at a discount from face value and redeemed by the Treasury at maturity for face value. The amount of the discount at which investors buy bills and the length of time bills have to be held before they mature together imply some specific yield that the bill will return if held to maturity.

T bills are currently issued in 3-month, 6-month, and 1-year maturities.[1] In issuing bills, the Treasury does not set the amount of the discount. Instead, the Federal Reserve auctions off each new bill issue to investors and dealers, with the bills going to those bidders offering the highest price, i.e., the lowest interest cost to the Treasury. By auctioning new bill issues, the Treasury lets currently prevailing market conditions establish the yield at which each new issue is sold.

The Treasury also issues interest-bearing *notes*. These securities are issued at or very near face value and redeemed at face value. Notes have an *original maturity* (maturity at issue) of 1 to 10 years.[2] Currently, the Treasury issues 2-, 3-, 4-, 5-, 7-, and 10-year notes on a regular cycle. Notes of other maturities are issued periodically depending on the Treasury's needs. Interest on Treasury notes is paid semiannually. Notes, like bills, are sold through auctions held by the Federal Reserve. In these auctions participants bid yields, and the securities offered are sold to those dealers and investors who bid the lowest yields, that is, the lowest interest cost to the Treasury. Thus, the coupon rate on new Treasury notes, like the yield on bills, is determined by the market. The last exception was a 1976 subscription offering in which the Treasury sold the famed 8s of 86.

In addition to notes, the Treasury issues interest-bearing negotiable *bonds* that have a maturity at issue of 10 years or more. The only difference between Treasury notes and bonds is that bonds are issued in longer maturities. In recent years the volume of bonds the Treasury can issue has been limited because Congress has imposed a 4.25 percent ceiling on the rate the Treasury may pay on bonds. Since this rate has for

---

[1] For tactical debt management purposes, the Treasury occasionally meets cash flow gaps by issuing very short-term "cash management bills."

[2] A 5-year note has an *original maturity* at issue of 5 years. One year after issue it has a *current maturity* of 4 years.

years been far below prevailing market rates, the Treasury is able to sell bonds only to the extent that Congress authorizes it to issue bonds exempt from the ceiling; the current exemption, which has been successively raised, is $110 billion. Treasury bonds, like notes, are normally sold at yield auctions.

Banks, other financial institutions, insurance companies, pension funds, and corporations are all important investors in U.S. Treasury securities. So, too, are some foreign central banks and other foreign institutions. The market for government securities is largely a wholesale market, and especially at the short end, multimillion-dollar transactions are common. However, when interest rates get extremely high, as they did in 1974 and again in 1978–82, individuals with small amounts to invest are drawn into the market.

Because of the high volume of Treasury debt outstanding, the market for bills and short-term government securities is the most active and most carefully watched sector of the money market. At the heart of this market stands a varied collection of dealers who make the market for *governments* (market jargon for government securities) by standing ready to buy and sell huge volumes of these securities. These dealers trade actively not only with investors but also with each other. Most trades of the latter sort are carried out through brokers.

Governments offer investors several advantages. First, because they are constantly traded in the *secondary market* in large volume and at narrow spreads between the bid and asked prices, they are highly *liquid*. Second, governments are considered to be free from credit risk because it is inconceivable that the government would default on these securities in any situation short of destruction of the country. Third, interest income on governments is exempt from state taxation. Because of these advantages, governments normally trade at yields below those of other money market instruments. Municipal securities are an exception because they offer a still more attractive tax advantage.

Generally yields on governments are higher the longer their *current maturity*, that is, time left to maturity. The reason, explained in Chapter 4, is that the longer the current maturity of a debt security, the more its price will fluctuate in response to changes in interest rates and therefore the greater the *price risk* to which it exposes the investor. There are times, however, when the yield curve *inverts*, that is, yields on short-term securities rise above those on long-term securities. This, for example, was the case during much of the period 1979–81. The reason for an inverted yield curve is that market participants anticipate, correctly or incorrectly, that interest rates will fall. As a result, borrowers choose to borrow short-term while investors seek out long-term securities; the result is that supply and demand force short-term rates above long-term rates.

FINANCIAL FUTURES AND OPTIONS MARKETS

In discussing the market for governments, we have focused on the *cash market,* that is, the market in which existing securities are traded for same- or next-day delivery. In addition, there are markets in which Treasury bills, Treasury notes, Treasury bonds, bank CDs, and other money market instruments are traded for *future* delivery. The futures contracts in Treasuries that are most actively traded are for 3-month bills with a face value of $1 million at maturity and for notes and long bonds with a par value of $100,000.

Interest rate futures markets offer institutions that know they are going to borrow or lend in the future a way to *hedge* that future position, that is, to lock in a reasonably fixed borrowing or lending rate. They also provide speculators with a way to bet money on interest rate movements that is easier and cheaper than going short or long in cash securities.

Since being introduced in 1976, futures markets for financial instruments have grown at an unforseen and astonishing rate. In fact, futures contracts for Treasury bills and bonds have been among the most successful contracts ever launched on commodities exchanges.

The newness and rapid growth of markets for financial futures, not surprisingly, has created situations in which the relationship between the rates on different futures contracts or between the rates on a futures contract and the corresponding cash instrument get, as the street would say, "out of sync," that is, out of synchronization or line. Thus, yet another major class of traders in financial futures has been arbitrageurs who seek to establish positions from which they will profit when a reasonable relationship between the out-of-line rates is inevitably reestablished.

FEDERAL AGENCY SECURITIES

From time to time Congress becomes concerned about the volume of credit that is available to various sectors of the economy and the terms on which that credit is available. Its usual response is to set up a federal agency to provide credit to that sector. Thus, for example, there is the Federal Home Loan Bank System, which lends to the nation's savings and loan associations as well as regulates them: the Government National Mortgage Association, which funnels money into the mortgage market; the Banks for Cooperatives, which make seasonal and term loans to farm cooperatives; the Federal Land Banks, which give mortgages on farm properties; the Federal Intermediate Credit Banks, which provide short-term financing for producers of crops and livestock; and a host of other agencies.

Initially, all the federal agencies financed their activities by selling their own securities in the open market. Today, all except the largest borrow from the Treasury through an institution called the Federal Financing Bank. Those agencies still borrowing in the open market do so primarily by issuing notes and bonds. These securities (known in the market as *agencies*) bear interest, and they are issued and redeemed at face value. Instead of using the auction technique for issuing their securities, federal agencies look to the market to determine the best yield at which they can sell a new issue, put that yield on the issue, and then sell it through a syndicate of dealers. Some agencies also sell short-term discount paper that resembles commercial paper (see below).

Normally, agencies yield slightly more than Treasury securities of the same maturity for several reasons. Agency issues are smaller than Treasury issues and are therefore less liquid. Also, while all agency issues have de facto backing from the federal government (it's inconceivable that the government would let one of them default on its obligations), the securities of only a few agencies are explicitly backed by the full faith and credit of the U.S. government. Finally, interest income on some federal agency issues is subject to state taxation.

The market for agencies, while smaller than that for governments, has, in recent years, become an active and important sector of the money market. Agencies are traded by the same dealers that trade governments and in much the same way.

FEDERAL FUNDS

All banks that are members of the Federal Reserve System are required to keep reserves on deposit at their district Federal Reserve Bank. A commercial bank's reserve account is much like a consumer's checking account; the bank makes deposits into it and can transfer funds out of it. The main difference is that while a consumer can run the balance in his checking account down to zero, each member bank is required to maintain some minimum average balance in its reserve account over the week. How large that minimum balance is depends on the size and composition of the bank's deposits over the third prior week.[3]

Funds on deposit in a bank's reserve account are referred to as *Federal funds* or *Fed funds*. Any deposits a bank receives add to its supply of Fed funds, while loans made and securities purchased reduce that supply. Thus, the basic amount of money any bank can lend out and otherwise invest equals the amount of funds it has received from depositors minus the reserves it is required to maintain.

For some banks, this supply of available funds roughly equals the amount they choose to invest in securities plus that demanded from them

---

[3] This will change when and if the Fed forces the banks to go to contemporaneous reserve accounting.

by borrowers. But for most banks it does not. Specifically, because the nation's largest corporations tend to concentrate their borrowing in big money market banks in New York and other financial centers, the loans and investments these banks have to fund exceed the deposits they receive. Many smaller banks, in contrast, receive more money from local depositors than they can lend locally or choose to invest otherwise. Because large banks have to meet their reserve requirements regardless of what loan demand they face and because excess reserves yield no return to smaller banks, it was natural for large banks to begin borrowing the excess funds held by smaller banks.

This borrowing is done in the *Federal funds market.* Most Fed funds loans are overnight transactions. One reason is that the amount of excess funds a given lending bank holds varies daily and unpredictably. Some transactions in Fed funds are made directly, others through New York brokers. Despite the fact that transactions of this sort are all loans, the lending of Fed funds is referred to as a *sale* and the borrowing of Fed funds as a *purchase.* While overnight transactions dominate the Fed funds market, transactions for longer periods also occur there. Fed funds traded for periods other than overnight are referred to as *term* Fed funds.

The rate of interest paid on overnight loans of Federal funds, which is called the *Fed funds rate,* is *the* main interest rate in the money market, and all other short-term rates are keyed to it. The Fed funds rate used to be closely pegged by the Fed. Starting in October 1979, however, the Fed, which still controls the general level of this rate, allowed it to fluctuate over a wide band.

EURODOLLARS

Many foreign banks will accept deposits of dollars and grant the depositor an account *denominated in dollars.* So, too, will the foreign branches of U.S. banks. The practice of accepting dollar-denominated deposits outside of the United States began in Europe, so such deposits came to be known as *Eurodollars.* The practice of accepting dollar-denominated deposits later spread to Hong Kong, Singapore, the Mid East, and other centers around the globe. Consequently today a *Eurodollar deposit is simply a deposit denominated in dollars in a bank or bank branch outside the United States,* and the term Eurodollar has become a misnomer. To make things even more confusing, in December 1981, domestic and foreign banks were permitted to open *international banking facilities* (*IBFs*) in the United States.[4] Dollars deposited in IBFs are also Eurodollars.

---

[4] See Chapter 6.

Most Eurodollar deposits are for large sums. They are made by corporations—foreign, multinational, and domestic; foreign central banks and other official institutions; U.S. domestic banks; and wealthy individuals. With the exception of *call money*,[5] all Eurodeposits have a fixed term, which can range from overnight to 5 years. The bulk of Euro transactions are in the range of 6 months and under. Banks receiving Eurodollar deposits use them to make loans denominated in dollars to foreign and domestic corporations, foreign governments and government agencies, domestic U.S. banks, and other large borrowers.

Banks that participate in the Eurodollar market actively borrow and lend Euros among themselves, just as domestic banks borrow and lend in the Fed funds market. The major difference between the two markets is that in the market for Fed funds, most transactions are on an overnight basis, whereas in the Euromarket, interbank placements (deposits) of funds for longer periods are common.

For a domestic U.S. bank with a reserve deficiency, borrowing Eurodollars is an alternative to purchasing Fed funds. Also, for a domestic bank with excess funds, a *Europlacement* (i.e., a deposit of dollars in the Euromarket) is an alternative to the sale of Fed funds. Consequently, the rate on overnight Euros tends to closely track the Fed funds rate. It is also true that, as one goes out on the maturity scale, Euro rates continue to track U.S. rates, though not so closely as in the overnight market.

CERTIFICATES OF DEPOSIT

The maximum rate banks may pay on savings deposits and time deposits (a time deposit is a deposit with a fixed maturity) is set by the Fed through *Regulation Q*. Essentially what Reg Q does is to make it impossible for banks to compete with each other or with other savings institutions for small deposits by offering depositors higher interest rates.[6] On large deposits, $100,000 or more, banks may currently pay any rate they choose so long as the deposit has a minimum maturity of 14 days.

There are many corporations and other large investors that have hundreds of thousands, even millions, of dollars they could invest in bank time deposits. Few do so, however, because they lose liquidity by making a deposit with a fixed maturity. The illiquidity of time deposits and

---

[5] Call money is money deposited in an interest-bearing account that can be called (withdrawn) by the depositor on a day's notice.

[6] The rates banks and thrifts may pay depositors are gradually being deregulated under the Banking Act of 1980. Also the Banking Act of 1982 permitted depository institutions to begin offering unregulated rates on super-NOW and money market deposit accounts. See Chapters 5 and 20.

their consequent lack of appeal to investors led banks to invent the *negotiable certificate of deposit,* or *CD* for short.

CDs are normally sold in $1 million units. They are issued at face value and typically pay interest at maturity. CDs can have any maturity longer than 14 days, and some 5- and even 7-year CDs have been sold (these pay interest semiannually). Most CDs, however, have an *original maturity* of 1 to 6 months.

The quantity of CDs that banks have outstanding depends largely on the strength of loan demand. When demand rises, banks issue more CDs to fund the additional loans they are making. The rates banks offer on CDs depend on their maturity, how badly the banks want to write new CDs, and the general level of short-term interest rates.

Most bank CDs are sold directly by banks to investors. Some, however, are issued through dealers for a small commission. The same dealers make an active secondary market in CDs.

Yields on CDs exceed those on bills of similar maturities by varying spreads. One reason for the higher yield is that buying a bank CD exposes the investor to some credit risk—would he be paid off if the issuing bank failed? A second reason CDs yield more than bills is that they are less liquid.

Variable-rate CDs

In the late 1970s banks introduced, on a small scale, a new type of negotiable CD, *variable-rate CDs.* The two most prevalent types are 6-month CDs with a 30-day *roll* (on each roll date, accrued interest is paid and a new coupon is set) and 1-year paper with a 3-month roll.

The coupon established on a variable-rate CD at issue and on subsequent roll dates is set at some amount (12.5 to 30 basis points depending on the name of the issuer and the maturity) above the average rate (as indicated by the *composite* rate published by the Fed) that banks are paying on new CDs with an original maturity equal to the length of the roll period.

Variable-rate CDs give the issuing bank the opportunity to make a rate play. They offer some rate protection to customers, but they also have the offsetting disadvantage of illiquidity because they trade at a concession to the market on other than roll dates. During their last *leg* (roll period) variable-rate CDs trade like regular CDs of similar bank name and maturity.

The major buyers of variable-rate CDs are money market funds. In calculating the average maturity of their portfolios, these funds treat variable-rate CDs as if they matured on their next roll date, a justifiable practice since such paper must trade at or above par on roll dates. Buying variable-rate CDs enables money funds to get a rate slightly above the prevailing rate for the relevant roll period while holding down the average maturity of their portfolios.

Discount CDs

CDs trade at a price equal to principal *plus* accrued interest. Dealers who make markets in CDs finance their CD inventory in the repo market (described below). Repos on CDs always cover principal but not accrued interest. A dealer that holds a CD inventory must therefore use its scarce capital to finance accrued interest on these securities.

To circumvent this problem and to facilitate comparisons by investors of yields on CDs with yields on discount paper—bills, bankers' acceptances (BAs), and commercial paper—some dealers proposed in the late 1970s that banks issue discount rather than interest-bearing CDs. A few banks did this, but it did not become general practice. One reason was a Fed ruling that a bank issuing a discount CD must treat it as a deposit whose size rises over the life of the CD by the amount of the discount at issue. The Fed also required that the issuing bank calculate its reservable deposits on the basis of the constantly rising value of the deposit associated with a discount CD. For banks issuing discount CDs, this created an accounting headache, which they chose to avoid by ceasing to issue such paper.

Eurodollar CDs

A Eurodollar time deposit, like a domestic time deposit, is an illiquid asset. Since some investors in Eurodollars wanted liquidity, banks in London that accepted such deposits began to issue *Eurodollar CDs*. These resemble domestic CDs except that, instead of being the liability of a domestic bank, they are the liability of the London branch of a U.S. bank, of a British bank, or of some other foreign bank with a branch in London.

Many of the Eurodollar CDs issued in London are purchased by other banks operating in the Euromarket. A large proportion of the remainder are sold to U.S. corporations and other U.S. institutional investors. Many Euro CDs are issued through dealers and brokers who also make a secondary market in these securities.

The Euro CD market is younger and smaller than the market for domestic CDs, but it has grown rapidly since its inception. For the investor, a key advantage of buying Euro CDs is that they offer a higher return than do domestic CDs. The offsetting disadvantages are that they are less liquid and expose the investor to some extra risk because they are issued outside of the United States.

The most recent development in the "Eurodollar" CD market is that some large banks have begun offering such CDs through their Caribbean branches. Note that a CD issued, for example, in Nassau is technically a Euro CD because the deposit is held in a bank branch outside the United States.

Yankee CDs

Foreign banks issue dollar-denominated CDs not only in the Euromarket but also in the domestic market through branches established there. CDs of the latter sort are frequently referred to as *Yankee CDs;* the name is taken from Yankee bonds, which are bonds issued in the domestic market by foreign borrowers.

Yankee, as opposed to domestic, CDs expose the investor to the extra (if only in perception) risk of a foreign name, and they are also less liquid than domestic CDs. Consequently, Yankees trade at yields close to those on Euro CDs. The major buyers of Yankee CDs are corporations that are yield buyers and fund to dates.

COMMERCIAL PAPER

While some cash-rich industrial firms participate in the bond and money markets only as lenders, many more must at times borrow to finance either current operations or expenditures on plant and equipment. One source of short-term funds available to a corporation is bank loans. Large firms with good credit ratings, however, have an alternative source of funds that is cheaper, namely, the sale of commercial paper.

Commercial paper is an unsecured promissory note issued for a specific amount and maturing on a specific day. All commercial paper is negotiable, but most paper sold to investors is held by them to maturity. Commercial paper is issued not only by industrial and manufacturing firms but also by finance companies. Finance companies normally sell their paper directly to investors. Industrial firms, in contrast, typically issue their paper through dealers. Recently foreign bank holding companies, municipalities, and municipal authorities have joined the ranks of commercial paper issuers.

The maximum maturity for which commercial paper may be sold is 270 days, since paper with a longer maturity must be registered with the Securities and Exchange Commission (SEC), a time-consuming and costly procedure. In practice, very little 270-day paper is sold. Most paper sold is in the range of 30 days and under.

Since commercial paper has such short maturities, the issuer rarely will have sufficient funds coming in before the paper matures to pay off his borrowing. Instead, he expects to *roll* his paper, that is, sell new paper to obtain funds to pay off the maturing paper. Naturally the possibility exists that some sudden change in market conditions, such as when the Penn Central went "belly up" (bankrupt), might make it difficult or impossible for him to sell paper for some time. To guard against this risk, commercial paper issuers back all or a large proportion of their outstanding paper with lines of credit from banks.

The rate offered on commercial paper depends on its maturity, on how much the issuer wants to borrow, on the general level of money market rates, and on the credit rating of the issuer. Almost all commercial paper is rated with respect to credit risk by one or more of several rating services: Moody's, Standard & Poor's, and Fitch. While only top-grade credits can get ratings good enough to sell paper these days, there is still a slight risk that an issuer might go bankrupt. Because of this, and because of illiquidity, yields on commercial paper are higher than those on Treasury obligations of similar maturity.

BANKERS' ACCEPTANCES

Bankers' acceptances (BAs) are an unknown instrument outside the confines of the money market. Moreover, explaining them isn't easy because they arise in a variety of ways out of a variety of transactions. The best approach is to use an example.

Suppose a U.S. importer wants to buy shoes in Brazil and pay for them four months later after he has had time to sell them in the United States. One approach would be for the importer to borrow from his bank; however, short-term rates may be lower in the open market. If they are, and if the importer is too small to go into the open market on his own, then he can go the bankers' acceptance route.

In that case, he has his bank write a letter of credit for the amount of the sale and sends this letter to the Brazilian exporter. Upon export of the shoes, the Brazilian firm, using this letter of credit, draws a time draft on the importer's U.S. bank and discounts this draft at its local bank, thereby obtaining immediate payment for its goods. The Brazilian bank, in turn, sends the time draft to the importer's U.S. bank, which then stamps "accepted" on the draft (that is, the bank guarantees payment on the draft and thereby creates an *acceptance*). Once this is done, the draft becomes an irrevocable primary obligation of the accepting bank. At this point, if the Brazilian bank did not want cash immediately, the U.S. bank would return the draft to that bank, which would hold it as an investment and then present it to the U.S. bank for payment at maturity. If, on the other hand, the Brazilian bank wanted cash immediately, the U.S. bank would pay it and then either hold the acceptance itself or sell it to an investor. Regardless of who ends up holding the acceptance, it is the importer's responsibility to provide its U.S. bank with sufficient funds to pay off the acceptance at maturity. If the importer fails to do so, the bank is still responsible for making payment at maturity.

Our example illustrates how an acceptance can arise out of a U.S. import transaction. Acceptances also arise in connection with U.S. export sales, trade between third countries (e.g., Japanese imports of oil from the Mid East), the domestic shipment of goods, and domestic or foreign storage of readily marketable staples. Currently, most BAs arise out of foreign trade; they may be in manufactured goods but more typically are in bulk commodities, such as cocoa, cotton, coffee, or crude oil, to name a few. Because of the complex nature of acceptance operations, only large banks that have well-staffed foreign departments act as accepting banks.

Bankers' acceptances closely resemble commercial paper in form. They are short-term, non-interest-bearing notes sold at a discount and redeemed by the accepting bank at maturity for full face value. The major difference is that payment on commercial paper is guaranteed only by the issuing company. In contrast, bankers' acceptances, in addition to carrying the issuer's pledge to pay, are backed by the underlying goods being financed and also carry the guarantee of the accepting bank. Consequently, bankers' acceptances are less risky than commercial paper and thus sell at slightly lower yields.

The big banks through which bankers' acceptances are originated generally keep some portion of the acceptances they create as investments. The rest are sold to investors through dealers or directly by the bank itself. Major investors in BAs are other banks, foreign central banks, money market funds, corporations, and other domestic and foreign institutional investors. BAs have liquidity because dealers in these securities make an active secondary market in those that are eligible for purchase by the Fed.

REPOS AND REVERSES

A variety of bank and nonbank dealers act as market makers in governments, agencies, CDs, and BAs. Because dealers, by definition, buy and sell for their own accounts, active dealers will inevitably end up holding some securities. They will, moreover, buy and hold substantial positions if they believe that interest rates are likely to fall and that the value of these securities is therefore likely to rise. Speculation and risk taking are an inherent and important part of being a dealer.

While dealers have large amounts of capital, the positions they take are often several hundred times that amount. As a result, dealers have to borrow to finance their positions. Using the securities they own as collateral, they can and do borrow from banks at the dealer loan rate. For the bulk of their financing, however, they resort to a cheaper alternative, entering into *repurchase agreements* (*RPs or repos,* for short) with investors.

Much RP financing done by dealers is on an overnight basis. It works as follows: The dealer finds a corporation or other investor who has funds to invest overnight. He sells this investor, say, $10 million of securities for roughly $10 million, which is paid in Federal funds to his bank by the investor's bank against delivery of the securities sold. At the same time, the dealer agrees to repurchase these securities the next day at a slightly higher price. Thus, the buyer of the securities is in effect making the dealer a one-day loan secured by the obligations sold to him. The difference between the purchase and sale prices on the RP transaction is the interest the investor earns on his loan. Alternatively, the purchase and sale prices in an RP transaction may be identical; in that case, the dealer pays the investor some explicit rate of interest.

Often a dealer will take a speculative position that he intends to hold for some time. He might then do an RP for 30 days or longer. Such agreements are known as *term* RPs.

From the point of view of investors, overnight loans in the RP market offer several attractive features. First, by rolling overnight RPs, investors can keep surplus funds invested without losing liquidity or incurring a price risk. Second, because RP transactions are secured by top-quality paper, investors expose themselves to little or no credit risk.

The overnight RP rate generally is less than the Fed funds rate. The reason is that the many nonbank investors who have funds to invest overnight or very short term and who do not want to incur any price risk, have nowhere to go but the RP market because (with the exception of S&Ls) they cannot participate directly in the Fed funds market. Also, lending money through an RP transaction is safer than selling Fed funds because a sale of Fed funds is an unsecured loan.

On term, as opposed to overnight, RP transactions, investors still have the advantage of their loans being secured, but they do lose some liquidity. To compensate for that, the rate on an RP transaction is generally higher the longer the term for which funds are lent.

Banks that make dealer loans fund them by buying Fed funds, and the lending rate they charge—which is adjusted daily—is the prevailing Fed funds rate plus a one-eighth to one-quarter markup. Because the overnight RP rate is lower than the Fed funds rate, dealers can finance their positions more cheaply by doing RP than by borrowing from banks.

A dealer who is bullish on the market will position large amounts of securities. If he's bearish, he will *short* the market, that is, sell securities he does not own. Since the dealer has to deliver any securities he sells whether he owns them or not, a dealer who shorts has to borrow securities one way or another. The most common technique today for borrowing securities is to do what is called a *reverse RP,* or simply a *reverse.* To obtain securities through a reverse, a dealer finds an investor holding the required securities; he then buys these securities from the investor under an agreement that he will resell the same securities to the investor at a fixed price on some future date. In this transaction, the dealer, besides obtaining securities, is extending a loan to the investor for which he is paid some rate of interest.

An RP and a reverse are identical transactions. What a given transaction is called depends on who initiates it; typically, if a dealer hunting money does, it's an RP; if a dealer hunting securities does, it's a reverse.

A final note: The FED uses reverses and RPs with dealers in government securities to make adjustments in bank reserves.

MUNICIPAL NOTES

Debt securities issued by state and local governments and their agencies are referred to as *municipal securities.* Such securities can be divided into two broad categories: bonds issued to finance capital projects and short-term notes sold in anticipation of the receipt of other funds, such as taxes or proceeds from a bond issue.

Municipal notes, which are an important money market instrument, are issued with maturities ranging from a month to a year or more. They bear interest, and minimum denominations are highly variable ranging anywhere from $5,000 to $5 million.

Most muni notes are general obligation securities; that is, payment of principal and interest is secured by the issuer's pledge of its full faith, credit, and taxing power. This sounds impressive, but as the spectacle of New York City tottering on the brink of bankruptcy brought home to all, it is possible that a municipality might default on its securities. Thus, the investors in evaluating this risk, publicly offered muni notes are rated by Moody's. The one exception is project notes, which are issued by local housing authorities to finance federally sponsored programs and which are backed by the full faith and credit of the federal government.

The major attraction of municipal notes to an investor is that interest income on them is exempt from federal taxation and usually also from any income taxes levied within the state where they are issued. The value of this tax exemption is greater the higher the investor's tax bracket, and the muni market thus attracts only highly taxed investors— commercial banks, cash-rich corporations, and wealthy individuals.

Large muni note issues are sold to investors by dealers who obtain the securities either through negotiation with the issuer or through competitive bidding. The same dealers also make a secondary market in muni notes.

The yield a municipality must pay to issue notes depends on its credit rating, the length of time for which it borrows, and the general level of short-term rates. Normally, a good credit can borrow at a rate well below the yield on T bills of equivalent maturity because of the value to the investor of the tax exemption on the municipal security. A corporation that has its profits taxed at a 50 percent marginal rate would, for example, receive approximately the same aftertax return from a muni note yielding 5 percent that it would from a T bill yielding 10 percent.[7] For a corporation subject to high *state* income taxes, the difference between the rate offered on a municipal note issued in the firm's state of domicile and the bill rate that would give the firm the same aftertax return would be substantially higher.

---

[7] We say "approximately" because most muni notes are sold on an *interest-bearing* basis while bills are quoted on a *discount* rate, so that the rates at which the two securities are offered are rarely directly comparable.

Chapter 4

Discount and interest-bearing securities

BANKS DEAL IN ESSENTIALLY TWO TYPES of securities, *interest-bearing securities* and *discount paper*. Yields on these two types of instruments are calculated and quoted in quite different ways. Thus, a discussion of banking should be prefaced by some simple math which shows how yields on these different instruments are calculated and how they can be made comparable. We start with discount securities.[1]

TREASURY BILLS

To illustrate how a discount security works, we assume that an investor who participates in an auction of new Treasury *year bills* picks up $1 million of them at 10%. What this means is that the Treasury sells the investor $1 million of bills maturing in one year at a price approximately 10% below their face value. The "approximately" qualifier takes a little explaining. Offhand one would expect the amount of the discount to be the face value of the securities purchased times the rate of discount times the *fraction of the year* the securities will be outstanding. In our

---

[1] For a complete description, see Marcia Stigum in collaboration with John Mann, *Money Market Calculations: Yields, Break-Evens, and Arbitrage* (Homewood, Ill.: Dow Jones-Irwin, 1981).

example, the discount calculated this way would equal $1 million times 10% times one full year, which amounts to $100,000. That figure, however, is incorrect for two reasons. First, the year bill is outstanding not for a year but for 52 weeks, which is 364 days. Second, the Treasury calculates the discount as if a year had only 360 days. So the fraction of the year for which the security is outstanding is 364/360, and the true discount on the security is:

$$\begin{pmatrix} \text{Discount on \$1 million of} \\ \text{year bills issued at 10\%} \end{pmatrix} = \$1,000,000 \times 0.10 \times \frac{364}{360}$$
$$= \$101,111.11$$

Because the Treasury calculates the discount as if the year had 360 days, our investor gets his bills at a discount that exceeds $100,000 even though he invests for only 364 days. The price he pays for his bills equals *face value minus the discount,* i.e.,

$$\begin{pmatrix} \text{Price paid for \$1 million of} \\ \text{year bills bought at 10\%} \end{pmatrix} = \$1,000,000 - \$101,111.11$$
$$= \$898,888.89$$

Generalizing from this example, we can construct formulas for calculating both the discount from face value and the price at which T bills will sell, depending on their current maturity and the discount at which they are quoted. Let

D = discount from face value
F = face value
d = rate of discount
t = days to maturity
P = price

Then

$$D = F\left(\frac{d \times t}{360}\right)$$

and

$$P = F - D = F\left(1 - \frac{d \times t}{360}\right)$$

EQUIVALENT BOND YIELD

If an investor lent $1 million for one 365-day year and received at the end of the year $100,000 of interest plus the $1 million of principal invested, we would—calculating yield on a *simple interest basis*—say that he had earned 10%.[2] Using the same approach—return earned divided by principal invested—to calculate the return earned by our investor who bought a 10% year bill, we find that, on a simple interest basis, he earned significantly *more than* 10%. Specifically,

$$\left(\begin{array}{l}\text{Return on a simple interest basis on}\\ \text{\$1 million 10\% year bills held to maturity}\end{array}\right) = \frac{\$101,000.11}{\$898,888.89} \div \frac{364}{365}$$

$$= 11.28\%$$

In this calculation, because the bill matures in 364 days, it is necessary to divide by the fraction of the year for which the bill is outstanding to annualize the rate earned.

Treasury notes and bonds, which—unlike bills—are *interest bearing*, pay the holder interest equal to the face value times the interest (i.e., *coupon*) rate at which they are issued. Thus, an investor who bought $1 million of Treasury notes carrying a 10% coupon would receive $100,000 of interest during each year the securities were outstanding.

The way yields on notes and bonds are quoted, 10% notes selling at *par* (i.e., face value) would be quoted as offering a 10% yield. An investor who bought these notes would, however, have the opportunity to earn more than 10% simple interest. The reason is that interest on notes and bonds is paid in semiannual installments, which means that the investor can invest, during the second six months of each year, the first semiannual interest installment.

To illustrate the effect of this on return, consider an investor who buys at issue $1 million of 10% Treasury notes. Six months later, he receives $50,000 of interest, which we assume he reinvests at 10%. Then at the end of the year, he receives another $50,000 of interest plus interest on the interest he has invested; the latter amounts to $50,000 times 10% times the one-half year he earns that interest. Thus, his total dollar return over the year is:

$$\$50,000 + (0.10)(\$50,000)(0.5) + \$50,000 = \$102,500$$

and the percentage return that he earns, expressed in terms of simple interest, is

$$\frac{\$102,500}{\$1,000,000} = 10.25\%$$

Note that what is at work here is *compound interest;* any quoted rate of interest yields more dollars of return, and is thus equivalent to a higher simple interest rate, the more frequently interest is paid and the more compounding that can thus occur.

---

[2] By *simple interest* we mean interest paid once a year at the end of the year. There is no compounding as, for example, on a savings account.

Because return can mean different things depending on the way it is quoted and paid, an investor can meaningfully compare the returns offered by different securities only if these returns are stated on a comparable basis. With respect to *discount* and *coupon* securities, the way yields are made comparable in the money market is by restating yields quoted on a *discount basis*—the basis on which T bills are quoted—in terms of *equivalent bond yield*—the basis on which yields on notes and bonds are quoted.

We calculated above that an investor in a year bill would, on a simple interest basis, earn 11.28%. This is slightly higher than the rate he would earn measured on an equivalent bond yield basis. The reason is that equivalent bond yield understates, as noted, the true return on a simple interest basis that the investor in a coupon security would earn if he reinvested interest. When adjustment is made for this understatement, the equivalent bond yield offered by a 10% year bill turns out to be something less than 11.28%. Specifically, it is 10.98%.

The formula for converting yield on a bank discount basis to equivalent bond yield is complicated for discount securities that have a current maturity of longer than 6 months, but that is no problem for investors and other money market participants because bill yields are always restated on dealers' quote sheets in terms of equivalent bond yield at the *asked* rate (Table 4–1).

TABLE 4–1
Selected quotes on U.S. Treasury bills, October 21, 1982

Billions outstanding	Days to maturity	Maturity	Discount (%) Bid	Discount (%) Asked	Dollar price	Equivalent bond yield
10.2	3	10/28/82	7.20	7.00	99.942	7.10
10.4	32	11/26/82	7.24	7.14	99.365	7.29
15.9	66	12/30/82	7.52	7.42	98.640	7.63
11.1	87	1/20/83	7.62	7.52	98.183	7.73
10.8	122	2/24/83	7.85	7.75	97.374	8.07
10.9	150	3/24/83	7.95	7.85	96.729	8.23
10.9	178	4/21/83	8.00	7.90	96.094	8.34
5.3	206	5/19/83	8.20	8.10	95.365	8.57
6.3	290	8/11/83	8.45	8.35	93.274	8.93
7.0	346	10/6/83	8.32	8.28	92.042	8.93

On bills with a current maturity of 6 months or less, equivalent bond yield is the simple interest rate yielded by a bill. Let

$$d_b = \text{equivalent bond yield}$$

Then, on a security quoted at the discount rate *d,* equivalent bond yield is given by

$$d_b = \frac{365 \times d}{360 - (d \times t)}$$

For example, on a 3-month bill purchased at 8%, equivalent bond yield is

$$d_b = \frac{365 \times 0.08}{360 - (0.08 \times 91)} = 8.28\%$$

From the examples we have considered, it is clear that the yield on a discount security is *significantly less* when measured on a discount basis than when measured in terms of equivalent bond yield. The absolute divergence between these two measures of yield is, moreover, not constant. As Table 4–2 shows, the greater the yield and the longer the maturity of the security, the greater the divergence.

TABLE 4–2
Comparisons, at different rates and maturities, of rates of discount and equivalent bond yields

Yields on a discount basis (%)	Equivalent bond yields (%)		
	30-day maturity	182-day maturity	364-day maturity
6	6.114	6.274	6.375
8	8.166	8.453	8.639
10	10.227	10.679	10.979
12	12.290	12.952	13.399
14	14.362	15.256	15.904

MONEY MARKET YIELD

Equivalent bond yield on a bill is calculated on the basis of a 365-day year. Bill rates are—to make them directly comparable to rates on CDs and other interest-bearing, money market instruments—often converted to a simple interest rate on a 360-day-year basis. That number, dubbed *money market yield,* is obtained by substituting 360 for 365 in the above equation for equivalent bond yield; specifically,

$$\binom{\text{money market yield}}{\text{on a bill}} = \frac{360 - d}{360 - (d \times t)}$$

FLUCTUATIONS IN A BILL'S PRICE

Normally, the price at which a bill sells will rise as the bill approaches maturity. For example, to yield 9% on a discount basis, a 6-month bill must be priced at $95.45 per $100 of face value. For the same bill three months later (three months closer to maturity) to yield 9%, it must have risen in price to $97.72. The moral is clear: If a bill always sold at the same yield throughout its life, its price would rise steadily toward face value as it approached maturity.

A bill's yield, however, is unlikely to be constant over time; instead, it will fluctuate for two reasons: (1) changes may occur in the general level of short-term interest rates, and (2) the bill will move along *the yield curve.* Let's look at each of these factors.

Short-term interest rates

T bills are issued through auctions in which discounted prices (yields) are bid. The rate of discount determined at auction on a new bill issue depends on the level of short-term interest rates prevailing at the moment of the auction. The reason is straightforward. Investors who want to buy bills at the time of a Treasury auction have two alternatives—to buy new bills or to buy existing bills from dealers. This being the case, investors will not bid for new bills a rate of discount lower than that available on existing bills. If they did, they would be offering to buy new bills at a price higher than that at which they could buy existing bills. Also, investors will not bid substantially higher rates of discount (lower prices) than those prevailing on existing bills. If they did, they would not obtain bills, since they would surely be underbid by others trying to get just a slightly better return than that available on existing securities. Thus, the prevailing level of short-term rates determines, within a narrow range, the discount established on new bills at issue.

However, the going level of short-term rates is not constant over time. It rises and falls in response to changes in economic activity, the demand for credit, investors' expectations, and monetary policy as set by the Federal Reserve System. Figure 4–1, which plots rates on 6-month T bills for the period 1970–82, portrays vividly the volatility of short-term interest rates. It shows both the sharp ups and downs that occurred in these rates as the Fed successively eased and tightened and the myriad of smaller fluctuations over the period in response to short-lived changes in other determinants of these rates.

If the going level of short-term rates (which establishes the rate at which a bill is initially sold) falls after a bill is issued, then this bill—as long as its price doesn't change—will yield more than new bills. Therefore, buyers will compete for this bill, and in doing so, they will drive up its price and thereby force down its yield until the bill sells at a rate of discount equal to the new, lower going interest rate. Conversely, if short-term rates rise after a bill is issued, the unwillingness of buyers to purchase any bill at a discount less than that available on new issues will drive down its price and thereby force up its yield.

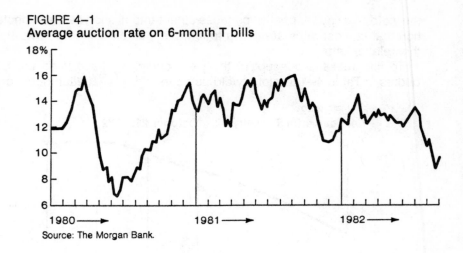

FIGURE 4–1
Average auction rate on 6-month T bills

Source: The Morgan Bank.

The yield curve

Even if the going level of short-term interest rates does not change while investors hold bills, it would be normal for the rate at which they could sell their bills to change. The reason lies in the *yield curve*. How this works is a function of several factors, described below.

Price risk. In choosing among alternative securities, an investor considers three things: risk, liquidity, and return. Purchase of a money market instrument exposes an investor to two sorts of risk: (1) *credit risk:* Will the issuer pay off at maturity? and (2) *price risk:* If the investor later sold the security, might he have to do so at a loss because interest rates had subsequently risen? Most money market investors are risk averse, which means that they will accept lower yields to obtain lower risk.

The price risk to which bills and other money market instruments expose the investor is *larger* the *longer* their current maturity. To see why, suppose that short-term interest rates rise a full percentage point across the board; then the prices of all bill issues will drop, *but the price drop will be greater, the longer an issue's current maturity*. For example, a 1 percentage point rise in market rates would cause a 3-month bill to fall only $2,500 in price per $1 million of face value, whereas the corresponding price drop on a 9-month bill would be $7,600 per $1 million of face value.

The slope of the yield curve. Because a 3-month bill exposes the investor to less price risk than a 9-month bill does, it will normally yield less than a 9-month bill. In other words, the bill market yield curve, which shows the relationship between yield and current maturity, normally slopes upward, indicating that the longer the time to maturity, the higher the yield. We say "normally" because other factors, such as the expectation that interest rates are going to fall, may, as explained below, alter this relationship.

To illustrate the concept of the yield curve, we have used the bid quotes in Table 4–1 to plot a yield curve in Figure 4–2; each dot is one

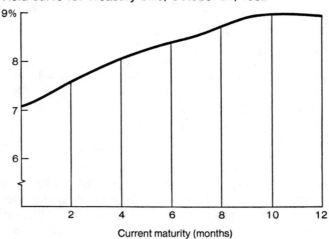

FIGURE 4–2
Yield curve for Treasury bills, October 21, 1982

Current maturity (months)

quote. Our results show a normal upward-sloping yield curve. Lest you try doing the same and be disappointed, we should admit that we cheated a bit in putting together our demonstration yield curve. On November 25, 1981, there were many more bill issues outstanding than those quoted in Table 4–1. Had we plotted yields on all of these in Figure 4–2, we would have found that yield did not rise quite so consistently with maturity; the points plotted for some bill issues would have been somewhat off a smooth yield curve. Yields may be out of line for various reasons. For example, a bill issue maturing around a tax date might be highly desired by investors who had big tax payments to make and, for this reason, trade at a yield that was relatively low compared to yields on surrounding issues.

While the yield curve for short maturities normally slopes upward, its shape and slope vary over time. Thus, it is difficult to pinpoint a "normal" spread between, say, 1-month and 6-month bills. Yield spreads between different securities are always measured in terms of basis points. *A basis point is 1/100th of 1 percentage point.* Thus, if 5-month bills are quoted at 10.45 and 6-month bills at 10.56, the spread between the two is said to be 11 basis points. A yield spread between two securities of 100 basis points would indicate a full 1% difference in their yields. A basis point is also frequently referred to as an 01.

Yield realized on sales before maturity

If an investor buys 1-year bills at 10% and holds them to maturity, he will earn, on a discount basis, precisely 10% over the holding period. If, alternatively, he sells the bills before maturity, he will earn 10% over the holding period only if he sells at 10%, a relatively unlikely outcome. If he sells at a lower rate, he will get a higher price for his bills than he would have if he had sold them at 10%, and he will therefore earn more than 10%. If, on the other hand, he sells at a rate higher than 10%, he will earn something less than 10%.

The holding period yield as a simple interest rate that an investor earns on bills purchased at one rate and subsequently sold at another can be calculated using the formula

$$i = \frac{\text{Sales price} - \text{Purchase price}}{\text{Purchase price}} \div \frac{t}{365}$$

where t equals the number of days held. To illustrate, assume that an investor buys \$1 million of 1-year bills at 10% and sells them three months later at 10.25%. His holding-period yield would be

$$i = \frac{\$924,166.67 - \$898,888.89}{\$898,888.89} \div \frac{91}{365} = 11.23\%$$

Bankers' acceptances and commercial paper

In talking about discount securities, we have focused on bills since they are the most important discount security traded in the money market. All we have said about yields on bills is, however, equally applicable to yields on BAs and commercial paper, both of which are sold on a discount basis with the discount being calculated on a 360-day year.

INTEREST-BEARING SECURITIES

The stock-in-trade of the money market includes, besides discount securities, a variety of *interest-bearing* instruments: Treasury and federal agency notes and bonds, municipal notes and bonds, and bank certificates of deposit. Notes, bonds, and other interest-bearing debt securities are issued with a fixed *face value;* they mature at some specified date and carry a *coupon rate* which is the annual interest rate the issuer promises to pay the holder on the security's face value while the security is outstanding.

Some notes and bonds are issued in *registered* form; that is, the issuer keeps track of who owns its outstanding IOUs, just as a corporation keeps track of who owns its common stock. Most notes and bonds, however, are issued in *bearer* form. To prove ownership of a bearer security, the owner must produce or bear it. An issuer with $50 million of bearer bonds outstanding does not know where to send interest when a payment date comes along. Consequently, such securities carry *coupons,* one for each interest date. On the interest date, the investor or his bank clips the appropriate coupon from the security and sends it to the issuer's paying agent, who, in turn, makes the required payment.[3] Generally, interest payments are made semiannually on coupon securities. Because notes and bonds carry coupons, the return paid on face value is called the *coupon rate* or simply the *coupon.*

Notes and bonds with a short current maturity are referred to as *short coupons,* those with an intermediate current maturity (2 to 7 years) as *intermediate coupons,* and those with a still longer current maturity as *long coupons.*

Call and refunding provisions

Once a bond issue is sold, the issuer might choose to redeem it early. For example, if interest rates fell, the borrower could reduce his interest costs by refunding his loan; that is, by paying off outstanding high-coupon bonds and issuing new lower-coupon bonds.

For the investor, early repayment on a bond is almost always disadvantageous because a bond issuer will rarely be tempted to repay early when interest rates are rising, a time when it would be to the bondholder's advantage to move funds out of the issuer's bonds into new, higher-yielding bonds. On the other hand, early payment looks attractive to the issuer when interest rates are falling, a time when it is to the investor's advantage to keep funds invested in the issuer's high-coupon securities.

To protect investors making long-term commitments against frequent refundings by borrowers out to minimize interest costs, most bonds contain call and refunding provisions. A bond issue is said to be *callable* when the issuer has the option to repay part or all of the issue early by paying some specified redemption price to bondholders. Most bonds offer some call protection to the investor. Some are noncallable for life, others for some number of years after issue.

Besides call protection, many bonds offer refunding protection. Typically, long-term industrial bonds are immediately callable *but* offer 10

---

[3] The procedure is different on Treasury and agency securities, which are now being issued in *book-entry* form; computerized records of ownership maintained by the Fed and banks have been substituted for actual securities.

years of protection against calls for refunding. Such a bond is referred to as *callable except for refunding purposes.* If a bond offered refunding protection through 1985, that would be indicated on a dealer's quote sheet by the symbol NR85.

Call provisions usually specify that the issuer who calls a bond must pay the bondholder a price above face value. The *call premium* frequently equals the coupon rate on early calls and then diminishes to zero as the bond approaches maturity.

Price quotes

Note and bond prices are quoted in slightly different ways depending on whether they are selling in the new issue or the secondary market. When notes and bonds other than governments are issued, the price at which they are offered to investors is normally quoted as a *percentage* of face value. To illustrate, the corporate mortgage bonds announced in Figure 4–3 were offered at a price of 99⅛%, which means that the investor had to pay $99.125 for each $100 of face value. This percentage price is often called the bond's *dollar price*. The security described in Figure 4–3 was offered below par, so the actual yield it offered exceeded the coupon rate of 16.25%.

Once a note or bond issue is distributed and trading in it moves to the secondary market, prices are also quoted on a percentage basis but always, depending on the security, in 32ds, 8ths, 4ths, or halves. Table 4–3 reproduces, by way of illustration, a few quotes on Treasury notes

TABLE 4–3
Quotations for selected U.S. Treasury notes, October, 21, 1982*

Publicly held ($ billions)	Coupon	Maturity	Bid	Asked	Yield to maturity	Yield value (1/32)
4.55.	13⅞	11/30/82	100–16	100–20	7.08	.3013
9.53.	12⅛	9/30/84	103–20	103–22	9.97	.0177
5.00.	12¼	9/30/86	105–16	105–18	10.48	.0096
9.00.	13¾	5/15/92	114–31	115– 3	11.14	.0049
4.49.	14	11/15/11–06	126–22	126–30	10.83	.0030

* The last issue quoted matures in 2011 but is callable in 2006. Its maturity, 11/15/11–06, indicates this.

and bonds posted by a dealer on October 21, 1982. The first bid is 100–16, meaning that this dealer was willing to pay $100¹⁶⁄₃₂, which equals $100.50 per $100 of face value for that issue. The advantage of dollar pricing of notes and bonds is that it makes the prices of securities with different denominations directly comparable.

FIGURE 4–3
Pricing announcement for corporate mortgage bonds

This announcement is neither an offer to sell nor a solicitation of an offer to buy any of these Securities. The offer is made only by the Prospectus.

$100,000,000

Louisiana Power & Light Company

First Mortgage Bonds, 16¼% Series Due December 1, 1991

Interest payable June 1 and December 1

Price 99⅛% and Accrued Interest

Copies of the Prospectus may be obtained in any State from only such of the undersigned as may legally offer these Securities in compliance with the securities laws of such State.

MORGAN STANLEY & CO. Incorporated — DEAN WITTER REYNOLDS INC.

THE FIRST BOSTON CORPORATION — MERRILL LYNCH WHITE WELD CAPITAL MARKETS GROUP (Merrill Lynch, Pierce, Fenner & Smith Incorporated) — SALOMON BROTHERS INC

BACHE HALSEY STUART SHIELDS Incorporated — BEAR, STEARNS & CO. — BLYTH EASTMAN PAINE WEBBER Incorporated

DILLON, READ & CO. INC. — DONALDSON, LUFKIN & JENRETTE Securities Corporation — DREXEL BURNHAM LAMBERT Incorporated

E. F. HUTTON & COMPANY INC. — KIDDER, PEABODY & CO. Incorporated — LAZARD FRERES & CO.

LEHMAN BROTHERS KUHN LOEB Incorporated — L. F. ROTHSCHILD, UNTERBERG, TOWBIN

SHEARSON/AMERICAN EXPRESS INC. — SMITH BARNEY, HARRIS UPHAM & CO. Incorporated — WARBURG PARIBAS BECKER Incorporated

WERTHEIM & CO., INC. — HOWARD, WEIL, LABOUISSE, FRIEDRICHS Incorporated

ATLANTIC CAPITAL Corporation — BASLE SECURITIES CORPORATION — ALEX. BROWN & SONS

MOSELEY, HALLGARTEN, ESTABROOK & WEEDEN INC. — OPPENHEIMER & CO., INC.

THE ROBINSON-HUMPHREY COMPANY, INC. — THOMSON McKINNON SECURITIES INC.

TUCKER, ANTHONY & R. L. DAY, INC. — ADVEST, INC. — ARNHOLD AND S. BLEICHROEDER, INC.

SANFORD C. BERNSTEIN & CO., INC. — JANNEY MONTGOMERY SCOTT INC.

LADENBURG, THALMANN & CO. INC. — NOMURA SECURITIES INTERNATIONAL, INC.

November 25, 1981

Treatment of interest in pricing

There's another wrinkle with respect to note and bond pricing. Typically, interest on notes and bonds is paid to the holder semiannually on the coupon dates. This means that the value of a coupon security rises by the amount of interest accrued as a payment date approaches and falls thereafter by the amount of the payment made. Since notes and bonds are issued on every business day and consequently have coupon dates all over the calendar, the effect of accrued interest on the value of coupon securities would, if incorporated into the prices quoted by dealers, make meaningful price comparisons between different issues difficult. To get around this problem, the actual prices paid in the new issue and secondary markets are always the quoted dollar price *plus* any accrued interest. For example, if an investor—three months before a coupon date—bought $100,000 of 12% Treasury notes quoted at 100, he would pay $100,000 plus $3,000 of accrued interest:

$$\$100,000 + 0.5\left[\frac{(0.12)(\$100,000)}{2}\right]$$

where (0.12)($100,000)/2 represents the $6,000 semiannual interest due on the notes.

Fluctuations in a coupon security's price

When a new note or bond issue comes to market, the coupon rate on it is, with certain exceptions, set so that it equals the yield prevailing in the market on securities of comparable maturity and risk. This permits the new security to be sold at a price equal or nearly equal to par.

The price at which the security later trades in the secondary market will, like that of a discount security, fluctuate in response to changes in the general level of interest rates.

Yield to maturity. To illustrate, let's work through a simple example. Suppose a new 6-year note with an 8% coupon is issued at par. Six months later, the Fed tightens, and the yield on comparable securities rises to 8.5%. Now what is this 8% security worth? Since the investor who pays a price equal to par for this "seasoned issue" is going to get only an 8% return, while 8.5% is available elsewhere, it is clear that the security must now sell at *less* than par.

To determine how much less, we have to introduce a new concept—*effective yield*. When an investor buys a coupon security at a *discount* and holds it to maturity, he receives a two-part return: the promised interest payment *plus* a capital gain. The capital gain arises because the security that the investor bought at less than par is redeemed at maturity for full face value. The investor who buys a coupon issue at a *premium* and holds it to maturity also receives a two-part return: interest payments due plus a capital *loss* equal to the premium paid.

For dollars invested in a coupon issue that sells at a discount or premium, it is possible to calculate the overall or effective rate of return received, which is the rate that the investor earns on his dollars when both interest received *and* capital gains (or losses) are taken into account. Naturally, an investor choosing between securities of similar risk and maturity will do so not on the basis of coupon rate but on the basis of effective yield, referred to in the financial community as *yield to maturity*.

To get back to our example, it is clear that once rates rise to 8.5% in the open market, the security with an 8% coupon has to be priced at a discount sufficiently great so that its yield to maturity equals 8.5%. Figuring out how many dollars of discount this requires involves complicated calculations. Dealers used to use bond tables, but all have now switched to bond calculators. A trader can thus determine in a few seconds that, with interest rates at 8.5%, a $1,000 note with an 8% coupon and a 3½-year current maturity must sell at $985.13 (a discount of $14.87) to yield 8.5% to maturity.

Current maturity and price volatility. A capital gain of $14.87. which is what the investor in our discounted 8% note would realize if he held it to maturity, will raise effective yield more the faster this gain is realized (the shorter the current maturity of the security). Conversely, this capital gain will raise effective yield less the more slowly it is realized (the longer the current maturity of the security).[4]

But if this is so, then a one-half percentage point rise in the yield on comparable securities will cause a larger fall in price for a security with a long current maturity than for one with a short current maturity. In other words, the discount required to raise a coupon security's yield to maturity by one-half percentage point is *greater* the *longer* the security's maturity.

By reversing the argument above, it is easy to see that if six months after the 6-year, 8% note in our example was issued, the yield on comparable securities *fell* to 7.5%, the value of this note would be driven to a *premium;* i.e., it would sell at a price above par. Note also that a one-half percentage point *fall* in the yield on comparable securities would force an outstanding high-coupon security to a *greater* premium the *longer* its current maturity.

As these observations suggest, when prevailing interest rates change, prices of long coupons respond more dramatically than prices of short coupons. Figure 4–4 shows this sharp contrast. It pictures, for a $1,000 note carrying an 8% coupon, the relationship between *current* maturity and the discount that would prevail if the yield on comparable securities rose to 8.5% or to 10%. It also plots the premium to which a $1,000 note with an 8% coupon would, depending on its current maturity, be driven if the yield on comparable securities fell to 6%.

---

[4] If you don't see this, just think—somewhat imprecisely—of the capital gain as a certain number of dollars of extra interest paid out in yearly installments to the investor as his security matures. Clearly, the shorter the security's current maturity, the higher these extra annual interest installments will be and, consequently, the higher the overall yield to the investor.

FIGURE 4–4
Premiums and discounts at which a $1,000 note with an 8%
coupon would sell, depending on current maturity, if market
yields on comparable securities were 6%, 8.5%, and 10%.

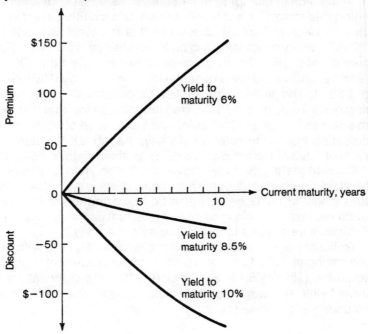

Coupon and price volatility.   The volatility of a note or bond's price in the face of changing interest rates also depends on its coupon; the *lower* the coupon, the *greater* the percentage change in price that will occur when rates rise or fall. To illustrate, consider two notes with 4-year current maturities. Note A has an 8% coupon and note B a 6% coupon. Both are priced to yield 8%. Suppose now that interest rates on comparable securities rise to 10% (the big credit crunch arrives). Note A will fall in price by $6.46; since it was initially priced at $100, that works out to a 6.46% fall in value. Note B's dollar price drops from $93.27 to $87.07—a $6.20 fall, which equals a 6.64% loss of value. The reason for the greater percentage fall in the price of the low-coupon note is that capital appreciation represents a greater proportion of promised income (capital appreciation plus coupon interest) on the low coupon than on the high coupon. Therefore, for the low-coupon note's yield to maturity to rise two percentage points, its price has to fall relatively *more* than that of the high-coupon note.

Yield value of 1/32:   Prices of government and federal agency securities are quoted in 32ds. The greater the change in yield to maturity that results from a price change of 1/32, the less volatile the issue's price will be in the face of changing interest rates. As a result, dealers include on their quote sheets for such securities a column titled *Yield value of 1/32*. Looking back at Table 4–3, we see that the yield value of 1/32 on the 137/8s Treasury notes maturing on November 30, 1982, was .3013, which means that a fall in the asked price on this security from 100–20 to 100–19 (a 1/32 fall) would have raised yield to maturity by 0.3013%, from 7.08 to 7.3813. The yield value of 1/32 drops sharply as current maturity lengthens. Thus, on the 133/4s Treasury bonds maturing on May 15, 1992 (the next to last line of the table), the yield value of 1/32 was only .0049, indicating that these notes would have had to fall in value by approximately 61.5/32 (1 point plus 28.5/32) for their yield to rise 0.3013%.

Current yield.   So far we have focused on yield to maturity, which is the yield figure always quoted on coupon securities. When the investor buys a note or bond, he may also be interested in knowing what rate of return interest payments per se will give him on the principal he invests. This measure of yield is referred to as *current yield*.

To illustrate, consider our earlier example of a note with an 8% coupon selling at $985.13 to yield 8.5% to maturity. Current yield on this note would be: ($80/$985.13) × 100, or 8.12%. On a discount note or bond, current yield is always less than yield to maturity; on a premium bond it exceeds yield to maturity.

THE YIELD CURVE

From the examples we have worked through, it is clear that investors in notes and bonds expose themselves, like buyers of discount securities, to a *price risk*. Moreover, even though longer-term rates fluctuate less violently than do short-term rates (Figure 4–5), the price risk associated with holding debt securities tends to be greater the longer the current maturity. Thus, one would expect the yield curve to slope upward over the full maturity spectrum. And often it does.

Price risk, however, is not the only factor affecting the shape of the yield curve. Borrowers' and investors' *expectations* with respect to future interest rates are also an important—at times dominant—factor.

If the general expectation is that interest rates are going to rise, investors will seek to keep their money in short coupons to avoid getting locked into low-yield, long coupons. Borrowers, on the other hand, will try to lengthen the maturity of their outstanding debt to lock in prevailing low rates for as long as possible. Both responses tend to force short-term rates down and long-term rates up, thereby accentuating the upward slope of the yield curve. The expectation that interest rates would rise

FIGURE 4–5
Short-term rates are more volatile than long-term rates: Rate
comparison—3-month T bill, 5-year note, and 20-year bond (monthly
averages through August 1982)

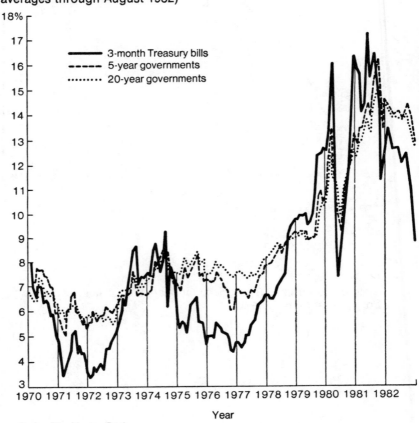

Source: The Morgan Bank.

was widespread in August 1975, the time of the yield curve pictured in
Figure 4–6, this expectation explains in part why the yield curve sloped
so steeply upward.

People, of course, may expect interest rates to fall. When this is the
case, investors respond by buying long coupons in the hope of locking
in a high yield. In contrast, borrowers are willing to pay extremely high
short-term rates while they wait for long rates to fall so that they can
borrow more cheaply. The net result of both responses is that, when
interest rates are expected to fall, the yield curve (or at least some part of
it) may be *inverted,* with short-term rates above long-term rates. Figure
4–7 pictures the yield curve on February 4, 1980, when people antici-

FIGURE 4–6
Yield curve for U.S. Treasury securities—bills, notes, and bonds—August 19, 1975*

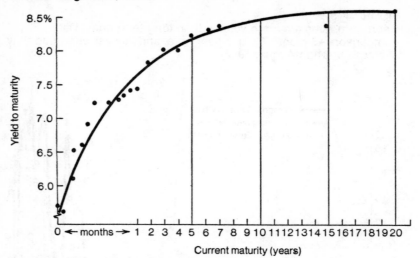

* Dots represent observed yields, yield curve is fitted to them.

FIGURE 4–7
Yield curve for U.S. Treasury securities—bills, notes, and bonds—February 4, 1980.

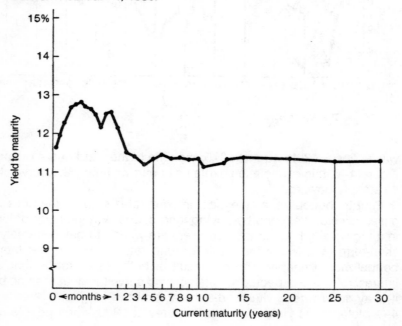

pated a fall in rates. Note that after a current maturity of 1 month, the slope of this curve becomes negative.

If, inspired by our yield curves, you start poring over dealer quote sheets on governments, you are bound to discover some out-of-line yields. The reasons are varied.[5] For one thing, sale of a large new issue may cause a temporary upward bulge in the yield curve in the maturity range of the new issue. Also, a security with an out-of-line yield may have some special characteristic. Some government bonds (*flower bonds* to the street) are acceptable at par in payment of federal estate taxes when owned by the decedent at the time of death. These bonds, which all sell at substantial discounts, have yields to maturity much lower than those on straight government bonds.

In calculating the yield on discount securities, we found a considerable discrepancy between yield measured on a discount basis and equivalent bond yield. There are also many discrepancies—albeit smaller ones—between the ways that interest is measured and quoted on different interest-bearing securities. For example, interest on Treasury notes is calculated for actual days on the basis of a 365-day year, while interest on CDs is calculated for actual days on the basis of a 360-day year. Thus, a 1-year CD issued at 10% would yield a higher return than a 10% year note selling at par. Partially offsetting this advantage, however, is the fact that a 1-year CD would pay interest only at maturity, whereas a 1-year note would pay it semiannually. This disadvantage disappears, however, on CDs with a maturity longer than 1 year, since such CDs pay interest semiannually.

Another discrepancy: When government notes and bonds are sold, accrued interest is calculated between coupon dates on the basis of actual days passed since a coupon date, while on agency securities it accrues as if every month had 30 days. Thus, for example, agency securities accrue no interest on October 31, but they do accrue interest on February 30!

These and the many other minor discrepancies among yields on interest-bearing securities have little importance for understanding the workings of the money market, but they are important to the market participant out to maximize return.

---

[5] One trivial reason may be a mistake in the quote sheet. These are typically compiled daily in great haste with the result that errors creep in. For this reason, such sheets often carry a footnote stating that the quotes are believed to be reliable but are not "guaranteed."

Part two

The major players

Chapter 5

The banks:
Domestic operations

THERE ARE VARIOUS PEOPLE, including bankers, who have an image problem. The first "crime" bankers are widely charged with is creating a situation in which interest rates range from high to damnably high. Their second alleged "crime" is that they periodically threaten the whole economy by acting so irresponsibly that some of them end up having problems or, worse still, failing.

Both charges reflect several serious misconceptions entertained by much of the public and more than a few politicians. First, low interest rates are always good for the economy. Second, it is bankers, not the Fed, that set the general level of short-term interest rates. Third, banking is riskless or, alternatively, riskless banking is what the country needs. Fourth, the Fed would permit or might not be able to avoid the failure of one or more major banks, which would indeed wreak economic havoc. None of these misconceptions is easy to correct; hence, bankers' rather intractable image problem. To be a banker is to be neither widely understood nor loved. It is not, however, to be unimportant. In the money market, in particular, bankers are players of such major importance that any serious discussion of the various markets that comprise the money market must be prefaced with a careful look at banking.

In the United States, unlike in most foreign countries, bank branching has always been severely restricted. Because bank charters were initially granted only by the states, banks have never been permitted to branch interstate, and in most states—California being a notable exception—even intrastate branching is severely restricted or prohibited.[1] As a result there are in the United States currently over 15,000 banks. Comparing the largest and the smallest, one might almost conclude that the most they have in common is the name *bank*. Actually that's extreme; all institutions called banks accept deposits, make loans, and have at least a few government securities on their balance sheets. There, however, the similarity between the largest banks and their smaller sisters ends.

A MONEY MARKET BANK

The nation's largest banks, true giants, are often referred to as *money market* or *money center banks*. The term *money market bank* is apropos, since activity in every sector of the money market is strongly influenced and in some cases even dominated by the operations of these institutions. Thus, to understand the money market, one has to begin by studying the great banks.

While it's easy to talk about a money market bank, it is not so easy to list just which banks are included in this category. The property of being a money market bank is, like liquidity, something measured in degrees. Certainly all of the nation's top 10 banks are important money market banks. As one goes further down the list of U.S. banks ranked by size, one continues to find banks that are active in some if not all sectors of the money market, but the smaller a bank's size and the narrower its range of activities, the smaller the likely impact of those activities. At some point as bank size diminishes, one encounters what is clearly a regional bank of secondary importance as opposed to a money market bank of primary importance. The Wachovia Bank and Trust Company, the 32nd largest bank in the country, is big and important; it's also clearly not in the same class as the Chase Manhattan, the third largest bank.

The activities of a money market bank encompass several separate but related businesses. All money market banks engage in traditional banking operations: lending, managing an investment portfolio, and running a trust department. In addition, a number act as dealers in government securities and as dealers in and underwriters of municipal securities, and several have extensive operations for clearing money market trades for nonbank dealers. A final important activity in which major banks engage is foreign operations. Banks operate abroad in two ways.

---

[1] A state may, as a few (South Dakota and Alaska) have done, pass legislation permitting out-of-state banks to enter the state. First Interstate, operating in a number of western states, benefits from grandfathering provisions.

They participate as lenders and borrowers in the broad international capital market known as the *Euromarket;* they also operate within the confines of other national capital markets, accepting deposits and making loans in local currency.

Of the various banking activities we have described, two—trust operations and clearing operations per se as opposed to granting dealer loans—could be described as largely off-balance-sheet profit centers. Both require capital in the form of space and equipment but do not require substantial funding from the bank. The trust department invests other people's money, and the clearing operation provides a service. In contrast, the banks' three other primary domestic activities—lending, running a portfolio, and dealing in securities—have to be funded, since each involves acquiring substantial assets.

To finance its operations, a money market bank draws funds from various sources. It starts with a fairly stable base of money—bank capital and the demand, savings, and small-denomination time deposits it receives in the normal course of its commercial banking activities. The total of these is typically far below the value of the assets the bank wants to finance, so there is a funding gap that the bank fills by buying money in the Federal funds market, the CD market, the RP market, and at times the Euromarket.[2]

As the above suggests, managing a money market bank involves a host of decisions concerning what assets to hold and what liabilities to incur. Before we say more about these, two comments are in order. First, one cannot separate a bank's domestic operations from its foreign operations, but we are going to try—treating domestic operations in this chapter and Euro operations in the next; the Euromarket is a fascinating and complex story that deserves a full chapter. Second, money market banks are, as indicated by Table 5-1, a disparate collection of animals. Some of their differences reflect differences in circumstances: The Bank of America (B of A) with more than 1,000 domestic branches is deposit rich; the Morgan with four domestic branches is, like most money market banks, deposit poor. Other differences reflect variations in historical patterns of development, areas of specialization, and management philosophy.

Profit and Risk

However heterogeneous the nation's largest banks may be, there still are strong similarities in the way that top management in these banks view and attack the problem of managing a large bank. First, their objective is, like that of management in any industrial, manufacturing, or other

_____

[2] See Chapter 3 for an introduction to these markets and the instruments traded in them.

TABLE 5–1
Top 10 U.S. banks, January 1, 1982 ($ millions)

	Total deposits		Equity capital	Net income	Total loans	Securities holdings*
	Amount	Percent foreign				
Bank of America.............................	$95,976.6	42.5%	$4,048.1	$429.8	$69,642.7	$7,402.0
Citibank.....................................	72,471.1	74.1	4,871.4	673.8	65,684.8	7,404.0
Chase Manhattan Bank........................	58,585.7	59.5	3,209.1	441.0	49,087.0	6,134.3
Manufacturers Hanover Trust Company...........	42,434.9	54.2	1,925.9	285.1	35,694.4	3,502.2
Morgan Guaranty Trust Company................	37,688.7	61.1	2,256.9	314.6	27,330.8	7,257.8
Chemical Bank..............................	31,203.7	42.5	1,545.1	200.0	27,797.5	3,756.5
Continental Illinois National Bank & Trust Company of Chicago	29,881.3	49.8	1,775.8	231.3	30,773.1	2,482.1
First National Bank of Chicago.................	25,867.6	50.3	1,149.6	109.9	19,790.2	1,868.7
Security Pacific National Bank.................	23,411.6	20.1	1,331.2	208.6	19,743.9	1,722.6
Bankers Trust Company.......................	23,276.9	58.5	1,342.3	174.9	17,248.2	3,127.5

* Securities holdings include U.S. Treasury securities, obligations of U.S. government agencies and corporations, obligations of states and political subdivisions in the United States, other bonds, notes, and debentures, federal reserve stock, corporate stock, and trading account securities.
    Source: December 31, 1981 call reports. Source of Bankers Trust data, *American Banker*, February 11, 1982.

business concern, to earn *profits.* Second, banks, like nonbank firms, operate under uncertainty and thus face *risk.* Risk in banking arises from several sources. On every loan a bank makes there is a credit risk; that is, the risk that the borrower won't pay back the money lent. Second, because of the mismatch, contrived or natural, that typically exists between the interest-rate maturities of the assets and liabilities on a bank's balance sheet (in banker's jargon, the *mismatch* or *gap* in the bank's book), a bank is exposed to *interest rate risk.* This second risk arises not only in connection with a bank's loans but as a result of its portfolio and dealer operations. A third risk a bank faces is *liquidity risk,* which is really the risk of illiquidity. Every money market bank continually buys large quantities of short-dated (short-term) funds to finance its operations. Liquidity risk is the risk that the bank might at some point be unable to buy the monies it needs at a reasonable price or, worse still, at any price.

Because any attempt by a banker to make profits involves risks, his objective inevitably becomes *to maximize profits subject to the constraint that perceived risks be held to some acceptable level.* Also since bank analysts, investors, and bank depositors all focus strongly on current income, bankers have a strong predilection for an earnings pattern that displays steady growth over time.

MANAGING A MONEY MARKET BANK

Economists' favorite term, *decision variable,* denotes something having a value that is the result of a conscious decision. *Exogenous variables,* in contrast, are things having a value more or less thrust on the decision maker by the outside world. On a bank's balance sheet, in the short run at least, both sorts of variables are found. Let's start with the exogenous ones.

Every bank establishes standards to limit credit risk. Once it has done this, a bank will normally do everything possible to meet the legitimate loan demands of any customer who meets these standards. Loans are a key source of bank profits, and loan customers normally provide a bank with deposits and other business as well. The quantity of loans demanded from a bank depends largely on the state of the economy and on what funds are available to would-be borrowers from other sources. These factors are beyond the control of the banks, so their loan volume is very much an exogenous variable. Bankers can wish they had more loans, but they can't decide to have them if demand for bank loans is weak.

In the short run, bank capital is also an exogenous variable, having a value that depends on past decisions. A third variable that is largely exogenous in the short run is the sum of demand deposits, savings deposits, and small-denomination time deposits received by the bank. Over time a bank will have built up a customer base that supplies it with a quite stable amount of such deposits. To significantly enlarge that base would take time and effort. A final important exogenous variable from the point of view of a bank is the reserves against deposits that it must keep with the Fed.

From a bank's viewpoint, the decision variables it faces in the short run are the size and composition of its investment portfolio, the dealer position it assumes, and the quantities and maturities of the monies it buys in the Fed funds market, the RP market, the CD market, and the Euromarket.

In assigning values to these decision variables, the bank is determining in part what asset portfolio it will hold and how it will fund that portfolio. In other words it is choosing a balance sheet that meets its goal of maximizing return subject to the constraint that perceived risks be held at an acceptable level.[3]

Several facts of life are of crucial importance for the bank in making these balance-sheet choices. One is that buying money is going to be a continuing way of life for a money market bank. Capital plus what we called *exogenous deposits* minus whatever reserves have to be held against such deposits are available to a bank for funding loans. However, since money market banks as a group tend to be deposit poor, it is common for these sources of funds to be insufficient to cover loans, not to speak of funding a securities portfolio and a dealer position.

Thus a second crucial fact of life for a money market bank is that it must have the preservation of liquidity as a concern of overriding importance. Here, by liquidity we mean the bank's ability to acquire money whenever it is needed in huge and highly variable sums. Since the principal, in fact almost the only, source of liquidity a money market bank has is its ability to buy money, maintaining access to its markets for bought money—RP to CD—becomes the *sine qua non* for the continued operation of such a bank.

A third fact of life facing a bank is the yield curve. As noted in Chapter 4, money market and bond yields are normally higher the longer the maturity of an instrument except when a downturn in interest rates is anticipated. This means, as any banker knows, that one path to profits and prosperity is often to acquire assets with maturities that are longer than those of the liabilities used to fund them—*borrowing short and lending long.* A domestic banker would refer to this as running a *gap* or *gapping.* A Euro banker would call this running a *mismatched* or *short*

---

[3] For an in depth discussion of bank asset and liability management, see *Managing Bank Assets and Liabilities: Strategies for Risk Control and Profit,* by Marcia Stigum and Rene Branch (Homewood, Ill.: Dow Jones-Irwin, 1982).

book. Gapping or mismatching contrasts with running a *matched book—* that is, funding every asset acquired with a liability of identical interest-rate maturity.

Asset and funding choices

The facts of life we have just discussed influence profoundly the asset and funding choices bankers make. Let's look first at loans. When loan demand increases, the shape of the yield curve often tempts bankers to fund those extra loans by buying the shortest-dated money they can. Yet bankers rarely do so except for short periods when they are waiting to see whether the increase in loans will be sustained. One reason is that regulators would frown on such a policy. A second and more important consideration is that funding loans with overnight money on a large scale would conflict with the bank's need for continued liquidity. As banker after banker will note: "If we tried to finance a big increase in loans by suddenly buying a lot more overnight money, that would be immediately visible in the market and later visible in our published statements. People, particularly suppliers of funds, would begin to question why we were getting out of line with 'safe practices' [roughly the average of what other banks are doing], and our ability to continue to buy money might be impaired. That is something we could not allow to happen." The upshot of all this concern is that bankers tend to fund loan increases largely through the purchase of additional CD money, 30 days and longer.

A bank's securities portfolio is a different breed of animal from its loan portfolio with respect to both acquisition and funding. On the funding side, the principal difference is that under present Fed regulations a bank can finance its holdings of governments and agencies in the RP market (by selling them under an agreement to repurchase on an overnight or longer basis) without incurring a reserve requirement.

Money market banks acquire portfolios of government securities for various reasons. First, there is a cosmetic motive. Traditionally *all* banks held governments for liquidity; as a result even today a money market bank that had no governments on its balance sheet would raise eyebrows. Second, some money market banks that are dealers in government securities feel that it would be awkward for them to sell governments if they did not themselves maintain large holdings of such securities. Third and most important, money market banks hold governments, sometimes large amounts, for profit. When economic growth slackens and interest rates are low or falling, money market banks used, at least, to increase their holdings of governments because at such times governments could be financed at an attractive positive spread in the RP market.[4] The trick, of course, in a hold-bonds-for-profit strategy is not to be holding too many when interest rates start their next cyclical upswing and bond prices begin to fall as financing costs rise. To the above, it should be added that in recent years, which have been characterized by a chronically inverted yield curve and by highly volatile interest rates, the case for a bank to hold any governments has weakened.

Bankers feel comfortable financing a large proportion of their government portfolios on an overnight basis because government securities, unlike loans, are highly liquid and the banks can and sometimes do sell large amounts of such securities over short periods. Consequently long-term funding of the portfolio, besides being expensive, is neither needed nor appropriate.

To the extent possible, banks use the RP market rather than the Fed funds market for funding their portfolios. Generally overnight RP money is cheaper than overnight Fed funds. Also the RP market, unlike the Fed funds market, is an anonymous market in the sense that no other banks or brokers are tracking how much a bank borrows there. Thus a bank can make substantial use of the RP market without impairing its liquidity.

Money market banks, like other banks, also hold portfolios of municipal securities. The principal advantage of such securities is that interest income on them is tax exempt. How large a portfolio of *munis* a given bank holds is thus largely a function of its effective tax rate. The disadvantage of municipals is that they can't be *RPed* (financed in the RP market) but instead must be financed with Fed funds or other monies.

Many money market banks act as dealers in government and municipal securities. Since a dealer by definition acts as a principal in all transactions, buying and selling for its own account, a bank running a dealer operation inevitably assumes both long and short securities positions. Bank dealerships also acquire securities holdings, at times quite large ones, because they are positioning for profit. Banks finance their dealer positions in governments and munis in the same way they finance their investment portfolios.

Mismatching the book

Earlier we said that banks have to be concerned with interest rate risk and liquidity risk. Matching asset and liability maturities to the extent possible would appear to be a way for a bank to limit both risks. However, it's impossible to find a banker who professes to follow this strategy. One reason is that it would be difficult if not impossible for a bank to do so. Few if any assets on a bank's balance sheet have a definite

---

[4] The *financing spread* is said to be *positive* if the cost of the funds borrowed is less than the yield on the securities financed.

maturity. A 10-year bond or a 2-year note in the bank's portfolio might be sold tomorrow. Term loans are often prepaid, and 3-month loans are frequently rolled (renewed). On the liability side of a bank's balance sheet, many items have specific maturities—RPs, CDs, Fed funds purchased—but a question arises as to how to view demand deposits. Technically, demand deposits can be withdrawn at any time, but in practice demand deposits in the aggregate provide a bank with a quite stable source of funds. Besides being impractical, any attempt to match asset and liability maturities would be expensive to a bank because lending long and borrowing short is a potential source of bank profits.

All bankers profess to follow the *pool* concept of funding; instead of matching specific assets against specific liabilities, they think of all the funds raised by the bank as a pool that in the aggregate finances the bank's assets. In the next breath, of course, the same bankers will say that they RP their governments and meet increases in loans with the sale of CDs. What is really going on?

The bank typically sets up a high-level committee, that, besides making general decisions about what sorts of assets the bank should acquire, attempts to measure in some fashion, however arbitrary, the average maturity of the bank's assets and liabilities and thereby the implicit mismatch in the bank's overall position. The committee's objective is to profit when possible from a maturity mismatch while also monitoring the size of the mismatch so that the mismatch never grows so large as to endanger the bank's liquidity or expose it to an undue rate risk. Under this approach, big increases in loans inevitably end up calling for the bank to write more CDs, while an increase in Treasury bill holdings can comfortably be accommodated by increased purchases of overnight money.

To this rough generalization several comments should be added. First, banks don't just react to current conditions. Management is constantly attempting to predict the future and to position itself so as to maximize future earnings. In particular, banks are constantly forecasting loan demand, deposits, and interest rates. On the basis of such forecasts, a bank might, for example, decide to issue more CDs than normally because it expects interest rates and loan demand to rise sharply. Or it might decide to rely more heavily on Fed funds purchased than normally because it expects loan demand and interest rates to fall. Interest rate forecasts also strongly influence the bank's decision about the size and maturity distribution of its portfolio and dealer positions.

The brief picture we have just presented of management of a big bank leaves much unsaid. The rest of the chapter attempts to fill in some of the missing subtleties. Also, banks are active in every market we describe, so they will be with us throughout the rest of the book.

BANK LENDING

Money market banks, like other banks, extend credit to consumers and make home mortgage and other real estate loans. However, the largest proportion of their domestic lending is to commercial and industrial (C&I) customers. The standard terms on which banks lent to their C&I customers were that they would make fixed-rate loans to top credits at the *prime rate* and to weaker credits at prime plus some markup. Borrowers were normally required to keep a percentage of loan proceeds, anywhere from 10 to 20%, on deposit as a *compensating balance* with the lending bank. Customers who choose not to hold compensating balances were charged a higher rate. The C&I sector of bank lending is of special importance to a discussion of the money market because bank C&I loans are highly volatile, and whether the volume of them is up or down is a crucial factor in determining the stance banks take in the money market.

Over the last 40 years the environment in which banks operate has been subject to constant, sometimes dramatic change. One result is that banks have had to continually alter their lending practices, searching for areas in which they have a real and potentially profitable role to play in supplying credit.

Before World War II much bank commercial lending was short term. Firms in wholesale trade and commodities needed financing, often on a seasonal basis, to fill their warehouses; and their bank supplied it. The normal arrangement was that the bank would look over the customer's books once a year and decide how large a line of credit it was willing to grant this firm. The firm could then borrow during the year any sum up to that amount, provided no material change occurred in its circumstances after the line was granted. The customer paid for its line with compensating balances, borrowed as necessary on the basis of 90-day notes and was expected to give the bank a *clean up* (pay off all its borrowings) at some time during the year.

When World War II came along, the situation changed. Defense contractors had to invest huge sums in new plant and equipment. They could have financed these investments by selling long-term bonds, the traditional approach, but that seemed inappropriate. They didn't expect the war to continue forever. Also, they believed they could pay for their new plant and equipment rapidly because they had a customer, Uncle Sam, who was sure to pay and because they could depreciate their plant and equipment at an accelerated rate. So they asked the banks for term loans. The banks provided such credits with amortization built-in, and while criticized at the time for doing so, banks ended up successfully entering the area of medium-term commercial lending.

After the war, borrowers who had become accustomed to 5-year credits asked for more flexibility. On a term loan they didn't always want to have to take down all the money right away; they also wanted the right to prepay some or all of their loan if their cash flow improved seasonally or permanently. So bankers said, "Alright that's a revolving credit. You can have it, but at some point, you'll have to give us a clean up." The final step in this evolution came when the customer said to his bank: "I'm not sure I will ever need to borrow from you, but I want to know that I can if I need to, not just now but for some number of years." In response bankers developed a *revolving line of credit;* the customer paid balances *plus a commitment fee;* in exchange for the latter, the bank promised to honor the line for the life of the agreement. A customer could turn such a *revolver* into a term loan simply by borrowing.

Rate risk

From the start of World War II until 1951, the Fed pegged yields on government bonds, and interest rates moved little. Then in 1951, after considerable infighting, the Treasury agreed that the Fed should be permitted to pursue an independent monetary policy.[5] This Treasury-Fed accord spelled the end of rate pegging, and interest rate began a secular climb punctuated with periodic ups and downs. The pace of this climb was, however, slow. As a result bankers rarely changed the prime rate that they charged their best customers, and they felt safe lending at a fixed rate not only on 90-day notes but on term loans; the rate risk in both sorts of lending seemed small. Then, as Figure 5–1 shows, things changed. Inflation became a problem, and to fight it, the Fed pushed up interest rates sharply and rapidly on a number of occasions starting in the mid-1960s.

The banks felt the impact of the initial credit crunch largely in terms of opportunity cost. At that point they were not buying huge amounts of money, so tight money did not dramatically raise their cost of funding. It did mean, however, that funds locked up in old low-interest term loans could not be lent out at the higher rates currently prevailing. Later, as banks began to rely more and more on bought money, tight money did significantly increase their cost of funding; and the rate risk implied in *fixed-rate* lending became more pronounced.

To minimize this risk, banks changed their lending practices. They began changing the prime rate more frequently, and they started altering the rate on existing as well as on new short-term loans whenever they changed prime. They also made it a rule to put term loans on a *floating-*

---

[5] See page 230.

FIGURE 5–1
Over time the volatility of interest rates has increased

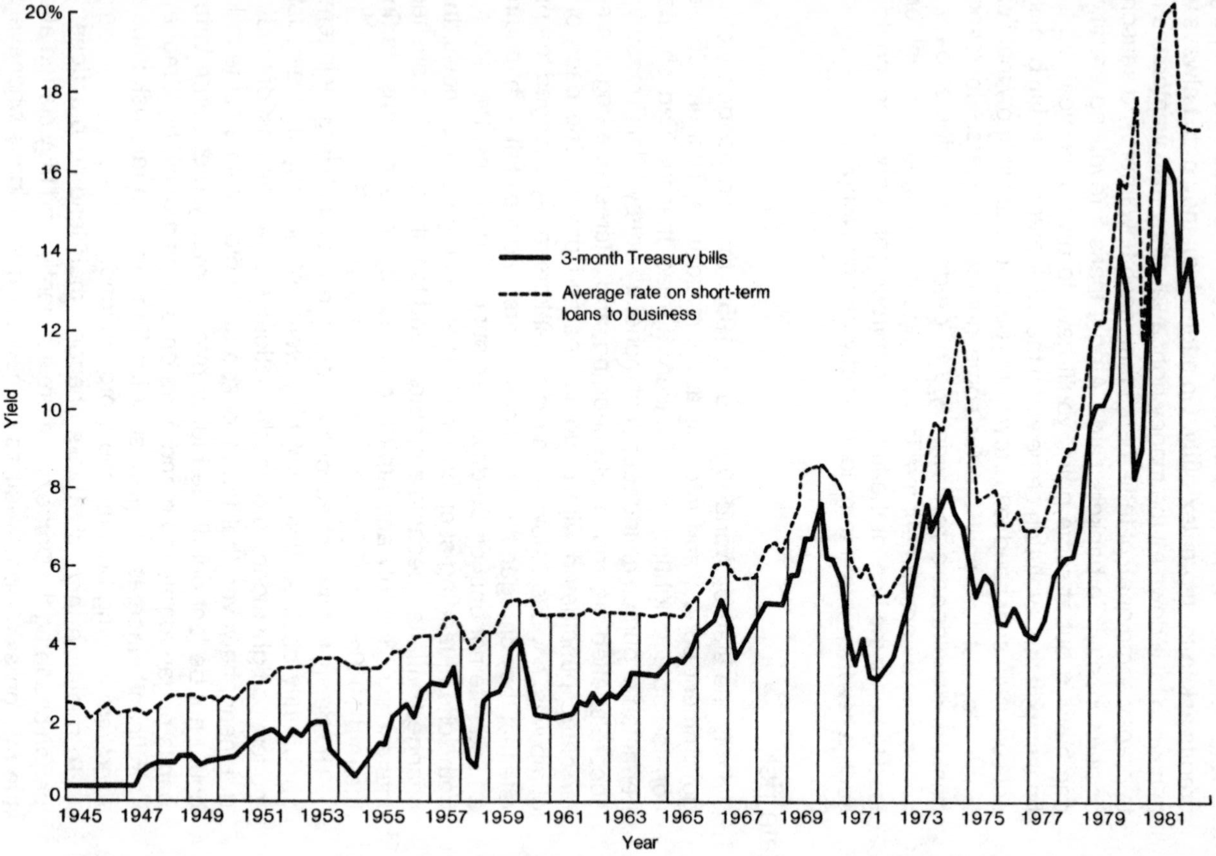
20%
18
16
14
12
10
8
6
4
2
0
Yield
3-month Treasury bills
Average rate on short-term loans to business
1945
1947
1949
1951
1953
1955
1957
1959
1961
1963
1965
1967
1969
1971
1973
1975
1977
1979
1981
Year

rate basis. The rule, of course, was not and is not always followed. As one executive noted: "We bankers are not as smart as we could be. When rates get near the peak and we ought to be making fixed-rate term loans, we shy away from doing so. Then when loan demand and lending rates decline and we are out scrambling for loans, we are tempted to make fixed-rate term loans at just the time when we shouldn't." Actually even fixed-rate term loans made when interest rates are high are not always as advantageous to banks as one might suppose. Once rates decline, the borrower of such money is likely to say to his banker, "You're my banker, and you know that the best thing for me would be to refinance this loan in the bond market or on other terms," and typically the banker lets the borrower do so without penalty, regardless of whether the loan agreement calls for one. On variable-rate term loans, the rate charged generally goes to an increasing spread above the prime rate during the later years of the loan. This maturity spread is supposed to compensate the banker for his long-term commitment, but he rarely earns it because of prepayment or renegotiation.

To some extent bankers tend to think of their special niche in commercial and industrial lending today as that of providers of flexible medium-term financing. Also, the money they provide is "warm" money in the sense that the lending arrangement is not only open to negotiation initially but also subject to renegotiation should the borrower's position change. While banks have done much to increase the attractiveness of bank loans, it is also true that by moving to floating-rate loans, they have shifted much of the rate risk involved in lending from their own shoulders to those of the borrower. This may, depending on borrowers' risk preferences and rate views, make bank loans appear less attractive to borrowers.

The prime rate, although viewed by some as a collusive price-fixing device, has always been responsive to open-market conditions. A fall in open-market rates attracts bank customers to the open market and to other nonbank financing sources, and thus puts pressure on banks to lower the prime, whereas a rise in open-market rates increases the cost of bank funding and the demand for bank loans and so does the opposite.

When the Fed tightens credit, the resulting increases in the prime rate, particularly if they are frequent and sharp, make bankers unpopular with politicians and the public. So gradually bankers have moved away from what appeared to be an arbitrarily set prime to one that is based on money market rates and fluctuates up and down with them. Citibank began the trend in 1971 by linking its prime to the 90-day commercial paper rate. Specifically Citi said that henceforth it would set its prime at the 90-day paper rate plus a spread, which fluctuated from as little as 1/8 to as much as 1 1/2 percentage points. Today banks change their prime rate frequently and always in response to changes in money market conditions.

While pricing loans at a flexible prime was supposed to eliminate a bank's rate risk on loans by tying its lending rate to its cost of funds, banks still encounter difficulties during periods of tight money. In the United States, as in many other countries, the prime rate has been so politicized that at times it may become impossible for the banks to raise it further. This happened, for example, in 1974. During such periods, banks can and have found themselves forced to make new loans at rates *below* their marginal cost of funds, that is, at rates below the cost of the extra money they had to buy to fund these loans.

The passing of prime

In recent years, the pace of change in bank lending practices has, if anything, accelerated. The world still keeps its eye glued on prime, but as one banker succinctly noted, "Prime is dead."

Bank lending terms used to be "10 plus 10." To get a line of credit, the customer had to put up 10% compensating balances; if he took down funds under the line—in addition to paying prime—he had to put up another 10% compensating balances on the amount of the loan. In those days, *prime was close to the banks' cost of funds, and what the banks really made money on was the free balances that granting lines and loans generated.* Then, competition began to whittle away at the balances. Instead of 10 plus 10, the terms became a straight 10% for the existence of the facility, and competition gradually cut that to 5%. By 1980, line and loan agreements for major loans were being written with no balance provisions.

As compensating balances vanished, banks found themselves earning on lines and loans just the rate charged on the funds taken down. Consequently, *banks had to administratively widen the spread between prime and their cost of funds so they could make some money.* Treasurers at major corporations, who push ever faster pens, reacted to a prime rate that floated at an increasing spread to banks' cost of funds by saying, "We won't borrow any more at prime except when it is to *our* advantage to do so. The spread between prime and other money market rates is so high that prime has become unrealistic. Worse still, we are being forced to accept the interest rate risk our bank used to take. And to top things off, banks always raise prime in step with money market rates, but when they misjudge the direction of rates and mistakenly fund loans with high-cost, long-term funds, banks are slow to lower prime as money market rates drop."

Either/or facilities. In bygone days, it was the practice that the terms on which major corporations could borrow from U.S. banks were as follows: they could get Eurodollar loans on Euro terms—LIBOR plus a small, fixed spread—to fund foreign operations, *but* they were supposed to borrow at prime to fund domestic operations.[6] The Euromarket is near perfect and consequently *very* efficient. Corporate treasurers, eyeing the terms they were getting from domestic banks on Euro loans booked outside the U.S. and on prime rate loans booked at the bank's head office, were quick to conclude that a Euro loan was often the better deal. So on large loans—particularly large syndicated loans, they literally forced their banks to give them line agreements that provided an *either/ or facility:* when the time came to take down funds, the corporate treasurer could choose—regardless of where the funds were to be spent— whether he wanted a Euro loan priced off LIBOR or a loan priced at prime. Since roughly 1980, every large-term loan negotiated by a major corporation with a money-market bank has contained an either/or option.

The either/or option gives a borrower two advantages: (1) he can, at times, use it to lower his funding cost by getting money in the market where the bank's spread is lower, and (2) he can use it to place his own bet on rates. If rates are on a plateau, the borrower may find that a Euro loan is cheaper than a prime loan and opt for the former on the ground. Alternatively, the borrower may anticipate a rise in rates and decide that his cheapest option is to fix his borrowing rate. In that case, he might take down 6-month money in the Euromarket even though the rate he pays, 6-month LIBOR plus a spread, exceeds prime. Finally, the borrower might ask for a loan at prime because he anticipates that money market rates will fall and wants to position himself so that his borrowing cost will fall with those rates.

Advances. After the advent of either/or facilities, the next change in bank lending practices was the introduction by major banks in the domestic market of short-term, fixed-rate loans priced off a bank's marginal cost of funds. On such loans, dubbed *advances,* a bank would price overnight funds at a spread over the Fed funds rate, 30-day money against 30-day CDs or 30-day term funds, and a 6-month advance against 6-month money. Advances in the domestic market are priced in much the same way as Euro loans are priced in the Euromarket, against money market rates.

It is a misconception that banks began making advances in the domestic market solely to compete with the commercial paper market. Another motive was to keep business that they would have lost had they insisted that borrowers pay prime at a time when borrowers felt that prime was unrealistically high. Big banks felt compelled to devise some

---

[6] See pp. 148–50 for Euro lending terms.

pricing mechanism that would give the borrower a rate he would view as a realistic; that is what really pushed banks into making loans at *sub-prime* rates.[7]

Initially, banks made only short-term advances, but pricing against a bank's cost of funds soon crept into longer-term agreements. Today, no corporate treasurer would sign an agreement with his bank saying that for the next seven years his bank will lend him money but that, when he borrows, he must always pay prime. He wants the option of paying prime or having a loan priced on an advance basis. Pricing of longer-term advances resembles Euro pricing. The borrower can choose the time period for which he wants to fix a rate; and over that period, the rate he is charged will be some fixed spread over the bank's cost of funds for money of that maturity.

Since Euros in any maturity range generally trade at a rate that equals the all-in cost—grossed up for reserve requirements and FDIC insurance—of money of the same maturity in the domestic money market, a borrower will get about the same deal from Euro pricing that he will on a domestic loan priced off money market rates. Only when U.S. and Euro rates are temporarily out of synchronization would he find that taking one option rather than the other will save him many basis points.

As would be expected, in choosing between a loan at prime and an advance, the borrower will take into account his rate expectations. If he believes rates are about to fall, rather than borrow at a fixed rate for 60, 90, or 180 days, he will take a prime loan on the expectation that prime will float down with other rates and that he will quickly realize the benefit of falling rates. Conversely, a borrower who thinks rates are going up will want to lock in a fixed rate on a 6-month advance. To illustrate, suppose the yield curve has a steep positive slope—from 10 to 14%—and prime is 11%; a borrower who is convinced that the yield curve is right and rates are about to rise sharply might opt for a 6-month advance priced off the current 14% cost of 6-month money rather than take a prime rate loan at 11%.

Not surprisingly, as corporate treasurers have been forcing their will upon banks with respect to lending terms, C&I lending at major banks has become more of an arms-length transaction. The relationships that these banks carefully cultivated with their customers are diminishing in importance.

Impact on funding.   Advances characterized by cost-plus pricing— short-term advances and floating-rate term loans that are priced at some fixed spread over the bank's marginal cost of funds—already represent

---

[7] Traditionally, prime rate loans were considered, implicitly, to be 90-day working capital loans. As corporate treasurers' borrowing needs began to be identified with greater precision (because of major advances in cash-flow projection techniques), the underlying rationale for traditional prime rate lending eroded.

10 to 15% of the total C&I loans made by large banks, and the amount is constantly increasing. With each day that passes, the domestic market for C&I loans comes to resemble Euro lending more closely.

This change in domestic lending practices promises to have significant effects on banking. It is already forcing large banks to rethink and restructure their funding strategies. Also it is creating pressure for a change in the structure of the banking industry because it places regional and smaller banks at a disadvantage.

Almost all banks used to (and most banks still do) think of themselves as financing most of their assets with a single, large, amorphous pool of funds. When a lot of bank assets were floating-rate prime loans, this concept was workable. If rates rose unexpectedly, banks quickly brought their lending rates into line with their funding costs by raising prime. Alternatively, if banks bought long-term money on the expectation that rates were going to rise and rates in fact fell, banks could and did respond by lowering prime slowly. It was, in part, against this asymmetry of changes in money market rates and changes in prime that corporate treasurers rebelled.

The growing trend toward cost-plus pricing of loans is forcing banks to abandon the pool concept of funding. To protect against the interest rate risk implied by booking a lot of loans at rates that are tied at a narrow spread to floating, money market rates in different maturity ranges, banks are being forced to think in terms of allocating specific pools of funds of specific maturities to support pools of assets of similar maturity. Within that framework, there remains room for a bank to choose to assume interest rate risk. A bank that faces a positively-sloped yield curve and is convinced that rates are going nowhere might opt to fund 30-day advances by rolling Fed funds. Or a bank that thought rates were about to rise might buy extra longer-term money in anticipation of making such loans at an attractive spread.

A second reason that cost-plus pricing is forcing a breakdown of the pool concept of funding is that a bank using this concept does not know how to price advances properly. A bank's current cost of funds depends on how successful it has been in the past in anticipating changes in interest rates. If the bank has taken a wrong view on rates, its cost of funds will be high; and if it then attempts to price fixed-rate advances off its current cost of funds, it will price itself out of the market. If alternatively the bank's cost of funds is low relative to market rates (the bank correctly forecasted rising rates and funded long), then if the bank prices fixed-rate advances off its current cost of funds, it will be competitive in getting loans and it will make money on them. The problem in this case is that, if the bank prices its loans off its current cost of funds, it will be charging rates so low as to give to its borrowers, instead of to its shareholders, the rewards of its past success at predicting rates.

Impact on the structure of banking. Cost-plus pricing has never caused a big interest rate risk problem for banks that are active lenders in the Euromarket. In the vast interbank market for Euros, banks of all sizes can freely bid for and get at the same or almost the same rate, funds in various maturity categories. In its Euro book, a bank always has the option of funding a matched position and thereby avoiding interest rate exposure, provided it respects an important caveat: A bank's presence in the market as a taker of funds must exceed that needed to support its present asset structure.

In the domestic market there exists no interbank market for funds over a wide range of maturities. Overnight Fed funds are traded actively among banks, but there is only a limited market for term Fed funds. A limiting factor on the demand side of the market for term Fed funds is that national banks must treat purchases of term Fed funds as borrowings rather than deposits.

The truly binding constraint on the growth of the market for term Fed funds lies, however, on the supply side of the market. The only way U.S. banks can get on their domestic books large deposits of money with a 1-month, 3-month, or longer maturity is by selling certificates of deposit to domestic institutional investors. Domestic CDs must, however, compete for investors' monies with a host of other short-term instruments: commercial paper, repo, T bills, municipal notes, and Europaper. In foreign countries, tne menu of short-lived, liquid securities available to institutional investors is much narrower than it is in the United States. Consequently, foreign banks get more large time deposits on their domestic books than do U.S. banks. These large time deposits form the basis of foreign interbank markets for funds over a range of maturities. Another factor is that foreign banks are generally not required, as are U.S. banks, to hold reserves against demand and time deposits. The absence of reserve requirements abroad permits foreign banks to compete more effectively than U.S. banks can for large domestic deposits. It also inhibits the growth of alternative methods of finance, such as the sale by corporations of commercial paper.

The lack in the U.S. of interbank markets for funds of differing maturities means that, if cost-plus pricing of loans grows and creeps down to loans of smaller size made by smaller borrowers, banks excluded from the national CD market—which means almost all banks—will be at a disadvantage vis-à-vis the elite few that can borrow in this market. The only source of funds a domestic bank can tap nationwide is the CD market. A bank that is excluded from this market and wants to participate in syndicated loans or make itself loans priced off CD rates will find no spread for itself in the deal.

A small bank with a $5 million lending limit can participate in a syndicated Euro loan because, if that bank goes to one of the brokers in the Euromarket and says it wants to bid for $5 million of 1-, 3-, or 6-month money, some bank or banks that have extended lines to this small bank will give it the money it wants in the maturity range it wants. If the same small bank chooses to participate in or itself extends a loan priced off domestic CD rates, it will find that it cannot buy funds in that amount in the domestic market. It could use Euros to fund domestic loans, but since they trade at a price grossed up for reserve requirements and FDIC premiums, it would, if it used Euros, earn no spread and under the new Reg D would also incur additional reserves.

A large regional bank with access to the domestic CD market might find that it could buy in the domestic CD market monies necessary to fund cost-plus priced advances, but only if it paid an extra 50 basis points above the rate money center banks were paying. Again, no spread.

The few small banks that might be able to deal in cost-plus priced loans at a profit are those banks that loom so large in their geographic sphere of influence that they have the advantages of a monopoly position working in their favor, one of those advantages presumably being the ability to sell small-denomination CDs to local businesses at submarket rates.

The trend toward cost-plus pricing of loans is forcing money market banks to rethink their funding concepts. It is also giving them a competitive advantage that is likely to cause a long-term shift of business toward them. Because of this, cost-plus pricing will add one more incentive to the host that already exist for bank mergers and some rationalization of the U.S. banking system.

Bank competition with commercial paper

Back in the 1930s, banks basically financed the working capital of corporate America. Today, the commercial paper market does so. While bankers once viewed the growing commercial paper market as threatening and unwanted competition, they no longer do so. Bankers realize that, if the $177-odd billion of business done in the commercial paper market were added to the $396 billion of C&I lending currently on their books, the impact on their capital ratios would be disastrous.[8] Also, bankers now perceive the commercial paper market as providing them with a tidy and steady flow of fee income for providing lines to paper issuers, lines that—because they are largely unused—have little or no impact on bank liquidity or interest rate risk. In effect, the commercial paper market provides banks with fees for doing next to nothing.

To create the appearance of liquidity necessary to sell commercial

---

[8] Figures are as of August 1982.

paper, almost all issuers back a very high percentage of their outstanding paper with *committed* facilities. Specifically the banks promise in exchange for balances and/or fees to provide commercial paper issuers with money should they encounter difficulties in rolling their paper.[9] This commitment gives the issuers the liquidity required to make their paper salable.

Initially, banks granting such lines tended to say to the issuer, "You can have the lines, but only if you commit to pay 1% over prime if you take down funds under it." The issuer responded by saying, "We'll give you 2% over prime." That was rational since, as the banks soon learned, most paper issuers make it a policy never to use their bank lines as a last resort source of funds if they can avoid doing so. When money is tight, commercial paper issuers would pay up rather than come into their banks for funds. So bankers said, "OK you can have the lines, but we want a fee," which they got and still get.

Two trends threaten the rather cozy income-for-doing-nothing situation that banks have gotten themselves into vis-à-vis the commercial paper market. First, the introduction and proliferation of short-term advances priced off short-term money market rates enabled banks to quote rates that are competitive or nearly competitive with short-term commercial paper rates, especially the all-in rates on dealer paper. Second, the Fed is reducing reserve requirements on time deposits and shortening their minimum length. This trend may well culminate in a situation where there are *no* reserves against time deposits and *no* minimum length on such deposits. If this happens, banks will be able to lend on truly competitive terms to corporations selling commercial paper. Should competition among banks drive banks to do so, the result will be a ballooning of banks' balance sheets and a concomitant deterioration of their capital ratios.

Bankers' acceptances

The closest banks come to competing directly with the commercial paper market is by issuing loans in the form of bankers' acceptances. On certain types of transactions—financing exports, imports, and the storage and shipment of goods at home and abroad—the bank can take the borrower's note, accept it (guarantee payment at maturity), and then sell it in the open market without incurring a reserve requirement. The interest rate charged the borrower is determined by rates prevailing in the bankers' acceptance market. These are normally less than commercial paper rates, but the banks' standard acceptance fee—currently ½ to 1%—adds additional cost, so the *all-in cost* to the BA borrower exceeds

---

[9] To *roll* paper means to repay maturing paper by selling new paper.

rates on commercial paper.[10] When loan demand is high, bankers normally sell the BAs they originate and take their spread, but when loan demand is slack, they may hold them as earning assets.

The real dilemma

While periods when loan demand is slack leave bankers feeling less than prosperous, some of the most difficult problems with respect to bank lending arise when money is tight. By accepting deposits from a firm and by building a customer relationship with it, a bank makes an often unwritten but nevertheless real commitment to lend to that firm when the latter needs funds. The bank, however, does not know when that need will occur or how large it will be. It can only be sure that the tighter money gets, the more loan seekers will be on its doorstep. To compound this problem, the one time that commercial paper issuers are likely to want to come or be forced to the banks for money is when money is tight. Thus a question arises as to whether banks will be able to honor all their written and unwritten commitments to lend when money tightens. Also, if they do honor them, will they be thwarting Fed policy by lending more at a time when the Fed is trying to contain overall bank lending?

Leasing

Banks and bank holding companies entered the leasing business in the early 1960s. It was a natural adjunct to their normal lending activities since a financial lease is the functional equivalent of a loan; under it the lessee is obligated to make a stream of payments to the lessor, the amount of which equals or exceeds the price of the asset leased.

Leasing is attractive to a bank. First, because a bank can take advantage of the investment tax credit and of accelerated depreciation on equipment it leases, leasing provides a tax shelter that permits the bank to *defer* taxes on current income. Second, leasing gives a bank protection against inflation; presumably the higher the rate of inflation, the greater the scrap value of the items leased will be at the end of the lease.

Because many lease agreements entered into by banks run for years, sometimes even several decades, a natural question is how banks control the rate risk that would seem to be inherent in making such indirect long-term loans. The answer varies with the segment of the market considered.

The leasing of small-ticket, short-lived items—autos, postage meters, and others—is normally not tax-shelter oriented, and the rates charged

---

[10] As noted in Chapter 17, there is in practice a lot of variation in the acceptance fees charged by banks.

are high. Even if allowance is made for the fact that some part of these high rates is compensation for the credit risks assumed, the rates are still sufficiently high, history suggests, to protect a bank's spread between its lending and borrowing rates.

In leasing big-ticket items, tax considerations are often of paramount importance. There are firms, not necessarily weak credits, that have such tremendous capital needs that they exhaust the tax benefits available to them under the investment tax credit and through accelerated depreciation before they make all the investments the require. If a bank that has taxable income leases equipment to such a firm, it can take advantage of tax benefits that the firm itself could not take on investment in the leased equipment.

Maturities on big-ticket, tax-oriented leases may run from 7 years on a computer to 25 years on a utility plant or oil loading dock. Such lease agreements always contain a clause that requires the lessees to pay a substantial penalty if they break the lease. Surprisingly a bank has little funding exposure on very long-term leases. The reason is that most leases are *leveraged leases*. The bank puts up 20 percent or more of the money required, enough to get the total tax benefits available; it then borrows the remaining funds required on a long-term basis from, say, an insurance company that has long-term funds available but, because of its low marginal tax rate, would not get the same tax benefits as a bank does from having the leased asset on its books. On a leveraged lease the bank's funding exposure lasts only 3 to 5 years. After that the rentals collected are used to repay the money borrowed and to build up a fund from which the taxes that the lease arrangement defers are eventually paid.

Balance sheet figures are misleading with respect to the importance of leasing to a bank or bank holding company. Only the lessor's equity in the item leased shows up as an asset, and in the case of leveraged leases, this equity drops to zero in a few years. However, the assets are still there; and even if the impact of leasing on the balance sheet is minimal, it may have a substantial impact on the bank's tax situation and on the return earned by the bank's stockholders.

THE BANK'S PORTFOLIO: TAXABLE SECURITIES

It used to be standard practice for a bank to invest some fraction of the funds deposited with it in government securities that could be sold off to meet increases in loan demand or depositor withdrawals. In other words, the bank's portfolio provided liquidity and some earnings on the side.

For the nation's largest banks, with the possible exception of the deposit-rich B of A, this began to change in the early 1960s. At that time many large banks, particularly those in New York, found that the secular uptrend in bank loans had eaten away most of the excess liquidity (bloated bond portfolios) with which they had emerged from World War II. At the same time, corporate treasurers began to manage their cash more actively, taking idle deposits out of the banks and investing them in commercial paper and other money market instruments. This too created liquidity problems. To solve them, the banks turned to the newly invented negotiable CD and other methods for buying money. Liability management was born, and the big banks' liquidity became in part their ability to buy money.

A second factor that discouraged banks from holding a bond portfolio primarily to provide liquidity was the ever-widening fluctuations that occurred in interest rates as a result of cyclical swings in economic activity and shifts in Fed policy. What the banks found was that, as loan demand slackened, interest rates would fall sharply; and as loan demand picked up, they would rise sharply. In this environment, using bonds as a source of liquidity meant buying bonds at high prices and selling them at low prices. Thus a bank that viewed its bond portfolio as a source of liquidity found the latter to be an automatic money loser; over time the portfolio provided some interest income and a lot of capital losses.

Today, since a large bank's government portfolio is financed in the RP market, it is more a *use* than a *source* of liquidity. Also, if such a bank sells securities, the RP borrowings used to finance them have to be repaid, so portfolio sales produce no money to fund loans or to meet other cash needs.

Maturity choice

Because the yield curve normally slopes upward, the yield on a 2-year note typically exceeds the overnight RP rate by more than does the yield on a 90-day bill. Thus a bank will get a better spread between the yield on its portfolio and its financing cost the longer it extends, in buying governments, along the maturity scale. This tempts a bank that is building up its portfolio to buy at least some governments and agencies with 2-year, 4-year, or even longer maturities, but doing so poses a risk.

An upturn in rates would cause not only a rise in financing costs but a fall in the value of the securities held; and the longer the maturity of these securities, the more dramatic that fall would be. Thus a bank with governments extending out on the maturity scale might end up in a position where rising financing costs tell it to sell governments at a time when it can do so only at a substantial loss.

To avoid getting into such a bind, banks use several strategies. One is to minimize the damage that rising interest rates can do by holding securities with short current maturities. Another is to match the maturity of the securities purchased with the time span over which interest rates are expected to be down—a policy that will result in a runoff of the portfolio as rates start up again. A third strategy is to count on being smart enough to know when to buy and when to sell. Both of the latter strategies will be successful only to the extent that the bank succeeds in predicting interest rate trends. That, however, is difficult. Thus it's not surprising that most large bank portfolios could have been managed better with hindsight than they were with foresight.

Portfolio management

Active portfolio management by a bank—a willingness to make judgments about interest rates trends and adjust maturities accordingly, to ride the yield curve, and to pursue other potentially profitable strategies—can significantly increase the return earned by the bank on its portfolio. Nevertheless, some large banks and many smaller banks do not engage in such management.

Under federal tax laws, net capital gains earned by a bank on its portfolio used to be taxed at the capital gains rate, while net capital losses were deductible from ordinary income. This created an incentive for banks to bunch capital gains into one tax year and capital losses into another. Managing a bank's portfolio thus boiled down to deciding whether the current year was a gain or a loss year; this wasn't difficult. If the market was up, it was a gain year; if it was down, it was a loss year. During a loss year a bank might find it had paper losses on securities it did not want to sell. That difficulty could be gotten around by selling these securities, taking the loss, and buying other securities that were similar but not so similar that the IRS would view the transaction as a wash sale.

At the end of 1969 tax laws were changed: All bank capital gains on portfolio transactions are now treated as ordinary income and all capital losses as deductions from ordinary income. This tax change created for the first time a profit incentive for banks to actively manage their portfolios.

One reason many still do not has to do with bank accounting practices. Table 5–2 presents in bare-bones style the format of a bank income statement. Note that *two* profit figures are given, *income before securities gains (losses)* and *Net income*. The first figure excludes capital gains and losses; the second reflects them as well as their effect on taxes due.

The special place given to securities gains and losses on a bank's income statement highlights them as an extraordinary item, and bank stockholders and stock analysts thus focus much attention on *Income before securities gains or losses*. Since interest income on securities is

TABLE 5–2
Typical format for a bank income statement

+Interest income
    (including interest income on securities held)
−Interest expenses
+Other operating income
    (including trading account profits)
−Noninterest operating expenses
    (including taxes other than those on capital gains)

Income before securities gains (losses)
+Securities gains (losses) net of tax effect

Net income

included in this figure but capital gains and losses on securities trades are not, bankers prefer interest income from their portfolio to capital gains. In addition, because stockholders and analysts like to see sustained earnings growth, bankers want this number to grow steadily from year to year.

That desire can at times discourage a bank from managing its portfolio. To illustrate, consider a bank that buys 3-year notes in a high-rate period. Two years later, interest rates have fallen substantially, and the 3-year notes, which have moved down the yield curve, are trading at a yield to maturity well below their coupon. At this point the bank might feel that, to maximize profits over time, it should sell these notes and buy new ones that have a longer current maturity and therefore sell at a higher yield. The logic of such an *extension swap* is that the capital gains earned immediately on the sale of the old notes plus the interest earned on the new notes would over time amount to more income than the interest that would have been earned by holding the old notes to maturity and then reinvesting. The swap, however, creates a capital gain in the current year and lowers interest income in the following year. To the banker who wants *Income before securities gains or losses* to rise steadily, such a redistribution of income often seems too great a price to pay for maximizing profits over time; so he doesn't do the swap.

A concern with steady earnings may also lead a bank to hold more governments or governments of longer maturity than caution would dictate. Conditions may suggest that loan demand is about to pick up, that interest rates are about to rise, and that the bank should therefore reduce its holdings of governments or the maturity of those holdings. Doing so in anticipation of the event would, however, mean a temporary earnings dip, something a bank may be unwilling to accept.

A bank can put some of its portfolio into a *trading account*. The advantage in doing so is that capital gains realized in the trading account are included in the top-line income figure. The disadvantage is that securities in this account have to be valued on the bank's balance sheet at the lower of market value or cost, whereas other securities in the bank's portfolio do not. At many banks one finds an anomalous situation. The bank works hard to earn profits on the 10–30% of its portfolio that is in a trading account, whereas it leaves the rest of its portfolio largely unmanaged.

No case for governments now

Banks, once big holders of governments and agencies, have over time tended to pare their holdings of these securities. This trend accelerated noticeably around the turn of the decade, a development that was hardly surprising. In the highly volatile rate environment that prevailed during the years 1979–82, *no* valid argument could be made for a bank to invest in taxable securities.

This contrasted sharply with the previously prevailing situation. From 1950 through roughly 1978, the economy experienced mild and predictable cyclical ups and downs; it was subject to what people call the *normal* business cycle. During that period, interest rates, following the business cycle, tended to decline to a trough over roughly a two-year period and then turn back up again and stay high for three years or so. This rate pattern made buying governments a sensible strategy for banks that could correctly call the turns in interest rates.

Since the end of World War II, the one good reason for a bank to buy governments was to protect its earnings against temporary, *cyclically predictable* declines in interest rates. Especially after October 1979, interest rates became cyclically unpredictable, and in 1980 in particular, rates took off on a roller coaster ride. Until there is a clear return of the normal business cycle, a *big* portfolio move by a bank would be extremely dangerous. That is what we mean by saying that from late 1979 to late 1982 *no* case existed for a bank to buy governments.

A government portfolio is often viewed as providing a bank with liquidity. In fact, governments are not a source of liquidity to large banks that finance them with RP. Governments also are a poor source of liquidity for small banks that buy them with their own money. Banks that thought otherwise had a rude awakening in August 1966. The economy was then passing through the worst credit crunch in decades, and there was *no* bid in the dealer market for Treasury bills. Banks that thought they had liquidity because they held bills found they had none.

A small bank, to the extent that it wants liquidity resident in its assets, should not buy bills; it should sell overnight Fed funds or Euros. The rate is always better, and the bank has no risk of ownership. A bank that sells funds can change the amount it invests not only day to day but during the day if need be. More and more banks have come to appreciate this.

Municipal portfolio

State and local securities (*municipals* for short) offer banks the advantage that interest income on them is exempt from federal taxation. It is also often exempt from state and local taxation if the securities held are issued by or within the state in which the bank is located. However, some states and localities (New York and New York City, in particular) impose a franchise tax on bank income that is based on total earnings, including tax-exempt income. Municipal securities, unlike governments, carry credit risk. Thus credit analysis plays a large role in a bank's decision about what municipal securities to buy.

While a bank's main objective in buying municipals is to obtain tax-exempt income, other motives may influence this decision. Banks receive large deposits from state and local governments, and these have to be collateralized. Sometimes the collateral used is governments, more often it is municipals. Also, a bank may invest in municipals because the issuer is a valued depositer.

The securities held in a bank's municipal portfolio typically range in maturity from short-term notes to bonds with a 10- or 15-year maturity. A bank often perceives its holdings of short-term muni notes as a true source of liquidity since their sale actually frees funds for other uses.

A bank's incentive for buying long-term munis is to obtain a higher yield by taking advantage of the upward slope of the yield curve. Long-term munis, however, expose the holder to a big price risk. In investing in municipal securities, many banks seek to compromise between price risk and yield by *laddering* the maturity of their portfolios out to 10 or 15 years (i.e., by buying something in every maturity range). However, in munis as opposed to governments, the investor is paid to extend maturity virtually to the end of the maturity spectrum. As a result some banks are willing to hold munis of very long maturity. In doing so they follow what's called a *barbell* strategy, buying muni notes for liquidity and buying, when they like the market, long-term munis for yield. This sounds risky, but practitioners argue that the supply of funds going into the far end of the market from fire and casualty insurance companies and from individuals is stable, whereas in the 10- to 15-year range dominated by the banks, it is highly cyclical; as a result, yields on medium-term munis go through large gyrations, and the medium-term investor who misplays his hand can be hurt as badly as the investor in long munis.

Generally banks do not actively trade their muni portfolios. One reason is tax considerations. A bank that buys tax-exempt issues when interest rates are high and later sells them at a capital gain when interest rates fall is trading future nontaxable interest payments for current taxable capital gains, a move that normally has an unattractive impact on after-tax income.

Industrial development loans. For years, states and municipalities have been permitted to issue tax-free bonds to finance various projects designed to promote the local economy. It is also possible for a private borrower to obtain a ruling from the Treasury that interest paid on a loan that will promote the economy of a particular area will be tax-free to the lender. Since banks began making floating-rate loans, they have sharply increased the volume of industrial development loans they make; such bank lending provides stiff competition to the purchase by banks of municipal securities.

For a bank, buying a bond is an arms-length transaction; the bond never knows who owns it. In contrast, a bank that makes an industrial development loan to a private borrower can expect to improve its relationship with that borrower and, as a result, to receive profitable balances and fee income.

Industrial development loans are a substitute for municipal securities because there is some limit on the quantity of tax-exempt income a bank can use. Buying municipals or making tax-free loans cuts a bank's effective tax rate on its total income. If a bank succeeds in getting that rate down to zero, then any additional tax-exempt investments it makes will yield it just the coupon not the taxable equivalent of the coupon.

DEALER OPERATIONS

Most money market banks have extensive dealer operations. The biggest part of their activity is in Treasury and federal agency securities, but banks are also big dealers in and underwriters of state and local general obligation securities. In addition some banks deal in the CDs of other banks and in BAs. Banks used to underwrite corporate issues, but since passage of the Glass-Steagall Act in 1936, they have been forbidden to do so.

Running a dealer operation makes sense for a large bank. A small bank often asks a money market bank with whom it has a correspondent relationship to buy securities both for its own portfolio and for its customers. Also large corporations, which are prime customers of money market banks and often have millions of dollars of short-term funds to invest, are ready customers for securities traded by bank dealerships. In this respect it should be noted that, while Glass-Steagall forbids banks from underwriting and dealing in corporate securities, banks can and do sell commercial paper issued by corporations. The big direct issuers of commercial paper post rates with the banks, which in turn quote these rates to customers; if a customer wants $1 million of General Motors Acceptance Corporation (GMAC) paper, the bank carries out the transaction between the customer and GMAC and safekeeps the paper for the customer until it matures.

Besides being a profit center, a bank's dealer department also provides it with useful, up-to-the-minute information on conditions in the money and bond markets. There's much to be said about how a dealer operation, bank or nonbank, runs. We turn to that in Chapter 9.

DEMAND DEPOSITS

Demand deposits have traditionally been a key source of bank funding, and as such they are an important and valuable raw material to banks. Yet in the United States, unlike in many foreign countries, banks are not permitted to pay interest on demand deposits. One exception is NOW accounts on which banks may pay to consumers passbook rates. Other more important and more recent (December 1982 and January 1983) exceptions are MMDA and Super-NOW accounts (see Table 2-5) on which banks may pay unregulated rates. So long as interest rates were low, forbidding the payment of interest on demand deposits caused bankers no problems; despite the fact that deposit balances offered a zero return, bank customers were willing to hold substantial demand deposits because the *opportunity cost* (forgone earnings opportunity) of doing so was negligible.

During the 1950s, however, things started to change. Interest rates began a secular climb, which, coupled with the periodic forays the economy made into the world of very tight money and high interest rates in the 1960s, drove home to corporate treasurers, state and local financial officials, and other holders of large short-term balances a new fact of life: The cost of holding idle balances was high and growing. In response depositors trimmed their demand balances to the minimum level possible and invested excess short-term funds in interest-bearing instruments including in particular money funds. In 1982 Congress permitted banks to offer MMDC and super-NOW accounts specifically to compete with money funds.

Because demand deposits are valuable to banks and because holders of such deposits incur a substantial opportunity cost, an elaborate system of barter has developed in which banks trade services to customers in exchange for deposits. On small accounts the barter involves imprecise calculations. It amounts to the bank giving free checking services to all customers or to those with some minimum balance.

On large accounts the barter is worked out more exactly; banks provide many services to corporate and other big customers: accepting deposits, clearing checks, wire transfers, safekeeping securities, and others. In providing these services, banks incur costs that they could recover by charging fees. Instead they ask customers to "pay" by holding demand deposits.

To determine the amount of deposit balances appropriate for each customer, the bank first costs each type of service it provides. It then sets up an activity analysis statement for each account, showing the types and volume of services provided and the costs incurred. Some of the demand deposits customers leave with a bank go to meet reserve requirements; the rest can be invested. Taking reserve requirements and current investment yields into account, the bank estimates the rate of return it earns on demand deposits. Finally, using that rate it determines what balance each account must hold so that the bank's earnings on the account cover the costs incurred in servicing it.

Banks also charge for credit lines by requiring compensating deposit balances; the standard formula used to be 10% of the unused portion of the line and 20% of any funds actually taken down.

As might be expected in a barter situation, the compensation arrangements worked out between banks and customers are subject to negotiation and vary not only from bank to bank but often from customer to customer at a given bank. Many customers obtain lines at less than the usual balance arrangement, and good customers may be able to get their banks to double-count balances for some purposes.

A bank that requires compensating balances on lines and loans is getting at zero interest deposits on which it can earn a return. An alternative way it could earn the same return would be to charge a fee for lines and higher rates on loans. Some customers prefer the latter approach, and in recent years it has become more common for banks to grant fee lines and to quote two loan rates, a standard rate for loans with balances and a higher rate for loans without. For some public utilities this approach is mandatory since regulators will not permit utilities to hold large idle balances.

To the extent that banks obtain demand deposits either from retail customers by establishing expensive branch networks or from large depositors by exchanging services or reducing lending rates, they are paying some implicit rate of interest on such deposits even though the nominal rate is zero. Moreover, the all-in cost of demand deposits is still higher than this implicit rate because, as Table 5–3 shows, the reserve requirement on demand deposits, which was 16¼% for large banks prior to the phasing in of new reserve requirements for all institutions accepting deposits under the Depository Institutions Deregulation and Monetary Control Act of 1980, will be 12% at the end of the phase-in period. This means that such a bank can invest only $88 of every $100 it takes in. Also, a bank has to pay the Federal Deposit Insurance Corporation (FDIC) a premium of ½ of 1% on all deposits it accepts.

However high the all-in cost of demand deposits may be, banks are eager to obtain all the demand deposits they can. One reason is that the quantity of such funds supplied to a bank is quite stable over time, and a bank can thus count on these deposits being there regardless of what happens to economic conditions or interest rates. Banks also attach importance to demand and time deposits for other reasons: regulators like to see a lot of deposits as opposed to bought money on a bank's balance sheet; banks are typically ranked by deposit size rather than asset size; and bank analysts attach what is probably undue importance to the share of deposits in a bank's total liabilities.

While exchanging services for deposits has enabled banks to retain substantial amounts of demand deposits, banks, until introduction of MMDA and super-NOW accounts, had no way to bid for additional funds from this source. The demand deposits they got were limited to the amounts consumers chose to leave with them plus the amounts needed to cover the services large customers chose to buy from them. This contrasted sharply and still does with the situation in the Euromarket where banks bid actively for deposits of all maturities, including call and overnight money (see Chapter 6).

Small-denomination time deposits

The all-in cost of time deposit money to a bank depends in part on the reserves the bank must hold against these deposits. As Table 5–3 shows, reserve requirements are much lower on savings and time deposits than on demand deposits; on time deposits, they used to be lower the longer the maturity of the deposit. Now they are a flat 3% on nonpersonal time deposits with an original maturity of less than 3½ years and 0% on nonpersonal time deposits of longer maturity. Reserve requirements on personal time deposits are also 0% regardless of original maturity.

The major competitors of banks in accepting time and savings deposits are savings and loan associations. When money becomes tight and interest rates soar, S&Ls are at a competitive disadvantage relative to banks. Because banks have many short-term and variable-rate assets on their books, they are able to capture rapidly rising interest rates on the asset side of their balance sheets. In contrast, the asset portfolios of S&Ls consist largely of fixed-rate, long-term mortgages.[11] It thus takes a

---

[11] This is changing. Under The Depository Institutions Act of 1982, S&Ls are permitted to invest up to 10% of their assets in commercial loans. S&Ls had already been empowered by the 1980 Banking Act to invest up to 20% of their assets in consumer loans, commercial paper, and company securities.

TABLE 5–3
Depository institutions reserve requirements (percent of deposits)[1]

Type of deposit and deposit interval ($ millions)	Member bank requirements before implementation of the Monetary Control Act		Type of deposit and deposit interval	Depository institution requirements after implementation of the Monetary Control Act[5]	
	Percent	Effective date		Percent	Effective date
Net demand[2]			*Net transaction accounts*[6,7]		
0–2.............................	7	12/30/76	$0–$26 million................	3	11/13/80
2–10............................	9½	12/30/76	Over $26 million.............	12	11/13/80
10–100..........................	11¾	12/30/76	Personal time deposits.......	0	11/30/80
100–400.........................	12¾	12/30/76			
Over 400........................	16¼	12/30/76			
			Nonpersonal time deposits[8]		
Time and savings[2,3]			By original maturity		
Savings.........................	3	3/16/67	Less than 3½ years...........	3	4/29/82
			3½ years or more.............	0	4/29/82
Time[4]					
0–5, by maturity			*Eurocurrency liabilities*		
30–179 days..................	3	3/16/67	All types...................	3	11/13/80
180 days to 4 years..........	2½	1/8/76			
4 years or more..............	1	10/30/75			
Over 5, by maturity					
30–179 days..................	6	12/12/74			
180 days to 4 years..........	2½	1/8/76			
4 years or more..............	1	10/30/75			

1. For changes in reserve requirements beginning 1963, see Board's *Annual Statistical Digest, 1971–1975* and for prior changes, see Board's *Annual Report* for 1976, table 13. Under provisions of the Monetary Control Act, depository institutions include commercial banks, mutual savings banks, savings and loan associations, credit unions, agencies and branches of foreign banks, and Edge Act corporations.

2. Requirement schedules are graduated, and each deposit interval applies to that part of the deposits of each bank. Demand deposits subject to reserve corporation, or family of U.S. branches and agencies of a foreign bank for the two statement weeks ending Sept. 26, 1979. For the computation period beginning Mar. 20, 1980, the base was lowered by (a) 7 percent or (b) the decrease in an institution's U.S. office gross loans to foreigners and gross balances due from foreign offices of other institutions between the base period (Sept. 13–26, 1979) and the week ending Mar. 12, 1980, whichever was greater. For the computation period beginning May 29, 1980, the base was increased by 7½ percent above the base used to calculate the marginal reserve in the statement week of May 14–21,

requirements were gross demand deposits minus cash items in process of collection and demand balances due from domestic banks.

The Federal Reserve Act as amended through 1978 specified different ranges of requirements for reserve city banks and for other banks. Reserve cities were designated under a criterion adopted effective Nov. 9, 1972, by which a bank having net demand deposits of more than $400 million was considered to have the character of business of a reserve city bank. The presence of the head office of such a bank constituted designation of that place as a reserve city. Cities in which there were Federal Reserve Banks or branches were also reserve cities. Any banks having net demand deposits of $400 million or less were considered to have the character of business of banks outside of reserve cities and were permitted to maintain reserves at ratios set for banks in reserve cities.

Effective Aug. 24, 1978, the Regulation M reserve requirements on net balances due from domestic banks to their foreign branches and on deposits that foreign branches lend to U.S. residents were reduced to zero from 4 percent and 1 percent respectively. The Regulation D reserve requirement on borrowings from unrelated banks abroad was also reduced to zero from 4 percent.

Effective with the reserve computation period beginning Nov. 16, 1978, domestic deposits of Edge corporations were subject to the same reserve requirements as deposits of member banks.

3. Negotiable order of withdrawal (NOW) accounts and time deposits such as Christmas and vacation club accounts were subject to the same requirements as savings deposits.

The average reserve requirement on savings and other time deposits before implementation of the Monetary Control Act had to be at least 3 percent, the minimum specified by law.

4. Effective Nov. 2, 1978, a supplementary reserve requirement of 2 percent was imposed on large time deposits of $100,000 or more, obligations of affiliates, and ineligible acceptances. This supplementary requirement was eliminated with the maintenance period beginning July 24, 1980.

Effective with the reserve maintenance period beginning Oct. 25, 1979, a marginal reserve requirement of 8 percent was added to managed liabilities in excess of a base amount. This marginal requirement was increased to 10 percent beginning Apr. 3, 1980, was decreased to 5 percent beginning June 12, 1980, and was reduced to zero beginning July 24, 1980. Managed liabilities are defined as large time deposits, Eurodollar borrowings, repurchase agreements against U.S. government and federal agency securities, federal funds borrowings from nonmember institutions, and certain other obligations. In general, the base for the marginal reserve requirement was originally the greater of (a) $100 million or (b) the average amount of the managed liabilities held by a member bank, Edge

1980. In addition, beginning Mar. 19, 1980, the base was reduced to the extent that foreign loans and balances declined.

5. For existing nonmember banks and thrift institutions at the time of implementation of the Monetary Control Act, the phase-in period ends Sept. 3, 1987. For existing member banks the phase-in period is about three years, depending on whether their new reserve requirements are greater or less than the old requirements. For existing agencies and branches of foreign banks, the phase-in ended Aug. 12, 1982. New institutions have a two-year phase-in beginning with the date that they open for business, except for those institutions having total reservable liabilities of $50 million or more.

6. Transaction accounts include all deposits on which the account holder is permitted to make withdrawals by negotiable or transferable instruments, payment orders of withdrawal, and telephone and preauthorized transfers (in excess of three per month) for the purpose of making payments to third persons or others.

7. The Monetary Control Act of 1980 requires that the amount of transaction accounts against which the 3 percent reserve requirement will apply be modified annually to 80 percent of the percentage increase in transaction accounts held by all depository institutions on the previous June 30. At the beginning of 1982 the amount was accordingly increased from $25 million to $26 million.

8. In general, nonpersonal time deposits are time deposits, including savings deposits, that are not transaction accounts and in which the beneficial interest is held by a depositor that is not a natural person. Also included are certain transferable time deposits held by natural persons, and certain obligations issued to depository institution offices located outside the United States. For details, see section 204.2 of Regulation D.

The category of time deposit authorized by the Depository Institutions Deregulation Committee (DIDC), effective Sept. 1, 1982 (original maturity or required notice period of 7 to 31 days, required minimum deposit balance of $20,000, and ceiling rate tied to the 91-day Treasury bill rate), is classified as a time deposit for reserve requirement purposes.

Note: Required reserves must be held in the form of deposits with Federal Reserve Banks or vault cash. After implementation of the Monetary Control Act, nonmembers may maintain reserves on a pass-through basis with certain approved institutions.

Author's note: Depository institutions were permitted to offer *money market deposit amounts (MMDAs)* with limited withdrawal privileges and *super-NOW accounts* with unlimited withdrawal privileges on December 14, 1982, and January 5, 1983, respectively. The new MMCA accounts are reservable as time deposits, the new super-NOW accounts as transactions accounts (Table 2–5).

long time for S&Ls to translate rising interest rates into rising revenues, and when money tightens, banks are therefore in a stronger position than S&Ls to bid for savings and time deposits by raising deposit rates.

To protect S&Ls from bank competition, the Fed, under Regulation Q, imposes lids on the rates that banks may pay on small-denomination savings and time deposits. These lids, which are periodically adjusted as economic conditions change, become higher as the maturity of the deposit lengthens (Table 5–4). The Federal Home Loan Bank Board, which regulates S&Ls, also establishes lids on the deposit rates S&Ls may pay; typically, these are set 0.25% above the rates banks may pay on the theory that, if S&Ls did not enjoy a rate advantage, consumers would, for convenience, opt to hold their savings accounts at commercial banks where they hold checking accounts. Other nonbank savings institutions enjoy the same rate advantage over banks that S&Ls do. Both banks and S&Ls are permitted to issue a wide, confusing, and constantly changing menu of variable and rate deposit accounts. S&Ls were permitted at the same time banks were to offer MMDA and super-NOW accounts free of any rate lid.

The Fed initially applied Reg Q lids to deposits of all sizes, but since 1973 it has exempted all deposits of $100,000 or more. Thus banks are currently free to bid whatever rate they choose for large time deposits, a freedom S&Ls also enjoy.

On June 1, 1978, the Fed authorized banks to pay on 6-month certificates with a minimum denomination of $10,000 the average return on T bills of the same maturity. S&Ls and savings banks were authorized to pay one quarter more on these certificates. The purpose of the new savings certificate, dubbed *MMC* for *money market certificate,* was to cushion the savings and loan industry against an outflow of funds into the money market and thereby protect the supply of funds flowing into home mortgages. Unfortunately, these certificates failed to accomplish the purpose and, in addition, by 1981 were threatening to bankrupt many S&Ls and savings banks.

By 1980, lids on the rates banks and thrifts were permitted to pay depositors were making it increasingly difficult for these institutions to compete with money market funds and other nonbank institutions for monies that used to be regularly deposited with them. As a result, the Depository Institutions Deregulation and Monetary Control Act of 1980 provided for the gradual deregulation of the rates paid by banks and thrifts. Rate decontrol was welcomed by large banks, which were long accustomed to buying money at market rates, but it was vehemently opposed by most thrifts and smaller banks, which saw it either as a threat to their existing profits if they were profitable or as a threat to their continued viability if they were unprofitable. By the end of 1980, the fight against rate deregulation had become so intense as to throw into question when, and even whether, rate deregulation would be carried out.

The issue was settled by passage of the Depository Institutions Act in September 1982. To help banks and thrifts compete with money funds, the new act required the Depository Institutions Deregulatory Committee to establish, which it did in December 1982, a new account—dubbed the *money market deposit account* (*MMDA*), that carries *no* interest rate lid and *no* withdrawal penalties. A depositor with such an account may each month make three preauthorized transfers from it and write three checks on it. The new account, whether at a bank or thrift, resembles in many respects a money fund account but has the added attraction to depositors of carrying federal insurance from the FDIC or the FSLIC on deposits up to $100,000. In January 1983, the DIDC also permitted depository institutions to offer checking accounts paying unregulated rates. These accounts, quickly dubbed *super-NOW accounts*, were initially available to consumers only. In January 1983 the DIDC was considering a proposal to permit corporations—already permitted to hold MMDA accounts—to hold super-Now accounts as well.

The 1982 Banking Act also stipulates that all interest-rate controls on bank accounts as well as the ¼% advantage S&Ls now enjoy over banks on the rates they may pay on time deposits must be phased out by January 1984, two years earlier than scheduled in the 1980 Banking Act.

FEDERAL FUNDS

Smaller banks typically receive more deposits than they need to fund loans, whereas large banks are in the opposite position. The logical solution to this situation, in which small banks have excess reserves and large banks suffer reserve deficiencies, would be for large banks to accept the excess reserves of smaller correspondent banks as deposits and pay interest on them, a practice that used to be common before banks were forbidden to pay interest on demand deposits.

To get around this prohibition, the Federal funds market, somnolent since the 1920s, was revived during the 1950s. In this market banks buy Fed funds (reserve dollars) from and sell Fed funds to each other. Since purchases of Fed funds are technically borrowings instead of deposits, banks buying Fed funds are permitted to pay interest on these funds. The all-in cost of Fed funds to the purchasing bank is the rate paid plus any brokerage incurred. Because Fed funds purchased are not deposits, there is no FDIC tax on them. They are also not subject to reserve requirements, since the reserve requirement has been met by the bank that accepted as a deposit the funds sold.

Most sales of Fed funds are made on an overnight basis, but some are for longer periods. Overnight transactions in Fed funds provide the purchasing bank with a cheap source of money and a convenient way to make sizable day-to-day adjustments in its reserves. For the selling bank, Fed funds sold provide a convenient form of liquidity. Small banks,

TABLE 5–4
Maximum interest rates payable on time and savings deposits at federally insured institutions (percent per annum)

Type and maturity of deposit	Commercial banks				Savings and loan associations and mutual savings banks (thrift institutions)			
	In effect September 30, 1982		Previous maximum		In effect September 30, 1982		Previous maximum	
	Percent	Effective date	Percent	Effective date	Percent	Effective date	Percent	Effective date
1 Savings	5¼	7/1/79	5	7/1/73	5½	7/1/79	5¼	(1)
2 Negotiable order of withdrawal accounts[2]	5¼	12/31/80	5	1/1/74	5¼	12/31/80	5	1/1/74
Time accounts[3]								
Fixed ceiling rates by maturity[4]								
3 14-89 days[5]	5¼	8/1/79	5	7/1/73	5½	7/1/79	(6)	....
4 90 days to 1 year	5¾	1/1/80	5½	7/1/73	6	1/1/80	5¾	1/21/70
5 1 to 2 years[7]	6	7/1/73	5½	1/21/70	6½	(1)	5¾	1/21/70
6 2 to 2½ years[7]	6½	7/1/73	5¾	1/21/70	6¾	(1)	6	1/21/70
7 2½ to 4 years[7]	6½	11/1/73	5¾	1/21/70	6¾	11/1/73	6	....
8 4 to 6 years[8]	7¼	11/1/73	(9)	....	7½	11/1/73	(9)	....
9 6 to 8 years[8]	7½	12/23/74	7¼	11/1/73	7¾	12/23/74	7½	11/1/73
10 8 years or more[8]	7¾	6/1/78	(6)	....	8	6/1/78	(6)	....
11 Issued to governmental units (all maturities)[10]	8	6/1/78	7¾	12/23/74	8	6/1/78	7¾	12/23/74
12 IRAS and Keogh (H.R. 10) plans (3 years or more)[10,11]	8	6/1/78	7¾	7/6/77	8	6/1/78	7¾	7/6/77
Special variable ceiling rates by maturity								
13 7- to 31-day time deposits[2]	(12)	(12)	(12)	(12)	(12)	(12)	(12)	(12)
14 91-day time deposits[13]	(13)	(13)	(13)	(13)	(13)	(13)	(13)	(13)
15 6-month money market time deposits[14]	(15)	(15)	(15)	(15)	(15)	(15)	(15)	(15)
16 12-month all savers certificates[16]	(16)	(16)	(16)	(16)	(16)	(16)	(16)	(16)
17 2½ years to less than 3½ years[17]	(17)	(17)	(18)	(18)	(17)	(17)	(18)	(18)
Accounts with no ceiling rates								
18 IRAs and Keogh (H.R. 10) plans (18 months or more)[19]	(19)	(19)	(19)	(19)	(19)	(19)	(19)	(19)
19 3½ years or more time deposits[20]	(20)	(20)	(20)	(20)	(20)	(20)	(20)	(20)

1. July 1, 1973, for mutual savings banks; July 6, 1973, for savings and loans.

2. For authorized states only. Federally insured commercial banks, savings and loan associations, cooperative banks, and mutual savings banks in Massachusetts and New Hampshire were first permitted to offer negotiable order of withdrawal (NOW) accounts on Jan. 1, 1974. Authorization to issue NOW accounts was extended to similar institutions throughout New England on Feb. 27, 1976, in New York State on Nov. 10, 1978, and in New Jersey on Dec. 28, 1979 and to similar institutions nationwide effective Dec. 31, 1980.

3. For exceptions with respect to certain foreign time deposits see the BULLETIN for October 1962 (p. 1279), August 1965 (p. 1084), and February 1968 (p. 167).

4. Effective Nov. 10, 1980, the minimum notice period for public unit deposits at savings and loan associations was decreased to 14 days and the minimum maturity period for time deposits at savings and loan associations in excess of $100,000 was decreased to 14 days. Effective Oct. 30, 1980, the minimum maturity or notice period for time deposits was decreased from 30 to 14 days at mutual savings banks.

5. Effective Oct. 30, 1980, the minimum maturity or notice period for time deposits was decreased from 30 to 14 days at commercial banks.

6. No separate account category.

7. No minimum denomination. Until July 1, 1979, a minimum of $1,000 was required for savings and loan associations, except in areas where mutual savings banks permitted lower minimum denominations. This restriction was removed for deposits maturing in less than 1 year, effective Nov. 1, 1973.

8. No minimum denomination. Until July 1, 1979, the minimum denomination was $1,000 except for deposits representing funds contributed to an individual retirement account (IRA) or a Keogh (H.R. 10) plan established pursuant to the Internal Revenue Code. The $1,000 minimum requirement was removed for such accounts in December 1975 and November 1976 respectively.

9. Between July 1, 1973, and Oct. 31, 1973, certificates maturing in 4 years or more with minimum denominations of $1,000 had no ceiling; however, the amount of such certificates that an institution could issue was limited to 5 percent of its total time and savings deposits. Sales in excess of that amount, as well as certificates of less than $1,000, were limited to the 6½ percent ceiling on time deposits maturing in 2½ years or more. Effective Nov. 1, 1973, ceilings were reimposed on certificates maturing in 4 years or more with minimum denomination of $1,000. There is no limitation on the amount of these certificates that banks can issue.

10. Accounts subject to fixed-rate ceilings. See footnote 8 for minimum denomination requirements.

11. Effective Jan. 1, 1980, commercial banks are permitted to pay the same rate as thrifts on IRA and Keogh accounts and accounts of governmental units when such deposits are placed in the new 2½-year or more variable-ceiling certificates or in 26-week money market certificates regardless of the level of the Treasury bill rate.

12. Effective Sept. 1, 1982, depository institutions are authorized to issue nonnegotiable time deposits of $20,000 or more with a maturity or required notice period of 7 to 31 days. The maximum rate of interest payable by thrift institutions is the rate established and announced (auction average on a discount basis) for U.S.

Treasury bills with maturities of 91 days at the auction held immediately before the date of deposit or renewal ("bill rate"). Commercial banks may pay the bill rate minus 25 basis points. The interest rate ceiling is suspended when the bill rate is 9 per cent or below for the four most recent auctions held before the date of deposit or renewal. The maximum allowable rate from Sept. 1 through Sept. 7 was 8.604 for commercial banks and 8.354 for thrifts. The interest rate ceiling was suspended for the remaining weeks in September.

13. Effective May 1, 1982, depository institutions were authorized to offer time deposits that have a minimum denomination of $7,500 and a maturity of 91 days. The ceiling rate of interest on these deposits is indexed to the discount rate (auction average) on most recently issued 91-day Treasury bills for thrift institutions and the discount rate minus 25 basis points for commercial banks. The rate differential ends 1 year from the effective date of these instruments and is suspended at any time the Treasury bill discount rate is 9 percent or below for four consecutive auctions. The maximum allowable rates in Sept. (in percent) for commercial banks were as follows: Sept. 8, 8.565; Sept. 14, 8.161; Sept. 21, 7.849; Sept. 28, 7.801; and for thrifts Sept. 8, 8.565; Sept. 14, 8.161; Sept. 21, 7.849; Sept. 28, 7.80.

14. Must have a maturity of exactly 26 weeks and a minimum denomination of $10,000, and must be nonnegotiable.

15. Commercial banks and thrift institutions were authorized to offer money market time deposits effective June 1, 1978. These deposits have a minimum denomination requirement of $10,000 and a maturity of 26 weeks. The ceiling rate of interest on these deposits is indexed to the discount rate (auction average) on most recently issued 26-week U.S. Treasury bills. Interest on these certificates may not be compounded. Effective for all 6-month money market certificates issued beginning Nov. 1, 1981, depository institutions may pay rates of interest on these deposits indexed to the higher of (1) the rate for 26-week Treasury bills established immediately before the date of deposit (bill rate) or (2) the average of the four rates for 26-week Treasury bills established for the 4 weeks immediately before the date of deposit (4-week average bill rate). Ceilings are determined as follows:

Bill rate or 4-week average bill rate	Commercial bank ceiling
7.50 percent or below	7.75 percent
Above 7.50 percent	¼ of 1 percentage point plus the higher of the bill rate or 4-week average bill rate

	Thrift ceiling
7.25 percent or below	7.75 percent
Above 7.25 percent, but below 8.50 percent	½ of 1 percentage point plus the higher of the bill rate or 4-week average bill rate
8.50 percent or above, but below 8.75 percent	9 percent
8.75 percent or above	¼ of 1 percentage point plus the higher of the bill rate or 4-week average bill rate

TABLE 5–4 Notes (Continued)

The maximum allowable rates in Sept. for commercial banks and thrifts based on the bill rate were as follows: Sept. 8, 9.855; Sept. 14, 9.954; Sept. 21, 9.693; Sept. 28, 9.446; and based on the 4-week average bill rate were as follows: Sept. 8, 9.79; Sept. 14, 9.76; Sept. 21, 9.874; Sept. 28, 9.737

16. Effective Oct. 1, 1981, depository institutions are authorized to issue all savers certificates (ASCs) with a 1-year maturity and an annual investment yield equal to 70 percent of the average investment yield for 52-week U.S. Treasury bills as determined by the auction of 52-week Treasury bills held immediately before the calendar week in which the certificate is issued. A maximum lifetime exclusion of $1,000 ($2,000 on a joint return) from gross income is generally authorized for interest income from ASCs. The annual investment yield for ASCs issued in Sept. (in percent) was as follows: Sept. 5, 8.15.

17. Effective Aug. 1, 1981, commercial banks may pay interest on any variable ceiling nonnegotiable time deposit with an original maturity of 2½ years to less than 4 years at a rate not to exceed ¼ of 1 percent below the average 2½-year yield for U.S. Treasury securities as determined and announced by the Treasury Department immediately before the date of deposit. Effective May 1, 1982, the maximum maturity for this category of deposits was reduced to less than 3½ years. Thrift institutions may pay interest on these certificates at a rate not to exceed the average 2½-year yield for Treasury securities as determined and announced by the Treasury Department immediately before the date of deposit. If the announced average 2½-year yield for Treasury securities is less than 9.50 percent, commercial banks may pay 9.25 percent and thrift institutions 9.50 percent for these deposits. These deposits have no required minimum denomination, and interest may be compounded on them. The ceiling rates of interest at which they may be offered vary biweekly. The maximum allowable rates in Sept. (in percent) for commercial banks were as follows: Sept. 14, 11.80; Sept. 28, 11.55; and for thrifts: Sept. 14, 12.05; Sept. 28, 11.80.

18. Between Jan. 1, 1980, and Aug. 1, 1981, commercial banks, and thrifts were authorized to offer variable ceiling nonnegotiable time deposits with no required minimum denomination and with maturities of 2½ years or more. Effective Jan. 1, 1980, the maximum rate for commercial banks was ¾ percentage point below the average yield on 2½ year U.S. Treasury securities; the ceiling rate for thrifts was ¼ percentage point higher than that for commercial banks. Effective Mar. 1, 1980, a temporary ceiling of 11¾ percent was placed on these accounts at commercial banks and 12 percent on these accounts at savings and loans. Effec-

tive June 2, 1980, the ceiling rates for these deposits at commercial banks and savings and loans was increased ½ percentage point. The temporary ceiling was retained, and a minimum ceiling of 9.25 percent for commercial banks and 9.50 percent for thrifts was established.

19. Effective Dec. 1, 1981, depository institutions were authorized to offer time deposits not subject to interest rate ceilings when the funds are deposited to the credit of, or in which the entire beneficial interest is held by, an individual pursuant to an IRA agreement or Keogh (H.R. 10) plan. Such time deposits must have a minimum maturity of 18 months, and additions may be made to the time deposit at any time before its maturity without extending the maturity of all or a portion of the balance of the account.

20. Effective May 1, 1982, depository institutions were authorized to offer ne-gotiable or nonnegotiable time deposits with a minimum original maturity of 3½ years or more that are not subject to interest rate ceilings. Such time deposits have no minimum denomination, but must be made available in a $500 denomination. Additional deposits may be made to the account during the first year without extending its maturity.

Note. Before Mar. 31, 1980, the maximum rates that could be paid by federally insured commercial banks, mutual savings banks, and savings and loan associa-tions were established by the Board of Governors of the Federal Reserve System, the Board of Directors of the Federal Deposit Insurance Corporation, and the Federal Home Loan Bank Board under the provisions of 12 CFR 217, 329, and 526 respectively. Title II of the Depository Institutions Deregulation and Monetary Con-trol Act of 1980 (P.L. 96-221) transferred the authority of the agencies to establish maximum rates of interest payable on deposits to the Depository Institutions De-regulation Committee. The maximum rates on time deposits in denominations of $100,000 or more with maturities of 30–89 days were suspended in June 1970; such deposits maturing in 90 days or more were suspended in May 1973. For information regarding previous interest rate ceilings on all types of accounts, see earlier issues of the FEDERAL RESERVE BULLETIN, the Federal Home Loan Bank Board Journal, and the Annual Report of the Federal Deposit Insurance Corporation.

Author's note: Depository institutions were permitted to offer money market deposit amounts (MMDAs) with limited withdrawal privileges and super-NOW accounts with unlimited withdrawal privileges on December 14, 1982, and January 5, 1983, respectively. Both types of accounts are free from rate lids so long as the depositor maintains a minimum balance of $2,500 (Table 2–5).

unlike large money center banks, cannot count on being able to buy funds whenever they need them. Therefore they must keep their liquidity resident in their assets, and because overnight sales of Fed funds can be varied in amount from day to day, they give such banks flexibility to adjust to the daily swings that occur in their reserve positions.

After the difficulties of the Franklin National were brought to light, banks have become acutely aware that, in selling Fed funds, they were making unsecured loans to other banks, and moreover they were doing so at one of the lowest rates prevailing in the money market.[12] This being the case, banks began to monitor more closely the credit risks they assume by selling Fed funds. They will sell Fed funds only to banks to which they have established lines of credit, and they will sell to these banks only up to the amount of the lines granted. In establishing a line to another bank, the selling bank will consider the other bank's reputation in the market, its size, its capital structure, and any other factors that affect its creditworthiness. The selling bank may also consider whether the buying bank is at times also a seller of funds. A bank that is always a buyer is viewed less favorably than one that operates both ways in the market. Selling funds is also important for a would-be buyer because the Fed funds market is one into which some banks have to buy their way. They do this by selling funds to a bank for a time and then saying to that bank, "We sell funds to you, why don't you extend a line to us?"

REPOS

The reemergence of the Fed funds market gave banks a back-door way to pay interest on demand deposits received from other banks. Corporations, state and local governments, and other big nonbank investors that have funds to invest for less than 30 days can't, however, sell that money directly in the Fed funds market because they are not banks.

---

[12] In the spring of 1974 the Franklin National Bank, then the 20th largest bank in the U.S., disclosed that it had sustained a $46 million loss through unauthorized speculation by traders in its foreign exchange department. The Fed, realizing the serious consequences that failure of the Franklin might have, particularly under the then prevailing tight conditions in the money and bond markets, promised immediately and publicly to support the Franklin by lending to it at the discount window whatever sums were necessary. Fed loans to the Franklin eventually reached an unprecedented $1.75 billion.

Had the Franklin's troubles been simply a temporary loss of confidence due to a single misstep, the Fed's actions combined with some minimal assistance from the FDIC might have sufficed to permit the Franklin to recover. Unfortunately as a result of chronically weak management, the Franklin also suffered from excessive leverage at unfavorable rates, an overloaded and badly depressed bond portfolio, and low-quality business loans. Thus, it was insolvent not only in the technical sense of having liabilities greater than assets but in a second and more serious sense—it was no longer able to operate profitably. As a result, by fall the FDIC felt compelled to force the Franklin to merge with another large and profitable bank, the European American Bank and Trust Co. In that merger the Franklin's depositors were fully protected.

Partly to meet the needs of such investors, the RP market has developed into one of the largest and most active sectors of the money market. In it, banks and nonbank dealers create each day billions of dollars worth of what resembles interest-bearing demand deposits. In fact an investor that does an RP transaction with a bank is making a loan secured by U.S. Treasury or other securities; investing in RPs thus exposes the investor to less credit risk than depositing funds directly in the bank would.

A large percentage of all RPs done by banks are on an overnight basis, but term RPs are also common. Since the yield curve typically slopes upward, the rate on term RPs normally exceeds the overnight rate, with the spread being larger the longer the maturity of the term RP. Thus, from a cost point of view, an overnight RP tends to be more attractive. However, excessive reliance on overnight RPs and purchases of Fed funds may create a shorter book (a greater mismatch between asset and liability maturities) than a bank wants to run. If so, the bank can use term RPs to snug up its book.

Since the RP money a bank buys is not deposits, it pays no FDIC premiums on such funds. It also incurs no reserve requirements on money purchased in the RP market provided that the collateral used is government or federal agency securities. However, on RPs done with other collateral, there is a reserve requirement.[13] RP transactions always involve some paperwork, and if the buyer of the securities wants them safekept by another bank, there is a clearing charge. Banks doing a lot of RPs carefully track these costs because they can raise significantly the all-in cost of RP money, especially if it is bought on an overnight basis. To avoid clearing charges, banks prefer to do RPs with customers who will safekeep with them the securities "purchased."

The overnight RP rate is normally lower than the overnight Fed funds rate for two reasons. Lenders in this market lack direct access to the Fed funds market. Also, doing RP does not expose the lender to the same credit risk that selling Fed funds would. The banks' main alternative to buying funds in the term RP market is buying term Fed funds. The decision between the two is likely to be made strictly on the basis of which sells at the lower all-in cost. Normally this will be term RP, which tends to trade below term Fed funds for the same reasons that overnight RP money is normally cheaper than overnight Fed funds.

Because RP money is cheap and because a money market bank buys lots of it, such banks carefully search out and cultivate big investors in RP. They make it a point to know the needs of their big customers—

---

[13] To be able to repo CDs and BAs in their dealer position without incurring a reserve requirement, a few banks have put their dealer operations into a GSI (Government Securities Inc.) subsidiary of the holding company. First Pennco, now defunct, was such a subsidiary of First Pennsy. Lombard-Wall, now in Chapter 11, was a dealer sub of Equimark in Pittsburgh.

whether they can buy commercial paper, repo, or what—and they call these customers every day to get a feel for what monies they have available. The banks also keep track of who is issuing bonds and who is therefore going to get big money. For example, if New York State floats a $2 or $3 billion bond issue to obtain funds that it intends to pay out to school districts two months hence, every money market bank will know that the state has money to invest in RP, and they will all be calling the state to get some of it.

Doing RP with customers is the way banks get most of the RP money they buy. However, banks that are primary dealers in government securities also frequently do RP transactions with the Fed and reverses as well. As explained in Chapter 8, the Fed relies heavily on repos and reverses with dealers in governments to make short-term adjustments in bank reserves.

NEGOTIABLE CDS

In the early 1960s the demand for funds at New York money market banks began to outstrip their traditional sources of funds. Moreover, these banks had no way to bid for funds outside their own geographic area, for example, to pull time deposits in from the West Coast. To solve this problem, Citibank introduced the negotiable CD, an innovation that became an instant success and was widely copied. Today CDs are a key funding instrument for every major bank.

The CD became important to top domestic banks not only because it allowed them to tap the national market for funds but because it provided them with a means, really the only one available, to bid for longer-term funds in volume. In the domestic market, unlike the Euromarket, the supply of large-denomination time deposits offered by investors is thin at best. Large corporations don't want to hear about time deposits; they want liquidity. State and local governments used to give large time deposits to banks, but they too have become increasingly interested in liquidity. Also, time deposits held by state and local governments have the disadvantage from the point of view of the accepting bank that they must be collateralized by Treasury or municipal securities.

In buying longer-maturity funds, the only alternatives a bank has to issuing CDs are to do term RP or buy term Fed funds. Term RP is a limited alternative because if a bank RPs any asset other than governments and agencies (banks have attempted to RP everything including loans), it incurs a reserve requirement. Purchases of term Fed funds are a viable alternative to the sale of CDs, but the market for such funds has nowhere near the breadth of the CD market.

The all-in cost to an issuing bank of CD money is the rate paid on the CD plus FDIC insurance plus the reserve cost plus the commission paid to the issuing dealer if one is used.[14] At times this all-in cost exceeds that of term Fed funds of comparable maturity. When it does, a bank will buy term Fed funds *but* within limits. All banks are conscious of their statements; term Fed funds are classified for statement purposes as borrowed funds, CDs as deposits. Thus cosmetic considerations guarantee that a bank will buy in the CD market some multiple of the funds it buys in the term Fed funds market.

The major choice a bank faces in issuing CDs is what maturity money to take. If a bank thinks its book is running too short or that interest rates and loan demand are likely to rise sharply, it will be tempted to buy longer-dated funds, say, 6-month rather than 3-month money. Because of availability and risk considerations, however, most of the money banks buy in the CD market is purchased at the short end of the maturity spectrum.

When a bank opts to issue longer-term (say, 6-month) CDs, it is typically gambling that interest rates will rise. With an upward-sloping yield curve, this is an expensive bet because in buying 6-month money, a bank forgoes the normally cheaper alternative of buying two consecutive batches of 3-month money. Thus interest rates have to rise sharply for a purchase of long-term money in anticipation of rising interest rates to pay off; banks therefore buy 6-month money in volume only if they believe strongly that the Fed is going to raise interest rates or if the yield curve is relatively flat.

When a bank buys long-term money, it gambles not only that rates will rise but that it will have some use for the expensive money it is acquiring. Should loan demand be less than anticipated, a bank that had bought 6-month money would find itself holding high-cost funds for which it had no high-yield use.

Availability is also a consideration in a bank's choice of CD maturities. The real depth in the CD market is in the 1- to 3-month range. There is a market for 6-month paper but it is thin, and the market for 1-year paper is still thinner. Thus banks have little choice but to buy the bulk of their money in short maturities.

This, moreover, becomes increasingly true during periods of tight money. When interest rates are rising and a bank expects them to continue to rise, it will be tempted to increase the average maturity of the CDs it sells. It is selling its CDs, however, to sophisticated investors who are likely to share its view on rates and who therefore want—just when the bank is trying to increase maturities—to decrease the maturity of the CDs they buy. Generally the investors get their way because banks can only sell paper that the market will accept. Thus tight money and rising interest rates tend to force *down* the average maturity of CDs sold.

---

[14] For the calculation of the all-in cost of CD money, see Chapter 15.

Variable-rate CDs. As noted in Chapter 2, variable-rate CDs became a big selling item largely in response to the demand of money funds for them.[15] Banks can sell variable-rate CDs to money funds whether rates are high or low because buying such paper does not constitute a bet on rates from the investor's point of view. However, selling a 6-month variable-rate CD, as opposed to selling a 6-month, fixed-rate CD, offers a bank protection against only liquidity risk, not rate risk. If rates rise, the rate a bank will have to pay on its variables will rise every time they hit a roll date.

Issuing CDs

In issuing CDs banks generally prefer to get these securities into the hands of investors who are likely to hold them at least for some time period, if not to maturity. That banks should attempt to sell an instrument, whose appeal by design is liquidity, to buyers who will rarely if ever trade it seems incongruous to the outside observer but not to bankers. A banker doesn't mind an investor selling a CD because of an unexpected cash need, but sales by trading accounts are something else. As the banker sees it, paper bought by trading accounts and subsequently dumped on the street could provide unwanted competition for any new paper his bank might later choose to write.

In their search for "warm nosed" money, most banks prefer to sell as many of the CDs they issue as possible through their own sales forces to their own customers. However, as noted in Chapter 15, a good portion of CDs are issued through dealers.

In the CD market, as in other sectors of the money market, a bank cannot buy unlimited quantities of funds. Not all investors in the money market are free to buy bank CDs because of either regulation or self-imposed investment parameters. Also, those that may limit their purchases of CDs to specific names and specific amounts for each name. Thus at any time there is some maximum amount of its paper that a bank can push into the market. That limit is one that banks attempt not to approach.

Several major banks have, however, breached this limit with unfortunate consequences. They suddenly found they could sell only small amounts of new paper to the market. Also the excess supply of their paper on the street drove down its price, which in turn soured investors who were holding that paper and threw questions on the bank's name. Once a bank gets itself into such a situation, it takes time to remedy. The bank may for awhile have to cut back sharply on the CDs it issues and attempt to selectively place these CDs, perhaps at a premium rate, with investors who will hold rather than trade them.

---

[15] See pp. 123–24.

EURODOLLARS

A final source of funding to which a bank may turn is the Euromarket, where it can bid for deposits (*take* money) of essentially any maturity from overnight on out. A bank can also invest (*place*) money it has raised in the domestic market in Euro time deposits. The reserve requirement on Euros is established under *Regulation D,* which currently requires a domestic bank to hold reserves equal to 3% of any *net* borrowings (borrowings minus placements) of Euros that is makes for its domestic book over a 7-day averaging period.[16] Because of Reg *D*, a bank that takes Euros of one maturity will often place Euros of some other maturity during the averaging period so that its reserve cost on the money borrowed is zero.

The head offices of money market banks are very active in the Euromarket for several reasons. First, they are constantly alert to the opportunities for arbitrage between the domestic and the Euromarkets that arise because of transitory rate discrepancies.[17] For example, if 6-month Euros are selling at 11.50% and 6-month money can be purchased at 10% in the domestic CD market, a bank will take domestic 6-month money and place it in the Euromarket through its London or Nassau branch. Doing so, besides locking in a spread for the bank, permits the bank to bring back short-dated Euros at no reserve cost. Such intrabank arbitrages play an important role in holding Euro and U.S. rates in line.

BANK CAPITAL ADEQUACY

In talking about bank capital adequacy, the first thing to note is that the essence of banking is to raise the return on equity earned by the bank through leverage. To illustrate leverage at work, let's use a simple example. Suppose an investor has $1,000 of capital to invest. He can borrow additional funds at 10% and he can invest at 15%. If he invests only his $1,000 of capital, he will earn $150 for a return of 15% on that capital. If alternatively he borrows $5,000 and invests a total of $6,000, he will have an investment income of $900, interest costs of $500, and profits of $400, which amount to a 40% return on his $1,000 of capital (Table 5–5). By borrowing funds at a low rate and investing them along with his capital at a higher rate, our investor has raised the return on his capital.

In an uncertain world, leverage can work against as well as for the investor. If, for example, our investor, who anticipated earning 15% on

---

[16] The 3% figure was to be phased in; the phase-in period has ended for member and foreign banks and will end for nonmember banks in 1987.

[17] Strictly defined to arbitrage means to buy something where it is cheap and to sell it where it is dear.

TABLE 5–5
Leverage at work: Investor has $1,000 of capital

Case I: No borrowed funds used; investment returns 15%:

Investment income = 15% × $1,000 = $150
−Interest cost = 4% × 0 =   0

Profit = $150

Rate of return on capital = $\dfrac{\$150}{\$1,000}$ = 15%

Case II: $5,000 of borrowed funds costing 10% used; investment returns 15%:

Investment income = 15% × $6,000 = $900
−Interest cost = 10% × $5,000 = $500

Profit = $400

Rate of return on capital = $\dfrac{\$400}{\$1,000}$ = 40%

Case III: $5,000 of borrowed funds costing 10% used; investment returns 5%:

Investment income = 5% × $6,000 = $300
−Interest cost = 10% × $5,000 =   500

Loss =   −$200

Rate of return on capital = $\dfrac{-\$200}{\$1,000}$ = −20%

his investment, earned only 5%, then his profit would be −$200, for a rate of return capital of −20% (Case III, Table 5–5).

Because bankers operate with borrowed funds that amount in total to a substantial multiple of their capital, they engage in leverage on a grand scale. Moreover, because assuming both a credit risk by lending and a rate risk by running a short book are fundamental elements of banking, the banker can never be sure either what average return he will earn on his assets or what his cost of funds will be. The purpose of bank capital is to cushion bank depositors and other suppliers of debt capital to banks against any losses the bank might incur due to unfavorable leverage—borrowing costs higher than return earned.

While it's easy to see that a bank needs capital, the question of how much is difficult, perhaps unanswerable. In attempting to measure bank capital adequacy, the yardstick used to be the ratio of a bank's deposits to its loans, its major risk assets. Then as banks became active buyers of money, focus shifted to the ratio of equity to total risk assets. However well or poorly this ratio may measure bank capital adequacy, it in no way solves the question of what minimum value the ratio should have. For every $1 of capital, should a bank borrow at most $10, $20, or what? Any intelligent answer to this question should probably be based on a bank's earning power as measured by certain historical indexes and modified to allow for the bank's bad-debt experience. Such numbers, however, vary from bank to bank, suggesting that no absolute industry-wide standard can or should be set.

As a practical matter, the capital ratios currently prevailing in banking in no way reflect reasoned decisions by either bankers or regulators as to what these ratios should be. To the contrary, what they are at any point reflects historical evolution and prevailing economic conditions. In particular during the post-World War II period, as loan demand surged and banks strove for continued earnings growth, bank capital ratios declined substantially. Moreover, no clear end to this downward trend is in sight.

The attitude of bankers toward the capital adequacy question is well illustrated by the words of one bank president: "Back in the credit crunch of 1974, because of inflation and an insatiable demand for credit, we got to the point where equity was about 4% of assets, so we had leverage of 25 to 1. At the peak we and a lot of bankers asked how far can this go, and we decided we had better slow down and tighten up. So we set a leverage maximum of 25 to 1." In the next breath the same banker added: "We of course have to forget all about that standard when we deal with foreign banks. The leading Israeli banks have about 1% capital ratios, and in Japan the figure is 1 or 2%." In effect this banker and other U.S. bankers measure capital adequacy in domestic and foreign banks by differing standards, a practice that suggests they have no absolute notion of what capital ratios should be.

Since the whole question of capital adequacy boils down to asking how much capital a bank needs to assure its survival under unknown future conditions, it is no surprise that neither bankers nor regulators have definitively answered this question. The typical banker's motto in determining what minimum capital ratio his bank should maintain seems to be: *Stay with the herd.* Banking tends to be a homogeneous industry and as such is characterized by pattern thinking. A banker judges his leverage ratio to be high or low in terms of where he is vis à vis his peers. If the pack lets their capital ratios fall, he is comfortable to follow, but he does not want to lead. This attitude makes sense because the Fed tends to judge banks against the pattern of what their competitors are doing. Also, bank customers who watch leverage carefully will penalize a bank that gets out of line.

Bank regulation

U.S. banks and foreign banks operating branches in the United States are highly regulated with respect to what they may do. As background, we present in an appendix to this chapter a short description of major U.S. banking acts.[18]

---

[18] Pp. 124–27

Banking in America is often referred to as a "dual" system because some banks operate under federal charters obtained from the Comptroller of the Currency, while others are chartered by the states. Banks operating under a federal charter are required to join the Federal Reserve System; state-chartered banks are not. State banks are more numerous than national banks, and the majority of them have not joined the Federal Reserve System primarily because reserve requirements make Fed membership expensive; this attitude will change as the 1980 Banking Act is implemented and all banks are required to hold reserves at the Fed. National banks are larger than state banks on the average, and as a result banks that are members of the Fed, while fewer in number, accept over 70% of the deposits received by domestic banks. Almost all banks in the country have opted to have their deposits insured by the Federal Deposit Insurance Corporation.

Bank regulation in the United States comes in layers. State banks are regulated by state banking authorities, national banks by the Comptroller. In addition, banks that are members of the Fed are regulated by the Fed, and the FDIC regulates insured banks. The overlap in bank regulation has led to periodic calls for a single unified system of bank regulation. However, movement in this direction seems unlikely because state banks, which are numerous and have considerable clout in Congress, are anxious to preserve a system in which the primary responsibility for regulating them lies with the local state banking authority; these banks fear being forced into a single national banking system.

Fortunately the regulatory overlap is less than appears on paper. Often the state regulators will focus on checking the accuracy of the bank's audited statements, whereas examiners from the Fed will be more concerned with whether the bank is being properly run.

The regulations under which U.S. banks, as opposed to British banks (see Chapter 6), operate are numerous, detailed, and complex; and they become more so all the time. Perhaps one reason is the checkered history of the U.S. banking system, which periodically experienced waves of failures and suspensions of payments right up into the 1930s. A second reason is that flexible regulation may be impractical in a country where there are 15,000 different banks, a situation unparalleled in any other major country.

Many people, particularly members of Congress, feel that, if the regulators were doing their job, no bank would have problems and that the existence of problem banks indicates the need for more or better regulation. Yet as one regulator noted, the same member of Congress who says there should never be problem banks is also quick to complain, when wheat prices are low and there is a big overhang in the wheat market, that Nebraska farmers are having trouble getting bank credit.

The nature of banking is taking risks by lending and by doing some maturity arbitrage. Good regulators see their job as trying to keep these risks prudent. They also recognize that the regulatory structure should not be such that no bank ever fails. If it were, banking as a creative force would be stifled.

When a bank experiences such severe problems that it ceases to be a viable institution, the regulators will normally arrange some sort of merger between that bank and another strong bank. This salvage operation may involve, as it did in the case of Franklin National, first substantial loans from the Fed to the ailing bank and later cash injections by the FDIC in exchange for some of the bank's less desirable assets.

The merger, if it occurs, is typically forced by events not by the regulators. As one regulator noted: "When a bank has problems, we try to save it so long as it's a viable institution. We will make suggestions to management, but it is their responsibility to right the situation. A bank ceases to be viable when public confidence in the bank weakens, usually due to some easily identifiable event. Before that occurs, we may look in the wings for potential marriage partners—act if you will as marriage brokers—but there is *no* shotgun for the marriage until public confidence is lost."

The fact that the Fed and the FDIC have not in recent decades permitted a *major* bank to fail with losses to depositors raises an interesting question: Would they ever? The answer, most observers believe (including some inside the Fed), is no.[19] The reason is that the economic consequences of permitting a major bank to fail with losses to depositors would be enormously more costly than acting to protect depositors. Still there is the *political risk,* that is, the possibility that a large bank might through its actions so arouse the public's ire that the Fed and the FDIC would not be permitted to save it.

BANK HOLDING COMPANIES

Almost all large banks and many smaller banks in the United States are owned by holding companies. Prior to the 1960s bank holding companies were used primarily to surmount restrictions on intrastate branching by bringing under a single organization a number of separately chartered banks. Formation of multibank holding companies was

---

[19] In 1982 the FDIC did permit the Penn Square Bank to fail with losses to depositors. Penn Square, with only a half billion in assets, was not, however, a *major* bank whose bankruptcy would bring down the system. The FDIC, however, normally bails out all depositors even when a small bank fails; it did not do so in the case of Penn Square presumably because that bank had suffered such huge losses that the cost to the FDIC of arranging a merger that would have protected all of Penn Square's depositors was more than the FDIC was willing to pay. Perhaps, too, the FDIC was trying to make a point to *yield buyers—* institutions looking for an extra ¼ or more on large-denomination CDs or time deposits: "Start doing some credit analysis instead of just grabbing the highest deposit rate a money broker can bring to you."

The story of the Penn Square failure is told at the end of this chapter.

brought under regulation by the Bank Holding Company Act in 1956. The purpose of this act, administered by the Federal Reserve Board, was twofold: to prevent the creation of monopoly power in banks and to prevent banks from entering via their holding company what were traditionally nonbank lines of activity.

In the late 1960s many of the nation's largest banks formed one-bank holding companies, which were not subject to the provisions of the 1956 act. One objective in doing so was to create a vehicle through which they could enter indirectly activities they could not carry out directly. The banks' ability to achieve such diversification was, however, severely limited by the Bank Holding Company Act of 1970. This act brought one-bank holding companies under regulation by the Federal Reserve Board, which is responsible for restricting their activities to those "which are so closely related to banking as to be a proper incident thereto."

A second reason banks formed one-bank holding companies was to achieve greater flexibility in liability management. During the late 1960s open-market rates rose on several occasions above the Reg Q ceiling, and banks had difficulty selling CDs. To solve the resulting funding problem, the banks segregated certain loans on their books, put them in the holding company, and issued commercial paper, which was not subject to Regulation Q, to fund these loans. The Fed's response to this end run around Reg Q was to impose a reserve requirement on any paper sold to fund such loans. This reserve requirement does not apply to other assets sold by a bank to its holding company.

Today bank holding companies enter the story of the money market primarily as issuers of commercial paper. They use the proceeds to fund various assets on their own books and on those of their nonbank subsidiaries (known as *subs*). These include bank credit card receivables purchased from the bank, assets leased, and loans extended through finance companies and other nonbank subs of the holding company.

EDGE ACT CORPORATIONS

A 1919 amendment to the Federal Reserve Act permits national banks and state banks that are members of the Federal Reserve System to establish international banking corporations, known familiarly as Edge Act corporations.

The operations of *Edge Act corporations* within the United States are restricted to activities that are incidental to the parent bank's international business—holding demand and time deposits received from foreign sources, issuing letters of credit, financing foreign trade, and creating BAs. Edge Act corporations are also permitted to engage in overseas operations, to provide certain types of specialized financing, such as loan syndication, and to make equity investments in foreign financial institutions.

Today all major U.S. banks have established an Edge Act corporation with branches in major financial centers around the country.[20] The principal function for which these subs are used is to carry out international banking business for the parent within the United States. The ability to set up an Edge Act sub, which because of its federal charter is exempt from state corporation and banking laws, gives banks a means to engage in interstate banking, albeit for limited purposes. This is particularly important to non-New York banks that use New York-based Edge Act subs to operate the equivalent of an international department in New York, the major domestic center for international banking. Edge Act corporations are also used by New York banks to participate in the regional markets for international banking that have developed in San Francisco, Chicago, Miami, and other commercial centers. For banks in high-tax states, Edge Act corporations offer an additional benefit—the ability to earn and book some income in lower-tax states.

With respect to the money market, Edge Act corporations are most prominent in the BA market. Currently a substantial fraction of all BAs outstanding are Edge Act corporation paper.

Domestic banks carry out the bulk of their foreign activities not through Edge Act corporations, but through foreign branches. The extensive activities of these foreign branches in the Eurodollar market are the topic of the next Chapter.

REGIONAL AND SMALL BANKS

In discussing bank management, our focus has been primarily on money market banks. We now shift to regional and small banks.

The first and most important point to be made is that our introductory remarks on profit and risk apply to *all* banks regardless of size. *Every* bank seeks to maximize profits subject to the constraint that perceived risk be held to some acceptable level. Also, in making asset and funding choices, *every* bank seeks to choose a balance sheet that meets this goal. Where money market banks and their smaller sisters differ is in the types of deposits and loan business they receive and in the funding options open to them.

Correspondent banking

Some of a large or regional bank's best customers are other smaller banks. Small banks look to a larger correspondent bank to provide them

---

[20] Banks used to have many separate Edge Act subs, one in each big financial center. Recently banks were permitted to merge their Edge Act subs into one corporation to increase the capitalization of Edge Act subs issuing BAs.

with various services: clearing checks, making wire transfers, buying and safekeeping securities, providing investment advice, offering participation in domestic and Euro loans, buying Fed funds in lots too small to be sold in the New York market, providing lines of credit, and buying and selling foreign exchange.

A bank using the services of a correspondent bank pays for many of these services by holding compensating balances at its correspondent bank. The correspondent bank relationship involves a form of barter, services for balances, that closely resembles the barter in which banks and their corporate clients engage. Both sorts of barter evolved because banks were forbidden by law from paying explicit interest on demand deposits.

Funding

Except in instances where it has done something to tarnish its good name, a money market bank has the option of buying huge sums of money in the Fed funds, repo, CD, and Euromarkets; and money market banks liberally exercise this option. A typical money market bank may finance over 60% of its assets with money bought in these markets. The corresponding figure for a regional bank would be 30 to 40%, and for a small bank, 0%.

Regional and small banks rely less heavily than money market banks on bought money for several reasons. Money market banks have many major corporations as customers; the latter are often big borrowers but seek to hold the smallest possible deposit balances at the banks from which they borrow. As a result, money market banks, excepting the B of A with its huge branch network, are deposit poor and must buy outside money to finance their basic asset structure. Most regional and all small banks do a lot of consumer business and consequently receive large amounts of demand and time deposits from consumers. Net consumers tend to deposit in demand and time deposits at banks more than they borrow from banks. Thus, regional banks and small banks, are often deposit rich.

Being deposit rich is especially common for a small bank. In fact, the single most important difference between small banks and other banks is that small banks may well have resources comprising capital, *hardcore* (won't go away) demand deposits and savings money that exceed their loan assets. To pluck some numbers out of the air, a small bank might have $30 million in capital and deposits and only $20 million in loans, leaving it with a surplus of $10 million. The bank might invest these funds by placing $5 million through its correspondent bank in the Euromarket and selling another $5 million of Fed funds, also through its correspondent bank.

A second reason that regional and small banks rely less on bought money than money market banks do is *market access*. A bank's ability to tap the national money market for funds, credit problems excepted, is directly proportional to its size. Money market banks that have preserved their good name can essentially buy all of the money they want; for them, the binding constraint on buying money and ballooning their balance sheet is the need to maintain a respectable capital ratio. Large regional banks have fair access to the national money market. Small regionals have only *very* limited access to this market, and small banks have no access at all.

CD money.   Technically, any bank can issue a large-denomination negotiable CD. However, a CD buyer desires liquidity and is therefore interested not just in negotiability but in *marketability*. He wants paper for which there is an active secondary market. Currently, there are only about 20 large domestic banks whose paper trades well in the secondary market. All other banks are shut out of the *national* market for CD money.

To sell CDs, banks that lack access to the national market—depending on their size—must look to regional or local customers in their economic sphere of interest.[21] This means that smaller banks cannot balloon their CD borrowings as a major bank can. It does not mean that such banks cannot sell CDs to anyone except consumers. Smaller banks do sell CDs in varying sizes to corporate customers that have insufficient cash to buy a $1 million CD issued by a major bank.[22] The advantage of buying a CD that is not marketable because of size or name for a corporation that might instead make a time deposit is that, if the corporation experiences an unanticipated need for money, it can always use the CD it has purchased from one bank as collateral for borrowing from another bank. Thus by buying a CD, the corporation gets liquidity a time deposit would not give it.

Small banks and other banks that do retail as well as corporate business also raise funds by issuing 6-month *money market certificates* (*MMCs*) and longer-term savings certificates. In 1978, the Fed gave banks authority to issue these consumer-oriented CDs so that they could compete more effectively for funds with money market funds and other instruments that offer consumers rates near or equal to the rates prevailing in the money market. MMCs now represent a substantial portion of the total time deposits received by banks doing a lot of retail business. The money banks raise by selling these certificates is expensive relative

---

[21] For sales by wire houses, such as Merrill, of CDs and BAs issued by smaller regionals, see Chapters 15 and 17.

[22] Major banks can and sometimes do issue CDs with a face value below $1 million to corporate customers. The problem with such CDs is that they trade at a concession in the secondary market, which is essentially a market for $1 million pieces of paper.

to the other deposits they receive; its high cost has forced small banks, and thrifts in particular, to make more sophisticated balance-sheet choices and to look for arbitrages that will permit them to utilize this money profitably. An attractive use—from the point of view of risk and return—that small banks and *thrifts as well* can make of money raised through the sale of 6-month MMCs and not required to support their basic asset structure is to make Euro time deposits of similar maturity. Because money funds tend to buy only paper issued by money market banks, the recent authorization of all banks to offer MMDA and super-NOW accounts has significantly increased the flow of funds to many regional and small banks that bid aggressively for such accounts.

Federal funds.   While the national CD market is open to only 20 or so top banks, the Fed funds market is broader; many regional banks buy Fed funds not only from their correspondents but in the New York market. All money market banks, with the exception of the deposit-rich B of A, are big net buyers of Fed funds; regional banks are smaller net buyers; and small banks are net sellers. Federal funds represent a source of liquidity both for banks that are net *buyers* of funds *and* for banks that are *sellers* of funds. For buyers, funds represent a source of liquidity because they are a liability that the buyer can expand at will. For sellers, funds also represent a source of liquidity because they are an asset the selling bank can liquidate without loss any time it needs money either to pay off deposit liabilities or to fund the purchase of a more attractive asset.

Euros.   All money market banks, all regional banks, and some small banks participate in the Eurodollar market. Large banks are net takers of funds in this market and so are large regionals. Smaller banks, to the extent that they participate at all, are lenders of funds.

Assets

Loans.   Banks, depending on their size, hold different types of loans on their books. A number of money market banks, the Irving Trust, Morgan, and Bankers Trust to name three, restrict their business largely to commercial and industrial (C&I) customers and to other financial institutions.[23] Regional banks generally do at least some retail business, and all small banks do a lot of retail business.

Banks making domestic loans to corporate clients typically price these loans either at a floating-rate prime or a fixed rate tied to their cost of funds. In contrast, banks that do retail business end up with a lot of 3- to 5-year *fixed-rate* paper that is financing car purchases and home improvements, and with long-term mortgages. The differences in maturities and pricing between C&I loans and consumer loans means that

---

[23] Trust department business with wealthy customers is an exception.

funding the loan portfolio has quite different implications for small and large banks with respect to liquidity and rate risk.

Size influences not only the types of borrowers that come to a bank but the size of the loan demand a bank faces relative to the total deposits it receives. Normally, loan demand at a money market bank far exceeds the bank's deposit base, and as a result, the bank has to finance some portion of its loans with bought money. Small banks, in contrast, sometimes find themselves with more deposits than loans. Banks in that position, instead of having to solve a funding problem, have to seek out attractive earning assets.

One way in which smaller banks acquire additional loan paper is by buying participations in loans made by their larger correspondent banks. Large banks sometimes *participate out* loans to their smaller correspondents as an accommodation to the latter and sometimes as a way to solve their own funding problems. Money market banks also participate Euro loans out to smaller regionals. These banks viewed such paper as highly attractive until 1982 when big Euro debtors, such as Mexico and Poland, ran out of dollars and had to negotiate rescheduling of their bank debts.

How attractive taking a participation in a loan will be for a given bank will depend not only on the national business situation—are business loans in the aggregate up or down—but on local conditions. Regional and small banks have to look to borrowers in their own sphere of interest for loans, and demand for loans there may be sluggish even when loan demand on the national level is strong. Such sluggishness might reflect depressed farm prices for a country bank or a downturn in local industry for a city bank.

Besides participating in other banks' loans, banks with excess deposits formerly used some of their surplus funds to buy commercial paper. That has become less common as the cost of funds to such banks has risen through introduction of MMCs and as the sophistication of such banks has increased. Many smaller banks now place funds in the Euromarket directly or through their correspondent. The spread between rates on short-term Eurodeposits and that on commercial paper is usually so wide that Euros are by far the more attractive investment.

Governments. For reasons described above, it is becoming less attractive for banks across the board to invest in government securities, but most banks still have at least some governments and agency paper. Money market banks never invest in governments because they are looking for an interest-bearing asset in which to park spare cash. These deposit-poor banks always finance their holdings of governments in the repo market, and their government portfolio, to the extent that it yields them profit, does so because they earn positive carry. Small banks, in contrast, often buy governments to absorb surplus funds. Regional banks, like large banks, are more likely to buy governments as an arbitrage.[24]

Because a repo transaction is backed by securities, more banks have access to the national repo market than have access to the national CD market. Besides doing repo in the national market, regional banks also do repo with their local customers. Even a few small banks now get into the act by doing RPs with consumers; this innovation was a product of high interest rates.

DOMESTIC BANKS THAT GOT IT WRONG

The year 1982 was tough for domestic banks. Several major banks encountered big problems; one regional failed with a splash. The shock tremor sent through financial markets by these events was disproportionately large because they occurred against a backdrop of troubles at other financial institutions. On the domestic side, S&L failures and bailout mergers occurred almost daily. On the international scene, failure of a subsidiary of the Banco Ambrosiano shocked the Euromarkets. That shock was followed by disclosure that the top Canadian banks had been mammoth lenders to a once-darling-of-investors but now near-bankrupt firm, Dome Petroleum. Finally, big sovereign loans syndicated in the Euromarket started souring at an alarming rate. Poland's debt was rescheduled, and before the dust had settled on that suspenseful-to-the-last-moment saga—to reschedule or to default—Mexico was demonstrating to its neighbors how to turn huge Euro and Gringo loans into nonperforming loans.

Penn Square failure

The Penn Square failure, the first since FDIC in which depositors lost money, was by far the most notable domestic bank failure of the year.[25] Fortunately it was not indicative of any widespread ill health in the U.S. banking system. Instead Penn Square was a sort of go go aberration. Its assets, $525 million in July 1982, were 17 times what they had been six years before, growth due largely to an energy-related loan binge.

Investors in anything from tulips to common stock are subject to crowd psychology. When a new investment becomes *the* hot fad, they *have* to get into it. Banks too are subject to crowd psychology. When REITS were the fad, most banks, to their later regret, got into REIT lend-

---

[24] The above describes what might be called normal operating procedure for a bank in a normal world. In the historically unusual circumstances that prevailed as the 1980s dawned, banks lost, temporarily at least, *all* rational reason to hold investment portfolios of government securities.

[25] See footnote, p. 114.

ing. Because energy-related loans were a fad until oil prices peaked, Penn Square not only made a lot of questionable energy-related loans but was able to peddle participations in those loans to big banks who should have known better: $1 billion to Continental, $200 to $300 million to Chase, $400 million to Seafirst, $200 million to Michigan National, and $125 million to Northern Trust.

Penn Square's demise was reported to have involved more than a misplaced enthusiasm for energy-related loans. Federal regulators investigating the failure of Penn Square had by September 1982 referred to the Justice Department at least 31 cases of possible criminal violations: embezzling or misapplying funds, taking kickbacks or illegal gifts, concealing assets, making false claims and statements, and offering bribes.

As early as April 1980, the Comptroller, during a routine audit of Penn Square, put the banks under special supervision. Subsequent examinations of Penn Square by the Comptroller showed that the bank's problems were continuing, even worsening. Questions must be asked in the wake of Penn Square's demise: What is supervision by the Comptroller worth? Why didn't the Comptroller blow the whistle that Penn Square was a troubled bank (1) to alert depositors who were placing uninsured monies (deposits in excess of $100,000) with Penn Square and (2) to alert banks that were buying loans generated by Penn Square? The answer to the second question seems to be that the tradition at the Comptroller's office is to protect a problem bank from publicity on the theory that, if a specific bank were named as a problem bank by the Comptroller, that would cause a run on that bank and its subsequent failure, which in turn might cause a general loss of confidence in the banking system, which in turn might set off a wave of bank failures like those that occurred during the 1930s. The Comptroller's logic is questionable. Banks failed in waves *only* before the FDIC was created to reassure depositors. Also, there is the recent example of the Franklin National Bank, which—thanks to federal assistance—was able to limp along for months under the burden of huge, well-publicized losses until it was merged into the European American Bank.[26]

Continental Illinois

During the spring and summer of 1982, Continental Illinois saw its image as one the nation's top banks sorely tarnished. Continental was a big taker of participations in the energy-related loans Penn Square was making; on these Continental had to take a second-quarter, pretax write-off of $220 million. Later in the summer Nucorp Energy—for which Conti-

[26] See footnote, p. 105.

nental, as leader of a group of nine banks, had put together a $300+ million revolving credit agreement—filed for Chapter 11 protection. Energy-related loans were not Continental's only problem. It had also made big loans to Penn Square, Braniff, International Harvester, Dome Petroleum, Wicks, and other firms that either went bankrupt or were experiencing severe financial problems.

The upshot of Continental's numerous sour and souring loans was that it faced a liquidity problem. To maintain liquidity, even a top-10 bank must make every effort to keep its name pure in the market place because, from everyone's point of view, there is *no* penalty for not lending to a bank that has let a shadow be cast over its good name.

Because of the large losses—real and potential—deriving from Continental's loan portfolio, investors by the summer of 1982 did not want and felt no need to hold Continental's paper. As a result Continental, the nation's seventh largest bank, was forced to ask CD dealers to remove its name from the list of top banks whose CDs traded—because they were viewed as all being issued by top credits—on a no-name basis. Continental was also forced to ask the IMM to delete its name from the list of banks whose paper was deliverable on a maturing futures contract for 90-day CDs; prior to doing so, Continental was the bank whose CDs were most frequently delivered at the expiration of a CD futures contract.

For a top bank, going through a period when it cannot sell its CDs in volume in the national market is not fatal: First of Chicago did it. Doing so, however, is costly to a bank because the inability to tap the national money market in volume inevitably raises the bank's cost of funds, which in turn has a negative impact on its profitability so long as the condition persists.

Fortunately for Continental, it continued to be able to buy Fed funds without having to pay up: Other banks knew Continental would not go bankrupt overnight. For a time, however, Continental did have to pay up for Euros.

To regain the confidence of investors and thereby liquidity—the ability to obtain money when it needs it at a *reasonable price*—Continental will have to do what First of Chicago did: take its lumps in the form of loan losses, slim its loan portfolio to creditworthy names, and regain a respectable and consistent record of profitability. Once it does this, investors will again be willing to lend to Continental on the same terms on which they lend to other top banks.

The Chase Bank

In 1982 the Chase managed a first of its own in American banking: It dropped slightly over a quarter of a billion pretax by fronting in the eyes of the street—acting as an agent in the eyes of Chase—for a small dealer, Drysdale. The story of the Drysdale debacle and Chase's involvement in it is told at the end of Chapter 9. Drysdale will go down in the history of dealers as the firm that managed to lose the most money on the basis of the least capital in the shortest period (three months from birth to death).

The Drysdale hit was the worst but not the only black eye Chase got in 1982. It also bought in roughly a quarter of a billion of questionable loans from Penn Square; and to add insult to injury, Chase had a $45 million unsecured claim against Lombard-Wall when the firm filed for bankruptcy in August 1982. (Lombard-Wall's voyage into Chapter 11 is also described at the end of Chapter 9.)

Thanks to Chase's well-publicized problems, Chase's paper—like Continental's—fell into disfavor with investors. As one money manager noted, ". . . people stay away from [Chase paper], not for investment reasons but because of a feeling of who needs it?" Like the Continental, Chase will restore its good name in due time as it reestablishes a record of respectable and stable earnings.

We have described the difficulties experienced by the Continental and Chase because these banks are mentioned frequently in later chapters as banks who, in various markets, had to either pay up for funds or lay back on issuing paper until the spotlight turned away from their difficulties. The money market is efficient; it is neither kind nor forgiving.[27]

APPENDIX TO CHAPTER 5

THE BANKING ACTS THAT MATTER*

Edge Act: 1919. Named after Senator Walter Edge of New Jersey, who played a prominent role in its passage, this act provided for federal chartering of corporations formed to engage solely in international or foreign banking. The hope was that these Edge Act corporations would play a key role in financing American exports.

McFadden Act: 1927. This prohibits interstate banking.

Glass-Steagall Act: 1933. This severed commercial from investment banking and forced banks to divest themselves of any security-

---

[27] For more on banks that got it wrong in recent years—The Franklin National Bank, The First Pennsylvania Bank (First Pennsy to the market), and The First National Bank of Chicago, see Chapter 7 of Marcia Stigum and Rene Branch, *Managing Bank Assets and Liabilities: Strategies for Risk Control and Profit* (Homewood, Ill.: Dow Jones-Irwin, 1982).

* From "A Survey of International Banking," *The Economist*, March 14, 1981, p. 19.

trading affiliates. The 1933 Banking Act also created the Federal Deposit Insurance Corporation and brought bank holding companies—except, as was discovered later, the one-bank holding companies—under the supervision of the Federal Reserve Board.

Douglas Amendment to the Bank Holding Company Act: 1956. This prohibits a bank holding company headquartered in one state from acquiring a bank in another state unless the second state specifically permits the acquisition.

Bank Merger Act: 1960. After a decade of debate over whether to apply existing antitrust laws explicitly to banking or to incorporate similar competitive standards into existing banking laws, this legislation plumped for the second course. It required the bank regulatory agencies (for the first time) to weigh the possible competitive effects of proposed mergers and acquisitions when considering applications.

Amendment to the Bank Holding Company Act: 1970. This brought one-bank holding companies under the same regulations as multibank holding companies.

International Banking Act: 1978. To bring foreign banks within the federal regulatory framework, the IBA introduced six major statutory changes:

It limited interstate domestic deposit taking by foreign banks. Previously, foreign banks had been free to open full-service branches wherever state law permitted. The new law required each foreign bank to elect a "home state" and restricted domestic deposit taking by offices outside that state.

Existing multistate branch networks of foreign banks were "grandfathered" (allowed to carry on as they were), a major concession since 40 of the 50 largest foreign banks were able to shelter under its wing.

It provided the option of federal licensing for foreign bank agencies and branches. Previously all foreign bank offices had state licenses and some states applied reciprocity rules which effectively barred banks from certain countries.

The federal licensing authority (the Comptroller of the Currency) has permitted foreign banks to establish offices without regard to whether the foreign bank's home country grants equivalent access to American banks.

It authorized the Federal Reserve Board to impose reserve requirements on agencies and branches of foreign banks with worldwide assets of more than $1 billion and to limit the maximum rates of interest such offices could pay on time deposits to the same as member banks.

It required federal deposit insurance (not previously available to foreign banks) for those branches engaged in retail deposit taking.

It amended the Edge Act to permit Edge corporations (which could conduct international banking out-of-state) to compete over a broader range of business and permitted foreign banks to set up such corporations.

It subjected foreign banks to the same prohibitions on nonbanking business as domestic bank holding companies. Once again, existing nonbanking activities (including securities underwriting from which domestic banks are excluded) were "grandfathered."

Depository Institutions Deregulation and Monetary Control Act: 1980. This "omnibus act" had four main aims:

To phase out (over a six-year period) interest rate ceilings on deposits and to eliminate the .25 percent favorable differential traditionally enjoyed by the thrifts. A Depository Institutions Deregulation Committee, with representatives from the main regulatory agencies, was set up to oversee the process. All the evidence points to the committee accomplishing its task in far less than six years.

To extend nationwide the authority (previously exclusive to the New England states) to offer NOW (negotiable order of withdrawal) accounts. The maximum rate to be offered on NOW accounts has been set initially at 5.25% for all institutions. This ends the prohibition on the payment of interest on demand deposits.

To grant new powers to the federally chartered thrifts. A number of states have passed parallel legislation for state-chartered institutions to discourage desertion from state to federal charter. Most importantly, these powers permit S&Ls to invest up to 20 percent of their assets in consumer loans, commercial paper, and company securities; to offer credit cards; and to exercise fiduciary powers.

To override state-imposed usury ceilings on mortgages. (Some states have already taken action to raise their ceilings.)

Depository Institutions Act: 1982.* This act was designed to aid failing thrifts and to permit both banks and thrifts to compete immediately for deposits with money funds.

To accomplish the first aim, the act created a scheme under which thrifts whose net worth drops below 3% of their assets can prop up their net worth by swapping paper they issue for promissory notes—to be counted as capital—from the Federal Savings and Loan Insurance Corporation, which insures deposits at S&Ls up to $100,000. For thrifts too sick to survive even with such aid, the act specially permits takeovers by

---

* Author's addition.

an out-of-state thrift or even a bank. The act also gives thrifts the new right to make commercial loans up to 10% of their total assets and to accept deposits from firms as well as individuals.

To help banks and thrifts compete with money funds, the new act required the Depository Institutions Deregulatory Committee to establish a new account that carried *no* interest rate controls and *no* withdrawal penalties and that permitted a depositor with such an account to make each month three pre-authorized transfers from it and to write three checks on it. The questions of whether unlimited withdrawals from such accounts would be permitted, of what minimum balance would be required, and of what if any reserve requirements would apply was left to the Depository Institutions Deregulatory Committee. The new account, whether at a bank or thrift, was to resemble a money fund account but have the added attraction to depositors of carrying federal insurance from the FDIC or FSLIC on deposits up to $100,000. The DIDC responded to this Congressional mandate by crediting first the new *money market deposit account* (*MMDA*) (December 1982) and then the new *super-Now account* (January 1983).

The law also stipulated that all interest-rate controls on bank accounts as well as the ¼% advantage S&Ls now enjoy over banks on the rates they may pay on time deposits must be phased out by January 1984, two years earlier than scheduled in the 1980 Banking Act.

Finally the act raised from 10% to 15% of capital and surplus the amount that nationally-chartered banks may lend to any one borrower. In general legal lending limits for state-chartered banks equal or exceed those for national ones.

Chapter 6

The banks: Euro operations

ACCORDING TO PROPAGANDISTS on both sides of the Iron Curtain, communists and capitalists are implacable enemies. It thus comes as a surprise to find that communist central banks bear as much responsibility as anyone for giving birth to one of the fastest growing, most vital and important capitalist institutions—namely, the international capital market known as the *Eurodollar market*. But then neither communist nor capitalist bankers had much idea of the long-run implications of what they were doing when the Euromarket was born.

EURO TRANSACTIONS IN T-ACCOUNTS

The best way to start a discussion of the Euromarket is by explaining the mechanics of Eurodeposits and loans, about which there is much confusion. First, a definition: *Eurodollars are simply dollars held on deposit in a bank or bank branch located outside the United States or in an IBF.*[1] If a U.S. investor shifts $1 million of deposits from a New York bank to the London branch of a U.S. bank, to Barclays London, or to the London branch of any French, German, or other foreign bank and re-

---

[1] International banking facilities (IBFs) are described at the end of this chapter.

ceives in exchange a deposit denominated in dollars, he has made a *Eurodollar deposit.* Such deposits came to be known as *Eurodollars* because initially banks in Europe were most active in seeking and accepting such deposits. Today, however, banks all over the globe are active in the Eurodollar market, and the term *Eurodollar* is a misnomer.[2]

The first important point to make about Eurodollars is that regardless of where they are deposited—London, Singapore, Tokyo, or Bahrain— they never leave the United States. Also, they never leave the U.S. regardless of where they are lent—to a multinational firm, to an underdeveloped country, or to an East European government. Let's work that out with T-accounts. As noted in Chapter 2, a T-account shows *changes in assets and liabilities* that result from a given financial transaction, as shown below.

T-Account	
Change in assets	Change in liabilities

To get our example going, suppose Exxon moves $10 million from its account at Morgan in New York to the London branch of Citibank. (You can think of Exxon as writing a check against Morgan New York and depositing it in Citi London, but the transaction is done by wire or Telex.) Clearing of this transaction, which normally occurs on the day after it is initiated, will result in several balance-sheet changes (Table 6–1).

Before we look at these changes, two preliminary remarks are in order. First, Citi's London branch is an integral part of Citibank; and when the bank publishes statements, it consolidates the assets and liabilities of head office and all foreign branches. However, on a day-to-day operating basis, Citi New York, Citi London, and Citi's other foreign branches all keep separate books. Second, Citibank has just one account at the Fed, that held by Citi New York, the head office.

Now let's look at Table 6–1. It shows that, as a result of the transaction, Exxon exchanges one asset, $10 million of demand deposits at Morgan New York, for another, $10 million of Eurodeposits at Citi London. To make this exchange, Exxon withdrew funds from Morgan and deposited them at Citi. This means, of course, that when the transaction clears, Morgan has to pay Citi the funds Exxon has transferred from one bank to the other. Morgan does this in effect by transferring money from its reserve (checking) account at the Fed to Citi's reserve account at the Fed.

---

[2] Some people refer to dollar deposits accepted in Singapore and other Far East centers as *Asian currency units* (ACUs) or *Asian dollars.* The natural extension of this practice would be to refer to dollar deposits accepted in Bahrain as Mid East dollars and dollar deposits accepted in Nassau as Caribbean dollars; that is, to use a multitude of terms to describe the same thing, an offshore deposit of dollars. The logical alternative to the term *Eurodollar* is an *international dollar,* a phrase that has never caught on.

TABLE 6–1
A Eurodeposit is made and cleared

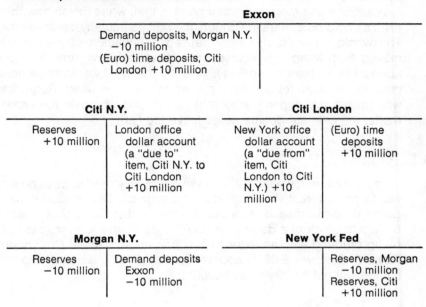

Exxon	
Demand deposits, Morgan N.Y. −10 million (Euro) time deposits, Citi London +10 million	

Citi N.Y.		Citi London	
Reserves +10 million	London office dollar account (a "due to" item, Citi N.Y. to Citi London +10 million	New York office dollar account (a "due from" item, Citi London to Citi N.Y.) +10 million	(Euro) time deposits +10 million

Morgan N.Y.		New York Fed	
Reserves −10 million	Demand deposits Exxon −10 million		Reserves, Morgan −10 million Reserves, Citi +10 million

Thus the transaction causes Morgan to lose reserves and Citi New York to gain them. At Morgan the loss of reserves is offset by a decrease in deposit liabilities.

At Citibank the situation is more complicated, as Table 6–1 shows. Citi London has received the deposit, but Citi New York has received the extra reserves. So Citi New York in effect owes Citi London money. This is accounted for by adjusting the *New York office dollar account*, which can be thought of simply as a checking account that Citi London holds with Citi New York. To Citi London, as long as this account is in surplus, which it normally would be, the account is a *due from* item, that it shows up on Citi London's balance sheet as an asset. On Citi New York's balance sheet the same account is a *due to* item, that consequently shows up on Citi New York's balance sheet as any other deposit would. With this in mind, it's easy to follow what happens on Citibank's books as a result of Exxon's deposit. Citi London gets a new $10 million liability in the form of a time deposit, which is offset by an equal credit to its account with home office. Meanwhile, home office gets $10 million of extra reserves, which are offset by a like increase in its liability to its London branch.

Note several things about this example. First, the changes that occurred on every institution's balance sheet were offsetting; i.e., net worth never changes. This is *always* the case in any transaction, the consequences of which can be illustrated with T-accounts.

A second and more important point is that, while Exxon now thinks of itself as holding dollars in London, the dollars actually never left the U.S. The whole transaction simply caused $10 million of reserves to be moved from Morgan's reserve account at the New York Fed to Citi's account there (see Table 6–1). This, by the way, would have been the case in any Eurodeposit example we might have used. Regardless of who makes the deposit, who receives it, and where in the world it is made, the ultimate dollars never leave the U.S.

A Euroloan

In our example we left Citi London with a new time deposit on which it has to pay interest. To profit from that deposit, Citi London is naturally going to lend those dollars out. Suppose, that Citi London lends the dollars to Electricité de France (EDF). Initially this loan results in EDF's being credited with an extra $10 million in deposits at Citi London, as Table 6–2 shows. EDF of course has borrowed the money, so the $10 million will not sit idly in its account.

TABLE 6–2
A Euroloan is granted to EDF

Citi London		EDF	
Loan, EDF +10 million	(Euro) deposits, EDF +10 million	(Euro) deposits Citi London +10 million	Loan, Citi London +10 million

Assume that EDF uses the dollars it has borrowed to pay for oil purchased from an Arab seller who banks at Chase London. Table 6–3, which should be self-explanatory to anyone who followed Table 6–1, shows the balance-sheet changes that will result from this transaction. Note that when EDF pulls $10 million out of Citi London, the latter, since it has no real dollars other than a deposit balance with Citi New York, must in effect ask Citi New York to pay out this money with dollars that Citi New York has in its reserve account at the Fed. As this is done, offsetting changes occur in the New York and London office dollar accounts at Citibank. Meanwhile opposite but similar changes occur on the books of Chase London and Chase New York.

It is important to note that in this Euroloan transaction, just as in the Eurodollar deposit transaction we worked through above, the dollars never leave New York. The transaction simply results in a movement of

TABLE 6–3
EDF uses its borrowed dollars to pay for oil

EDF		Arab Oil Seller	
(Euro) deposits −10 million	Accounts payable −10 million	Accounts receivable −10 million (Euro) deposits, Chase London +10 million	

Citi London		Chase London	
New York office dollar account −10 million	(Euro) deposits EDF −10 million	New York office dollar account +10 million	Time deposits, Arab oil seller +10 million

Citi N.Y.		Chase N.Y.	
Reserves −10 million	London office dollar account −10 million	Reserves +10 million	London office dollar account +10 million

New York Fed	
	Reserves, Citibank −10 million Reserves, Chase +10 million

$10 million from Citi's reserve account at the New York Fed to that of the Chase. One might argue that we have not yet gone far enough—that the Arab oil seller is going to spend the dollars he has received and that they might then leave the U.S. But that is not so. Whoever gets the dollars the Arab spends will have to deposit them somewhere, and thus the spending by the Arab of his dollars will simply shift them from one bank's reserve account to another's. In this respect it might be useful to recall a point made in Chapter 2. The only way reserves at the Fed can be increased or decreased in the aggregate is through open-market operations initiated by the Fed itself. The one exception is withdrawals of cash from the banking system. If the Arab oil seller were to withdraw $10 million in cash from Chase London and lock it up in a safe there or elsewhere, the dollars would have actually left the U.S. However, no big depositor would do that because of opportunity cost: Eurodeposits yield interest, cash in a vault would not.

A Europlacement with a foreign bank

In the Euromarket banks routinely lend dollars to other banks by making deposits with them and borrow dollars from other banks by taking deposits from them. People in the Euromarket and people in New York with international experience always refer to the depositing of Eurodollars with another bank as a *placement* of funds and to the receipt of Eurodollar deposits from another bank as a *taking* of funds. Other people in the U.S. money market are likely to use the jargon of the Fed funds market, referring to placements of Euros as *sales* of funds and to takings of Euros as *purchases* of funds.

To illustrate what happens when a foreign bank ends up holding a Eurodollar deposit, let's work through the mechanics of a placement of Eurodollars with such a bank. Assume that Chase London places a $20 million deposit in the London branch of Crédit Lyonnais.

The special feature of this example is that Crédit Lyonnais, unlike an American bank, is not a member of the Federal Reserve System. This used to mean that the bank, because it was foreign, did not have a reserve account at the Fed and therefore had to keep its dollars on deposit in a U.S. bank. Since passage of the 1978 International Banking Act, foreign bank branches operating in the U.S. are required to hold reserves at the Fed and consequently must have an account there. These branches have, however, continued to make and receive the bulk of their payments through a deposit account they maintain at their U.S. correspondent bank. One reason is that the Fed will not permit foreign bank branches to run a daylight overdraft in their Fed account (see Chapter 16).

To continue our example, suppose that the dollars placed by Chase London with the London branch of Crédit Lyonnais are deposited in a Crédit Lyonnais account at Morgan New York. Then, as Table 6–4 shows, the net effect of the transaction will be that Crédit Lyonnais ends up with dollars on deposit in New York, and reserves move from Chase's account at the Fed to Morgan's account. Note again that the dollars remain in New York, even though they are now held by the London branch of a French bank.

In constructing our example, we tried to keep things simple and so ignored an important detail, namely, how Euro transactions are cleared. In the U.S. it is customary for banks to make payments between each other in Federal funds, that is, by transferring funds on deposit at the Fed over the Fed wire; all large payments in the money and bond markets are

TABLE 6–4
A Eurodollar interbank placement

Chase London		Crédit Lyonnais, London	
(Euro) time deposit, Crédit Lyonnais, London +20 million New York office dollar account −20 million		Deposit, Morgan N.Y. +20 million	Time deposit, Chase London +20 million

Chase N.Y.		Morgan N.Y.	
Reserves −20 million	London office dollar account −20 million	Reserves +20 million	Deposits, Crédit Lyonnais, London +20 million

New York Fed	
	Reserves, Chase −20 million Reserves, Morgan +20 million

also made in Fed funds. In contrast, in the Euromarket money transfers are made and settled through the New York Clearing House, known as *CHIPS*—an acroynm for the computerized Clearing House Interbank Payments System. Payments made through CHIPS used to result in the receipt of *clearing house funds,* which became Fed funds only on the day after receipt. The distinction between Fed funds (good money today) and clearing house funds (good money tomorrow) did several things: It set the stage for banks to engage in profitable technical arbitrages between the two sorts of funds; it also was the source of no end of confusion for foreigners dealing for the first time in the Eurodollar market; and finally, as volume on CHIPS grew, it created an overnight credit risk that both CHIPS and the Fed eventually deemed unacceptable.

Reacting to this risk, CHIPS moved on October 1, 1981, to same-day settlement. Despite a great deal of trepidation by U.S. bankers, who feared a grand-scale, computer snafu, the switch by CHIPS to same-day settlement went so smoothly that all Euromarket participants termed it a nonevent.

For more about CHIPS—its history, method of operation, and relationship to the Fed wire—see Chapter 16.

HISTORY OF THE MARKET

Anyone following Tables 6–1 through 6–4 is likely to wonder what the rationale is for carrying on outside the U.S. huge volumes of dollar deposit and loan transactions in what seems to be a rather complicated fashion. The best way to answer is to describe briefly the stimuli that gave birth to the Euromarket.

Long before World War II it was not uncommon for banks outside the U.S. to accept deposits denominated in dollars. However, the volume of such deposits was small, and the market for them had little economic significance. During the 1950s things began to change. One reason was the activities of the communist central banks. Since Russia and other communist countries imported certain goods that had to be paid for in dollars and exported others that could be sold for dollars, the central banks of these countries ended up holding dollar balances. Initially these balances were held on deposit in New York, but as Cold War tensions heightened, this practice became less attractive to the communists, who feared that at some point the U.S. might block their New York balances. As a result they transferred these balances to banks in London and other European centers. The value of the dollar goods the communist countries wanted to import often exceeded the amount of dollars they were earning on exports, so these countries became not only important lenders to the Eurodollar market but also important borrowers in this market.

While the Cold War may have kicked off the Euromarket, other factors stimulated its development. Historically the pound sterling played a key role in world trade. A great deal of trade not only within the British Commonwealth, but between Commonwealth nations and the rest of the world and between third countries was denominated in British currency, the pound sterling, and financed in London through borrowings of sterling. After World War II this began to change. Britain ran big balance of payments deficits (that is, spent more abroad than it earned), and as a result devaluation of the British pound—a decrease in the amount of foreign exchange for which a pound could be traded—was a constant threat and in fact actually occurred several times during the period of pegged exchange rates. The chronic weakness of the pound made it a less attractive currency to earn and to hold, which in turn stimulated the trend for more and more international trade to be denominated in dollars. It also caused the British to restrict the use of sterling for financing international trade. Specifically in 1957 the British government restricted the use of sterling in financing trade between non-sterling-area countries, and in 1976 it restricted the use of sterling in financing trade between Commonwealth countries and non-sterling-area countries. Because of the increased use of dollars as the availability of sterling financing decreased, importers began borrowing Eurodollars to finance trade, and the Euromarket emerged first as a nascent and then as a fast-growing and important international capital market.

In the early days of the Eurodollar market, it was British banks, not U.S. banks, that played a leading role. Historically British banks had a dominant place in financing world trade, so they had expertise other banks lacked. Given that expertise, British banks shrewdly took the view that they could finance international trade in whatever currency was available and acceptable—beads or, as happened to be the case, dollars.

U.S. banks entered the Euromarket step-by-step and always *defensively*—their fear being that their London activities would undercut their domestic operations. One U.S. banker, who was in London during the market's formative years, noted, "The story of how the U.S. banks entered the Euromarket reflects rather poorly on us because we did not think out where the market was going. It just sort of grew up on us."

During the early 1950s when the Russian and East European banks began depositing dollars outside the U.S., the London branches of U.S. banks were *not* taking Eurodollar deposits. They began to do so very hesitantly several years later when some of their good U.S. customers said to them, "Can't you take our dollar deposits in London? The foreign banks do, and they give us better rates than you can in New York because of Reg Q." For several years this worked out satisfactorily because the head offices of the U.S. banks involved could profitably use in the U.S. the dollars deposited with their London branches. This was so because the structure of the loan and other interest rates in the U.S. was such that U.S. banks could well afford to pay higher rates than those permitted under Reg Q.

Then the London branches of U.S. banks began getting 3- and 6-month money, that the head offices of U.S. banks did not want because it did not fit their books (asset and liability structures). So, again very defensively, the London branches of the U.S. banks began making Eurodollar loans to commercial customers and placements of deposits with foreign banks. In doing so they said, "We are giving you this money but don't count on our continuing to do so because we don't know how long we will continue getting this funny money called Eurodollars." For years U.S. banks did not view their Eurodollar activities with a customer as traditional, ongoing banking relationship.

In its initial stages, the growth of the Euromarket was hampered by the myriad of exchange control regulations that all nations except the U.S. imposed on their residents with respect to (1) the use of domestic currency to acquire foreign exchange and (2) the disposition of foreign exchange earning. This changed in 1958 when the major European countries, with the exception of the U.K., substantially liberalized their foreign exchange controls as a first step toward making their currencies fully convertible.

A fourth factor that stimulated the growth of the Euromarket was the operation of Regulation Q during the tight money years of 1968 and 1969. At that time U.S. money rates rose above the rates that banks were permitted to pay under Reg Q on domestic large-denomination CDs. To finance loans, U.S. banks were forced to borrow money in the Euromarket. All this resulted in a sort of merry-go-round operation. A depositor who normally would have put his money in, say, a Chase New York CD gave his money (perhaps via a Canadian bank because of U.S. controls on the export of capital) to Chase London, which then lent the money back to Chase New York. In effect Reg Q forced a portion of the supply of bought money that money market banks were coming to rely on in funding to move through London and other Eurocenters. The operation of Regulation Q also encouraged foreign holders of dollars who would have deposited them in New York to put their dollars in London. Thus, for example, surplus German dollars borrowed by Italians ended up passing through London instead of New York.

Another important stimulus to the Euromarket was the various capital controls that were instituted during the 1960s to improve the U.S. balance of payments, which was in deficit. The first of these, the Interest Equalization Tax passed in 1964, was designed to discourage the issuance by foreign borrowers of debt obligations in the U.S. market. This measure was followed in 1965 by the Foreign Credit Restraint Program, which limited the amount of credit U.S. banks could extend to foreign borrowers. Finally in 1968 the government passed the Foreign Investment Program, which restricted the amount of domestic dollars U.S. corporations could use to finance foreign investments. Whatever the wisdom and effectiveness of these programs (they were eliminated in 1974), there is no doubt that they substantially increased the demand for dollar financing outside the U.S., that is, for Eurodollar loans.

The persistent balance of payments deficits in the U.S. have often been given substantial credit for the development of the Euromarket; by spending more abroad than it earned, the U.S. in effect put dollars into the hands of foreigners and thus created a natural supply of dollars for the Euromarket. There is some truth to this, but it should be noted that U.S. balance of payments deficits are neither a necessary nor a sufficient condition for a thriving and growing Euromarket. After all, foreigners can deposit dollars in New York, *and* domestic holders of dollars can place them in London. Where dollars are held need not be a function of who owns them. It is often a function of the relative attractiveness of the domestic and the Euromarkets to depositors. What has made the Euromarket attractive to depositors and given it much of its vitality is the freedom from restrictions under which this market operates and in particular the absence of the implicit tax that exists on U.S. domestic banking because of the reserve requirements imposed by the Fed.

A final important stimulus was given to the Euromarket by the hike in the price of oil that occurred in 1974. Due to that rise member nations in the Organization of Petroleum Exporting Countries (OPEC) suddenly found themselves holding massive balances of dollars, which they deposited in the Euromarket. Meanwhile many countries that were importers of oil experienced severe balance of payments difficulties and were forced to borrow dollars in the Euromarket to pay for oil imports.

Just as dollars can be deposited in banks and bank branches outside the U.S. to create Eurodollars, the currencies of European countries can be deposited outside their country of origin and thereby give rise to other types of *Eurocurrency deposits.* For example, German marks deposited in London in exchange for a mark balance are *Euromarks.* The major currencies other than dollars in which Eurocurrency deposits are held are German marks, the British pound, and Swiss francs (*Swissy* to the irreverent). There is also a limited market in Dutch guilders and rather difficult markets in other currencies. While the Euromarket is still primarily a dollar market, Eurodeposits of other currencies are an important and growing part of the market.

THE MARKET TODAY

From the inception of the Eurodollar market, London has been its biggest and most important center. That this role fell to London is hardly surprising. London has a long history as a world center for a host of financial activities: international lending, trade financing, commodities trading, stock trading, foreign exchange trading, insurance, and others. In truth, that square mile of London known as *the City of London,* or more often as just *the City,* is and has been since the 19th century the financial capital of the world.

Some of the many factors that contributed to London's development as an international financial center were the freedom and flexibility with which financial institutions were permitted to operate there. That freedom and flexibility still prevail, and because they do, London—with its huge concentration of financial expertise—was the logical place for the nascent Euromarket to develop and flourish. Throughout London's history as a Eurocenter, foreign banks have been permitted to open London branches and subsidiaries with ease and operate these branches and subsidiaries with a minimum of regulation. The Bank of England has imposed no specific capital requirements on the London branches of foreign banks, and it has imposed no reserve requirements on the Eurocurrency deposits they accept. Britain *taxes the profits* earned by foreign banks' branches and subsidiaries but has imposed *no withholding taxes* on the interest banks pay to nonresident depositors.

While London has remained the preeminent center of the Euromarket, other centers have also developed. The Euromarket is, after all, a worldwide market. In the Far East in particular, Singapore and Hong Kong have both become important centers for Asian trading in Eurodollars. These centers suffer the disadvantage that the natural sources of dollar supply and demand arising from trade and other activities in the Far East are less than those that focus on London, so their role remains secondary.

From the banks' point of view, one growing disadvantage of basing Euro operations in London is the high taxes that must be paid on profits earned there. Largely to avoid these taxes, *booking centers* have developed in several localities offering favorable tax treatment of profits— Bahrain in the Mideast, Nassau, and Grand Cayman, to name the most important. Banks that operate branches in these centers book there loans negotiated and made in London, New York, or elsewhere. They fund these loans either by having their branch buy money in its own name in the Eurodollar market or by funding the operation with dollars purchased in the name of their London branch. Nassau and Grand Cayman offer one important advantage over Bahrain; they are in the same time zone as New York and only one hour ahead of Chicago. Thus it is easy for management in U.S. money market banks to direct their operations in these centers during normal working hours.

Next to London the second most important center of the Euromarket is New York. Until the opening of international banking facilities (IBFs) there, New York banks could not accept Eurodeposits, but New York was still an important center in Euros trading for several reasons. First, New York banks and the branches established in New York by major foreign banks are active takers of Euros in the names of their Nassau and Grand Cayman branches. A second reason New York is an important trading center for Euros is that New York and the other banks actively arbitrage between Euro and "domestic" dollars (see Chapter 16). A final reason for the prominence of New York as a Eurocenter is that many of the nation's largest banks direct their worldwide Euro operations from New York.

In the formative years of the Euromarket, U.S. banks felt compelled to establish a London office to participate in this market. So, too, did the other major foreign banks around the world. At that time London was the preeminent center of the Euromarket. Gradually the importance of New York relative to London as a Eurocenter increased for all of the reasons cited above. Consequently in recent years foreign banks having London branches but no New York branch have felt compelled to open a New York branch. Fed figures on the explosive growth in the number of foreign bank branches and agencies in New York and on the total deposits held by them tell the story (Table 6–6 at the end of the chapter).[3]

In addition to the major centers of the Euromarket we have described, there are numerous centers of lesser but growing importance, for example, Paris, Frankfurt, and Luxembourg in Europe. Many financial centers that would seem logical candidates to become Eurocenters have not done so. Generally, the reasons have to do with local exchange controls, bank regulations, taxation, or other inhibiting factors. The Japanese banks, for example, are important participants in the Euromarket, but Tokyo has never become an important center of this market in part because Japanese businesses have been restricted from incurring dollar-denominated liabilities.

From rather meager beginnings the Euromarket has developed into a huge market. Unfortunately, it is impossible to say just how huge because there is no worldwide system for collecting data on the Eurocurrency market. The best figures available are probably the estimates made by the Morgan Bank. Its figures (Table 6–5) cover Eurodeposits in all significant Eurocenters. The gross numbers in Table 6–5 include sizable amounts of interbank placements. Using estimates, Morgan eliminates these placements to get figures on the net amounts of Eurodollars and other Eurocurrencies that nonbank depositors have placed with banks in the reporting countries. From these net figures, it is evident that both Eurodollar and Eurocurrency deposits have grown phenomenally over the last decade.

Overview of bank Euro operations[4]

In a very real sense the Eurodollar market is a true international market without location, which means that for no bank is it a domestic market. Thus every bank active in the market tends to compartmentalize its activities there, to think in terms of what Eurodollar assets and liabilities it has acquired. In the jargon of the market, every Eurobanker is running a Eurodollar book. In the case of foreign banks, the reason is obvious; they are dealing in a foreign currency, the dollar, which has limited availability to them at best. In the case of U.S. banks, the distinction between domestic and Euro operations arises from a less fundamental but still important consideration, namely, the fact that Fed reserve requirements and other factors create a real distinction between Eurodollars and do-

---

[3] The U.S. operations of foreign bank branches and agencies are described at the end of this chapter.

[4] For an in-depth discussion of how U.S. and foreign banks run their Euro books as well as their books in non-native currencies (e.g., Morgan's French franc book at its Paris office), see *Managing Bank Assets and Liabilities: Strategies for Risk Control and Profit,* by Marcia Stigum and Rene Branch (Homewood, Ill.: Dow Jones-Irwin, 1982).

TABLE 6–5
Eurocurrency market size, end of period ($ billions rounded to nearest $5 billion)

	1973	1974	1975	1976	1977	1978	1979	1980	1981	1982 Mar[r]	1982 Jun[p]
Estimated size											
Gross	315	395	485	595	740	950	1235	1525	1860	1930	1900
Liabilities to nonbanks	55	80	90	115	145	190	260	345	440	455	n.a.
Liabilities to central banks	40	60	65	80	100	115	145	150	130	120	n.a.
Liabilities to other banks[a]	220	255	330	400	495	645	830	1030	1290	1355	n.a.
Net	160	220	255	320	390	495	590	730	890	900	905
Claims on nonbanks	70	105	130	165	210	265	330	425	530	540	n.a.
Claims on central banks and on banks outside market area[b]	70	95	105	130	150	185	200	230	275	275	n.a.
Conversions of Eurofunds into domestic currencies by banks in market area[c]	20	20	20	25	30	45	60	75	85	85	n.a.
Eurodollars as % of gross liabilities in all Eurocurrencies	74	76	78	80	76	74	72	75	78	79	n.a.

Note: Based on foreign-currency liabilities and claims of banks in major European countries, the Bahamas, Bahrain, Cayman Islands, Netherlands Antilles, Panama, Canada, Japan, Hong Kong, and Singapore.
[a] Includes unallocated liabilities.
[b] Includes unallocated claims.
[c] In European market area only.
[r] Revised.
[p] Preliminary.
Source: World Financial Markets (New York: The Morgan Bank, November 1982)

mestic dollars, one that is of varying importance depending on economic conditions and on the maturities of the domestic and Eurodollar assets and liabilities compared. While all U.S. bankers continue to speak of their Eurobook, as distinct from their domestic book, a growing number of them view their job as managing a single, unified *global bank*.[5]

Banking ground rules in the Euromarket differ sharply from those prevailing on the U.S. banking scene, with the result that U.S. bank operations in the Euromarket also differ sharply from their operations in the domestic money market. Thus we will present a quick overview of bank Euro operations before we talk in detail about their deposit-accepting and lending activities in this market.

The first important distinction between U.S. banks' domestic and Euro operations is in the character of their liabilities. In the Euromarket all deposits, with the exception of call money, have a fixed maturity (*tenor* in British jargon) which may range anywhere from 1 day to 5 years. Also, interest is paid on *all* deposits, the rate being a function of prevailing economic conditions and the maturity of the deposit. While most bank Euro liabilities are straight time deposits, banks operating in the London market also issue Eurodollar CDs. Like domestic CDs, these instruments carry a fixed rate of interest, are issued for a fixed time span, and are negotiable.

A second important distinction between banks' domestic and Euro operations is that no reserve requirements are imposed against banks' Eurocurrency deposits. Thus every dollar of deposits accepted can be invested.

Banks accepting Eurodollar deposits use these dollars to make two sorts of investments, loans and interbank placements. All such placements, like other Eurodeposits, have fixed maturities and bear interest. The market for Eurodollar deposits, nonbank and interbank, is highly competitive, and the rates paid on deposits of different maturities are determined by supply and demand. Since the Euromarket operates outside the control of any central bank, there are no Reg Q or other controls limiting or setting the rates that Eurodollars can command. As one might expect, Euro rates are volatile: rising when money is tight, falling when it is easy.

The rate at which banks in London offer Eurodollars n the placement market is referred to as the *London interbank offered rate, LIBOR* for short. In pricing Euro loans, LIBOR is of crucial importance.

In the Euromarket, unlike the domestic market, all loans have fixed maturities, which can range anywhere from a few days to 5 years or

---

[5] The practice by some banks of viewing their domestic and offshore books as a single global book is described later in this chapter.

longer. The general practice is to price all loans at *LIBOR plus a spread.* On some term loans the lending rate is fixed for the life of the loan. By far the more usual practice, however, is to price term loans on a *rollover basis.* This means that every 3 or 6 months the loan is repriced at the then-prevailing LIBOR for 3- or 6-month money plus the agreed-upon spread. For example, a 1-year loan might be rolled after 6 months, which means that the first 6-month segment would be priced at the agreed-upon spread plus the 6-month LIBOR rate prevailing at the time the loan was granted, while the second 6-month segment would be priced at the same spread plus the 6-month LIBOR rate prevailing 6 months later. On Euro loans banks never require the borrower to hold compensating balances.

Running a bank's Eurodollar book boils down to much the same thing as running its domestic book. The bank must decide what assets to hold and what liabilities to use to fund them. In making these decisions, the bank faces the same *risks* it does in its domestic operations—credit risk, liquidity risk, and rate risk. In its Euro operations, as in its domestic operations, a bank's objective is to maximize profits subject to the constraint that risks are held to an acceptable level.

In a bank's Euro book, credit risk exists both on ordinary loans and on interbank placements, which—like sales of Fed funds—are unsecured loans. To control risk on ordinary loans, banks impose credit standards on borrowers as well as limits on the amount they will lend to any one borrower. On placement with other banks, credit risk is controlled, as in the case of Fed funds sales, by setting up lines of credit that limit the amount the bank will lend to any other banking institution. As noted below, banks also use lines to limit what is called *country risk.*

Because most of a Eurobanker's assets and liabilities have fixed maturities, it would be possible for a Eurobanker, unlike a domestic banker, to run a *matched book;* that is, to fund every 3-month asset with 3-month money, every 6-month asset with 6-month money, and so on. If he did so, moreover, he would reduce his rate risk to zero because every asset would be financed for its duration at a locked-in positive spread. He would also minimize his liquidity risk; but he would not eliminate it, since on rollover loans he would still have to return periodically to the market to obtain new funding.

While running a matched book would reduce risk, it would also limit the bank's opportunity to earn profits in an important and traditional way: by lending long and borrowing short. Eurobankers are aware of the profit opportunities that a mismatched book offers, and to varying degrees they all create a conscious mismatch in their Eurodollar books: one that is carefully monitored by head office to prevent unacceptable risks. How great a maturity mismatch a given bank will permit in its Euro book depends on various factors: the shape of the yield curve, its view on interest rates, and its perception of its own particular liquidity risk. If a bank is running a global book, the size and nature of the mismatch it will want in its Euro book will depend partly on the mismatch in its domestic book.

THE INTERBANK PLACEMENT MARKET

The pool of funds that forms the basis for the Eurodollar market is provided by a varied cast of depositors: large corporations (domestic, foreign, and multinational), central banks and other government bodies, supranational institutions, such as the Bank for International Settlements (BIS), and wealthy individuals. Most of these funds come in the form of time deposits with fixed maturities. The banks, however, also receive substantial amounts of *call money,* which the depositor may withdraw on a day's notice. Banks normally offer on call money a fixed rate, which they adjust periodically as market conditions change. The major attraction of a call deposit to the holder is liquidity. Time deposits pay more, but a penalty is incurred if such a deposit is withdrawn before maturity. From the banks' point of view, call money is attractive because, with a positively-sloped yield curve, it is cheap. Also, despite its short-term nature, call money is a fairly stable source of funds, so much so that a big bank might, in running its Euro book, feel comfortable viewing half of its call deposits as essentially long-term funds.

For reasons discussed below, banks receiving Eurodeposits frequently choose to place some portion of these deposits with other banks, often while simultaneously taking deposits of other maturities. As a result of all this buying and selling, a huge and highly active market in interbank placements has developed. This market is worldwide. It also has a large number of participants, which reflects two facts. First, banks from countries all over the world participate in the market. Second, every one of a bank's foreign branches (and many U.S., European, and Japanese banks have many of them) participates in this market as a separate entity. This means, for example, that Citibank's foreign branches in London, Singapore, Bahrain, Nassau, and elsewhere all take and place Eurodollars in their own names.

Because there are so many players in the Eurodollar market and because they are scattered all over the globe, it would be difficult and costly for all of them to communicate their bids and offers for deposits directly to each other. To fill the gap, a number of firms have gone into the business of brokering Euro time deposits.

While a high proportion of total Europlacements is brokered, not all such placements pass through the brokers' market. In particular some money is sold by continental banks direct to big London bidders, with the London bidders quoting rates based on those prevailing in the brokers' market. Also, a bank branch normally won't trade with another branch of the same bank through brokers since the two communicate directly with each other.

A bank placing funds in the interbank market faces two risks. First, there is the *credit risk,* which banks seek to control through the use of credit lines. In establishing lines to foreign banks, a U.S. bank will look at the normal criteria of creditworthiness, such as size, capitalization, profitability, and reputation. In addition, a bank will be concerned about *country* or *sovereign risk.* Specifically, it will consider various factors about the bank's country of origin that might influence either the bank's viability or its ability to meet commitments denominated in a foreign currency. Of particular interest would be factors such as whether the country of origin was politically stable, whether nationalization on terms unfavorable to foreign depositors was a possibility, and whether the country's balance of payments was reasonably strong.

There's also a second aspect of sovereign risk that banks placing Eurocurrency deposits with other banks worry about. A bank selling Euros to, say, the London branch of the Bank of Tokyo must be concerned not only about the creditworthiness of that bank and the Japanese country risk but about the economic and political climate in London: Is it conceivable that by nationalizing foreign bank branches, freezing their assets, or some other action the British might render it impossible for these branches to honor their commitment to repay borrowed dollars? Questions of this sort are less of a concern with respect to London than with respect to smaller and newer Eurocenters, such as Bahrain and Nassau. Banks seek to limit the sovereign risk to which they are exposed by imposing country limits on their lending and interbank placements.

The administration of these limits is complex. First, two sets of limits apply, country limits and limits to individual banks. Second, for Bank A to track how much credit in the form of Eurodollar placements it has granted to Bank B, it must track the Euro sales of *all* its branches to *all* Bank B's branches. Third, at the same time that Bank A is selling Euros to Bank B, it will also be granting credit to Bank B in other ways, for example, through the sale of Fed funds or via letters of credit.

Granting lines to buyers of Eurodollars used to be more casual and less cautious than it is now. In 1974 the Bankhaus I.D. Herstatt, a medium-sized German bank, failed under conditions that left several banks standing in line along with other creditors to get funds due them. This event, along with the difficulties experienced during the same year by the Franklin National Bank, sent shock waves through the Euromarket and caused banks to review with an air of increased caution the lines they had granted to other banks. The upshot was that many smaller banks lost the lines they had enjoyed, and they experienced difficulty buying Euros; some were even forced out of the market. *Tiering* also developed in market rates, with banks that were judged poorer credit risks being forced to pay up. In particular, the Japanese banks, which are consistently big net takers of Euros, had to pay up 1–2% and so did the Italian banks because of unfavorable economic and political developments within Italy. Several years after the Herstatt crisis, the Euromarket regained much of the confidence lost in 1974, and lines were again enlarged. Tiering, however, has remained a phenomenon in the market, being more pronounced the tighter money gets and the higher rates rise. As noted elsewhere, the various financial crises, including the failure of Banco Ambrosiano Holdings, that rocked the financial world in 1982 caused tiering to again become more pronounced in the Euromarket and changed its pattern.[6]

Most banks, because of their size, nationality, and customer base, tend to be natural net sellers or buyers of Euros. However, it's important for a bank that wants to buy Euros to sell them some of the time since one way a bank gets lines from other banks is by placing deposits with them. In the Euromarket, as in the Fed funds market, some banks have to buy their way in.

There is much more to be said about how Euros are quoted and traded in the brokers' market and about arbitrage between Eurodollars and domestic dollars. These topics are covered in Chapter 16.

EURO CERTIFICATES OF DEPOSIT

Because Eurodollar time deposits, with the exception of call money, have fixed maturities, from the point of view of many investors they have one serious disadvantage, namely, illiquidity. To satisfy investors who needed liquidity, Citibank began issuing *Eurodollar certificates of deposit* in London. Its example was quickly followed by other U.S. and foreign banks with London branches.

Because of the liquidity of Euro CDs, banks issuing them are able to sell them at rates slightly below those offered on time deposits of equivalent maturity, ¼ to ⅛% less when the market is quiet. While Euro CDs were originally designed for corporations and other investors who wanted real liquidity, following the Herstatt incident an interesting development occurred in the Euro CD market. Many smaller U.S. banks and foreign banks as well felt the need for the appearance of greater liquidity in their Eurodollar books. To get it, they bought Euro CDs from other banks with the understanding that the bank buying the CD would never trade that CD and that it would moreover permit the selling bank to safekeep the CD to ensure that this understanding was honored. CDs

---

[6] See pp. 121–24 and end of this chapter.

sold on these terms, known as *lock-up CDs,* are close to a time deposit from the point of view of the issuing bank, and normally the rate they pay is close to the time deposit rate. While no figures are available, it is estimated by some that as much as 50% of all Euro CDs sold are lock-up CDs; others put the figure much lower. Some of the remaining Euro CDs sold are purchased by Swiss banks for investors whose funds they manage; these CDs are rarely traded. Most of the rest of the Euro CDs issued in London are sold to investors in the U.S.: corporations, domestic banks, and others.

Since the major advantge to the issuing bank of writing Euro CDs is that CD money is cheaper than time deposit money, banks issuing such CDs carefully limit the amount they write so that the spread between the rates at which they can buy CD money and time deposit money is preserved. To issue CDs, the banks normally post daily rates, the attractiveness of which reflects both their eagerness to write and the maturities in which they want to take money. Occasionally when the banks are anxious to write, they will also issue through either London CD brokers or U.S. money market dealers who have set up shop in London. These brokers and dealers also make a secondary market for Euro CDs, without which these instruments would have liquidity in name only.

The Euro CD market is smaller than the domestic CD market, and Euro CDs are less liquid than domestic CDs. More about that and the mechanics of Euro CD trading in Chapter 15.

EURO LENDING

Today the Eurodollar market is *the* international capital market of the world, which is very much reflected in the mix of borrowers that come to this market for loans. Their ranks include U.S. corporations funding foreign operations, foreign corporations funding foreign or domestic operations, foreign government agencies funding investment projects, and foreign governments funding development projects or general balance of payments deficits.

Lending terms

All Euro loans are priced at LIBOR plus a spread. Since different banks may be offering Eurodollars at not quite the same rates, the LIBOR rate used in pricing a loan is usually the average of the 11:00 A.M. offering rates of three to five reference banks, the latter always being top banks in the market.

How great a spread over LIBOR a borrower is charged depends on risk and market conditions. In a period of slack loan demand, a top borrower might be able to get funds at LIBOR plus as little as ½%. In contrast, a second-class credit shopping for a loan when money was tight might have to pay as much as LIBOR plus 2½%.

On rollover loans, which most Euro loans are today, the bank normally allows the borrower to choose whether to take 3- or 6-month money each time a rollover date occurs. Banks will also grant a 1-year rollover option to good customers but try to discourage the inclusion of this option in loan agreements because to match fund maturities beyond 6 months can be difficult due to the thinness of the market in longer-term deposits. What choice of maturity the borrower makes on a rollover date depends on whether he expects interest rates to rise or fall.

The bank may, at the borrower's request, also include in a rollover loan agreement a *multicurrency clause* that permits the borrower to switch from one currency to another—say, from dollars to German marks—on a rollover date. Multicurrency clauses usually stipulate that nondollar funds will be made available to the borrower conditional upon "availability." This clause protects a bank from exchange controls and other factors that might dry up the market and prohibit the bank from acquiring the desired funds, even in the foreign exchange market.

While fixed-rate, fixed-term loans do occur in the Euromarket, they are uncommon. Banks are generally unwilling to make them unless they match fund, a policy that makes such loans so expensive that the borrower is likely to conclude that his funding cost over the life of the loan would be less with a rollover loan. Also a prime borrower willing to pay up to lock in a fixed borrowing rate may find a Eurobond issue cheaper than a fixed-rate term loan.

The maximum maturity that Eurobankers will grant on term loans generally is around 7 years, although some banks are willing to go to 10. In judging what maturity it will grant on a specific loan, a bank will consider the borrower's underlying need (what is he financing?), his ability to repay, and—if the loan is to be shared by several banks—what the market will accept. Typically the slacker loan demand, the longer the maturity that is acceptable.

Often term loans extended to finance capital projects have an availability *period* during which the borrower receives funds according to some prearranged schedule based on his anticipated needs. The availability period may be followed by a grace period during which no repayment of principal is required. After that the normal procedure is for the loan to be amortized over its remaining life. Some *bullet loans* with no amortization are granted, but they are the exception not the rule.

On Euro loans the standard practice has been to disallow prepayment, but some agreements do permit it on rollover dates with or sometimes without payment of a penalty. To gain greater flexibility the borrower can negotiate a *revolving facility*, which permits him during the life of the loan agreement to take down funds, repay them, and take them down again as he chooses.

The fact that Euro loans are made to borrowers all over the world could create considerable legal complications for lenders, especially in the case of default. To minimize these, Euro loan agreements generally specify that the loan is subject to either U.S. or British law.

Many Euro loans granted to U.S. corporations by U.S. banks are negotiated at the bank's head office in the United States. This is most likely to be the case if the loan is granted to a foreign subsidiary that is kept financially anemic because it is operating in a weak-currency country or if management of the overall firm is strongly centralized. If, on the other hand, the sub is financially strong and its management is largely autonomous, negotiation for a Euro loan will occur abroad, frequently in London because the expertise is there.

Loan syndication

Over time syndication of Euro loans has become increasingly common. There are various reasons a bank might choose to syndicate a loan. On corporate loans for big projects (e.g., development of North Sea oil) the amount required might exceed a bank's legal lending limit, or the bank might not choose to go to that limit in the interests of diversification of risk. On country loans the basic chip can be $1 billion or more, and no bank could write that sort of business alone. Country loans often are for such huge amounts these days because certain borrowers, especially underdeveloped countries, are financing big development projects. Other countries with substantial borrowing needs are financing balance of payments deficits that they have incurred in part because the price of oil has risen, while prices of other raw materials they export have been weak in recent years.

Big Euro loan syndication agreements are negotiated in London. Often the lead bank is a top U.S. bank, but German banks have also become more aggressive in this area. While many of the banks that participate in a typical Euro syndication are based in London, it is not uncommon for continental banks and even domestic U.S. banks with no London branch to take a piece of such loans. Doing so may provide them with both a good rate and a chance to diversify their assets.

Loan syndication normally starts with the borrower accepting the loan terms proposed by a bank and giving that bank a mandate to put together a credit for it. Most such agreements are on a *fully underwritten basis*, which means that the lead bank guarantees the borrower that he will get all of the money stipulated in the loan proposal.

Since the amount guaranteed is more than the lead bank could come up with alone, it selects *comanagers* that help it underwrite the loan. Once the lead bank and the comanagers have split up the loan into shares, they have about two weeks to sell off whatever portion of their underwriting share they do not want to take into portfolio. At the end of this selling period, the lead bank advises the borrower as to what banks have participated in the syndication. Then the borrower and these banks attend a closing at which the final loan agreement is signed. Two days later the borrower gets his money. From the point of view of the lender, participation in a syndicated loan carries a commitment to lend for the life of the loan, since such participations are rarely sold by one bank to another.

Various fees are charged on a loan syndication. First there is the management fee, which may run from as low as ⅜% up to 1% or more, depending on market conditions and the borrower's name. Normally the lead bank shares some portion of this front-end fee with the banks that take significant portions of the total loan into portfolio.

A second fee the borrower pays is a spread over LIBOR on whatever funds he takes down. The borrower also pays a commitment fee, generally around ½%, on any monies committed but not drawn. Finally, there is an agency fee that goes to the bank responsible for interfacing between the lending banks and the borrower, that is, for the receipt and disbursement of loan proceeds and for general supervision of the operation of the credit agreement.

Merchant banks. While loan syndication can be done directly by a bank, it has become increasingly common for large U.S. banks to set up separate merchant banking subsidiaries with the principal function of syndicating loans. Loans are also syndicated by consortium banks, that is, by banks set up and jointly owned by several banks, frequently of different nationalities.

A British bank may engage in a much wider range of activities than a U.S. bank may. There has, however, tended to be some degree of specialization between different British banks. In particular the so-called merchant banks have specialized primarily in providing not loans of their own funds, but various financial services to their customers. These include accepting bills arising out of trade, underwriting new stock and bond issues, and advising corporate customers on acquisitions, mergers, foreign expansion, and portfolio management.

One reason why several top U.S. banks have opened merchant banking arms in London is that these subs may engage in activities, such as bond underwriting, that the branch itself could not because of Glass-Steagall. Another reason is that some U.S. banks feel that merchant banking activities, including loan syndication, are a different sort of business from commercial banking—one that requires deals-oriented money raisers and more continuity of personnel than is found in commercial banking. As one banker put it, "Merchant banking is using other people's assets and getting paid a fee for it; the other people in this case may be anyone in the market, including the parent bank. In loan syndications where we add value is by taking a view on price, terms, conditions, and amounts that can be done for a borrower and by then assembling the group that will manage and sell the issue."

Most U.S. banks' merchant banking subs keep little of the loans they syndicate on their own books. Their objective is to provide the parent bank with the portion of the loan it wants and sell the rest. One reason is that the parent bank has a comparative advantage over the sub in funding. It has a stronger name in which to buy funds, and it has experienced dealers and funding personnel that the merchant bank could duplicate only at considerable expense.

Consortium banks. A number of U.S. banks, in addition to or instead of setting up a merchant banking subsidiary, have joined with other banks to form consortium banks. These carry out many of the same activities as their merchant banking subs do. The objectives of U.S. banks in joining such groups have been mixed, depending on the size and experience of the bank. Some smaller banks joined to be able to participate in medium-term Euro financings. Other banks joined to gain experience in international financial markets in general, in specific geographic markets, or in new lines of business. Consortia formed by large banks provide a large standing capability for syndicating loans, and these institutions are active in this area.

Eurolines

In addition to granting straight loans, Eurobankers grant lines of credit to a varied group of borrowers, including both domestic and foreign firms issuing commercial paper in the U.S. market.

Eurolines, unlike U.S. lines, are granted on a strict fee basis; no compensating balances are required. Many Eurolines are revolvers that legally commit the bank to provide the line holder with funds if it requests them. Eurobankers, however, have also granted Eurodollar and multicurrency lines on a more or less no-change-in-material-circumstances basis.

Generally speaking, the Euromarket is more transactions oriented than the customer-oriented U.S. market. One result of this is that when money is easy, Eurolines are often cheaper than lines of credit in the U.S. In contrast, when money tightens, Eurolines tend either to dry up in terms of availability or to rise dramatically in price.

In the Euromarket and in foreign banking in general, some of the most important lines granted by banks are not lines to customers but lines to other banks. A French bank operating a dollar book in London or New York is running a book in a foreign currency, and so is a U.S. bank running a French franc book in Paris or a sterling book in London. All these banks worry with good reason about liquidity; that is, about their ability to fund on a continuing basis in a foreign currency the various assets they have acquired that are denominated in that currency.

To reduce the risks in running books denominated in foreign currencies, many major world banks have set up reciprocal line agreements. Under such an agreement a big French bank that naturally has better access than a U.S. bank to the domestic French franc market agrees to provide a U.S. bank with francs in a time of crisis. In exchange the U.S. bank promises to supply the French bank with dollars.

Another way foreign banks operating in the Euromarket enhance their dollar liquidity is by purchasing for a fee backup lines from U.S. banks. The attractiveness of such lines depends in part on the shape of the yield curve. Assume, for example, that such a line cost 0.5%. If the foreign bank could take 1-year dollars at 12% and lend them day to day at 11.75%, borrowing long and lending short in the placement market would be a cheaper way to acquire liquidity than taking out a line, and it might also do more for the foreign bank's balance sheet. If, on the other hand, the yield curve were steep, buying lines would be the more attractive alternative.

Euroloans for domestic purposes

While the bulk of Euro lending is to foreign borrowers or to U.S. corporations funding foreign operations, a growing number of U.S. corporations have been borrowing money in the Euromarket for domestic purposes. Their major incentive in doing so is to reduce borrowing costs. Frequently the rate quoted on a Euro loan by a bank's London branch will be cheaper than the *all-in* cost (prime plus compensating balances) quoted by the same bank on a domestic loan, a situation that one top U.S. bank executive described as "sillier than hell."

There are several reasons for this price discrepancy. First, reserve requirements, which prevail in domestic banking but not in Eurobanking, in effect constitute a tax on domestic banking that tends to force domestic lending rates above Euro rates. Second, U.S. banks have only a single prime based on 90-day money market rates. With an upward-sloping yield curve from 1 day out to 90, this arrangement naturally penalizes borrowers who want short-term money. In the Euromarket there is no such penalty. A 1-month loan is priced at LIBOR for 1-month money plus a spread, an all-in rate that may be significantly less than LIBOR on 3-month money plus the same spread. In effect Eurobankers charge *money market rates* on loans, while domestic bankers until recently did not.[7]

The potential advantages of borrowing in the Euromarket have led some large U.S. corporations to exert pressure on their banks to grant them *either/or facilities,* that is, to permit them to borrow from their bank's head office or a foreign branch as they desire. Generally the banks resisted, citing the importance of customer relationships, loyalty, and other factors. They did so for two reasons. First, their profit margin was likely to be larger on a domestic loan than on a Euro loan. Second, they knew they could not be competitive in the market for Euroloans. When a U.S. bank lends Eurodollars to a domestic borrower for domestic purposes, it incurs under Reg D a small reserve requirement, which forces it to raise the Euro rate it quotes to a domestic borrower a slight fraction over the rate it quotes to foreign borrowers. Foreign banks lending into the U.S. used to incur no such reserve requirement and thus were in a position to consistently underprice U.S. banks on such loans. Today foreign bank branches in the U.S. are subject to reserve requirements, and either/or facilities have become a common feature of U.S. bank lending agreements to large borrowers.

RUNNING A EURO BOOK

In running their Eurodollar books, the big U.S. banks have taken several decades to develop strategies that are sophisticated and with which they feel comfortable. One reason is that the top executives of money market banks were often people with little experience in international business. Also during the early years of the Euromarket, no one really understood it or knew where it was going. Gradually market expertise developed in London, but that spread only slowly across the Atlantic. Thus when the London branches of the big U.S. banks began running dollar books, the edict went out from home office that asset and liability maturities were to be matched to minimize rate and liquidity risks.

The emphasis on matching continued for some time. In fact, it has only been since the early 1970s that U.S. banks have become willing to mismatch their Euro books aggressively to increase profits. Oddly enough the Herstatt crisis probably contributed to their willingness to do so. As it blew over, bankers concluded that, if the Euromarket had survived Herstatt, it was mature enough to survive anything.

Today all the major U.S. banks have several foreign branches running Euro books, so their overall exposure to risk in the Euromarket is the sum

---

[7] See pp. 81–82.

of the risks associated with several separate branch books. With respect to liability management, head office's main concern is with the rate and liquidity risks that are created through the mismatch of the bank's consolidated Euro position. To control these, management sets up guidelines within which each branch is supposed to operate.

There is no precise way to compare the risk associated with funding, say, a 3-month loan with overnight money versus lending 6-month money and funding the first 4 months with 4-month money. So head office guidelines take arbitrary and quite different forms. Their purpose, however, is always the same: to limit the mismatch a branch may practice.

Eurobankers often refer to the practice of lending long and borrowing short as running an *open book*. Head office might, for example, control the mismatch on a branch's book by setting limits on the open positions that the branch could assume beyond 2 months, 4 months, and 6 months. An alternative approach is to apply different weights to the mismatches in different maturity ranges (larger weights, the longer the maturity range) and then require that the weighted sum of all mismatches be less than some dollar figure.

The job of operating the branch's book under these guidelines falls to local funding officers. In the London branch of a large U.S. bank, there will be several senior people responsible for making overall policy decisions and a number of dealers under them who actually buy and sell money. Much of the work of the senior people involves formulating a view on what is likely to happen to interest rates and then deciding, in light of that view and current market conditions, what strategies to follow in taking and placing deposits.

In making decisions of this sort, the Euro liability manager is in a position quite different from that of his domestic counterpart. As a London Eurobanker, now at New York head office, put it, "In the U.S. a bank doesn't have to work very hard on liability management; if the cost of money goes up, the bank puts the prime up. Thus buying long money involves taking a view that the bank doesn't really have to,[8] and the typical practice is for the bank to fund the bulk of its domestic loans with short or very short money. In the Euromarket, in contrast, the only assets the bank can take on are fixed-rate, fixed-maturity assets. Thus, the Eurobanker who mismatches incurs a real rate risk, and the existence of this risk forces him to constantly make interest rate predictions and to structure his asset and liability maturities accordingly."

If a Eurobanker expects interest rates to stay steady or fall, he will lend long and borrow short, i.e., run a *short* book, assuming a positively-shaped yield curve. How short depends in part on the slope of the yield

---

[8] *Taking a view* is a London expression for forming an opinion as to where interest rates are going and acting on it.

curve. As one banker noted, "There's no incentive to take money at call and put it out for 3 or 6 months for a ¼ or ⅜ spread. With a flat yield curve like that, you are taking a tremendous risk for little reward; if rates back up, you are left with a negative carry. But when the yield curve is steep—a 1% spread between call and 1-year rates—there is a real incentive to overlend and take the spread."

As interest rates became high and highly volatile at the end of the 1970s, banks began imposing much tighter limits on the mismatch positions branch treasuries could assume. Also, the growing tendency for banks to globalize their world book led to a situation in which the head offices of a number of banks were dictating to their branches the positions the latter should run.

The dealers

Once a decision about the maturity structure of the branch's assets and liabilities is made, the responsibility for implementing this decision falls on the chief dealer and his assistants. The London dealing room of a large bank is a fascinating and busy place, populated during trading hours by a bevy of time deposit and foreign exchange traders engaged in rapid-fire, nonstop conversations with brokers and large customers.

The "book" that is thrust into the chief dealer's care is a sheet of data giving the current amounts and maturities of all the branch's assets and liabilities. The salient features of this book are something a good dealer keeps in his head—the mismatch in different maturities, the amounts of funds he is likely to have to buy or sell in coming days, and when and in what maturity ranges rate pressures might develop from big rollovers. On the basis of this information, the overall guidelines established for the branch, and the strategies set by local funding officers, the dealer's job is to do the necessary taking and placing of funds as profitably as possible. This sounds simple but leaves much room for the exercise of tactics and judgment.

On every Eurodollar loan a bank makes and funds, it has three potential sources of profit. First, there is the spread the bank gets over LIBOR, which compensates it for operating expenses and the credit risk it is assuming. Second, there is the extra ¹⁄₁₆ or ⅛% that the bank may be able to make if its dealers can pick up the needed funds a little below LIBOR, for example, through astute timing of the purchase. A third way a bank can profit from a loan is through mismatching its book.

While major decisions about mismatch are made by senior funding officers, the dealer has and needs some leeway in implementing them. When a big syndicated loan rolls over and many banks are in the market trying to "match fund" their participation in the loan, a good dealer may be forced to mismatch—buy funds in anticipation of need or pick them up later—if he does not want to overpay for his money.

In this respect it's worth noting that when the Eurodollar market was younger, a big rollover could cause a perceptible, if temporary, upward bulge in Euro rates. This is less true today because of banks' increasing willingness to mismatch and because of the market's depth. In fact, today $1 billion loan rollovers occur with no impact on market rates.

Eurobankers take time deposits from two sources, bank customers and the interbank market. A major bank branch in London will have several people whose job is to contact big depositors, such as major corporate customers (e.g., the oil companies), certain central banks, and other big depositors. Unlike the time deposit dealers, these customer representatives have time to chat with depositors about market conditions and rates. The banks like to pick up money this way, since it saves them brokerage. Also at times such money may be cheaper than what they could pick up in the interbank market. That depends on the sophistication of the depositor.

Banks that are large takers of funds also try to cultivate direct relationships with other banks. Banks, unlike corporations, can go into the brokers' market to place Eurodollars. Thus a bank attempting to pick up money direct from other banks to save brokerage normally tries to post fair bid rates for different maturities and to suggest indirectly at least that sellers go elsewhere on days when it is posting noncompetitive rates because it does not need money. A major bank that posts noncompetitive rates may still pick up deposits either because the lender has lines to only a few banks or because his lines to other banks are full.

While large banks prefer to get money direct to save brokerage, brokers are extremely useful to them. Although brokers have to be paid, they save banks money on both communications and personnel. A funding officer of one of the largest U.S. banks estimated offhand that without the brokers, he would need 200 telephone lines and 50 dealers to run the London dealing room. The brokers are also useful to a bank that suddenly discovers it has an hour to raise $200 million of short-dated funds, an amount that might take some time to dig out directly. A third advantage the brokers offer is the cloak of anonymity. As a funding officer at the London branch of one of the largest U.S. banks put it, "Suppose I want to sell $50 million and I call a bank direct, one who would have been prepared to do that transaction in the brokers' market. He sees that it is my bank on the other side and he gets nervous and wonders—what are they trying to do, $50 million or $200 million? So he does a $10 million deal and now not only have I not done the transaction, but I have disclosed the amount I am trying to do." Anonymity in this respect is useful for all the top banks. They are a bit like bulls in a barnyard; whenever they move, their smaller companions get nervous.

Europlacements

One of the curious things about the Euromarket, at least to the uniniti-ated, is that many participants in the market are busily taking deposits with the right hand and placing them with the left. In the beginning, interbank placements may have been made partly out of a concern for balance sheet cosmetics. In domestic operations, it's not considered proper for a bank to loan out all the funds it takes in, the idea being that this would leave the bank with no bonds to sell and thus with a potential liquidity problem. For a money market bank, this notion makes little sense, but no U.S. bank, big or small, is going to get caught with no securities on its balance sheet. In their Euro operations banks pick up few salable securities unless they run a Euro CD portfolio. Thus, espe-cially in the early days of the Euromarket when matched funding was the rule, a book in which all assets were loans would have been logical and would have posed no liquidity threat. It would, however, have looked bad according to the traditional criteria of bank management. Placements, which are not classed as loans but can be just as illiquid, do not present this difficulty. Thus cosmetic considerations were one incentive for Euro-placements. Once banks became willing to mismatch, *profits* became another incentive.

A domestic bank that has a strong view on where interest rates are going is hard put to place a big bet based on that view. If it expects interest rates to fall, there is no interbank market in which it can sell long-dated money, and since a savvy corporate treasurer is likely to have the same interest rate view that the bank does, he will be unwilling to take out a fixed-rate term loan at such a time. If alternatively a domes-tic banker expects rates to rise, he will want to buy long-dated money, but he has no place where he can do this in volume. Whatever his expectations, his options for structuring maturities are limited.

In the Euromarket things are different. A bank can't order its customers to take fixed-rate term loans whenever it would like them to, but in the placement market a bank can buy and sell funds in reasonable volume over a wide range of maturities. There are several reasons for the con-trast in maturity options between the U.S. market and the Euromarket. First, the Euromarket is traditionally more accustomed to dealing in longer dates. On the deposit side in particular there have always been some suppliers of funds who were concerned primarily with preservation and safety of principal as opposed to maximizing return and were willing for a spread to supply long-dated funds to creditworthy banks. The ranks of such depositors have been joined in recent years by the Arabs, who are willing to offer top banks deposits with maturities as long as 5 years to stockpile oil income earmarked to finance planned investments.

The contrast in maturity options between the U.S. market and Euro-market also reflects differences in the positions of banks operating there.

The natural customer base of a foreign bank, for example, will include firms that lack the same access to dollar financing that U.S. firms have in the domestic capital market, and that therefore may choose to borrow on terms different from those on which a large U.S. corporation would. Also, because the dollar is not their domestic currency, foreign banks are and should be more anxious to match fund than U.S. banks are. Smaller regional U.S. banks are in a somewhat similar position to foreign banks; they do not have the assurance that, say, Citi or Morgan has that they will be able to buy whatever money they need whenever they need it. Liquidity considerations are a final reason that a foreign bank might want to buy long-dated funds whereas a top U.S. bank would not. Especially since the Herstatt crisis, foreign banks operating in the Euromarket have been concerned with liquidity, and one way they can get it is by buying, say, 1-year money and lending it short term.

Placements are generally less profitable than loans because they offer no built-in spread over LIBOR. But because of the maturity options in the placement market, at times they offer attractive possibilities for speculating on interest rate changes. Assuming a positively-sloped yield curve, such speculation is more attractive when interest rates are expected to fall than when they are expected to rise. A bank that expects interest rates to fall will lend long and borrow short. In doing so it gets paid for taking a view (the spread between the long lending rate and the lower short borrowing rate), *and* if the bank is right, it earns something extra as the borrowing rate falls.

Alternatively, if a bank expects rates to rise, the natural strategy is for it to lend short and borrow long. Doing so, however, will cost the bank money, so it will come out ahead only if it is right and rates do rise sharply. Some banks, when they expect rates to rise will, instead of borrowing long and lending short, continue the pattern of lending long and funding short. Or they will fund in a barbell fashion, taking both short and long (6-months and over) deposits. The success of this strategy depends on the speed and extent of the rate rise. Studies have shown that, during a period of rising rates, the barbell strategy often provides funds at the cheapest cost because rates do not rise quickly or sharply enough to offset the advantages of the cheap short-dated funds used.

While there is a lot of variability, it would not be unusual to find the London branch of a large U.S. bank holding 50% of its Euro assets in placements and 50% in loans.

Mismatch strategies

Because of rollovers most assets that a bank in the Euromarket is financing have original maturities of 3 or 6 months, although some may go longer. In financing these, a bank can mismatch in various ways. The most extreme approach would be to rely on overnight money. Doing so would normally create the greatest positive spread from mismatch, but it would also expose the bank to the greatest rate risk. An alternative would be to fund a new asset for part of its life. For example, a bank might fund a 6-month asset with 4-month money (*buy 4s against 6s* in the jargon of the trade) and then fund the remaining 2 months with overnight money or a purchase of 2-month Euros. One consideration in plotting this sort of strategy is the maturities that are most actively traded in the Euromarket. Funding a 6-month asset with 1-month money would leave a bank that planned to match fund the tail of the asset in need of 5-month money, a maturity in which the market is thin.

If a bank buys 4s against 6s or pursues some similar strategy, it creates an open position in its book and thereby assumes a rate risk. One way it can eliminate that risk while simultaneously locking in a profit from the mismatch is by entering into a *forward forward* contract; that is, *buying money of a fixed maturity for future delivery.* In the example above, the appropriate forward forward contract would be for 2-month money to be delivered 4 months hence. In the Euromarket there is some trading in forward forwards, but the market is thin.

The seller of a forward forward assumes a rate risk because he cannot be sure how much it will cost him to fund that commitment. Therefore he will enter into such a contract only if he is compensated for his risk. In our example, the seller of 2-month money 4 months hence will want to get something more than the rate he expects to prevail on 2-month money 4 months hence. For his part, if the borrower is locking up a profit on his mismatch, he might be willing to pay some premium on the forward forward contract. Another reason a buyer and seller might strike a forward forward deal is that they entertain diverse opinions on where interest rates are headed.

In an interesting book on Eurobanks, Steven Davis, a Eurobanker, statistically tested the results over the time of several arbitrary strategies for mismatching. His conclusion was that, while mismatching is common in the Euromarket, it is unprofitable over the long run.[9] This conclusion surprises funding officers who have long experience in the market. Most claim that over time they can and have made money through mismatching. Perhaps one reason is that they follow more flexible strategies than those tested by Davis.

In the game of mismatching, the big U.S. banks have an advantage over their competitors in forecasting Euro rates. One reason is that Euro rates, as shown in Chapter 16, tend to track U.S. rates closely, with U.S. rates generally doing the leading, Euro rates the following. This gives banks that are active in the U.S. money market and have a close feel for

---

[9] Steven I. Davis, *The Euro Bank; Its Origins, Managements and Outlooks* (London: MacMillan Press, 1976).

developments there (i.e., domestic banks) an edge over their foreign brethren in predicting Euro rates.

Also, the bigger the bank, the better the input it is likely to get from head office and the more intimate the contact between London and head office is likely to be. As the chief dealer in the London branch of a top U.S. bank put it, "We get tremendous input from New York. I speak to people there two hours every afternoon on the phone. Also, the foreign exchange desk next to mine has a direct line open to New York at all times, and we have direct telex, too. All that information permits us to quickly build up a feel for conditions in the U.S. market. There's no way a smaller bank or a foreign bank can get access to the same information. They can read it tomorrow in the paper, we get it right away. That's important because in this market half an hour sometimes makes a crucial difference."

The information flow between London and New York is not one way. At times London sees things New York does not, and the two have differing rate views. For example, at a time when New York anticipated continued ease, a London dealer looking at his book might conclude that both Euro and domestic rates in a certain maturity range were likely to firm up temporarily at least due to a confluence of scheduled Euro rollovers. Alternatively, if New York foresaw an upturn in rates because domestic loan demand was beginning to revive, London might temper that view by arguing that no parallel increase in loan demand was occurring outside the United States.

Role of Euros CDs

In talking about bank funding in the Euromarket, we have relegated the issuance of Euro CDs to the end of our discussion. The reason is that CD money is much less important in Euro funding than in domestic funding. In the U.S. large investors are not in the habit of making time deposits, and the market for term Fed funds is thin. Thus the domestic banker who wants to take 3-, 6-, or 9-month money is more or less forced to go to the CD market to get it. In the Euromarket, in contrast, a banker can obtain time deposits of any maturity either directly from nonbank depositors or in the interbank market.

Because of the availability of time deposit money, a bank will issue Euro CDs only if there is a distinct rate advantage in doing so. Also, because the overall market for such CDs is thin and the market for any one bank's CDs is thinner still, a bank is cautious about the quantity of Euro CDs it writes, particularly if the CDs issued are likely to turn out to be *trading paper* as opposed to lock-up CDs. The danger of overwriting is not only that the bank will lose its rate advantage in the CD market but that it may block actions it may want to take in the future. For example, if a bank writes a lot of 9-month CDs and then 3 months later wants to take 6-month money, it may find that it can't do so unless it pays up because there is so much of its old 9-month paper, which now has a 6-month current maturity, in the hands of dealers and investors. A similar fear may also inhibit a bank from writing very short-maturity Euro CDs. The treasurer reasons that writing a 1-month CD will not save his bank enough money to compensate for the fact that the presence of such securities in the market might during their life block his bank from seizing an attractive opportunity to writer longer-term CDs. Investors after all will be willing to hold only so much of any one bank's paper in their portfolios.

Most Euro CDs have a maturity at issue of 1 year or less, but it is much more common for CDs with longer maturities—2, 3, or even 5 years—to be issued in the Euromarket than in the domestic market. While a bank will normally take any short-dated CD money offered to it by a nonbank customer, it may be unwilling to issue long-term CDs unless it has a specific use for such funds, for example, to match fund a long-term asset coming onto its book.

Buyers of Euro CDs are highly selective. As a result only major U.S. banks can raise money in real volume in this market. Other banks, U.S. and foreign, do issue CDs to their customers, sometimes at the same rates a Citi or Morgan would pay, but were they to try to really write in volume, they would be forced to pay up, how much depending on the name, nationality, and size of the bank. As noted in Chapter 15, tiering is pronounced in the secondary market for Euro CDs.

Arab dollars

In the Euromarket the top U.S. banks, because of their size, reputation, and customer base, have always been the recipients of large deposits from nonbank depositors. Both because they could earn profits by laying off such deposits in the interbank market and because the maturity structure of the deposits they received was not necessarily what they desired for their Euro book, these banks became big sellers as well as takers of funds. In effect they came to act as dealers in Eurodeposits.

After the OPEC nations dramatically increased the price of oil in 1974, the dealer banks rapidly became recipients of huge short-term deposits from Arab oil sellers. As they assumed responsibility for recycling petro dollars, their balance sheets changed dramatically, with placements becoming much more important than previously relative to loans.

Their new role as recyclers of petro dollars created problems for the big banks. One concerned liquidity; in taking a lot of short-term money from the Arabs, these banks were violating two basic rules of liability management: (1) a bank should not take a significant portion of its deposits from a single depositor or group of depositors, and (2) a bank should not accept big deposits of volatile short-term (*hot*) money. The one comfort that the big banks could take in this matter was that, regardless of what the Arabs did with their dollars, these dollars could not disappear from the system. If the Arabs pulled a lot of money out of one bank, that bank could certainly buy back the lost dollars in the interbank market from the bank or banks in which the Arabs subsequently redeposited their dollars.

A second problem created by big Arab deposits was credit risk. By taking huge deposits of Arab money and redepositing it with other banks, the dealer banks were forced to assume a credit risk that they thought properly belonged to the original depositor. To compensate for this risk, the dealer banks attempted to buy Arab money as cheaply as possible, a policy the Arabs seem to have understood. A final problem for a bank receiving big Arab deposits was that the resulting $2 or $3 billion increase in deposits and redeposits on its balance sheet tended to perceptibily erode the bank's capital ratios. Such erosion was something that a big bank might willingly have accepted to increase bread-and-butter loan business but not to earn a small margin in the placement market. To cope with these problems, a few big banks sought to limit the size of their Eurodollar book, a policy that offered the side benefit of enabling them to buy money more cheaply than other banks could.

Over time the problems created by Arab dollars have eased, partly because the Arabs gradually became more willing to place funds with the bottom end of the triple-A banks and the top end of the double-A banks. Whereas a decade ago 10 or 15 banks were receiving the bulk of Arab deposits, the list has now expanded to 50 or 60 banks, and it includes more non-U.S. names. In addition to expanding the number of banks with which they were willing to place money, the Arabs also became more willing to give top banks longer-term deposits, out to as long as 5 years. Thus the price advantage to the top banks of buying Arab money tended to slip from the shorter to the longer end of the maturity spectrum. This occurred, however, at a time when bank borrowers were loath to take down long-term, fixed-rate loans, so the development was of less advantage to the big banks than it might otherwise have been.

More recently the problems associated with recycling petro dollars have diminished because of weakness in the price of oil. This weakness has caused the balance-of-payments positions of a number of oil-exporting countries—Mexico and Nigeria to name two—that had undertaken huge development programs on the basis of anticipated oil revenues to turn from surplus to deficit.

One fact that seems to surprise many people is that, as the Arabs acquired so many dollars, the Mid East did not expand into a major Eurocenter. Bahrain, is primarily a booking center funded to a significant degree out of London. Part of the explanation is that the Mid East has always been viewed as an area of political instability, so people there prefer to keep their funds elsewhere. Also the Arabs have displayed little talent for the sort of cooperation that would be required to develop a major Mid East Eurocenter. In addition, unlike the Chinese of Singapore, the Arabs have never displayed great interest in or aptitude for banking and finance.

Worldwide funding

As noted, the major U.S. and foreign banks participating in the Euro-market all have branches running their own separate Eurodollar books in each of the major market centers and in newer peripheral centers as well. This proliferation of Euro activity naturally raises a question as to how centralized a bank's overall Euro activities should be.

In the past it was typical for a bank's branches in different dealing centers to act in a highly independent way, each creating its own dollar book under guidelines set by home office. Some banks now see benefits in greater coordination of the Euro activities of their different branches and are attempting to achieve it. Others, however, prefer to stick to decentralization. In this respect, Citibank and Chase are probably at extreme opposite poles: Citi having a reputation for decentralization, Chase for increasing coordination.

One argument for giving branches a high degree of autonomy is that funding at each is headed by senior and experienced officers who expect to accept responsibility and need it to develop. Also, if funding officers in some branches are bullish while others are bearish, letting each put his money where his mouth is has a pro side as well as a con. While the bank will not make as much money as it would have if every branch had acted on a *correct* rate view promulgated by head office, the bank also won't lose as much money as it would have if every branch had acted on an incorrect view. Another argument for branch autonomy is that, in a huge worldwide organization, coordination of what everyone is doing is infeasible or, alternatively, if feasible, would be costly and might take so long that the bank would be handicapped in taking advantage of constantly changing opportunities.

One advantage of coordinating the activities of a bank's individual branches and thereby creating a global Euro book for the bank is that doing so permits the bank to take its maximum open position in the most advantageous tax areas, for example, to run a very short book in Nassau and compensate by *snugging up* (decreasing the mismatch in) its London book. To the extent that the yield curve is upward sloping, this policy has the advantage of shifting the most expensive funding to the highest-tax areas. A second argument for coordination is that a bank may feel so confident in its rate predictions that it wants to make all its bets in the same direction. A third and, by the 1980s, crucial reason for a bank to run a worldwide Euro book was that, because of interest rate volatility, head office wanted to tightly control the bank's overall interest rate exposure by running a single global book in which its worldwide Euro and its domestic books were combined.

Another question concerning the funding of a bank's worldwide Euro operations is the extent to which each branch should be expected to finance its operations by buying funds in its own name. This question arises for two reasons. First, the *natural* (local) supply of and demand for Eurodollars is unbalanced in different Eurocenters; Singapore, Bahrain, and the Caribbean centers, for example, all tend to be big net buyers of funds. Second, lenders of dollars perceive the country risks associated with net buying centers outside London as being greater than those associated with London and are therefore unwilling to lend as much to banks in these centers. Together these two factors create a situation in which a bank's branches outside London may have to pay more for funds than the same bank's London branch would: whereas the London branch might be able to buy in the middle of the market or at the bid side, the non-London branch might have to buy at the offered side.

While this price differential does not amount to much, $1/16$ to $1/8$% typically, to the extent that it exists, there is a natural temptation for a bank to have its London branch buy extra funds in its name and then relend them to its branches in other centers. The only real cost to this operation is that the British Inland Revenue requires that the London branch make some small taxable profit on such transactions. Currently the minimum acceptable markup is $5/64$. Since this figure is modest, many banks do fund—sometimes to a large degree—the operations of their branches in other centers with funds bought in London.

However, there are banks that think every branch should stand on its own feet and do its own funding. One argument is that centers outside London will never be built up as meaningful entities in the global Euromarket unless they are seen to perform in the market in their own names. A second argument is that "sourcing" in London huge quantities of funds that are destined to be used in other centers makes London appear to be a much bigger buyer of Euros than it really is and may thereby impinge on London's sovereign value.

Earlier we said that there was a lot of dealing in New York and elsewhere in the U.S. in Euros for funding the assets of bank branches located in the Caribbean. This funding is all done in the name of the branch, since if a New York bank bought Euros in the name of head office, these dollars would become "domestic" dollars and as such would be subject to a reserve requirement. The fact that the funding and lending operations of the Caribbean branches of U.S. banks are carried out mainly by personnel at head office naturally raises the question of whether the profits of such branches should be treated as domestic income subject to domestic taxation or as foreign-source income. This tax question is one reason New York banks had for establishing IBFs.[10]

Eurocurrency swaps

The bulk of the Eurocurrency market consists of Eurodollar deposits, but it also includes Eurodeposits of German marks, sterling, Swiss francs, Dutch guilders, Belgian francs, French francs, and other currencies. The uninitiated might think of a bank accepting deposits in all of these currencies as ending up with a mixed bag of different kinds of money. Not so the Eurobanker; he knows that he can turn one currency into another through the simple device of a *swap*. To him money is money whatever its country or origin.

In the foreign exchange market, currencies are traded for each other on two bases, *spot* and *forward*. In a spot transaction, say, deutsche marks (DM) for dollars, the currencies exchanged are normally delivered two days after the trade is made. In a forward transaction the exchange occurs at some specified date further in the future, perhaps months later. *A swap is a pair of spot and forward transactions in which the forward transaction offsets or unwinds the spot transaction.* For example, if a holder of marks traded them for dollars in the spot market and simultaneously entered into a forward contract to sell these dollars for marks 3 months hence, he would have engaged in a swap. Note that the effect of this transaction is to permit the holder of marks to go into dollars for 3 months without assuming a *foreign exchange risk*. Specifically, by locking in a selling rate for the dollars he acquires, the swapper eliminates the risk that he might suffer a loss due to a fall in the exchange value of the dollar against the mark while he holds dollars.

Most large banks act as dealers in foreign exchange. The individuals who run this part of the bank's operations take speculative positions long and short in various currencies as part of their normal dealing activities—making markets and servicing customers' buy and sell orders. Also, based on their expectations of probable changes in exchange rates, they will assume speculative positions in foreign exchange designed to earn profits for the bank. Such activities expose the bank to foreign exchange risk. This risk, however, is one that the bank is prepared to assume within limits because the people in the foreign exchange department are experts in this area.

Funding officers, in contrast, have their greatest expertise in areas other than foreign exchange. As a result, banks in their Euro operations confine their speculation in foreign exchange to the foreign exchange

---

[10] See end of chapter.

department and require that funding officers match their Euro book in terms of currencies (e.g., use dollar liabilities to fund dollars assets). Thus, when a Eurobanker receives a deposit of a currency other than the dollar, he will either sell that deposit in the interbank market or swap it for dollars. Also if he is asked to extend a loan denominated in a currency other than the dollar, he will fund that loan either by buying a deposit of that currency or by swapping dollars into that currency.

Most of the time the spot and forward rates at which any currency trades against the dollar will differ. In particular the dollar price that a foreign currency commands in the forward market will be higher than the spot rate if this currency can be borrowed more cheaply than the dollar or if it is expected to appreciate in value relative to the dollar. The opposite conditions will cause the currency to sell at a discount in the forward market.

If a currency is selling at a premium in the forward market, a swap out of the dollar into that currency will yield some gain, while a swap out of that currency into the dollar will produce some loss. If, alternatively, a currency is selling at a discount in the forward market, the result will be the reverse. The gain or loss inherent in any swap, the amount of which can be calculated at the time the transaction is arranged, can be expressed as an annualized percentage rate of gain or loss through the use of a simple formula.[11] This rate of gain or loss is a crucial element in a bank's decision about what rates to charge on nondollar loans and to pay on nondollar deposits.

For example, suppose that a corporation offers a bank a 3-month DM deposit and that the forward mark is selling at a premium. If the bank accepts the deposit, it will swap these marks into dollars and in doing so will incur some loss. It will, however, also earn the going 3-month LIBOR rate on the dollars it obtains from the swap. Thus the rate that the bank offers the depositor will equal roughly 3-month LIBOR minus the annualized rate of loss on the swap. In costing a nondollar loan, the bank follows a similar approach.

On swap transactions, interest payments generate a residual foreign exchange exposure. For example, if a bank takes in a 3-month DM deposit and swaps it into dollars, the bank assumes a foreign exchange risk because it is committed to pay interest in DM on the DM deposit at maturity, while it will earn interest at maturity in dollars on the dollars it has loaned. If the bank chooses to avoid this risk, it can lock in a fixed spread on the overall swap by buying DM (selling dollars) *forward* in an amount equal to the interest to be paid in DM.

Several large banks that receive many deposits of Euromarks and Swiss francs and also receive many requests for loans denominated in

---

[11] For a numerical example of a swap, see Chapter 16.

those currencies have departed from the swap-everything-into-dollars approach we have just described. Specifically they have begun to run books in each of these currencies, matching off deposits in these currencies against loans and placements in the same currencies. Doing so eliminates transactions costs associated with swaps into and out of dollars—the foreign exchange dealers' spreads between bid and asked prices in the spot and forward markets and some bookkeeping and ticket costs. Banks running books in Euromarks and Euro Swissy feel that this reduction in costs permits them to offer depositors and borrowers of these currencies slightly better rates than they could if they consistently swapped all the *natural* DM and Swiss franc business they received into dollar assets and liabilities.

We have talked about banks using swaps to match their Euro books (in terms of currencies held and lent). Banks also use swaps another way, to minimize funding costs. Suppose, for example, that a bank wants to fund a 6-month dollar loan. To any funding officer, every Eurocurrency deposit is nothing but a Eurodollar deposit with a swap tagged on. Thus, in shopping for 6-month money, a bank dealer will price out not only 6-month dollar deposits but 6-month dollars obtained by swapping deposits of other currencies into dollars. If 6-month dollars can be obtained more cheaply by buying 6-month Euromarks and swapping them into dollars than by buying dollars, the dealer will go the swap route.

Because all banks in the Euromarket seize every opportunity available to reduce their borrowing costs through swaps, the all-in cost of dollars obtained by swapping any actively traded Eurocurrency into dollars tracks closely the yield on dollar deposits of the same tenor. Thus the rate saving that a bank can obtain by using a swap to obtain dollars usually amounts to only a narrow spread. However, when the foreign exchange market moves dramatically, short-lived opportunities for saving ⅛ or ¼% through a swap do occur.

THE TAX CUSHION PROBLEM AND SHELL BRANCHES

Because of the rapid buildup in recent years of the Euro books run both by U.S. *and* by foreign banks in the Caribbean, and because of the increasing importance as a Eurocenter given to New York by the running of such books from New York, we need to expand our earlier sketchy remarks on *booking centers,* or *shell branches* as they are also known. A U.S. bank is given a credit against its federal taxes for any foreign taxes it pays on profits earned abroad. A bank seeking to *maximize* its *aftertax* return must manage its affairs carefully so that it doesn't end up with more foreign tax credits than it can use against its federal tax bill. Because of foreign tax credits, major U.S. banks normally have no trouble working their federal tax liability down to zero. In fact, such banks do so much international business in London and other high-tax centers that they often end up with excess tax credits. In that case, the bank faces what is known as *the tax cushion problem.*

To illustrate, consider for simplicity a bank that has just two offices, head office and a London branch. If the bank gets into a position where it has booked so much profitable business in London office that the tax credit it gets from paying a 52% tax on profits in the U.K. exceeds 46% of its total taxable income, it will have excess tax credits against its U.S. federal taxes. In this case, the ratio of foreign taxes paid to its total taxable income will exceed 46%, that is,

$$\frac{\text{Foreign taxes paid}}{\text{Total taxable income}} \times 100 > 46\%$$

and the bank has a tax cushion problem.

To solve this problem, the bank needs to earn more foreign profits without increasing foreign taxes paid. A simple way to do this is for the bank to open a branch in a tax haven, such as Nassau or Grand Cayman, which imposes no profits tax. Such branches are referred to as *shell branches* because no decision making occurs at the branch and no senior bank personnel are stationed there. Instead, the branch is run directly from head office, which books loans and accepts deposits on the shell's behalf. A U.S. bank that has a shell branch in Nassau or some other tax haven will generate a lot of paperwork at the branch; this work is done by some local bank, and the resulting rise in local employment is the benefit the country sponsoring the tax haven gets out of doing so. U.S. banks run a lot of shell branches in the Caribbean because this area is in a time zone that makes it easy for U.S. banks to deal on the shell's behalf during normal working hours.

While some investors feel comfortable placing deposits at the Caribbean branch of a U.S. bank, many do not. This is because most investors don't understand sovereign risk. However, the educational process is ongoing, and the more that people become acquainted with the subject of sovereign risk and realize how small it is with respect to the Caribbean, the more they are encouraged to invest there. Doing so is easier than investing in London because of time-zone considerations.

Sovereign risk has to do with the danger posed to depositors at a foreign branch by possible expropriation of the branch's assets. Many investors fear that, if Nassau or some other tax haven country suddenly turned communist and expropriated the assets of bank branches there, deposits in these branches would not be repayable.

By law, a U.S. bank is responsible for all deposits in its foreign branches unless (1) there is a change in government in a country where it has a branch, and (2) the new government is inimical to the U.S. Even if a new government is unfriendly, a U.S. bank is relieved of its liability to repay depositors at the expropriated branch only to the extent that the new government succeeds in seizing the branch's assets. If 95% of the loans a bank booked in a branch were to major U.S. and multinational companies, these companies would—in the event of expropriation of the branch—pay off their loan obligations not to the branch but to the bank's head office. This would protect 95% of the branch's assets, and thereby 95% of its deposits, from expropriation. If the other 5% of the branch's total loans were to communist countries that recognized the new government's claim on the branch's assets and repaid their loans to the expropriated branch, the maximum loss depositors at the branch could sustain would be 5%. As a matter of practice, the loss would probably be zero since a major U.S. bank would be loath to have depositors lose any money placed with it.

A bank that books assets in a tax haven where the political tide might turn is careful to place only safe loans there—loans to corporations and other entities that would pay off to head office any loans outstanding at an expropriated branch. Because of this, the sovereign risk attaching to deposits in Caribbean tax havens is minimal to zero. Citibank officers who have booked over $20 billion of assets at their Nassau branch sleep soundly; so, too, should depositors who have placed funds there.

U.S. banks should (and most do) book the large loans they make to communist countries at head office or in a branch in a politically stable country; London office is a natural choice.

A GLOBAL BOOK

All U.S. banks running Euro books used to think of themselves as running two distinct positions: a domestic book and a Euro book. In recent years some banks have departed sharply from this practice and begun to think of themselves as running a single global book.

One reason for adopting a global-book strategy is that doing so will prevent a bank from getting into a position where it has a natural hedge going for it that doesn't know about: New York is running a short domestic book, the foreign branches a long book. A bank should also avoid the oppositive extreme where both the domestic book and the Euro book are geared the same way, but so much so that the bank is taking an unacceptable risk against its interest rate outlook. A bank can avoid either extreme by aggregating its positions worldwide and then implementing strategies with respect to its global position.

A little history

The head office of every U.S. bank that started operations in the Euromarket in the early 1960s initially instructed its foreign branches to accept *no* interest rate exposure in their Euro operations. A branch that acquired a 3-month, fixed-rate asset was expected to buy 3-month money against it and then sit tight and earn its spread. This situation lasted until the early 1970s. Then, gradually, U.S. banks began to allow their branches to mismatch. In those days, this almost always meant borrowing short and lending long because the yield curve was usually positively sloped.

As the 1970s progressed, head office at many banks became concerned about the risk to which the mismatch limits it imposed on the branches exposed the bank. Often these limits were couched in percentage terms. Consequently, as a bank's Euro book grew, the absolute amounts represented by these percentages became large. The mismatch risk in a bank's Euro book, which initially had been minimal, became significant.

At this point, the major banks began to track their branches' mismatch regularly from head office and to set tighter mismatch limits based on absolute dollar amounts. By 1975, it was not unusual for a bank to impose a whole set of limits on each foreign branch with respect to various mismatches it could have: overnight against 1-month, 1s against 3s, and so on. Coupled with this, many banks instituted a system whereby all the branches would report to head office weekly on their positions. Head office would then aggregate these reports so that it could determine at a glance the interest rate exposure on its worldwide Euro book. It would also compare that exposure with the exposure it was taking in its domestic book. For a time, banks permitted their foreign branches to operate more or less autonomously within the confines of the risk parameters set by head office.

Running a global book

Then, in the late 1970s and early 1980s, as interest rates became higher and more volatile, a number of banks decided to tighten up still further on the freedom given to the branches: to require that the branches act in conformity with rate views formulated at head office and communicated regularly to them. The path by which banks arrived at this decision was long and less than direct. Nonetheless, the decision itself was extremely important. For the first time, banks were controlling their global book from a central point.

By doing so, a bank got not only the obvious benefit of being better able to control its total exposure; it also got additional flexibility in adjusting that exposure. For example, a bank that has a lot of floating-rate loans on its domestic book is always vulnerable to a decline in interest rates. If the bank is running a global book, it can offset this vulnerability by running a short Euro book. For a major bank that fears a fall in rates and wants to run a neutral position, running a short Euro book is the way to achieve such a position.

At top banks that operate a global book, the absolute limit on running a short day-to-day position in the Euro book is liberal—several or more billion dollars. If a bank ran just a Euro book and nothing else, this limit would be so large as to permit the bank to take a tremendous risk. However, when the bank's domestic and Euro books are viewed as a whole, the offset to a huge, short Euro position is all the bank's floating-rate loans on which rates can change at the drop of a hat. Given these loans, a short Euro book can be consistent with a bank's desire to be neutral overall. As this example illustrates, a bank should never look at its domestic book on Tuesday, its Euro book on Friday. In a volatile rate environment, a global view pays.

This is a conclusion that Citibank did not used to accept. In this respect, it is interesting to note that it was Citi's London office that incurred in the fourth quarter of 1980 a staggering loss that offset much of the profit earned by the rest of the bank.[12]

BANK OF ENGLAND REGULATION

Since London is the preeminent center of the Euromarket, it is important to ask who regulates what goes on in the London market, how they do it, and how well they do it.

The first important point to make is that regulation of domestic banking has always been much less formal in Britain than in the U.S. or on the Continent. Unlike many U.S. bank regulators, the Bank of England proceeds on the assumption that bankers are prudent, honest people who know as much if not more about banking than regulators do. Thus their approach has not been to impose regulations and ratios on the banks; instead they ask for periodic reports from the banks. On the basis of these, they discuss informally with each bank's top management the quality of the bank's loans, their liquidity, any features of the bank's condition that the Bank of England views as unusual or out of line, and any suggestions that the Bank of England might make with respect to the bank's operations.

Passage of the Banking Act of 1979 has done little to change this situation. One reason for passage of the act was that other EEC (European Economic Community) members regarded it as anomalous that the U.K. had no statutory backing for the regulation of banks. British bankers are proud of how well self-regulation under the eye of a benign regulator, the Bank of England, has worked in the U.K. and view pressure for

---

[12] To properly run a global book, a bank must solve some tricky people problems and appropriately alter its profit center analysis. See Stigum and Branch, *Managing Bank Assets and Liabilities,* pp. 312–16.

harmonization of banking regulation among EEC members with a mix of suspicion and sadness. Said one long-term market participant, "In a highly regulated market, participants spend all their time counterproductively: trying to find ways around the regs. There is now pressure from the EEC to have London conform more closely to their pattern of regulated financial markets. They are trying to force written regulations on London; this will close the gap between us and them a bit—move us down towards their level."

When foreign banks come to London, they are treated in much the same way as domestic British banks. If the Bank of England recognizes a bank as reputable in its home country, it will permit that bank to open a London branch with a minimum of red tape. The bank does not have to put in any capital; all it has to do to open an office is to agree to comply with certain regulations, and it is granted the same right to engage in banking that any other bank in the U.K. has. Foreign banks establishing independent entities, merchant banking subs or banking consortia, do have to put in capital, but again if the parentage is reputable, the red tape is minimal. As an executive of a large U.S. bank noted, "When we went to the Bank of England for permission to open a merchant banking arm, they said, 'You need a foreign exchange trader, someone who knows British exchange control regulations, some capital, and since you are asking to be recognized as a bank, at least a window where you could take deposits whether you do or not. Oh, and one other thing. We'd like you to locate in the City of London. The rents are high which keeps out the riffraff.' "

In justification of the Bank of England's rather casual regulation of foreign banks, it might be added that the bank operates on the quite logical assumption that foreign bank branches are an inextricable part of the parent, which implies two things. First, it is difficult if not impossible to regulate these branches as independent entities. Second, the natural assumption is that these branches are being regulated indirectly by banking authorities in the parent country, which regulates the activities of the parent bank as a whole.

The ease with which foreign banks can enter the London market and the minimal regulations imposed on their activities there have encouraged the entry of several hundred foreign banks into London. It has also permitted the rapid *growth* and constant *innovation* that have been characteristic of the Euromarket.

To a U.S. regulator the British approach to bank regulation might seem like a time bomb guaranteed to create monumental difficulties at some time. Yet the record shows that the British approach to bank regulation has been at least as successful, if not more so, than the U.S. approach. One reason is that there is a lot of mutual respect between banks operating in Britain and the Bank of England. Because of this and because of the real powers the Bank of England possesses, banks don't fight "The Old Lady (of Threadneedle Street);" instead they take her suggestions seriously. Another reason the Bank of England approach has been so successful is that it is responsible for overseeing the operations of only a limited number of banks, about 100 domestic and 200 foreign banks. In contrast, U.S. regulators have to cope with over 15,000 banks. As one Bank of England official noted, the limited number of banks in Britain has permitted the Bank of England to know on an almost personal basis the managers of these institutions and thus whether they do or do not need closer supervision.

Naturally with the entry of so many foreign banks into London, it is becoming more and more difficult for the Bank of England to pursue its brand of personal regulation. As a result, in recent years the Bank of England has asked banks to report to it with increasing frequency and has visited them more often.

Sovereign risk in London

Investors, both bank and nonbank, depositing dollars in a bank or bank branch located in a foreign country are always concerned with *sovereign* or *country risk.* U.S. investors, particularly those with little experience in international business, used to display a lot of concern over the sovereign risk associated with making dollar deposits in London. As these investors saw it, at least before the U.K.'s emergence as an oil producer, the periodic crises through which the pound sterling passed and the chronic weakness of the British economy both suggested that at some time the British might be tempted to block payment on the dollar liabilities of London banks. While one cannot say this could never happen, there is only one conclusion that anyone who has studied the London market carefully can reach: The sovereign risk attached to dollar deposits in London is *very* close to zero.

One practical reason is that Britain would gain nothing from blocking payment of the Eurodollar liabilities of London banks during a sterling crisis. From the end of World War II until the U.K. became an oil producer, the pound sterling was a weak currency; to prop up its value, the British maintained tight controls on the use of sterling by domestic holders. Because of these controls, the Euromarket in London, which would in any case have been largely a market in offshore funds, was strictly a market in offshore funds. With the few exceptions permitted by the British exchange control authorities, all the Eurodollars that flowed into London were owned by foreign depositors, and all the Eurodollars that flowed out went to foreign borrowers. In effect London acted and still does largely as a conduit through which dollars flow from foreigners to foreigners. Thus inflows of Eurodollars to London do not add to British foreign exchange reserves, and outflows do not subtract from them, which means in turn that blocking payment on the Eurodollar liabilities of London banks would have done nothing to stem the loss by Britain of foreign reserves during a sterling crisis. Actually, in 1980 sterling was so strong that the U.K. fully dismantled its exchange control apparatus.

The financial activities centered in the City of London, including Eurodollar transactions, earn Britain large amounts of foreign exchange, provide thousands of jobs, and add vitality to the whole economy. A second reason Britain would not block payment on Eurodollar deposits is that, if it did, it would lose these advantages. As a Bank of England official noted, "If the British interfered with the payout of Eurodollars, nationalized foreign branches, or whatever, that would kill more than the Euromarket, it would kill London. Any action taken against Euro operations in London would immediately spread to London as a banking center; and if London is not a banking center, then it isn't a commodity market, it isn't an international insurance center, it isn't a stock or investment market generally. In London these things dovetail closely: if you damage one, you damage the lot. The game would not be worth the candle."

Had Britain during a sterling crisis been willing to do something dramatic and potentially dangerous to its economy, the logical step would have been to block the large sterling balances held by Commonwealth nations. That would have directly stemmed the loss by Britain of foreign exchange reserves by preventing conversion of these balances into foreign exchange. Blocking sterling balances is a course of action that was open to Britain during every sterling crisis. Yet the British never took it, presumably in part because of the effect doing so would have had on London's role as a world financial center.

LENDER OF LAST RESORT

Another question that troubles some Euromarket watchers is: Who is to act as lender of last resort if some event much more shaking than the failure of the Herstatt hits it? This question really involves two separate questions: Who lends if the supply of Eurodollars dries up? Who lends if the solvency of a major bank or group of banks in the Euromarket is threatened through bad loans or other losses?

As noted, dollars can't disappear, but they can move from place to place. Thus it's conceivable, though highly unlikely, that the supply of dollars in the Euromarket could dry up because holders of dollars for some reason decided to move their deposits from banks in Eurocenters to banks in New York or elsewhere in the United States. Such an eventuality would not cause U.S. banks severe liquidity problems with respect to their Euro operations; they could always buy back in the U.S. market the dollars they had lost in the Euromarket and use them to fund their

Euro assets. The major inconvenience to them in doing so is that they would incur a reserve cost on domestic dollars funneled to the Euromarket. To some extent foreign banks could do the same thing, buy more dollars in New York and funnel them abroad, but in doing so they would face a crucial problem: Most of them would be able to buy in the U.S. market only a fraction of the dollars they were accustomed to buying in the Euromarket. Thus, in the unlikely event of dollars drying up in the Euromarket, foreign banks could face a liquidity crisis. Foreign banks negotiate standby lines with U.S. banks to protect against this risk.

Central banks have discussed at length, in meetings in Basel, Switzerland, the question of lender of last resort to the Euromarket and have reached the conclusion that each looks after his own. Thus the Fed is the appropriate lender of last resort to a U.S. banker whether its troubles arise from its New York or London operations, and the Bank of England stands behind the operations of its domestic banks both at home and abroad. The logical thrust of this philosophy is that, if foreign banks experienced liquidity problems with respect to their dollar operations, it would be up to their respective central banks to provide them with dollars, something that the central banks of major countries could do either from their own reserves or by obtaining dollars through swaps from the Fed.

With respect to the second question concerning the possible failure by a major Eurobank or group of banks, the comment of a German banker is relevant. In speaking of the Herstatt failure, which sent shock waves through the Euromarket, he said, "The Bundesbank [German central bank] will never admit that they made a mistake, but in retrospect they know they did. They should not have permitted the Herstatt to fail; instead they should have merged it into one of the larger German banks. A bank failure on that scale will, I guarantee, never occur in Germany again."

The development of the Euromarket as an international capital market has made a significant contribution over the last several decades to the world economy by providing financing for a huge expansion in international trade and investment. The development of this market has also tied in ways hitherto unknown the economies, capital markets, and fortunes of many free-world countries, including all of the major ones. Thus to allow this market to falter or fail would create economic havoc on a world scale. Central bankers know this, and the almost universal opinion among bankers is thus that no central bank in a major country will again let one of its key banks fail. Moreover, if a group of banks were threatened, say, by defaults on loans to underdeveloped countries, the central banks standing behind those banks would undoubtedly keep them afloat through individual or coordinated actions. As a foreign banker noted,

"No central bank will ever commit itself publicly to keeping all domestic banks above size X afloat, but they know—and we know they know—that, should a major bank be threatened, the economic costs of inaction on their part would *far exceed* the cost of action. Therefore they would act." Another foreign banker echoed this thought, "If any of the top 50 banks in the world went under, none of us would survive. No central bank will say, 'We will support the top X banks.' They do not want to draw a line, but in practice the line is drawn: you'll get central bank support if you're so big that by failing you would drag everyone else down with you."

The question of who is the lender of last resort in the Euromarket has particularly troubled the Bank of England because of the extensive Euro operations carried out in London by foreign banks. The understanding under which foreign banks are permitted to open branches in London has always been that the parent would stand behind the branch, whatever difficulties it might encounter. In the case of merchant banking subs and consortium banks, this understanding was implicit but perhaps less formal. During the nervous and anxious period that prevailed after the Herstatt failure, the Bank of England acted to formalize this commitment by asking for "comfort letters" stating that each parent of a merchant banking sub or consortium bank would provide support, if required, to that entity up to its share of ownership.

Clouds on the Horizon

In the years following Herstatt, the Euromarket grew and matured in a general atmosphere of confidance both in the big banks and in the market itself. All this changed in 1982, which turned out to be a year marked by one financial calamity after another. At the end of Chapter 6, we noted some of the problems that arose at Chase, Continental, and several other big U.S. banks. At the end of Chapter 9, we describe the failures of two U.S. dealers, Drysdale and Lombard-Wall. Here we pause to tell briefly the stories of the major problems that arose in the Euromarket during 1982.

THE FAILURE OF BANCO AMBROSIANO HOLDINGS

In June 1982, the Italian central bank requested that the chairman, Mr. Robert Calvi, of the Banco Ambrosiano, then Italy's 11th largest bank and largest private bank, provide it with details concerning the $1.4 billion of loans that the Banco Ambrosiano Holdings S.A., a Luxembourg financial holding company, had extended through its Latin American subsidiaries to a number of Panamanian companies. Shortly thereafter,

Mr. Calvi was found hanging from a London bridge in a position that suggests that, unless he was an extraordinary athlete, his death was not suicide.

From there on, the Ambrosiano story unfolded like a good yarn spun by Paul Erdman. Unfortunately for Eurobankers, however, the story was fact not fiction.

On July 12, the Midland Bank—agent for a syndicate of banks that had lent $40 million to Banco Ambrosiano Holdings (BAH)—declared BAH in default because of long-overdue payments of interest and principal. Other banks in other syndicates followed suit; and on July 14, BAH's assets were frozen by a Luxembourg court.

Subsequent investigations revealed that the $1.4 billion of loans extended in early 1980 by the Latin American subsidiaries of BAH and financed by BAH and other Ambrosiano subsidiaries were to paper corporations that were nominally owned by the Vatican Bank. The operations of this bank, known officially as the Instituto per le Opere de Religione (IOR), have, until recently, been shrouded in total secrecy; IOR owns at least 1.58% of the Banco Ambrosiano and is suspected of owning much more. Apparently in many matters—the full story has yet to be told and may never be—the Vatican Bank acted as a *de facto* partner in various ventures with the Banco Ambrosiano. Certainly Calvi was known in Italian circles as "God's banker."

A most peculiar aspect of the loans financed by BAH in Latin America is that Archbishop Paul Marcinkus, the American-born president of the Vatican bank, signed "letters of patronage" for the Panamanian ghost companies that received loans from BAH. Marcinkus's letters stated that the companies were controlled by the Vatican bank and were apparently written to serve as references or guarantees for the lender. However, after the letters were written, Calvi secretly rendered them legally worthless by absolving the Vatican Bank from any responsibility in these loan transactions. As of fall 1982, no one knew what had happened to the $1.4 billion lent by Ambrosiano subsidiaries to paper companies in Panama.

The declaration by the Midland Bank that BAH was in default and the subsequent disclosure of the irregular activities in which the Banco Ambrosiano had engaged (often in confusing partnership with the IOR) caused the Banco Ambrosiano to face a *liquidity* crisis. When it became apparent that this bank could no longer meet its obligations, the Bank of Italy, working with a consortium of major Italian banks, put together an aid package designed to permit the Banco Ambrosiano to make timely payments on its obligations. This arrangement continued until early August when the Bank of Italy stated that the remnants of the Banco Ambrosiano's assets would be reconstituted into a new bank controlled by the consortium formed in July to bail out Ambrosiano. By reorganizing the Banco Ambrosiano into a new bank rather than declaring it bankrupt, the central bank permitted Ambrosiano to continue its normal banking activities without interruption.

In announcing the establishment of the new bank, called the Nuovo Banco Ambrosiano, the Italian Treasury minister stressed that this bank would in no way assume the liabilities of BAH or of its Latin American subsidiaries. The support given by the Bank of Italy to the Banco Ambrosiano is in line with what one would expect. Since the failure of the Herstatt, no major free-world country has permitted one of its top banks to fail with losses to depositors.

While the fate of the Banco Ambrosiano has been settled, the question of what institution, if any, would assume responsibility for paying off BAH's liabilities remained an open issue in the fall of 1982. As Italian authorities sought to pierce the veil of secrecy and diplomatic immunity surrounding the operations of the Vatican Bank and threatened to bring fraud charges against three of its directors, the IOR, for its part, refused to accept any liability for the debts of BAH, which as a practical matter the IOR could not pay off in full since these debts exceeded its net worth.

The Bank of Italy argued that it was under no legal or moral obligation to pay off the debts of BAH because the company was a holding company located in Luxembourg. For its part, Luxembourg washed its hands of responsibility for BAH's debts on the grounds that BAH was a holding company, not a bank.

All this was troubling to Eurobankers for several reasons. First, they stood to lose $526 million on loans to and notes issued by BAH and perhaps a good bit more on deposits with its Latin American subsidiaries.[13] Second, Eurobankers feared that default by BAH might ring the death knell of the Basle concordate, which many of them had viewed as providing a general, lender-of-last-resort underpinning for the Euromarket.

The Basel concordate. Following the failure of Herstatt, governors of the top ten central banks of the free world met in Basle in 1974 and issued, after considered deliberation, the delphic statement:

> While it is not practical to lay down in advance detailed rules and procedures for the provision of temporary support to banks experiencing liquidity difficulties, the means are available for that purpose and will be used if and when necessary.[14]

---

[13] The miasma of intergroup transactions that linked the Banco Ambrosiano, the numerous subsidiaries of its holding company, the Vatican bank, and other Eurodollar market participants are portrayed schematically in the *Financial Times,* August 5, 1982. A lot of the dollar flows in the chart that lead to the Vatican bank are marked with question marks.

[14] The Group of Ten consists of the U.S., Canada, Japan, the U.K., France, Germany, Italy, Belgium, the Netherlands, and Sweden; Switzerland is an honorary 11th member. The G10 overlaps in membership but is distinct from the BIS whose directors are all governors of European central banks: Belgium, the Netherlands, France, the U.K., Germany, Switzerland, Sweden, and Italy.

The Bank of Italy concluded that this initial statement by the Group of Ten, together with its subsequent dictums, concerned banks; BAH was not a bank; *ergo* the Bank of Italy bore no responsibility for bailing out BAH. Luxembourg also disavowed responsibility for BAH because of its foreign parentage.

All this resulted in much hew and cry in the Euromarket, especially from the 250 banking institutions that had lent BAH a half billion or so, which they stood to lose.

The aftermath.   Post BAH's plunge into bankruptcy, the Euromarket suffered a good case of jitters, but it survived with nothing much worse happening than some cutting back of bank lines and some temporary pronouncing of rate tiering in the interbank market.

The failure of BAH led to none of the dire consequences initially feared for several reasons. First, sophisticated Euromarket participants took the view that anyone with ears to hear or eyes to read should have known for several years prior to the failure of BAH that Calvi and his foreign operations were in trouble. Said one banker, "If BAH had been a bank and a big bank, its failure would have had a huge impact on credit lines and market liquidity. But BAH wasn't a bank; it was an Italian financing sub operating out of Luxembourg, which everyone accepts as something risky in the first place. If BAH's failure caused you to pull in your reins [cut lines], you must have been shooting without looking. Ambrosiano was to be expected. If you had loans to BAH on your book, and it took the failure of that institution to tell you you had a problem, I don't want to own shares in your bank."

While the failure of BAH did not cause even a near crisis in the Euromarket, it imprinted indelibly in the minds of lenders the distinction between a branch and a sub. Lending to a sub in London might be a safe bet because in London, where there are lots of foreign-owned subs in the form of consortium banks, such entities are supervised by the Bank of England, which also has—just in case—a file drawer of comfort letters from their parents. Luxembourg, following the Bank of England's example, asked belatedly—after BAH failed—for comfort letters from the parents of the many foreign-owned financial subs operating in Luxembourg.

Presumably Luxembourg had no trouble getting such letters from the top German banks, all of whom operate big subs in Luxembourg. These banks do so because the stringent capital and liquidity rules imposed on them by German authorities would preclude German banks from participating on a significant scale in the Euromarket if they did not use the ruse of booking their Eurobusiness on the books of their Luxembourg subs.

The failure of BAH caused a lingering concern in the Euromarket over subs located in places such as Panama and Grand Cayman where central bank supervision and support is likely to range from weak to nonexistent. Why are those subs there, and what are they doing?

BAH, like Penn Square, was paying up to borrow. That led one banker to comment, "If a guy is paying up to borrow that doesn't mean he is a bad credit, but you had better ask why he is paying up. If he's Soc Gen's holding company paying up in the U.S. commercial paper market, you know he is doing so because U.S. investors don't know the name and don't like to lend to a nationalized bank, even if the credit is that of a sovereign nation, France. If, on the other hand, the guy who is paying up is—you learn with one, well-placed call—a guy with a credit problem, that's a different story. You lend in the first case, not in the second."

East European Lending

A final cloud over the banking scene in the summer of 1982 was the huge loans U.S. and foreign banks had outstanding to East European countries. Certainly in the case of Poland, there was no realistic hope that it could or would repay its loans in the foreseeable future. Yet bankers clung to the hope of rescheduling Poland's debts to obviate the necessity of huge loan writeoffs.

In this respect, it is interesting to note that the German banks, which are among the most heavily regulated of Western banks, had made, relative to their size, the biggest loans to East European countries and that they had done so partly at the behest of German authorities who were anxious to further the cause of detente.

Strict bank regulation and sound banking do not necessarily go hand in hand for two reasons. As the case of Germany demonstrated, strict regulation in no way prevents a government from encouraging domestic banks to take imprudent actions if the government feels it is in the national interest that domestic banks do so.

Dome Oil and the Canadian Banks

Canada provides a second case in point. While U.S. banks were making or otherwise participating in energy-related loans to their later regret, the same was occurring north of the border on an even grander scale. In Canada, energy-related lending became a fad not only because energy prices were rising but because Trudeau convinced Canadians—economic theory to the contrary notwithstanding—that a massive capital outflow resulting from the buyout by Canadian companies of American properties in Canada would be in the long-run economic interest of Canada. This created an atmosphere in which Dome Petroleum, the giant of the Canadian energy industry, could, with the aid of bank loans, attain a leverage ratio of $30 of debt to $1 of capital. To put things in proportion, note that Dome is a nonfinancial business corporation not a bank that is supposed to make money by being highly leveraged; if Citibank or any other major U.S. bank were to attain a 30-to-1 capital ratio, the regulators would be knocking on its door asking bank management just what they thought they were doing and what their plans were for reducing their debt or bolstering their capital.

At the end of 1982, Dome, which was in dire financial straits, had outstanding from the major Canadian banks loans equal to roughly 40% of the total equity and reserves of these banks. The Canadian government, which could not permit widescale collapse of its domestic banking system, was in the position of having to decide whether to bail out Dome or the Canadian banks.

Unease in the Euromarket

It is fair to say that until 1982 most knowledgeable participants in the Euromarket—however diverse their roles might be—felt that the informal regulation imposed on this market by the Bank of England and other central banks together with the implicit support provided by each nation's central bank to its own banks would give the international Euromarket sufficient strength to weather any forseeable storm.

Then came 1982. One financial calamity piled on top of another: the failure of Penn Square and the $1 billion of questionable loan participations it left on Continental's book (Chase held at least another quarter of a billion); the Drysdale debacle, which cost Chase a tarnished image and over ¼ of a billion pretax; the failure of Lombard-Wall; the failure of BAH; the possible failure of Dome Petroleum to which Canadian banks had loaned huge sums; the rescheduling of the Polish and Mexican debts; and the threats of more reschedulings of country loans or of outright country defaults.

No one of these events alone would have sufficed to cast a broad shadow of doubt and unease over the Euromarket, but coming together as they did, they raised uneasy questions in the minds of many: Were the big banks as safe as they had been thought to be? Was the international capital market more fragile than had been thought, so fragile that it might be unable to withstand the shock of defaults by several major debtor nations?

One result of these doubts was a pronounced flight to quality. Tiering in the Euromarket increased, and spreads widened between Euro rates and U.S. rates and between rates on bank CDs and rates on credit-risk-free Treasury bills.

How long the uneasiness about the major banks and the Euromarket would last was unclear. Perhaps all that was required to brush the clouds from the sky and to restore a brighter perspective was an easing of interest rates and a revival of the depressed world economy.

In retrospect, Ambrosiano was little more than a costly lesson to the international banking community: Know thy customer. Souring country loans were a more serious problem. In the past country loans were regarded as safe. Companies might and did default, but countries did not because, unlike companies, they were destined to remain in business; and a country that defaulted on its debts would be ostracized from the international capital market. With oil-rich Mexico literally bankrupt, country loans seemed less sacrosanct.

Bankers and others called for the International Monetary Fund (IMF) to create a major bail-out facility for country debtors. Some nations proposed that the IMF be given the resources to act as lender of last resort to bankrupt countries, a solution that would have bailed the major world banks out of their country-loan problems. Other nations—the U.S. in particular—set more modest goals for the IMF.

Perhaps this time around at least all that is needed is an upswing in economic activity and modest help from the IMF. In brighter moments bankers argued that it was unrealistic to expect underdeveloped countries to pay off their debts in the foreseeable future. Being capital poor, it would always make economic sense for them to borrow more rather than less as their economies grew. After all—here analogy is brought to bear—doesn't AT&T borrow more each year?

That analogy has a ring of plausibility, but it should be born in mind that AT&T is a profitable company that is expanding capacity in a capital-intensive industry in a politically stable and wealthy nation. Also, to service its debts, AT&T does not have to force street rioters back to work (Poland), nor does it have to impose further austerity measures on millions of poor people threatening a leftist revolution (Mexico), nor has it recently seen fit to devote scarce resources to waging war on Great Britain (Argentina).

FOREIGN BANK OPERATIONS IN THE UNITED STATES

Foreign banks have used various organizational vehicles to enter the U.S. market (Tables 6–6 and 6–7). A few have set up wholly owned subsidiaries operated under a domestic banking charter. Of these, a handful are long-standing operations like Barclays' banking network in California. Others are of recent origin.

A second way commonly used by foreign banks to enter the U.S. market is to set up *agencies* in U.S. financial centers. By far the largest agencies in the U.S. are those of Canadian banks. An agency cannot accept deposits in its own name, and it cannot hold loans on its own books. Instead it acts as a loan production office and funding agent for

TABLE 6–6
Foreign banking offices in the United States by type and parent country

Location of parent bank	Agencies	Branches	Subsidiaries	Total assets ($ billions)
Japan	22	36	12	100.1
United Kingdom	12	20	8	49.7
Canada	18	12	8	23.2
Hong Kong	7	7	1	14.9
France	7	15	2	14.6
Switzerland	4	7	1	12.3
Italy	7	10	1	11.0
Germany	6	14	0	7.9
Other countries	104	106	22	37.3
Total	187	227	55	271.0

Source: Federal Reserve Board.

TABLE 6–7
Foreign banking offices in the United States, offices and assets by state

U.S. location	Agencies	Branches	Subsidiaries*	Total assets ($ billions)
New York	46	141	29	168.0
California	96	7	22	80.5
Illinois	—	39	2	10.0
Florida	31	—	2	1.7
Other	14	40	—	10.8
Total numbers	187	227	55	271.00

* Includes U.S. commercial banks majority owned by foreign banks, New York State investment companies majority owned by foreign banks, U.S. offices of banking Edge or agreement corporations majority owned by foreign banks.
Source: Federal Reserve Board.

the parent bank. It arranges loans and then books them at some branch of the parent, for example, Nassau or at head office. It also acts as an agent for the parent in the New York money market, buying and selling Fed funds and Euros for head office's account.

The principal reason why foreign banks initially set up agency offices rather than branches in New York was that, under New York State law, a foreign bank was permitted to set up a New York branch only if its country of origin permitted U.S. banks to establish branches there. Canada precluded foreign banks from establishing branches in Canada, so the big Canadian banks all established New York agencies. Because Canada has since changed its law, Canadian banks could now convert their New York agencies to branches. In fact only one of the top five Canadian banks has done so.

A second reason some foreign banks set up a U.S. agency instead of a branch was to avoid the overhead they would have incurred in setting up a branch with facilities for accepting deposits. Finally, prior to the passage in 1978 of the *International Banking Act* (*IBA*), foreign bank agencies were subject neither to U.S. regulation nor to reserve requirements. Under the 1978 act, Congress took the view that agencies were, in effect, branches and, as such, should be treated in a fashion similar to that specified for foreign bank branches.[15]

A third way a foreign bank can enter the U.S. market is by setting up a branch. In recent years the growth of such branches in New York has been explosive (Table 6–6). Prior to the passage of the IBA in 1978, foreign bank branches operated exclusively under state banking laws and were regulated solely by state banking authorities. Most are located in New York, California, and Illinois, which have specific legislation permitting the establishment of branches by foreign banks. Generally such branches can engage in the full range of domestic banking activities.

Setting up a branch in the United States is expensive for a foreign bank not only in terms of overhead but in terms of taxation. Once a foreign bank establishes a U.S. branch, all of its income on loans into the United States becomes subject to U.S. taxation. Yet the U.S. market, and more particularly the New York market, acts as a magnet drawing in more and more foreign bank branches.

Foreign banks setting up U.S. branches do so for several reasons. First, they are attempting to follow their customers to the U.S. just as U.S. banks followed their customers abroad; the growth of international banking is in part a response to the emergence of multinational firms. Foreign banks are also attempting to develop relationships with large U.S. corporations; most of these have foreign operations, and a foreign bank can therefore provide them with special services and expertise. A third reason foreign banks have set up New York branches is to obtain access to the huge domestic reservoir of dollars. Finally, New York is a convenient place for foreign banks to run and fund a Nassau or Grand Cayman Eurodollar book.

Most foreign bank branches are primarily wholesale operations servicing large as opposed to retail accounts. For example, the customers of one big foreign bank branch in New York include a large proportion of

---

[15] The IBA also granted the Comptroller the power to override New York State's reciprocity restriction by granting a national charter to a nonqualifying foreign bank wishing to establish a New York branch. The Comptroller's power to do so was upheld in court when the Comptroller granted a national charter to an Australian bank wanting to open a New York branch.

the Fortune 500, big European corporations, Japanese trading corporations, large firms trading in commodities, and foreign banks for which the branch acts as a clearing agent. Foreign bank branches fund themselves much as domestic money market banks do, by accepting deposits and by purchasing monies in the Fed funds, Eurodollar, and CD markets. There are, however, differences. One is that CDs issued by foreign bank branches have only limited acceptance in the U.S. market. Another is that for a foreign bank branch there was no distinction between Eurodollars and "domestic" dollars because foreign bank branches did not have to hold reserves against any of the funds they received in deposit or purchased. This changed with passage of the IBA.

The position of a foreign bank operating a New York branch is much the same as the position of the London branch of the same bank in the Eurodollar market. It is acquiring assets and incurring liabilities in a foreign currency, the dollar, and it thinks of itself as running a dollar book. In running this book, moreover, the New York branch, like the London branch, is concerned about mismatch and is subject to guidelines from home office with respect to the degree of mismatch it may run. One difference, however, is that foreign bank branches in New York, like domestic U.S. banks, make a lot of variable-rate loans, so mismatch on their books can't be measured or controlled in quite the same way in New York as in London.

The U.S. is the home of the dollar, so having a U.S. branch provides a foreign bank with additional funding and liquidity for its overall Eurodollar operation because the U.S. branch can directly tap the vast domestic market for dollars. Setting up a U.S. branch also permits a foreign bank to establish an entity to which other branches in the bank's international network can turn to make adjustments in their dollar books; for example, if one of the bank's non-New York branches were getting short-term dollar deposits but had to fund longer-term dollar loans, it might ask the New York branch to lay off its short-term deposits and buy it longer-term money.

A final way in which foreign banks are currently entering the U.S. market is by buying U.S. banks. Two prominent examples are the purchase of Marine Midland Bank of Buffalo, N.Y., by the Hong Kong & Shanghai Banking Company of London and the purchase of Crocker National Corporation in San Francisco by Midland Bank of London. Acquisition of U.S. banks follows a trend common in other industries. Managers of large foreign firms and of large foreign pension and other funds view the U.S. as an attractive place in which to invest and diversify because—as compared to other countries—the U.S. ranks high in terms of economic and political stability and of potential for continued economic growth.

Competition with U.S. banks

When they were able to buy money without incurring a reserve requirement, foreign bank branches had a certain cost advantage over U.S. banks in making loans to domestic firms for domestic purposes. This cost advantage, which has now disappeared, was always partially offset by the fact that foreign bank branches have to pay up slightly for money they buy in the domestic market and by the fact that any Euros they buy are more expensive than domestic money of the same tenor. Despite this, for years foreign bank branches in major financial centers quoted loan rates to domestic corporations at LIBOR plus a spread, which worked out to a rate below the U.S. prime plus balances. This put pressure on domestic banks in these centers to lend to prime customers at sub-prime rates and eventually to offer fixed-rate advances.

Regulation of foreign branch operations

State regulation of the operations of foreign bank branches in the U.S. has always been stricter and more detailed than the regulation to which foreign bank branches are subject in London. In New York State, for example, foreign banks are subject to all the detailed provisions of the state's banking law. In addition, they are required to hold qualifying assets equal to 108% of their total liabilities (intrabank deposits excepted); of this, 5% must be held in T bills or certain other instruments in a special account with a depository bank. Since the qualifying assets that a foreign bank branch may use to satisfy the 108% requirement include a wide range of instruments—loans on its New York book, CDs bought, deposits at other banks, Fed funds sold, BAs held in its portfolio, and broker/dealer loans—this requirement imposes no cost on foreign banks as do Fed reserve requirements. On the other hand, the 108% requirement does mean that a foreign bank's branch has to net borrow funds from the rest of the system—funds that constitute, in effect, the branch's U.S. capital base. The New York State 108% rule is designed to ensure that a foreign bank branch will always have sufficient assets to meet its deposit and other liabilities. As such, it has been viewed abroad as a model for foreign bank branch regulation and has been widely copied.

In the eyes of some foreign bankers, however, the New York State regulation is anything but a model. One British bank commented, "It's far too complex and to some extent outdated. In these days when funds can be moved rapidly, a foreign bank in trouble could rape its New York branch before the regulators smelled trouble. The only regulation that makes sense and that is going to be effective over the long run is to grant branch licenses only to banks that are credit- and trustworthy."

One advantage that foreign banks used to enjoy over domestic banks is that they could open branches in several different states, whereas domestic banks were not allowed to engage in interstate banking. Because of this and other issues, a lot of pressure was exerted on Congress to pass new foreign bank legislation putting foreign and domestic banks on an equal footing.

The International Banking Act of 1978. This pressure resulted in passage, in 1978, of the *International Banking Act (IBA)*. The major statutory changes provided by the act with respect to foreign banks are: (1) foreign agencies and branches now have the option of federal licensing; (2) foreign branches and agencies engaged in retail banking are required to buy FDIC insurance; (3) foreign branches and agencies are subject to reserve requirements imposed by the Fed in exchange for which they now have access to the discount window and other services provided by the Fed to domestic banks; (4) foreign banks may no longer branch into more than one state; and (5) the Fed is authorized to act as an examining agency to police the activities of those foreign banks that established multistate branches prior to IBA passage and that were permitted, under a "grandfather clause" in IBA, to keep these branches.[16]

INTERNATIONAL BANKING FACILITIES (IBFS)[17]

On December 1, 1981, domestic banks and foreign bank branches in New York and 11 other states that had passed enabling legislation were permitted to open *international banking facilities (IBFs)*. The hope in New York was that introduction of these facilities would put New York on a par with London as an international banking center; the chance of this occurring, however, was diminished by the restrictions that the Fed imposed on IBF activities.

The concept behind IBFs is to create a species of free trade zone for international money—primarily Eurodollars. An IBF offers a bank several advantages: Deposits in the facility are subject to no reserve requirements, and the IBF need not pay FDIC insurance premiums; also, income earned by the facility enjoys, in New York and nine other states, special provisions for relief from state taxes.[18]

---

[16] The details of the International Banking Act are spelled out in a mimeographed report by the Board of Governors of the Federal Reserve System entitled *The International Banking Act of 1978* and dated September 17, 1980.

[17] The following section is excerpted in part from Marcia Stigum, "A Free Trade Zone for New York? IBFs to Be Allowed, but Fed Restrictions May Limit Growth," *Pensions & Investment Age,* September 28, 1981, pp. 20–21.

[18] For more details on IBFs and tax provisions covering them, see "International Banking Facilities," by Sydney J. Key in the *Federal Reserve Bulletin,* October 1982, pp. 556–77.

For depositors, one attraction of IBFs is that any interest they pay to foreigners is exempt from withholding taxes; another advantage is that the depositor will get U.S. as opposed to U.K., Bahrainian, or some other sovereign risk. U.S. sovereign risk won't attract Iranian depositors, but it should attract institutions that are loath to place funds in the shell branches that major U.S. banks have opened in Nassau and other tax havens because they don't like the sovereign risk that they perceive attaches to deposits there.

The origin of IBFs goes back to the days when New York City was tottering on the brink of bankruptcy. At the time, the state and the city zeroed in on the banks as the culprits. The city's problems were the banks' fault because the banks kept selling the city's debt whereas they should have told the city it was bankrupt. To add injury to insult the city and the state raised their tax rates on bank income earned within New York State, and the city topped off its tax hike with a tax surcharge.

The imposition of punitive state and city taxes gave New York banks a tremendous incentive to book international business in offshore tax havens, primarily Nassau and Grand Cayman, which are located in a time zone that permits New York banks to deal on the shell's behalf during normal business hours. Once this trend asserted itself and serious defections among New York banks became a distinct possibility, the state passed legislation to permit the creation in New York of IBFs. These were supposed to draw huge amounts of business back from London and the offshore shells to New York City.

For the IBFs to get off the ground, the Fed had to give them its blessing. The latter was slow in coming because out-of-town banks opposed New York IBFs as unfair competition. The Fed has a history of not making rules that favor a particular group of banks; to permit the New York IBFs to go ahead, it had to come up with a rationalization: this was that any state could pass the same legislation New York had. A second concern of the Fed was with leakage: the movement of domestic deposits and loan business into the Euromarket. The Fed fears that further leakage would weaken its control over domestic credit and the domestic money supply.

This concern sounds legitimate but is, in fact, somewhat ludicrous since the horse in question left the barn years ago. Today, treasurers at major domestic corporations actively and freely ferry their loan and deposit business between the domestic and the Euromarket on the basis of what best suits their needs. When the Fed, in 1975, wrote a letter to the banks reiterating its instructions to them not to solicit Eurodeposits from domestic depositors, it forgot to send a copy to corporate America which currently buys half the Euro CDs issued in London.

Despite the fact that leakage has become a torrent, the Fed—to prevent its further growth—imposed severe restrictions on what IBFs may do; specifically, it ruled that IBFs may not pay interest on overnight money, may not issue CDs, and may not take deposits from or make loans to domestic entities. These restrictions sharply limit the value of IBFs to banks. No corporate depositor will settle for a two-day notice account when he can earn interest on a Euro call account at a London or Caribbean branch. Also, corporate treasurers will not make time deposits with IBFs when they can buy liquid Europaper in London.

Bereft of corporate deposits, IBFs have had to rely for most of their funding on the interbank market for Euros and on deposits from central banks that have large dollar holdings and that, because they wanted to diversify their sovereign risk, were already holding some dollar deposits in the U.S.

This contrasts sharply with the situation at U.S. banks' Caribbean branches where half of the funding comes from U.S. depositors. The restrictions imposed by the Fed on IBFs are sufficiently stringent to make New York unattractive compared with London and other Eurocenters.

Nonetheless, since IBFs were permitted, every major New York bank and a large number of foreign banks with New York branches or agencies have opened such a facility. The banks that have bid most aggressively through their IBFs for Eurodollars are, interestingly enough, not the New York banks who originally wanted the facilities but Japanese banks. The explanation is simple: Japanese banks are forbidden by their Ministry of Finance from running shell branches in the Caribbean and other tax havens; thus IBFs gave the Japanese banks their first opportunity to participate in the shell-branch game that all the other banks had been playing for years.

By September 1982, 395 IBFs had been opened (Table 6–8). Of these, New York IBFs were by far the most numerous and held 78% of the

TABLE 6–8
Numbers of IBFs and total IBF assets by state and establishing institutions

State	Number of IBFs				Assets of IBFs ($ billions)
	U.S.- chartered banks	Foreign bank branches and agencies	Edge Act corporations	Total	
New York	36	125	15	176	118.2
California	12	48	10	70	19.7
Florida	21	19	20	60	9.1
Illinois	6	13	4	23	3.0
Other*	52	9	5	66	1.5
Total	127	214	54	395	151.5

* Fourteen other states have IBFs.
Source: *Federal Reserve Bulletin.*

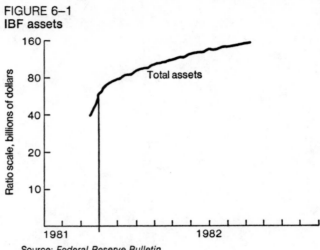

FIGURE 6–1
IBF assets

Source: *Federal Reserve Bulletin.*

total assets in IBFs. Since the inception of IBFs, those established by foreign bank agencies and branches have played a dominant role. IBFs at agencies and branches of foreign banks account for 70% of the IBFs in New York; nationwide they hold slightly over half of total IBF assets. Of the foreign-held share of IBF assets, three-fifths were in Japanese-owned facilities.

The big increase in IBF assets, which currently total $151.5 billion, came in December 1981 when these facilities were first permitted to accept deposits (Figure 6–1). Since then IBF assets have grown slowly but steadily.

Chapter 7

The Treasury and the federal agencies

THE SINGLE MOST IMPORTANT ISSUER of debt in the money market is the U.S. Treasury. It is closely followed in importance by federal agencies as a group.

U.S. GOVERNMENT SECURITIES

In mid-1982, the U.S. government had $1.08 trillion of debt outstanding. As Table 7–1 shows, about 6¼% of the Treasury's outstanding debt is represented by Series E and H bonds, which are *nonnegotiable savings bonds* sold to individuals. The Treasury also issues substantial amounts of special *nonnegotiable* issues to (1) foreign central banks that have accumulated dollars through their foreign exchange operations, through the sale of oil for dollars, or in other ways, (2) federal agencies and trust funds that have surplus funds to invest, and (3) state and local governments.[1]

---

[1] The reason the Treasury issues special debt series to state and local governments is explained on p. 210.

TABLE 7–1
Gross U.S. public debt, June 1982 ($ billions)

Bills	256.0
Notes	406.9
Bonds	101.1
Total marketable	764.0
Savings bonds	67.4
Special issues to U.S. government agencies and trust funds	206.0
State and local government series	23.4
Foreign issues	17.5
Other	2.3
Total gross debt	1,079.6

The remainder of the Treasury's outstanding debt is *negotiable* issues, all of which are actively traded in the money and bond markets. Currently the Treasury issues three types of negotiable securities:[2]

1. Noninterest-bearing *bills* that have an original maturity of 1 year or less.
2. Interest-bearing *notes* that have an original maturity of 1 to 10 years.
3. Interest-bearing *bonds* that have an original maturity of more than 10 years.

Volume outstanding

A huge expansion has occurred in recent years in total Treasury debt outstanding (Figure 7–1). The principal cause of the increase is the enormous deficits that the federal government has consistently rung up since 1975 (Table 7–2). A second factor contributing to the increase in Treasury debt outstanding is that the Treasury began in 1974 to borrow money in its own name to fund the lending activities of the Federal Financing Bank, discussed later in this chapter.

The recent sharp increase in Treasury debt has caused a substantial rise in the amount of marketable Treasury securities outstanding (Figure 7–2). Most of this rise has occurred though increases in the amounts of notes and bills outstanding. Negotiable bonds represent the smallest component of the Treasury's total marketable debt (Figure 7–2).

Treasury debt management: Some history

Over the last two decades the Treasury has made substantial changes in the types of marketable securities it offers and in the way it sells these

---

[2] The Treasury used to issue interest-bearing *certificates* with an original maturity of 1 year or less. It has not done so since 1967.

FIGURE 7–1
Treasury debt outstanding

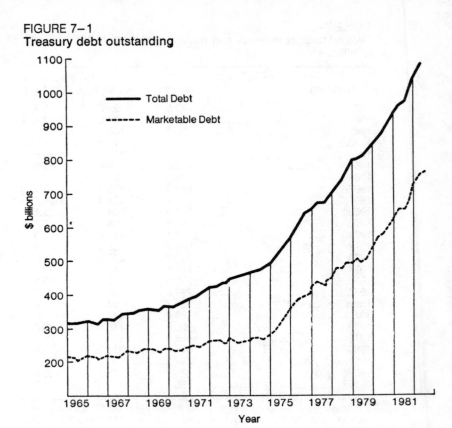

securities. These changes were made in response to several pressures: the Treasury's need to be able to market its debt in the face of increasingly volatile interest rates, its need to be able to market rapidly growing amounts of debt, and its need—perceived by the mid 1970s—to lengthen the average maturity of its outstanding debt (Figure 7–3).

In the mid-1960s the Treasury funded the debt by selling 3-month and 6-month bills at weekly auctions and 9-month and 1-year bills at monthly auctions; in addition, there was a quarterly financing in the middle of each quarter when the Treasury sold notes and bonds. The bills were sold as they are today through auctions, the notes and bonds through exchange and subscription offerings.

Bill auctions. In a bill auction, money market banks, dealers, and other institutional investors who buy big amounts of bills submit *competitive* bids; that is, for the bills they want to buy, they bid a discounted price expressed on the basis of 100. For example, a dealer who wanted to buy $100 million of 3-month bills might bid a price of 97.865, which is

TABLE 7–2
Federal budget receipts and outlays, fiscal years 1960–1978
($ billions)

Fiscal year	Receipts	Outlays	Surplus or deficit (−)
1960.	92.5	92.2	.3
1961.	94.4.	97.8	−3.4
1962.	99.7	106.8	−7.1
1963.	106.6	111.3	−4.7
1964.	112.7	118.6	−5.9
1965.	116.8	118.4	−1.6
1966.	130.9	134.7	−3.8
1967.	149.6	158.3	−8.7
1968.	153.7	178.8	−25.1
1969.	187.8	184.5	3.2
1970.	193.8	196.6	−2.8
1971.	188.4	211.4	−23.0
1972.	208.6	232.0	−23.4
1973.	232.2	247.0	−14.8
1974.	264.9	269.6	−4.7
1975.	281.0	326.1	−45.1
1976.	299.2	365.6	−66.4
Transition quarter*	81.7	94.7	−13.0
1977.	356.9	401.9	−45.0
1978.	399.6	448.4	−48.8
1979.	463.3	491.0	−27.7
1980.	517.1	576.7	−59.6
1981.	599.3	657.2	−57.9
1982†.	626.7	725.3	−98.6
1983†.	666.1	757.6	−91.5

* Under provisions of the Congressional Budget Act of 1974, the fiscal year for the federal government shifted beginning with fiscal year 1977. Through fiscal year 1976, the fiscal year ran from July 1 through June 30; starting in October 1976 (fiscal year 1977), the fiscal year ran from October 1 through September 30. The 3-month period from July 1, 1976, through September 30, 1976, is a separate fiscal period known as the *transition quarter*.
  † Estimates.
  Source: *Economic Report of the President,* January 1982.

equivalent to a yield of 8.446 on a discount basis.[3] The prices dealers and investors bid for bills depend both on the rates yielded by outstand-

[3] Rearranging the formula

$$D = F\left(\frac{d \times t}{360}\right)$$

which was given on p. 46, we get

$$d = \frac{D \times 360}{F \times t}$$

In the above example D equals 2.135 per \$100 of face value, and t equals 91 (13 weeks × 7 days per week). Thus

$$d = \frac{2.135 \times 360}{100 \times 91} = 8.446\%$$

FIGURE 7–2
Composition of the U.S. government's marketable debt

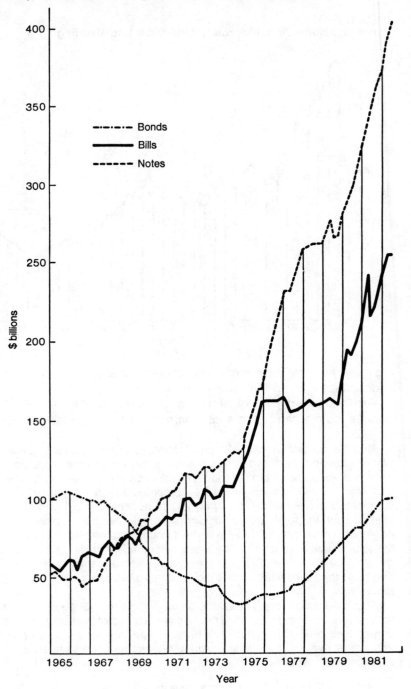

FIGURE 7–3
Average maturity of marketable Treasury debt outstanding

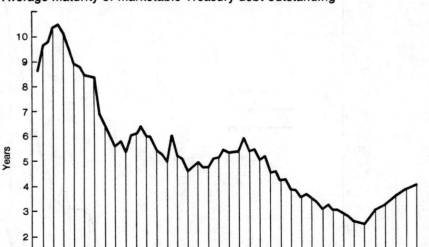

ing money market instruments and on what (if any) movement they think is occurring in short-term rates.

The less expert investor who is not prepared to work out a bid to three decimal points can put in a *noncompetitive* bid that states no price.

After the auction closes, bids are forwarded to the Treasury Department in Washington and tabulated for each issue. First, the volume of noncompetitive awards is subtracted from the total amount to be issued. Government and Federal Reserve Bank tenders, which are noncompetitive, are accepted in full. Noncompetitive tenders of private investors are accepted in full up to [the current limit on such tenders]. The remainder is allocated among competitive bidders beginning with those that bid the highest prices and ranging down in price until the total amount is issued. The lowest accepted price is called the *stop-out* price. Since a number of bids may have been entered at the stop-out price, the Treasury may award each of the bidders at this price only a portion of the amount requested.

After the auction on Monday, the amount and price range of accepted bids are announced, and competitive bidders are advised of the acceptance or rejection of their tenders. Competitive bidders pay the price that they bid while noncompetitive entries pay the weighted average price to three decimals of accepted competitive bids.[4]

---

[4] Margaret Bedford, "Recent Developments in Treasury Financing Techniques," *Monthly Review*, Federal Reserve Bank of Kansas, July–August 1977, p. 17.

Exchange offerings. When the Treasury sold bonds through exchange offerings, it used two techniques. In a *straight exchange offer,* the Treasury sought to refund maturing securities by offering their holders new securities with the same par value. In an *advance refunding* or *pre-refunding,* the Treasury offered holders of an outstanding issue the opportunity to exchange their securities for new securities of the same par value before maturity.

Holders of eligible securities who did not wish to invest in the new issue could sell their *right* to the new issue to other investors or turn in their maturing securities for cash. The purpose of straight exchange offerings was to encourage existing bondholders to roll their bonds, thereby permitting Treasury refundings to be carried out with minimal disruption to the market. In the case of pre-refundings, an additional objective was to reduce Treasury borrowing costs by taking advantage of the interest rate cycle; the Treasury would pre-refund when interest rates were expected to rise and pre-refunding looked cheap relative to refunding at maturity. Exchange offerings were usually made on generous terms so that issues for which exchange offerings were made rose in value, reflecting the *rights* value they acquired through the exchange offering. The practice of exchange offerings also led to speculative demand for issues that were considered likely candidates for pre-refunding.

Subscription issues

In a subscription offering [which the Treasury has used to raise new cash], the Treasury announces the amount to be sold, the interest coupon on the issue, and the price of the issue. The Treasury reserves the right to change the amount sold and the allotment procedures after all subscriptions have been submitted. Additional amounts are issued to Federal Reserve and Government accounts after allotments to the public.

Investors enter subscriptions for the amount of securities they wish to purchase at the Treasury's given price and yield. Since investors may enter subscriptions totaling more than the amount offered by the Treasury, the allotment procedure becomes important for limiting the size of the issue. Allotments can be made by awarding a percentage of the amount of each tender or by setting a maximum dollar amount to be accepted for each tender.

The Treasury usually offers to accept some tenders in full on a preferred allotment basis. preferred tenders are limited in size (up to $500,000 in recent offerings) and must be accompanied by a deposit of 20 percent of the face value of securities applied for.[5]

The rate lid on bonds. Congress permits the Treasury to pay whatever rate of return is necessary to sell bills and notes but bars the Treasury from paying more than 4.25% on bonds. This rate lid created no problem when long-term rates were below 4.25%. But in the mid-1960s

[5] Ibid., p. 23.

rates rose above this level, making it impossible for the Treasury to sell new bonds.

In the early 1970s Congress granted the Treasury permission to sell $10 billion of bonds exempt from this rate ceiling. Congress raised the amount of this exemption on several occasions but always kept the amount small relative to the Treasury's total marketable debt. The 4.25% rate lid, despite its popularity with members of Congress who favor low interest rates, does nothing to hold down interest rates. It does, however, bar the Treasury from competing directly with private corporations and municipal borrowers in the long-term market and from pulling funds directly out of the mortgage market, which explains some of the support for retaining the lid.

Introduction of price auctions. The fact that, for a period starting in the mid-1960s, the Treasury could sell no long-term bonds left it in the position where the longest-maturity security it could sell was a 5-year note. As a result, the average maturity of the debt began to decline at a disturbing rate (Figure 7–3). To counter this trend, the Treasury sought and received from Congress in 1967 permission to raise the maximum maturity of notes from 5 to 7 years.

As interest rates became more volatile in the late 1960s, it became increasingly difficult for the Treasury to issue new debt through subscription issues on which both the price and the coupon were announced several days before the date on which investors tendered for the issue. In a 1970 refunding the Treasury experimented, using for the first time a *price auction* instead of the subscription technique to sell new notes and bonds to the general public.

In the price auction, the Treasury announces the amount to be sold to the public, and a few days prior to the auction sets a coupon rate and a minimum acceptable price. Competitive bidders state the price they are willing to pay on the basis of 100 to two decimals. These bids may be at par ($100 per $100 face), at a price below par (at a discount), or at a price above par (at a premium). The price bid would reflect the investor's judgment as to how attractive the coupon rate is compared to other market rates. The rate associated with a price of par is the coupon rate; paying a premium will result in a lower effective yield than the coupon rate; and buying at a discount will yield an effective return higher than the coupon rate. As in the Treasury bill market, the noncompetitive tenders are subtracted from the amount to be sold and the remainder is distributed by accepting the highest price bid on down until the amount of the issue is taken. Competitive bidders pay the price that they bid, and noncompetitive bids are accepted in full at the average price of competitive bids. However, since the competitive bids are not necessarily at par, the average price paid by noncompetitive bidders may be more or less than par and thus they will receive an effective yield somewhat different from the coupon rate.[6]

---

[6] Ibid., p. 22.

Switch to yield auctions. In 1973 the Treasury further changed its policies of debt issuance. It again sought and received from Congress permission to raise the maximum maturity on notes, this time from 7 to 10 years. Also, because of its increasing cash needs, it discontinued exchange offerings with the February 1973 refunding and began to rely solely on price auction sales. The Treasury also began to issue 2-year notes on a regular cycle but later discontinued this cycle; it also discontinued issuing 9-month bills because of a lack of investor acceptance of this maturity.

The year 1974, which was characterized by high and volatile interest rates, was a difficult time for the Treasury to sell debt. To ease its problems, the Treasury increased the size of the noncompetitive bids that could be tendered for notes and bonds to $500,000 in order to appeal to a wider class of investors. It also began to issue on an occasional basis special longer-term bills issued for nonstandard periods when it needed additional funds.

The final and most important change the Treasury made in 1974 was to switch its auctions of notes and bonds from a price to a yield basis. Under the price auction system, at the time a new issue was announced, the Treasury set the coupon on the issue in line with market rates so that the new issue's price, determined through auction, would be at or near par. If rates moved away from the levels prevailing on announcement day, the prices bid on auction day would, reflecting this, move away from par. For example, if rates fell between the announcement of an issue and the auction, bid prices would be above par, whereas if rates rose, bids would be below par. As interest rates became more volatile, deviations of bid prices from par became a problem. In August 1974 one Treasury issue was sold at 101 while another failed to sell out because the Treasury received too few bids at or above the minimum price it would accept. The Treasury feared that above-par prices would discourage some bidders and that below-par prices would place purchasers in an unanticipated tax position (the amount of the discount at issue being taxable at maturity as ordinary income). Another problem with price auctions was that, when the Treasury set coupons, the market tended to move to them, so that price auctions disturbed the market. To solve both problems and to ensure that its issues sold out, the Treasury moved in late 1974 to a new technique in which would-be buyers bid *yields* instead of prices.

In a yield auction for notes and bonds, the Treasury announces the new issue a week or more before the auction. At that time it tells the market what amount of securities it will issue, when they will mature, and what denominations will be available. *Competitive* bidders bid yields to two decimal points (e.g., 10.53) for specific quantities of the new issue. After bids are received, the Treasury determines the stop-out bid on the basis of both the bids received and the amount it wishes to borrow. It then sets the coupon on the security to the nearest ⅛ of 1 percent necessary to make the average price charged to successful bidders equal to 100.00 or less. Once the coupon on the issue is established, each successful bidder is charged a price (discount, par, or premium) for his securities; the price is determined so that the yield to maturity on the securities a bidder gets equals the yield he bid. *Noncompetitive* bidders pay the average price of the accepted competitive tenders.

TABs, strips, and cash management bills. In 1975, when the Treasury faced the problem both of refunding huge quantities of maturing debt and of financing a burgeoning federal debt, it changed its policies of debt issuance.

From time to time the Treasury finds it necessary to sell special bill issues to meet short-term borrowing needs. Prior to 1975 the Treasury used *tax anticipation bills* (TABs) and bill *strips* for this purpose.

Tax anticipation bills were issued to help the Treasury smooth out its tax receipts, and they could be submitted in payment of income taxes. Commercial banks were usually permitted to make payment for TABs by crediting Treasury tax and loan accounts and thus became underwriters for these issues. About 28 TAB offerings were made during the 1970–74 period, and they ranged in maturity from 23 to 273 days.

A bill strip is a reopening of a number of issues of outstanding bill series. Strips enabled the Treasury to raise a large amount of short-term funds at one time rather than spreading out receipts through additions to weekly bill auctions. In the 1970–74 period, nine strips of bills were issued ranging from additions to 5 series to additions to 15 series and averaging 22 days to 131 days in maturity.[7]

In 1975 the Treasury discontinued the use of TABs and strips and replaced them with *cash management bills*. Cash management bills are usually reopenings of an outstanding issue and often have quite short maturities. When they are auctioned, the minimum acceptable bid is $10 million, and only competitive bids are accepted. Cash management bills are usually bought by banks and dealers at some spread to their cost of money and held to maturity.

Regularization of debt issuance

The year 1975 was an important one in the evolution of debt management policy. In that year the Treasury adopted a program of *regularization of debt issuance*. Under this program, the Treasury began to issue 2-year, 4-year, and 5-year notes on a regular cycle. A 2-year note was issued at the end of each month, a 4-year note in the middle of the second month of each quarter, and a 5-year note in the middle of the first

---

[7] Ibid., p. 18.

month of each quarter. The normal quarterly refunding, at which the Treasury offers a mix of notes and bonds to refund maturing issues and raise new cash, occurs at the middle of the second month of each quarter. Thus in the late 1970s the Treasury was issuing coupons on a regular schedule of six dates a quarter.

The Treasury began its policy of regularizing debt issuance for several reasons. First, in the mid-1970s it was obvious, against a background of large and then record deficits, that the government was going to have huge financing requirements for the foreseeable future. Therefore, Treasury officials concluded that, both to minimize the cost of issuing Treasury debt and to maximize the capacity of the market to absorb such debt, it was crucial that debt issuance be made as predictable as possible.

Before the Treasury sought to regularize debt issuance, it operated on a sort of ad hoc basis. It used to be that at a quarterly financing the Treasury might come with anything from a 1- to 10-year note or with a long bond if they had authority to sell them. Dealers, never knowing what to expect, had two choices: to come into an auction with a position because they were willing to bet on something or to come in naked to avoid risk.

A second reason for regularizing debt issuance was to avoid bunching too much Treasury debt in the quarterly financings. There is a limit on how much debt the market can absorb and dealers can distribute at any time; it was thought that, if the Treasury continued to issue most of its coupon debt on four dates a year, that limit would be breached and the Treasury would be forced to pay higher rates than it would have had to if bunching were avoided. Under the current program the market has a chance to digest one issue before it girds up to take another.

A third reason the Treasury began issuing debt on a regular schedule was that doing so was viewed as a means to lengthen the average maturity of marketable Treasury debt outstanding; in 1977 such lengthening did in fact occur for the first time in years (Figure 7–3).

EXCEPTIONS TO THE GENERAL PATTERN

Since 1975 the Treasury had relied primarily on yield auctions to sell new coupon securities. It has made exceptions to this practice for several purposes. First, the Treasury sometimes *reopens* (sells more of) an already outstanding note or bond issue. In that case the coupon on the issue has already been determined in a previous auction; therefore the new securities offered must carry that coupon and must be sold through a *price* auction.

Second, several times in 1976 the Treasury had so much new debt to place that it feared it would strain the underwriting and distribution capacity of the street if it used the normal auction procedure; so it issued notes carrying an attractive coupon at a fixed price through subscription offerings. This strategy enabled the Treasury to reach beyond its normal market directly to individual investors. A coupon of 8% was then thought to be a magic number: Whenever the Treasury put an 8% or higher coupon on an issue, individuals—comparing that rate with what they could get on savings accounts and time deposits—would rush out to buy it, and typically they then held the issue to maturity.

More recently, as part of the February 1978 quarterly financing, the Treasury offered a 6-year note with an 8% coupon through a price auction. The Treasury's objective in fixing the coupon instead of using a yield auction was to sell an out-sized issue by appealing to individuals as well as institutional investors. Since then the Treasury has offered no subscription issues.

While debt regularization offers obvious advantages, critics have suggested that the program may also have drawbacks.

Too many issues.   Since the Treasury began its program of debt regularization, one question frequently raised on the street is whether the Treasury is creating a situation in which Treasury issues are too numerous to be tradable. Opinions vary.

One dealer commented, "The Treasury should start reopening issues. Currently they have so many outstanding that it is impossible to keep track of them all. This puts a premium on active issues; people will buy and be active only in current, on-the-run issues, because to get off the run, is to forgo so much liquidity as to be painful."

A second dealer argued, "Debt regularization is a necessity. You can't have the Treasury just popping in selling 5 billion of this or that and the market never knowing what is coming. It is not good for the market to know that the Treasury has a 15 billion financing job to do in a quarter and to have no idea of where [in the maturity spectrum] or when the issues will come. It would be easier for the traders to have fewer issues, but for the market and the Treasury—it is better to have a debt regularization."

TREASURY DEBT MANAGEMENT TODAY

Treasury officials who are today responsible for debt management are quick to point out that responsibility for making the tax and expenditure decisions that determine the size of the current deficit and of projected deficits belong to other economic policymakers. As one debt manager noted, "We are told what the financing requirements of the federal government are going to be. Our job is to decide, based on our market expertise, what is the least disruptive way of handling that financing requirement."

In recent years the Treasury has been forced to fund the debt under increasingly difficult circumstances. Half of the national debt—currently a trillion dollars—matures and must be refunded through Treasury sales of new debt each year. In addition the Treasury must sell new debt to fund the federal government's rapidly increasing deficits. Selling so much debt would have been no small job for the Treasury under normal market conditions. Money and bond market conditions have, however, been anything but normal since the Fed's switch to monetarism in October 1979. During the period 1979–82, interest rates—short and long—reached historic highs with respect to both level and volatility.

Focusing on debt regularization

Throughout this period, debt management has been a nonpartisan issue. The Treasury's agreed-upon objective has been to get its debt sold in the least expensive and the least disruptive way possible, given the constraints placed upon it by external forces in the form of congressional mandates and market conditions and by internally imposed constraints, such as its decision to issue no instrument that would compete directly and favorably with savings deposits at banks and S&Ls.

The policy of regularization of Treasury debt issuance, begun in the mid-1970s, has been continued. As noted earlier, the Treasury started its policy of debt regularization by instituting 2- and 4-year note cycles. Over time as the Treasury had more and more debt to finance, it responded by adding more coupon cycles (Table 7–3) and by building up

TABLE 7–3
Quarterly schedule of Treasury coupon offerings

Quarterly dates	*Issue offered*
First month	
Middle	7-year note
End	2-year note
Second month	
Middle	Quarterly refunding (3- and 10-year notes, 30-year bond)
End	2-year note, 5-year note*
Third month	
Middle	2-year note
End	4-year note, 20-year bond*

* Week between auctions of these two new issues.

those it already had. To further regularize debt issuance, the Treasury has sought to make its mix of offerings at the quarterly refunding as predictable as possible. Normally this mix includes a new long bond; the June 1982 refunding was an exception because the Treasury had at that time used up its exemption from the 4¼% lid and was petitioning Congress to increase it.

Since debt regularization was adopted, the major focus of debt management has been on decisions with respect to coupon issues: which coupons and how much of each to issue? This was inevitable given the big deficits the federal government was running. Whenever the Treasury must meet a big cash drain, it goes first to the bill market (Figure 7–4).

FIGURE 7–4
Treasury net market borrowing*

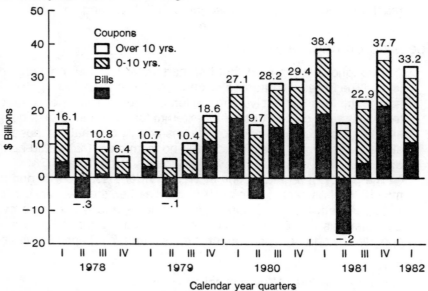

Calendar year quarters

* Excludes Federal Reserve and government account transactions.
Source: U.S. Treasury.

Continuing deficits would thus result in an enormous buildup of bill issues if the Treasury made no attempt to expand its coupon issues.

A second objective of debt regularization has been to lengthen the average maturity of the debt, which in 1975 dropped under 3 years. A short average debt maturity forces the Treasury to sell an enormous quantity of debt each year just for refunding purposes. It also makes the interest component of federal debt service highly sensitive to the current level of market rates. During the period 1979–82, the cost of financing the national debt rose 60% (from 55.5 to 99.1 billion), while the debt itself rose only 21%, in part because the short average maturity of the debt forced the Treasury to constantly refund huge sums of maturing debt at ever increasing rates.

Debt regularization ought to reduce in several other ways the cost of financing the debt. By reducing uncertainty of the sort that prevailed when the Treasury came to the market on an ad hoc basis, regularization ought to reduce the yields at which dealers and investors are willing to bid for new Treasury issues. It should also decrease borrowing costs because, when the Treasury creates a security and keeps selling it, the security creates its own demand after a time.

The Treasury for this reason makes it a policy to regularly issue long-term bonds at each quarterly financing. Its rationale is that if portfolio managers know the Treasury is coming with a long bond issue once a quarter—as they know that the telephone company does, they will adjust their portfolios so that, when the new government bonds come to market, other bonds will have been swapped out to make room for them. This gives the Treasury a share of the market under all conditions—a share that the Treasury can and does increase when conditions are favorable and rates are down.

The Treasury is conscious of the problem of issue proliferation because of debt regularization. Particularly in the case of long coupons, it would like to include in its quarterly financing reopenings of existing issues. Noted one Treasury official, "It makes sense to reopen an issue if possible especially in the longer issues where we normally would have come with an issue of 2 to 2½ billion. That is a rather small issue to develop active trading. By reopening the issue and enlarging its size, we would enhance its liquidity. Unfortunately, we do not often get the opportunity to reopen recent issues because the volatility of rates has been such that the market tends to get away from us [e.g., the level of a 10-year coupon changes markedly] between refundings."

Even keeling.   In the old days it used to be that around Treasury auction dates, the Fed would *even keel;* that is, keep conditions in the money market as stable as possible. Some argued that, if the Treasury kept increasing the number of dates on which it offered coupons, the Fed would be forced to even keel all the time and consequently be left with no window during which it could alter monetary policy. In fact this has not been a problem. Even keeling died an untolled death, one that was facilitated by the Treasury's switch from price to yield auctions and by the Treasury's decision to sell small amounts of coupon debt frequently rather than huge sums quarterly. Today the Fed pursues monetary policy with little or no concern over the impact of its actions on the success of a particular Treasury offering.

Rate lid on bonds

Once the 4¼% lid on the rate that the Treasury could pay on long bonds became a binding constraint, the Treasury issued fewer long bonds than it would otherwise have done. While Congress has granted the Treasury exemptions from this lid, the latest of which raised the exemption from $70 to $110 billion, it has refused to remove the lid

FIGURE 7–5
Use of authority to issue Treasury bonds with interest rate over 4¼%

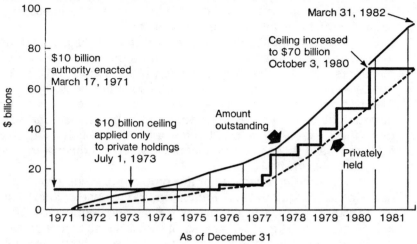

As of December 31

Source: U.S. Treasury.

(Figure 7–5). Congress wants to retain some control over Treasury debt management policies, to not give the Treasury carte blanche authority to issue long-term securities at any rates. Congress does not want the taxpayers locked in forever at what it views as high rate levels.

Ironically, the moment has never seemed right in the past for the Treasury to sell long bonds although by doing so it would have saved a lot of money. Back in the 1950s and 60s when rates reached cyclical lows, it was argued that the Treasury should not sell long bonds because, by doing so, it would put upward pressure on long rates and thus discourage private capital spending needed to speed economic recovery. On the other hand, when the economy became bouyant and rates moved to cyclical highs, it never seemed appropriate for the Treasury to sell long bonds because at such times rates were always at historic highs due to the upward secular trend in interest rates that has prevailed over the last three decades.

Under the Reagan administration, the question arose whether the government should continue to sell long bonds at historically high rates when the then new administration was implementing supply-side economic policies that were supposed to generate economic growth while reducing inflation and interest rates. Undersecretary of the Treasury, Beryl Sprinkel, argued that, for the government to sell long bonds carrying coupons in the teens demonstrated a lack of faith in the administration's policies and forecasts.

Those who thought that the Treasury should continue to sell long bonds retorted that the Treasury should not seek, as private borrowers do, to pick its spots in issuing long bonds. The Treasury, they argued, is no more able than anyone else to predict the trend in long rates. Second, due to the inevitable cyclical ups and downs in interest rates, the Treasury, which has so much debt maturing all the time anyway, would have plenty of opportunity to benefit from low rates when they prevailed. Third, the Treasury must finance somewhere; if they financed less in the long market, they would *have to finance more in the short market,* which would run counter to their intent to lengthen the debt. The Treasury could reconcile heavy reliance on short issues with its intent to lengthen the average maturity of the debt only if the government were running surpluses and the size of the debt were declining.

Capacity of the market to absorb Treasury debt

The constantly increasing amount of Treasury debt outstanding and the increasing volatility of rates have caused some to wonder if Treasury debt issuance might at some point breech the limit on the amount of Treasury debt dealers are able to underwrite or on the amount investors are willing to absorb. So far Treasury officials have seen no signs that either eventuality is occurring. As one Treasury official noted, "Rate volatility helps make the market because traders make more money when markets are volatile than when they are not. It is true that the street is taking smaller positions than they once did, but we have had no problem in auctioning our securities. One reason is that unrecognized dealers probably represent a larger proportion of the total underwriting than they did before; you have a lot of speculators who are not primarily government dealers but rather futures market participants who are now bidding directly in government auctions. Also, in bill auctions it is currently not the dealers who are the largest factor but rather the money funds. The amount of government financing has grown rapidly over the last few years, but financial markets have grown with it. Certainly we have had no problem with coverage in auctions, and there seems to be no shortage of capital to back auction bids."

The Treasury has also experienced no difficulty in finding a sufficient supply of investors to buy its debt. What has occurred is that, as the level and structure of rates has changed, the mix of investors has also changed.

On the minus side, the Treasury has lost a number of offbeat sources of funds that used to total a lot of money (Figure 7–6). Sales of savings bonds have diminished; in fact redemptions have outpaced sales since 1978. Also, until 1978 the dollar was weak, and foreign central banks were always buying dollars to prevent unwanted appreciation of their

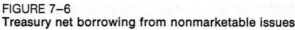

FIGURE 7–6
Treasury net borrowing from nonmarketable issues

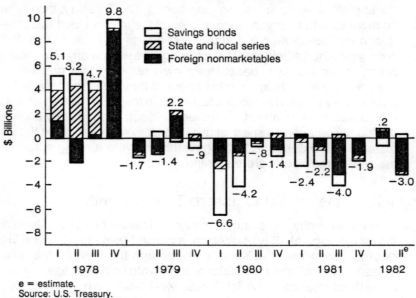

e = estimate.
Source: U.S. Treasury.

currencies and then investing these dollars in Treasury bonds. This trend reversed as high interest rates in the U.S. and other factors strengthened the dollar. A third source of funds lost to the Treasury has been investments in Treasury issues by state and local governments. It used to be that, when interest rates declined to cyclical lows, a number of such muni issuers would find it attractive to pre-refund outstanding, high-coupon bonds by selling a new, lower-coupon issue. They would then invest, until the pre-refunded issue reached its refunding date, the proceeds of the new issue in specially tailored, nonnegotiable Treasury issues designed to prevent them from profiting from the potential arbitrage. This source of funds, which accounts in part for the $23.4 billion of Treasury debt that state and local governments held in 1982 (Table 7–1), has, because of high interest rates, provided few new funds to the Treasury in recent years.

Offsetting these losses have been gains from other sources. Money funds, unheard of a decade ago, today constitute a major source of demand in bill auctions. The strength of the dollar combined with high U.S. interest rates has made the market for U.S. Treasuries attractive both to OPEC countries investing oil surpluses and to wealthy foreigners.

Also the innovative new zero-coupon securities created out of Treasury long bonds by Merrill Lynch and others may, depending on market conditions, create a huge new demand from individuals, especially those having nontaxable IRA and Keogh retirement accounts, for Treasury bonds.

Despite the fact that the Treasury has experienced no visible difficulty in selling its debt, people keep putting forth to Treasury officials their pet ideas on how the Treasury should borrow. The most conservative—in the sense that it has been done before—is that the Treasury should offer a big subscription issue. The Treasury, which has not utilized the subscription technique since 1978 and has no intention of reviving it, has doubts about the technique, not the least of which is whether it is cost effective. As one Treasury official noted, "We have been able to raise the amount of money needed off the market. From time to time we pay a concession of 3, 4, or 5 basis points, but the market does not appear so overburdened that we should come and offer, say, a 50-basis-point premium to get off a big subscription issue. That is expensive. Also in doing such an offering, the Treasury would essentially be admitting that the market was too small to accommodate its financing at anything close to current market levels. I have seen no evidence that we are in that sort of environment yet."

It has also been proposed that the Treasury issue a variable-rate security. The Treasury has resisted this idea on several grounds. In its view it already offers a variable-rate security in the form of bills that can be rolled. Bills, moreover, are more liquid than any new variable-rate Treasury security would be. The Treasury tries to appeal to all market segments. If investors want a variable-rate security, they can buy bills. If they want a fixed-rate security, they can buy notes or long bonds.

Another gimmick proposed to the Treasury has been that it sell gold-backed bonds. The Treasury's answer to that proposal is that it is equivalent to nothing more than a sale of gold attached to the sale of a Treasury obligation; why not just sell the gold outright? Another proposal has been to sell bonds backed by oil in the strategic reserve pool. Treasury officials dismiss this proposal with scorn, "They talk as if we were a company that could not get any money except by selling collateral-secured debt."

Treasury debt managers, who seek to fund the government debt as cheaply and nondisruptively as possible, see no need for what they view as gimmicks. One official said, "The U.S. Treasury is issuing the finest paper in the world in terms of liquidity and credit quality. Every theory I know indicates that the Treasury sells its debt to the investor at the lowest expected return and therefore *a priori* at the lowest expected cost to the issuer of any security issued in the world. Why should we clutter up this great market by throwing in gimmicks that no one will know how to price—by creating securities that will have limited marketability, at least at first, and for which buyers will therefore demand a higher return?"

FEDERAL AGENCIES ISSUING SECURITIES

In Chapter 2 we talked about financial intermediaries, which are institutions that act as conduits through which funds are channeled from consumers, firms, and other spending units with funds surpluses to spending units (consumers, firms, and government bodies) running funds deficits. Most financial intermediaries in the U.S. are private (albeit government regulated) institutions: commercial banks, savings and loan associations, credit unions, life insurance companies, and private pension funds, to name a few.

In addition to these private institutions, there is also a large and growing number of government credit agencies that act as financial intermediaries. These agencies borrow funds and then use them to make various types of loans to specific classes of borrowers. The reason for all this government competition to private intermediation is that Congress has periodically taken the position that for some groups of borrowers, the available supply of credit was too limited, too variable, or too expensive. In each instance remedy was Congress's to set up a federal agency charged with providing a dependable supply of credit at the lowest cost possible to these disadvantaged borrowers. Some federal agencies are owned and directed by the federal government, and their debt obligations are backed by the full faith and credit of the U.S. government. Others are federally sponsored but privately owned. The obligations of federally sponsored agencies presumably have *de facto* backing from the federal government.

The largest government credit agencies specialize in providing mortgage money for housing and agriculture, two favored children of policymakers. In addition, there are agencies that provide credit to small business firms, students, communities financing development projects, and so forth.

Most federal agencies are supposed to set their lending rates so that they at least cover their borrowing costs and perhaps even earn a modest profit. Since each agency's function is to supply funds to borrowers at minimum cost, the rational approach would have been to have the agencies borrow from the cheapest possible source. Because its securities carry zero risk of default and are so liquid, the Treasury can always borrow at lower rates than any other issuer, municipalities excepted. Thus, having the Treasury lend to the agencies funds that it had borrowed in the open market would have been the least-cost way to fund agency lending.

This approach, however, was not taken. Instead, until 1974 almost all agencies issued their own securities, each carrying some degree of backing from the federal government. The main reason for taking this approach was that, if the agencies had all borrowed from the Treasury, the Treasury's outstanding debt would have gone up commensurately. Today it would be $139 billion greater than the $1.08 trillion figure quoted earlier in this chapter.

Such an increase in Treasury debt could have created problems for several reasons. First, Congress imposes a statutory limit on Treasury borrowing. This limit has no perceptible impact on government spending because Congress always pauses—between passing spending bills—to raise it. Nevertheless Congress has at times been stubborn and slow about raising the debt limit, with the result that in practice it might have been difficult for the Treasury to borrow sufficient funds to meet *all* the agencies' needs. Also there are voters who lose sleep over the size of the national debt. In this respect, it is important to note that agency and federal debts differ sharply with respect to both source and character. Most Treasury debt is the result of government deficits, a true national debt. In contrast, agency debt is incurred to make loans, largely to creditworthy borrowers.

THE FEDERAL FINANCING BANK

As federal agencies proliferated, their borrowings from the public caused several problems. One had to do with calendar scheduling. Each year federal agencies issue substantial quantities of new debt. Agency issues compete with each other and with Treasury issues for investors' funds, and an uneven flow of agency and Treasury issues to the market could result in rates being driven up one week and down the next. To avoid this, the Treasury schedules the timing and size of both its own and agency issues to ensure a reasonably smooth flow of federal issues to the market. In 1973 minor federal agencies made 75 separate offerings, so many that it made Treasury calendar scheduling of new issues difficult. Another problem resulting from the proliferation of federal agencies was that the new small agencies constantly being created by Congress were not well known to investors; and because of their small size, their issues were less liquid than Treasury issues. Consequently, small agencies had to pay relatively high borrowing rates.

To deal with these problems, in 1973 Congress set up the *Federal Financing Bank* (FFB), a government institution supervised by the Secretary of the Treasury. The FFB buys up the debt issues of the smaller agencies, and its clientele currently includes about 20 separate agencies, essentially all federal agencies except for the seven major ones described below.

The FFB was supposed to obtain funds by issuing securities fully backed by the government in a fashion similar to the way the Treasury issues its securities. It tried this approach once with an offering of short-term bills. This offering was bid for by dealers and others at yields close to those prevailing on T bills, but the issue fell in price in the secondary market, which was discouraging to both dealers and the Treasury. Some dealers felt that, if the FFB had continued to issue its securities, they would—after five or six issues—have been accepted by investors as equal to Treasury issues and would have sold at yields no higher than those on Treasury issues. The Treasury, however, seems to have doubted this; one reason was that FFB offerings would have been smaller than Treasury offerings and consequently less liquid. In any case, the FFB discontinued its public offerings and now borrows from the Treasury. Today only seven major federal agencies still issue new securities to the market. Some of the smaller agencies, which now borrow from the FFB, do, however, still have a few long-term issues outstanding.

As Figure 7–7 shows, the FFB's borrowings from the Treasury have risen from a zero base in 1974 to almost $139 billion in mid-1982, and the trend is steadily upward.

FIGURE 7–7
Borrowings of the Federal Financing Bank from the U.S. Treasury

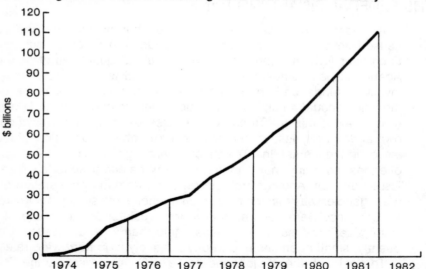

AGENCY SECURITIES

Among the agencies still issuing securities to the public, practices and types of securities issued vary considerably. One can, however, make a few generalizations. Each federal agency establishes a fiscal agent through which it offers its securities, all of which are negotiable. Agency issues are not sold directly to investors by these fiscal agents. Instead they are sold through a syndicate of dealers, who distribute the agency's securities to investors and participate in making a secondary market for these securities.

Agency securities come in varying forms: short-term notes sold at a discount and interest-bearing notes and bonds. Agency bonds are frequently issued with the title *debenture*. Any bond is an interest-bearing certificate of debt. A *mortgage bond* is a bond secured by a lien on some specific piece of property. A debenture is a bond secured only by the general credit of the issuer.

Interest on agency securities and principal at maturity are usually payable at any branch of the issuing agency, at any Federal Reserve bank or branch, and at the Treasury. Agency bonds are typically not callable.

Like Treasury securities, agency securities are issued under the authority of an act of Congress. Therefore, unlike private offerings, they are exempt from registration with the Securities and Exchange Commission (SEC). Typically agency issues are backed by collateral in the form of cash, U.S. government securities, and the debt obligations that the issuing agency has acquired through its lending activities. A few agency issues are backed by the full faith and credit of the U.S. A number of others are guaranteed by the Treasury or supported by the issuing agency's right to borrow funds from the Treasury up to some specified amount. Finally, there are agency securities with no direct or indirect federal backing.

HOUSING CREDIT AGENCIES

The major federal agencies still offering securities differ considerably in mission and method of operation, so we have organized our survey of them by function: first the mortgage-related agencies and then the farm credit agencies.

Federal Home Loan Banks

Behind the nation's commercial banks stands the Federal Reserve System, which regulates member banks, acts as a lender of last resort, and otherwise facilitates a smooth operation of the banking system. Behind the nation's S&Ls stands a somewhat similar institution, the *Federal Home Loan Bank* system. The FHLB, created in 1932, is composed of 12 regional banks and a central board in Washington.

S&Ls, savings banks, and insurance companies may all become

members of the FHLB system; federally chartered S&Ls are required to do so. Currently about 3,400 S&Ls belong to the FHLB system; these S&Ls hold over 98% of the total assets of all S&Ls in the country.

The Federal Home Loan banks are owned by the private S&Ls that are members of the system, just as the 12 Federal Reserve banks are owned by their member banks. The private ownership, however, is only nominal since the FHLB, like the Fed, operates under federal charter and is charged by Congress with regulating member S&Ls and with formulating and carrying out certain aspects of government policy with respect to the savings and loan industry. Thus the Federal Home Loan banks are in fact an arm of the federal government.

In addition to overseeing member S&Ls, the FHLB also lends to member S&Ls just as the Fed lends to commercial banks. Here, however, the similarity ends. The Fed obtains money to lend to banks at the discount window by monetizing debt. The Federal Home Loan banks have to borrow the money they lend to member S&Ls. Most of the money S&Ls provide to home buyers comes from their depositors. The FHLB lends to member S&Ls primarily to augment this source of funds. In a nutshell, the FHLB borrows money in the open market, then relends it to S&Ls, which in turn either relend it again to home buyers or, in recent years, use it to offset deposit outflows.

One purpose of this involved operation is to aid S&Ls with a temporary liquidity problem. A more important function is to channel money into the S&Ls when money is tight and rate lids cause a slowdown of the inflow of funds into S&Ls or even generate a net outflow of funds from such institutions. During such periods the FHLB has to pay more to borrow in the open market than S&Ls are permitted to pay depositors. Since the rate S&Ls have to pay on FHLB loans is set sufficiently high to cover the FHLB's borrowing costs, such loans are not a cheap source of funds to S&Ls. Also, the FHLB's borrowings in the open market create an interesting (disturbing to the FHLB) possibility for disintermediation: S&L depositors, seeking a higher return on their funds, might take money out of S&Ls and buy FHLB securities. To preclude this short-circuiting of the S&Ls, the FHLB raised the minimum denomination on its bonds from $5,000 to $10,000 in 1970.

The main security issued by the FHLB is consolidated *bonds,* "consolidated" referring to the fact that the bonds are the joint obligation of all 12 Federal Home Loan banks. FHLB bonds have a maturity at issue of 1 year or more, pay interest semiannually, and are not callable. They are issued in book entry form[8] and are now sold in denominations of

---

[8] Under the *book entry* system, to which the Treasury and the major federal agencies are moving, securities are not represented by engraved pieces of paper but are maintained in computerized records at the Fed in the names of member banks that in turn keep computerized records of the securities they own as well as those they are holding for customers. The book entry system is described in Chapter 13.

$10,000, $25,000, $100,000, and $1 million. FHLB bonds often appear on dealers' quote sheets as *FHLB notes*. The FHLB used to issue short-term, interest-bearing notes, but it switched some time ago to the sale of discount notes to raise short-term money. These discount notes have a minimum denomination of $50,000 and maturities under one year.

FHLB securities are backed by qualified collateral in the form of secured advances to member S&Ls, government securities, insured mortgages, etc. FHLB securities are *not* guaranteed by the U.S. government. However, they are the obligation of the FHLB system, which plays a key federal role in regulating and assisting the S&L industry. Given this role and the importance of the S&L industry to the economy, it is inconceivable that the U.S. government would ever permit the FHLB to default on outstanding securities.

Interest income from FHLB securities is subject to full federal taxes but is specifically exempt from state and local taxation.

Federal National Mortgage Association

Most money market instruments are extremely liquid (commercial paper being the main exception). The reason is not simply that these securities are stamped *negotiable* but more importantly that they have a broad and active secondary market. One of the major factors contributing to the existence of this secondary market is the homogeneity (one unit is just like another) of bills, bonds, and notes. Because mortgages lack homogeneity, a wide secondary market for mortgages has never developed in the United States. The lack of a secondary market for mortgages makes these instruments illiquid, which in turn diminishes the flow of funds into the mortgage market.

The *Federal National Mortgage Association* (FNMA), popularly known as "Fannie Mae," was set up in 1938 by Congress to create a secondary market in FHA mortgages (mortgages insured by the Federal Housing Administration). Initially Fannie Mae was wholly government owned, and its funds came from the Treasury. Later in 1954, Fannie Mae was split into three separate divisions: secondary market operations, special assistance functions, and management and liquidating functions.

The secondary market division was supposed to attract money to the mortgage market by providing liquidity for government-insured mortgages. To do so, it bought and sold mortgages insured or guaranteed by the Federal Housing Administration, the Veterans Administration, and the Farm Home Administration. Until February 1977 institutions dealing as buyers or sellers in mortgages with Fannie Mae were required to buy small amounts of Fannie Mae stock, thereby permitting the secondary market division of Fannie Mae to be converted from government ownership to private ownership.

In 1968, Congress completed its partition of Fannie Mae by putting its special assistance and management and liquidating functions into a new government-owned corporation, the *Government National Mortgage Association.* The remaining secondary market division of Fannie Mae, which retained the title Federal National Mortgage Association, was converted into a privately owned corporation. The corporation's private ownership is, however, to some degree nominal since the government retains broad powers to direct and regulate the operations of Fannie Mae through the Secretary of Housing and Urban Development (HUD). In 1977 the question of how much control HUD could exercise over Fannie Mae was disputed by both parties. HUD sought more control, suggested that Fannie Mae's profits were too high, and attempted to force the agency to funnel more funds into mortgages on inner-city housing.

Currently Fannie Mae's function is to buy government-insured or guaranteed mortgages (also conventional mortgages since 1970) when mortgage money is in short supply and to sell them when the demand for mortgage money slacks off. It does this through auctions at which it buys and sells some preannounced total of mortgages. For a fee Fannie Mae also extends advance commitments to buy mortgages. In the recent years of tight money and recurring shortages of mortgage funds, Fannie Mae has more often bought than sold mortgages. Nevertheless, this agency and others created to serve the same purpose have made significant progress toward increasing the liquidity of mortgages and attracting into mortgages funds that would otherwise have flowed elsewhere.

To finance its mortgage purchases, Fannie Mae relies primarily on the sale of debentures and short-term discount notes. The latter have maturities ranging from 30 to 360 days, and the minimum purchase is $50,000. Fannie Mae periodically adjusts the rates if offers on its discount notes so that they are in line with T bill rates. Fannie Mae debentures, which (with one exception) are not callable, are issued in book-entry form. They pay interest semiannually, and are available in denominations starting at $10,000 with $5,000 increments thereafter. Fannie Mae debentures are not backed by the federal government, but given the association's role as a government policy tool and its government supervision, it seems highly improbable that the government would permit a default on Fannie Mae obligations.

Interest income on Fannie Mae securities is subject to full federal, state, and local taxation. The large volume of Fannie Mae securities outstanding makes availability and marketability in the secondary market excellent.

Government National Mortgage Association

The 1968 partition of the old Federal National Mortgage Association spawned yet another financial lady, "Ginnie Mae," more formally known as the *Government National Mortgage Association* (GNMA), Ginnie Mae, a wholly government-owned corporation within the Department of Housing and Urban Development, took over the special assistance and the management and liquidating functions that had formerly been lodged in FNMA. These functions involve activities that could not be profitably carried out by a private firm. Ginnie Mae's mission is also to make real estate investment more attractive to institutional investors, which it has done by designing and issuing—partly in conjunction with private financial institutions—mortgage-backed securities for which an active secondary market has developed.

Under its management and liquidating functions, Ginnie Mae sold mortgages—some inherited from FNMA's earlier operations as a three-division organization and some acquired in the mid-1960s from other government agencies. It did this by creating pools of mortgages and selling participations in these pools to private investors. No such GNMA participation certificates have been issued since 1968.

Under its special assistance function, Ginnie Mae provides financing for selected types of mortgages through mortgage purchases and commitments to purchase mortgages. Under one program, for example, Ginnie Mae provides funds for the rehabilitation of deteriorating housing, which is subsequently resold to low-income families. Ginnie Mae finances its special assistance operations partly with funds obtained from the Treasury. To limit its borrowings from this source, Ginnie Mae currently operates most special assistance projects under a tandem plan. As Ginnie Mae acquires mortgages or mortgage purchase commitments, it resells them at market prices to other investors. Typically, under its special assistance function, Ginnie Mae buys mortgages at prices above prevailing market levels. Thus, to resell under the tandem plan, it has to absorb some loss, making it in effect a source of subsidy for certain types of mortgages.

Under the pass-through approach, private mortgage lenders assemble pools of mortgages acquired through Ginnie Mae auctions or from other sources and then sell certificates backed by these mortgages to investors. These certificates are referred to as *pass-through securities* because payment of interest and principal on mortgages in the pool is passed on to the certificate holders after deduction of fees for servicing and guarantee. Pass-through certificates have stated maturities equal to those of the underlying mortgages. However, actual maturities tend to be much shorter because of prepayments, the average life on single-family mortgages being approximately 12 years.[9] On pass-through securities,

---

[9] This used to be the standard average life quoted. As interest rates rose—especially in the period 1979–82—and mortgage money became prohibitively expensive or unattainable, home resales declined, and the average life of pass-throughs lengthened reflecting the concomitant decline in prepayments.

principal and interest are paid *monthly* to the investor. Because payments are made monthly and because the amount passed through varies from month to month due to mortgage prepayment, pass-throughs are issued in registered form only. Pass-through certificates have a minimum denomination of $25,000. They carry Ginnie Mae's guarantee of timely payment of both principal and interest and are backed in addition by the full faith and credit of the U.S. government.

Federal Home Loan Mortgage Corporation

The *Federal Home Loan Mortgage Corporation* (FHLMC) was created in July 1970 through enactment of Title III of the Emergency Home Finance Act of 1970. The organization's purpose is to promote the development of a nationwide secondary market in conventional residential mortgages. To accomplish this, the FHLMC buys residential mortgages and then resells them via the sale of mortgage-related instruments. The FHLMC's operations are directed by the Federal Home Loan Bank system, which provided the new agency with its initial capital.

To some extent the FHLMC duplicates the activities of Fannie Mae. But it has a special feature; it may purchase mortgages only from financial institutions that have their deposits or accounts insured by agencies of the federal government. The requirement that it deal with only regulated institutions (whereas Fannie Mae also buys mortgages from mortgage bankers) permits the FHLMC to cut documentation and paper requirements on mortgage purchases and thereby operate at lower cost. Unlike Fannie Mae, which has borrowed over $60 billion to finance its mortgage holdings, the FHLMC has pursued a course similar to that of Ginnie Mae—namely, selling its interest in the mortgages it purchases through mortgage-backed, pass-through securities.

Specifically the FHLMC sells two types of pass-through securities, *mortgage participation certificates* (PCs) and *guaranteed mortgage certificates* (GMCs). PCs resemble Ginnie Mae pass-throughs. Each PC represents an undivided interest in a pool of conventional residential mortgages underwritten and previously purchased by the FHLMC. Each month the certificate holder receives a prorated share of the principal and interest payments made on the underlying pool. The FHLMC guarantees timely payment of interest on PCs and the full return of principal to the investor. While PCs technically have a maturity at issue of 30 years, their average weighted life is assumed to be 12 years or less.[10]

Guaranteed mortgage certificates also represent an undivided interest in conventional residential mortgages underwritten and previously purchased by the FHLMC. These certificates pay interest semiannually

---

[10] See previous footnote on p. 219.

and return principal once a year in guaranteed minimum amounts. The final payment date on GMCs is 30 years from the date of issue, but the expected average weighted life of these securities is around 10 years.[11] Certificate holders may require the FHLMC to repurchase certificates at par 15 to 25 years (the put date varies with the issue) after they are issued.

Both PCs and GMCs are issued in registered form. PCs are sold in denominations of $25,000, $100,000, $200,000, $500,000, $1 million, and $5 million. While GMCs are issued in amounts of $100,000, $500,000, and $1 million. Currently the FHLMC has approximately $19.8 billion of such securities outstanding.

In addition to selling pass-through securities, the FHLMC has also sold $2.2 billion of bonds guaranteed by Ginnie Mae and backed by FHA and VA mortgages.

Finally in 1981 the FHLMC began issuing its own discount notes and debentures. FHLMC debentures are issued in book-entry form only; they have a minimum denomination of $10,000. FHLMC discount notes are offered with maturities of 1 year or less and a minimum face value of $25,000. At the end of 1981, FHLMC had a total of $1.3 billion of discount notes and debentures outstanding.

All securities issued by and through the FHLMC are subject to full state and federal taxation on income.

FARM-CREDIT AGENCIES

The production and sale of agricultural commodities require large amounts of credit. So too does the acquisition by farmers of additional land and buildings. To assure an adequate supply of credit to meet these needs, the government created over time the Farm Credit Administration. This administration, which operates as an independent agency of the U.S. government, oversees the Farm Credit System, which operates in all states plus Puerto Rico. Under this system, the country is divided into 12 farm credit districts. In each, there is a Federal Land Bank, a Federal Intermediate Credit Bank, and a Bank for Cooperatives; each bank supplies specific types of credit to qualified borrowers in its district.

Until January 1979, the 36 banks plus a Central Bank for Cooperatives obtained funds by issuing their own securities. After that the Farm Credit Banks decided to issue securities on a consolidated basis under the name of the Federal Farm Credit Bank. These consolidated discount notes and bonds are the secured joint obligations of the 37 Farm Credit Banks. Discount notes are issued with a minimum face value of $50,000

---

[11] See footnote on p. 219.

and have maturities ranging from 5 to 270 days; they provide the banks with interim financing between bond sales. Each month, the FFCB issues bonds with maturities of 6 and 9 months. It also issues long-term bonds about eight times a year.

All bonds and notes issued by the Federal Farm Credit Bank must be secured by acceptable collateral in the form of cash, Treasury securities, and notes or other obligations of borrowers from these banks. Also, each bank is examined at least annually by the Farm Credit Administration. Although FFCB securities are not guaranteed either directly or indirectly by the U.S. government, nevertheless, given the semiofficial status of the Federal Farm Credit Banks and the government's high degree of concern for agriculture, it is inconceivable that the government would permit the FFCB to default on its securities.

Banks for Cooperatives

The 12 district *Banks for Cooperatives,* organized under the Farm Credit Act of 1933, make seasonal and term loans to cooperatives owned by farmers, purchase farm supplies, provide business services to farmers, and market farm output. These loans may provide working capital or finance investments in buildings and equipment. The Central Bank for Cooperatives participates in large loans made by individual district banks. Initially the Banks for Cooperatives were owned by the U.S. government. Since 1955, however. government capital has been replaced by private capital, and ownership is now private.

Interest income from debentures issued by the Banks for Cooperatives is subject to full federal taxation but is specifically exempt from state and local income taxes.

Federal Land Banks

The 12 *Federal Land Banks* were organized under the Federal Farm Loan Act of 1916. These banks extend first mortgage loans on farm properties and make other loans through local Federal Land Bank (FLB) associations, which now number 700. Mortgage loans must be made on the basis of appraisal reports and may not exceed 65 percent of the appraised value of the mortgaged property. Maturities on FLB loans may run from 5 to 40 years, but most have original maturities of around 20 years. Although the Federal Land Banks were set up under government auspices, all government capital in these banks has been replaced by private capital, and they are now owned by the FLB associations, which in turn are owned by the farmers who have obtained FLB loans through these associations.

The Federal Land Banks obtain funds to lend out primarily by issuing Consolidated Federal Farm Loan bonds and by occasional short-term borrowings between bond issues. Since 1963 all FLB bond issues have been noncallable. These securities range in maturity from a few years to 15 years. Most have an original maturity of longer than 1 year. Securities with a maturity of less than 5 years are issued in bearer and book-entry form. Those with a maturity of more than 5 years are also issued in registered form. Interest on FLB bonds is payable semiannually. The smallest denominations available are $1,000, $5,000, and $10,000.

S&Ls are placed in an uncomfortable position whenever interest rates rise because the nature of their businesss is to borrow short and lend long. Federal Land Banks are in a somewhat similar situation since maturities on the loans they extend tend to be longer than the original maturities of the bonds they issue. To avoid the danger inherent in this position, Federal Land Banks now write only *variable-rate* mortgages. This approach enables them to keep loan income in line with borrowing costs whether interest rates rise or fall.

FLB bonds must be backed with collateral in the form of cash, Treasury securities, or notes secured by first mortgages on farm properties. Federal Land Banks are examined at least annually by the Farm Credit Administration. Their securities are not guaranteed either directly or indirectly by the U.S. government. However, their semiofficial status makes it unlikely that the government would ever permit default on their securities.

Income from FLB bonds is subject to full federal taxation but is exempt from state and local taxation.

Federal Intermediate Credit Banks

The 12 *Federal Intermediate Credit Banks* (FICB) were organized under the Agricultural Credit Act of 1923. Their job is to help provide short-term financing for the seasonal production and marketing of crops and livestock and for other farm-related credit purposes. These banks do not lend directly to farmers. Instead they make loans to and discount agricultural and livestock paper for various financial institutions that lend to farmers.[12] These institutions include commercial banks, production credit associations organized under the Farm Credit Act of 1933, agricultural credit corporations, and incorporated livestock loan companies. Originally, Federal Intermediate Credit Banks were government owned, but today their ownership is wholly private.

FEDERAL AGENCY SECURITIES

Federal agency securities have been around in significant volume for only two decades, but during that time, the outstanding volume of them

---

[12] *Discounting agricultural paper* means buying up farmers' loan notes at a discount.

FIGURE 7–8
Outstanding volume of selected federal agency securities*

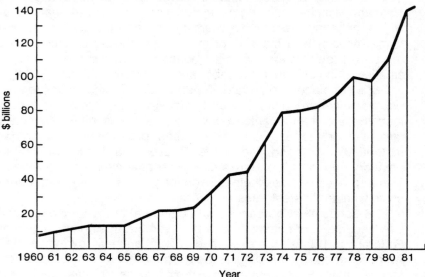

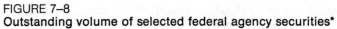

Year

* Issuers covered: the Federal Home Loan Banks, the Federal Home Loan Mortgage Corporation, the Government National Mortgage Association, the Federal National Mortgage Association, the Federal Land Banks, the Federal Intermediate Credit Banks, and the Banks for Cooperatives. (Excludes pass-through securities: these instruments are not debts of the agencies through which they are marketed.)
Source: *Federal Reserve Bulletin.*

has grown rapidly (Figure 7–8). In June 1982, marketable Treasury issues equaled $1.08 trillion, while agency securities (excluding pass-throughs) totaled $139 billion.

Attraction to investors

Federal agency securities are attractive for several reasons. Most agency issues are backed either *de jure* or *de facto* by the federal government, so the credit risk attached to them is zero or negligible. Also, many agency issues offer the tax advantage that interest income on them, like interest income on governments, is exempt from state and local taxation.

A third advantage of many agency issues is liquidity. Agency issues are smaller than Treasury issues so they do not have the same liquidity Treasury issues do, but their liquidity compares favorably with that of many other money market instruments.

Normally agencies trade at some spread to Treasuries of the same maturity. This spread varies considerably depending on supply conditions and the tightness of money. The difference between the rates at which agencies and governments trade apparently reflects almost solely differences in the liquidity of the two sorts of instruments since capital-rich institutions like the Federal Home Loan banks must, to borrow, pay the same rates that more poorly capitalized federal agencies pay.

Controlling federal agency debt

There are two sorts of federal agencies that get involved in the credit market: those such as the student loan program, which provide government guarantees of loans, and sponsored agencies such as Fannie Mae, which, although they have been largely "privatized," are regarded by most people who lend them money as the government in disguise. The Treasury has approval rights but no explicit control over the issuance of debt by sponsored agencies. The current administration would like to make such agencies as close to private as possible. In their view, having sponsored agencies lend, for example, to the housing market makes it appear as if the private sector is doing the job whereas in fact the government really is. Seen in this light, the sponsored agencies amount to a subterfuge that make sense only to the extent that they are able to operate more efficiently than a strictly government body would.

To make the sponsored agencies truly private, the government would have to cut them off from all government ties: no more government borrowing lines, no more government oversight, no more government assistance, implicit or explicit. The government is unlikely to make such dramatic and direct changes because it would meet determined opposition from both the agencies and the sectors they serve. Turning sponsored agencies into private firms would not suit the sectors they serve because the current system gives them a lower cost on borrowed funds. It also would not suit the agencies, who do not want to be subject to competitive market forces.

While the government has made little headway in further privatizing sponsored agencies, it has been able to increase public awareness of government guarantee programs. In fiscal 1982 the guarantee authority of federal agencies was cut back by $21 billion; the government also sought to develop with Congress a binding credit budget, one that would constrain both the guarantee and credit activities of agencies just as the regular budget constrains their direct outlays. So far no perceptible showdown has occurred in most agency off-budget borrowing.

Agency programs, like any political program, are there because they are a goody that some special interest group got. Any attempt to cut back on that goody results in an outcry. In 1982 students complained that a cutback in the student loan program would deny them a college education. Farmers complained that any cutback in their subsidy program would come in the worst farm income year in history. Everyone always has an ax to grind. Agency outlays, like any other government outlays, are easy to make for the first time and easy to increase; cutbacks, however, are nigh impossible.

The Treasury wants to cut back on agency borrowing to pare the government deficit and the amount of government debt offered in the market. Treasury officials also argue that off-budget expenditures and guarantees distort the federal budget, an important function of which is to act as an allocation index for resources used by government.

Congress sees things differently. For Congressmen, making sharp distinctions among direct government expenditures, agency loans, and agency guarantees is hard; they think of guarantees in particular as the government just giving a little aid. The unsurprising outcome is that guarantee programs have grown by leaps and bounds.

Chapter 8

The most watched player:
The Fed

THE FEDERAL RESERVE SYSTEM, the nation's central bank, was established by act of Congress in 1913. The Federal Reserve Act divided the country into 12 districts and provided for the creation within each of a *district Federal Reserve bank.* Responsibility for coordinating the activities of the district banks lies with the Federal Reserve's *Board of Governors* in Washington, D.C. The board has seven members appointed by the President and confirmed by the Senate.

The main tools available to the Fed for implementing policy are open-market operations, reserve requirements, and the discount rate. On paper authority for policymaking at the Fed is widely diffused throughout the system. In practice, however, this authority has gradually been centered in the *Federal Open Market Committee* (FOMC), which was established to oversee the Fed's open-market operations. Members of the FOMC include all seven governors of the system, the president of the New York Fed, and the presidents of 4 of the other 11 district banks; the latter serve on a rotating basis. Every member of the FOMC has one vote, but it has become tradition that the chairman of the Board of Governors plays a decisive role in formulating policy and acts as chief spokesman

227

for the system, which is why that position is viewed as one of power and importance.

In establishing policy, the Fed enjoys considerable independence on paper from both Congress and the executive branch. Members of the Board of Governors are appointed to 14-year terms so that a President has only limited control over who serves on the Board during his term of office. The chairman of the board, who is designated as such by the President, serves in that capacity for only 4 years, but his term is not coincident with that of the President, so an incoming President may have to wait until well into his first term to appoint a new chairman.

Congress, like the President, has no lever by which it can directly influence Fed policy or the way it is implemented. In creating the Fed, Congress endowed this institution with wide powers and granted it considerable leeway to exercise discretion and judgment. Having said that, one must hasten to add that the autonomy enjoyed by the Fed is in reality much less than it appears. Presidents who are concerned that the Fed is forcing interest rates too high (Presidents *never* seem to be concerned over interest being too low) attack the Fed subtly and not so subtly from the White House. Also the Fed is well aware that Congress, should it become too distressed over high interest rates, might take away the Fed's autonomy.

The perception that its independence is limited can and has influenced Fed policy. In particular during times when the Fed was tightening and it appeared that interest rates might reach unacceptable levels, the Fed has more than once attempted to force a contraction in bank lending while simultaneously preventing interest rates from rising to market-clearing levels. "It is not always politically feasible," commented one banker in 1977, "for the Fed, when it wants to curtail bank lending, to allow interest rates to go where they must to do so. The Fed would never admit or write this down, but they know they are a creature of Congress, and Congress would never let the prime go to 15 percent—one way or another it would remove in one fell swoop the so-called independence of the Fed. That is why the Fed forced the banks to institute a two-tier prime in 1971. We could raise the prime to big corporations but not on small loans. It was a terribly populist policy, but the Fed in instituting it was recognizing political reality." So much for predictions. In the grand monetarist experiment it began in October 1979, the Fed unhinged interest rates from its control, and the prime soared over 20%. Congress did not "react in one fell swoop" to limit the independence of the Fed, but by 1982 it was tiring of historically high interest and threatening to mandate a change in the focus of Fed policy from controlling money supply back to pegging interest rates. Politicalization of the prime has occurred not only in the United States but in Britain and other countries as well.

SOME HISTORY

The primary policy tool available to the Fed is open-market operations, the ability to create bank reserves in any desired quantity by monetizing some portion of the national debt.[1] The Fed could in theory monetize anything—scrap metal to soybeans—but it has stuck largely to Treasury IOUs because there has never been any shortage of them in the market, and in addition they are highly liquid so the Fed can sell them with as much ease as it buys them. In formulating policy, the first question the Fed faces is what macroeconomic *targets* to pursue. There are various possibilities: full employment, price stability, or a stable exchange value for the dollar. The achievement of *all* of these targets is desirable. However, since the Fed has only *one* powerful string to its bow—the ability to control bank reserves and thereby money creation by the private banking system—it is often forced to make hard choices between targets, to choose for example to pursue policies that would promote price stability but might increase unemployment.

Once the Fed has chosen its policy targets, it faces a second difficult question: What policies should it use to achieve these targets? If it wants to pursue a tight money policy to curb inflation, does that mean it should force up interest rates, strictly control the growth of the money supply (if so, which money supply), or what?

Not surprisingly the Fed's answers to the questions of what targets it should pursue and of how it should do so have changed considerably over time. One reason is that external conditions—the state of the domestic and world economy—have been in constant flux. A second reason is that central banking is an art form that is not fully understood, and the Fed's behavior at any time is therefore partly a function of how far it has progressed along its learning curve.

Before we look at how the Fed operates today, a few words on history. During World War II inflation was one extra disruption that the nation could do without. Thus during the war the appropriate stance for monetary and financial policy would have been for the federal government to raise taxes to cover as much of the war expenditures as possible and for the Fed to pursue simultaneously a policy of restraint to discourage private spending. This, however, was not done. Taxes were held down so as to not discourage incentives, and rationing and price controls were used to contain private spending and control the price level. Meanwhile the Fed assumed responsibility for pegging interest rates at the low levels that prevailed when the country entered the war. The rationale was to encourage individuals and institutions to buy bonds by eliminating the price risk that would normally attach to holding such securities. The

---

[1] See Chapter 2 for an explanation of debt monetization.

policy had the additional advantage of minimizing the cost to the Treasury of financing the burgeoning national debt.

In guaranteeing to buy whatever quantity of government securities was necessary to peg both long- and short-term interest rates at low levels, the Fed lost all control over the money supply; and its policy permitted a big buildup of private liquidity. In retrospect this buildup was not totally undesirable because the liquid assets acquired by citizens during the war permitted them to finance at the war's end the purchase of cars and other goods that had been unavailable during the war. The resulting spending spree prevented a much-feared postwar slump.

Inflation, however, did arrive on the scene. By 1948 the Fed was feeling uncomfortable about its obligation to peg bond prices, since that left it with no tool to fight inflation. The recession of 1949 provided some relief, but inflation again become a problem during 1950 when the Korean War broke out. Again, the Fed wanted to tighten but the Treasury resisted, arguing that higher interest rates would disrupt Treasury refundings, increase the cost of financing the national debt, and inflict capital losses on those patriotic individuals and institutions that had bought bonds during the war.

Finally the Fed threw the gauntlet down to the Treasury in September 1950 by raising the discount rate. The Treasury retaliated by announcing a 1-year financing based on the old discount rate of 1.25%. Rather than allowing the financing to fail or rescinding the rate increase, the Fed bought the Treasury's new issue, stuck to its higher discount rate, and then resold the issue to the market at a slightly higher rate. This started a 6-month battle with the Treasury, ending in the famous March 1951 *accord* between the Fed and the Treasury, which read:

The Treasury and the Federal Reserve System have reached full accord with respect to debt management and monetary policies to be pursued in furthering their common purpose to assure the successful financing of the Government's requirements and, at the same time, to minimize monetization of the public debt.

This statement, despite the fact that it appears to be a prime example of "governmentese" that says nothing, was important. Its key phrase, "to minimize monetization of the public debt," gave the Fed the right to henceforth pursue an independent monetary policy. The following year the Fed, to protect its flank, adopted a policy of *bills only;* in the future the Fed would confine its purchases of governments largely to bills. In adopting this policy, the Fed was saying to the market and the Treasury that henceforth the market would set the yield curve and in particular the yields on Treasury bonds.

As a price for its accord with the Treasury, the Fed agreed to stabilize credit-market conditions during Treasury financings. This policy, known as *even keeling,* was pursued for years. The reason such stabilization was required was that the Treasury used to fix both the coupon and the price at the time it announced a new issue on Wednesday. Thus if anything important had happened after the announcement of an issue but before it was sold the following week, that would have killed the auction; that is, the Treasury would have been unable to sell its securities—something that neither the Treasury nor the Fed could risk.

While even keeling prevailed, the Fed tried to plan major moves so that the market would have time to react to them before a Treasury financing. It insisted, however, that Treasury financings meet the test of the market; the Treasury could not rely on direct support from the Fed.

In the 1970s even keeling gradually died an untolled death. One reason is that the Treasury adopted the policy of selling almost all of its coupon issues through yield auctions. Also, the Treasury's new policy of auctioning notes of different maturities on a regular cycle created a situation in which the Treasury is in the market twice a month with new coupon issues. If the Fed were to even keel, it would have no "windows" during which it could decisively shift policy.

Before the accord the Fed was forced to focus almost solely on interest rates. After the accord, the Fed's focus gradually shifted to *free reserves*—excess reserves minus borrowed reserves. The Fed reasoned that the stance of monetary policy would be sufficiently easy during a recession if free reserves were increased, thereby promoting additional bank lending and falling interest rates; and that, during periods of excessive demand for output, the stance of monetary policy would be appropriately tight if free reserves were decreased, thereby promoting a reduction in bank lending and a rise in interest rates.

This reasonable-sounding policy contained a fatal flaw. During a recession, interest rates are likely to fall by themselves as the demand for bank credit diminishes, so increases in free reserves may be consistent with a falling money supply and a tight monetary policy. In an overheated economy, in contrast, limiting free reserves to some small sum need not mean tight money. So long as the Fed continues to supply banks with reserves and the banks use them, a policy of holding free reserves to a low figure is consistent with a rapidly expanding money supply.

After a decade of obsession with free reserves, the Fed in the early 1960s shifted focus to interest rates. At the time the economy was recovering sluggishly from a severe recession, and the Fed wanted to stimulate investment spending by lowering long-term interest rates. However, the U.S. was also experiencing a big deficit in its balance of payments, and defense of the dollar therefore called for the Fed to maintain high short-term interest rates. In response to both needs, the Fed adopted *operation twist:* It started buying bonds instead of bills in an attempt to force up short-term interest rates while simultaneously lowering long rates.

Whether operation twist was successful in altering the slope of the yield curve, in stimulating investment, or in decreasing the balance of payments deficit has been much debated. The policy died in 1965, a victim of the Vietnam War, which set off inflationary pressures in the economy and caused the Fed to focus on curbing inflation. In 1966 the Fed introduced the first of several credit crunches that drove interest rates to historical highs.

As fighting inflation came to be a key target of Fed policy, another change was also occurring—a gradual shift in the Fed's attention away from interest rates toward growth of the money supply. The level of interest rates does not necessarily indicate how tight or easy monetary policy is because interest rates respond not only to what the Fed is doing but to general economic conditions. During a recession interest rates can fall, as occurred in early 1960, even though bank reserves and the money supply are shrinking. Similarly during an expansion, rising interest rates are compatible with rapid increases in bank reserves, bank credit, and money supply. A second reason why the Fed gave increased attention to the monetary aggregates was the increasing popularity of monetarism: a view that the rate of growth of the money supply plays a dominant role in determining the rate of inflation.

In the decade following 1966, during which the Fed continued to be concerned much of the time with controlling inflation, it gradually put, in measuring monetary tightness and ease, more emphasis on the rate of growth of the money supply and less on that of free reserves. This switch in focus was encouraged by Congress, which in a 1975 joint resolution required the Fed to set and announce targets for monetary growth.

While the Fed set such targets at each meeting of the FOMC and attempted to keep growth of the monetary aggregates at targeted levels, the Fed never fully bought the monetarist doctrine, at least until October 1979. Prior to that time, the Fed seemed to be unconvinced that money matters as much as Milton Friedman, the leading monetarist, argues. Also, the Fed perceived that as a practical matter it could not control the growth of the then monetary aggregates—M1 to M whatever—with the precision envisioned in textbooks.[2]

---

[2] Because it has difficulty controlling precisely—even gauging precisely—the size of the money supply by any measure, the Fed in 1972 adopted as an operating policy target bank *reserves available to support private deposits (RPDs).* The idea was that, by controlling this aggregate, the Fed could control closely, albeit indirectly, the money supply available to the private nonbanking sector, that is, the total money supply minus Treasury

IMPLEMENTING MONETARY POLICY TODAY

Before we turn to monetary policy in the last few years, we need to look at the mechanics of and problems in implementing such policy and at the operation of the discount window.

The Fed's ultimate policy goals today are what they have always been: price stability, high employment, and a stable dollar. However, as economic conditions shift, so too does the focus of Fed policy. That was demonstrated by the jolt the Fed gave to the capital markets in early 1978 when it tightened, unexpectedly in the face of a sluggish economy, to defend the exchange value of the dollar. It was again demonstrated with even more vigor when, in October 1979, the Fed switched to monetarism, pure and simple, in a last-ditch effort to wring out of the economy a high and obdurate rate of inflation. By late 1982 the Fed appeared to have taken the pragmatic decision to declare that the inflation battle had been won for the moment and to focus on stimulating a severly depressed economy.

Whatever its ultimate macro economic goals may be, the Fed currently states its immediate policy objectives in terms of desired rates of growth over several months for the monetary aggregates, M1 and M2 (Table 8–1). Should the attempt to limit money supply growth cause Fed funds to trade persistently outside a quite *wide* band, then the money supply bands might be reconsidered.

The FOMC directive

Approximately once a month the FOMC meets to review economic conditions, its macro goals, and the guidelines it has set with respect to open-market operations for achieving those goals. At the end of the meeting, it issues a directive to the manager of the system's open-market account in New York. The August 24, 1982, directive read as follows:

The information reviewed at this meeting suggests only a little further advance in real GNP in the current quarter, following a relatively small increase in the second quarter, while prices on the average are continuing to rise more slowly than in 1981. In July the nominal value of retail sales rose somewhat from a sharply reduced June level; housing starts increased substantially, though from a relatively low rate; and industrial production and nonfarm payroll employment were essentially unchanged. The unemployment rate rose 0.3 percentage point to 9.8%. Over the first seven months of the year the advance in the index of average hourly earnings was considerably less rapid than during 1981.

balances at commercial banks and interbank deposits, both of which are excluded from Fed money supply figures. After several years, the Fed gave up on its experiment to use RPDs as a target because RPDs proved as difficult to control and measure as money supply.

TABLE 8–1
The Fed's changing definitions of money supply

Prior to February 1980
M1:   Currency in circulation plus demand deposits
M2:   M1 plus small-denomination savings and time deposits at com-
        mercial banks
M3:   M2 plus deposits at nonbank savings institutions
M4:   M2 plus large-denomination CDs
M5:   M3 plus large-denomination CDs
February 1980
M1A: Currency in circulation plus demand deposits
M1B: M1A plus other checkable deposits, including NOW accounts
M2:   M1B plus overnight RPs and money market funds and savings
        and small (less than $100,000) time deposits
M3:   M2 plus large time deposits and term RPs
L: M3 plus other liquid assets
January 1982
M1:   Currency in circulation plus demand deposits plus other checka-
        ble deposits, including NOW accounts
M2:   M1 plus savings and small (less than $100,000) time deposits at
        all depository institutions plus balances at money funds (exclud-
        ing institutions-only funds) plus overnight RPs at banks plus
        overnight Euros held by nonbank U.S. depositors in the Carib-
        bean branches of U.S. banks
M3:   M2 plus large (over $100,000) time deposits at all depository
        institutions plus term RPs at banks and S&Ls plus balances at
        institutions-only money funds
L: M3 plus other liquid assets such as term Eurodollars held by
        nonbank U.S. residents, bankers' acceptances, commercial pa-
        per, Treasury bills and other liquid governments, and U.S. sav-
        ings bonds.
December 1982
        The Fed included the new money market deposit accounts
        (MMDAs) that depository institutions were permitted to offer on
        December 14, 1982, in M2.
January 1983
        The Fed included the new super-Now accounts that depository
        institutions were permitted to offer on January 5, 1983, in M1.

The weighted average value of the dollar against major foreign currencies,
while fluctuating over a wide range, has changed little on balance since late
June despite a sharp decline in U.S. interest rates relative to foreign rates. Demand for dollars appeared to reflect concern about economic and financial

difficulties abroad. The U.S. foreign trade deficit in the second quarter was somewhat below the first-quarter deficit, with petroleum imports down substantially.

M1 declined slightly in June and July, while growth of M2 moderated somewhat from its average pace earlier in the year. Business demands for credit, especially short-term credit, remained generally strong. Market interest rates have declined sharply since around midyear, reflecting a shift in market sentiment about the outlook for interest rates against the background of strains in financial markets, relatively weak economic indicators, and legislative action on the federal budget. The Federal Reserve discount rate was reduced in three steps from 12% to 10½% during the period.

The Federal Open Market Committee seeks to foster monetary and financial conditions that will help to reduce inflation, promote a resumption of growth in output on a sustainable basis, and contribute to a sustainable pattern of international transactions. At its meeting in early February, the Committee had agreed that its objectives would be furthered by growth of M1, M2, and M3 from the fourth quarter of 1981 to the fourth quarter of 1982 within ranges of 2½ to 5½%, 6 to 9%, and 6½ to 9½%, respectively. The associated range for bank credit was 6 to 9%. The Committee began a review of these ranges at its meeting on June 30–July 1, and at a meeting on July 15, it reaffirmed the targets for the year set in February. At the same time the Committee agreed that growth in the monetary and credit aggregates around the top of the indicated ranges would be acceptable in the light of the relatively low base period for the M1 target and other factors, and that it would tolerate for some period of time growth somewhat above the target range should unusual precautionary demands for money and liquidity be evident in the light of current economic uncertainties. The Committee also indicated that it was tentatively planning to continue the current ranges for 1983 but that it would review that decision carefully in the light of developments over the remainder of 1982.

In the short run, *the Committee continues to seek behavior of reserve aggregates consistent with growth of M1 and M2 from June to September at annual rates of about 5% and about 9%, respectively.* Somewhat more rapid growth would be acceptable depending on evidence that economic and financial uncertainties are leading to exceptional liquidity demands and changes in financial asset holdings. *The Chairman may call for Committee consultation if it appears to the Manager for Domestic Operations that pursuit of the monetary objectives and related reserve paths during the period before the next meeting is likely to be associated with a federal funds rate persistently outside a range of 7 to 11%.*[3]

The first thing to note about this directive is that target rates of growth are stated not for one monetary aggregate but for several. Also the target rates of growth for the aggregates are stated in terms of *bands*. One reason is that, as economic conditions change, the public responds by altering the form in which it chooses to maintain its liquidity. Rising interest rates in particular encourage people to shift funds out of demand

---

[3] *Federal Reserve Bulletin,* October 1982. Italics are the author's.

deposits into time deposits, which slows the growth of M1 but does not affect that of M2. This trend has been accelerated and made less predictable by the phenomenal growth of money funds (Table 8–2), by the spate of new time deposit accounts that the DIDC has permitted banks and thrifts to offer, and more recently by the new money market accounts authorized under the Depository Institutions Act of 1982.[4] A second reason for stating monetary rates of growth in terms of bands is that seasonal factors, shifts in money balances between the Treasury and the public, and changes in the volume of trading in financial markets can and do have dramatic short-term effects on the growth of the monetary aggregates. There is, moreover,

. . . no really good way [for the Fed] to detect when short-run deviations in monetary growth from longer run targets are truly temporary and when they reflect more fundamental developments. Judgment, and the concomitant risk of error, is unavoidable in these situations. To avoid overreacting to short-term developments, the Federal Reserve has in practice tended to "tolerate" short-run swings in monetary growth rates over fairly wide ranges. The limits to such "toleration" have usually been expressed as upper and lower limits on two-month average growth rates—known, obviously enough, as "tolerance ranges." These ranges are set at levels that reflect the Open Market Committee's estimates of the various short-run influences that may be impinging on the monetary aggregates at any given time. As a result, the short-term tolerance ranges for any particular two-month period may differ significantly from the underlying one-year target ranges. . . . Moreover, reflecting the highly unpredictable nature of short-term movements, the percentage point spread embodied in the two-month tolerance ranges have normally been set wider than the spreads contained in the one-year target ranges.[5]

Since 1977 when this was written, the difficulty in interpreting short-run swings in the monetary aggregates has, if anything, increased.

A second point to note about the FOMC's current directives to the manager of the open market account is that they specify a *wide* band within which Fed funds may trade. This is a *sharp* break with pre-1979 practice when the Fed, despite the monetarist hue of its policy, tightly pegged the funds rate.

Day-to-day operations of the open market desk

As noted, the FOMC gives the account manager in New York two sorts of directives: target ranges for monetary growth and a target range for

---

[4] Note that by August 1982 total money fund balances almost equaled demand deposits at banks.

[5] Richard G. Davis, "Monetary Objectives and Monetary Policy," *Federal Reserve Bank of New York Quarterly Review* 2 (1977), pp. 35–36.

TABLE 8–2
Money stock measures and components ($ billions, averages of daily figures)

Measures	1976 Dec.	1977 Dec.	1978 Dec.	1979 Dec.	1980 Dec.	1981 Dec.	1982 Dec.
M1	316.1	341.3	372.5	398.8	424.6	451.2	454.0
M2	1,169.1	1,295.9	1,408.5	1,524.7	1,662.5	1,829.4	1,938.7
M3	1,303.8	1,464.5	1,637.5	1,789.2	1,973.9	2,199.9	2,342.3
L	1,527.1	1,718.5	1,946.6	2,162.8	2,380.2	2,653.8	n.a.
Selected components							
1. Currency	82.1	90.3	99.4	108.2	118.3	125.4	130.0
2. Demand deposits	231.3	247.0	261.5	270.1	275.1	243.3	229.3
3. Other checkable deposits	2.7	4.1	8.4	17.0	27.2	78.4	89.8
4. Overnight RPs and Eurodollars	13.6	18.6	24.1	26.3	35.0	38.1	44.7
5. Savings deposits	444.9	483.2	478.0	420.5	398.0	343.0	346.2
6. Small-denomination time deposits	393.5	451.3	531.1	649.7	748.9	851.7	919.9
Money market mutual funds							
7. General purpose and dealer/broker	3.4 }	3.8 }	7.1	34.4	61.9	151.2	180.0
8. Institution only			3.1	9.3	13.9	33.7	43.1
9. Large-denomination time deposits	119.7	147.7	198.6	226.0	262.3	305.4	333.5

Source: *Federal Reserve Bulletin.*

Fed funds.[6] The account manager's job is to keep money supply growth within the target ranges by adjusting through open market operations the reserves available to banks and other depository institutions.

In implementing the FOMC's directive, the desk tends to view M1 as the more important operating target because it is M1, not M2, that is composed primarily of reservable deposits (Table 8–1).

Having picked its primary operating target, the desk, with the aid of staff at the Board in Washington and at the New York Fed, estimates what reserves depository institutions will need to support the level of deposits implied by the M1 target. The desk then adds to this figure an estimate of the excess reserves that banks will hold and deducts from it an estimate of what appropriate borrowings from the discount window will be. The *net* of these figures is the amount of reserves that the desk seeks to supply on average over the week through its open market operations (Table 8–3).

TABLE 8–3
**Calculating the desk's
reserve target**

Reserves needed to support deposits
consistent with M1 Target
+ Appropriate borrowings at the
discount window
− Estimated excess reserves

= Reserve target to be supplied
by the desk

The desk's task sounds straightforward but in practice is tricky to carry out. First the numbers upon which its reserves target is based are estimates, which may prove incorrect, of what excess reserves and borrowings at the discount window will be. Second, the quantity of reserves actually available on any day to depository institutions is influenced not only by actions taken on the desk but by unpredictable changes in Treasury balances and float that together can easily total $1 billion.

Treasury balances. Because of tax collections and securities sales, the Treasury holds huge and highly variable deposit balances. It used to keep these balances primarily in commercial banks in what are called *Treasury tax and loan accounts*. When it did so, the Treasury as it needed to make disbursements, would transfer funds from its TT&L accounts into its account at the Fed and write checks against that.

---

[6] People at the Fed distinguish between quarterly *targets* and *tolerance ranges* that are permissible within any month; the latter are wider because the shorter the period, the more difficult it is to tightly control the rate of monetary growth.

Then in 1974 the Treasury adopted a new policy: It began to hold most of its deposits at the Fed. Its primary reason for doing so was to raise its revenues. By depositing huge sums in its account at the Fed (which drained bank reserves, see Table 8–4), the Treasury forced the Fed to

TABLE 8–4
When the Treasury transfers funds from an account at a commercial bank to its account at the Fed, this decreases bank reserves.

The Treasury

	Demand deposits at Citibank −10 million Deposits at the Fed +10 million

Citibank

Reserves −10 million	Treasury tax and loan account −10 million

The Fed

	Reserves, Citibank −10 million U.S. Treasury deposits +10 million

expand its portfolio via additional open market purchases, and the result was that the Fed earned more profit. All Fed profits above a small amount are paid to the Treasury. So by holding its balances at the Fed, the Treasury turned them in effect into interest-bearing deposits.

After the Treasury began holding the bulk of its funds at the Fed, movements of funds into and out of its account there became both huge and difficult to predict. The sheer size of the shifts in Treasury balances created operational problems for the Fed, which had a hard time offsetting smoothly these flows through normal open market operations. To alleviate this problem, Congress—prodded by the Fed—acted to permit banks beginning in 1978 to pay the Treasury interest on demand balances held with them. For its part the Treasury starting paying banks for services which banks had previously provided free to it in exchange for non-interest-bearing deposits.

Float. Whenever a check is cleared through the Fed, the Fed first credits the reserve account of the bank at which the check is deposited by the amount of the check and then debits the reserve account of the bank against which the check is drawn by a like amount. Sometimes the reserve credit is made before the reserve debit, which results in a temporary and artificial increase in reserves. This increase is referred to as *float*. Since the size of float can be affected by such factors as the weather (when planes can't fly, movement of checks and reserve debiting are slowed), float has been and remains a difficult variable to estimate.

Adding and draining. By comparing its estimate of reserves available to depository institutions with its reserve target, the desk determines each day what amount of reserves it needs to inject or drain from the system. To add reserves, the Fed either buys securities *or* does repos with dealers in government securities. To drain reserves, it either sells securities *or* does reverses with the dealers. As Table 8–5 shows, when

TABLE 8–5
The Fed adds to bank reserves by doing a repo with a bank dealer

The Fed

Bills bought under repurchase agreement +10 million	Reserves, Continental Bank +10 million

Continental Bank of Chicago

Reserves +10 million	Securities sold under agreement to repurchase +10 million

the Fed does a repo with a bank dealer, this adds to bank reserves just as an outright purchase of bills would; a repo done with a nonbank dealer would have the same effect on bank reserves. Reverses done by the Fed are repos in reverse gear, they drain reserves.

The securities the Fed buys vary from day to day depending partly on availability. Bills and notes can usually be easily bought in size, and the Fed holds a large proportion of its portfolio in such securities (Table 8–6). Much of the rest is in bonds; which, due to changes in Treasury debt management policy, represent a slowing growing portion of the Treasury's outstanding debt.

The Fed also buys federal agency securities, in part because it was directed to do so by Congress in 1971 to help support the market for these securities. The Fed imposes guidelines on what agency issues it will buy; currently an agency issue, to be eligible for purchase, must be

TABLE 8–6
**The Federal Reserve's portfolio, beginning of September 1982
($ millions)**

Loans		
Member bank borrowings		449
Acceptances		
Bought outright.		0
Held under repurchase agreements		565
Federal agency obligations		
Bought outright.		8,955
Held under repurchase agreements		229
U.S. government securities		
Bought outright		
Bills.	51,387	
Notes.	62,018	
Bonds	18,264	
Total		131,669
Held under repurchase agreements		1,189
Total U.S. government securities		132,858
Total loans and securities		143,056

Source: *Federal Reserve Bulletin.*

at least $300 million in size if its maturity is less than 5 years and $250 million in size if its maturity is more than 5 years. Since the Fed created these guidelines, the agencies have ensured that their new issues comply. The Fed no longer buys securities issued by agencies that may obtain funds from the Federal Financing Bank. Thus the agencies whose securities the Fed now buys are limited to the FHLB, the farm-credit agencies, and Fannie Mae; the Fed does not buy pass-throughs. In recent years the Fed has deemphasized its purchases of agency securities as the Figures in Table 8–6 show.

The Fed used to buy BAs as part of its program to encourage the growth of the domestic BA market (Chapter 17). However, now that the market has grown and matured, the Fed no longer purchases BAs for its own portfolio. It does, however, still do repo against BAs (Table 8–6).

The Fed sometimes buys governments and agencies for same day settlement; more typically, however, it buys for regular or skip-day settlement because, when it buys on those terms, it gets better offerings from the dealers.[7]

When the Fed wants to reduce reserves by selling securities, it sells securities of short maturity. Said someone at the Fed, "I do not remember a time in the last 20 years that we have sold coupon issues longer than 2 years. The market would be shocked and bewildered if we did so; it is

---

[7] A skip-day trade is settled two business days after the trade is made. A cash trade is settled on the day it is made.

taken as a given fact that we do not, so—to do so—we would have to educate the market."

In carrying out open market operations, the Fed constantly has two objectives in mind: (1) the need to offset short-term fluctuations in reserves due to changes in float and other variables, and (2) the need to gradually and secularly increase bank reserves so that the money supply and bank credit can expand—within the bands set by the FOMC—in step with economic activity and national output. In making day-to-day short-term adjustments in reserves, the Fed relies primarily on repos and reverses, which it does against governments, agencies, and BAs (Table 8–7). Permanent injections of reserves are done through purchases of bills, notes, and bonds.

The line between Fed actions that are a reaction to short-term fluctuations in reserves and those designed to add permanent reserves is difficult to draw because the two often mesh. Also, because of uncertainty with respect to reserve availability, the Fed is often forced to switch gears. Here's a scenario of how things on the desk might go during reserve week: "Our research department does projections of available reserves, and some are done in Washington at the Board. We compare notes on these projections during our morning conference call with the Board. Mostly we focus on our projections for the current week, but to give perspective to any action we might want to take, we give projections for the next several weeks. Then we build up a program for the day based on what we think the need is and on the information flowing in from the market.

"Say it is Thursday and we figure we need $39.4 billion of reserves on average over the week.[8] We think excess reserves will run $400 million, and the FOMC directive takes $500 million to be an appropriate level of borrowed reserves. Then we have a reserve target of $40 billion of which $500 million is expected to come from borrowings. Say our projections tell us that—unanticipated changes in Treasury balances, float, and currency in circulation aside—there would be $38 billion of nonborrowed reserves in the system if we took no action. That would leave us with $1.5 billion of nonborrowed reserves to add for that week on average.

"We would proceed to add those reserves; and if all went well—the banks did end up with $600 million of excess reserves and so on—that would result in the level of nonborrowed reserves being just about consistent with that needed to support the level of deposits the committee

---

[8] As explained in Chapter 11, settlement by the banks is based on their average reserve balances over the settlement week. So the Fed's concern is with the average reserve balances available daily to the banks over the settlement week. Which banks get or lose reserves as a result of Fed open market operations is of no concern to the Fed because banks with surpluses sell funds to banks with reserve deficits in the Fed funds market.

wanted. If the level of deposits were greater, there would be a bigger reserve requirement that would be met through borrowing at the discount window. If deposits required an extra $400 million of reserves and the desk had done its job just right, borrowings at the window would be not $500 million, but $1 billion.

"We do not hit each week so precisely. If we fall short in one week—have too few reserves and too many borrowings—we would, if the aggregates were in line with what the committee wanted, take account of that in future weeks and put in a little extra to counter the shortage in the previous week.

"If alternatively the aggregates grew in excess of what the committee wanted, then we would not provide additional reserves to meet those reserve requirements; and borrowings at the window would rise. If growth in the aggregates were sufficiently strong, we might want to make an extra adjustment—reduce by $500 million the nonborrowed reserves made available to the system. That would produce still more borrowings and presumably cause a swifter reaction."

One problem the Fed faces in hitting its reserve target is that the distribution of reserves within a week can be highly skewed, with a lot of reserves being available early or late in the week. Because most banks are unwilling to run big reserve deficits or surpluses on a day-to-day basis, this creates artificial tightness or ease, which the Fed feels compelled to offset and can do only with difficulty. Said one person at the Fed, "A major and not widely recognized problem is the distribution of reserves within the week. If early in the week there is a shortage of reserves, even if we pump in reserves, the market may still be tighter than we like. And by pumping in all those reserves, we may be creating a problem because we are putting in more reserves than we can take out at the end of the week. The market is often incapable of handling a large amount—either because on the repo side they lack collateral or because on the reverse side we have exhausted the supply of banks that want to do reverses.

"Banks who do reverses with us are not as welcome at the discount window as they would be if they did not. So banks are reluctant to do reverses because they fear the money market might tighten and they might have to come into the discount window. The rationale for this policy is that a bank should not borrow from us money that they have in fact lent us. The banks are discouraged from doing reverses and borrowing at the discount window even when they would be taking a loss on the *net* transaction, which at times they would be."

Another difficulty the Fed may experience in trying to hit its target is that it may be forced at times to engage in large open market operations to offset shifts in Treasury balances or float. The danger is that the large resulting injections or withdrawals of reserves may—depending on mar-

TABLE 8–7
Federal Reserve open market transactions ($ millions)

Type of transaction	1977	1978	1979	1980 Feb.	Mar.	Apr.	May.	June	July	Aug.
U.S. GOVERNMENT SECURITIES										
Outright transactions (excluding matched sale-purchase transactions)										
Treasury bills										
1 Gross purchases	13,738	16,628	16,623	187	1,370	2,428	838	322	0	0
2 Gross sales	7,241	13,725	7,480	1,590	0	108	232	0	2,264	47
3 Exchange	0	0	0	0	0	0	0	274	0	0
4 Redemptions	2,136	2,033	2,900	400	0	0	0	0	950	0
Others within 1 year[1]										
5 Gross purchases	3,017	1,184	3,203	0	292	109	155	121	0	137
6 Gross sales	0	0	0	0	0	0	0	0	0	0
7 Maturity shift	4,499	−5,170	17,339	1,822	921	179	1,670	412	311	2,423
8 Exchange			−11,308	−2,177	−809	−459	−5,276	−1,479	−788	−3,134
9 Redemptions	2,500	0	2,600	0	0	0	0	0	0	0
1 to 5 years										
10 Gross purchases	2,833	4,188	2,148	0	355	373	405	465	0	541
11 Gross sales	0	0	0	0	0	0	0	0	0	0
12 Maturity shift	−6,649	−178	−12,693	−374	−921	−179	−1,302	−412	−311	−720
13 Exchange			7,508	1,377	809	459	3,000	1,479	788	1,750
5 to 10 years										
14 Gross purchases	758	1,526	523	0	107	62	133	164	0	236
15 Gross sales	0	0	0	0	0	0	0	0	0	0
16 Maturity shift	584	2,803	−4,646	−1,364	0	0	−25	0	0	−1,703
17 Exchange			2,181	450	0	0	1,300	0	0	1,000
Over 10 years										
18 Gross purchases	553	1,063	454	0	81	64	216	129	0	320
19 Gross sales	0	0	0	0	0	0	0	0	0	0
20 Maturity shift	1,565	2,545	0	−84	0	0	−342	0	0	0
21 Exchange			1,619	350	0	0	976	0	0	384

All maturities[1]										
22 Gross purchases	20,898	24,591	22,950	187	2,206	3,036	1,747	1,200	0	1,234
23 Gross sales	7,241	13,725	7,480	1,590	0	108	232	0	2,264	47
24 Redemptions	4,636	2,033	5,500	400	0	0	0	0	950	0
Matched transactions										
25 Gross sales	425,214	511,126	626,403	54,541	55,658	57,316	49,934	50,590	48,370	72,315
26 Gross purchases	423,841	510,854	623,245	54,584	54,636	57,479	50,965	52,076	46,023	71,645
Repurchase agreements										
27 Gross purchases	178,683	151,618	107,374	5,407	6,682	3,029	7,717	12,810	10,719	2,783
28 Gross sales	180,535	152,436	107,291	4,787	6,379	3,952	4,811	15,258	10,110	3,016
29 Net change in U.S. government securities	5,798	7,743	6,896	-1,140	1,486	2,168	5,452	238	-4,952	284
FEDERAL AGENCY OBLIGATIONS										
Outright transactions										
30 Gross purchases	1,433	301	853	0	0	668	0	0	0	0
31 Gross sales	0	173	399	0	0	0	0	0	0	0
32 Redemptions	223	235	134	*	5	2	0	2	2	*
Repurchase agreements										
33 Gross purchases	13,811	40,567	37,321	2,403	1,883	483	1,611	3,035	1,737	1,082
34 Gross sales	13,638	40,885	36,960	2,372	1,834	563	1,258	3,351	1,242	1,132
35 Net change in federal agency obligations	1,383	-426	681	31	45	586	353	-318	492	-50
BANKERS ACCEPTANCES										
36 Outright transactions, net	-196	0	0	0	0	0	0	0	0	0
37 Repurchase agreements, net	159	-366	116	205	-34	-171	366	7	-64	-33
38 Net change in bankers acceptances	-37	-366	116	205	-34	-171	366	7	-64	-33
39 **Total net change in System Open Market Account**	**7,143**	**6,951**	**7,693**	**-903**	**1,497**	**2,582**	**6,171**	**-73**	**-4,523**	**202**

Note. Sales, redemptions, and negative figures reduce holdings of the System Open Market Account; all other figures increase such holdings. Details may not add to totals because of rounding.

1. Both gross purchases and redemptions include special certificates created when the Treasury borrows directly from the Federal Reserve, as follows (millions of dollars): September 1977, 2,500; March 1979, 2,600.

Source: *Federal Reserve Bulletin.*

ket conditions—be mistakenly interpreted by the market as a signal of a shift in Fed policy.

Problems of this sort are the reason the Fed lobbied to have the Treasury hold the bulk of its deposit balances in TT&L accounts at private banks. Despite the Treasury's new deposit arrangements, the Treasury must still keep sizable balances at the Fed. Any time these run below $1 billion, the Treasury runs a risk, unless it puts in more money, of ending up *OD* (*overdrawn*) at the Fed. When this occurs, the Treasury issues the Fed special certificates, which are usually on the Fed's books for no more than a day or two.

A go-around

The Fed goes into the market to do open-market operations after the morning conference call between the New York desk and the board in Washington. Usually this is around 11:30 to 12.

When the Fed goes into the market to do normal, daily, open market operations, the size is usually large. A typical bill operation for the open market account currently varies from $700 million to a billion or two. In Treasury coupons and agencies, it will run from $500 million to a billion. Repos and reverses can run from $1 to $4 billion.

Once the Fed decides what it wants to do in the way of open market operations, it does what is called a *go-around*. It calls all of the primary dealers in government securities and tells them that it wants to buy securities, sell securities, do repo, or do reverses and asks them for bids and offers, as the case may be.

On securities purchases and sales, the Fed compares dealers' bids and offers with current market quotes and determines on which issues yields are most attractive and on which of these issues it has gotten the best quotes. It then does business with those dealers who have given it the highest bids or lowest offers on those issues.

To get current market quotes on governments and agencies, the Fed asks five of the primary dealers in governments to give it, hourly or more frequent, quotes for a wide range of securities. Providing such quotes is a nuisance for the dealers, so the Fed rotates the job.

The word that a go-around is being done is flashed out to all the dealers within 30 seconds. Thereafter the process slows. It takes the dealers time to get back to the Fed with their offerings or bids, and then it takes the Fed time to compare the dealers' propositions and select the most favorable. Particularly in agencies, the process can easily consume over an hour. To cut this time, the Fed plans to move to a computer system that will permit dealers' bids and offers to be directly transmitted to the Fed's computer, which may eventually be programmed to select the best bids or offers. Developing and installing such a system, however, is a large job that is unlikely to be done for some time.

In addition to its normal open market transactions with the dealers, the Fed uses transactions with foreign central banks that hold dollars as a way to affect bank reserves. Such transactions are marginal on a long-term basis but can be significant in the day-to-day control of reserves. "Foreign accounts have buy and sell and repo orders every day," said one person on the desk. "We can choose to be on the other side of any one of those transactions, which gives us flexibility. Say there is a big excess of reserves in the market. If we try to drain reserves, the market may conclude we are tightening further. But if we do transactions internally with foreign accounts, no one sees them, and no one is upset. Such transactions do what a market transaction would do without providing any signal." Foreign account transactions on an average day in 1982 amounted to $100 to $500 million on the buy side and the same amount on the sell side. The repo amounts ran from $1.2 to $2.5 billion a day.

THE DISCOUNT WINDOW

When a bank borrows at the discount window, reserves are created just as they are when the Fed does repos in the course of open market operations (Table 8–8). Back in the 1920s granting banks loans at the

TABLE 8–8
When a bank borrows $50 million at the discount window it increases bank reserves by a like amount

The Fed

Member bank borrowing +50 million	Reserves of borrowing bank +50 million

The Borrowing Bank

Reserves +50 million	Borrowing from the Federal Reserve +50 million

discount window was the Fed's main technique for creating bank reserves. Gradually this technique of reserve creation was replaced by open market operations, and the primary function of the discount window today is to provide member banks and other depository institutions that encounter any one of a range of possible difficulties with a means to adjust in the short run.[9]

An institution's borrowings at the discount window must be collateralized. According to the old commercial loan theory of banking, it was proper for banks to make only *short-term* loans because their liabilities were short-term in nature. Also, bank loans were supposed to be *self-liquidating;* that is, to fund an activity that would automatically generate funds required to repay the loan. Finally, bank loans were to be *productive;* that is, to fund the production and marketing of goods not, for example, the carrying of securities. Influenced by this doctrine, the authors of the Federal Reserve Act stipulated that only notes arising from short-term, self-liquidating, productive loans were *eligible* as collateral at the discount window. Notes not meeting these conditions are deemed to be *ineligible* collateral.

Currently the Fed classifies (reflecting various congressional amendments to the Federal Reserve Act) as eligible collateral: Treasury securities, federal agency securities, municipal securities with less than 6 months to run, and commercial and industrial loans with 90 days or less to run. What banks use as collateral at the window has varied over time. There was a time when banks borrowed at the discount window almost exclusively against governments. Then large banks began RPing their government portfolios and using customer promissory notes as collateral. Major banks try to always hold at the Fed adequate collateral against possible borrowings.

When a bank borrows against ineligible collateral, it used to have to pay a rate at least ½% above the posted discount rate. The Monetary Control Act eliminated this penalty rate and thus made the concept of ineligibility historically important but irrelevant for today's discount window. This change pleased the Fed, which viewed the penalty rate as an anachronism and had been asking Congress to eliminate it for a decade or more. Historically banks made short-term, self-liquidating loans; now banks make many other sorts of loans as well. The Fed's purpose in asking for collateral loans at the window is not to promote short-term lending but to limit its credit risk. Thus the Fed should be and is more interested, when it takes in loan paper, with the creditworthiness of the borrower than with the maturity of the loan.

In 1974 Congress amended the Federal Reserve Act to exempt 1-to-4-family mortgages used as collateral at the window from the ½% penalty rate. In 1978 the New York Fed facilitated the use of mortgages as collateral for loans at the window by saying that banks in its district need

---

[9] It used to be that just member banks could borrow at the discount window. Then foreign banks were given access to the window by passage in 1978 of the International Banking Act. Finally all domestic depository institutions were given access to the window by passage in 1980 of the Monetary Control Act.

not transfer the physical documents to it; instead all the New York Fed requires is that a bank segregate mortgages used as collateral at the window and give it a custody receipt. Since 1978 New York district banks with big mortgage portfolios have made substantial use of mortgages as collateral for loans at the window. The New York Fed still requires that other sorts of readily marketable collateral be lodged with it or with a third party. What types of collateral the Fed will take under off-premise custody varies from district to district; generally Federal Reserve District Banks are viewed as being more lenient the farther west they are.

NEW FACES AT THE WINDOW

With passage of the IBA in 1978 and of the Monetary Control Act in 1980, the borrowing constituency of the Fed was raised from 5,000 member banks to 40,000 institutions—the new faces being foreign banks and all nonmember domestic depository institutions.

Foreign banks

Since most foreign banks having U.S. branches or agencies are large, one would have expected them to do at least a test borrowing at the Fed to learn the procedure in preparation for the day they really needed a loan from the window. A few have done so, but the number is small. Most foreign banks still rely on their domestic correspondent bank as a lender of last resort. Presumably that will change over time as foreign banks learn that the window is truly open to them and, more important, that at times it would be both appropriate and cheaper for them to borrow there.

Since foreign banks must hold reserves at the Fed only against the deposits they book in the U.S., their required reserves are small compared to those of domestic banks of similar size. Whereas a Citi or Chase might have required reserves of $1 billion, the comparable figure for the Crédit Lyonnais might be only $10 million. Yet when they both need to borrow at the window, the size of the borrowing needs of both classes of banks is likely to be similar. The Fed recognizes this and has said in effect to the foreign banks, "We are as willing to lend you $100 million as we are to lend the same amount to Citi, but since you hold much smaller reserves on average than Citi, we'd expect you to come to the window much less often than they do." That is the Fed's way of respecting the IBA requirement that loans made at the discount window to a bank be related in size to the reserves held by that bank at the Fed.

Nonmember banks and thrifts. Most nonmember banks and thrifts tend to be highly liquid institutions and are normally sellers, not buyers, of Fed funds. As noted below, an institution that sells Fed funds is not supposed to simultaneously borrow at the discount window as this practice could often result in a profitable arbitrage. The purpose of the window is not to increase profits of depository institutions by creating the opportunity for them to engage in risk-free, for-profit arbitrages. So far, in the New York district at least, few of the institutions who were first given access to the discount window by the Monetary Control Act of 1980 have taken advantage of the opportunity to do so.

After passage of the 1980 Monetary Control Act, the Fed published a pamphlet, *The Federal Reserve Discount Window,* to acquaint its new borrowing constituency with discount-window practices. At that time the Fed reviewed its lending practices and tightened them but only in ways so marginal that the New York Fed felt no need to tell banks who had been borrowing from it that any changes had been made.

Bank attitudes toward discounting

The Fed takes the position that access to the discount window is a privilege and that institutions should borrow there only when they have a legitimate need and then only for reasonable amounts and periods. The discount rate is sometimes set above money market rates, but often it is set at a level such that it is cheaper for an institution to borrow at the discount window than to buy overnight Fed funds (Figure 8–1).[10] The discount rate, unlike the Fed funds rate, is not typically a major beacon pointing up the direction of Fed policy; it is normally changed only after other short-term rates have moved up or down. However, occasionally a change in the discount rate may be interpreted by the market and intended by the Fed as a signal. An example is the cut below market rates that the Fed made in the discount rate on November 19, 1982. (Figure 8–1).

The Fed's guideline on use of the discount window is vague at best, and not surprisingly there is a wide range of views among potential borrowers with respect to the window and its proper use.

At one extreme are some small institutions that feel that a stigma is attached to use of the discount window. Other institutions, which take a less extreme point of view, have very conservative senior management who regard it as a sign of weakness to borrow at the window; they are happy and proud to say that they have not found it necessary to borrow at the window in 5 years, or whatever. This attitude led one bank during the

---

[10] In 1971 the Fed switched from actually discounting paper at the window to making straight loans against collateral. As a result the discount rate is not quoted on a discount basis as Treasury bill rates are; instead the discount rate is an add-on rate that is directly comparable to the Fed funds rate, which is also an add-on rate. In making the 1971 switch in window practice, the Fed's motive was to simplify lending at the window. The change also permitted banks to borrow more dollars against a given amount of collateral.

FIGURE 8–1
Relationship of the discount rate to the Fed funds rate

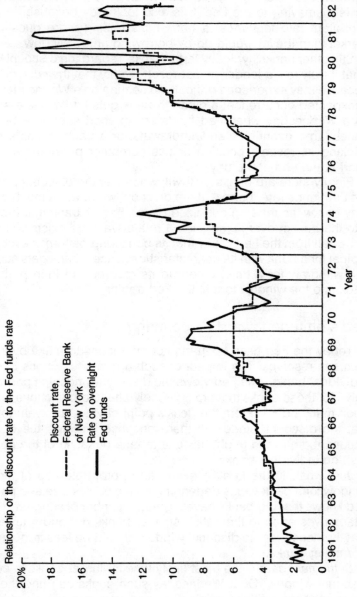

Relationship of the discount rate to the Fed funds rate

Discount rate,
Federal Reserve Bank
of New York

Rate on overnight
Fed funds

Year

Source: *Federal Reserve Bulletin.*

1974 credit crunch to pay, on a settlement day when Fed funds were tight, 25% for overnight funds rather than go to the window. Such behavior is dismaying to the Fed. It is also foolhardy because, in paying an exorbitant rate for funds, a bank risks raising more questions in the market than it ever would do by borrowing at the window.

Still other banks, typically large banks, regard the discount window as what it truly is—a lender-of-last-resort facility that they use occasionally because they experience difficulty in settling on a Wednesday due to an unexpected occurrence: a clearing bank gets hit by dealers loans late on a Wednesday when Fed funds are in short supply; a bank experiences large unanticipated withdrawals; or a bank makes a mistake in tracking its reserve position or has computer problems and ends up short at the end of the day.

Finally there are banks that will, whenever the discount rate is below the Fed funds rate, borrow at the discount window, as much as they feel they can without being criticized by the Fed. A bank that dips its ladle into the bucket every time such a rate advantage exists will eventually get a call from the Fed to say that its borrowing pattern is exceeding that typical for a bank with its characteristics. Once a bank gets such a call, it will withdraw for a time, clean up its record, and then perhaps come back into the window to test the Fed again.

The Fed's attitude toward discounting

Today the Fed uses open market operations to make overall adjustments in reserves. The impact of such aggregate actions can differ for individual banks. The Fed views the discount window in part as a safety valve for those banks that are adversely affected by actions taken on the open market desk. From the desk's point of view, it is valuable to know that the discount window is there because it allows the desk to take actions it otherwise might hesitate to take because of the potential impact on individual banks.

Just what, in the Fed's view, is an appropriate use of the discount window for a bank varies depending on the bank's size and position. The Fed knows that big banks have a greater number of short-term borrowing alternatives open to them than smaller banks do, and it takes the view that their need for the discount window should be less frequent than that of smaller banks.

Settlement date is the most likely time for larger banks to come to the discount window. On a Wednesday such banks can find their position much shorter than they anticipated, and rates can get out of hand in the Fed funds market on Wednesday afternoon. The reserve week ends on Wednesday so that is the day banks make final settlement with the Fed (see Chapter 11). The Fed takes the position that if the choice facing a bank on a Wednesday is between paying an "exorbitant" rate for funds and coming to the discount window, it should come into the window. This view, however, still leaves room for judgment. If the discount rate is 9 and Fed funds are at 11, is 11 a bandit rate? If not, what about a 3-point spread? Whether use of the discount window is legitimate on a Wednesday also depends on how available funds are in the market, how late in the day it is, how much a bank needs, and the lines available to it in the Fed funds market.

A small bank has less access to the Fed funds market than a large bank; it lacks access to the Euromarket; and it may have few repo possibilities. When such a bank experiences a sudden run-off in deposits (the school district withdraws balances) or increased local demand for loans, it may be unable to immediately react to that development. It may not have liquid assets to pay off deposits that are running off; it may not have short-term liquidity to fund a big increase in loan demand. In that type of situation, the Fed would view short-term use of the discount window by the bank as appropriate, and it would carry the bank for as long as it took the bank to make the fundamental adjustment required in its asset and liability structure. Normally the Fed would expect this to take no longer than several months, but that is a flexible number.

"Informational" and other calls

To encourage the notion that a loan at the discount window for a legitimate purpose is available on request, the Fed did not use to call an institution that was borrowing for the first time to ask why it was borrowing. Now the Fed does make this call, partly because it wants to get to know the needs of the many new institutions that have been added to its borrowing constituency.

If an institution continues to borrow at the window, the Fed—taking into consideration the amount of the borrowing, the bank's past borrowing record, its frequency of borrowing, and conditions affecting banks of its type at that time—may eventually conclude that the borrowing is getting out of range of the typical need.

Then it would make an *informational call*. This, from the Fed's point of view, has no stigma attached to it. The Fed is trying to get a fix on where the bank is and on how much longer it expects to rely on the Fed. The call lets the bank know that it has reached a point where the Fed is taking an interest in it, and it gives the bank an opportunity to tell the Fed what its problems are and what it is doing to cope with them. Normally this suffices, and within a few weeks the bank will have taken steps to cope with its problems—cut its loans or sought out new deposits.

But if an additional period goes by and no improvement occurs, the Fed will make a second *administrative counseling call*. The purpose of this call is to tell the bank that its borrowing pattern is becoming atypical or excessive and that it is time for the bank to terminate its borrowing. Normally such a call will end the borrowing. It is rare that the Fed has to make a final call to say that the bank must terminate its borrowing as of a certain date.

Reverses and loans at the window

The Fed has an administrative rule that an institution should not do reverses with the Fed if it expects at the time that it might borrow from the Fed during the settlement week. The rationale is to prevent banks from using the window to fund a profitable arbitrage. However, there are qualifications to this rule. If a bank thinks it is in good shape with respect to its reserve position and does reverses and then something changes in the interim—operational problems or whatever—the Fed would not object to the bank borrowing at the window. Also there is no problem in borrowing if a bank acts as a conduit for customer funds in doing reverses.

The Fed has an additional rule that an institution should not be a net seller of Fed funds during a period in which it borrows at the discount window. This again is to prevent borrowing at the discount window from being part of a for-profit arbitrage.

Extended credit

Banks. Besides granting loans at the window to facilitate short-term adjustments, the Fed will grant longer-term financing to institutions encountering fundamental problems. There are two situations in which the Fed provides such emergency aid. One is when an act of God—flood, hurricane, or whatever—adversely affects a group of banks, their borrowers or their depositors. For example, a hailstorm wipes out a crop and causes farmers to withdraw deposits from local banks. Such a situation would call for prolonged loans to the affected banks and a program to restore them to financial health.

The Fed will also grant emergency long-term financing to a single bank if in its judgment the risks to the banking system as a whole of not doing so are sufficiently great to warrant providing credit to that bank while another solution is worked out. This is the primary reason the Fed got into the Franklin Bank loan and let it get up to $1.7 billion; the Penn Central and the Herstatt had already failed. Thus, failure of the Franklin—the 20th largest bank in the U.S.—at that time might have threatened the public's confidence in the whole banking system.

Even if a single bank's failure would not threaten to bring down the whole house of cards, the Fed feels a responsibility to help out a bank that gets into trouble if it is in fact salvageable. In the Fed's view, a bank that holds reserves has paid its dues, and help in time of need is one of the benefits that it gets.

Thrifts.   Following passage of the Monetary Control Act of 1980, the Fed instituted an extended credit program for thrifts designed to carry them through periods of disintermediation. The program however, is not the general industry-wide bail out that the thrifts wanted. The Fed put a lot of restrictions on what institutions borrowing under this program may do. These restrictions, which include a prohibition of new lending, have made borrowing under this program so unattractive that few institutions have used it. For long-term adjustment needs, the Fed thinks it appropriate that S&Ls continue to think first of the FHLB as their special lender of last resort; it is, and the Fed does not want to compete in this area with the FHLB.

Historically the bulk of the loans that the Fed has made at the discount window have been to help borrowing institutions meet *temporary* liquidity needs. The Monetary Control Act opened the discount window to a lot of institutions, thrifts included, who normally do not have this sort of problem and therefore are not natural borrowers at the discount window.

Others.   The Fed also has limited statutory authority to grant emergency loans to individuals, partnerships, and corporations. This authority was used during the 1930s to grant about 125 loans totaling a mere $1 million; it has not been used since. However, questions have been raised at to whether the Fed could or should use this authority to bail out the Penn Central, Lockheed, and more recently New York State agencies and New York City. In the case of the latter, the Fed's response was that—if the federal government *broadly defined* were going to provide assistance to states, municipalities, and their agencies individually—it should do it directly by decision of Congress and the administration. Had the Fed gotten into the business of lending to New York City, it would also have faced the question of whether to lend to Detroit and other troubled cities.

Seasonal credit

In 1973 the Fed instituted a program for providing seasonal credit to smaller banks that lack access to the national money market. The purpose of the program was to meet anticipated borrowing needs for banks in resort communities, agricultural centers, and other areas where local businesses need to borrow funds early in the seasonal cycle and make their profits later. Loans made under this program represent only a small proportion of the total credit granted by the Fed at the discount window.

Collateral

Banks make uncollateralized loans to their customers on the basis of their financial position. So it is natural to ask why the Fed, instead of demanding collateral at the discount window, should not make unsecured loans to member banks that it regulates and whose condition it knows well.

The answer is that many inside and outside of the Fed would like to do away with collateral at the discount window because doing so would reduce record keeping, securities transfers, and other paperwork associated with discounting, which in turn would make discounting cheaper and simpler both for the Fed and for institutions that borrow at the window. For the collateral requirement on loans at the discount window to be eliminated, however, Congress would have to amend the Federal Reserve Act. Passage of such an amendment appears politically impossible because many members of Congress would view such a change as subjecting the Fed to a risk of loss. That risk, however, is one to which the Fed is already exposed because its responsibility to provide emergency aid to troubled institutions, presumably might force it to lend against questionable collateral, as in the Franklin Bank situation.

MONETARY POLICY IN RECENT YEARS

While from 1975 on, the Fed publicly described its policy as one of controlling the growth of the monetary aggregates; its method of seeking to do so was indirect, to say the least. At that time and even today, the FOMC's directives to the New York *open-market desk* contain two sets of targets: a target range for the Fed funds rate and target ranges of growth for various measures of the money stock. To the uninitiated, an FOMC directive that says the desk shall carry out open-market operations so that Fed funds trade at X and money supply grows at rate Y sounds tidy and reasonable. As noted in Chapter 2, however, the Fed has only one policy tool, adjusting bank reserves—the impact of which it can augment by changes in the discount rate and in required reserve ratios. An institution charged with implementing policy that is given only one tool can, as economists have long noted, *hit only one target.* If it manages to hit two, the event is fortuitous.

Thus, Fed policymakers, whatever their public pronouncements may be, must view achieving one target—interest rate levels or money supply growth—as *the* binding constraint on how open-market operations shall be run; they must view achieving the second target as something which they hope—pray—will occur as a stroke of luck due to the well-intentioned. The alternative of foundering back and forth to achieve both goals is a recipe for achieving neither.

Prior to 1979, the Fed sought to control the growth of the monetary aggregates by controlling the Fed funds rate. If the monetary aggregates were growing too fast, the FOMC would instruct the open-market desk to raise the Fed funds rate, and vice versa. At the time, the market was accustomed to having the Fed fine tune the funds rate; and the desk could, by making a few signals to the market, get funds to trade where it wanted them to. No highly precise adjustments of reserves was required.

During this period, Fed policy was not noticeably successful. A major problem was that the FOMC always moved the Fed funds target rate by only small amounts, ½ or ¼%. Moving the funds rate from 10 to 10¼% affected a few holders of securities but not much else. Fed policymakers were loath to move the funds rate by large amounts partly because they always took the view that things were *uncertain* and that maybe a month later they would know better where things stood, which they never did. Consequently, they never acted decisively to control spending either by tightly controlling the growth of the money supply or by sharply raising interest rates. Whereas changing the Fed funds rate by ¼% had no major impact on either money supply growth or spending, raising it from 10 to 13 or even 15% might have had. That experiment was one that the Fed was unwilling to make.

Prior to August 1979, William Miller was Chairman of the Fed, and Carter was in the White House. Miller, a team player, lacked strong convictions on what monetary policy should be, and Carter, elected by a party filled with populists, was not about to suggest that the play his monetary quarterback call be to control the growth of the money stock so tightly that monetary policy would slow spending and inflation, strengthen the exchange value of the dollar, and, in all probability, also induce a sharp rise in interest rates and a recession. By August of 1979, indirection in macro policymaking was becoming intolerable. The dollar was in crisis, and Carter, in choosing a new chairman for the Fed, had to pick a strong person who would command the respect of foreign central bankers and of the international financial community in general. His choice was Paul Volcker, then Chairman of the New York Fed.

The "Saturday night special." In October 1979, Volcker instituted a dramatic change in Fed policy. Previously, the Fed attempted to control the supply of nonborrowed reserves so that Fed funds would track a target level that in turn was supposed to induce the money supply to grow within the Fed's target bands. Volcker switched gears 180°; he declared that henceforth the Fed would seek to control the growth of the monetary aggregates directly by holding the growth of nonborrowed reserves on a strict target path. To do so, the Fed necessarily had to relinquish its hitherto tight control over the Fed funds rate. In a nutshell, the new Volcker policy was to tightly control the growth of reserves, which form the basis of the money supply, and let funds trade where they would.

In the same month, the Fed also sought to directly curtail the expansion of bank lending by imposing an 8% marginal reserve requirement on increases in the managed liabilities of large banks. The market responded dramatically to these policy changes—dubbed Volcker's "Saturday night special" because it was announced on Saturday, October 6. Interest rates, which on October 5 had already risen in anticipation of further tightening by the Fed, moved sharply up again in response to the Fed announcement on the following day of changes in its policy; and the rates continued to move higher through March 1980 (Figure 8–2).

FIGURE 8–2
The yield curve before and after the Fed's "Saturday night special"

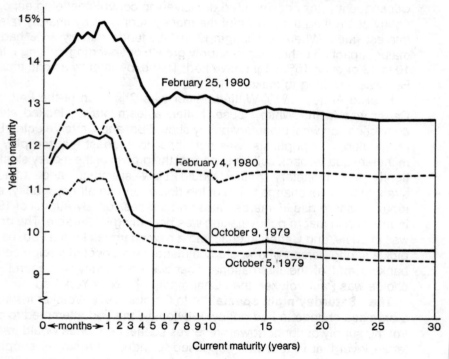

Ironically, the Fed, in the name of strictly controlling the money supply, began for the first time to experiment with the impact that tight money—in the form of high and sharply rising interest rates—would have on the economy. The new Fed policy is often described as a *reserves-oriented operating procedure*. The FOMC chooses a rate of growth for the monetary aggregates. Then the staff of the Washington Fed and the FOMC decide, in consultation with the manager of the system account in New York, what level of reserves is required to support the prescribed growth in the aggregates. The New York desk then supplies that level of reserves. The desk takes estimates of excess and borrowed reserves as given, and focuses on nonborrowed reserves, a residual variable. If the Fed's pursuit of its targets tightens credit-market conditions, borrowed reserves will rise, forcing up short-term interest rates. The Fed may seek to offset the effect of increased borrowings by reducing the nonborrowed reserves it supplies to the market, a move that will, in turn, reinforce the upward trend in short-term rates. Under the new system of pegging reserves rather than the funds rate, the Fed needs to and does, in fact, intervene much less frequently in the market than it did prior to October 1979.

Revolutions normally occur in steps, and the change in monetary policy instituted by Volcker was no exception. After October 1979, the Fed continued, as it still does, to set target bands for the rates within which Fed funds should trade. Until December 1980, the desk had to consult with the chairman if pursuit of the reserve target seemed likely to push the funds rate out of the enlarged band in which funds were permitted to trade. During the period from October to December, movements of the funds rate outside the prescribed bands put only temporary and modest constraints on the implementation of the Board's new reserves operating procedure. In December, the desk was directed to continue to aim for its reserve objective regardless of where funds traded, with the proviso that the chairman be notified if funds traded outside their prescribed range. Currently that range, which has varied from 4 to over 8 percentage points, is so wide as to place no constraint on the desk's efforts to achieve its reserve target.

What is money?

That the Fed's attempt, beginning in October 1979, to control the monetary aggregates *strictly* resulted in a policy any good Keynesian could have prescribed for controlling inflation—a sharp rise in interest rates—was not the only irony the Fed faced in the winter of 1980. It was simple for Congress to instruct the Fed to control the growth of the money supply. The difficult task was and is for the Fed to define precisely what money is, particularly in recent years when the strains imposed on deposit-accepting institutions by various regulations, in particular by controls placed on the rates they may pay depositors, have spawned a variety of new and rapidly growing institutions and instruments: new NOW and ATS accounts, new time deposit certificates (including MMCs), money market funds, and further growth of the Eurodollar market. Rate deregulation promises to further complicate the task of defining money supply; it in fact did with the introduction of MMDAs and super-NOW accounts.

In February 1980, the Fed abandoned its old definitions for a new, expanded set (Table 8–1, p. 234). The new M1B recognized the growing importance of NOW accounts, which are, in effect, interest-bearing checking accounts. M2 recognized, in addition, that a lot of small-denomination time deposits (money market certificates in particular) and money fund shares are instruments that individuals and corporations currently use for holding what amount to money balances.

Finally, the large money supply measure, L, recognized that individuals and, to a greater degree, institutional investors rely on a host of highly liquid instruments for holding their money balances. Contemplation of the scope of L and of the fact that even it is not all-inclusive is sobering. To theorize in the ivory towers of academia about the role of the money supply in economic activity is easy. To even measure, let along control, money supply in the real world may be impossible.[11]

A final irony is that granting permission to all deposit-accepting institutions to offer NOW accounts caused M1A to start to decline in November 1981, as deposits shifted out of it into M1B which consequently grew more rapidly than it would have otherwise (Figures 8–3 and 8–4). In January 1982, the Fed, recognizing this, scrapped M1A and dubbed what had been M1B simply M1. Definitions of money supply began the decade of the 1980s displaying a rapid rate of obsolescence.

The Fed's problem in measuring money is not only in defining money but in getting accurate numbers on whatever it has defined money to be. Every Friday afternoon, the Fed announces money supply figures.[12] It is the dream of monetarists that these figures fall neatly along a prescribed growth path. In practice, they fall all over the lot. Weekly money supply numbers, which are always revised—often by substantial amounts—are full of "noise" and sometimes contain large errors. In addition, the seasonal adjustments the Fed makes in these numbers at times loom *very* large relative to week-to-week changes in the money supply; worse still, because of the rapidly changing way in which people hold their money balances, the validity of these adjustments is dubious.

The upshot of all this is that there is a large random element in week-to-week changes in the money supply figures announced by the Fed.

---

[11] This prospect is not disturbing to all economic theorists. Many would argue that outsized increases in the money supply, however it is measured, are the *result* rather than the *cause* of excessive aggregate demand and of the inflation it induces. A hyperinflation, during which the government's presses print money literally full-time, seems to be one case in which monetarism's supposed causal chain works. But even in a hyperinflation the root cause of the problem is not the rolling of the presses but rather government spending, unmatched by tax revenues, that causes them to roll.

[12] The Fed announces a figure for M1 every Friday afternoon. It announces figures for M2, M3, and L only on the last Friday of each month.

FIGURE 8–3
M1A (discontinued in January 1982) grew erratically week to week and was rarely within the Fed's target bands

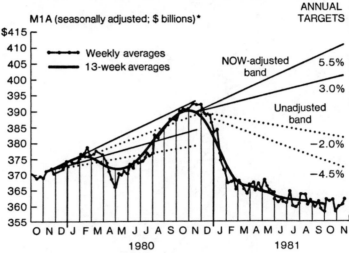

* Data not adjusted for effects of NOW accounts.
Source: The Morgan Bank.

Consequently, announcement of these figures, to which the market always reacts sharply, has become the basis for a weekly crap game on Wall Street. More important, the weekly money figures give the Fed a questionable yardstick for measuring what its policies have wrought. This is why the Fed always says it never bases policy on a single week's or on several weeks' money supply figures.

March 1980: Credit controls

By March 1980, interest rates had reached what were then regarded as astronomical levels, and the Carter administration directed the Fed to impose credit controls in an attempt to curb spending directly. At the same time, the Fed increased from 8 to 10% the marginal reserve requirement, imposed in October 1979, on the managed liabilities of large banks, and it reduced the base upon which this reserve requirement was calculated. The Fed also imposed a similar reserve requirement on monies bought by large nonmember banks, a new 15% reserve requirement on increases in the assets of money market funds, and a surcharge on borrowings by large banks at the discount window.

The Fed's actions in March 1980, threw the growth rates of M1A and M1B into a tailspin (Figures 8–3 and 8–4). Bank lending fell off because the Fed mandated that it do so. In addition, the economy slipped into a

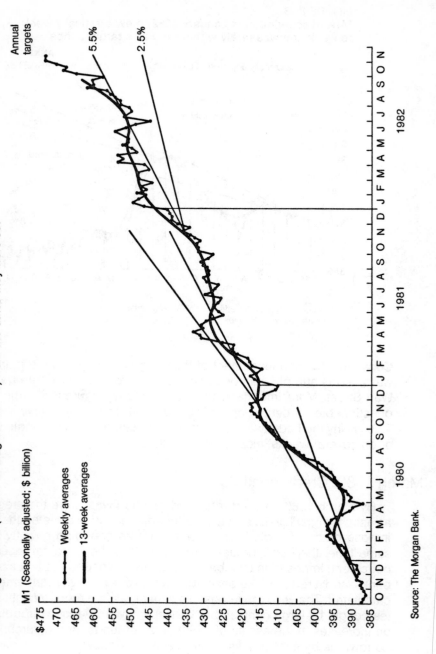

FIGURE 8–4
M1B, which in January 1982 became simply M1, has grown erratically week to week and was often outside the Fed's target bands (shown in diagram as <s) from the dates they were set

M1 (Seasonally adjusted; $ billion)

●—— Weekly averages
—— 13-week averages

Annual targets

5.5%

2.5%

$475
470
465
460
455
450
445
440
435
430
425
420
415
410
405
400
395
390
385

O N D J F M A M J J A S O N D J F M A M J J A S O N D J F M A M J J A S O N
        1980   1981   1982

Source: The Morgan Bank.

mini recession. At the same time, interest rates started to plummet, first because credit controls forced the banks to reduce the amount of funds for which they were bidding in the market and second because the economy began to weaken (Figure 8–5). By June, short-term rates had fallen 1,000 basis points. In this environment, the Fed phased out credit controls between May and July.

In reaction to the sharp decline in money supply numbers, the Fed also pumped nonborrowed reserves into the system (Figure 8–6). It continued to do so until midsummer, at which time interest rates were again on the rise and M1A and M1B were back in their target ranges. At that point, money supply again began growing at outsized rates, the basis for this growth being the excessive reserves the Fed had pumped into the system in previous months.

In late 1980, interest rates hit historical new highs. Then in January 1981, they fell off sharply but quickly rebounded to their previous peak levels and stayed there for four months, after which they began a gradual decline. During this period, the Fed first sopped up the excess reserves it had supplied to the banks and then allowed reserves to again expand (Figure 8–6).

By 1981, it was clear that interest rates were determined by the Fed's reaction function. The unanswered question was to what was the Fed reacting? After all deposit-accepting institutions were permitted to offer NOW accounts in late 1980, M1A plunged, as was to be expected. From then on, the Fed had to be focusing on M1B and M2. During much of 1981, M1B, renamed M1 when the old M1A was dropped in January 1982, looked at on the basis of a 13-week moving average, was behaving— moving within or below its prescribed growth bands—and thus providing no basis for historically high interest rates. At the same time, however, M2 was growing much more vigorously (Figure 8–7). Finally, in the fall of 1981, as the economy showed signs of moving into a recession, the Fed eased by starting to supply more reserves to the banking system (Figure 8–6). Short-term interest rates declined rapidly, long-term rates more slowly; both, by historical standards, remained high in both nominal and real terms.

The major difference between the events of the fall of 1981 and those following the imposition of credit controls is that the Fed moved less rapidly to expand bank reserves in the fall of 1981 than it did following the imposition of credit controls. Also, it permitted interest rates to fall more slowly and to bottom out at a higher level (Figure 8–5). Presumably the Fed had learned a lesson in the spring of 1980. This time around it was seeking not to repeat the mistake it had made then; it was trying to avoid pumping into the system reserves that would establish the basis for subsequently outsized growth of the money supply and a new, sharp rise in interest rates.

FIGURE 8–5
Since October 1979, the pursuit of monetarism by the Fed has created high and highly volatile short-term interest rates.

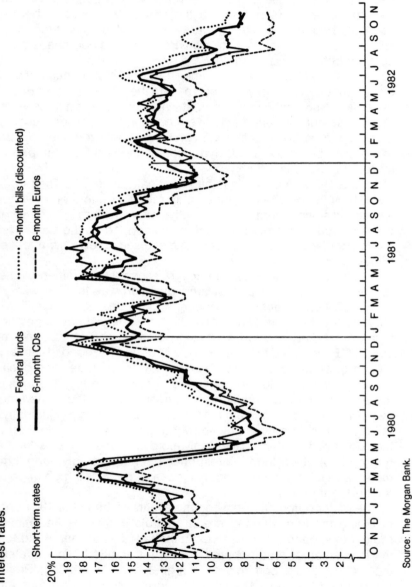

Source: The Morgan Bank.

FIGURE 8–6
The Fed's attempt to control the growth of M1 (old M1B) has caused it to widely vary the rate at which it increases the supply of reserves available to the banking system.

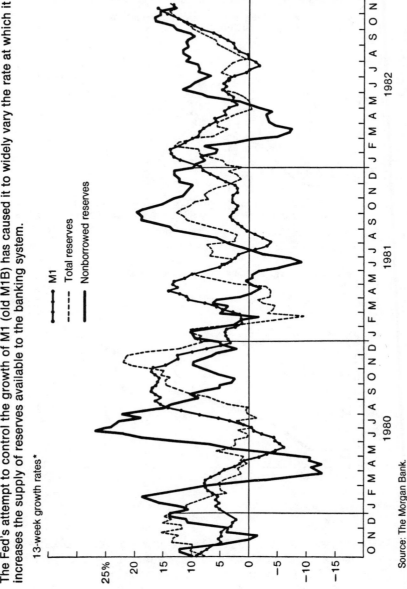

13-week growth rates*

●—● M1
---- Total reserves
—— Nonborrowed reserves

Source: The Morgan Bank.

FIGURE 8–7
In recent years, M2 has grown much more rapidly than M1

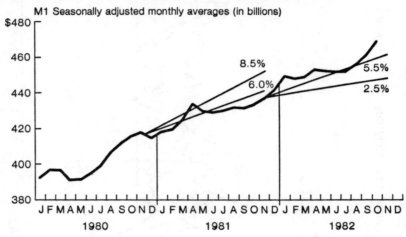

M1 Seasonally adjusted monthly averages (in billions)

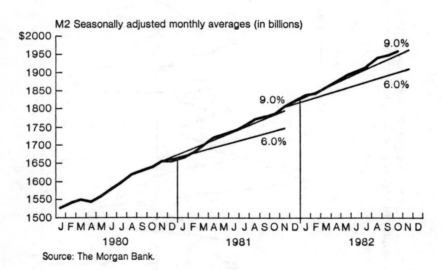

M2 Seasonally adjusted monthly averages (in billions)

Source: The Morgan Bank.

Nonetheless, by late 1981 M1 was growing well above the Fed's target band for it and continued to do so throughout the first half of 1982 (Figure 8–7). At the same time, M2 was growing at or above the upper band of 9% that the FOMC had established for it. In response the Fed sharply cut, from the end of 1981 through the spring of 1982, the rate at which it was increasing nonborrowed reserves (Figure 8–6). This caused interest rates to surge and then to remain high into the early summer of 1982.

In July 1982 the growth of M1 on a moving-average basis (Figure 8–7) again got within the Fed's target bands, and M2 growth was close to target range. From then on, the Fed supplied reserves to the banking system on an increasingly generous basis; and interest rates declined sharply (Figure 8–5). By late summer 1982, M1 was again growing sharply above the Fed's upper band, while M2 growth noticeably exceeded the upper band set by the FOMC (Figure 8–7).

Some time in the second half of 1982, the Fed decided, temporarily at least, to pay less attention to the aggregates. Whether this change was temporary or permanent remained to be seen. What was clear was that Volcker was a pragmatist. Had the Fed followed a policy of strictly controlling the aggregates, it would have been forced, during the fall of 1982, to follow an absurd path: to tighten at a time when the economy had weakened and seemed unable to get moving and when inflation appeared well under control, for the moment at least.

Instead of tightening, the Fed continued to feed nonborrowed reserves into the banking system at a generous pace, and short-term rates continued to decline sharply. Long-term rates also declined, and a huge rally occurred in the bond market. This rally, however, left real interest rates at historical highs reflecting investors' fears that the defeat of inflation might prove temporary, that the huge overhang of long-term financing that needed to be done by both public and private borrowers might again push up long rates, and that the Fed—having shifted gears so often from easing to tightening—might do so again. Noted one bond trader, "It took the Fed five years to destroy the long bond market; it will take them another five to recreate it."

Officially the Fed never abandoned its monetarist stance. Initially it defended its easing in the summer of 1982 on the basis of the good behavior of money supply figures. However, at its October 1982 meeting, the FOMC concluded that M1 would "inevitably be distorted" during the final months of 1982 by the billions of dollars in maturing all-savers certificates and by the introduction of the new money market deposit account; consequently it would temporarily pay less attention to the aggregates and in particular to any outsized growth in them. All of this seemed to leave the Fed for the moment, perhaps for good, back where it was pre-October 1979, controlling interest rates—but with one key difference: In 1979 inflation was out of control; as 1983 began, it was under control.

The new money market accounts

A further reason for the Fed to demphasize in late 1982 the aggregates in charting its policies was the anticipated introduction of the new money market deposit accounts authorized by Congress, which in the

1982 Banking Act specifically stipulated that depository institutions were to be enabled to offer accounts on terms competitive with those of money funds. These new accounts were described in Chapter 2 (pp. 23–25).

How the new federally insured accounts would affect the money holding habits of consumers and of business firms was impossible to predict. In the past consumers have displayed little inclination to take their money out of money funds once they put them there. Certainly any big shift of funds out of money funds into the new MMDAs and super-NOW accounts at depository institutions, besides substantially increasing the cost structure of smaller institutions, would increase M1 at the price of diminishing M2. In the words of Chairman Volcker, "We're on our way to destroying M1."

What was/is the Fed really doing?

It is hard, in fact impossible, to find any informed person in the money market who believes that someone who really understands the money market and commercial banking could be a monetarist. That raises the question of how monetarist the Fed truly is.

Since passage of the Humphrey-Hawkins Act and more especially since the arrival in Washington of the Reagan administration with its monetarists—including Beryl Sprinkel at the Treasury—the Fed has had no choice but to publicly espouse monetarism. That in no way means that the Fed may not be Keynesian in the closet. The Keynesian prescription for a high rate of inflation is high real rates of interest; during 1981 and the first half of 1982, Fed policy had, in fact, a very Keynesian hue.

A major goal of monetarism is to reduce—preferably to zero—the discretion the Fed has always exercised in implementing monetary policy. The great irony of the public espousal of monetarism by the Fed is that, by proclaiming itself to be monetarist, the Fed has vastly increased its range of discretion. As Arthur Burns realized some years ago the Fed can—by picking and choosing among the various money growth rates and among the different periods over which these rates can be measured—justify almost any action it wants to take.

Moreover, since setting targets for the monetary aggregates is highly technical, the Fed can—without fear of dispute from Congress—set targets for whatever M it likes, even if those are targets that the Fed realizes will drive interest rates to historical peaks.[13] If, alternatively, the Fed said to Congress, "Our objective is to have funds trade in the 18 to 19% range," a hue and cry would arise not only from Congress, but from one end of the land to the other.

---

[13] Serious threats by Congress to dictate that the Fed focus on stabilizing interest rates at "reasonable levels," did not materialize until the fall of 1982.

As these observations suggest, it is possible that what the Fed was doing in 1981 and early 1982 was pursuing a tight money policy in the form of *high interest rates:* a policy that it justified by looking at whatever money figure supported its actions. Conceivably, Volcker felt that, with a strong Republican administration in power—one dedicated to cutting government spending and slowing inflation—there was a chance, perhaps the last in a generation, to break the back of inflation by using high interest rates to brake the economy and to hold down the price indexes for a sufficient period to kill inflationary expectations; expectations that—so long as they persisted—were bound to reignite the fires of inflation.

The Bank of England, which over the last several decades has jounced interest rates up and down a good bit more than the Fed has, never espoused monetarism to the degree that the Fed has. In the Bank of England's view, their job is to be central bankers not ideologues. An interesting question: How many ideologues sit on the Fed's Board? To the chagrin of monetarists, the number could be zero.

WATCHING THE FED

In the money market there is tremendous substitutability between instruments for both borrowers and lenders. Banks that need funds can go to the Fed funds market, the Euromarket, the repo market, and the CD market, or they can sell off BAs and other securities. Investors have in every maturity range a variety of instruments among which to choose, and depending on their needs and their rate forecasts, instruments of different maturity can also be close substitutes for them. Because of all this substitutability, changes in the Fed funds rate are immediately transmitted to every other sector of the money market.

Because a change in the Fed funds rate affects in a quite predictable way all other short-term rates, everyone in the money market has a tremendous stake in predicting the next move in the funds rate. Banks base the maturity structure of their liabilities in part on where they anticipate funds will trade, and dealers and portfolio managers position on the basis of where they think funds will trade. When either the banks or the dealers position on the basis of a correct prediction, the payoff can run into tens, even hundreds, of millions of dollars; and when they are wrong, the losses can be equally staggering.

Everyone on the street watches the Fed in much the same way. They read the minutes of FOMC meetings, which are released a month after each meeting, to learn the Fed's current targets for money supply growth and secondarily the Fed funds rate. Then they track what has actually been happening to money supply figures against the Fed's target rates of growth. If money supply growth is exceeding the Fed's targets, they anticipate a possible tightening and higher interest rates; if it has been sluggish, they anticipate an easing and lower interest rates.

"Watching the Fed is," said one dealer, "very easy if one can read. There are sunshine laws available. All one has to read is how they go about what they do—and get some experience in watching their little points of finesse such as how they handle customer repo." There is, of course, a 30-day lag between when the Fed sets targets and when the street can read what those targets are. But the street attempts to compensate for this by taking into account everything they know about economic trends and developments in the capital market when they surmise what changes in targets the FOMC might have made at its last meeting.

However easy some dealers may consider watching the Fed, it is still a tricky game. The Fed is looking closely at *two* money supply figures, M1 and M2, which don't always behave in the same way relative to the Fed's target rates of growth for them. Also the Fed tends to respond with a *lag* to out-of-bounds growth rates in the money stock because it waits to see whether a given month's figures reflect a temporary aberration or a longer-term trend that must be counteracted.

Besides watching the Fed in what might be called the big-picture way—focusing on trends over time—the street also watches the Fed on a moment-to-moment basis, looking for some clue as to whether a change in policy might be underway. To do so, the resident Fed watchers at the banks and the dealers make their own estimates of shifts in Treasury balances, of changes in reserve availability, and of the adding or subtracting job the Fed must do. On the basis of these, the street interprets every open market move the Fed makes. If the Fed is doing reverses, they want to know whether it is draining reserves to meet a temporary need or initiating a new tightening.

The street's attempts to read a signal into even the Fed's smallest moves reminds one of a gypsy reading tea leaves. And when carried to extremes, these attempts probably have about the same level of reliability. A common comment on the desk is that the street constantly attributes motives and levels of sophistication to Fed actions that simply do not exist. This is not surprising, since the Fed itself is groping on a moment-to-moment basis to determine what, if anything, needs to be done in the *very* short run.

THE M1 GAME

Every week the Fed compiles and publishes on Friday afternoon figures on the size of the money supply according to the M1 measure defined in Table 8–1; on the last Friday of the month it publishes figures on M2, M3, and L. These figures are at best estimates and are later subject to *substantial* revisions.

There are various reasons for the unreliability of weekly and monthly figures on the money supply. One fourth of all demand deposits are held by nonmember banks that report their deposits on only four call dates a year; the rest of the time the Fed has to estimate what deposits they hold. Also, seasonal factors are important but so erratic that it is difficult to build up enough experience to tell what the seasonal adjustment factors should be. It is also hard to adjust for changes in float, Treasury balances, tabulating errors, and the like.

However worthless figures on weekly changes in the money supply may be, they are taken *seriously* by the street. The Fed claims that errors and random changes in weekly money supply figures are so great that it never bases its actions on one week's numbers; therefore it is absurd for the street to place great emphasis on them. But the street believes that one week's figures can make a difference. There is probably some justification for this view because, while just a week of high or low monetary growth won't stir the Fed to action, every now and then one week's numbers turn out to be the straw that broke the camel's back—that caused the Fed to conclude that a trend that must be counteracted was under way.

There is also another element to the street's attitude. The street needs a benchmark, and it always picks one. In that selection it is not the least dogmatic. It used to look at free reserves, now it looks at money supply figures.

Because the street watches money supply figures so closely and has so much faith that they influence Fed policy, the reaction of the street to Friday afternoon announcements of money supply figures is *violent*. If money supply growth is way down, a buying panic occurs; if it is way up, a selling panic occurs.

Because the stakes are huge, every large bank and dealer on the street has someone tracking money supply figures and making in-house predictions of how the money supply will change over the week. The incentive is that real money can be made and losses avoided by basing short-term positions on correct predictions of money supply figures.

However, no matter how much information and manpower street firms put into their money supply projections, and some put in a lot, these projections turn out to be poor. Said a top practitioner of the art, "I predict money supply figures every week, but the traders in the shop treat my predictions with some reservation. I get lucky at times, at other times I am not. On the whole I do not know of anyone doing this sort of work whose record is good." This is unsurprising given the many random elements and errors that affect the weekly money supply figure published by the Fed.

Because money supply figures are considered to be so important by the street and because no one can predict them accurately, Friday afternoon has come to be a giant crap game on the street. It is as if the Fed every Friday afternoon threw dice and all the dealers and banks bet on the outcome. Commented one dealer with slight exaggeration, "It's crazy what goes on. The stakes are getting so large that it is coming to the point where we are inviting the mafia to come in and find out ahead of time what the M1 figure on Friday will be."

The Fed would like to remedy this situation, but there seems to be no way it can. "We do not know," said one thoughtful observer at the Fed, "what to do about the Friday afternoon crap game. The market looks at the numbers because we do. The market is not the least bit doctrinaire and will look at anything we look at. They do not care about the relationship of money supply to economic activity. We are the source of the problem. I do not know of any way out, and I think that the market would like to get out from this situation. We cannot publish the numbers less frequently, and the numbers are unlikely to get a lot better in the next few years. So unless we abandon the monetary aggregates as targets, we are never going to solve this problem."

FORECASTING INTEREST RATES

Every bank, dealer, and investor is busily predicting interest rates over various time spans. Money market participants base many of their decisions on relatively short time horizons, and they are most concerned with and have the most confidence in quite short-term predictions of interest rates. A good many of them believe that interest rate levels can be predicted with better than 50% accuracy for short periods—a month or two or three—but that somewhere beyond that their predictability diminishes sharply.

In predicting short-term interest rates, Fed watching is a big input in everyone's calculations. There are, however, other inputs. Interest rate predictors are voracious readers of every bit of news on economic trends and the ups and downs of economic indicators. In addition, they estimate the funds that borrowers are likely to demand and lenders are likely to supply; more demand than supply means that rates are likely to be forced up. One important element in such estimates is the Treasury's projected borrowing needs. The Treasury estimates them, but the street feels that the Treasury's figures are often unrealistic because of political considerations—the Treasury has to stick with the official projection of GNP in predicting its revenues and with the official projection of the inflation rate in predicting its expenditures. Other problems also crop up. For example, Defense Department expenditures may run for months below projected levels due to unanticipated delays in procurement.

People on the street predicting interest rates also plug into their calculations the predictions of interest rates produced by the major economic models—the Wharton model and the models constructed by Data Resources, Chase Econometric Associates, and others. In addition, many banks, dealers, and even large investors have their own sophisticated computer models for making interest rate predictions. The time span of econometric projections of interest rates tends, however, to be much longer than that on which money market participants base their decision. So the economists and econometricians who are employed by banks and dealers—and they are legion—are by and large kept politely but firmly out of the trading room.

The yield curve as a predictor

Another predictor of interest rates that many people on the street look at is the yield curve. The argument for the yield curve as a predictor of interest rates is best illustrated with an example. In October 1982 the 3-month bill was trading at 7.62, the 6-month bill at 8.00, and the 9-month bill at 8.40 (see Figure 8–8). Presumably many people holding the 3-

FIGURE 8–8
The yield curve in the bill market, November 1982

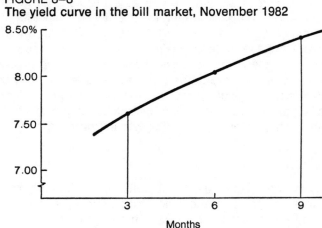

month bill had longer-term money to invest and could therefore have bought the 6-month bill, which was yielding 38 basis points more than the 3-month bill. For them not to have done so implies that they expected that the 3-month bill 3 months hence would yield 8.38, i.e., that by rolling the 3-month bill they could earn the same *average* return over 6 months as they could by buying the 6-month bill.[14] Similarly, the fact that the 9-

---

[14] For the formula to precisely calculate the *forward* rates implied by cash bill rates, see Stigum and Mann, *Money Market Calculations,* pp. 54–57.

month bill yielded 8.40 implies that investors expected the 3-month bill 6 months hence to also trade at 8.80. This sort of argument can be applied to any stretch of the yield curve, so that throughout its length the shape of this curve reflects the street's expectations as to what future interest rates will be and thus provides implicit consensus predictions of future rates.

How good these predictions are is debatable. Presumably they have a bearish cast, because the farther the investor goes out along the maturity scale, the greater the price risk to which he is exposed. The amount of that bearish bias is impossible to measure, but the assumption used to be that it works out in ordinary times to be 1% over the length of the yield curve. Since 1979 ordinary times have not prevailed.

Whether the yield curve is a good or bad predictor of interest rates, the investor cannot ignore the implicit rate predictions made by it. In the situation described above, an investor who bought the 3-month bill when he had 6-month money to invest would be implicitly betting that the 3-month bill 3 months hence would be yielding at least 8.80. He should know that this is his bet and should ask whether it is a good bet, not make it randomly.

With respect to the yield curve as a predictor of interest rates, it is amusing and perhaps revealing to note that Ralph Nader, in a freedom of information suit, forced the Fed to make public an internal memo that observed that the yield curve had a better track record at predicting interest rates than the Fed's own model. Depending on one's opinion of the yield curve as a predictor, this can be taken to imply that econometric models are abysmally poor at predicting interest rates, that the yield curve is a better predictor of interest rates than most people on the street believe, or that interest rates simply can't be predicted!

M1 OR WHAT?

We have noted the importance attached by the Fed in policymaking to the impact of its actions on the money supply and the importance attached by the street to changes in money supply.

All the prominence given to the money supply raises the question of just what money is. Clearly the Fed is unsure, since it mentions in the FOMC directive several measures of money, and it keeps redefining them.

Economists are of no more help in providing a definitive answer as to what money is. Monetarists argue that money is whatever balances the public holds to make transactions. Such balances include all demand deposits and should perhaps include savings deposits. They should not, however, include long-term time deposits (which are included in M2) because they are illiquid. But these balances should probably include large-denomination short-term CDs held by money market investors because they are highly liquid. *And* they should probably include all the various highly liquid short-term instruments (*near monies*), such as overnight RP, Euro call deposits, and short-term commercial paper, that corporations and other investors hold to fund anticipated payments for taxes, to suppliers, and to others. No definition of the money supply, other than L, comes near to being that inclusive.

Economists who are not monetarists argue that money is demanded not only for transactions purposes but as a financial asset. This position opens the door to a very inclusive measure of money supply, but it is impossible to say just what that measure should be; the attraction of money as a financial asset lies in its liquidity, a property that assets possess in degrees.

The facts that it is impossible to measure the money supply at any time and that what serves as money undoubtedly changes over time throw into question the validity of making the growth of the money supply a major policy target. In this respect the comment of one of the street's most astute Fed watchers is of interest, "There is no question but that the Fed responds to short-run gyrations in the money supply. But the Fed is eclectic. I think they align their 2-month growth targets to give them the policy that most closely follows the policy they want to implement based on the fundamentals of the economy—the unemployment rate, the inflation rate, and so forth. I think the Fed now realizes the unimportance of short-run changes in money supply and uses them as a basis to change policy merely as a front to insulate its policies from criticism by Congress." This comment made in 1977 may just possibly be as appropriate now as it was then. Is a pragmatic Fed now setting interest-rate targets on the basis of fundamentals such as the rate of inflation and the level of economic activity?

Perhaps—an intriguing possibility—money supply isn't so important after all.

Chapter 9

The market makers:
Dealers and others

THE COLLECTION OF MARKETS described in this book is called *the* money market. This suggests that the market's participants trade in a single market where at any time one price reigns for any one instrument. This description is accurate, but that is startling. Money market instruments, with the exception of futures contracts, are traded not on organized exchanges but strictly over the counter. Moreover, money market participants, who vary in size from small to gargantuan, are scattered over the whole United States—*and* throughout Canada, Europe, the Mid East and the Far East. Thus one might expect fragmentation of the market, with big New York participants dealing in a noticeably different market from their London or Wichita counterparts. However, money market lenders and borrowers can operate almost as well out of Dearborn, Michigan, Washington, or Singapore as they can from Wall Street. Wherever they are, their access to information, bids, and offers is (time zone problems excepted) essentially the same. That the money market is a single market is due largely to the activities of the dealers and brokers who weld the market's many participants into a unified whole and to the modern communication techniques that make this possible.

THE DEALERS

Money market dealers are, like bankers, a mixed bag. Some are tiny, others huge. Some specialize in certain instruments, others cover the waterfront. One is also tempted to say that some are immensely sharp and others not so sharp, but the not-so-sharp players lead short lives. Despite dealers' diversity, one can generalize about their operations.

Activities

The hallmark of a dealer is that he buys and sells for his own account; that is, trades with retail and other dealers off his own position. In addition, dealers engage in various activities that come close to brokering.

The prime example of the latter is commercial paper dealers. Each day they help their customers borrow hundreds of millions of dollars from other market participants. Commercial paper dealers' responsibilities are: (1) to advise their clients on market conditions, (2) to ensure that their clients post rates for different maturities that give them the lowest possible borrowing costs but are still high enough to get their paper sold, and (3) for a ⅛ commission, to show and sell that paper to retail. Positioning is part of a commercial paper dealer's operation but only marginally so. Paper dealers will position any of their clients' paper that goes unsold, but amounts to little. One reason is that dealers are careful to ensure that their clients post realistic rates. A second reason is that commercial paper dealers as a group feel that it is not in their best interests or in that of their clients for them to position large amounts of paper. Commercial paper dealers do, however, stand ready to bid for paper bought from them by retail and thus make a secondary market in paper. Such activity leads them at times to position paper, but the amounts are small because the secondary market in commercial paper is not active. Thus dealers in commercial paper act more like brokers than like true dealers.

Dealers also act at times like brokers in the CD market. A bank that wants to do a large program in one fast shot may call one or more dealers and offer then an 05 (5 basis points) on any CDs they can sell to retail. Finally, smaller dealers who are hesitant about the market or who are operating outside their normal market sector at times act more or less as brokers, giving a firm bid to retail only if they can cross the trade on the other side with an assured sale.

As noted, however, brokering is not what dealing is all about. The crucial role dealers play in the money market is as market makers, and in performing that role, they trade off their own positions.

Part of the dealers' role as market makers involves underwriting new issues. Most large municipal note issues are brought up at issue by dealers or syndicates of them who take these securities into position and sell them off to retail. In the market for governments there is also underwriting, though of a less formal nature; frequently dealers buy large amounts of new government issues at auction and then distribute them to retail.

In the secondary market dealers act as market makers by constantly quoting bids and offers at which they are willing to buy and sell. Some of these quotes are to other dealers. In every sector of the money market, there is an *inside market* between dealers. In this market dealers quote price *runs* (bids and offers for securities of different maturities) to other dealers, often through brokers. Since every dealer will *hit* a bid he views as high or take an offering he views as low, trading in the inside market creates at any time for every security traded a prevailing price that represents the dealer's consensus of what that security is worth.

Dealers also actively quote bids and offers to retail. In doing so they consistently seek to give their customers the best quotes possible because they value retail business and they know that other shops are competing actively with them for it. This competition between dealers ensures that dealers' quotes to retail will never be far removed from prices prevailing in the inside market. Thus, all the money market's geographically dispersed participants can always trade at close to identical bids and offers.

As the above suggests, through their trading activities, the dealers give the secondary market for money market instruments two important characteristics. First, they ensure that at any moment a single price level will prevail for any instrument traded in it. Second, by standing ready to quote firm bids and offers at which they will trade, they render money market instruments liquid.

Profit sources

Dealers profit from their activities in several ways. First, there are the 05s and $\frac{1}{8}$s they earn selling CDs and commercial paper. Particularly for firms that are big commercial paper dealers, these commissions mount up to a substantial sum, but in total they represent only a small part of dealers' profits.

A second source of dealers' profits is *carry*. As noted below, dealers finance the bulk of their long positions (muni notes excepted) in the repo market. Their RP borrowings are of shorter maturity than the securities they position. Thus their financing costs are normally less than the yields on the securities they finance, and they profit from *positive* carry.

Carry, however, is an undependable source of profit because, when the yield curve inverts, carry turns negative.[1] As one dealer commented:

---

[1] The yield curve is said to be *inverted* when short-term rates exceed long-term rates. For an inverted yield curve, see Figure 4–7.

"Back in 1974 when Fed funds were 10 to 14%, there was nothing you could position at a positive carry. You might position because you thought rates were going to fall, but not for carry. And you knew *ex ante* that, if you positioned and the market did not appreciate, you would lose money on two levels: carry and depreciation of values. This led to the phenomenon of the Friday night bill trader. At one point, to carry bills over the weekend cost 5 basis points. So traders would attempt on Friday to sell the 90-day bill for càsh settlement and buy it back for regular settlement." The historically unusual period 1979–82 was also characterized much of the time by negative carry.

A third source of dealer profits is what might be called day-to-day trading profits, buying securities at one price and reselling them shortly at a slightly higher price, or shorting securities and covering in at a slightly lower price. How traders seek to earn 02s and 32nds from such trading is discussed later.

The sources of profit mentioned so far suffice to pay dealers' phone and light bills—to cover their overhead. Dealers earn really big money on position plays, that is, by taking into position huge amounts of securities when they anticipate that rates will fall and securities prices will rise or by shorting the market when they are bearish.

Being willing to position on a large scale is characteristic of all dealers, although the appetite of some shops for such *speculation* is stronger than that of others.[2] One might argue that positioning done specifically to speculate as opposed to the positioning that arises out of a dealer's daily trading activities with retail and other dealers is not an inherent part of being a market maker. But such speculation serves useful functions. It guarantees that market prices will react rapidly to any change in conditions, economic or in demand, supply, or rate expectations. Also, and more important, the profits dealers can earn from correct position plays are the prime incentive they have for setting up the elaborate and expensive operations they use daily to trade with retail and each other. In effect position profits help to oil the machinery that dealers need to be effective market makers.

Dealers possess no crystal balls enabling them to perfectly foresee the future. They position on the basis of carefully formulated expectations. When they are right, they make huge profits; when they are wrong, their losses can be staggering. Thus the successful shops and the ones that survive are those that are right on the market more often than wrong.

---

[2] The term *speculation* as used here and throughout the book is *not* meant to carry pejorative connotation. *Speculation is taking an unhedged position, short or long.* A homeowner who buys a house financed with a mortgage is assuming a speculative, levered position in real estate. A dealer who buys governments with RP money is assuming a speculative, levered position in governments. The only difference between the two is that the dealer knows he's speculating; the homeowner used not to think of it that way.

DEALER FINANCING

The typical dealer is running a highly levered operation in which securities held in position may total 500 or 600 times capital. Some dealers rely heavily on dealer loans from New York banks for financing, but as one dealer commented: "The state of the art is that you don't have to." RP money is cheaper, and sharp dealers rely primarily on it to meet their financing needs. For such dealers the need to obtain RP money on a continuing basis and in large amounts is one additional reason for assiduously cultivating their retail customers. The money funds, corporations, state and local governments, and other investors that buy governments and other instruments from them are also big suppliers of RP money to the dealers.

Much of the borrowing dealers do in the RP market is done on an overnight basis. The overnight rate is typically the lowest RP rate. Also, securities "hung out" on RP for one night only are available for sale the next day. Nonbank dealers have to clear all their RP transactions through the clearing banks, which is expensive. As a result they also do a lot of *open repos* at rates slightly above the overnight rate. Open or demand repos have an indefinite term; either the borrower or the lender can each day choose to terminate the agreement.

Banks prefer to do overnight repos with customers who will permit them to safekeep the securities bought. This saves clearing costs and ensures that the bank will have the securities back at 9:00 A.M. the next day. If repoed securities are transferred out of the bank, there is always the possibility that the securities will be delivered back to the bank too late the next day for the bank to repo them again or to make timely delivery if they have been sold. To make RP as convenient an investment as possible, some banks have minimum balance arrangements with customers under which any excess deposit balances the customer holds with them are automatically invested in RP In effect what such a bank is doing is getting around Reg Q and paying the customer interest on any demand deposits he holds in excess of the minimum compensating balance the bank requires him to maintain.

The financing needs that nonbank dealers do not cover in the RP market are met by borrowing from banks at the dealer loan rate. Even dealers who look primarily to the RP market for financing will use bank loans to finance small pieces they hold in inventory. A typical nonbank dealer commented, "The smallest RP ticket I will write is 2 [million]. On a transaction of less than 2, writing the tickets and making deliveries is not worth the cost and trouble. I can combine small pieces, but generally I let such junk just sit at the bank."

In financing, bank dealers have one advantage over nonbank dealers—they can finance odd pieces they do not RP by buying Fed funds.

While much dealer financing is done using open or very short repos, dealers will sometimes finance speculative positions they anticipate holding for some time with term RP, taking in money for 30, 60, or 90 days, or even longer.

Fails and the fails game

If, on the settlement date of a trade, a seller does not make timely delivery of the securities purchased, delivers the wrong securities, or fails in some other way to deliver in proper form, the trade becomes a *fail*. In that case the buyer does not have to make payment until proper delivery is made, presumably the next day; *but* he owns the securities as of the initially agreed-upon settlement day. Thus, on a fail the security buyer (who is *failed to*) receives a one-day free loan equal to the amount of the purchase price, that is, one day's free financing. And if the fail persists, the free loan continues. Fails occur not only in connection with straight trades but in connection with repos; on a repo the lender has to make timely return of the collateral he is holding to unwind the transaction and get his money back.

Dealers often play some portion of their financing needs for a fail; that is, they estimate on the basis of past experience the dollar amount of the fails that will be made to them and reduce their RP borrowing accordingly. If their estimate proves high, more securities will end up in their box at the clearing bank than they had anticipated, and that bank will automatically grant them a box loan against that collateral.[3] On such last-minute loans the clearing banks charge the dealer a rate that's a tiny margin above their posted dealer loan rate to encourage dealers to track their positions and run an orderly shop. A dealer who plays the *fails game* is in effect using his clearing bank as a lender of last resort.

A DEALER'S BOOK

A dealer who takes big positions is operating like a banker. He acquires assets of varying types and maturities and incurs liabilities of varying maturities to finance them. And like a banker, he faces *risks:* credit risks, a rate risk, and a liquidity risk.

Because dealers confine themselves to buying high-grade paper, as opposed to making loans to LDCs, dealers assume fewer and smaller credit risks than banks do. But because they borrow so much short-term money and are so highly levered, the rate risk they assume is substantial. This is especially true because the classic way dealers make a bullish bet is not only to buy *more* securities but also to *extend* to longer maturities where they get more bang for the buck from rate movements.

---

[3] See discussion of dealer loans by clearing banks, pp. 311–14.

With respect to rate risk, a dealer has one advantage over a bank. A bank that makes a fixed-rate loan can't readily sell off that asset to cut its losses if rates start to climb. In contrast, a dealer who positions the 11⅝s of 02 has acquired a liquid asset that can always be sold at some price no matter how bad the market gets.[4] Every dealer, because he is exposed to a large rate risk, is very conscious of the fact that he is running a large *unmatched book.* Moreover, he seeks, like a bank, to profit from that mismatch while simultaneously monitoring it to ensure that it does not become so large that it exposes him to *an unacceptable level* of risk. Noted one dealer, "Any guy who can run a large dealer operation on leverage could run a bank, not the esoterica of loans to Zaire, but the nuts and bolts of asset and liability management."

While bankers talk about managing the mismatch in their book, dealers talk about *tail management,* by which they mean the same thing. Dealers also talk about *indices,* where an index is some average of asset and liability maturities that indicates the rate risk to which they are exposed.

One difference between dealers and banks is that there is much more pressure on the dealer to be right and to be right in the short run. One reason is that dealers mark their assets to market daily and track daily their profits and losses overall and by instrument. A second reason is that dealers' annual compensation is tied closely to performance through bonuses or other devices. As one dealer noted, "If we buy at the wrong moment, we cannot hold a 2-year note, let alone a 10-year bond, to maturity not only because of profit considerations but because of the emotional and psychological damage that holding that security and marking it to market would have on the work group. We have to be right on balance, and we don't have the luxury of being able to wait for the long run to prove us right." A bank, in contrast, while it marks its dealer and trading portfolios to market, may or may not track the performance of its investment portfolio daily, and it certainly does not attempt to mark its loans to market. Thus, in managing its overall position, a bank is confronted less frequently than a dealer with the consequences of its actions, and it can brush under the carpet the consequences of ill-conceived plays by lumping their impact on profit in with overall profits instead of isolating them.

INTEREST RATE PREDICTIONS

The key rate in the money market is the Fed funds rate. Because of the role of this rate in determining dealers' cost of carry (the RP rate is

---

[4] The 11⅝s of 02 are an actively traded Treasury bond that carries an 11⅝% coupon and matures in 2002.

usually slightly below the funds rate), the 90-day bill rate settles close to the Fed funds rate, and other short-term rates key off this combination in a fairly predictable way (Figure 9–1). Thus when a dealer positions, he does so on the basis of a strongly held view with respect to where money

FIGURE 9–1
Other short-term money rates key off the Fed funds rate

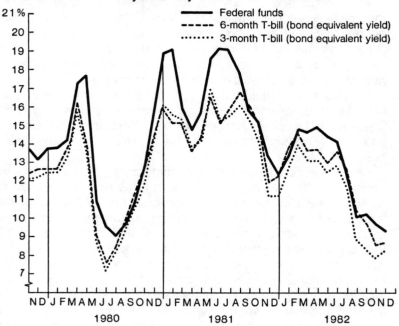

Source: *Federal Reserve Bulletin.*

supply numbers and Fed policy are headed; and *every long position he assumes is, in particular, based on an implicit prediction of how high Fed funds and other money market instruments might trade* within the time frame of his investment. In formulating expectations about the funds rate, dealers engage in constant and careful Fed watching of the sort described in Chapter 8.

CONFIDENCE LEVEL IN POSITIONING

Positioning is a form of gambling, and the dealers most skilled in this art attempt first to express their expectations about what might occur in terms of probabilities of various outcomes and second to estimate the payoff or loss that a given strategy would yield if each of these outcomes were to occur. Then on the basis of these numbers, they decide whether to bet and how much to bet.

Probabilists who have theorized about gambling like to talk about a fair gamble or a *fair game.* A fair game is one that, if played repeatedly, will yield the player neither net gains nor losses. For example, suppose a person plays the following game: A coin is flipped; if it lands heads up, he wins $1; if it lands heads down, he loses $1. The probability that the coin will land heads up is ½. So half the time he bets our player will lose $1; half the time he will win $1; and his *expected winnings* or *return,* if he plays the game repeatedly, is *zero.*

There is nothing in it for a dealer to make a fair bet. What he looks for is a situation in which expected return is *positive;* and the more positive it is, the more he will bet. For example, if a dealer believed: (1) that the probabilities that the Fed would ease and tighten were 60 percent and 40 percent, respectively, and (2) that a given long position would return him $2 if the Fed eased and would cause him to lose $1 if the Fed tightened, then his *expected* winnings would be

$$0.6 \times \$2 - 0.4 \times \$1 = \$0.80$$

In other words, the gamble is such that, if the dealer made it 10 times, his expected winnings would be $8. That degree of favorableness in the bet might suffice to induce the dealer to position.

If the game were made still more favorable, for example by an improvement in the odds, then he would gamble still more. For example, if the dealer believed: (1) that the probabilities that the Fed would ease and tighten were 70 percent and 30 percent, respectively, and (2) that a given long position would again return him $2 if the Fed eased and lose him $1 if the Fed tightened, then his expected winnings would be

$$0.7 \times \$2 - 0.3 \times \$1 = \$1.10$$

In other words, the gamble is such that, if he made it 10 times, his expected winnings would be $11. That's the sort of gamble that might cause the dealer to pull up the delivery trucks and position securities in size.

All this may sound a bit theoretical, but it is the way good dealers think, explicitly or intuitively; and such thinking disciplines them in positioning. As one dealer noted: "The alternative is a sloppy operation in which a dealer runs up his position because he sort of likes the market now or runs it down because he doesn't like the market."

Quantifying his thinking about the market also helps a dealer provide retail with useful suggestions. Most customers can find fair bets on their own. What they appreciate is a dealer who can suggest to them a favorable bet, that is, one on which the odds are out of synchronization with the payoff and the expected return is therefore positive.[5]

In quantifying expectations and payoffs and acting on them, fleet-footedness is essential. Everyone on the street is playing the same game, and the market therefore frequently anticipates what the Fed is going to do. Thus the dealer who waits until the Fed is ready to move will probably be too late to make money, the market having already discounted much or all of that move.

THE MATURITY CHOICE

We suggested that the more favorable the gamble a dealer faces, the more securities he's likely to position. And this is precisely the way dealers talk about what they do; specifically, dealers frequently comment, "The higher our *confidence level,* the more we will position." Translated into the jargon we've used, this means simply that the higher the probability associated with gain and the lower that associated with loss (that is, the higher the expected return), the more the dealer will bet.

There is, however, one more wrinkle to the dealer's positioning decision. As noted, a classic part of a bullish strategy is for a dealer to extend to longer maturities. The reason he is tempted to extend is that the longer the maturity of the securities he positions, the more price play he will get. To illustrate, suppose that a dealer believes that the probability that the average Fed funds rate will fall by 1 point is 70% and the probability it will rise by 1 point is 30%. If the dealer positions the 90-day bill, which has a yield that is likely to move roughly as many basis points as the Fed funds rate does, he will be making a bet on which his potential gains and losses per $1 million of securities positioned are $2,500. If alternatively—to make the example extreme—he invests in the 15¾s of 2001, his potential gains and losses will be in the range of $15,000 per $1 million even if a 1-point move in the Fed funds rate is assumed to move the yield on these securities only 15 basis points. Whether he positions 90-day bills or the 15¾s of 01, the dealer is making a favorable bet. However, positioning the 15¾s of 01 is a much *riskier* bet because, if

---

[5] To keep things simple we assumed in our examples that only two interest rate outcomes were possible. More might be, each with its own associated payoff; Let p_1 equal the probability of the first interest rate outcome and x_1 the associated payoff; p_2 the probability of the second interest rate outcome and x_2 the associated payoff; etc. Then the expected return or value (EV) on a bet in which it is assumed that the Fed might peg Fed funds at any one of three possible levels would be:

$$EV = p_1x_1 + p_2x_2 + p_3x_3$$

Using this approach, one can easily generalize the technique to any number of possible outcomes.

rates rise, the dealer will lose much more owning the 15¾s of 01 than he will owning the 90-day bill.

Dealers are very conscious that extending to longer maturities exposes them to greater *price risk*. They also tend to think that extending to longer maturities exposes them to greater risk for another reason; namely, the predictability of long-term rates is less than that of short-term rates. Short rates relate directly to Fed policy; long rates do so to a much lesser extent because they are also strongly influenced by the *slope* of the yield curve. Thus the dealer who extends must be prepared not only to predict Fed policy but to predict shifts in the slope of the yield curve—an art that is separate from and, in the eyes of many dealers, more difficult than successful Fed watching.

To protect against the risks posed by extending maturity, some dealers confine their unhedged positions largely to securities of short current maturity. A dealer typical of this group noted, "We are accused of being an inch wide and a mile deep—the mile deep being in securities with a maturity of a year and under. There are various arts in this business: predicting spreads, predicting the yield curve, predicting the trend in interest rates. You go with the learning curve of the organization you have, and ours is very strong in predicting short-term spreads and yields."

Other dealers are more willing to extend maturity to reach for gains, but in doing so they seek to control carefully the price risk they assume. The guidelines used to control price risk—frequently they take the form of smaller position limits on longer maturities—vary considerably from shop to shop. One reason is that there is no objective way a dealer can compare the risk he assumes in holding 6-year notes to that he assumes in holding 6-month bills. Another is that in establishing position limits by instrument and maturity, a dealer is inevitably making subjective judgments about the ability of each of his traders.

SHORTING

When money market dealers are bullish, they place their bets by positioning securities: when they are bearish, they do so by shorting. One might expect that the quantity of securities a dealer would short, if he believed that the probability of a fall in securities prices was 80%, would be as great as the quantity of securities he would position if he believed that the probability of a rise in securities prices was 80%. But in fact dealers will, at a given confidence level, short smaller amounts of securities than they would position. There are several reasons. First, the only instruments dealers can short are governments and agencies; other instruments, such as commercial paper, BAs, CDs, and muni notes, are too heterogeneous with respect to name, maturity, and face amount to short. Second, shorting securities tends to be more cumbersome and expensive than going long because the short seller must find not only a buyer but—since the shorted securities must be delivered—a source of these securities.

In recent years it has become increasingly common for dealers to *reverse in* securities shorted rather than to borrow them. One reason is that the reverse may be cheaper. When a dealer borrows securities, he give up other securities as collateral and pays the lender a borrowing fee, which typically equals ½ of 1% but may be more if many people want to short an issue at once. On a reverse the dealer obtains the securities shorted by buying them from an investor with an agreement to repurchase. In effect the dealer is extending a collateralized loan to the owner of these securities. The owner takes the loan because he needs cash or, more typically, because he can reinvest the loan proceeds at a higher rate, and the reverse thus becomes to him part of a profitable arbitrage.

Whether a dealer borrows securities or reverses them in, he must make an *investment*—in the first case in collateral, in the second case in a loan to the institution on the other side of the reverse. To figure which investment would yield more, he compares the rate he could earn on the collateral *minus* the borrowing fee with the reverse rate. For example, suppose a dealer has some short-dated paper yielding 9.25% he could use as collateral. If he did so, he would own that paper at 9.25% minus the 0.5% borrowing fee; that is, at an effective rate of 8.75%. If the reverse rate were 9%, he would do better on the reverse.

A dealer's overall cost on a short is (1) the interest that accrues on the securities shorted (rise in value in the case of a discount security) over the period the short is outstanding, *minus* (2) the yield on the offsetting investment he makes. If the reverse rate exceeds the net rate he could earn on collateral backing a borrowing, reversing will be the cheaper way to support his short.

A dealer who borrows securities to support a short can never know with certainty how long he can have those securities because borrowed securities can be called by the lender on a day's notice. If, alternatively, a dealer reverses in securities for a fixed period, he knows he will have the securities for that time. Thus a dealer who anticipates maintaining a short for some time may choose to cover through a reverse rather than a borrowing not only because the reverse is cheaper but because it offers him certainty of availability.

In this respect it should be mentioned that a dealer can borrow securities from the Fed. He is supposed to do so only when he can't make delivery on securities he has sold because he has experienced a *fail;* that is, because the firm from which he bought the securities he has sold failed to deliver them to him. Dealers who experience difficulty covering a short sometimes stretch a point and borrow the securities shorted from the Fed. However, the Fed's borrowing rate, which increases sharply the longer the borrowing is maintained, is higher than anyone else's, so dealers view borrowing securities from the Fed as a last resort.

RP AND REVERSE BOOK

A large dealer who is known to the street can borrow more in the repo market and at better rates than can a small dealer or a corporate portfolio manager. Thus a large dealer finds knocking at his doors not only customers who want to give him repo money but would-be borrowers who want to reverse out securities to him because that is the cheapest way they can borrow. In response to the latter demand, large dealers have taken to doing repo and reverse not just to suit their own needs but as a profit-making service to customers. In providing that service, the dealer takes in securities on one side at one rate and hangs them out on the other side at a slightly more favorable (lower) rate; or to put it the other way around, the dealer borrows money from his repo customers at one rate and lends it to his reverse customers at a slightly higher rate. In doing so, the dealer is acting like a bank, and dealers know this well. As one noted, "This shop *is* a bank. We have customers lining up every morning to give us money. Also we are in the business of finding people who will give us securities at a little better rate than we can push them out the repo door. So we are a bank taking out our little spread, acting—if you will—as a financial intermediary."

A dealer who seeks to profit by borrowing in the repo market and lending in the reverse market ends up in effect running a *book* in repo. And, like a bank, he can mismatch that book to increase his profit, that is, borrow short and lend long. A dealer who runs a short book in RP incurs not only a rate risk but other risks as well. What these risks are and how different shops seek to control them is a topic left to Chapter 12, where we look closely at the repo and reverse markets.

POSITIONING AND PROFITS

Ever since the Fed turned monetarist with a vengeance in October 1979, interest rates—short- and long-term—have displayed a degree of volatility far exceeding anything experienced in past years (Figure 9–1). As one dealer noted, "Once the Fed switched focus, that meant that the funds rate could fluctuate 200, 300, or even 400 basis points over a 30-day period, whereas five or six years ago that was a huge move that took a long time. Long bonds used to move 3 points over a cycle; now they sometimes move 14 points over three days."

The recent volatility in interest rates has altered both the relative importance which many dealers assign to positioning as a source of profits and also the size and ways in which they are willing to position. Five years ago, it was hard to find a big dealer who did not claim to make his real profits from big position plays that were on the mark. There are still shops that operate this way: They might be satisfied to lose money for four months in small amounts and then to make it big in the fifth month.

Among dealer shops today, however, a more typical attitude is that the first step in building a successful, long-term operation is to establish a mix of dependable profit sources that can be counted on to be there in good markets and bad. For such a shop, position profits are icing on the cake not the cake itself. Typical of this attitude is a bank dealer who noted, "Our focus has changed from one where we were always trying to make large amounts of money from guessing right the big swings in the market to one where we are trying to develop in our department a base of operations that makes money day in and day out. If you can build a business that makes money consistently, then you can afford to speculate with money that you have made as a department, as opposed to speculating with the bank's capital."

One base for earning consistent profits that is getting much attention from dealers these days is retail business. In describing operations, one dealer after another will stress the importance they place on building a solid retail business by providing good markets to retail. Noted one manager, "For us to make money, we had to focus on the real nuts and bolts of the business—service. We look at our business as one in which we provide our clients access to the market, investment advice, risk transfer, and execution."

No dealer can stand ready to make markets with customers without holding inventory and being willing to take securities into position on which customers want to bid. Shops that stress making markets to retail realize this and emphasize techniques to minimize the risks inherent in being a market maker. One technique is hedging. Hedging, which used to be a sometimes affair, now gets a lot of attention especially with the development in Chicago of large and liquid futures markets in governments and other securities. Using these markets, a dealer can transfer the risk generated by customer business back into the markets a lot faster than formerly, and agile shops do just that.

Dealers trying to make money regularly on retail business also strive to develop techniques to anticipate order flow. Said one dealer, "We put a lot of effort into developing relations with major buyers and sellers of securities so that they will give us the inquiry. When we look at the brokers' screens and there is a lot of activity in a sector, we want to know who is participating and what they are doing. This is a crucial part of our business. Now we *all* know what the Fed is doing. What is really tough is to keep on top of and anticipate what retail is or will be doing."

Arbitrage is another base that more dealers are seeking to develop as a source of consistent profits—not spectacular gains but 10 basis points here and 30 there earned by observing an anomaly in the market, taking a position against it, and then having the patience to wait until natural market forces eliminate that anomaly and permit the arbitrage to be unwound at a profit.

Having noted that there is more talk today among dealers about risk control and less bravado about risk taking, we should be quick to add that big differences in attitude still exist among dealer shops. These reflect in part how different firms are organized and the role some dealer operations play in a larger firm that is active in many areas of business. Banks, as highly visible, publicly owned institutions, have always operated under a lot of pressure from bank analysts to generate a *steadily* growing earnings stream; they earn no brownie points for making half a billion this quarter and nothing the next. Some publicly owned nonbank dealers are getting to sound just like bankers. Said one, "As a highly visible public firm, we have had to begin to look at leverage and consistency of earnings because we want to maintain the high perceived value our debt has in the market, and we want the market to view our stock not as cyclical but as blue chip."

Such pressures do not characterize every dealer. Some are privately held firms with a lot of staying power whose mission remains more to be position takers than market makers. They can afford to wait for the moment to make a big play and also to absorb a big loss if, one time out of five, that play proves wrong. There are also firms running dealer operations that are sufficiently large and diversified so that they can afford to take the view that, if their government department makes a lot of money one year, that is pure gravy; if, in another year, it makes nothing, the firm can live with that too.

ARBITRAGES

Strictly defined, the term *arbitrage* means to buy at a low price in one market and simultaneously resell at a higher price in another market. Some arbitrages in this strict sense do occur in the money market. For example, when a Canadian agency bank accepts an overnight Eurodollar deposit from a U.S. corporation and resells the funds at ⅛ markup in the Fed funds market, it is (besides offering the corporation backdoor entry to the funds market) also engaging in arbitrage in the strict sense of the term. Another example of pure arbitrage would be a dealer who takes in collateral on a reverse for a fixed period and RPs it a lower rate for precisely the same period, that is, a matched transaction in repo.

Money market participants use the term *arbitrage* to refer not only to such pure arbitrages but to various transactions in which they seek to profit by *exploiting anomalies* either in the yield curve or in the pattern of rates established between different instruments. Typically the anomaly is that the yield spread between two similar instruments is too wide or too narrow; that is, one instrument is priced too generously relative to the other. To exploit such an anomaly, the arbitrager *shorts* the expensive instrument and goes *long* in its underpriced cousin; in other words, he shorts the instrument that has an abnormally low yield relative to the yield on the instrument in which he goes long.

If the arbitrager is successful, he will be able to unwind his arbitrage at a profit because the abnormal yield spread will have narrowed in one of several ways: (1) the security shorted will have fallen in price and rise in yield, (2) the security purchased will have risen in price and fallen in yield, or (3) a combination of the two will have occurred.

In the money market, yield spread arbitrages are often done (1) between identical instruments of similar maturity (one government is priced too generously relative to another government of similar maturity) and (2) between different instruments of the same maturity (an agency) issue is priced too generously relative to a government issue of the same maturity).

Note that in a strictly defined yield spread arbitrage (the long and the short positions in similar maturities), the arbitrager exposes himself to *no market risk*. If rates rise, the resulting loss on his long position will be offset by profits on his short position; if rates fall, the reverse will occur. Thus the arbitrager is not basing his position on a prediction of the direction of market rates; he is concerned about a possible move up or down in interest rates only insofar as such a move might alter yields spreads in the money market.

An arbitrage in the purest sense of the term involves *no* risk, since the sale and purchase are assumed to occur simultaneously or almost so. An arbitrage based on a yield spread anomaly involves, as noted, no market risk, but it does involve risk of another sort: The arbitrager is speculating on a yield spread. If he bets that a given spread will narrow and it widens, he will lose money. Thus even a strictly defined yield spread arbitrage offers no locked-in profit.

Most money market dealers, with the exception of commercial paper and muni note dealers, actively play the arbitrage game. They have stored in a computer all sorts of information on historical yield spreads and have programmed the computer to identify anomalies in prevailing spreads as they feed into it data on current yields. Dealers used the resulting "helpful hints to the arbitrager" both to set up arbitrages themselves and to advise clients of arbitrage opportunities.

Generally in a dealer shop arbitrage is done in an account that is separate from the *naked trading* account. Arbitrage and naked trading are distinctly different lines of business. The trader who seeks to profit from a naked position long or short is a specialist in one narrow sector of the market, and the positions he assumes are based on a prediction of interest rate trends and how they are likely to affect yields in his sector of the market. The arbitrager, in contrast, has to track yields in a number of market sectors, and if he engages in strictly defined yield-spread arbitrage, he is not much concerned with whether rates are likely to rise or fall.

Anomalies in yield spreads that offer opportunities for profitable arbitrage arise due to various temporary aberrations in market demand or supply. For example, if the Treasury brings a big 4-year note issue to market, it might trade for a time at a higher rate than surrounding issues because investors were loath to take the capital gains or losses they would have to in order to swap into the new issue. In this case the cause of the out-of-line yield spread would be, for the time it persisted, that the new issue had not been fully distributed. Alternatively, an anomaly might be created by a particular issue being in extremely scarce supply.

Example of an arbitrage

Here's an example of an arbitrage along the yield curve. The dealer put it on at a time when the yield curve was flat. His general expectation was that the Fed would ease causing the yield curve to steepen. Also, he anticipated that the spread between the 3- and 4-year notes would widen because the Treasury normally now includes a new 3-year note in its quarterly financing, the announcement of which was scheduled for early November.

In late October 1981, the yield curve in the 3- to 4-year area was relatively flat. Thus buying the current 3-year note and shorting the current 4-year note appeared to be an attractive arbitrage. Here's how one dealer did this arbitrage. On October 21, for settlement on October 22, he bought the current 3-year note, 13⅛N 8/15/85, at a yield to maturity of 10.95. Simultaneously he shorted the current 4-year note, 12¼N 9/30/86, at a yield to maturity of 11.00.

The current 3-year note was trading at a dollar price of 105− 3+, and the yield value of ¹/₃₂ on it was 0.126.[6] The current 4-year note was trading at a dollar price of 103−28+, and the yield value of ¹/₃₂ on it was .0096. The smaller yield value of ¹/₃₂ on the 4-year note meant that, for a given movement up or down in interest rates, the 4-year note would move 131% as far up or down in price as the 3-year note would.[7] This in turn meant that, if the arbitrage were established on a dollar-for-dollar

---

[6] The + in the quote equals ¹/₆₄.

[7] The calculation is

$$\frac{.0126}{.0096} = 131\%$$

basis, that is, if the amount of 4-year notes shorted equaled the amount of 3-year notes purchased, the arbitrage would expose the dealer to market risk. In particular, if rates should fall while the arbitrage was on, the dealer would lose more on his short position in the 4-year note than he would gain on his long position in the 3-year note. To minimize market risk, the dealer set the arbitrage in a *ratio* based upon the yield values of ¹⁄₃₂ on the two securities. Note that this procedure insulated the arbitrage against general movements up or down in yields but not against a relative movement between yields on the two securities.

Table 9–1 shows precisely how the arbitrage worked out. The dealer bought for October 22 settlement $1.31 million of the current 3-year note and financed these securities by RPing them at 7.50%. Simultaneously he reversed in $1 million of the 4-year note at the lower 7.15 reverse repo rate and sold them. Thirty-one days later when the dealer's expectations had come true—the Fed had eased, and the yield curve steepened, the dealer was able to unwind his arbitrage, which he put on at a *5-basis-point* spread, at a *16-basis-point* spread (Step 2, Table 9–1). The dealer's total return on the arbitrage was, as Step 3 in Table 9–1 shows, $2,611 per $1 million of securities arbitraged.

On an arbitrage of this sort, risk is limited to the spread relationship, so the size in which dealers do such arbitrages depends only upon their ability to finance the securities purchased and to borrow the securities shorted. In practice such arbitrages are commonly done for $50 or $100 million.

Risk: The unexpected occurs

When a strictly defined yield spread arbitrage fails to work out, the reason is usually that something unexpected has occurred. Here's a dated but still valid example. On several occasions in the spring of 1977, the old 7-year note and the current 7-year note, whose maturities were only 3 months apart, traded at a 10-basis-point spread. This made no sense since it implied that, at the 7-year level, the appropriate spread between securities differing by 1 year in maturity was 40 basis points— an impossible yield curve. One dealer successfully arbitraged this yield spread three times by shorting the high-yield, current note and going long in the old note. On his fourth try the unexpected occurred. In his words, "We stuck our head in the wringer. We put on the 'arb' at 10 basis points, and while we had it on, the Treasury reopened the current 7-year note. That did not destroy the productive nature of the arbitrage, but it did increase the time required before it will be possible to close it out at a profit. The costs of shorting the one issue and being long in the other (especially delivery costs on the short side) are high so at some point we will probably have to turn that arbitrage into a loss trade. Had the Trea-

TABLE 9–1
An arbitrage along the yield curve

Step 1: Set up the arbitrage for settlement October 22, 1982.

A. Buy $1.31 million of the current 3-year note, 13⅛ 8/15/85, at 105– 3+ (10.95 yield)

Principal...........................	$1,376,933
Accrued interest....................	31,771
Total purchase price	$1,408,704

Repo these securities at 7.50

B. Reverse in and sell $1 million of the 4-year note, 12¼ 9/30/86, at 103–28+ (11.00 yield)

Principal...........................	$1,038,906
Accrued interest....................	7,445
Total sale price.....................	$1,046,351

Reverse rate 7.15

Step 2: Unwind the arbitrage for settlement on November 22, 1982.

A. Sell out the long position in the 3-year note at 106– 2+ (10.49) yield:

Principal...........................	$1,389,623
Accrued interest....................	46,255
Total sale price.....................	$1,435,878

Pay financing cost at 7.50 repo rate for 31 days: $9,098.

B. Cover the short position in the 4-year note at 105– 1 (10.65 yield):

Principal...........................	$1,050,323
Accrued interest....................	17,935
Total purchase price	$1,068,258

Receive return on reverse at 7.15 for 31 days: $6,442.

Step 3: Calculate net return on arbitrage.

Return on long position in the 3-year note:

Sale price..........................	$1,435,878
Purchase price......................	−1,408,704
Cost of repo	− 9,098
Total return	$ 18,076

Return on short position in 4-year note:

Sale price..........................	$−1,068,258
Purchase price......................	1,046,351
Income on reverse	6,442
Total return	$− 15,465

Net return on overall arbitrage:

Return on long position	$18,076
Return on short position..............	−15,465
	$ 2,611

sury reopened some other issue, we would have made $200,000 bang. Instead we're looking at a $40,000 paper loss."

The arbitrage in this example comes close to being a strictly defined yield arbitrage. Many money market arbitrages do not. Dealers will often go long in an issue of one maturity and short another issue of quite different maturity. An arbitrage of this sort resembles a strictly defined yield spread arbitrage in that it is a speculation on a yield spread. But it is more risky than such an arbitrage because, if interest rates move up or down, the price movement in the longer-maturity security will normally exceed that in the shorter-maturity security; thus the arbitrage exposes the investor who puts it on to a *price risk.*

Dealers are not unaware of this, and they attempt to offset the inherent price risk in an arbitrage involving securities of different maturities by adjusting the sizes of the two sides of the arbitrage, as in the arbitrage example above. If, for instance, the arbitrage involves shorting the 2-year note and buying the 7-year note, the arbitrager will short more notes than he buys. Such a strategy, however, cannot completely eliminate market risk; a movement in interest rates may be accompanied by a change in the slope of the yield curve, and the difference in the price movements the two issues would undergo if interest rates changed can therefore only be estimated.

Bull and *bear market arbitrages* are based on a view of where interest rates are going. A bull market arbitrager anticipates a fall in interest rates and a rise in securities prices. Thus he might, for example, short 2-year Treasuries and go long in 10-year Treasuries on a one-for-one basis, hoping to profit, when rates fall, from the long coupon appreciating more than the short coupon. If, alternatively, the arbitrager were bearish, he would do the reverse: short long governments and buy short ones.

An arbitrage can also be set up to profit from an anticipated change in the slope of the yield curve. For example, an arbitrager who anticipated a flattening of the yield curve might buy notes in the 7-year area for high yield and short notes in the 2-year area not necessarily on a one-to-one basis. If the yield curve flattened with no change in average rate levels, the 7-year note would appreciate, the 2-year note would decline in price, and the arbitrage could be closed out at a profit.

Money market practitioners are wont to call any pair of long and short positions an arbitrage; as the maturities of the securities involved in the transaction get further and further apart, however, price risk increases, and at some point the "arbitrage" becomes in reality two separate speculative positions, a naked long and a naked short.

Money market arbitragers normally put on both sides of an arbitrage simultaneously, but they rarely take them off simultaneously. As one dealer noted, "The compulsion to *lift* a leg [unwind one side of an arbitrage before the other] is overwhelming. Hardly anyone ever has the discipline to unwind both sides simultaneously. Instead they will first unwind the side that makes the most sense against the market. If, for example, the trader thinks the market is going to do better, he will lift a leg by covering the short."

Arbitrages today

Some traders argue that in the volatile markets characteristic of the late 1970s and early 1980s, arbitraging became more difficult because markets were less liquid in the sense that spreads between bid and asked prices had widened and the size that could be done at those spreads had diminished. Most traders disagree. Said one, "Execution is perhaps more of a problem, but you can get an arb done if you wait for the opportunity. You can't just go and decide to execute an arb. You have to wait for these spreads to come into you, which they will when supply is really there. Then you put on the arb and wait for the supply to leave. A month ago I did a yield-curve play. I was buying the 2-year note and selling the 10-year at 20 basis points less. One day I could have done that trade all day long because someone was going the other way. I did up to what was comfortable to me. Then I had to sit on that trade for a month, but it worked out well."

One sort of arbitrage that has increased tremendously in volume since the opening of futures markets in bills, notes, bonds, and other fixed-income instruments is between cash securities and futures (see Chapter 14). Also, to an agile arbitrageur, a sale of a futures contract is a substitute for a short of a cash security, and purchase of a futures contract is a substitute for purchase of a cash security; so to him, futures have opened up new ways to do arbitrages he'd been doing for years strictly in the cash market.

A good arbitrageur is always alert to opportunities for trading around one leg of his arb to pick up a few basis points here or there. That trading around used to involve moving from one cash security to another; now it may involve moving from cash to futures or vice versa depending on how spreads move.

If the arbitrageur has any problems these days, it is that there are so many cash securities on the quote sheet and so many futures contracts that the choice among alternatives is getting hard. Said one trader, "Say I want to do a yield-curve trade—long on the front end, short on the back end: Do I go long bill futures, cash bills, CDs, the RP market [collateral], or bond spreads; and on the back end, do I short the 10-year note, the note contract, bond futures, or cash bonds—and if cash bonds, do I choose current coupons or the discounts out there." The arrival of options on fixed-income securities has further widened the menu of opportunities and made the choices more difficult.

Support personnel play an important part in any arbitrage operation. As one dealer noted, "The one thing in an arbitrage account that can force a paper loss to become a realized loss is if you lose control of your ability to support your short side. You don't want your traders worrying about when securities are due back, so you need someone else who assumes responsibility for making sure that people doing RP and reverse keep the needed supply of securities you have shorted on hand."

Money market dealers seek out promising arbitrage opportunities not only because they can profit from them in their own trading but because arbitrage suggestions passed on to customers are a source of customer business. As one dealer commented, "We're in a competitive business, and the customer looks for the guys with the best ideas and information. If we supply them, he trades with us."

The persistence with which dealers and their customers arbitrage every out-of-line yield spread they find has an important impact on the money market; it ensures that spreads relationships never get far out of line or, to put it another way, that the differences in the yields on instruments of different types and maturities consistently mirror differences in the liquidity of and credit risk, if any, attached to these instruments.

Given all the arbitrage on the street, the question arises: How can there be anything left to arbitrage? The answer seems to be that opportunities continue to exist partly because of the constantly increasing size of the market and partly because of the constant entry of new investors, some of whom are unsophisticated players. As would be expected, opportunities for arbitrage increase noticeably in volatile markets.

TAILS

Dealers who were bullish used to create tails as a way to pick up a profit if rates did in fact fall or, in some cases, just stayed flat. When carry is positive and the expectation is that rates won't rise, traders still do this. As often or more often, however, traders create tails as part of what has come to be known as a *cash and carry trade:* the purchase of a cash security which is simultaneously sold in the futures market and financed until expiration of the futures contract with term repo.

Tails can be confusing. The easiest way to explain what is involved is with an example. We will do so here with a cash-market trade. In Chapter 14, we work out a cash-and-carry trade involving futures.

Assume a dealer is operating in an environment in which the 90-day bill is trading at a rate 1/8 below the Fed funds rate. Assume also that Fed funds are trading at 8.075, the 90-day bill at 7.95, and 30-day term RP at 7.50.

If in this environment the dealer were to buy a 90-day bill and finance it with 30-day term RP, he would earn over the 30-day holding period a positive carry equal to

7.95 − 7.50

or a profit equal to 45 basis points over 30 days. He would also have created a *future* 60-day bill, namely, the unfinanced *tail* of the 90-day bill purchased.

If he thought, as dealers do, of the carry profit over the initial holding period as raising the yield at which he in effect buys the future security, then by purchasing the 90-day bill at 7.95 and RPing it for 30 days at 7.50, he would have acquired a future 60-day bill at a yield of 8.05.[8] The 45-basis-point carry, which is earned for 30 days, adds only 10 basis points to the yield at which the future security is effectively purchased because the latter has a maturity of 60 days, which is twice as long as the period over which positive carry is earned.

Faced with this opportunity the dealer would ask himself: How attractive is it to contract to buy a 60-day bill at 8.05 for delivery 30 days hence? Note the dealer would precisely break even, clearing costs ignored, if he were able to sell that future bill at a rate of 8.05. Thus contracting to buy the future bill will be attractive if he believes he can sell the future bill at a rate below 8.05.

The dealer's answer to the question he has posed might run as follows: Currently the yield curve is such that 60-day bills are trading 15 basis points below the rate on 90-day bills. Therefore, if the 60-day bill were to trade at 8.05 one month hence and if yield spreads did not change, that would imply that the 90-day bill was trading at 8.175 and Fed funds at 8.30, that is, at a level approximately ¼ above the present rate. I do not believe that the Fed will tighten or that yield spreads will change unfavorably, therefore I will do the trade.

If the dealer were correct and the Fed did not tighten and yield spreads did not change, he would be able to sell 30 days hence the future 60-day bill he had created at 7.80, which is the rate that would be the prevailing rate at that time on the 60-day bill, if his predictions with respect to yield and yields spread were correct.[9] In doing so, he would make a profit equal to ¼ (the purchase rate 8.05 minus the sale rate 7.80) on a 60-day security.

Of course, the dealer's predictions might prove to be favorable. Note, however, he has some built-in margin of protection. Specifically, if he is able to sell his future bills at any rate above 7.80 but still below 8.05, he will make some profit, albeit less than he would if he sold at 7.80. If, on the other hand, rates or rate spreads move so unfavorably that he ends up selling his future 60-day bill at a rate above 8.05, he will lose money.

For the benefit of those who like to look at dollar numbers rather than

---

[8] Note that the *higher* the yield at which a discount security is purchased, the *lower* the purchase price. So buying the future security at 8.05 is, from the dealer's point of view, better than buying it at 7.95.

[9] Recall the 60-day bill was assumed to be trading at a rate 15 basis points below the rate on the 90-day bill, at 7.95 − .15 = 7.80.

yields, we have reworked the example presented in dollars in Table 9–2. Recall the 60-day bill was assumed to be trading at a rate 15 basis points below the rate on the 90-day bill, at 7.95 − .15 or 7.80.

In deciding whether to buy securities and finance them for some period, dealers invariably "figure the tail," that is, determine the effective yield at which they are buying the future security created. Whether the security financed is a discount security or an interest-bearing one, this yield can be figured approximately as follows:[10]

$$\begin{pmatrix} \text{Effective yield} \\ \text{at which future} \\ \text{security is} \\ \text{purchased} \end{pmatrix} = \begin{pmatrix} \text{Yield at} \\ \text{which cash} \\ \text{security is} \\ \text{purchased} \end{pmatrix} \times \begin{pmatrix} \dfrac{\text{Rate of profit} \times \text{Days} \\ \text{on carry} \quad \text{carried}}{\text{Days left to maturity} \\ \text{at end of carry period}} \end{pmatrix}$$

Applying this formula to our example, we get:

$$7.95 + \frac{.20 \times 30}{60} = 7.95 + .10 = 8.05$$

Risk. A dealer who engages in the sort of transaction we have just described incurs a rate risk. He might end up with a loss or a smaller profit than anticipated because the Fed tightened unexpectedly, because bill rates rose relative to the Fed funds rate due to, say, heavy bill sales by the Treasury; or because a shift in the yield curve narrowed the spread between 60- and 90-day bills. Thus whether a dealer who thinks such a transaction would be profitable decides to take the position and the size in which he takes it will depend both on the confidence he has in his rate and spread predictions and the amount of risk to which he thinks it would expose him.

The same sort of transaction could also be done in other securities: BAs, commercial paper, or CDs. In each case the yield spreads that would have to be estimated would differ from those estimated in our bill example. If the instrument purchased and financed were CDs, the risk would be perceptibly greater than if the instrument were bills because supply is more difficult to predict in the CD market than in the bill market, and CDs back up faster than bills.

RELATIVE VALUE

We have said that a dealer will position securities if he is bullish. In choosing which securities to buy, he considers relative value.

Every rational investor is interested in risk, liquidity, and return. Specifically he wants maximum return, maximum liquidity, and minimum

---

[10] There is bias in this approximation. For a formula giving the precise yield calculation on a tail, see Stigum and Mann, *Money Market Calculations* (Homewood, Ill.: Dow Jones-Irwin, 1981), pp. 41–45.

TABLE 9–2
Figuring the tail: An example*

Step 1: The dealer buys $1 million of 90-day bills at a 7.95% rate of discount

$$\text{Discount at which bills are purchased} = \frac{d \times t}{360} \times F = \frac{0.795 \times 90}{360} \times \$1,000,000$$
$$= \$19,875$$

Price at which bills are purchased $- F - D = 1,000,000 - 19,875$
$$= \$980,125$$

The dealer finances the bills purchased for 30 days at 7¾%

$$\text{Financing cost}\dagger = \frac{.0775 \times 30}{360} \times \$1,000,000$$
$$= \$6,458$$

Step 2: At the end of 30 days the dealer owns the bills at a net cost figure. Determine what yield this cost figure implies on the future 60-day bills created

Net cost of future 60-day bills = Purchase price + Financing cost
$$= \$980,125 + \$6,458$$
$$= \$986,583$$

Net discount at which 60-day bills are owned = F − Net cost
$$= \$1,000,000 - \$986,583$$
$$= \$13,417$$

$$\text{Rate at which future 60-day bills are purchased}\ddagger = \frac{360 \times D}{t \times F} = \frac{360 \times \$13,417}{60 \times \$1,000,000}$$
$$\doteq 0805$$
$$= 8.05\%$$

Step 3: Future 60-day bills created are sold at 7.80% discount rate. Calculate dollar profit

$$\text{Discount at which bills are sold} = \frac{d \times t}{360} \times F$$
$$= \frac{0.0780 \times 60}{360} \times \$1,000,000$$
$$= \$13,000$$

Profit = Net purchase discount − Discount sale
$$= \$13,417 - \$13,000$$
$$= \$417$$

Step 4: Figure the annualized yield on a discount basis that $417 represents on a 60-day security

$$d = \frac{360 \times D}{t \times F} = \frac{360 \times \$417}{60 \times \$1,000,000}$$
$$= .0025$$
$$= \tfrac{1}{4}\%$$

---

* For explanation of formulas used, see page 46.
† Actually less than $1 million has to be borrowed, which is one reason why the dealer's approach to figuring the tail is only an approximation. A second reason is that the bill rate is a discount rate, the RP rate is an add-on rate.
‡ Solving the equation

$$D = F\left(\frac{d \times t}{360}\right)$$

for d, gives us

$$d = \frac{360 \times D}{t \times F}$$

risk. When he shops for securities, however, he finds that the real world presents him with nothing but trade-offs; securities offering higher returns tend to be riskier or less liquid than securities offering lower returns. That is as true in the money market as elsewhere, and it is the reason money market dealers think first of *relative* value when they decide to position.

If the spread at which one security is trading relative to another more than adequately compensates for the fact that the high-yield security is riskier or less liquid than the low-yield security, the high-yield security has greater relative value and should be bought in preference to the low-yield security. If, alternatively, the spread is inadequate, then the low-yield security has greater relative value and should be bought in preference to the high-yield security. When dealers talk about relative value, they are really talking about the management of credit risk, market risk, and liquidity.

How relative value considerations affect a dealer's decisions as to what to position was put rather nicely by one dealer, "When we are all bullish, my bill trader, my CD trader, and my BA trader all want to take on stuff, and my reverse trader wants to take on 90-day collateral. At that point we have to sit down and get our heads together about relative value theory. Say we want to position $100 million in 6 months and under. Our most obvious options are CDs and bills. If, because of unusual supply conditions in the CD market, CDs are trading at a narrow spread—8 basis points—to bills, we are not going to buy CDs. Now picture a slightly different situation. Loans are not increasing at major New York banks, and additionally CDs are trading in the 6-month area 35 basis points off bills. We expect market rates to fall, and we also expect the spread between CDs and bills to narrow. In this situation CDs have greater relative value, so we will buy some. *But* putting all our eggs in one basket might be terribly unwise because we can only make an intelligent guess about supply in the CD market. Morgan might do a large Euro loan and fund the first 6 months with domestic CDs. If so, bing, we get knocked out of the water. We do not get the price action we expected out of the CD market even though the market as a whole rallies. Because that's possible, we might go 60 percent CDs and 40 percent bills—hedge our bets by diversifying. That way we will not miss the entire flip. I have seen it happen on numerous occasions, when we have done half bills and half CDs, that bills rallied 30 basis points—a nice flip we had anticipated—and CDs just sat there like a rock."

Relative value considerations arise not only in choices between different instruments but in choices between different maturity sectors of the same market. A dealer might ask whether he should position 6-month or 1-year bills. If the yield curve were unusually steep out to 1 year and the dealer expected it to flatten, then the year bill would have more relative value than the 6-month bill.

Relative value analysis, besides guiding a dealer in deciding what securities to position or short, is also useful for generating business with customers, and dealers use it that way constantly. To take an example, suppose BAs and bills in a given maturity range are normally spread 5 basis points. The spread is now 20 basis points, which more than compensates for the extra risk and lesser liquidity of the BAs. Moreover, the dealer anticipates that the spread at which BAs trade to bills will narrow. Then the BAs have greater relative value than the bills, and by pointing this out to retail customers holding bills, the dealer could probably induce some of them to *swap* for a yield pickup out of their bills into BAs (to sell their bills and buy BAs).

RUNNING A DEALER OPERATION

We have talked a lot about how money market "dealers" operate, but a dealership, of course, consists of many people. At its heart are a position manager, who is invariably a highly savvy street person, a group of specialized traders, and a sales force that contacts retail.

The position manager (or managers—in large firms responsibility is layered) has various responsibilities. First, he has to establish guidelines to limit the total risk the firm assumes at any one time. Second, it is his responsibility to develop a forecast of short-term interest rates—using inputs from his resident Fed watcher, his traders, and retail. Then he must decide, based on the level of confidence he has in that forecast, whether his firm should make a market play, how big that play should be within the firm's position limits, and the instruments and maturity range in which the play should be made.

Establishing position limits

As interest rates have become more volatile and position risks concomitantly greater, dealers—with their limited capital—have begun to pay a lot more attention to risk management and in particular to the setting of position limits overall and at different points along the yield curve. Since risk defies precise measurement, different dealers set such limits in different ways. A typical approach is for a dealer to start by saying: The most we are willing to lose in one day is X million. Next, for securities at different points along the yield curve, the dealer constructs volatility indices based on the past price behavior of these securities. The firm might then use indices to establish maximum positions it is willing to assume at different points along the yield curve. Or, alternatively, the firm might say: Given the current market environment, the maximum total position we will assume is $1 billion. Our index tells us that long bonds are 7 times as volatile as the year bill, so if we make our play at the short end, we are willing to go up to a billion, but if we make our play in long bonds, we'll do only 1/7th of that.

Listening to a dealer talk about volatility indices and limits, one gets the feeling of déjà vu. It all sounds very reminiscent of a Euro trader describing how he seeks to control risk in his placement book. This is not surprising because a Euro trader and a securities dealer both face the same problem: controlling unquantifiable risks.[11] Also, both inevitably come up with guidelines that are arbitrary at best, which is not to say that they are without purpose. Said one dealer, "We know our position limits are arbitrary, but they give us the comfort of knowing, when we go home at night, that we will still be in business tomorrow."

In implementing position limits, a dealer faces a delicate task. If he wants good traders, he has to give them some freedom, but he can't give them so much that he loses control over the size and composition of the firm's position. One manager described the problem well, "Every trader is entitled to trade his markets, to have a certain degree of free hand. Traders are big boys. Sometimes, however, I find, much to my dismay, that our bill futures trader is short, our bill trader long, our CD trader even to a little long, and our coupon trader short. Thanks to the grace of God, it often all works out because our traders know their markets and the technicals in them. But when we are making a major position play, my allowance for each trader doing his own thing in his own market no longer holds. Then I have to set the positions and the limits."

The traders

Because there are so many types of money market instruments, because they trade so differently, and because they vary so in maturity, money market dealers all have a bevy of traders, each trading a single *narrow* sector of the market: short bills, long bills, 2–4-year notes, CDs, BAs, short agencies, and so on.

Trading on an hour-to-hour, day-to-day basis is a fine art that those with the inherent knack pick up through on-the-firing-line training. A good trader bases every trade he makes on his feel about the levels at which every instrument in which he deals ought to be trading. That feel will tell him, for example, that a 6 bid for one instrument is the same as a 13 bid for another, in other words, that he should be *indifferent* between selling one instrument at 6 and the other at 13; also if his market trades at a 2/32 spread, he should be indifferent between buying the one instrument at 8 and the other at 15. So the trader will quote these two markets, 6–8 and 13–15. If someone hits his bid at 13 and takes his offer at 8, he will, if his indifference levels are correct, have earned 2/32 and estab-

---

[11] See Chapter 6, pp. 154–56.

lished a position (long in the one security and short in the other) that he can with patience unwind for another ²⁄₃₂. The unwinding is, of course, likely to occur one leg at a time. Retail might pick up the securities in which he is long, then he would have to buy something else to keep his *net* book even. And if such *chain trading* caused a maturity gap in his book, he would seek out other trades to close it—tell the sales force to look to buy this one or sell that one. The essence of successful trading is to be able to set correct indifference levels and then keep the position moving—buying here, selling there, and picking up 32nds along the way.

Of course, at times the firm may take a strong view with respect to where interest rates are going and want the trader to run a net long or short position in his book. To establish that position, he will have to be a net buyer or seller, but once he has established the position, trading again becomes calculating indifference levels and trading off them in a fashion that keeps his book where he wants it.

A trader is a highly paid professional whose life is his market. Most traders are young; they have to be since they operate under a lot of pressure, both because of the hectic pace of the market and because the results of what they do get thrown at them daily in the form of a profit and loss statement on their previous day's trades. Most traders are also highly competitive. As one dealer noted, "A trader is the archetype I-will-kill-you player of tennis, backgammon, and other games. He knows this is a killer business, and to him winning is everything—it's his mission in life, and when he wins, he won't even be nice about it."

A trader's job is to work not to manage. He has to quote markets, write tickets, and make things happen, all the while interjecting his personality into what he is doing. Few traders have any academic training for what they are doing, and in seeking out potential traders, dealers more often eschew than seek out those with such training. Said one dealer of MBAs, "The universities send us a bunch of academically oriented capons who don't know what it is to bitch, sweat, live, and die with positions of hundreds of thousands of dollars. There are a lot of bright guys down here with degrees, and they construct models on the computer of future interest rates, but when Sali's trader says to them. 'The 6-month bill is 29–28, what do you want to do?' they face a whole different class of decision. There may be beneficial sorts of training that could be given them beforehand, but there is no possible training for meeting that sort of situation well."

Creating a trading team

In the recent environment of high rate volatility, it has become increasingly important to dealers seeking to control risk closely to achieve a high degree of discipline among their traders. In a firm that wants both to service retail and to limit risk, there is a natural, constant conflict between the firm and its traders. Traders do not want to be functionaries who buy here and sell there to satisfy either the needs of the firm's retail customers or the demands of its position manager. Traders want to be creative people who earn money by taking big positions and by being right on the market; they also have sensitive egos that get them into trouble.

One position manager, describing his efforts to control both risk and his traders, said, "We thought having a bunch of traders along the yield curve all trying to decide whether the market was cheap or expensive was a poor way to manage risk. We had to retrain our traders—to get them a lot more comfortable with a team environment where we tell some guys that they have to sit out a rally because we are not going to make our play in their sector. I think we now have the most effective trading desk on the street. To get it, we had to get traders to think that the good trader is not the guy who buys a billion but the guy who makes consistent profits during the year. We found that a trader feels a need to belong; he does not want to be out there all alone. As management, we share the risk with him all the way, which reduces the stress in his job. We want our traders around for a long time. The most disruptive thing to a trade or sales organization is continuous turnover—a condition endemic on Wall Street—that we have stopped temporarily.

"Steinbrenner's Yankees are a good model for what you find in a lot of undisciplined trading outfits. There are a lot of high-priced ball players all trying to wing a home run, but the team has not won too many games. Our objective is not to have one winning season but to build a number of steady revenue streams. If you don't have such revenue streams, you are always going to be speculating instead of having the freedom to pick your spots. Since we have tried to speculate less, our record of making good speculations has improved. This year was our best ever."

The last comment throws an interesting perspective onto our earlier observation that rate volatility has shifted the focus at more than one dealer shop from earning profits on speculation to finding consistent sources of revenue. The discipline of doing the latter may improve a dealer's ability to do the former.

Sales force

There is a lot of variability from dealer to dealer in the size of the sales force and its function. At one extreme are houses that are big in commercial paper and put their sales force to work selling Amco Credit and have them do repo as an afterthought. At the other extreme are the position houses that look to their sales force first as sellers of repo, second as a source of information on how retail is behaving in and views the market, and third as an outlet to retail business when the firm wants it. A few such firms even reward their sale force according to the amount of repo they do, which is fairly unusual.

The level of sophistication among sales personnel varies considerably. It takes little expertise to sell commercial paper to the average corporate treasurer but a lot to deal with some of the sharper players in the market.

In most corporations, running the short-term portfolio is a rookie job, in a scant few it is done by highly paid professionals.[12] The dealers staff accordingly; rookies talk to and advise rookies, and pros talk to pros. Said one dealer, "It works fine hiring a rookie to talk to a rookie. They relate to each other and have a good time. I can't have a hot-shot trader of mine talking to the money trader for some average corporation. They're separated by an unbridgable cultural gap."

Controls

The topic of personnel brings up a housekeeping detail—controls. There is no way a dealer can protect against fraud (a trader or salesman, for example, selling something to a customer and buying it back if it does not appreciate) except by bonding. He can, however, give his firm protection against traders overstepping their trading authority by having traders confirm all trades on the phone *and* in writing, with the written confirms going at the end of the day to the confirmation or auditing department where they are balanced out. Such controls are standard practice. Still it does happen, albeit infrequently, that a trader oversteps his bounds, perhaps in collusion with someone in the cage, and loses large sums through unsuccessful and unauthorized trading.

THE CONTRAST IN SHOPS

We have noted throughout this chapter the variability that exists between the different money market dealers, a point that's hard to overemphasize. In terms of size, there are at one extreme Merrill Lynch and Salomon Brothers, both with enormous market-making capability and, particularly in the case of Merrill Lynch, with a superb distribution system. At the other extreme are some small highly specialized shops that deal in only a single instrument, BAs or muni notes.

Money market shops also vary tremendously in their attitude toward positioning. Salomon is known for its willingness to take risk, to assume huge positions, and to be prepared to take huge losses. Aubrey Lanston

---

[12] See chapter 10.

is another house with a reputation for positioning. One dean of the market described it as "a firm willing and able to engage in brilliant and massive speculation in governments when it likes the market and to disappear when it doesn't." Among the banks, there are also players willing to take on huge positions, Citi in particular. At the opposite extreme, one encounters customer-oriented firms like Carroll McEntee & McGinley, which was built first to service retail (the small portfolio manager as well as the large), second to take positions.

Another difference between houses is the maturities that they trade and position. Some houses are equally active in all sectors of the government and corporate securities market. Others feel comfortable taking on positions only in securities of relatively short maturity. Said the manager of one such firm, "What is a long bond worth, 10.80 or 10.90? Who knows? Yet the price difference is enough to wipe you out."

As noted, some dealers are banks and others are nonbank firms. Each has its advantages and disadvantages. Bank dealers can carry municipal securities tax-free, nonbank dealers cannot; also banks have direct access to the Fed funds market for financing but incur a reserve cost if they repo CDs or BAs. Nonbank dealers, on the other hand, can deal in commercial paper, corporate bonds, and municipal revenue bonds, which banks are forbidden to do by the Glass-Steagall Act.

There are also other more subtle differences between bank and nonbank dealers. Banks are in the business of commercial banking, and all else is collateral. Everything they do is designed to serve the customer rather than the bank, and their government bond trading operations are no exception. They were created to serve correspondent banks and the emerging corporate treasurer who was trying to utilize cash balances he had previously held idle. The trading operation in a bank was and is directed predominantly toward customer satisfaction, whereas the nonbank dealer is likely to feel some compulsion to profit on every transaction since he has no other function. Also, whether a bank would admit it or not, it makes better markets to its best banking customers than it does to strangers. There is, however, a counterpart to this among the nonbank dealers. A dealer that is also a big investment banking house is not going to hold at arms' length in its dealer operation a huge corporation that is one of its prime investment banking customers. Corporate finance is to investment banking firms what commercial banking is to a bank, only it is less wide and deep.

Another difference between the bank and nonbank dealers lies in the quality and continuity of personnel. The industry standard in the nonbank dealer shops and even in the bank dealers is that personnel get some form of incentive pay: a year-end bonus based on the firm's profits. At a nonbank dealer it is common for a good trader to get a base salary of $70 or $100,000 and to leave the firm at the end of the year with a W-2 form that reads $200, $300, or even $400,000. These numbers tend to create a situation in which aggressive, comparatively seasoned, and terribly smart people with a bent for the money market are drained out of the banks and corporations, which compensate less generously, unless they are people who aspire to be a high bank or corporate executive. Big banks and corporations could, of course, afford to pay traders and port-folio managers the same salaries nonbank dealers pay them, but it is hard for them to defend paying somebody who is nowhere on the firm's organizational chart the same salary an executive vice president gets. Because of this, bank trading rooms tend to be a training ground for traders, from which many of the best entrants move on to nonbank shops in search of more money once they have mastered their skill. Some bright bank traders, of course, remain but for them a trading room posi-tion, whatever it is, tends to be an interim assignment. In a bank, as in a corporation, good people have to be given room to move up.

THE CLEARING BANKS

We have described at length the role of dealers as market makers in the money market. There are also other institutions that play a vital role in this process—the clearing banks and the brokers. The *clearing banks* clear trades for nonbank dealers in governments, agencies, and other money market instruments. The bank with by far the largest clearing operation is Manufacturers Hanover Trust (*Manny Hanny* or just *Manny* to all who know her). The next largest clearing bank is the Bank of New York; they are followed in importance by Irving Trust and Marine Mid-land. Other banks—Morgan, Chase, and Citi—have also become active in clearing in recent years.

In acting as a clearing agent, a clearing bank makes payments against securities delivered into a dealer's account and receives pay-ments made to the dealer against securities delivered out of its account. It also safekeeps securities received by a dealer and makes payments into and out of the account that the dealer holds with the bank. Finally, a clearing bank provides dealers with any financing they require at its posted *dealer loan rate.*

Volume

Clearing, which sounds simple in theory, turns out in practice to be a huge and complex operation because of the tens of thousands of trades and RP transactions that occur daily in the New York market. The vast majority of money market instruments traded in the national money mar-ket are payable in New York regardless of where the issuer is located and are safekept in New York regardless of where the investor is located.

The volume figures at a big clearing bank are staggering. Manny's average trade is close to $5 million. On a record day it has cleared over the Fed wire almost 12,000 transactions and done another 1,500 pair off transactions. A pair off occurs when, for example, Sali and Merrill, which both clear through Manny, do a trade with each other; Manny clears such trades simply by moving securities from desk A to B through its internal system. On an average day Manny alone processes $70 billion of transactions to its general ledger, and the figure on some days has been well in excess of $100 billion of which $8 billion might reflect the trades of a single dealer!

The Fed wire

Putting governments and agencies into book entry form and making transfers of them over the Fed wire possible was supposed to make life simpler and more comfortable for everyone. Initially wire transfers did this. However, it is fair to say that the existence of book entry system and of the Fed wire make today what would otherwise be a completely manageable situation barely tolerable.

The problem is simple. Volume over the Fed wire has grown over the last several years to such unbelievable levels that the wire system in its current form is taxed to the point of bursting. By mid-1983 the Fed is supposed to have a new state-of-the-art system in place. Meanwhile, it will have to continue to deal with overload by extending the hours the wire is open for securities transactions.

Large dealers have a computer-to-computer link-up with their clearing bank. Smaller houses deliver trading tickets by hand to their clearing bank, often the night before clearing if the trade is for regular settlement. As securities are delivered to a clearing bank, the bank matches them up with a dealer's purchase tickets, and payment is made against receipt. When securities go out, the procedure is reversed. Despite all the computerization that has been applied to securities clearing (all governments are delivered and paid for over the Fed wire), a clearing operation still involves a great deal of labor. Five years ago Manny Hanny had 11 people on the desk handling the Merrill Lynch account alone; today they have 14 people to handle twice as many trades. The size of Manny's clearing floor, which is jammed with computer terminals making and receiving messages, rivals that of a football field.

The Fed wire is supposed to close down at 2:30 P.M. for buys and sells and at 3 P.M. for reversals to correct mistakes. If those deadlines are not met, which is most of the time, extensions are granted. Said the head of one clearing operation, "Last Tuesday evening we went home at 8:30. In my report to management about overtime, I noted that from January through September 1982 there were over 500 unscheduled extensions of the Fed wire for securities transfers. Extensions come in increments of half an hour, so that was roughly 3 extensions per day, which means an average closing time for securities transactions of 4:30." As noted in Chapter 11, congestion on the Fed wire for securities transfers and the resulting extensions inevitably cause frequent late closings of the wire for funds transfers. Congestion on the Fed wire and the movement to same-day settlement of funds have combined to convert the workweek of Fed funds traders and brokers, who used to view their jobs as fun, into a series of unbearably long days.

Turnaround times. Several years ago it was common for dealers to get securities into their clearing bank on time but for that bank to be unable to make timely redelivery of those securities. The dealers asked for and got a two-minute turnaround time from their clearing bank. Then the issue went to the Fed, which finally decided that dealers deserved some privilege as makers of the market in governments and adopted a formal *turnaround time* in those cities where it was considered necessary: New York, Chicago, San Francisco, and Los Angeles. Now a customer in those cities has until 2:15 to deliver securities to a dealer, and a dealer has until 2:45 to deliver securities to a customer or to a dealer bank in those cities.

To illustrate, say Chrysler has bought governments from Merrill. If Chrysler clears at Morgan, Manny for the account of Merrill has until 2:45 to deliver to Morgan for the account of Chrysler. However, if Chrysler clears at the National Bank of Detroit, the cutoff time for delivery is the normal 2:30 cutoff for securities transfers. This distinction is widely misunderstood. To many operating people in the dealer community, a customer is a customer, and he takes delivery until 2:45. The fact that the cutoff is 2:30 for firms that clear at banks located in a city that has no formal turnaround time puts firms such as Chrysler in a position to pick up extra fails by clearing at a local bank. The obvious solution is nationwide cutoff times.

Dealer loans

Extending dealer loans is an inherent and important part of a bank's clearing operations. When securities come into a clearing bank for a dealer's account, the banks pay for them whether or not the dealer has funds in its account, and it takes in any payment made to the dealer on security sales. Then at the end of the day, the bank net settles with each dealer. Since payments out of a dealer's account are made against the receipt of securities and payments in are made against the delivery out of securities, if a dealer ends up net short on cash for the day, he will have bought more securities than he sold, and the bank will have collateral against which to lend to him. Dealer loans are always made on an overnight basis. The collateral is returned to the dealer's account the next morning, and his account is charged for the loan amount plus interest.

Because overnight repo is cheaper than dealer loans, most dealers use dealer loans only to finance odd pieces and securities they hold because they failed on a delivery. There are, however, some dealers who work the RP market less hard than most and use dealer loans regularly. At one extreme is a firm like Kidder that repos everything. In contrast there are firms that move a billion a day and feel good if they leave only $100 million in the box at their clearing bank.

The clearing banks are happy with the relatively small reliance dealers place on dealer loans for their financing; in fact, they tell the dealers not to think of them as a primary supplier of position financing; an exception is when a bank has an excess of cash and calls the dealers to tell them it is looking for loans. The size of dealer's positions is so huge that these positions could not be financed in toto by the clearing banks or even by the whole New York banking community. Despite the fact that dealers eschew bank financing, dealer loans can reach large proportions. A big clearing bank lends on average as much as $250 to $300 million overnight to dealers. Some days, however, the figure goes as high as $1.5 billion of which—top side—$400 million might go to a single dealer.

Normally clearing banks post their dealer loan rate at around 11:00 A.M. It runs ¼ to ⅜ above the Fed funds rate when money is easy and as much as 1 point above Fed funds when money is tight. This rate typically prevails for the rest of the day, but if the level at which Fed funds trade alters sharply, it will be changed. This occurs most often on Wednesdays when the banks are settling with the Fed.

Clearing banks attempt to get estimates from the dealers of their anticipated borrowings as early as possible so that they can adjust their Fed funds positions accordingly. A dealer may end up needing much less financing than he anticipated or significantly more. Thus a clearing bank does not know the full size of its loans to dealers until after the national money market has closed, the Fed wire has closed, and sometimes the bank itself has closed. This causes the major clearing banks no problem in settling with the Fed because they have automated their wire to the Fed and know their reserve balance instantaneously even if they can't identify as quickly the sources and uses of funds that led to that balance.

If a clearing bank gets hit with big dealer loans late on a Wednesday and Fed funds are very expensive, it may go to the discount window for funds. This is something about which the Fed used to be quite understanding but no longer is. The clearing banks manage to accommodate the wide fluctuations that occur in their loans to dealers only because they are large banks with big reserve positions and the ability to buy huge and highly variable sums of money in the Fed funds market. A smaller bank without that ability could not function as a major clearing bank. The Bank of New York, second only to Manny in clearing, is an exception in this respect. BNY is heavily committed to one customer, FBI. This firm, which is a *blind broker* (i.e., acts as principal in trades it brokers), pumps through BNY an unbelievable number of trades. These never require financing by BNY except when fails occur.

On dealer loans the clearing banks normally require collateral plus some margin, 2 percent on most short-term instruments and maybe 5 percent on a longer-term instrument, such as a Ginny Mae pass-through. If a dealer ends up with insufficient collateral, the clearing bank still makes all payments due out of his account and gives him an overdraft, for which it charges a rate higher than its normal dealer loan rate.

Clearing banks are not the only banks that provide dealers with overnight money. If other banks happen to find themselves with excess funds, perhaps because they have been hosed with money by correspondent banks that sell them Fed funds, they will call the dealers and offer them dealer loans at an attractive rate. Said one such banker, "We do not finance the dealers on an ongoing basis, but when we do it, we do it at a very nice rate. We are either all the way in or all the way out." For such a bank, making dealer loans is an attractive alternative to selling excess funds in the Fed funds market.

Clearing charges represent an important part of every dealer's costs. Clearing banks used to set their fees on the basis of the par value of the securities cleared. Then, as automation reduced their costs, they switched to a per-ticket pricing structure, and as they did, the net cost of clearing to dealers fell. Fees for clearing vary from bank to bank, and also at a given clearing bank they may vary for different dealers. As one dealer noted, "We have a sweetheart relationship with our clearing bank, and whatever the banks may say, such relationships are common."

Mistakes

Clearing banks make mistakes. Sometimes the problem results from delivery instructions. Said one clearing officer, "What is a good delivery instruction? Chase Manhattan Bank, 1 Chase Plaza, 43rd floor, Att. Al Clark. That is terrific, it says everything, but it does not fly on the wire. I need something that says Chase/Cust or Chase/Dealer, a system-recognizable mnemonic. Problems with respect to delivery instructions arise when a dealer gets a new sales person who sends something back to operations, which sends us God knows what. Sometimes a dealer has to take a fail for us to make the point to him. At a lot of shops, the operations side tends to be ignored in terms of resources until things start to go not so well."

"Also, we make mistakes, maybe half a dozen on a 12,000-trade day.

An operator pushes the inquire button instead of transmit. We hope the mistake is on a 1 million not a 20 million trade. Naturally $100 million problems always arise on Fridays or before a long weekend. On the day before Labor Day weekend, we found a $65 million problem because an operator failed to push transmit. The trade was an outright sale to a receiver who had the securities going out to 7 or 8 different places. Fortunately we saved about $40 million of it. In a situation like this, we end up giving someone a free dealer loan on whatever we can't save; at 11% for four days that can be a big hit."

THE BROKERS

A broker is a firm that brings buyers and sellers together for a commission. Unlike dealers, brokers by definition do not position. Brokers are everywhere in the money market. They are active in the *interdealer* markets in governments, agencies, CDs, bankers' acceptances, repo, and reverse, and in the *interbank* markets for Fed funds and Euro time deposits.

Volume and commissions

The volumes of funds and securities that are brokered each business day are staggering. Unfortunately, because statistics on brokered trades are not collected in most sectors of the market, it is impossible to put precise dollar figures on these amounts. It is possible, however, to give a few suggestive numbers. On an active day one of the top Fed funds brokers, who is in competition with nine other brokers of varying size, may broker over $6 billion of funds! Currently almost all interdealer trades in governments and agencies are done through brokers.

Brokers could not survive without a huge volume of trades because the commissions they receive per $1 million of funds or securities brokered are so small. In the bill market, brokerage on 90-day bills works out to $12.50 per $1 million; in the Fed funds market, on overnight trades it's only $0.50 per $1 million. In some sectors of the market (Fed funds and Euros) brokerage is paid by both the buyer and the seller; in others (governments and agencies), it is paid only by the dealer who initiates a trade by either hitting a bid or taking an offer quoted by the broker.

The service sold

Much of what a broker is selling his clients is a fast information service that tells the trader where the market is—what bids and offers are and how much they are good for. Speed of communication is thus crucial to a money market broker, and each has before him a board of direct phone lines through which he can contact every important trader he services by merely punching a button. Over those lines brokers constantly collect bids and offers throughout the day. They pass these on to other traders either by phone calls or more commonly over display screens, referred to throughout the industry as *CRTs*—short for cathode ray tubes.

In many sectors of the market (governments, Euro time deposits) the broker gives runs: bids and offers for a number of issues or maturities. In others (the market for overnight Fed funds) just one bid and offer are quoted. In some sectors of the market, bids and offers are good until withdrawn; in others they are understood to be good for only a few minutes.

The pace at which brokering is done in all sectors of the money market is hectic most of the time and frantic at certain crucial moments— in the Fed funds market on Wednesday afternoon when the banks settle with the Fed, in the government market on Friday afternoon after the Fed announces money supply figures.

Brokerage operations vary a lot in size. Since shops dealing in CDs have a single CD trader, CDs can be brokered by just a couple of people sitting in a small room with a battery of direct phone lines. Brokering governments or Euros takes more personnel because there are many more traders to be covered and many more bids and offers to be quoted. Some brokerage outfits are large because they broker a number of different instruments. A Euro broker, for example, often brokers foreign exchange, and some firms that broker Fed funds also broker a potpourri of other instruments.

A broker has to be not only quick but *careful* because he is normally expected to substantiate any bid or offer he quotes. This means that if he quotes a market inaccurately to a trader, he must either (1) pay that trader an amount equal to the difference between the price he quoted and the price at which the trade can actually be got off or (2) buy securities from or sell securities to that trader at the quoted price and then cover, typically at a loss, his resulting long or short position.

The ethics of brokering are strict in all sectors of the money market. A broker is not supposed to and never will give up the names of the dealers or banks that are bidding or offering through him. He simply quotes prices and size. However, in certain markets, once a bid is hit or an offer taken, names are given up. In the Fed funds market, for example, before the seller can agree to a trade, he must know to whom he is selling because he has to check that he has a line to the buyer and that it is not full. Also, the buyer has to know who the seller is because the two institutions clear the transaction directly with each other over the Fed wire. In many brokered securities trades, in contrast, the seller never knows who the buyer is, and vice versa.

There are certain rules of ethics that brokers' clients are expected to observe. In particular, in markets in which names are given up, the customer is not supposed to then go around the broker and do the trade direct. Also, brokers feel it is unfair of a trader to use them as an information service and just do small trades through them. Traders who make a practice of this get to be known and ignored by brokers.

Usefulness of brokers

In recent years brokerage has been introduced to almost every sector of the money market; and in those market sectors where it did exist, the use of brokers has increased dramatically. One reason is that in all sectors of the market the number of dealers has expanded sharply; as a result, it has become increasingly difficult for a trader to know where other traders are quoting the market and to rapidly disseminate his own bids and offers other than through the communications network provided by the brokers. In the government market, there are over 35 primary dealers, and no bill trader can possibly keep in touch with his counterparts at other shops by talking to each of them directly.

Another important reason brokers are used is anonymity. A big bank or dealer may operate in such size that simply by bidding or offering, he will affect either market quotes or the size for which they are good. A trader who would be willing to buy $15 million in bills through a broker might, for example, be leery of buying the same amount at the same price from a big position house like Salomon Brothers for fear that Sali might have a lot more of these bills to sell.

A second reason anonymity is valued by traders is the "ego element." In the words of one dealer, "Anonymity is very important to those giant egos on Wall Street. When they make a bad trade, they just do not want the whole world to watch them unwind it at a loss."

Still another reason the brokers are used is because a lot of traders literally hate each other, usually because of some underlying ethical issue, real or perceived. As one trader noted, "There are guys I would not deal with personally, but if it happens through a broker, well OK. Money is green whatever the source."

A final reason brokers are used, particularly in the government market, is that the brokers' screens provide an arena in which a trader can paint pictures and play other trading games.

Blind brokering

Blind brokering has been a common practice in many areas of the money market for years. In plain English the term means simply that the broker does not give up the name of the other side of a trade to either party in the trade. Customers often prefer the practice because, especially if they are big players, they want anonymity; they do not want the world to know they are big buyers or sellers of, say, bills, especially if they are only part way through doing a big job. In a few areas of the money market blind brokering works to the advantage of the broker; if a special issue is being brokered by a repo broker, he'd rather do it blind because that way the securities borrower won't know next time he needs the security where to go direct to get it.

In a blind brokering operation, the broker, by acting as agent for an undisclosed third party, assumes, in the opinion of most lawyers (it is never the case that all lawyers agree on anything), all the responsibilities of a principal. Some brokers acknowledge this and say they are acting as principal. Others claim to be acting as agents.

After the Drysdale debacle (described at the end of this chapter), blind brokering got an undeserved bad name because Chase did what amounted to a lot of blind brokering for Drysdale and then tried to get off the hook when Drysdale defaulted by saying it had acted merely as agent, a position which it later reversed.

There are a lot of safeguards for all concerned built into the system of blind brokering as it is practiced by traditional brokers. First, the brokers protect themselves against credit risk by being *extremely* careful about with whom they deal. Second, dealers are extremely careful about (1) who a broker's other clients are and (2) how much capital the broker has. Whether a blind broker says he is principal, agent, or whatever, a dealer will set some limit on the exposure he will take to that broker—the amount depending both on the broker's capital and his other clients.

For a broker of securities, there is no delivery risk since delivery is always made against cash. Risk of loss does occur because of mistakes a broker makes; however, the elaborate internal controls brokers impose to prevent mistakes ensure that these are usually small in number and only for small amounts.

Consolidation of brokers

In recent years there has been a strong tendency for brokers to merge. The reasons are various. For a big blind broker, a marriage that adds to capital can look extremely attractive. A second reason for broker mergers is that a shop that handles a wide menu of securities has a better chance of getting its foot into a dealer's door and, once there, can better service the dealer's needs. Institutions that reverse out securities often do so, for example, as part of an arbitrage in which they invest in another security; a broker that offers one-stop shopping can put together the whole arbitrage package.

In Euro and foreign exchange brokering, both cross-market and trans-Atlantic mergers made sense. The foreign exchange and Euromarkets could not be separated, and no broker could provide an international service without having an office or tie of some sort in at least both New York and London.

Personnel

Brokering is much more than quoting rates. As brokers are wont to note, it's a highly professional business. The broker is often required to make split-second decisions about difficult questions. If a trader offers at a price and the broker has x bids at that price on his pad, with which buyer does he cross the trade? Technically he attempts to decide who was there first, but the choice is often complicated by the fact that the offer is for one amount, the bids for others.

Also, in some sectors of the money market, a broker does more than quote rates. The buyer or seller may look to him for information on the tone of the market, and it's the broker's job to sense that tone and be able to communicate it—to say, for example, to a bidder, "The market's 5/16– 3/8, last trade at 5, but I think it could be worth 3/8."

Being a broker is also part salesmanship, to get a buyer or seller who has done one trade to let the broker continue to work for him. This is especially the case in markets, such as those for Fed funds and Euros, where a dealer who does a trade is likely to have a lot more business to do in the same direction during the day. In one area of brokering, the reverse market, salesmanship is crucial. To get a bank or an S&L to reverse out securities, the broker almost always has to point out a profitable arbitrage and then sell the institution on doing that arbitrage.

Being a good broker requires a special mix of talents. As noted, salesmanship is one. In addition, a broker has to be able to listen with one ear on the phone and keep the other tuned to bids and offers coming in around him, to maintain a feel for his own market and for other related markets as well. A good broker also has to be able to think on his feet and often use his own personality to put trades together. As one broker noted, "Brightness is not enough; anyone can quote a market."

Many brokers are ex-traders, people who have the advantage when they come to brokering of knowing a market and how traders in it operate. One reason traders become brokers is the pressure under which traders operate. Another is their own inability to do what many good traders do, forget their position when they go home. Said one successful broker, "Trading is a problem. You track the things you think might impact the market and then buy. All too often the unexpected—war in the Mid East—happens and you end up being right for the wrong reason, or vice versa. Once as a trader, I was down three-quarters of a million. I made 2 million the next month, but accepting the fact that I had done something stupid at one point in time was too much. It's part of the reason I became a broker."

COMMUNICATIONS

In a discussion of the makers of the money market, ignoring the phone company, Telexes, CRTs, computers, and other communications facilities would be a serious omission. Without Ma Bell and her foreign counterparts, the money market would be an utterly different place. That the money market is a single market that closely approaches the economist's assumption of perfect information is currently due in no small part to the fact that New York brokers and traders are one push of a direct-phone-line button away from the B of A and often only a four-digit extension from London, Singapore, and other distant spots. All this is extremely expensive. Banks spend well over half a billion on phone bills; and the nonbank dealers and brokers spend huge amounts in addition to that. To cut costs, the banking industry has considered setting up a private interbank phone network, which would be the most ambitious private phone network in the country.

The phone bill is one reason for the concentration of the money market in New York. The brokers in particular have to be there to minimize communications costs. It is cheaper to be in New York with one direct phone line to the B of A than to be in San Francisco with 30 direct lines to New York.

Phones, while ubiquitous, are not enough. Giving and receiving quotes over the phone takes more time than money market participants have; thus the growing role of CRTs.

Only a few years ago the only way money market participants could get current quotes was by calling brokers and dealers. Moreover, to get a range of quotes they had to make several calls because no quote system covered the whole market. In 1968 a new organization, *Telerate,* began to remedy this situation by quoting commercial paper rates on a two-page, cathode-ray-tube display system; it then had 50 subscribers. From this modest start, the system was quickly expanded because people wanted more information.

Today several hundred pages of information on credit market quotes and statistics are available to Telerate subscribers; the subscriber gets the page he wants by pressing a series of numbered buttons. Information on current quotes, offerings, and bids are inputted into the system through computers around the country, and the system is dynamically updated; that is, if GMAC changed its posted rate while a viewer is looking at the commercial paper quotes, the quotes change as GMAC inputs its new rates into the system. A wide range of institutions now use Telerate; its advent has not only eliminated a lot of phone calls but vastly improved communications within the money market. On the international scene, there is a similar *Reuters* system that flashes information on the Euromarket, the foreign exchange market, and other related markets into foreign countries and the United States. Since the money market is international in scope, it was to be expected that both Telerate and Reuters invaded each others' turf both geographically and in terms of information provided.

Many brokers in the government and other markets have also replaced endless phone quotes with CRTs that they have placed before the traders at dealer shops. Today every trading room is literally strewn with CRTs.

While impressive, the present CRT systems are not the ultimate state of the art. In the view of some participants, the money market is on the threshold of a communications revolution. One London dealer noted, "We are working on a system by which we will show our offerings and rates on a CRT. Say Ford in Dearborn, Michigan, hits our code. They will be to type on a machine, like a Telex, a message that will come up on our CRT in London: 'Want to buy your 5 million Chases, Oct. 17th, bid you 7/8.' We are offering at 13/16 and decide to take hit their bid. So we type in, 'OK, done.' Then they type in, 'Deliver to Morgan,' and the confirmations come out of the machine. We are going to put on the screen actual offerings; Cantor Fitzgerald already does that in governments, but they do not trade off the machine."

Said another dealer, envisioning much the same sort of development, "The firms like us without branch offices will introduce machines to the world to undercut the branch office franchises of the Merrills and the Salis. It is clear that for firms like us that lack branch offices, this is the cost-effective way to compete. We will trade off those machines; the black box is coming, and when it does, the market will go central marketplace."

DEALERS THAT GOT IT WRONG

In the spring and summer of 1982, two money market dealers, Drysdale Government Securities Inc. and Lombard-Wall Inc., went bankrupt. Their stories are important for several reasons. First, the two bankruptcies, one coming on the heels of the other, gave the market—already troubled over the condition of the banking system—a first class case of jitters and caused many market participants to examine their procedures for monitoring and controlling their exposure to credit risk. Second, these failures again brought up a host of questions—raised seven years earlier by the failure of Financial Corp.—with respect to the precise nature of a repo transaction. Third, the Drysdale debacle caused the Fed to order a change in the way collateral is priced on repo transactions and raised the specter of further regulation of the government market and of dealers in it.

Financial Corporation

People on the street were first made acutely aware of the risks involved in repo and reverse transactions because of the sobering experience to which Eldin Miller, who headed Financial Corporation of Kansas City, treated them in 1975.

"Eldin," said a dealer who knew him well, "was a guy who made a fortune in trucking. He came to New York looking like a church deacon. He didn't drink, he didn't smoke, and his personality was such that people tended to trust him."

Eldin rapidly built up a huge portfolio—eventually totaling $1.8 billion—of governments financed almost solely in the RP market. He bought first bills and later coupons. So long as interest rates were falling or flat, there was a profitable arbitrage in this: Eldin borrowed short, invested long, and raked in positive carry. Eventually, however, interest rates moved against him, and carry on his position turned negative. This caused a cash drain, which Eldin met by RPing out at par to unsophisticated investors, including some state and municipal investment officers, T bills selling at 94. He was able to do this because, as one dealer notes, "Eldin ran into some real dummies who said, "OK he has $100 million of bills: The dollar price on them is 94, but we will lend him par because it is too difficult to write funny number tickets."

As interest rates continued to go against him and his cash drain continued, Eldin—who learned street games fast—started reversing in Treasury bonds and then shorting them. Since it was then normal on a reverse to ignore accrued interest in pricing collateral on a reverse, Eldin was able to generate cash equal to roughly the amount of the accrued interest on a bond every time he reversed in a bond and then sold it.

Even that ploy, however, did not suffice to meet Financial Corp.'s cash needs, and eventually the firm failed. The people who had loaned the firm money against bills had collateral, but its market value was often less than the amount of the loan. Meanwhile the people who had borrowed money from the firm against collateral in the form of coupons found that the amount of money they had was often smaller than the market value (accrued interest included) of the securities they had reversed out to Financial Corp.

Many of those—whom Eldin reminded, by his dealings with them, that the prudent deal only with those they know and trust—were large, respectable, normally astute institutions. That Eldin could fool them made him the object of some admiration among street traders. Said one, "The guy in Kansas had class. There are people who have embezzled $5 or $10 million. He did $1.8 billion!" Actually that's an exaggeration; when he went belly up, Eldin was estimated to owe a mere $15 to $24 million to his unpaid creditors.

The failure of Financial Corp. raised crucial questions: Is a repo (or reverse) a true sale-repurchase *or* a collateralized loan? If it is the former and the side owing the money fails to execute the repurchase, does the side holding securities have the right to sell them? If so and there is *overage*—the securities sale produces proceeds that exceed the loan plus accrued repo interest—to whom is the overage due?

It seems startling that people waited until the repo market had become a huge sector of the money market to question the true nature of a repo. In fact it was a situation the street slipped into naturally and gradually. Neither Congress nor any other body had ever defined in law what a repo is. That technicality notwithstanding, a repo transaction seemed, first to a few and then to many money participants, a convenient way to do something they wanted to do—be it finance securities, lend securities, or do one leg of an arb; and the repo market grew like Topsy with only a few participants evidencing concern, until Miller came along, over the risk that the transaction might involve.

Miller's failure left in its wake a host of suits in courts around the country, suits that took years to settle. The street's initial presumption concerning where things stood and probably would stand when the legal dust settled coincided by and large with the opinion expressed in 1977 by one RP dealer, "My position is that, if I have your bonds and you do not pay me back, it is my prerogative to sell those bonds and sue you for any difference. The distinction between RP and a collateralized loan is that in an RP transaction I own those bonds, whereas on a collateralized loan there are release agreements and certain legalities I have to go through before I can handle the underlying collateral as if I owned it."

After some years, the Miller bankruptcy generated rulings on a number of suits. A problem is that these lack consistency and so set no precedents. Currently it is impossible to predict the outcome of a case in any jurisdiction except in the rare instance where a case is exactly like one already tried there. The outcomes of the suits against Miller have thus led to a confusing situation: When the borrower of money defaults, in some jurisdictions investors feel they can keep the securities and even any excess collateral; in other jurisdictions, investors feel they can't keep the collateral; in most jurisdictions investors don't know where they stand.

The first ruling arising from the Miller bankruptcy was on a suit brought by Miller against the state of Florida for overage that resulted when the state sold bonds it had held as collateral in a reverse on which Miller defaulted. The Florida court ruled that Miller had forfeited the securities when he failed to pay the state money due it at the end of the 30-day transaction.

Miller grabbed this ruling and took off for California where an oil company was suing him for the difference between the market value of the securities it held and the larger amount of money owed it by Miller. Miller cited the Florida ruling as a precedent for claiming that the oil company owned the bonds at market, period.

The county of Los Angeles had a contract with Miller which stipulated that it could sell any securities that it might be left holding in the event of default by Miller. When Miller did default, LA County did exactly what Florida had done: sold out the collateral it held, came out ahead on the deal, and said to Miller, "Sue us if you want the overage."

For most people who had deals with Miller on their books when he went bankrupt, things went less pleasantly. Institutions that had loaned him par against year bills worth 94 had a choice: sell out at a loss or hold the securities to maturity and forget about Miller paying any interest on the reverse. There were also many investors who had reversed at market price to Miller bonds that had 3 months of accrued interest on them. It was on trades of this sort that the biggest sums were lost in the Miller bankruptcy. People involved in such trades lost both interest accrued on their bonds at the time the reverse transaction occurred and interest accrued during the life of the reverse.

While the initial rulings on suits arising from Miller's bankruptcy set no overriding precedents, they suggested that the street had some justification in operating on the working hypothesis that, in the case of default by the borrower of money, the position of the securities holder was: if you've got them, you can sell them.

Drysdale Securities

When Financial Corp. went under, people assumed that money market participants had been so chastened by its failure and by the Winters debacle in Ginnie Mae forwards which preceded it that they would henceforth either institute new credit controls or strictly enforce controls already in place. Drysdale proved this presumption incorrect.

In its brief—three months—career, Drysdale is estimated to have shorted $4 billion of bonds and to have gone long another $2.5 billion on the basis of a mere $20 million in capital. Drysdale's basic game was to reverse in through agent banks—Chase and others—high-coupon securities nearing a coupon date; for collateral, Drysdale put up cash close to the dollar prices at which these securities were trading; it then sold the borrowed securities for principal *plus* accrued interest and in the process garnered for itself significantly more cash than it had paid out.

By the time Drysdale started playing Miller's final game, high interest rates had ballooned enormously the sums that could be generated from it. For example, a firm shorting $500 million of a bond carrying a 12%

coupon five months into a coupon period could pick up $25 million of cash for a month. Drysdale saw this; its sin, if any, was to abuse the system to its logical conclusion, to say, "Why do this for $500 million? We will do it for $5 billion."

A time-honored street convention was that, when a firm borrows bonds, it must pass onto the lender of these securities any coupon interest paid on them. When the May coupon date arrived on the bonds Drysdale had borrowed, it was—to the shock of the street—unable to come up with cash to pay the agent banks through which it had borrowed these securities the coupon interest owed to the ultimate lenders of the bonds.

Then the fun started. Chase said it would not make good on the $160 million of coupon interest owed to investors whose bonds it had loaned to Drysdale on the grounds that it had acted only as agent not principal. Manny, which was hit for a much smaller amount ($29.3 million), and U.S. Trust, which lost a "nonmaterial" amount, paid up right away.

Dealers on the street reacted with shock to Chase's action fearing not only that they would lose money but that the Drysdale failure might set in motion a *domino* effect that would bring other dealers on the street tumbling down with it. Nonreceipt of some portion of the $160 million of missing interest might have been a big hit against the capital of some small firms, especially since at the time a lot of firms were doing poorly anyway because the market was running against them. If some other firms had gone down, their inability to meet their commitments to still other firms might in turn have forced those firms to fail as well. In a worst-case scenario, a scramble by many firms on the street to raise cash to meet their obligations might have caused a lot of selling of securities, which in turn would have depressed their prices and caused still greater losses for firms with big long positions.

After Chase announced its refusal to pay out the $160 million of interest due from Drysdale for whom it had acted as agent, the NY Fed hastily convened a meeting of Chase and the other dealers. It was widely rumored that at that meeting the Fed did some arm twisting to get the Chase to honor what other dealers thought was its obligations and to prevent possible calamity on the street. Merrill, whose Readi Assets Trust Fund then held $736 million of Chase BAs and CDs, was also reported to have done a little arm twisting on its own.

In the end Chase agreed to come up with the $160 million of interest due and to take responsibility for that portion of Drysdale's position assumed through trades on which it had acted as agent. At the same time Chase reserved the right to pursue future legal actions against third parties.

Chase's decision caused sighs of relief on the street. At the same time it left important questions unanswered: What was Chase's real role and responsibility in the Drysdale debacle, and how did it get itself into such a mess? How did the supposedly savvy street firms with all their controls on credit exposure allow themselves to get caught in such a snafu? How did Drysdale lose so much money so fast? It cost Chase $285 million pretax to meet Drysdale's interest payments and unwind its positions.

The story runs—as best as can be determined—like this: Drysdale wanted to short a lot of high-coupon bonds carrying big sums of accrued interest for two reasons—to generate cash and because it thought rates would move higher permitting it to profit on the shorts it intended to establish. It got some lower-level officers in Chase's securities lending department to provide it with securities that Chase obtained from Button-wood and C&W, firms that specialize in finding and borrowing stocks and bonds for a fee.

In taking in these securities, Chase had the delivery tickets made out Chase NY/Cust/Special loan account, as opposed to, say, Chase/Inv, which would have indicated that the securities were destined for Chase's portfolio (inventory), or Chase/dealer, which would have indicated that the securities were destined for its dealer operation.

The way the tickets were made out should have immediately alerted securities lenders to the fact that a third party other than Chase was involved in the deal. Shops that saw this warning signal reacted in several ways. Some refused outright to deal with Chase on those terms unless it revealed the name of the third party involved, which it would not. Others asked Chase for a letter assuring them that Chase was acting as principal; Chase refused to give this letter, which caused these firms to refuse to deal with Chase. Still other firms seeing the Chase ticket took the view that, by not disclosing the third party for whom it was acting, Chase was assuming de facto—and de jure should the case ever come to court—the role of principal and that, this being the case, they willingly dealt with Chase. Finally, there were other investors, probably the majority, who paid no attention to what was on the ticket and simply did the trade assuming that Chase was the principal.

The prevailing legal opinion after the dust started to settle on the Drysdale case was that Chase, by acting as agent for an undisclosed third party, had assumed 99.9%, if not all, of the responsibilities of principal. Therefore if it had continued its initial refusal to pay out the $160 million of interest due to bond lenders, the courts would eventually have forced it to do so.

This observation raises the question of how Chase, the nation's third largest bank, allowed itself to get into the position where it had a credit exposure of over a quarter of a billion dollars to a small new dealer with $20 million in capital. The answer seems to be that the people in Chase's securities lending department who were doing the business were in over their heads; they thought they were acting as agent not principal; and consequently they did not realize the credit risk to which their actions exposed the bank. What they did perceive was that their activities were generating some nice fee income that would add to Chase's return on assets and presumably lead to their earning some recognition in terms of remuneration or stature within the bank. Also, it is has been widely reported that at least some people at Chase were being paid under the table by Buttonwood and C&W for taking in and funneling securities to Drysdale.

Stripping the Drysdale transactions down to bare bones, what Chase was doing was acting as a *blind broker.* The catch phrase, blind broker, immediately acquired a pejorative connotation, and regulators wondered if they should not act in some way to stop the practice. Actually the bad name that Chase's actions gave to blind brokering was totally undeserved. There are a number of large and highly reputable blind brokers operating on the street without whose services major dealers could not operate as effectively as market makers as they currently do.

As one blind broker of RP noted, "If it had been me instead of Chase fronting for Drysdale, the situation could never have occurred. My customers know the net worth of my firm [less than $50 million], and they limit their exposure to us. If I were to take $500 million of coupons in from a customer and put $25 back out to them, they would have to my firm a net-accrued-coupon exposure on $475 million of bonds; that could be $10 or $20 million of accrued interest. A huge amount. People are not going to take a $20 million exposure with me."

How Drysdale managed to lose as much money as it did playing around for all of three months with $20 million of capital remains something of a mystery. As one astute trader noted, "I find it puzzling that Drysdale could lose so much so fast. If you charged me to lose ¼ of a billion, I think it would be hard to do; I would probably end up making money some of the time because I would buy something I thought was going down and it would go up. They must have been extraordinarily good at losing money."

In fact Drysdale did make money on some of its trades. Noted another trader, "Drysdale did a lot of good trades. From what I saw in the market, I know they bought the 2-year note in February and March—a lot of them—great trades on which they have to make a huge profit no matter when they sold them; they could not have done otherwise."

The upshot of Drysdale was that Chase lost a lot of money and presumably tightened controls; other dealers lost nothing; securities lawyers spent a lot of time delving into the finer points of the distinction between agent and principal; and the Fed was finally stirred into action. In a letter to all recognized dealers, the New York Fed ordered them to begin in October 1982 to include accrued interest in pricing securities used as collateral in repo and reversed transactions. The reactions of dealers to the switch to *full-accrued pricing* and its ramification for the way repo transactions are now done are discussed in Chapter 12.

It was reported in *Barron's* that Drysdale was put out of business by a street conspiracy. Traders laugh at this. Traders are out to make a buck, and if they perceive that another trader has gotten out on a limb, they will gouge him ruthlessly, but they won't saw off the limb. When traders saw Drysdale trying to establish big shorts, they let him but always by hitting one down bid after another with the result that Drysdale set some sloppy shorts. Later when Drysdale was trying to cover by borrowing issues and everyone knew it, traders said, "Sure we will loan these issues to you [Drysdale], but they are very rare; that is 8% never mind that the RP market is trading around 14%." That is not conspiracy; it is just trading with your archetype competitor who's out to win big and has no intention of being nice about it.

Lombard-Wall's downfall

The failure in May 1982 of Drysdale cast doubt on the creditworthiness of small dealers in general. In this climate it was not hard for Lombard-Wall, another small dealer, to add its name to the casualty list, which it did in August 1982. Unlike Financial Corp. and Drysdale, Lombard-Wall did not abuse the repo market to raise cash to finance speculations. It got into trouble by offering flex repos to its customers, a legitimate transaction but one that requires an ability, which Lombard-Wall apparently lacked, to perceive the full market risk in a position and to manage asset and liability maturities accordingly.

A specialty of Lombard-Wall was to do *flex repos* with housing and other authorities. These authorities floated bond issues to pay for construction projects that required cash payouts over several years; they then invested the bond proceeds over the payout period in flex repos. These repos were often done as part of a package in which the dealer agreed to do the bond underwriting provided the borrower promised to do with him a repo lasting several years. Under a flex RP, it was understood that the borrower would draw funds out of the RP according to some prearranged schedule. A safe way for a dealer to quote a fixed rate on a flex repo lasting several years would be to buy securities with maturities matching the time spans for which varying amounts of cash were to be lodged by the bond issuer with the dealer: to run—in the jargon of asset and liability managers—a *matched book* on which it locked in a small spread. Lombard-Wall did not do this; instead it mismatched its book on the basis of incorrect predictions of interest-rate trends; this eventually caused it to lose substantial amounts of money.

A common problem with flex repos is that the bond issuer, while required to provide a draw-down schedule, need not adhere to it and often does not. The draw-down schedules of some borrowers are quite predictable, those of others less so. Because uncertainty often exists concerning a borrower's draw-down schedule, the only shops that should be doing flex repos are those that understand the risk and can afford to take it. A large shop doing a flex repo—and large shops do do this business because it is big business—will, in quoting a rate on a flex repo, take into consideration not only the shape of the draw-down schedule but both the predictability of the borrower in sticking to it and any provisions written into the repo contract limiting the flexibility of the timing of draw-downs.[13]

When Lombard-Wall failed, the NYS Dormitory Authority ended up with a $55 million unsecured claim against Lombard. How this arose out of a repo transaction remains unclear. Presumably Lombard gave the Dormitory Authority not collateral but a safekeeping receipt, which, as it lost more and more money, Lombard was unable to back with securities having a market value equal to that indicated by the receipt.

On a flex repo the dealer normally has unlimited right of substitution with respect to collateral, and safekeeping receipts are not uncommon. Such receipts also make sense on an open repo on which dealers commonly ask for the right of substitution because they like to throw into such repos odds and ends too small to repo alone. A safekeeping receipt amounts to a guarantee that securities have been segregated in a bank account for the repo investor. Most investors, who have an on going safekeeping-receipt relationship with a dealer, periodically send their auditor to check that the securities that are supposed to be in their account are in fact there. One can only guess that the Dormitory Authority failed to do so.

The Dormitory Authority's well-publicized potential losses led some people to argue that flex repos should be banned. However, it was the Dormitory Authority that chose for a few extra basis points to deal with a poorly capitalized firm like Lombard when it could have struck a similar deal with a highly capitalized, well-regarded dealer—DLJ, Goldman, or the B of A to name a few—that have been around a long time.[14]

At the time it went into Chapter 11, Lombard had an unsecured debt of $45 million to the Chase Bank. Every dealer needs a line of credit. As noted, dealers are highly leveraged: as high as 500 or 600 times capital. To finance in the repo market positions equal to a large multiple of their capital, dealers need a safety net in the form of a bank line of credit.

---

[13] Flex repos are done not only in connection with municipal issues but also for corporations issuing bonds to finance the construction of plant equipment.

[14] The Dormitory Authority was reported to have entrusted $305 million of idle funds to Lombard-Wall early in 1982 after taking bids from 15 financial institutions offering various interest rates. For an investor to shop for yield without regard to credit risk and the size of its exposure to a single dealer is to invite trouble.

Should interest rates rise and the value of the securities financed therefore fall, normal market practice is that the securities RPed will be repriced to reflect their now lower market value. Such repricing reduces the amount of money a dealer can borrow against his securities and thereby eats into his capital. At some point, to hold its securities, the dealer may have to fall back on its line of credit. Presumably its losses forced Lombard-Wall to draw on its line from Chase.

Repo: A sale-repurchase or a collateralized loan?

The events following the failure of Lombard-Wall cast serious doubt on the widely prevailing street presumption that a repo would be regarded in court as a sale-repurchase agreement. When Lombard filed for Chapter 11 status in early August, it argued that federal bankruptcy law prohibited its customers from selling securities it had reversed out to them as part of the repo transaction.

Specifically, Lombard asked the court for and got a stay in bankruptcy. This means that the firm received the protection of the court and that all of its transactions were *stayed*. If the court interprets repo, which it seemed to be doing, as a collateralized loan, then an investor holding collateral as part of a repo transaction on the books with Lombard at the time of its failure becomes a secured creditor, someone to be treated preferentially in bankruptcy proceedings but someone who could also have to wait out years of litigation to get his money back.

The judge in the Lombard-Wall case permitted several hardship cases, Reserve Fund (a money fund) in particular, to sell securities held as collateral, but by and large he seemed inclined to the interpretation that a repo transaction is a secured loan.

As noted in Chapter 12, this creates a situation that repo market participants cannot live with. Two possible solutions to the dilemma exist: One is to obtain a binding definition of repo as a sale-repurchase agreement; the other is to get Congress to amend the 1978 bankruptcy law to make special provision for repo transactions. More about this in Chapter 12.

Chapter 10

The investors:
Running a short-term portfolio

MONEY MARKET INVESTORS include a wide range of institutions: commercial banks, savings and loan associations, insurance companies of all sorts, mutual savings banks, other financial institutions, federal agencies, nonfinancial corporations, international financial institutions, such as the World Bank, foreign central banks, and foreign firms—financial and nonfinancial. Also, when interest rates get sufficiently high, individual investors make forays into certain sectors of the money market.

One might expect most institutional portfolios to be managed with considerable sophistication, but "the startling thing you would find, if you were to wander around the country talking to short-term portfolio managers [bank and corporate], is the basic underutilization of the portfolio." These are the words of the sales manager of the government department in one of the nation's top banks. Another dealer described portfolio management practices similarly but in slightly different terms, "Most portfolio managers would describe themselves as 'conservative,' by which they mean that the correct way to manage a portfolio is to look to your accounting risk and reduce that to zero. The opportunities thereby forgone are either ignored or more frequently not even perceived." Most short-term portfolios are poorly managed, many are not managed at all. Before we talk about that, let's look first at how a liquidity portfolio should be managed.

CONTRAST OF A PORTFOLIO MANAGER WITH A DEALER

In Chapter 9, we noted that dealers' biggest profits result over time from well-chosen position plays and that a crucial ingredient in a successful dealer operation is therefore the ability to manage a highly levered portfolio well.

Much of what we said in Chapter 9 about how a good dealer manages his portfolio applies to bank and corporate portfolio managers as well. There are, however, important differences in perspective between the two. First, a dealer is likely to be *much* less risk averse than the typical manager of a liquidity portfolio because it is the dealer's job to speculate on yields and yields spreads, whereas the portfolio manager's job is first to ensure that the funds he invests will be available whenever his firm needs them and only second to maximize the return he earns on these funds. A second difference in perspective is that, whereas the portfolio manager has free funds that he has to invest, the dealer has no such funds, and his decision to invest is therefore always based on a view of the market. A third difference in perspective is the time horizon. A dealer often buys securities on the expectation that he will be able to resell them at a higher price within a few hours or a few days. The portfolio manager, in contrast, is normally looking for instruments that he would be comfortable holding for some longer period—how long depends on the type of portfolio he is running.

THE PARAMETERS

A liquidity portfolio is always managed within certain investment *parameters* that establish limits with respect to: (1) the types of instruments the portfolio may buy; (2) the percentage of the portfolio that may be invested in any one of these instruments (in T bills the limit might be 100%, whereas in CDs, which are less liquid, it might be much lower); (3) the kind of exposure to names and credit risk the portfolio may assume (which banks' CDs and which issuers' commercial paper it may buy and how much of each name it may buy); (4) whether the portfolio may invest in Euros and foreign names; (5) how far out on the maturity spectrum the portfolio may extend; (6) whether the portfolio may short securities or repo securities; and (7) whether the portfolio may use futures and options.

The investment parameters within which every liquidity portfolio operates are set by top management. Because senior management delineates the portfolio manager's playing field and thereby the kinds of winnings—return on investment—that he can seek to earn through managing the portfolio, it is important that management take time to learn what the game is about before establishing such guidelines. Another input in this decision should be an evaluation of the kind of money that the firm is likely to have to invest short term: How big is it likely to be? How variable will it be? A third important input is the firm's management style. There are swinging corporations and there are very conservative corporations, and that difference should be reflected in their styles of portfolio management. A fourth factor is the caliber of the personnel the firm hires to manage its short-term portfolio. Investment parameters are meant to limit the portfolio manager's freedom of judgment, and inevitably they will at times prevent him from pursuing strategies that he correctly believes would increase return. For example, tight restrictions on the amount a portfolio manager could invest in BAs might prevent him, when BAs were trading at an attractive spread to bills, from making a profitable swap out of bills into BAs. The more qualified the personnel the firm anticipates hiring to run its liquidity portfolio, the wider guidelines should be set and the greater the latitude the portfolio manager should be given to exercise judgment.

MANAGING A LIQUIDITY PORTFOLIO

In large institutions a portfolio manager is often given several portfolios to manage—one for the firm itself, another for its financing sub, still others for self-insurance funds, and so forth. With respect to each portfolio, the manager has to ask: What are the size, variability, and predictability of the money I am investing? The answer obviously depends in part on the purpose for which the funds are held. For example, the short-term portfolio of a manufacturing firm that experiences big seasonal fluctuations in cash flows, as auto firms and food packers do, will be more variable and less predictable in size than a portfolio supporting a self-insurance fund. A second element in the portfolio manager's evaluation of the sort of money he is investing is the cash forecasts the firm gives him—their frequency, the periods for which they are available (these might be tomorrow, the next week, the next month, and the current quarter), and the confidence that experience suggests he can place in these forecasts. The portfolio manager's assessment of the sort of money he is investing tells him how long he is likely to be able to hold securities he buys and thus the planning horizon—30 days, 90 days, 1 year, or longer—upon which he should base investment decisions.

Relative value

Once he has determined his planning horizon, the portfolio manager asks, just as a dealer does: *Where is relative value?* Answering this question requires knowledge, experience, and feel for the market.

On a purely technical level, the portfolio manager first has to face the problem that yields on money market instruments are not quoted on comparable bases. The problem is not just that yields on discount securities are quoted on a discount basis whereas yields on interest-bearing instruments are quoted on another basis. There are also all sorts of other anomalies with respect to how interest accrues, how often it is paid, whether the security is U.S. or Canadian (Canadian CDs trade on a 365-day-year basis, domestic CDs on a 360-day-year basis), whether it is a leap year, whether a security happens to mature on a holiday, and other factors. These anomalies, moreover, are *not* reflected in the yield to maturity figures on dealers' quote sheets.[1]

A number of portfolio managers, who run such large sums of money that the cost is justified, have developed sophisticated computer programs that permit them to calculate yields on a wide range of securities on a comparable basis. One such portfolio manager noted, "I developed a program that incorporated a day algorithm which I got from a mathematician. I wanted the computer to know when a weekend occurs and to skip it in evaluating yield on a Friday trade I do for regular settlement. I also wanted the computer to recognize that in agencies July 31 is a nonday [in terms of interest accrued], that February 29 exists whether or not it actually does, and so too does February 30; there's an arbitrage from February 28 to March 1 in agencies, and I want the computer to recognize this. The computer also knows a Canadian security from a U.S. security."

In evaluating the relative value of different instruments, being able to calculate their yields on a comparable basis is just a starting point. In addition, the portfolio manager has to have a good feel for the *liquidity* of different instruments, under both prevailing market conditions and those he foresees might occur. This can involve subtle distinctions. The manager of a large portfolio commented, "I buy only direct issue [commercial] paper that I know I can sell to the dealers—GMAC but not Prulease. It's a question of liquidity, not quality. Also I buy paper from dealers only if they are ready to take it back."

To determine relative value among different instruments, the portfolio manager must also have a good feel for *yield spreads:* what they are, and how and why they change. This too involves subtleties. Here's an example given by one investor, "Lately the 6-month bill has been trading

---

[1] See Marcia Stigum and John Mann, *Money Market Calculations: Yields, Break-evens, and Arbitrage* (Homewood, Ill.: Dow Jones-Irwin, 1981).

above Fed funds. I ask, 'Why?' The technical condition of the market has been excellent with little supply on the street [in dealers' hands]. So the 6-month bill should have done better, but it didn't. The reason is that we've got a pure dealer market. The retail buyer, who is scared and going short, is simply not there."

Finally, to determine where relative value lies among different *maturity* sectors of the market, the portfolio manager must explicitly predict interest rates *and* the slope of the yield curve over at least the time span of his planning horizon. Such predictions will, as noted in Chapter 8, be based on a wide range of factors, including a careful tracking of the Fed's stated objectives and whether it is currently achieving these objectives.

Relative value, in addition to depending on all the factors we have enumerated, may also depend partly of the temperament of the portfolio manager—whether he has the psychology of a trader, as a number of top portfolio managers do, or is more inclined to make a reasoned bet and let it stand for some time, an attitude characteristic of other successful portfolio managers. As one investor noted, it makes a difference, "The 9-month bill will, except in very tight markets, trade at yield levels close to the corresponding long issue, which is the 1-year bill. So if you are looking for the most return for your dollar on a buy-and-hold strategy, you buy the 9-month bill and ride it for 3 months. If, however, you want to trade the portfolio—to buy something with the idea that its price will rise—you are better off staying in the active issue, which would be the current year bill."

Credit risk

Most companies, when they have money and are trying to increase yield, will start reaching out on the credit spectrum—buying A-2 or P-2 paper.[2] A few do so in an intelligent and reasoned way, devoting considerable resources to searching out companies that are candidates for an upgrading of their credit rating to A-1 or P-1 and whose paper thus offers more relative value than that of A-1 and P-1 issuers.

The average firm, however, would probably be well advised not to take this route. As the sales manager of one dealership noted, "We tell a company doing this, "It's the wrong thing for you to do because you do not know how to do it. You have no ability to track these companies. Also their financial statements are not worth much, and you of all people should know this because you know what you do to your own.' They sort of look at us with jaundiced eyes, and say, 'Oh, yes, I guess that's so.' "

---

[2] Commercial paper, as noted in Chapter 18, is rated by several rating services. A-2 and P-2 paper are a grade off top-rated A-1 or P-1 paper.

The ablest portfolio managers tend as a group to steer clear of credit analysis. As one of the sharpest commented, "We are not interested in owning anything that does not have unimpeachable credit because, on an instrument that does not, credit will tend to dominate the performance of the instrument more than interest rates. Also, I am a one-man band, and I simply do not have time to evaluate credit risk."

Among large portfolio managers, the exception to this attitude is most often found in those in insurance companies, which are a different breed. They are far more comfortable than most with credit exposure. This is an offshoot of their purchase of long corporate bonds. Because of these purchases, insurance companies are following many corporations and consequently they can and do knowledgeably buy a lot of lesser-grade commercial paper that other portfolios would not touch.

Maturity choice

While a good portfolio manager can, as many do, refuse to get into credit analysis, he *cannot* avoid making explicit interest rate predictions and basing his maturity choices upon them. As one portfolio manager pointed out, "The mistake many people make is to think that they do not have to make a forecast. But buying a 90-day bill and holding it to maturity *is* making a forecast. If you think that rates are going to move up sharply and soon, you should be sitting in overnight RP; and then when rates move up, you buy the 90-day bill."

Making rate predictions is important not only because an implicit rate prediction underlies every maturity choice a portfolio manager makes, but because good portfolio managers feel as a group that the way yield on a large portfolio can most effectively be increased is by positioning correctly along the maturity spectrum—by recognizing which maturity sectors of the market are cheap (have relative value), which are expensive, and by buying or selling accordingly.

Riding the yield curve. The best way to illustrate the kind of dividends yielded by maturity choices based on an explicit prediction of how interest rates might move is with a few concrete examples. Let's start by illustrating how a technique commonly used to raise return— namely, *riding the yield curve*—must be based on an explicit prediction of how short-term rates might change. The idea of riding the yield curve is to increase return, when the yield curve is positively sloped, by buying a security out on the shoulder of the yield curve and holding that security until it can be sold at a gain because its current maturity has fallen and the yield at which it is currently trading has consequently decreased. Note that the main threats to the success of such a strategy are that short-term rates might rise across the board or that the yield curve might invert at the very short end.

Assume that an investor has funds to invest for 3 months. The 6-month (180-day) bill is trading at 7.90, and the 3-month (90-day) bill is trading at 7.50 (Figure 10–1). The alternatives the investor is choosing between are: (1) to buy the 90-day bill and mature it and (2) to buy the 6-month bill

FIGURE 10–1
Yield curve in an example of riding the yield curve

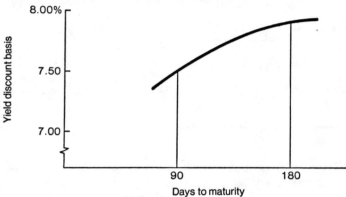

and sell it 3 months hence. To assess the relative merits of these two strategies, the investor does a *break-even analysis*.

On $1 million of bills, a 90-day basis point (a basis point earned for 90 days) is worth $25.[3] If the investor bought the 6-month bill, he would earn 40 basis points more than if he bought the 3-month bill. Thus he could sell out the 6-month bill after 3 months at a rate 40 basis points above the rate at which he bought it, that is, at 8.30, and still earn as many *dollars* on his investment as he would have if he had bought and matured the 3-month bill (Table 10–1). Therefore the rate on the 3-month bill 3 months hence would have to rise above 8.30 before holding the 6-month bill for 3 months would pay out fewer dollars than buying and maturing the 3-month bill.

How likely is this to occur? Note that because of the slope of the yield curve (a 40-basis-point drop between the 6-month and 3-month bill rates), the rate at which the 3-month bill trades 3 months hence would be

---

[3] The formula used (see page 46) is:

$$D = \left(\frac{d \times t}{360}\right) (\$1,000,000)$$

The calculation is as follows:

$$\left(\frac{0.0001 \times 90}{360}\right) (\$1,000,000) = \$25$$

TABLE 10–1
Dollar calculations of return in example of riding the yield curve

I. Buy $1 million of 90-day bills at 7.50% and hold to maturity.

Face value	$1,000,000		Discount at purchase	$18,750
−Purchase price	981,250		−Discount at maturity	0
Return	$ 18,750		Return	$18,750

II. Buy $1 million of 180-day bills at 7.90% and sell at breakeven yield of 8.30%.

Sale price	$979,250		Discount at purchase	$39,500
−Purchase price	960,500		−Discount at sale	20,750
Return	$ 18,750		Return	$18,750

III. Buy $1 million of 180-day bills at 7.90% and sell at 7.50%.

Sale price	$981,250		Discount at purchase	$39,500
−Purchase price	960,500		−Discount at sale	18,750
Return	$ 20,750		Return	$20,750

7.50 if no change occurred in interest rates, 80 basis points below the break-even rate of 8.30. Thus the investor has 80 basis points of protection, and the question he has to ask in making his choice is: How likely is it that the Fed will tighten in the next 3 months so sharply that the 3-month bill will rise 80 basis points, from 7.50 to 8.30? If his answer is that it is highly unlikely, then he would buy the 6-month bill and ride the yield curve.

Note that if the investor buys the 3-month bill and matures it, he will earn $18,750 on each $1 million of bills he buys (see Table 10–1). If, alternatively, he opts to ride the yield curve and does so successfully (i.e., buys the 6-month bill and is able, because the Fed does not tighten, to sell out at 7.50), he will earn $20,750, which exceeds $18,750 by $2,000. This $2,000 equals the extra 80 90-day basis points he earns: 40 because the 6-month bill is bought at a 40-basis-point spread to the 3-month bill and 40 because he is able to sell it 3 months later at a rate 40 basis points below the rate at which he bought it.

Actually the investor riding the yield curve in our example has more protection than we indicated. The reason is that, when he buys the 6-month bill, he invests fewer dollars than when he buys the 3-month bill. So on a *simple interest basis,* he would earn an annualized return of 7.75 if he bought and matured the 3-month bill, whereas if he bought the 6-month bill at 7.90 and sold it as the break-even level of 8.30, he would earn an annualized return, again on a simple interest, 365-day-year basis, of 7.92, which is greater.[4] To earn an annualized return of only

---

[4] The formula is:

$$\left(\begin{matrix}\text{Annualized return on a} \\ \text{simple interest basis}\end{matrix}\right) = \left(\frac{\text{Dollar return}}{\text{Principal invested}}\right) \div \left(\frac{\text{Days held}}{365}\right)$$

7.75 on the funds invested in the 6-month bill, the investor would have to sell it out after 3 months at a discount of 8.46, which is 96 basis points above 7.50. The first break-even calculation we made on a dollar-return basis is easier to make, but this second more refined calculation is the one the investor who wants to maximize yield should make.

Another maturity decision. Here's a second example of how a conscious prediction of interest rates over the investor's time horizon can help an investor increase yield. The example is dated, but the point it illustrates still holds. When it appears that the Fed might tighten, the reaction of many portfolio managers is to retreat in panic to the base of the yield curve. Whether doing so is wise depends on the opportunities available and on how fast and how far the Fed is likely to tighten.

In April 1977, it was felt that the Fed was tightening. Funds were trading at 4¾ and no one was sure where that rate was going. It was the feeling in the market that a ¾ point move was needed and that 5½ would probably be the top side, but some in the market suggested 5¾. Just prior to this period, 6-month BAs had risen in yield from 5.20 to 5.85 because of a lack of demand on the part of investors; the yield on 3-month BAs was 5.45. At this point a portfolio manager with 3-month money to invest faced a choice. One alternative, assuming he was managing an S&L portfolio, would have been to adopt the bearish strategy of selling overnight Fed funds in anticipation of eventually getting a 5½ overnight rate.[5] Alternatively, he could have decided to buy 6-month BAs and sell them after 3 months.

Using the same sort of break-even analysis illustrated in the previous example, one investor facing this choice concluded that if he bought 6-month BAs at 5.85, he could after 90 days sell them at 6.30, and do as well as he would have if he had invested in overnight Fed funds and the Fed funds rate had in fact immediately moved to 5½.[6] In other words, he could sell 6-month BAs 3 months hence at 85 basis points above the rate at which 3-month BAs were then trading and still earn as many dollars as he would have by rolling funds overnight at 5½. That 85 basis points of protection seemed more than sufficient, so he bought the 6-month BAs. As things turned out, the Fed's target for funds was only 5¼–⅜, so the BAs were by far the better investment. An investor who did not use this analysis would probably have missed this opportunity.

Asymmetric positions of the investor and the issuer. The two maturity-choice examples we worked through involved a choice between riding the yield curve and making an alternative investment: in

---

[5] The alternative facing a corporate portfolio manager would have been to invest in overnight RP at a slightly lower rate.

[6] The calculation assumes that the same number of dollars would have been invested in both instruments. It also allows for the fact that the investor of large sums in Fed funds in effect gets daily compounding of interest. The Fed funds rate is quoted on a 360-day-year basis.

one case buying and maturing the 3-month bill and in the other case rolling funds in the overnight market.

With respect to riding the yield curve, note that a bank liability manager issuing CDs or a firm issuing commercial paper is playing precisely the opposite ball game from the investor—one is trying to minimize interest paid, the other to maximize interest earned. If the issuer of paper finds that, from a cost point of view, it makes sense to roll 3-month CDs, then the investor should be buying 6-month paper and riding it for 3 months rather than rolling 3-month paper.

Stability of return

As one good portfolio manager after another will note, "Real money is to be made by positioning correctly along the maturity spectrum—by making conscious market judgments and acting on them."

Such positioning does not, however, guarantee *steady* high return. One reason is that sometimes the portfolio manager will be wrong in his rate predictions. A second reason is well described by one manager, "If you can invest out to 2 years and you feel strongly that rates are going to fall, you might choose to have an average 9- or 12-month maturity—not everything out in the longer spectrum. If you are correct and the market rallies, the proper response is to shorten the portfolio—not just to sit there and hold this apparent book yield, but to recognize it. The reason you sell is that the market eventually gets to a point where you think it has reached a peak and might go lower. If after you sell you decide that you were wrong and believe—on the basis of a new rate forecast—that rates are likely to go still lower, you buy in again long term."

It's hard to produce a stable income pattern with that sort of portfolio management, and thus it would be criticized by some. But the basic assumption is that the firm is a going concern. Therefore, the portfolio manager's primary goal should be long-term profitability not stability of income.

In this respect the track record of the World Bank's liquidity portfolio is interesting. The managers of this portfolio are constantly making maturity choices of the sort described above. In February 1977, their treasurer noted that over the previous 29 months, they had earned on their dollar portfolio a high average return, 9.32%, but their monthly annualized returns had fluctuated from a low of −0.67% in one month to a high of almost +32% in another.[7]

As that track record suggests, in evaluating the performance of a managed portfolio, monthly figures are meaningless. A portfolio manager needs to look at his average record for 6 months or longer to get a true feel for his performance.

---

[7] *The Money Manager,* February 14, 1977, p. 3.

Time horizon and maturity of securities purchased

In the example we gave of why the return on a managed portfolio is likely to fluctuate from month to month, the portfolio manager—believing that rates were likely to fall—might well have extended maturity into the 2-year area. In this respect it's important to note that such an extension does not imply that either the portfolio manager's planning horizon or his interest rate forecast extends anywhere near 2 years. It simply implies that he is confident that rates will fall during some much shorter period and that he is willing to sell and realize his gain once this occurs.

Good managers of short-term portfolios, who have wide parameters, frequently buy Treasury notes and other longer-term instruments in the hope of realizing short-term gains. Said an ex-portfolio manager, "If I liked the market, I'd buy a 10-year bond even if I needed the money tomorrow." That's an extreme example, but this portfolio manager had the inborn instincts of a good street trader, which he eventually became.

Changing relative value

The search for relative value is not a one-time affair. The money market is dynamic; changes in demand, supply, expectations, and external events—announcements of the latest money supply figures, changes in tax laws the souring of country loans, or the failure of a dealer—are constantly having an impact on it. And as they do, yield spreads and rates change. Thus relative value may reside in one sector today, in another tomorrow.

A good portfolio manager must reassess his position each day, asking not only whether his expectations with respect to interest rates have changed but whether transitory anomalies have arisen in spreads or distortions in rates from which he could profit.

One cause of transitory rate distortions is overreactions by investors. Said one portfolio manager, "When I saw the huge money supply figures last Friday [$2.7 billion for M1, $13 billion for M2], I started buying, knowing that in a few days the market would come back. This sort of overreaction has been much more common since '74, in part because there are so many more players in the market today."

Here's an example of another transitory rate situation from which a corporate portfolio manager could benefit. Capital gains are taxed as ordinary income for banks at the capital gains rate for corporations. Thus a longer-term municipal note selling at a discount from par offers a double-barreled tax advantage to a corporation but not to a bank.[8] Banks, however, are such big investors in this market that at times discount muni notes are priced to the bank market rather than to the corpo-

---

[8] This assumes that the corporation is in a position to benefit from tax-exempt income. See Chapter 19.

rate market. When they are, a corporation can earn a much higher after-tax return on such notes than it could from taxable securities of comparable maturity and risk.

Tracking changes in relative value takes time and effort, but as a portfolio manager gains experience, it becomes almost second nature. Also, a portfolio manager can rely on the dealers for help. Once a portfolio manager recognizes that a change in relative value has occurred between instruments or maturity sectors, his response should be to *swap* or *arbitrage*.

As one portfolio manager with wide parameters observed, "Arbitrating a portfolio is one way to make money, whether it's a complete arbitrage or a swapping arbitrage between sectors of the market. Money market instruments oscillate in relative value for very good reasons; and as you get experienced, you can with not too much time keep asking why one sector of the market is out of line with where it should be—the latter judgment being more than an extrapolation of a historical average. Once you have convinced yourself that the reason is transitory, then not to own the instrument that is undervalued and be short in the other instrument that is out of line is foolhardy."

Extension swaps

We discussed various arbitrage strategies in Chapter 9. One very simple swap strategy many portfolio managers use, when markets are calmer than they have been in recent years, is to do *extension swaps*. They pick a maturity sector of the market they like, say 2- or 3-year governments, and then, for example, adopt the strategy of *extending* (lengthening maturity) a few months whenever they can pick up 5 basis points and of *backing up* (shortening maturity) a few months whenever that costs only 3 basis points. If market conditions are such that many such swaps can be done, a portfolio manager can pick up basis points this way. Note that, whereas a 90-day basis point is worth only $25 per $1 million, a 3-year basis point is worth $300.[9]

A similar practice used by some investors in bills to pick up basis points is to roll the current 3-month or 6-month bill each week when new bills are auctioned. If conditions are such that new bill issues, which the market has to absorb, are priced in the auction cheap relative to surrounding issues, then by rolling his bills the investor may be able to pick up each week two or three $25 or $50 basis points by doing this. A second advantage of this strategy is that it keeps the investor in current bills, which are more liquid than off-the-run issues.

---

[9] The calculation is:

$$3(0.0001)(\$1,000,000) = \$300$$

In swapping and trading generally, "it's important," as one portfolio manager noted, "to know what dealer will deal in what and who will make the best markets. Say a bank has a big writing program and uses the dealer community—Becker, Sali, and Goldman. The bank sells the dealers 70 million, and they resell them to retail. If I have some of that bank's CDs, I would not go to Goldman, since I know their customers are stocked up on those CDs. Instead, I would go to some fourth dealer whose customers are light in that bank's CDs."

Leverage

Like a dealer, a portfolio manager can repo securities he owns.[10] If the portfolio is that of a fair-sized bank, the portfolio manager will probably be able to repo securities directly with retail customers. If, alternatively, the portfolio is that of a corporation or other institution that does not have direct contact with suppliers of repo money, the portfolio manager can always RP his securities with the dealers, who will in turn hang them out on the other side (see Chapter 12).

The ability to repo securities can be used by a portfolio manager in various ways. If an unanticipated short-term need for cash arises at a time when the portfolio manager has established a position he wants to maintain, he can bridge that gap by RPing his securities instead of selling them. Said one corporate portfolio manager, "We never fund to dates. We fund to market expectancy—what we think is going to happen to interest rates. We can repo the portfolio so we never have problems raising money for short periods. If we have to raise money for a long period to meet a portfolio embarrassment [securities in the portfolio can only be sold at a loss], that means we made an error and had better face up to it."

Another way a portfolio manager with wide parameters can use the RP market imaginatively is to buy a security, finance the first part of its life with term RP, and thereby create an attractive future security. That is a technique of portfolio management, the rewards and risks of which we discussed in Chapter 9. A corporate manager can use it as well as a dealer, and some do.

Still another way a portfolio manager can use the RP market is to out and out lever his portfolio—buy securities at one rate, turn around and RP them at a lower rate, and then use the funds borrowed to buy more

---

[10] Jargon in this area is confusing. Dealers talk about "doing repos" when they are financing their position and about "doing reverses" when they are borrowing securities. Some portfolio managers who use repurchase agreements—just as dealers do—to lever, talk about doing repo, others talk about doing a reverse (i.e., reversing out securities). We have opted to use the word *repo* when the initiative comes from the side wanting to borrow money, and *reverse* when the initiative comes for the side wanting to borrow securities.

securities. Or the portfolio manager can simply buy securities for which he has no money by doing a repo against them at the time of purchase. A portfolio manager who uses this technique commented, "I repo the portfolio as an arbitrage technique everyday and probably run the biggest matched sale book in American industry. We RP anything we can, even corporates. In doing RP, I am either financing something I have or buying something I don't have any money for. We take the RPs off for quarter ends because they might comprise the aesthetics of our statement." Avoiding repos across quarter ends is common among those corporations that use repos, so it is impossible from looking at financial statements to determine whether a corporation uses repos to borrow.

To the corporate portfolio manager who can use repos, it is, in the words of one, "the most flexible instrument in the money market. You can finance with repo, you can borrow using it, and you can ride the yield curve using it—buy a 2-month bill, put it out on repo for a month, and then sell it or do a 30-day repo again. And you can use repo to create instruments: put a 6-month bill out on a 2-month repo, and you have created a 4-month bill 2 months out."

Despite the many and reasonable ways in which the ability to borrow in the repo market can be used, it is rare for a corporate short-term portfolio manager to be able to hang out any of his portfolio on repo.

In large banks, the practice of RPing the government portfolio is almost universal. As noted in Chapter 5, such a bank views its government portfolio as a massive arbitrage rather than as a source of liquidity. Among smaller banks, practices with respect to the use of repo vary widely.

Arbitrages based on a term repo. In discussing the use of the repo market by portfolio managers to borrow, a distinction should be made between portfolio managers who are using the market consciously to borrow and lever, and those who are, so to speak, coaxed into doing reverses. As noted in Chapter 9, when dealers want to short securities they will often cover their short by reversing in securities. If the security is not one that is readily available, the dealer will go to a broker of repo who knows what securities various banks, S&Ls, and other institutions have in their portfolios. The broker will attempt to get an institution that holds the needed securities to reverse them out by showing that institution an attractive arbitrage. Such a transaction looks like an ordinary repo, but the initiative comes not from the institution that is borrowing but from the dealer who wants to cover a short. Many banks, S&Ls, and other institutions that would never use the repo market to borrow to meet a temporary cash need or to lever will reverse out securities that they intend to hold indefinitely, probably to maturity, to pick up basis points on an arbitrage.[11]

---

[11] For an example see Chapter 11, p. 393.

Break-even rate on a reverse to maturity. Frequently an institution that holds a government note or bond in its last coupon period will find that, by swapping out of that security into CDs, term Fed funds, or some other instrument, it can pick up 50 basis points or more. On a $1 million swap, a pickup of 50 basis points is worth approximately $2,500 if earned over 6 months, half as much if earned over 3 months. Thus such swaps are attractive. Many institutions, however, cannot do such a swap on an outright basis if the security they want to sell is trading, due to a rise in interest rates, below the book value their accountant assigns to it.

Institutions in this situation have to resort to doing swaps indirectly. Instead of selling the maturing notes or bonds, they *reverse them out to maturity* to a dealer; that is, they borrow money against the securities. They then invest that money in a higher-yielding instrument, often one that matches in current maturity the security being reversed out. An institution that does this type of transaction is in effect arbitraging between the low term RP rate at which it can borrow on a collateralized basis and the higher rate at which it can invest.

Normally a dealer who is doing a reverse to maturity will try to charge a reverse rate at least 10 basis points above his break-even rate. When a security's true yield to maturity—which measures the dealer's interest cost on the reverse—is significantly less than its yield to maturity on the quote sheet, the dealer will try for more. Thus it is worth an investor's time to calculate a dealer's *break-even reverse rate.* When a short government is sold and the proceeds are reinvested in some higher-yielding instrument, some $X of extra earnings will be picked up; how many go to the dealer and how many to the investor depends on where the reverse rate is set.

This point can perhaps be made with more punch by using a dollars-and-cents example. In one riskless-to-both-sides trade that a dealer made with a large but sleepy S&L, there was an $8,000 profit to be divvied up. The dealer set the reverse rate so that $5,000 went to him and $3,000 to the S&L doing the arb. Had the S&L treasurer known how to calculate the dealer's break-even reverse rate, he would have been in a position to bargain for a more equitable arrangement. By taking one minute to calculate this rate, the S&L could probably have captured another $3,000 of the profit to be made on the trade, leaving the dealer with $1,000—not bad pay for selling a security at the bid side of the market and writing a few tickets.[12]

Caveat. When nothing calamitous has happened of late in the repo market, there is a tendency for lenders and borrowers in this market to regard repos and reverses as riskless. In fact such transactions expose

---

[12] For an off-the-quote-sheet example that illustrates a reverse to maturity and the calculation of a dealer's break-even reverse rate, see Stigum and Mann, *Money Market Calculations,* pp. 93–95.

both parties to a credit risk, as the failures of Financial Corporation, Drysdale, and Lombard-Wall (see end of Chapter 9) well illustrate.

Because of credit risk, no portfolio manager should do repos or reverses with a dealer or broker before carefully checking the latter's creditworthiness. Also, he should set dollar limits on the exposure he will take to any one dealer or broker, with the limit depending in part on that institution's capital. The NYS Dormitory Authority, which had invested over $300 million of its own spare cash and of that of other state agencies with Lombard-Wall, is a good example of an institution that got into trouble by putting a lot of eggs in one basket: in this case a smallish dealer that had inadequate capital to support the risks it was taking.

Use of the futures markets

Portfolio managers who may use futures and options are currently in the distinct minority, but to those who may, these contracts offer an array of opportunities to lock in yields, to arbitrage, to hedge, and to speculate. A few portfolio managers use futures contracts extensively as one more tool of portfolio management. We discuss that in Chapter 14, which focuses on futures contracts for and options on fixed-income securities.

Shorting securities

It's unusual for the manager of a corporate portfolio to be authorized to sell securities short but less rare than it used to be. The ability to short securities can be useful to a portfolio manager in several ways. For one thing, it permits him to arbitrage as dealers do—going long in an undervalued security and short in an overvalued security—as a speculation on a yield spread. A few corporate portfolio managers do this quite actively.

As one portfolio manager noted, there are also tax reasons for shorting, "Say you have ballooned maturities in part of your portfolio out to 10 years. You were right on the market and have only 30 days to go to get a long-term capital gain. But you think the market might back up and you want to take some of the risk out of your position. To do so is easy—you short something similar. In the corporate tax environment, the tax on long-term capital gains is 28%, while the tax on ordinary income is 46%. With that sort of 18-point advantage, you have to be badly wrong on the short not to come out ahead shorting." For banks there is no incentive to short for tax purposes because their long-term capital gains are taxed as ordinary income.

Still another reason a corporate portfolio manager might want to short is because borrowing through a short seems less expensive than selling an attractive investment. Said one portfolio manager, "If we decided, yes, the market is in here [in a given maturity sector], then we would look for the cheapest thing [the instrument with most relative value] on a spread basis—CDs, BAs, or bills—and buy that. Even though bills might yield less than, say, Euro CDs, we might buy them because the spread on Euros into bills was too tight. We'd decide whether to buy or not and then buy the cheapest thing. When we decided to sell, we would sell the most expensive thing. But we could not short so we were sort of up against it at times when we had to sell. I had already bought the cheapest thing around, so generally I had to sell something cheap. It bothered me a lot not to be able to short when we needed cash, but it might have raised questions with stockholders."

The big shooters

We have drawn in this chapter and the last a distinction between dealers and portfolio managers that is perhaps too sharp. There are in the U.S. money market a number of huge liquidity portfolios taking positions that rival those taken by more than one dealer, and a few of those are very actively managed. The people who run these portfolios utilize every tool of portfolio management that the dealers do—from creating future securities and figuring tails to shorting to do speculative arbitrages. Some also trade their positions as actively as a dealer does. Said an individual who ran one such portfolio, "I sometimes bought securities today that I knew I would have to sell for cash the next day. I might even buy if I was bullish for the next few hours—I have bought securities on the day cash was needed and sold them later in the day if I thought the market would go up a couple of 32nds." The major differences between portfolios of this sort and a dealer operation are first that retail business is important to a dealer, and second that, whereas dealers are highly levered, a leverage ratio of 3 to 1 is highly unusual and probably top side for a liquidity portfolio.

Investing when rates are high and highly volatile

A number of the portfolio strategies we have described make sense in "normal" markets when rates display some stability and predictability and when the yield curve slopes upward. In the period October 1979 to at least mid-1982, investors were playing in a very different ball park. Rates were historically high, historically volatile, and cyclically unpredictable; also, much of the time the yield was negatively sloped.

Noted one portfolio manager in the fall of 1981, "Riding the yield curve and tails are no longer interesting. One had better forget them. I have resisted the temptation to extend maturities, and I have been amazed when I compare my rate of return to what it would have been had I attempted to extend and either hold to maturity or ride the yield curve.

During periods of intense rate volatility, what you must do is to make the proper maturity decision because the impact of that decision on total return dwarfs that of all others; right now the correct decision is to opt for the shortest maturity you can. If you can live with day-to-day rollovers, you should do it even though you may have to accept lower rates on Wednesdays."

Compounding. Until recently neither investors nor borrowers thought much about the impact of frequent rolling of investments or borrowings on the return earned or the cost incurred. To fail to do so in a period of high rates can be an expensive mistake since the impact of compounding on a rate earned or paid increases not only the more often compounding occurs but the higher the rate being compounded is.

To illustrate, suppose, for example, that the yield curve is flat at 14% from overnight to 6 months. If an investor opts to buy a 6-month CD and roll it once, his total return over the year will be 14.49% assuming no change in interest rates. If, alternatively, he rolls overnight funds on the 255 business days that typically occur during a year, he will—again assuming no change in rates—earn a total return of 15.02%, 53 basis points more than by rolling a 6-month CD. On a $20 million investment, this would amount to $106,000 of extra earnings over a year.

Our simple example is not meant to suggest that interest rates, when they reach 14%, are likely to stay there for a year and that a portfolio manager should act accordingly. Rather, our intent is to illustrate the power of compounding to raise total return when rates are high and to suggest that, during such periods, the portfolio manager, in making maturity choices, start by making benchmark calculations of the sort illustrated by our example to get a feel for how compounding would affect his total return under different rate and maturity-choice scenarios.

If a portfolio manager opts to roll overnight funds, from a rate point of view the most attractive place for him to invest is typically the Euro-market. Banks do not go out of their way to ensure that a money manager will get daily compounding on short-term funds deposited at, say, its Caribbean shell. To get daily compounding, the investor in effect must mature his investment each day and then reinvest. This can be easily done if the task is approached systematically. Describing his procedure, one portfolio manager said, "If we put money overnight in Morgan, Cayman, we instruct them at the time the investment is started where to repay the money. A reliable bank should not have to be reinstructed. We check the next day with Chase, our clearing bank, to see that the money has in fact come in, and then we reinvest it at the most attractive rate quoted."

Trading. Volatile markets offer the portfolio manager opportunities for making huge profits is he guesses right on rates. They may thus tempt him to trade his portfolio. Noted the same portfolio manager quoted above, "To trade in volatile markets, you must be very nimble: psychologically prepared to buy at one moment and, if necessary to protect yourself, to unload your position the next moment. Recent fluctuations in interest rates have been mind-boggling. Imagine that on a position in short-term paper you could take a 3% capital loss in 3 weeks. The trading game has become so dangerous in terms of the money you can lose that you must be very attentive to the market and a very skillful trader to take positions on the long side and make money. In an environment like the current one, most corporations ought not to trade. We are not staffed to nor expected to trade securities as dealers are. And even dealers today often do nothing in effect but broker securities. They are scared to death and have reduced their trading positions to the lowest levels possible. It has been quite a market, as we again go up the side of the mountain!"

Euro floating-rate notes

U.S. investors as a group tend to be rather provincial. They shy away from Euros and frequently refuse to even consider foreign names. Investors who fail to understand sovereign risk, who therefore overestimate it, and who think Dai-ichi is a dread disease whereas it is in fact one of the world's largest and most creditworthy banks create what might be called a provincialism premium that sophisticated investors willing to invest in Euros and to take foreign names are pleased to reap.

Recently a number of such investors have discovered an attractive investment that most short-term money manager overlook, *Euro floating-rate* notes. Most of these issues pay interest semiannually although some are quarterly pay issues. The rates Eurofloaters pay are set at a spread over 6-month LIBOR if they pay interest twice a year; at a spread over 3-month LIBOR if they pay interest quarterly. The normal spread is 1/8 over LIBOR or 1/4 over the mean of the bid and offer, which is equivalent to 1/8 over LIBOR.

Most of the issuers in this market are top credits: major U.S. and foreign banks and sovereign credits such as the Kingdom of Sweden, New Zealand, and some French government agencies.

While most Eurofloaters mature in the late 1980s to the mid-1990s, this paper trades within a 2-point range either side of par and very close to, if not at, par on its coupon-reset date. The reason is that investors view buying such paper as the equivalent of making a 3- or 6-month time deposit except that the rate is slightly better.

The markets in top bank and in sovereign risk Eurofloaters are very liquid. One active investor in this market noted that, "In a good market, you can, on Kingdom of Sweden quarterly pays, get dealers down to a nickle spread which is as good as you can do in the domestic CD market."

Eurofloaters should be distinguished from domestic floating-rate notes. The latter, introduced in the mid- to late 1970s were typically priced at a spread off T bills, and because of the wide swings that occur in the spread of CDs to bills, domestic floaters have traded all over the map; the Chase 09s, for example, have been down as low as 80. When they were initially issued, it was envisioned that domestic floaters would trade near par at all times.

Eurofloaters, like variable-rate CDs, do trade near par because they are priced over LIBOR, which is the true cost of money for the banking system and should continue to be so in the future.

So far the only time there has been price volatility in a Eurofloater is when a sovereign country or its agencies did issues at a time when the country was considered a sound credit and then the situation surrounding that country changed dramatically: Mexican issues are the most notable examples of this.

While risk—price and credit—associated with a carefully chosen portfolio of Eurofloaters is minimal, it is still the more venturesome investor who buys it. Noted one of these, "An in-house joke is: If we can't spell it or pronounce it, we would probably like to buy it—but seriously speaking, only after we have looked at the credit carefully." This company's philosophy is: Why discriminate against a company with an A rating, especially if it is paying up, just because it has a funny—to American ears—name?

Marking to market

In well-run short-term portfolios, it is common practice to mark the whole portfolio to market each day. The objective of running a portfolio is to maximize over time not interest accured, but *total financial return*—interest earned plus capital gains realized minus capital losses realized. A portfolio manager who has this objective will, if he buys a 2-year note with a 9% coupon and then finds that yields on the 2-year have risen to 10%, view his decision to have bought the 9% coupon as a serious mistake. Moreover, if he anticipates that rates will rise still further, he will sell that security at a loss (convert his paper loss into a realized loss) and wait to recommit long-term until he thinks rates have stabilized.

The use of this tactic in portfolio management calls for a willingness to book capital losses, and that willingness is a hallmark of every good portfolio manager. Realizing losses is, however, difficult to do psychologically; it is something a trader must discipline himself to do. One advantage of marking a portfolio to market each day is that it helps get the focus of those who buy and sell for the portfolio off book value. As one portfolio manager noted, "If market value declines today and you book to market, tomorrow you start at that market value. And your gain or loss will be a function of whether tomorrow's price is better than today's." Said another, "If you mark to market, the past is gone. You've made a mistake, and the point now is not to make another one."

Tracking performance

Active management can substantially increase yield on a short-term portfolio. "You can as much as double yield on a short-term portfolio," said one practitioner of the art, "by arbitraging sectors and by changing maturities in response to interest rate forecasts."

In an institution where the short-term portfolio is actively managed, there are always people in top management who understand the credit market and who are therefore comfortable with creative management of the institution's portfolio. It is also the case that the focal point in management of the portfolio is on yield earned rather than on when money is needed. In other words, the portfolio manager's main concern in investing is with where relative value lies not with when he needs cash; specifically he does not *fund to dates*—buy 3-month bills because he needs money 3 months hence.

Performance in every liquidity portfolio managed to maximize return is carefully tracked. A key element in this tracking is marking the portfolio to market so that the return-earned calculation incorporates not only realized but unrealized capital gains and losses.

Once performance is tracked, it is compared against a variety of yardsticks. A portfolio manager might, for example, compare his performance with what he could have achieved had he followed any one of several naive strategies: rolling overnight funds, rolling 3-month bills, or rolling 6-month bills. If the portfolio invests longer-term funds, the yardstick might be the yield on 2- or 3-year notes.

Another standard often used is the performance achieved by various money funds, each of which runs in effect a large-liquidity portfolio. Comparing the performance of two portfolios is however, difficult. One has to ask about the differences in the parameters: in maturity restrictions, in percentage restrictions, and in name restrictions. Also differences in the time flow of funds through two portfolios may affect their relative performances.

Still another approach used in evaluating performance achieved is to compare actual results with the optimal results that could have been achieved. In other words, to ask: How high was the return we earned compared with what we could have earned if our market judgements had always been correct?

Tracking performance and comparing it against various yardsticks are important not only because they give the portfolio manager a feel for how well he is doing but because they give management some standard against which to evaluate his performance. As one portfolio manager noted, "I'm a money market specialist working for an industrial concern so it's hard for management to evaluate what I do unless I give them some frame of reference."

In a few rare cases, the portfolio manager is not only judged but paid, according to how well he performs. That sort of arrangement is typically found only in a corporation or a bank that has a large short-term portfolio and has recognized that, to get professional management, it must hire a street-oriented person who will never do anything but run money or work at a related job.

THE WAY IT'S DONE

We have discussed so far how an elite minority of portfolio managers who have wide latitude in what they may do and who possess the skill and judgment to make good use of that latitude manage their portfolios.[13]

Most liquidity portfolios—be they owned by corporations, banks, S&Ls, or other institutions—are managed with little sophistication; perhaps it would be more correct to say they are barely managed at all. The problem is often that top management has never focused on what portfolio management is all about and how it should be done. In the case of corporations, management will often adopt the attitude: We're in the business of manufacturing widgets, not investing. Having done that, they fail to appy to managing of their short-term portfolio the principles they daily apply to managing the whole corporation. Banks and S&Ls that daily assume carefully calculated credit risks in the course of their normal business operations quite often simultaneously run their securities portfolios according to the guiding principle: Buy Treasuries and mature them.

Restrictive guidelines

The failure of top management to be interested in and to have knowledge of what managing a liquidity portfolio involves almost invariably results in the establishment of extremely tight guidelines on what the portfolio manager may do, guidelines that reflect, as one portfolio manager noted, "the attempt of a bunch of guys who know nothing about securities to be prudent."

---

[13] One observer in a position to know puts the number of really well-managed liquidity portfolios in corporate America at half a dozen. If people on the street (Wall Street, that is) were asked to compile their lists of those six corporations, no one would fail to mention Ford, which has portfolios universally viewed as being aggressively and astutely managed. Another portfolio that consistently gets kudos from the street is that of the World Bank.

Tight guidelines make it impossible for a portfolio manager to use almost any of the strategies of portfolio management discussed earlier in this chapter. In particular, tight maturity guidelines can create a situation in which a portfolio manager has almost no leeway to raise yield by basing his investments on market judgments. For example, one giant U.S. corporation, which has volatile cash flows, will not permit its portfolio manager to extend further than 30 days; that still leaves him some room to make choices, but none are going to be very remunerative because he is working at best with $8 basis points.[14] Not atypically, there is no one in his corporation who cares and no one who tracks his performance.

Another problem with tight guidelines is that they are sometimes written in terms of amounts rather than percentages. This can make a large portfolio difficult to manage and may lead to false diversification. An extreme example of such guidelines is provided by a corporation that went so far as to limit the amount of bills its portfolio could hold.

The accounting hang-up

The failure of top management to understand or interest itself in the management of the liquidity portfolio also results in what might be called the *accounting hang-up.* Specifically, it has created a situation in which the majority of portfolio managers, all of whom would describe themselves as *conservative,* believe that the correct way to manage a portfolio is to reduce their accounting risk to *zero.* In other words, they attempt to run the portfolio in such a way that they will *never* produce a book loss.

This means that they can take no market risk: They can't do swaps that would produce a book loss regardless of how relative value shifts; when they need cash, they can't decide what to sell on the basis of relative value; they can't arbitrage; in fact, they are literally reduced to rolling overnight money and buying securities they intend to mature.

To fully appreciate how the decision never to take a loss restricts a portfolio manager, it is necessary to understand that when a portfolio acquires a discount security, such as bills or BAs, each day the accountant accrues interest income on that security at the discount rate at which it was purchased, so when the security is redeemed at maturity for full face value, all of the difference between the purchase price and the face value (i.e., the discount at purchase) will have been accrued as interest. This seems reasonable, but it means, for example, that if a portfolio manager buys 6-month bills at 7.90 and resells them 3 months later at

---

[14] The calculation:

$$(0.0001) \left(\frac{30}{360}\right) (\$1,000,000) = \$8.33$$

8.30, that is, at a rate *above* that at which he bought the bills, *he will have incurred a capital loss even though in dollar terms he has earned money.* Table 10–2 spells out the mathematics of this. Note that by buying $1 million of the 6-month bill at 7.90 and holding it for 90 days, the portfolio

TABLE 10–2
Accounting treatment of $1 million of 6-month bills bought at 7.90 and sold 3 months later at 8.30

Book value at purchase	$960,500
+ Interest accrued over 90 days	19,750
Book value at sale	$980,250
Price at sale	$979,250
− Book value at sale	980,250
Accounting capital gain (loss).	(1,000)
Price at sale	$979,250
Price at purchase	960,500
Actual gain	$ 18,750

has earned $18,750 and the $1,000 capital loss occurs only because the accountant has accrued $19,750 of interest over the holding period.

The yields and maturities in this example were purposely chosen so that they are identical with the yields and maturities used in the example of riding the yield curve presented earlier in this chapter (see Table 10–1). Once these numbers are seen in the context of that example, it is clear that the unwillingness to take an accounting loss (to expose the portfolio to an accounting risk) rules out even the most basic investment strategy based on market judgment; namely, riding the yield curve. In this respect, note that in our example the portfolio manager who rode the yield curve stood to gain—if interest rates did not rise—an extra $2,000 of return, *and* he had a lot of protection against losing in terms of dollars earned but *not* against incurring an accounting loss.

Portfolio managers preoccupied with accounting losses and gains are encountered by dealers frequently. Said one, "It cracks me up when someone comes to me with BAs or bills and says, 'What's your bid?' and I say, '7.60,' and he says, 'I can't sell because I bought at 7.50 and I can't take a loss.' It makes no sense if he has held the instrument for awhile, but I do not question people any more. I figure they just don't understand the concept. Still it's crazy, if you have to generate cash, to say that you cannot sell the instrument it is best to sell because you cannot take a 10-basis-point loss." Said another dealer, "I talk to portfolio managers about this problem and encounter nothing but resistance. They do not care if they could earn more money, they are just not going to take a loss. It's an organizational not a rational constraint."

The whole accounting problem applies not only to discount securities but to CDs and other interest-bearing securities, because the accountant accrues interest on them just as he does on discount securities; in addition, he amortizes over the time to maturity the premium on coupons purchased at a price above par and accretes the discount over the time to maturity on coupons purchased at a discount from par.

A negative sum game

The aversion to book losses and the failure to track performance that are characteristic of many institutions create a negative sum game for the portfolio manager. If he invests on the basis of market judgment, he ends up in a position where, if his judgment is wrong, the resulting losses—even if they are losses only by accounting standards—will be highly visible and criticized, whereas if his judgment is correct, the resulting gains will not be perceived by senior management.

The obvious response of the portfolio manager put in this position is to make no attempt to predict interest rates and to invest so as to avoid all market risk. If such a portfolio manager reaches for yield at all, he does so by buying P-2 paper or Euro CDs because they offer relatively high yields without ever asking whether they have *relative value.* Such portfolio managers think of themselves as sophisticated because they know a lot about many different markets, *but* when they need cash 3 months hence, they buy a 3-month instrument instead of making a conscious market decision.

Opportunity cost

The typical "conservative" portfolio manager thinks of himself as never having lost a penny or at least as not having lost very many, and his accountant will confirm this. But in fact an institution with a portfolio run on the principle that it funds to dates and never takes a market risk incurs a large *opportunity cost,* namely, the earnings forgone because the responsibility to manage funds in the portfolio has been abnegated. An example is provided by the example of riding the yield curve given earlier in this chapter. The portfolio manager who rides the yield curve with a lot of basis points of protection built into his gamble need not be right more than half the time to noticeably increase yield. Thus, to refuse to do so to avoid the risk of an accounting loss implies a cost, one no less real because it goes unperceived by most institutions.

There is also a more subtle aspect to opportunity cost. As one portfolio manager commented, "Most people you talk to will buy a 6-month bill and hold it to maturity and say that they are taking no risk because they know what they are going to earn. That is farcical. They *are* taking a risk, one that is not measured by the accounting system but is measured in terms of opportunity cost. And the institution may in reality be affected by this risk. If rates rise sharply and the money invested could have been used elsewhere, there is a cost to having bought those securities. Either the institution has to finance them somehow or it may be forced into other business decisions that are suboptimal."

Many common portfolio practices can be pursued only at a considerable opportunity cost. One is to say that, if money is needed in 30 days, cash on hand should be invested in a 30-day instrument even though predictable cash flows will more than suffice to cover that need. Another is to invest a large sum of money in short-term instruments when it is clear that most of that money will not be needed in the short run or even in the long run. A corporation that pursues such a strategy, as some triple-A credits do, pays a large premium year in and year out to ensure that it can survive even a severe credit crunch without mild discomfort.

With respect to the opportunity cost associated with the latter policy, one sales manager noted, "If stockholders realized what was going on in some corporations with cash holdings that are large relative to their total assets, what amount of money it is costing the company to not manage money, you might have some stockholder suits. I found one company that could go no longer than 90 days; they had a roughly $500 million portfolio; and the average life of their investments was 60 days. They could never buy and sell, never swap. I figured that in 1976 the fact they could not extend to the 1-year area probably cost them 1½ to 2% in yield. On half a billion that could add significantly to the bottom line [$10 million if the increase in yield was 2%]. And there was *no* call for the funds."

It is sometimes suggested that the reason some large corporations do not manage their portfolios is that they have too much money; that is, it is impossible within the confines of the money market to actively manage $3 or $4 billion. Sums of that magnitude are, however, actively managed; the World Bank's $6 billion portfolio is a prime example. So, too, are the actively traded portfolios of some multibillion-dollar money funds.

As noted, there is an opportunity cost to not managing money. The counterpart is that it costs money to have someone manage a portfolio, consequently there is some level below which benign neglect—rolling commercial paper or investing surplus cash in a money market fund—is the preferable alternative. That cutoff point is hard to pinpoint; estimates put it anywhere from $20 to $40 million. Somewhere up from that, between $100 and $150 million, there are solid benefits to be reaped from having someone watch the market daily.[15]

---

[15] See Chapter 20 for a more detailed analysis of this point.

For the firm at the opposite pole, one with hundreds of millions to be managed in one or a number of portfolios, the optimal solution may be one that a few institutions in this position have adopted—namely, to hire a professional, give him wide guidelines, monitor his performance, and pay him on an incentive basis so that making market judgments is for him a positive sum game. A side benefit of doing so is that the same individual can be used, as is done in many corporations, to manage the parent's or its financing sub's commercial paper operations. Anyone who can manage a short-term portfolio well can manage a commercial paper operation equally well, since the latter is nothing but a *negative* portfolio.

Ignorance of opportunity cost and extreme risk aversion are not the only reasons why many large institutions have failed to opt for professional management of their portfolios. Another is that they would have to pay a professional money manager in toto what a senior executive earns. A third reason is that corporations, especially if they are headquartered in outlaying places, have difficulty attracting and holding street-oriented people.

For a large corporation that wants to aggressively manage its portfolio, the commonly practiced alternative tactic of having one fast-track rookie do the job for awhile and then train another to do it does not always work out. Said a portfolio manager who traveled that route, "Trading is an art form which I could not succeed in teaching my peers who had come through the system as I did. I would have done better to take on some kid hustling on the streets of Marrakesh."

Part three

The markets

Chapter 11

The Federal funds market

SCENE: Late Wednesday afternoon on the Fed funds desk of a major New York bank.

"Where is that 150 million we bought?"

"The bank swears they sent it."

"Then why the hell hasn't the transfer gone through the San Francisco Fed?"

"The bank says their computer broke down. They had to deliver the transfer request by hand."

"Is that money coming or not? Call the New York Fed! Ask them if they'll keep the wire open or let us do an 'as of' tomorrow. Damn! This is enough to make an atheist out of a priest."[1]

---

[1] This actual situation resulted from something happening that was *never* supposed to happen. A wire transfer of Fed funds got lost in the Fed's computer network. The San Francisco Fed sent out the notice of the transfer of funds, but that message was not received by the New York Fed; it simply disappeared in the Fed's switching center at Culpepper, Virginia.

SETTLING WITH THE FED

Wednesday afternoon settlement with the Fed creates a lot of tension for bankers, brokers, and the Fed. To understand why requires some knowledge of the rules by which banks settle.

All banks that are members of the Federal Reserve System, and since 1980 other depository institutions, are required to maintain reserves in the form of deposits at the Fed. Any vault cash such institutions hold also counts as reserves. The reserves that a bank must maintain during the current settlement week are currently based on the average daily deposits it held over a 7-day period two weeks earlier. The ratios used in calculating required reserves were given in Table 5–3. The Fed has declared its intent to modify this system by going in February 1984 to *contemporaneous reserve accounting*. At that time the reserves that a depository institution must maintain during the current settlement week will be based on the average daily deposits it held over that week. Monetarists have been pushing for contemporaneous reserve accounting on the theory that it would reduce short-term fluctuations in money supply by forcing banks to adjust their level of reserves and thereby their lending to their current week's deposits. This notion seems naive at best since major banks all adjust their loans not to what deposits that receive but rather to whatever loans their creditworthy customers demand of them; banks then fund these loans to the extent necessary by buying money in the money market.

A second problem bankers see with contemporaneous reserve accounting was put quite succinctly by one banker, "I pay $145 billion every day. If my error rate is ½%, which is reasonably good, I have made $750 million of mistakes. If I don't have time to identify and correct those errors, all my reports to the Fed will be wrong. The Fed tells me they are going to fine tune control of the money supply by getting information faster from me. They are wrong. They are going to get more current, but less accurate, information."

For reserve calculation purposes, the week begins on Thursday and ends on Wednesday. Thus, to a Fed funds trader, Friday is always "early" in the week.

In settling with the Fed, a bank starts with a certain *required* average daily level of reserves. It need not hit its required level everyday, but its average daily reserve balances over the week must equal this figure.

To make it easier for banks to settle, the Fed permits a bank to offset a deficiency (up to 2% of its required) in one reserve week with a surplus run in the previous or following week.[2] The carry-over privilege is, how-

---

[2] The 2% surplus or deficiency that a bank may carry forward equals 2% of the *total* reserves it must hold over the week, which in turn equals the bank's required reserves times seven; this is so because a bank's required refers to the *average* balance it must

ever, limited to one week. A bank cannot go *red* (have a reserve deficiency) two weeks in a row; and if it goes *black* (runs a reserve surplus) two weeks in a row, the second week's surplus becomes excess reserves for which it gets no credit. Thus a bank's settlements with the Fed tend over time to follow a pattern, alternating red and black weeks.

With the exception of the B of A, the dollar total of the assets most large banks choose to fund far exceeds their deposits. The reverse is true of most smaller banks. Thus, large banks have a chronic need to obtain funds to settle with the Fed, whereas smaller banks have a chronic need to invest excess funds to avoid running a surplus. The needs of both sorts of banks are well met in the Fed funds market. In this market, reserve-short banks buy Fed funds (funds on deposit at the Fed), and reserve-rich banks sell them. Since the open-market desk at the New York Fed works hard each settlement week to ensure that the quantity of reserves the banks need to settle is provided to them, all the banks do manage—via the mechanism of the Fed funds market—to settle more or less within a whisker of where they meant to be each Wednesday.

THE FED WIRE

The operation of the Fed funds market and related activities requires tens of thousands of transfers of dollars daily among thousands of banks and other depository institutions. This is possible in large part because of the Fed wire system. Under this system an individual bank's computer is linked by wire to the computer at its district Federal Reserve Bank, which in turn is linked to the Fed's central computer in Culpepper, Virginia; that computer switches interdistrict messages between Federal Reserve district banks.

When a commercial bank wants to transfer funds from its reserve account to that of another bank, it types out a computer message that goes directly to the Fed, and the required payment is automatically made. For example, if the B of A sold $50 million of Fed funds to Chase, it would send through its computer the appropriate message to the San Francisco Fed, which would debit B of A's account and relay the payment message via Culpepper to the New York Fed, which would credit Chase's account and notify Chase (Table 11–1).

The Fed wire began to assume its present form only 15 years ago. Before that, even the big New York banks had to exchange checks to make payments to each other. Now they are linked by wire to the New York Fed, and all interbank payments in New York, with the exception of

---

maintain over a 7-day period. Thus if a bank's required were, for example, $1 billion, it could carry forward a reserve surplus or deficit equal to:

$$\$1 \text{ billion} \times 7 \times 2\% = \$140 \text{ million}$$

TABLE 11–1
The B of A sells Chase $50 million of Fed funds

Bank of America		**Chase**	

Reserves
  −50 million
Fed funds sold
  +50 million
		Reserves
		  +50 million
			Fed funds
			  purchased
			  +50 million

San Francisco Fed		**New York Fed**	

	Reserves, B of A
	  −50 million
			Reserves, Chase
			  +50 million

Euro transactions (see Chapter 16), go over the Fed wire. The New York Fed was the first district bank to be linked by wire to member banks within its district. Until 10 or 11 years ago, the way the principal banks in St. Louis, which were across the street from the St. Louis Fed, communicated with the Fed was to walk across the street and deliver a slip of paper. Now all the Federal Reserve District banks and most of their branches have extended access to the Fed wire to member banks having volumes of transactions justifying such access.

Banks use the Fed wire not only to handle their transactions in the Fed funds market but for other transactions. Each major bank has hundreds of correspondent—domestic and foreign—banks that keep accounts with it, and it keeps accounts at other banks. Throughout the day monies are constantly being paid into and out of these accounts over the Fed wire in connection with securities transactions, collections, and so forth.

Also, corporations and nonbank financial institutions are constantly requesting banks to make *wire transfers* of funds for them. For example, a large corporation might wire money from its account in a West Coast bank into its account at Citibank and then later in the day have those funds wired from that account to the account at Manny Hanny of a nonbank dealer from which it had bought governments. The money market, which is largely a cash-settlement market (payment is made on the day of a trade with "good"—*immediately available*—funds), generates a huge volume of traffic on the Fed wire.

The bank wire

In addition to being linked by the Fed wire, banks are also linked by *the bank wire*. This wire, which is a secure, closed-loop Telex system supported by a computer switch, could not be used for making payments until recently; it is an *advice medium* for about 185 member banks; the major traffic on it consists of messages advising the receiving banks of some action that has occurred. For example, Morgan gets an instruction from a corporate client to pay or transfer to the Continental Bank $5 million, perhaps in connection with the purchase of commercial paper. Morgan debits the account of the corporate client and credits the account of Continental at Morgan. At the same time, it sends a message over the bank wire to Continental saying that it is crediting their account for $5 million. Such transfers and wire advice continue throughout the day. Meanwhile Continental tracks these advices and at some point might wire back to Morgan: "You have credited our account six times for a total of $30 million today. Transfer $29 million to our account in Chicago at the Fed." By doing this Continental would get effective use of the funds in its account in New York. Or Continental might instruct Morgan to transfer the funds in its account through the Fed to some other New York bank to make a money market investment.

The gradual perfecting of the Fed wire has caused big changes in the way banks make payments. In particular the Fed wire has in recent years provided competition to the use of correspondent bank accounts. Banks have begun to conclude that there is no sense in running bank balances all over the country when they can have everyone exchange funds with them through the Fed over the wire. Use of the Fed wire is faster and simpler because the bank has to track only one position rather than many balances all over the country.

One difficulty posed by the increased use of the Fed wire is that banks get jammed up processing wires because wire activity severely peaks late in the afternoon, due in part to the many settlements that have to be made in connection with commercial paper transactions. Because of this traffic jam, every afternoon there are some payments that don't get made before the Fed wire shuts down.

The Fed wire has also provided competition to the bank wire. When a bank opts to make and receive all payments in Fed funds over the Fed wire, it has less need of the bank wire, and traffic has been falling constantly in recent years. While competition from the Fed wire was the initial reason for declining traffic on the bank wire, the forecast of further declines in such traffic has become a sort of self-fulfilling prophecy. The scarcest resources available to people directing the wire transfer operations of major banks are systems people. One bank officer noted, "Since we do the majority of our traffic over the Fed wire and CHIPS, we dole out more of our systems people to improve the ways we interface with those systems than the bank wire.[3] This in turn makes the two major competi-

---

[3] CHIPS, which is used to clear Euros, is described in Chapter 16.

tors of bank wire more efficient so bank wire loses more volume." To counter the decline in its traffic, bank wire has started a settlement system. However, the major banks who do only a small portion of their transactions—5% or so—over the bank wire are unlikely to invest enough in interfacing with this new capability to make it a viable service in the long run.

Breakdowns

Because of the vast number of messages that pass daily over the Fed wire and the bank wire, it is essential, if the banking system is to continue to operate, that every bank's computer and the Fed's computer keep running. To prevent breakdowns, the Fed relies on redundancy and backup equipment. Still, on occasion, the Fed wire goes "down." When this occurs, it is held open longer than usual. Because the major banks could not tolerate a long breakdown in their computer operations, they have all designed their internal systems to that the maximum down time for a breakdown is no more than a few minutes.

Amusingly, the big New York banks, which had all supplied their computer systems with emergency generators years ago, woke up one day to ask, "What the hell would our computer centers, humming away in the midst of a blackout, be working on with the rest of the bank shut down in darkness?" So they supplied auxiliary power to all the major departments that provide inputs to their computer system: check collections, money transfer, and the trading room. Said the manager of one bank computer operation, "We have got that capacity and," reaching into his desk, "I keep a flashlight, too."

HISTORY OF THE MARKET

In 1921 some member banks were borrowing at the discount window, while others had surplus reserves for which they had trouble finding an outlet due to depressed market conditions. After informal discussions, the banks that were borrowing from the Fed began purchasing balances from the banks that had excess reserves, and the Fed funds market was born.

Trading in Fed funds continued throughout the 1920s but fell into disuse during the 1930s, when most banks had excess reserves for a long period. During the early 1940s the banks purchased large amounts of the $400 billion of new government debt issued to finance the war, and they adopted the practice of settling their reserve positions by trading short-term Treasury bills for cash settlement.

Gradually, it became clear that there was an easier way for the banks to settle—instead of selling bills among themselves, they began in the early 1950s to sell 1-day money among themselves.[4] And as they did, the Fed funds market—dormant since the 1920s—was revived. Another reason for the revival of the funds market was that, as interest rates started to rise after the Treasury-Fed accord, everyone became more conscious of the value of money left idle, and banks in particular began to see the merit in keeping their excess funds fully invested. The revival of the Fed funds market was particularly attractive for retail banks with a customer base consisting largely of consumers. These banks needed an outlet for their surplus funds, and they took up the practice of selling Fed funds everyday to their large-city correspondents.

By 1960 these developments led to a situation where the big New York and Chicago banks began to deliberately operate their basic money positions so that they were always short, on the ground that they needed room to buy all the Fed funds that were coming into them from smaller correspondents. This was an attractive situation for the large banks because Fed funds were the cheapest money around, and they naturally asked: Why not use it for 10 percent of our overall needs?

In the late 1950s when the big banks sold to their correspondent banks the "service" of buying up the latter's excess funds, they said, "Of course if you ever need Fed funds, we will be happy to sell them to you." This commitment came back to haunt them in 1963 when interest rates started to take off in the aftermath of the Kennedy tax cut. By then the smaller correspondent banks had developed an insight into the money market; they began buying Treasury bills, which were then trading at a higher yield than the discount rate, and financing them first with their own surplus funds and then by purchasing Fed funds from the big banks.

At that time Fed funds had *never* traded higher than the discount rate. Since banks bought Fed funds only to settle their reserve positions and then only as an alternative to borrowing at the discount window, bankers feared that any bank that was willing to pay more than the discount rate for Fed funds would be subject to the accusation that for some reason it could not borrow at the window.

Gradually the situation became critical for the big banks because all their correspondents were buying T bills at 4%, financing them with Fed funds purchased at 3½% (the level of the discount rate), and raking in the spread. This continued for more than a year, during which time the big banks became huge net sellers of Fed funds. To fund the sales, these banks were issuing CDs at rates higher than the rate at which they were selling Fed funds to their "valued" correspondents.

Something had to give. Finally, in 1964 Morgan decided that if any bank could get away with paying more than the discount rate for Fed

---

[4] This development was fostered by Garvin Bantel (now Garvin GuyButler), a firm that once brokered call loans to brokers and was an important broker of listed bonds. Garvin is now a major broker of several money market instruments, both domestic and Euro.

funds, it could, and on October 4 of that year it bid 3⅝ for funds at a time when the discount rate was 3½ and funds were trading at 3½. The $500 million estimated to have been traded at this higher rate that day was a small sum by today's standards, but the gambit succeeded and began a new era in the funds market. Rapidly funds began to trade at a market rate that was determined by supply and demand and was affected by the discount rate only insofar as that rate influenced demand.

After funds began to trade at a market rate, the Fed funds market mushroomed, and more and more banks got into it. Regional banks that at the inception of the market were selling funds to large banks began to operate their own regional markets. Before this development, most trading in Fed funds was done in New York and Chicago, with perhaps a little in San Francisco. Small outlying banks with only a little money to sell were excluded from the market because it made no sense for a bank with $100,000 of overnight money to sell to telephone New York when the rate it would get was 3 or 3½%.[5] However, when the regional banks began to buy Fed funds, it paid for a bank in Joplin, Missouri, to call St. Louis for $0.30 to sell even $50,000 of Fed funds. In the Fed funds market now, regional banks buy up funds from even tiny banks, use what they need, and resell the remainder in round lots in the New York market. Thus, the Fed funds market resembles a river with tributaries: Money is collected in many places and then flows through various channels into the New York market.

As the Fed funds market developed, some regional banks that entered it felt they were not in close enough contact with the market to call the last ¼ or ⅛; they adopted the practice of asking brokers to sell or buy money for them at whatever price the brokers thought was the best available. The amount of such *discretionary money* amounted at one time to a sizable sum. There is less of it around today because "most of the regionals," in the words of one broker, "like to believe they are a Chase or a Morgan. Also they are becoming more sophisticated."

In the days when Fed funds were first traded, "the market was," said one ex-trader from a large bank, "a travesty, a joke as far as being a real market. There were six or eight real decision makers in the entire market—a couple of brokers and the guys on the money desks of the top banks. When a top broker walked in on Thursday morning at the start of a new settlement week and said, 'Funds are 1¹⁄₁₆–¾,' the market pretty much formed up around that. Few people would challenge that view because they knew a lot of banks had given that broker money to buy or sell at his discretion. On Broadway the *New York Times* drama critic can close a show. In every area you have opinion makers, and the Fed funds market was, and is, no exception."

---

[5] At a 3½% rate, $100,000 of overnight Fed funds is worth $9.72.

Over time, the Fed funds market had evolved considerably. Initially Fed funds traded at ¼s of a percent; then, as more participants entered the market and it became more competitive, funds began trading at ⅛ths and then at 1/16ths. For a time the Fed let the funds rate fluctuate in a wide band. Then in the late 1960s, it began to peg that rate tightly. How tightly is indicated by a comment made in 1977 by a person on the Fed desk, "When we are in a period when our Fed funds target is not changing, money supply is growing at a steady rate, and we are at peace with the world, we are inclined to be more relaxed about the funds rate and to let it fluctuate within a ¼ band. But in a delicate situation where we want to give signals to the market—when they are misunderstanding our posture and we want to be sure they get the message—we might narrow that spread to 1/16."

All that changed in October 1979 when the Fed switched to monetarism pure and simple. At that time, the Fed decreed that the rate at which funds traded would be wherever market forces took it, which turned out to be all over the lot. Whereas in pre-1979 days a move during the day, other than Wednesday, in the Fed funds rate of one quarter was unusual, intraday swings of 200, 300, even 400 basis points in the rate became common after the Fed switched the primary focus of its policy from tight control of the funds rate to tight control of the rate of growth of money supply.

A funds broker, commenting on the change, noted, "Years ago when funds were trading at 4, if they fell to 3¹⁵/16, you knew the Fed would come in and do reverses. Then they were rate oriented. Today there's a different scenario. Fed intervention is not a predictable reaction to changes in the funds rate."

In recent years, the Fed funds market, like every other sector of the money market, has undergone a huge expansion. Everything has increased in size: the number of buyers and sellers, the size of the trades they do, the volume of funds they trade, and the number of brokers who service them.

Sophistication is also on the upswing. Six or seven years ago when rates were low and rarely moved much, some regional banks thought all they needed for a Fed funds trader was an order taker who bought and sold at the market. Today, with rates high and highly volatile, the cost of being wrong and the rewards of being right are much greater than ever before. In response, Fed funds traders at regional banks have become increasingly sophisticated; today most are acutely aware of and follow closely not only statistics on money supply and economic indicators but any and all other factors that might impact the funds market. Whatever the value of such information, the regionals today track it as closely as do the majors who always used such information.

Not many years ago, the Fed funds market could have accurately been described as a largely domestic market in which some foreign bank branches and agencies participated. Today that is untrue. In the last few years, the number of foreign banks opening branches in the U.S., principally in New York, has increased dramatically. As London drew foreign bank branches in the 1960s and early 1970s, New York draws them today.[6] Because of their increasing number and the widening scope of their U.S. activities, foreign bank branches and agencies have become major players in the Fed funds market; currently they account for ¼ to ⅓ of total market volume.

RUNNING A FED FUNDS DESK

The primary job of the manager of a bank's Fed funds desk is to ensure (1) that the bank settles with the Fed *and* (2) that in doing so it holds no more excess reserves than the amount, if any, that it can carry into the next week. This is a tricky job at a major bank because each day such a bank experiences huge, highly variable, and difficult-to-predict inflows and outflows of funds. These all influence the bank's balance at the Fed and so they must be carefully monitored by the desk, which at the same time is buying or selling funds as necessary to develop the balance it wants for the day at the Fed.

The flows that affect a major bank's funds position come from various sources. Its correspondents sell it huge sums of money, and sometimes they will ask to buy funds from it. Additional flows result from changes in correspondent (domestic but more especially foreign) bank deposit balances, changes in customer deposit balances (firms wiring money into and out of the bank), changes in the Treasury's balance in its tax and loan account, big loans coming on or going off the bank's books, purchases and sales made by the bank's portfolio and by the bank's dealer department, changes in the amount of CDs the bank has outstanding, changes in the level of RPs it does, flows from and to foreign branches, and—in the case of clearing banks—fluctuations in dealer loans.

Normally a bank's Fed funds desk starts the day with a sheet on which it projects the inflows and outflows that will affect its bank's reserve account at the Fed during the day. Some, such as flows generated by maturing RP and big loans going on or off its books, are known. The rest it estimates on the basis of past experience and any additional information available. The desk *heads out* (adds up and compares) all these figures to get its first estimate of what money it will need to buy or sell during the day. Then, as the day progresses and actual inflows and outflows occur, someone on the desk tracks these flows and their effect

---

[6] This development is both part and consequence of the increasing importance of New York as a Eurocenter. See Chapter 6.

on the bank's balance at the Fed. This is boring and tedious work but must be done if the bank is to keep a handle on its position. As one Fed funds trader after another will note, the traders on the desk are only as good as their backup people. When one of the latter makes an error, the bank may inadvertently end up way black or way red, a situation that can create a problem on any day and a major bust on a Wednesday.

Here's one trader's scenario of the sort of difficulty that could crop up: "Say on Thursday we think we are $2 billion short and buy $2 billion, but actually we are only $1.5 billion short. We start Friday half a billion black on the accumulated. Now say the same thing happens again on Friday, so we end up going black again half a billion, only this time it's times three [because of the weekend]. That means we start Monday with a $2 billion accumulated black. Technically a bank is not supposed to go below 50 percent of its required; it's a technicality the Fed does not strictly enforce but they do remind you that you have gone below. Suppose that Monday to Wednesday we need only $600 million a day in our reserve account. If we respected the 50 percent rule, we would end up with $900 million of that $2 billion black we could not use up. Actually we would drain down our balance at the Fed as low as we dared and get rid of that money, but we prefer not to get in that position."[7]

At most major banks the Fed funds desk is managed conservatively. The desk knows what average daily balance it must have to settle for the week, and it attempts each day to be within 10% of that figure. The reason used to be that, since Fed funds traded in a narrow range—except when the Fed was moving the rate, there was not much profit to be earned by playing the rates, going long on a day when funds seem cheap and short on a day when they seem expensive. Now with the funds rate being volatile and hard to predict, a conservative stance still seems appropriate to most banks.

Another reason banks are disinclined to play around on the Fed funds desk is that most of them are either big natural sellers or buyers of funds, and they work best—because of line problems—when operating from their natural stance. With the exception of B of A, most large banks are net buyers of funds. A bank will sell funds only to a bank to which it has extended a line and only up to the amount of that line. Thus, if a bank that is normally a net buyer of funds accumulates a big surplus position, it may have difficulty working off that surplus because it has insufficient lines to sell it.

Some state-chartered banks have an additional problem. The Comptroller of the Currency has ruled for national banks that funds purchases and sales are not to be treated as borrowings and loans for purposes of

---

[7] The 50 percent rule was established by the New York Fed for banks within its district. This rule was subsequently dropped, a fact of which not all banks are aware.

regulation. Thus there is no legal limit on the amount of Fed funds a national bank may sell to another bank. In some states, however, sales of Fed funds are treated as a normal loan. In such states, a state-chartered bank can extend to another bank a line equal to only a small percentage of its capital.

A bank that cannot get rid of excess funds because of line problems can always sell these funds in the RP market, that is, provide dealers with secured loans. But in doing so it will typically get a lower rate than it would by selling funds, and it may end up selling off excess funds at a rate below that at which it purchased them from its correspondents.

Line problems can also constrain the amount by which even the largest and most well-thought-of banks can go red early in the week. When Franklin and Herstatt failed, banks were suddenly reminded of something they had almost forgotten—that the sale of Fed funds is an unsecured loan. In response, banks cut back on their lines for selling funds, which in turn diminished the leeway banks have to vary their daily purchases of Fed funds. Said one dealer, "If you think at the beginning of the week that the Fed is going to do a lot of adding and that funds are going to trend down, you might borrow a little less than you otherwise would have. But at a large borrowing bank you have such a big job to do that you cannot get far behind. You cannot borrow nothing on Thursday and hope to make it up the rest of the week. It cannot be done."

Conservative Fed funds traders, while they will not try to make money by dealing aggressively in funds, attempt to do what they can for the bank's profit and loss (P&L) statement in other ways. Said one typical of the breed, "We are not supposed to be a profit center. We do, however, usually make money if we sell funds or finance dealers loans. The dealer loans give us a better spread 3/16 to 1/4 over Fed funds, and it's a secured loan. But the real nature of our game is to buy cheaper than the effective funds rate. We make the bank money by saving it. A 16th is only $1.74 on $1 million but, with the amounts we borrow, 16ths can mount up."

Dealing aggressively

While most Fed funds traders are conservative, and well advised to be so because that is what management wants, there are a few sharpshooters in the crowd. One trader of this genre, who was quite comfortable going above or below his daily required by 50%, commented, "I don't like to just pick up the phone and buy or sell. If I feel that there is strength in the market, I will wait to sell even if I have a lot to sell. Then in the early afternoon, there is the moment of truth. I have to make some sort of decision. You get a good sense of accomplishment when you wait and it turns out you were right. When it does not, you have to scramble. But that is part of the fun of doing it. The fun is to have a conviction and at times buy yourself long or sell yourself short."

Said a trader who liked to play even more: "Some guys act as if they settled every night. That is what you call a *day position*. I have a different philosophy. Say I need $100 million a day for seven days, that is, a $700 million cumulative. If I think rates are high one day, I might buy just $50 million and then pick up $150 million the day after if rates are more reasonable. Also I go where the money is cheapest. If it is cheaper to buy Euros, I buy Euros not Fed funds. If Euros are cheap, I will buy Euros and sell Fed funds.

"When I got this job, they tended to think that you need $100 million a day. I said, OK, if I can get money cheap, I will buy $200 million and sell $100 million off at a profit and reduce my effective cost of funds. Not many people do that. I ask: How can a bank not leverage down their cost of funds by using this route? It takes extra work to buy and sell, but in the end you reduce your cost of money. Over the first quarter of this year, if I had just bought money all the time from our correspondents, as I should have, I would have had an effective cost on the $500 million to $1 billion, which I had to buy, that was 25 basis points higher than the actual effective cost of money I achieved. And I managed that savings in a market in which you have a ⅛ spread.

"A lot of banks look at the Fed funds guy as custodian of a checking account whose prime function is to make sure that the bank does not go OD at the Fed. The Fed funds market has not progressed as far as other markets have, and it should. This is where the action is, where the basic position of your bank is settled.

"Too many people are stodgy. The way I look at it, Babe Ruth only hit .342, and he was a superstar. Ty Cobb, who had the best batting average ever, hit .367. So if you are right 75 percent of the time, you are going to make a lot of money. If you are gambling, you have to take the big loss to make the big win. Lots of guys say to me, 'I never took a big loss,' but they never made a big win either."

This quote illustrates well an attitude that is common on the street and characteristic of aggressive traders, dealers, and portfolio managers: There are plenty of gambles around in which you can count on being right more than half the time; if you are, you'll make money, so to not gamble is expensive and foolish.

Personnel and sophistication

Most of the traders on the funds desks of large banks have no special academic training for their job. They are people with a good memory, which a Fed funds trader requires, who started out in operations and just picked up trading. In a few banks the trading slot on the Fed funds desk is one that fast-track MBAs are passed through for a year.

At small banks the Fed funds desk is often run with much less sophistication than at large banks because the person who does the job is the treasurer of the bank and also has to handle governments, repos, and whatever. Sophistication, however, is not only a function of size. A trader at a bank that ranks 150th may be quite sophisticated, whereas one at a somewhat larger bank is merely an order clerk—when he has $10 million to sell, he calls the broker, gets a quote, hits the bid, writes a ticket, and thinks of himself as a trader.

Glamor

While a Fed funds trader may handle huge sums everyday, there is little glamor or recognition attached to the job, as is the case with most money market jobs. Said one trader who handles several billion dollars everyday, "I went out to dinner the other night with a fellow from Price Waterhouse. He said, 'What do you do?' I said, 'Trade overnight funds.' He said, 'Oh, how does your wife like your working nights?' "

Overnight money

The bulk of the money sold in the Fed funds market is overnight money. Much of this money is traded directly between the selling and buying banks.

Because they depend heavily and persistently on purchases of Fed funds to cover their basic funding needs, most large banks go out of their way to cultivate smaller correspondents that find it convenient to sell their surplus funds on an ongoing basis to one or several large banks. A smaller bank could, of course, shop in the brokers market and try to pick up an extra $1/16$, but most don't because the amounts they sell are so small that the cost of trying would outweigh the potential gain. Overnight $1/16$ on $10 million is only $17, and that's before the phone bill is paid.

To cultivate correspondents that will sell funds to them, large banks stand ready to buy whatever sums these banks offer, whether they need all of these funds or not. If they get more funds than they need, they sell off the surplus in the brokers market. also they will sell to their correspondents if the latter need funds, but that occurs infrequently. As a funding office of a large bank noted, "We do feel the need to sell to our correspondents but we would not have cultivated them unless we felt that they would be selling to us 99 percent of the time. On the occasional Wednesday when they need $100,000 or $10 million, OK. Then we would fill their need before we would fill our own."

When the Fed funds market was younger and less competitive and the smaller players were relatively unsophisticated, it was not uncommon for buying banks to pay their smaller correspondents a rate well below the New York rate. Today, however, most large banks pay correspondents that sell to them regularly some formula rate—the opening rate, the average rate for the day, or whatever. And even though they know that they may well have to sell off some of the funds they purchase from correspondents, they do not try to arbitrage—buy low and sell high. A banker typical of this attitude said, "We will pay a bank in Cedar Rapids the same rate for $100,000 that we would pay the B of A selling us $100 million. We do that because we want the bank in Cedar Rapids to be coming back to us. Relative to other sources of funds, Fed funds are cheap, and we try to cultivate this funding source."

A few big banks, however, still see a potential arbitrage, "trading profits," in selling off funds purchased from smaller banks and attempt to profit from it to reduce their effective cost of funds. Also a few tend to bid low to their correspondents. Said a trader typical of the latter attitude, "We have a good name in the market so I often underbid the market by a $1/16$. A guy with a few million to sell doesn't care. He's happy to get his money sold and get on with other banking business." The tendency to shave rates is particularly pronounced on Fridays because a Friday purchase is for three days. At the opposite end of the spectrum are majors who will offer a small bank an extra $1/4$ to pick up correspondent bank business with them.

One of the striking things about the Fed funds market is the wide access all banks have to it. A tiny bank with $50,000 of overnight money to sell won't be able to sell to one of the top money market banks because such a bank would not bother with such dribbles. But at a rate slightly off the market, it can sell its funds to a regional bank that is happy to take in small amounts either to fund its own position or to resell in larger blocks. In recent years even S&Ls have gotten into the Fed funds game. Small thrifts sell funds through their Federal Home Loan Bank. Bigger thrifts go directly into the brokers' market when they have funds to sell. The national market for borrowing CD money is open in real volume only to the top 25 banks or so in the country. But regional banks much smaller in size can and do buy large sums in the Fed funds market. The market is also open to foreign bank branches and foreign agencies, which use it extensively.

There is some tendency in the Fed funds market for banks to expect banks they sell to be willing to sell to them, and a handful of banks will sell funds only to banks with whom they have reciprocal lines. However, the need to "buy one's way in" is less pronounced in the Fed funds market than in the Euromarket because banks in the Fed funds market tend to be one way most of the time—either consistent buyers or consistent sellers.

THE BROKERS' MARKET

In addition to the large volume of funds traded *directly* between big banks and their correspondents, there are huge amounts of overnight funds traded through *brokers*. Large banks lay off any excess funds they take in from their correspondents in the brokers market. Also, if their needs exceed the amounts they receive from their correspondents, they will buy funds through brokers. There are many regional banks, foreign banks, and foreign agency banks that also buy and sell funds through brokers. And those few funds desks manned by traders who *deal* in funds—buying and selling to pick up 1/8—add to the volume in the brokers market. Finally, there is the deposit-rich B of A, which everyday sells vast amounts of funds through brokers.

The major brokers in the market are Garvin GuyButler, Mabon Nugent & Co., George Palumbo & Co., Lasser Brothers, and Noonan, Astley, and Pierce. In addition to these, there are a number of minor brokers. Also, the Irving Trust runs a matching service for correspondents buying and selling Fed funds; this service is not precisely brokering, and Irving does not charge for it.

The Fed funds rate is an add-on rate quoted on a 360-day-year basis. Thus if funds were trading at 9¾, a purchase of $50 million of overnight funds would cost the buyer

$$0.0975 \times \$50{,}000{,}000 \times \left(\frac{1}{360}\right) = \$13{,}541.67$$

In addition, he would pay brokerage costs equal to $0.50 per $1 million per day, which works out to slightly less than 1/50 of 1 percentage point. Brokerage is paid by both the buyer and the seller.

The volume going through the brokers varies from day to day. Friday transactions are particularly attractive to a broker because he earns a three-day commission on them; a Friday sale is unwound on Monday. On an active day, a top broker with a staff of 25 may handle more than $15 billion of overnight funds.

Function of the broker

The major function of the Fed funds brokers is communications. There are so many participants in the brokers market—all the top 500 banks plus a lot of foreign banks—that, in the absence of brokers, the banks would need a host of traders and telephones on their Fed funds desk to get their job done.

Each broker has a particular set of names that use him. There is, however, considerable overlap between the clients of the top brokers since many banks use two or even three brokers on a regular basis. The brokers put in direct phone lines to any bank having a volume of trading through them that justifies the cost. They communicate with the rest over WATS lines. The phone bill for a broker is necessarily huge: He is providing a communications network, and doing so is not cheap.

In addition to communications, brokers also provide the banks with anonymity. A top bank that has a big job to do values this because it fears that if it were a bid for or offer huge sums in its own name in the market, it might move the market.

The brokers market is really open to only those banks that buy and sell in volume. In Fed funds anything under $5 million is an odd lot. A small bank in Iowa that wants to buy $500,000 is better off going to its regional correspondent, since the New York brokers are not set up to handle trades of that size. Noted one broker: "We have a guy who sells through us $300,000 to $1 million everyday. He asks, "What is the market?' We say, '5/16–3/8.' He says, "What do I get for $1 million?' We have to say, '1/8.' "

Today the average trade in the brokers' market for overnight funds is $25 million. A few of the major banks won't take 5s [$5 million] any more, and some won't even take 10s. A lot of regionals, however, both take and give 10s.

Trading the sheet

A Fed funds brokering operation today is a rather impressive sight to view: 25 people sitting around a desk, each constantly talking on one of a battery of direct phone lines facing him, and each constantly scribbling down bids and offers on a sheet of paper. That sheet, however bedraggled it may look, is a key part of the operation since each person on the desk, by glancing at it, can see what banks are bidding and offering through the firm and what the amounts are.

Brokers will often describe what they do as *trading the sheet.* "We do not," said one broker, "trade in the sense of taking a position. But when someone acts in the market, how do we react? That is our trading decision. Thursday always used to be difficult because it was a slow day. We'd end up with a sheet cluttered on both sides with bids and offers. If a name then came in and said he wanted to sell $20 million at the bid, we might have 25 names to choose from; ethically the best we could do was to decide who was there first. When the market is moving you do not have to worry about this because everyone will be satisfied. Wednesday is easy because it moves so fast."

Brokering is very much a team effort. Commented the head of one brokering operation, "This job takes concentration and coordination. To run an efficient shop, you cannot have two people on the phone saying the market is going down and three others saying it's going up. Avoiding that is hard because our thoughts on the market may change 20 times a day."

Many Fed funds brokers come out of the banks, and a number are ex-Fed funds traders. Such experience is valuable: an ex-trader knows how to quote the market and understands how to react to what the banks do.

Quoting the market

Broker: Hello, ¾ bid on 50. I am offered at 6 in two spots, 75 firm, 50 under reference.

Bank: I'll take 50.

Broker: OK, 50 done. Can I make it a C note?

Brokering occurs at a breakneck pace. The top New York banks do not want a lot of information, and a broker makes a fast quote to them. In a minimum of words he attempts to convey the tone of the market. He might, for example, quote the market: "5/16–3/8, last at 5/16," or "5/16–3/8, quiet," or "Market last at 3/8 looking like it might go to 9." Some regional banks want a slower quote and a little more information on market developments. Said one broker, "The worse even ask what the *handle* is."

In the Fed funds market, banks, in addition to putting *firm* bids and offers into the brokers, will also make *subject* bids and offerings. When a bank's bid or offer is subject or *under reference,* before the broker executes a trade for that bank, he has to go back and ask it if they will make their bid or offer firm. When the Fed goes into the market to do open-market operations, it creates uncertainty, and the brokers, in courtesy to their customers, treat all bids and offers as subject until they are renewed.

Part of the fun and the frustration of brokering funds is that the market is constantly changing throughout the day. Because of this, an important part of a broker's job is to get a line on the market, a feel for its tone and where it is moving. In doing so, he looks not only at his own market but at related markets. What is the rate on overnight repo? Where are Euros trading? The top Fed funds brokers also broker Euros and a variety of other instruments, so their people have constant and easy access to information on developments in related markets as they occur.

Fine tuning quotes

In the Fed funds market, whenever a buyer takes a seller's offering, the broker has to go back to the seller and tell him the name of the buyer and ask him if he will do the trade. The ethics of the game are such that the seller is supposed to do the trade unless he does not have a line to the buyer or his line to the buyer is filled. If the seller can do the trade, the broker then tells the buyer the seller's name, and the buyer and the seller clear the trade directly over the Fed wire. Brokerage bills are sent and paid at the end of the month.

Line problems and other subtleties make brokering more than just quoting two rates. A good broker knows what lines various banks have extended to other banks and how big they are. And he tries to guess during the day how much of those lines have been used up. Said one broker: "I know the B of A's lines better than they do. It's not that they tell me, but if they keep selling some guy *x* million day after day, I know pretty quickly what their line to him is."

Because of line problems," commented the same broker, "the quote to each bank is individualized." Line problems become especially acute on Wednesdays when the banks settle and trading is active. "The quote will be one thing to Manny if they have been in the market all day long buying up everything in sight and another story to Chase if they have been selling all day. A broker is foolish if he says, '9¼–⅜,' when there is nothing on the offer side good to the guy on the phone who wants to buy. We may have an offering but we say none. Or I can say, 'I am 9¼–⅜, but my offer is not good to you. I will work for you at that price.' "

Lines are particularly a problem for small regional banks, agency banks, and foreign banks that don't have the line coverage of big domestic banks and that consequently have to pay up to get money on occasion.

Another factor that individualizes the market is size. If a prime New York bank comes in and wants to buy $300 million, the broker is naturally tempted to do the whole trade with the B of A in one fast shot. Also, buyers occasionally want to buy in block size and won't mess around with nickels and dimes ($5 and $10 million pieces). This makes it difficult to sell for banks that for one reason or another have small lines to other banks.

Part of being a good broker is the ability to be a good salesman—to anticipate a customer's needs and to nudge him subtly into a trade. One broker noted, "This is a pattern market in the sense that many names do not change in their posture in the market very much. They are constantly one way or the other. You often know with a good customer what he is going to do and when he is going to do it. A good broker will anticipate what the bank is going to do without letting the bank know and without being pushy. The minute you see a borrowing bank's line ring, you get your people on the phones with the accounts that are going to be selling. So when the bank says, "I will take 200,' you have the offers all lined up and can say, 'Sold 25,' 'Sold 50,' and so on."

The same broker went on to observe that "when you have a big buyer on the phone, you try to get a round number out of him. If he asks me how much I might be able to bring down [get for him] and I say 350, my next question might be: 'Do you want 500?' This is a volume market; we can put through a single trade for half a billion a lot easier than we can do five $1 million trades."

Knowing what a bank might want to do is also important because some big banks fear that showing all they want to do might distort the market. So a bank that is looking for $1 billion might bid for only $100 million. When a broker sells money to such a bank, he always tries to keep the trade going by asking: "Can I work some more for you?"

The Garban, Telerate, and Reuters screens show constantly updated quotes on Fed funds so that buyers and sellers can use them to track what the market is doing.[8] However, a given broker's quotes may at any moment differ from those on the screen because the market moves so fast. Also, each broker has a somewhat different clientele so that quotes coming out of different brokers may vary slightly.

The banks

It costs a bank money to buy and sell through a broker, but using a broker saves the bank time and cuts its phone bill. Said one trader: "When I have funds to sell, it is easier for me to go into the brokers and hit 10 or 15 bids than for me to call individual banks." Also there is the human factor. The same trader continued: "If I sell through the broker and then the rates fall, I feel, well, that bank was in there bidding at that rate. If I go in and sell direct and then the rate falls off, often the guy who sold will feel I knew something he did not. And the next time I call he bids below the market."

Most large banks use several brokers. One reason is that the more brokers a bank uses, the more exposure it gets. Another is that a bank with a big job to do may be able to operate faster by using several brokers.

A third reason some sharp traders use two brokers is that now and then the quotes at two major brokers will differ long enough to allow a profitable arbitrage. Said one trader: "The last time the Fed did reverses, Garban was at 3/16, Mabon at 1/8. I bought through Mabon, sold through Garban, and picked up 1/16 on every buck I passed through."

Finally, there is the embarrassment factor. One dealing trader commented: "If on a Wednesday I buy funds at 10 through Mabon and now want to sell at 8, I will go to another broker. I made a mistake and it's

---

[8] Garban brokers governments and agencies. See Chapter 13.

embarrassing. The guy at Garban says, 'Hey, you are going to sell before the bottom falls out.' He does not know I took in the money at 10."

The banks will also use the brokers to play games with each other. A bank may try to influence where funds are trading by posting high bids when they want to sell and vice versa.

The opening

In the early morning the chatter in a broker's office is likely to run:

"Work for you? OK, I show you out."

"¼–⅜, the bid at 5 is junk. Japanese at 6. No opening yet."

"Light opening at ⁵⁄₁₆, a regional name. I am at ¼–⅜."

Calling an opening is a touchy affair for a major broker because a lot of big banks pay their correspondents the opening rate. Years ago the big New York banks tried on occasion to distort this rate. One broker said: "They were paying correspondents the opening rate at Mabon or Garvin. So to ensure they were not getting ripped off, they used to come into the market and hit the bids, and they had an official opening. That was a distortion since the market opened on the bid side. We stopped that because we thought it was unethical. They might sell $100 million at that price when they had $500 million that they were committed to buy at that price. We told the banks that if they satisfied every bidder on our sheet, we would call an opening. If not, we would not. That stopped that."

Sometimes the major brokers open ⅛ apart because one opens on the bid side of the market, the other on the offered side.

TIERING

Currently there is almost a two-tier market in Fed funds, with foreign banks paying a higher rate than domestic banks. The spread between the rates established foreign banks and top domestic banks pay varies from almost zero in good markets to ⅛; harder foreign names have to pay up more: ¼, ⅜ or even ½. Foreign banks have to pay up in the funds market because they lack the lines at many regional banks that big American banks have. Also, the newer the foreign bank is on the U.S. scene, the less recognized its name will be, the fewer the lines that will be extended to it, and the more it will have to pay if it bids aggressively for funds. Over time as a new bank's name gets exposed, that bank will be able to buy more funds and to buy them at a better rate. An exception is the Japanese banks; they have had U.S. branches for a long time and are perceived as good credits, but because they bid so aggressively for funds, they continue to have to pay up for funds.

Some small regionals, because they are less well known, also must pay up ⅛ of so for funds. Major banks are infrequent givers of funds to regionals. Thus it is not surprising that a lot of regionals trade with each other in the brokers' market. Also, one sees many foreign banks selling in this market to other foreign banks.

Whenever a big domestic bank does something to sully its good name, as Chase and Continental did in the summer of 1982, some of their regional correspondents who had habitually sold them anywhere from $10 to $50 million daily will cut back their lines to these banks.[9] At the same time, the lines extended to a problem bank by banks that sell funds in the brokers' market will also be cut back. Simultaneously the problem bank will be demanding, if anything, more money in the brokers' market because it will feel a need to cut back the amount of negotiable paper, CDs, and BAs that it issues into the market to keep from paying up in markets where tiering is visible to all money market participants. Inevitably the law of supply and demand comes into play, and the rates a problem bank has to pay for funds rises. Normally such tiering is temporary, diminishing as the affected bank solves whatever problems had plagued it.

VOLUME

In recent years the volume of trading in the overnight market for funds has picked up substantially; there is more money around, and a lot more foreign banks have entered the market. One broker of overnight funds estimates that between 1978 and 1982, the market in overnight funds doubled and that $60 billion of trades now pass on an average day through the brokers' market. There is no Fed statistic against which to check these estimates because the figures the Fed now collects and publishes on the overnight borrowings of banks include their transactions in both Fed funds and repo.

Figures published by the Fed until 1979 on bank transactions in Fed funds were revealing. They showed that week in and week out, the top 46 banks met close to 100% (give or take a little) of their reserve requirements by buying Fed funds and borrowing at the discount window. The figures were slightly smaller for top New York banks, but they were much larger for the top Chicago banks, which daily borrowed 300–400% of their required reserves in the Fed funds market. The Fed figures also

---

[9] Continental had its name sullied because of all the bad loans it had on its books, including a lot of energy-related loan participations it had bought from the Penn Square Bank before that bank failed. Chase lost over ¼ of a billion pretax because of the prominent and questionable role it played in the Drysdale debacle; it also had more than its share of bad loans and other problems.

showed that the top 46 banks as a group bought about twice the quantity of funds that they sold. Most banks in the group were net buyers of funds; no top New York or Chicago bank was a net seller of funds. The Fed's figures also showed that the top New York banks played a prominent role in dealer financing relative to other large banks. Presumably all these relationships still prevail in the funds market. Only the numbers have changed; today they must be much larger.

THE DAILY PATTERN

On October 1, 1981, the Fed required that CHIPS go to same day settlement.[10] At that time the Fed introduced a new schedule of cutoff times for money transfers over the Fed wire; it also changed the old pattern under which the Fed wire closed for interdistrict and intradistrict transfers on a geographic basis: early in New York, later on the West Coast. Today cutoff times apply nationally.

CHIPS is scheduled to settle by 4:30 New York time, and by 4:35 the New York Clearing House banks and other participating members should have a printout indicating their bank's gross and net positions with CHIPS, the gross and net positions for each bank for whom they settle, and finally their *net net*—the dollars they must send out or will receive due to CHIPS settlement.

At the same time that CHIPS settles, the Fed wire closes for commercial (nonsettlement) transactions. From 4:30 to 6:30 is *the settlement period;* a *settlement transaction* is one in which both parties are subject to reserve requirements under the 1980 Banking Act.

Together with same day settlement of CHIPS, the new Fed wire schedule has turned daily trading in Fed funds into a sort of two-phase affair. From the opening of the market at 8:30 A.M. until about 2 or 2:30 P.M., banks busily trade funds to get themselves roughly into the position in which they want to end the day.

Then at 4:30 the CHIPS figures hit the major banks, and a new burst of activity occurs. No small amount of this activity is on the part of foreign bank branches and agencies, which make and receive most of their payments through an account at a correspondent bank, typically a top New York bank. Once these banks get their CHIPS figure, they will have at their clearing bank either a surplus that they want to unload or a deficit that they must cover. As foreign banks make transfers into and out of their clearing bank accounts—for French and Japanese banks the sums can be huge—each clearing bank must in turn buy or sell funds to fine tune its reserve position which is affected both by its net net from CHIPS and

---

[10] For reasons, see Chapter 16.

by subsequent transfers into and out of foreign bank and other correspondent bank accounts held with it. The cutoff time for transfers out of correspondent bank accounts is traditionally 6 P.M. The time from then to 6:30 is reserved for banks on line with the Fed to adjust their accounts there by buying and selling amongst themselves.

The above scenario of trading hours and cutoff times sounds well organized and reasonable, except perhaps to New York traders for whom it means a 10-hour day: 8:30 A.M. to 6:30 P.M.. In practice, however, the schedule is more fantasy than fact, since it is a rare day when all cutoff times are respected. For one thing, the Fed has agreed that, if CHIPS settles late due to machine problems, it will extend wire hours to accommodate banks that settle through CHIPS.

A second, more common—in fact almost daily—problem is that the Fed wire gets so jammed up in the early afternoon with securities traffic that the cutoff times cited in Chapter 9 for securities transactions have to be extended. This in turn requires that the banks be given more time to settle. Consequently New York traders and brokers of Fed funds frequently work until 7 to 7:30 P.M., and on really bad days the Fed wire closes hours later than that.

Once the Fed's new computer network—scheduled to go into operation in 1983—is in place, it should be possible for wire cutoff times for both securities and funds transfers to be respected most of the time. However, that will still leave the New York banks and funds brokers with a big staffing problem. No institution can expect employees regularly to work 50-hour weeks. Yet a 10-hour day is awkward to break into shifts. Noted one broker, "If they went to 24-hour-a-day trading, that would make my job easier. Right now I am in limbo. The pace of the desk is such that you just do not sit down; 8:30 to 6:30 is a *long* day."

WEDNESDAY CLOSE

The most exciting and volatile time in the Fed funds market is Wednesday afternoon when all depository institutions settle.

On Wednesday a bank's Fed funds trader will try to determine as early as possible what the bank's position is. At 5:30 he starts putting numbers together. He knows his final net CHIPS number and his number for securities transactions; everything else is pretty well cleaned up and steady. The big unknown—a hardship same day settlement has imposed on the clearing banks—is what monies foreign banks will transfer into and out of the bank late in the day. Foreign banks, who do a lot of volume after they get their CHIPS position to work off that position, can cause tremendous changes late in the day in a clearing bank's position. Sometimes on a Wednesday, this will create real problems for such a bank.

Extensions and as ofs

On Wednesday the loss of a transaction in the system, a mistake by a bank, or a mistake by a broker can set off a panic on a bank's Fed funds desk; they thought they had settled and suddenly find they have not. A bank in this position may ask the Fed to hold the wire open until the mistake is righted or may ask the Fed to permit them to do an *as of* transaction, that is, to do a transaction the next day and be credited for it as if the transfer had occurred on the previous day.

In the scenario that introduced this chapter, a bank was searching wildly for $150 million that had been lost in the system. The Fed is tough about doing "as of" transactions in such situations because, as someone at the Fed noted, "The way things work out is that if a West Coast bank is supposed to have sent Chase money and Chase did not get it, through no fault of either bank [something went wrong with the wire system or a computer], and if we then credit Chase as if the transfer had been made, there will be no offsetting debit for the West Coast bank; it will be a one-sided adjustment, and we end up giving money away free. The reason is that the West Coast bank will argue that they knew they had sent the money, and when they saw their balance [at the Fed], they assumed that this money had already been taken out and managed their balance accordingly. So to take the money from them now would cause them to end up short through no fault of their own."[11]

"When people reported things by hand, there was no such thing as 'as of' adjustments. The advent of computers gave rise to them—obliged us to give money away free because of mistakes that lie with the technology. The same thing occurs when governments and agencies [securities] are transferred over the Fed wire."

A slightly different situation in which a bank might ask for an "as of" transfer is if it had made a mistake in tracking its own balance or if a mistake had been made by a broker. Here is an example of the latter. When the Fed wire still closed by districts, a broker commented late one Wednesday afternoon "We are in trouble. We thought a bank was willing to give up ⅛ to sell. He says he was not. They misunderstood me and I misunderstood them. Now we have a bank that is short $25 million. We will try to find someone outside the district and arrange an 'as of' sale.

"The Fed can be a son of a bitch about this sort of thing. This is an ethical business, so it is sad that when an honest mistake is made, they

---

[11] Because of the huge volume of transfers being made into and out of a major bank's account at the Fed, it is not uncommon for such a bank to reconcile its balance at the Fed, which it can track throughout the day, with transfers into and out of that account after both it and the Fed have closed. Thus a bank could make the honest mistake of assuming that its closing balance reflected an outward transfer that had not gone through.

do not give much leeway. But if they are not strict about cutoff times, abuses occur. Still they do make allowances for size.

"For a small bank in Tulsa, losing $5 million is like Chase losing $250 million. The Fed thinks of the small banks as less sophisticated so it is more likely to let them do an 'as of' to cover a mistake than they are to let a New York bank do so."

It is the current understanding of the major banks that the Fed will not permit them to do an as of (*reserve adjustment*) transaction unless failure to do so would cause the bank to be OD at the Fed. A bank that is overdrawn at the Fed at the end of the day incurs a stiff penalty.

On a bank's desk

Settling on a Wednesday is tricky for a bank's funds desk. A bank can offset large and unanticipated inflows to or outflows of funds from its reserve account right up to the moment the Fed wire closes by selling or buying additional Fed funds. However, the Fed funds rate sometimes gets out of hand late Wednesday when either bids or offers may be scarce. This has been particularly true for the large New York banks, which clear for major international banks. The latter may, after they get their CHIPS figures at 4:30, make tremendous transfers into and out of their clearing bank account until the 6:00 cutoff for such transfers. That leaves the clearing banks only half an hour to clear up their own positions at the Fed.

A bank that finds itself unexpectedly in the red can, in addition to buying funds, go to the discount window. But if it is way red, it may have a collateral problem, that is, need to borrow more than the amount of collateral it has at the Fed. In that case, it either must scurry to find funds or, if worse comes to worse, ask for an unsecured advance at the window. In the short run the Fed has to grant such an advance, but asking for it is a black mark against a bank, and the Fed will expect that bank to be more careful and conservative in the future.

The fact that a bank can run 2% short or long on its reserve balance and carry that over into the next reserve week gives it some leeway in settling. How much depends on whether it settled on the nose during the previous week. If, for example, it was red in the previous week, then in the current week it has to settle on the nose or run an excess.

Sometimes on a Wednesday, many banks end up with reserves imbalances in the same direction—they are all red or all black. This occurs because the Fed has misestimated the reserves available to the banks, and there are either too many or too few in the aggregate. When this occurs, the funds rate will start to move.

Late on a Wednesday, when the Fed can no longer act, the Fed funds rate can go anywhere and sometimes does. As one trader noted, "When rates were at 18, I have seen funds go from 1 to 30 with no in between. Now [September 1982] you might see a range of 10 to 18 during the Wednesday close. When an extreme is reached, not a lot of money trades at that level. If a high occurs around 6 P.M., you know that banks buying at that late hour are doing so to get into their borrowing range [at the discount window] or because they had not truly bought their position. Once such banks cover, there is no further interest, and the rate will fall off." A bank that pays 25% on a Wednesday afternoon is probably a bank that has a country-bank philosophy: We won't go to the window.

Part of the reason the funds market becomes so volatile late on Wednesday is that volume can get so *thin* that a $10 million purchase will move the market up ½. A bank may also have to pay high rates late in the day because, while funds are still offered in the market, they are not being offered by banks with lines open to it.

That the funds rate sometimes falls so low on Wednesdays is due to the way the carry-over provision operates. Suppose a few banks, the B of A included, end up late Wednesday way black due to bad numbers. As they pump out money, the funds rate will start to fall; this ought to attract buyers because banks can carry a reserve surplus from the current week forward into the following week, and sometimes the banks will bid for the surplus funds to carry them forward. It may, however, happen that most of the big banks were black the week before, If so, then if they go black again, they will get no credit for the current week's surplus. A bank in this position will bid for additional funds only if the rate is very low and only if it can buy more money than the black it is erasing. For example, if a bank were $80 million black in the previous week and planned to be $80 million short in the current week, it would pay it to decrease that short only if it bought more than $80 million and only if it bought that money very cheaply.

If a bank in such a position bids for funds, it will probably put in an *all or none* (AON) bid. An AON bid does not mean that the money all has to come from the same source, only that it has to equal in total the amount bid for and be offered at the rate bid.

Weekly pattern in excess reserves

Because banks can carry forward reserve deficiencies and excesses in limited amounts, one would expect a pattern in banks' excess reserves; namely, that if they were *positive* one week, they would be *negative* the next. Figures in Table 11–1 show that in 1980 (the last year for which the Fed collected such data) precisely such a pattern existed in the excess reserves run by *large* banks in New York, Chicago, and elsewhere. However, for the banking systems as a whole, excess reserves are consistently positive (Table 11–2, line 9). The reason is that

TABLE 11–1
Reserves and borrowings of member banks: Weekly averages of daily figures, 1980 ($ millions, end-of-week dates)

Reserve classification	May 7	May 14	May 21	May 28	June 4	June 11	June 18	June 25	July 2
All member banks									
Reserves									
1 At Reserve Banks........	32,904	31,869	33,754	32,461	32,830	31,487	31,799	32,336	32,615
2 Currency and coin........	11,415	11,410	10,196	10,925	11,114	11,254	11,407	10,695	11,257
3 Total held............	44,530	43,488	44,159	43,595	44,151	42,948	43,413	43,240	44,069
4 Required............	44,202	43,453	43,880	43,614	43,766	42,809	43,268	43,080	43,778
5 Excess.............	328	35	279	−19	385	139	145	160	291
Borrowings at Reserve Banks									
6 Total.............	1,331	1,020	838	1,124	459	401	396	318	349
7 Seasonal............	155	47	41	29	21	15	11	8	7
Large banks in New York City									
8 Reserves held	7,649	7,320	8,006	7,471	8,118	7,368	7,611	7,391	7,664
9 Required............	7,495	7,445	7,829	7,661	8,007	7,478	7,619	7,352	7,680
10 Excess	154	−125	177	−190	111	−110	−8	39	−16
11 Borrowings..........	0	89	0	48	0	0	8	0	0
Large banks in Chicago									
12 Reserves held	1,947	1,876	1,985	1,838	1,888	1,848	1,908	1,820	1,900

13 Required	1,921	1,903	1,955	1,859	1,871	1,857	1,902	1,825	1,891
14 Excess	26	-27	30	-21	17	-9	6	-5	9
15 Borrowings	11	0	0	108	11	0	0	0	21
Other large banks									
16 Reserves held	17,936	17,571	17,363	17,439	17,285	17,097	17,158	17,209	17,518
17 Required	17,934	17,555	17,460	17,401	17,282	16,994	17,210	17,203	17,433
18 Excess	2	16	-97	38	3	103	-52	6	85
19 Borrowings	861	831	774	899	393	378	291	297	298
All other banks									
20 Reserves held	16,580	16,204	16,325	16,310	16,304	16,028	16,301	16,415	16,602
21 Required	16,448	16,085	16,193	16,175	16,103	15,902	16,132	16,335	16,412
22 Excess	132	119	132	135	201	126	169	80	110
23 Borrowings	459	100	64	69	55	23	27	21	30
Edge corporations									
24 Reserves held	315	329	321	350	367	390	375	347	343
25 Required	302	297	295	328	341	368	355	315	326
26 Excess	13	32	26	22	26	22	20	32	17
U.S. agencies and branches									
27 Reserves held	103	188	159	187	189	217	60	58	39
28 Required	102	168	148	190	162	210	50	50	36
29 Excess	1	20	11	-3	27	7	10	8	3

TABLE 11–2
Reserves and borrowings, depository institutions ($ millions)

Reserve classification	1981 Dec.	1982 Jan.	Feb.	Mar.	Apr.	May	June	July	Aug.
		Monthly averages of daily figures							
1 Reserve balances with Reserve Banks..	26,163	26,721	25,963	24,254	24,565	24,207	24,031	24,273	24,471
2 Total vault cash (estimated)............	19,538	20,284	19,251	18,749	18,577	19,048	19,318	19,448	19,500
3 Vault cash at institutions with required reserve balances	13,577	14,199	13,082	12,663	12,709	12,972	13,048	13,105	13,188
4 Vault cash equal to required reserves at other institutions	2,178	2,290	2,235	2,313	2,284	2,373	2,488	2,486	2,518
5 Surplus vault cash at other institutions..........	3,783	3,795	3,934	3,773	3,584	3,703	3,782	3,857	3,794
6 Reserve balances + total value cash.....	45,701	47,005	45,214	43,003	43,142	43,255	43,349	43,721	43,971
7 Reserve balances + total vault cash used to satisfy reserve requirements	41,918	43,210	41,280	39,230	39,558	39,552	39,567	39,864	40,177
8 Required reserves (estimated)..........	41,606	42,785	40,981	38,873	39,284	39,192	39,257	39,573	39,866
9 Excess reserve balances at Reserve Banks............	312	425	299	357	274	360	310	291	311
10 Total borrowings at Reserve Banks.....	642	1,526	1,713	1,611	1,581	1,105	1,205	669	510
11 Seasonal borrowings at Reserve Banks............	53	75	132	174	167	237	239	225	119
12 Extended credit at Reserve Banks....	149	197	232	309	245	177	103	46	94

there are many smaller banks in the system that consistently run excess reserves either because they don't find it worthwhile to sell off the last penny of their surplus reserves or because they do not ever want to end up at the discount window and so manage their funds positions very conservatively.

THE FORWARD MARKET

So far we have been talking about the market for overnight funds for *immediate* delivery. Before CHIPS went to same day settlement, there was a lot of trading in overnight funds for forward delivery (a sale on Friday for delivery on Monday), mostly in connection with Euro arbitrages. One of the Fed's objectives in mandatory same day settlement on CHIPS was to eliminate the possibilities for technical arbitrages between Euros and Fed funds that next day settlement of CHIPS created. Such arbitrages, which were profitable and therefore were carried out for huge sums, cost the Fed money; they also resulted in big overdrafts in clearing house funds and therefore a big potential risk.[12]

TERM FED FUNDS

Most transactions in the Fed funds market are for overnight (over the weekend in the case of Friday sales) funds. There is, however, a big and rapidly growing market for what are called *term Fed funds.* On term transactions the funds are normally sold for a period of time, normally in the range of a week to 6 months. Occasionally longer term transactions of 1, 2, or even 3 years also occur. There is no way to measure precisely the volume of transactions in term funds outstanding. One broker estimates it to be in the tens of billions.

The main advantage to a domestic bank of buying term funds is cost. A bank that wants to get some longer-term money on its book has a choice between CDs and term Fed funds. From the point of view of cost, term Fed funds have the attraction of being classified as a borrowing, not a deposit, so a bank buying term Fed funds incurs no reserve requirements and need pay no FDIC insurance. This means that, if term Fed funds were trading at $\frac{1}{32}$ spread or less above CD money of the same maturity, term Fed funds would be cheaper to the buying bank than CD money.[13] Another advantage of term Fed funds is that they can be bought for a maturity of less than 30 days, which CD money cannot.

---

[12] See Chapter 16.
[13] The all in cost to a bank of CD money is, assuming the bank pays 3% reserves, 1.03173 times the rate paid (for calculation see Chapter 15.)

$$\frac{1}{32} = .03125$$

On a bank's statement, money that a bank has bought in the CD market shows up as "time deposits," whereas money a bank has purchased in the term Fed funds market shows up as "other borrowing." Banks like to have a lot of deposits to preserve the aesthetics of their balance sheet, so they limit the amount of term Fed funds they will buy even when there is a rate advantage to doing so. This is particularly true over the year-end statement date.

Foreign bank branches and agencies also buy large amounts of term Fed funds for two reasons. First, for them as for domestic banks, it is typically cheaper to buy term Fed funds than to buy money in the CD market. Second, given their appetite for dollars and the limited acceptance of their names by domestic investors, foreign banks are anxious to take advantage of every source of funds open to them in the domestic market.

Some of the money sold in the term Fed funds market is sold by small domestic banks that might alternatively have invested in CDs issued by large banks. A small bank selling Fed funds loses the liquidity it would have if it purchased a CD, but it gains extra return. Foreign bank branches and agencies also appear in the term funds market as sellers of funds.

Many small banks that consistently sell overnight Fed funds do not sell term funds. One reason is that for a small bank, *selling* Fed funds everyday is its liquidity.[14] Even small banks have to settle with the Fed, and their money positions change from day to day. They might have $300,000 available to sell one day, $350,000 the next day, and only $100,000 the day after that. If such a bank sold term Fed funds, it would be acquiring a fixed-rate term asset that it could not liquidate. Sales of day-to-day money, in contrast, give it great flexibility.

In 1970 the Fed ruled that Fed funds purchased by banks from agencies of the U.S. government, savings and loan associations, mutual savings banks, and agencies and branches of foreign banks operating in the United States were, like purchases of Fed funds from commercial banks, not subject to reserve requirements. Commercial banks at that time had already been buying Fed funds from some of these institutions, so the Fed's action simply made official what the banks had assumed to be Fed policy.

For a savings and loan association, a sale of term Fed funds with a maturity of no longer than 6 months is a qualifying asset for purposes of meeting short-term liquidity requirements. Because the rate on term Fed funds is quite attractive relative to other short-term rates, S&Ls have

---

[14] Note the contrast between small banks and large banks. For the large bank, the ability to *buy* overnight money is its major source of liquidity.

become major sellers of term funds to the banks. Some of these sales are made directly to banks and others through the Federal Home Loan Bank system, which collects small amounts of overnight and term funds from individual S&Ls and resells them in round-lot amounts in the New York market. The FHLB also invests funds from its own liquidity portfolios by selling term funds.

A lending institution does not have to have spare cash in the till to participate in the term funds market. The country is full of banks and S&Ls who are sitting on low-coupon government and agency paper that they would like to sell but won't because they will not take a capital loss. One way such institutions can and do raise the total return on their portfolios is by reversing out securities—trading their securities for money at the repo rate—and then investing the money received (borrowed) in a higher yielding instrument. Normally the spread between the rate at which governments can be repoed and that at which term funds can be sold runs about 50–60 basis points in the 6-month area. In early October of 1982 a bank holding governments could, for example, have reversed them out to 6 months at 9.15 and simultaneously sold 6-month funds at 9.75 for a 60-basis-point pickup in total return on the securities reversed out. For those who like to think in terms of dollars, we note that, had the institution done this trade using governments with a market value of $10 million, it would have earned over 6 months an extra $60,000.

A more venturesome bank doing this arb might have chosen to go for a wider spread by selling term funds to a foreign banks branch or agency or by selling Euros. S&Ls, who are big sellers of funds obtained by reversing out securities, have recently been authorized to lend Euros but only to FDIC-insured banks. Being restricted to selling to FDIC-insured institutions means that S&Ls may not sell either term funds or Euros to many foreign banks that have U.S. branches or agencies.

Term Fed funds are actively brokered by several shops: Palumbo, Garban, Maybon, Lasser, Noonan, and Dominion Securities to name the largest. Besides quoting rates, as brokers of overnight funds do, brokers of term funds keep an eye on which securities their customers own and are quick to point out to a customer any arbitrage into term funds that they think might be attractive to that customer. An arbitrage need not involve the sale of term Fed funds; it might call for a purchase. A broker, for example, might suggest that a bank buy term funds and sell, at a spread, Euros of the same tenor.

Because brokerage on Fed funds is paid on a per-day basis, sales of term Fed funds are attractive to a broker. Also when arbitrage is involved, the broker may—depending on how wide a range of instruments his shop brokers—be able to pick up brokerage on both sides of the transaction.

The repo market

The market for Fed funds is one in which *immediately available* funds are lent on an unsecured basis. A market closely related to the Fed funds market is the *repo* market, in which immediately available funds are lent on a *secured* basis. We turn to the repo market in the next chapter.

Chapter 12

Repos and reverses

IN RECENT YEARS the repo market has become one of the fastest growing sectors of the money market. This is unsurprising: There is so much more debt around to be financed; there are so many more arbs, including cash against futures, being done; new strategies are constantly being developed in which a repo or a reverse play a role; and finally dealers' matched books, which used to be run as a sideline to financing the firms' positions, have become in many shops a big trading and profit center in which term-collateral is the vehicle traded.

There are no figures on volume transacted in the repo market. One repo broker hazarded the guess that, "Trading in overnight Fed funds runs between 75 and 80 billion a day, and the comparable figure for the overnight RP market is probably twice that size. The amount of term RP outstanding—transactions for 1-week, 3-months, or longer—is in the 200–300 billion range." Whatever the true numbers are, the market is enormous.

Transactions in this market are referred to by various terms: a *sale-repurchase agreement,* a *repo* (*RP* for short), or a *reverse.*[1] The term

---

[1] Much has already been said in this book about repos, reverses, and their uses. This chapter builds on and amplifies this earlier discussion.

sale-repurchase agreement accurately describes how the transaction most typically is done. It calls for writing two tickets: a *sale* ticket for current settlement and a *repurchase* ticket for settlement at some latter date (Figure 12–1). Because the term, sale-repurchase agreement, is a multisyllable mouthful, street people talk about doing repos and reverses. Also, and more important, most people who do repo think of themselves as engaging in what amounts—whatever the technicalities may be and however the tickets are written—to a *collateralized loan.*

In talking about the sale-repurchase market, we will use the terms repo and reverse because most of the practices in this market are more consistent with the transaction being a collateralized loan than with its being a strict sale-resale.

Even the terms repo and reverse are confusing because they are used on the street with no consistency. The essential definition to bear in mind is this: A repo or a reverse—*one firm's repo is necessarily another's reverse*—is a loan secured by collateral in the form of securities. One side lends money, the other side lends (or *reverses out*) securities. At the risk of adding confusion, we note that the party lending money is sometimes said in street jargon to be *reversing in* securities.

Since the failures of Drysdale and Lombard-Wall in 1982, street people, who used to be much too busy doing repos and reverses to give much thought to whether they were engaging in a sale-repurchase transaction or a collateralized loan, have given that and related questions much thought.[2] Precisely what is a repo transaction: a buy-sell or a collateralized loan? What are the rights of the borrower and of the lender? Who bears what responsibilities if an agent is interposed between the borrower and the lender?

It may seem peculiar to the outsider that these questions had not been definitively answered previously and, more specifically, that repo transactions had never been strictly defined in a legal sense. The explanation lies in the history of the market. Repo transactions, like Eurodollar transactions, began to be done in volume after World War II because they suited the needs of a lot of money market participants.

Regulation Q prevented banks from paying interest on time deposits having a maturity of less than 30 days and in particular on overnight and call deposits. Banks dealing with other banks circumvented this prohibition by buying and selling Fed funds. Nonbank institutions—corporations, municipalities, and so on—that dealt with banks could not sell them Fed funds so they turned to doing repo as a way to put their money to work short-term for a fee. As one banker noted, "Nothing spurs innovation like a regulation." This is especially true of one that assigns a zero price to a commodity—in this case the use of money—that would in a free market command a positive price.

---

[2] The failures of Drysdale and Lombard-Wall were described at the end of Chapter 9.

FIGURE 12–1
Confirmations on a term repo agreement (pre-October 1982)

A. Sale confirmation

MORGAN GUARANTY TRUST COMPANY OF NEW YORK	23 WALL STREET, NEW YORK, N.Y. 10015

AS PRINCIPAL, WE HEREBY CONFIRM **SALE TO YOU.**

DATE PREPARED	TRANSACTION NUMBER		TRADE DATE	SETTLEMENT DATE
6/21	RS-0001		6/21/74	6/21/74

ACCOUNT / DELIVERY INSTRUCTIONS

ABC CORPORATION
INVESTMENT A/C

WE	QUANTITY	CUSIP NUMBER	SECURITY DESCRIPTION
SLD	10,000,000	912827 BN 1	U S A TREASURY NOTES

ACCRUED INTEREST PERIOD		
10.00% FOR DAYS	A-77	8.00% DUE 2/15/77

PRICE	PRINCIPAL	ACCRUED INTEREST	SERVICE CHARGE	TOTAL COST
98.00	9,800,000.00			9,800,000.00

DUPLICATE CONFIRMATION   FORM 51-4-1 D   GOVERNMENT BOND DEPARTMENT

B. Repurchase confirmation

MORGAN GUARANTY TRUST COMPANY OF NEW YORK	23 WALL STREET, NEW YORK, N.Y. 10015

AS PRINCIPAL, WE HEREBY CONFIRM **PURCHASE FROM YOU.**

DATE PREPARED	TRANSACTION NUMBER		TRADE DATE	SETTLEMENT DATE
6/21	RP-0001		6/21/74	7/11/74

ACCOUNT / DELIVERY INSTRUCTIONS

ABC CORPORATION
INVESTMENT A/C

WE	QUANTITY	CUSIP NUMBER	SECURITY DESCRIPTION
BOT	10,000,000	912827 BN 1	U S A TREASURY NOTES

ACCRUED INTEREST PERIOD		
10.00% FOR 20 DAYS	A-77	8.00% DUE 2/15/77

PRICE	PRINCIPAL	ACCRUED INTEREST	SERVICE CHARGE	TOTAL PROCEEDS
98.00	9,800,000.00	54,444.45		9,854,444.45

DELIVERIES ARE TO BE MADE TO OUR CUSTODY DEPARTMENT, 17TH FLOOR, 15 BROAD STREET, N.Y.C.

DUPLICATE CONFIRMATION   FORM 51-4-1 D   GOVERNMENT BOND DEPARTMENT

At the beginning of the repo market there were just a few shops doing it, and repo was what they said it was. "That," noted one dealer, "is the way it should be. Now there are layers of lawyers and judges trying to tell us what we have been doing low these many years. We left it purposely vague because doing so fit our needs. If a customer said, 'I can't do repo,' we said, 'OK, we will sell you securities and buy them back.' If another customer said he could not buy securities, we said, 'Fine, we will borrow money from you and give you collateral.' It was all very convenient, and now they [the lawyers and judges] have messed it up."

The undefined and unregulated nature of the repo transactions seemed untidy to say the least to the SEC. It tried to call a repo transaction a security that had to be cleared through the SEC each and every time it was done. The dealers objected on the grounds that such a requirement would make it impossible for them to use repo to meet their daily financing needs. The Fed, this time in the dealers' corner, argued that the SEC's requirement would also deprive the Fed of an extremely useful tool for day-to-day implementation of monetary policy.

Today, with all the questions that have been raised about repo transactions, every big participant in the market—borrower or lender—has his lawyer trying to sort out the precise legal nature of the transaction. Borrowers' counsels are seeking to substitute old confirm slips with newly drawn documents that stipulate precisely the rights of each party should the other fail to execute his role in unwinding the transaction. Lenders' counsels are wondering whether, under the 1978 bankruptcy act, any written RP document—no matter what it says—will give collateral holders who fail to get back funds lent a position any stronger than that of being just one more secured creditor who must—to get all or part of his money back—participate in an orderly and lengthy distribution, overseen by a bankruptcy court, of the debtor's assets.

More about this at the end of the chapter. While the failures of Drysdale and of Lombard-Wall—coming one on the heels of the other—put a big crimp in repo activity, that crimp proved short lived. Soon the street was back to business as usual with one proviso: Everyone was paying a lot more attention to the old maximum, know thy customer. The pretty much universal reasoning was, "If I am careful about the credit of those I deal with, I will never end up down in Foley Square [the Federal court house] trying to collect money or securities in a bankruptcy court. And so long as I don't end up in the Square, what the judges and lawyers say about the status of repo—and they all seem to be saying different things—won't matter."

NATURE OF A REPO TRANSACTION

In any repo or reverse transaction, whatever the courts may decide it is, there is first a sale of securities, subsequently a repurchase. On the day the transaction is initiated, securities are sold against money; on the day the transaction is unwound, these flows are reversed—the money and the securities are returned to their original holders with the money holder getting something extra in the form of interest for the use of his money during the term of the transaction.

Sale-repurchase agreements are always quoted in the market in terms of the interest rate paid—the *repo rate.* This jibes with the interpretation of a sale-repurchase agreement as being a secured loan to the seller of securities with the securities sold serving as *collateral.*

Pricing prior to October 1982

Until October 1982, the normal practice on an RP agreement was for pricing to be *flat,* that is, on coupon securities the coupon interest that accrues over the life of the transaction was ignored.[3] Figure 12–1 presents confirmations from the borrower, a bank, on a term repo priced flat. Note that the purchase price (*principal amount*) on the sale confirmation is the same price that appears on the repurchase confirmation. The agreed-upon repo rate is 10%, so the repurchase confirmation shows that the amount due to the lender at the time of repurchase is the principal sum plus $54,444.45 of accrued interest.

The repo rate is a straight add-on interest rate calculated on a 360-day-year basis. So interest due is figured as follows:

$$\text{Interest due} = \left(\begin{matrix}\text{Principal} \\ \text{amount}\end{matrix}\right) \times \left(\begin{matrix}\text{Repo} \\ \text{rate}\end{matrix}\right) \times \left(\frac{\text{Days repo is outstanding}}{360}\right)$$

Applying this formula to the example presented in Figure 12–1, we get

$$\$9,800,000 \times 0.10 \times \frac{20}{360} = \$54,444.45$$

which is the accrued interest appearing on the repurchase confirmation.

Credit risk and margin

Even on a repo transaction priced flat (i.e., with no account taken of accrued interest), the lender was exposed to risk. Interest rates might rise, forcing down the market value of the securities he had taken in; if the borrower then went bankrupt and the repurchase was not executed, the lender might be left holding the securities with a market value, in-

---

[3] Coupon securities, except when the issuer is in default, are sold in *outright* purchases at the quoted dollar price *plus* accrued interest. When a bond is in default and no interest payments are being made, it trades *flat;* that is, unpaid interest is not billed to the buyer but is his if the issuer later resumes interest payments. Given this use of the term *flat,* it was natural for participants in the repo market to describe repo transactions on which accrued interest is ignored in the pricing as being *priced flat.*

cluding accrued interest, less than the amount he had lent. Assuming the securities RPed has not been trading above par, the lender could make himself whole by maturing these securities, but if he needed the money he had lent, that might be impossible or it might be expensive because it forced him into other suboptimal decisions.

The borrower in a repo transaction also incurs a risk. Interest rates might fall during the life of the agreement, forcing up the market value of the securities he had sold. If the lender then went belly up, the borrower would be left holding an amount of money smaller than the market value of the securities he had sold. So by retaining the money lent to him instead of effecting the agreed-upon repurchase, he would incur a loss.

In every repo transaction, no matter how the collateral is priced, both the lender and the borrower are exposed to risk. The lender can seek to protect himself by asking for *margin,* that is, by lending less than 100 percent of the market value of the securities he takes in, but in doing so he *increases* risk for the borrower. Alternatively the borrower might seek to reduce his risk by asking for *reverse margin,* that is, by asking the lender to buy his securities at a price above their market value, but that would increase risk for the borrower. No strategy exists to simultaneously reduce risk for both the borrower and the lender.

Margin in practice

Traditionally on a repo transaction, the lender of money, because it is lending the more liquid asset, receives margin. To provide that margin, securities used as repo collateral are priced at market value minus a *haircut;* the size of the haircut varies depending on the maturity, scarcity value, and price volatility of the underlying collateral, on the term of the repo, and on the credit of the customer.

On transactions of short maturity, the amount of the haircut (difference between market value measured at the *bid* side of the market and value used in the RP agreement) is typically ¼ of a point. Thus if a coupon for which the bid was "par 8" were RPed, the investor would lend only par.[4] If, alternatively, the securities RPed were 6-month discount paper (bills) quoted at 8% and therefore trading at a dollar price of 96.10, they would be priced at 95.85 in a repo agreement.

Pricing on an RP agreement depends both on the length of the transaction and on the current maturity of the securities RPed. An investor in a 6-month RP collateralized by long bonds might want more margin.[5] Sometimes on term repo transactions, dealers demand the right to reprice; more about that later.

---

[4] A bid of par 8 means the bid is 100⁸⁄₃₂.

[5] Not all long bonds are acceptable as collateral on an RP transaction. Normally only securities with a current maturity of 10 years or less are used.

On coupon securities, the lender also used to get a second sort of margin, because in the pricing of securities RPed, no account was taken of interest already accrued at the time the transaction was undertaken. As one dealer commented when flat pricing still prevailed, "If I have coupons on which $350,000 of accrued interest is due in five days, they are still priced at the bid side of the market less ¼. Doing so is less time-consuming than figuring the accrued interest, adding it to the securities' dollar price, and then deducing ¼, but from a dollar and cents points of view, this practice makes no sense at all."

The abuse of flat pricing

Under flat pricing of coupons used as collateral in a repo deal, problems—viewed as "opportunities" by Drysdale and Miller—occurred because undercapitalized dealers who wanted to assume huge positions could do the following: reverse in, or "buy," securities nearing a coupon date, short them, and thereby generate cheap, borrowed money that the high-flying dealers could then use to finance speculative positions.[6]

By the time Drysdale got into the reverse-them-in-and-short-them-out act, the sums that could be generated by playing this game had ballooned enormously because of high interest rates. For example, a firm shorting $500 million of a 12% bond five months into a coupon period could pick up $25 million of cash for a month.

As long as Drysdale and Miller bet correctly on interest rates, the game kept going. Eventually, however, wrong guesses on interest rates broke the bank at both Miller and Drysdale.

At the end of its brief—three month—career, Drysdale was reported to have shorted $4 billion of bonds and to have gone long another $2.5 billion on the basis of a mere $20 million in capital. The street, always wary of credit risk, would never have permitted Drysdale, acting in its own name, to build up positions of this size. It was able to do so only because Chase, the nation's third largest bank, fronted for it—acted as Drysdale's agent without disclosing Drysdale's name to those it dealt with on Drysdale's behalf.

The Drysdale default—given its magnitude, the involvement of Chase, the threat of substantial losses to other dealers, and perhaps the failure of other dealers via a domino effect—made the Fed determined to change the way the repo market operated so as to guarantee that in the future no firm would be able to repeat Drysdale's performance. The one, obvious, and only way the Fed could do this was by requiring dealers to go to *full accrued pricing;* that is, to include full accrued coupon interest in pricing notes and bonds used as repo collateral.

---

[6] The failure of Eldin Miller's Financial Corp. was also described at the end of Chapter 9.

Since Drysdale was doing nothing Financial Corporation had not done several years earlier, one might ask why the Fed took so long to act. Part of the answer is lack of authority. While the outside world views the Fed as having surveillance authority over dealers in governments and over the government market in general, in practice the Fed has no statutory authority to regulate either dealers or trading practices in this market.

To force dealers to adhere to any rule it lays down, the Fed can make only one threat, that it will stop trading with a dealer it has recognized (i.e., agreed to do business with). In ordering recognized dealers to include accrued interest in pricing repo collateral, the Fed used its ultimate weapon: it threatened to pull its wire out of the shops of noncomplying dealers. Presumably the Fed felt that the Drysdale failure had so damaged its image of competence that it had to act or face possible congressional action or an attempt by the SEC to extend its scope of regulation. Either eventuality might have brought into the government market regulators who did not understand the nature of the business; and that in turn might have altered for the worse the market environment in which the Fed carries out open market operations, its basic tool for implementing monetary policy.

The switch to full accrual pricing

In a letter to all recognized dealers, the Fed ordered them to begin, by October 1, 1982, to include accrued interest in pricing securities on repo and reverse transactions. The Fed's action was precipitated by the Drysdale debacle, but it addressed a risk of abuse in the repo market that the Fed and the dealers had recognized ever since the failure of Financial Corporation in 1975. In calling for full accrued pricing on repo collateral, the Fed required dealers to change a long-standing practice.

To foster the move to full accrued pricing, the Fed began in August 1982 to include accrued interest in pricing its securities when it did repo with dealers as part of its open market operations. It also urged the government securities Dealer Association to make it a rule that a dealer doing repo either with another dealer or with retail use full accrued pricing. Most dealers agreed with the principle of full accrued pricing, but they were unable to agree on precisely how it should be implemented. Frustrated with the dealers' endless deliberations over full accrued pricing, the Fed finally gave up on self regulation by the dealers and decided to dictate that every dealer must implement this method of pricing no later than October 1, 1982.

The reactions of individual dealers to the Fed's dictate were varied. Most viewed the move as long overdue and were supportive. As one broker noted, "Drysdale made people aware of where their true exposure lay. Banks, even the big ones, used to think of a repo done by them as a loan to them. They took the attitude, 'You can lend me money, but you won't get my cash.' In fact because of accrued interest, the securities they were giving out to get cash were worth substantially more than the cash they were getting. Drysdale made people aware that, under the old pricing method, your exposure was not to the people who had your cash but to the people who had your bonds."

While most dealers were supportive of the Fed's dictate that they move to full accrued pricing, some were troubled by the operational problems, including reprogramming of computers, that they believed the switch in collateral pricing would cause. A few were irate that the Fed told them to go to full accrued pricing without telling them precisely how to do it. In the absence of a specific directive from the Fed, the dealers pretty much followed the suggestions made by the Dealer Association's subcommittee on repo pricing.

Under previous practice, on a coupon date, the lender of money, who also held the securities used as collateral, received the coupon interest and passed it on to the lender of these securities, who in turn, if he had reversed them in, passed on the coupon to the ultimate owner of the securities. The Dealer Association proposed that this be changed. Specifically it proposed that, when a coupon is paid on a security used as collateral for a repo, the holder of the security keep the coupon and the lender of the security deduct the full amount of the coupon from the amount of the repo loan. So far so good, except for extra accounting.

The committee, however, went on to suggest that on the coupon date accrued interest on the repo be added to the amount of the repo. This sounds fair and innocuous, but on a term repo incorporating a coupon date, it calls for prepayment of interest and thereby makes the repo rate—until now a simple interest rate—a compound rate.

As one dealer noted, "If I do a 60-day deal with Bear Sterns, and he calls me back 20 minutes later and says that the collateral he is giving me has a coupon date in 15 days, that would—assuming a 12% repo rate—raise the effective rate on the transaction by 4½ basis points." This sounds insignificant, but on a repo done as part of an arbitrage designed to lock a 10-basis-point profit, compounding of the repo rate—depending on in whose favor it worked—could almost halve or increase by 50% the actual profit realized on an arb calling for a 60-day repo.

Current pricing practices

Currently, in pricing coupons securities used as repo collateral, the dealers add accrued interest to the bid price for the security and then round the resulting total to the nearest dollar price at which a bond or note would be quoted. From this amount they deduct a haircut, the size of which the Fed directive did not indicate. Since full accrued pricing reduced the average amount of margin given to lenders of money, it is not surprising that, after the adoption of full accrued pricing, investors tended to ask for and dealers were willing to give larger haircuts. Ironically the Fed, in doing repo with the dealers, has always asked for much larger haircuts than those given by dealers on trades with each other and with retail.

Most dealers did not adopt the Dealer Association's suggestion with respect to precollection of repo interest.

Protecting the wrong group?

Well-capitalized dealers who use repo primarily to finance their positions were more than willing to grant repo customers larger haircuts. One such dealer argued that the Fed's dictate protects the wrong group. In his view excluding accrued interest in pricing repo collateral provided margin to staid investors, such as money funds, who could be counted on to tuck away in a safe-keeping account any securities taken in on repo transactions.

Full accrued pricing on the other hand will protect supposedly sophisticated dealers who were big lenders of hundreds of millions of dollars of securities to Drysdale. Also, by permitting dealers to finance accrued interest on coupons they buy, the new pricing rule will permit dealers, should they choose, to assume long positions larger than those their capital would otherwise have permitted. Finally the new rule may encourage speculation, for example, by enabling traders who do cash and carry trades "against the board" (i.e., the CBT bond futures contract) to do those trades without putting up their own capital to cover the accrued interest on bonds they buy and finance as part of such trades.

The Fed, by its dictate, may have quelled the calls for further regulation of the government market and the dealers in it, but it has not and—because of the nature of a repo transaction—could not act so as to ensure that risk in the repo market was consistently shifted from the weaker and less sophisticated party in a transaction to the stronger and more sophisticated party. One ironic result of the varied uses to which the repo market can be and is put is that the conservative money funds and the Drysdales of this world end up on the same side of the repo fence: as lenders of money and borrowers of securities.

GROWTH OF THE MARKET

Dealers first began to use the RP market to finance their positions shortly after World War II. Later, as large banks began to practice active liability management, they joined the dealers in the RP market, using it to finance not only their dealer positions but their government portfolios. In the last few years the market, which was initially small, has grown dramatically. In 1969 the Fed amended Regulation D to make clear that RPs done by banks against governments and agencies (banks were already doing them) were borrowings exempt from reserve requirements. The same amendment also specified that RPs done by banks against other instruments—CDs, BAs, and loans in particular—were subject to reserve requirements; the amendment thus killed banks' use of the RP market to finance such instruments.

A second factor contributing to the rapid growth of the RP market was the Treasury's decision in 1974 to shift the bulk of its deposits from TT&L accounts at commercial banks to accounts at the Fed. This shift freed billions of dollars worth of governments and agencies that the banks had been holding as collateral against Treasury deposits for use as collateral in the RP market.

Acceptance by investors of repo as a money market instrument has grown in step with the increased use of the market by borrowers. The historical highs to which the Fed pushed interest rates on several occasions beginning in the late 1960s made corporate treasurers acutely aware of the opportunity cost of holding idle balances. In response they became big investors in RP, which offered them a way to invest highly variable amounts of money on a day-to-day basis. By the mid-1970s most corporations, including many that a few years earlier did not know what RP was, had amended their bylaws to permit them to invest in RP.

State and local governments and their agencies have in recent years also become huge investors in RP. Such government bodies are frequently required by law to hold their excess cash in bank deposits or to invest it in governments and agencies. Also, they are typically not permitted to take a capital loss on their investments, which means that they cannot invest in a security that they are unsure they will be able to hold to maturity. RP collateralized by governments and agencies offers state and local governments—whose regulations permit them to use it instead of outright purchases of governments—a way to invest tax receipts and proceeds of note and bond issues in *any* amount for *any* period. The volume of money going into the repo market from state and local governments can be huge. If New York State sells $3 billion of bonds, all that money is immediately invested in the repo market and stays there until it is needed.

A lot of banks made the pitch to foreign central banks, who traditionally gave any dollars they held to the Fed to invest for them, that their money would be better managed outside the Fed. One result is that a lot of foreign central bank money is now in the repo market. Quasi-international funds like the World Bank also supply funds to this market.

The newest and one of the biggest investors in repo is money funds.

The ex-manager of one of the largest such funds noted, "The repo market is tremendously fluid and deep. Right after a Treasury refunding in which the dealers have taken down enormous positions, the amount of collateral on the street is huge, and it is cheap to buy because the dealers are all looking for money. At times like that I sometimes did $2 billion a day in RP with one firm."

A final important stimulus to growth of the RP market has been the development of a big market in flex repos. These were described at the end of Chapter 9 where we discussed the problems Lombard-Wall got into doing such RPs.

Dealer RP financing

It is impossible to measure the size of the repo market because bank borrowings in the repo market are lumped with purchases of Fed funds for reporting purposes, and RP borrowings of other institutions (government securities dealers excepted) are not tracked by the Fed. An idea of the rate of growth of the RP market can, however, be gleaned from the figures the Fed collects on the RP borrowings (technically repurchase agreements) of U.S. dealers in government securities. These figures are plotted in Figure 12–2. RP borrowings by dealers equal roughly the difference between the repurchase agreement they make and the securi-

FIGURE 12–2
Average daily financing by U.S. government securities dealers ($ billions)

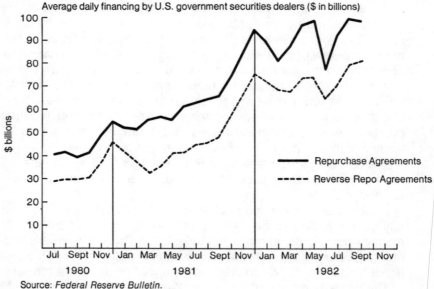

Source: *Federal Reserve Bulletin.*

ties they reverse in. The large amount of reverses dealers do reflects not only their covering of shorts but the substantial growth, discussed later in this chapter, of the matched books that they run in repo and reverse.

RP and market decisions

The RP market gives investors who are willing to base their investments on market judgments tremendous flexibility with respect to where along the yield curve they want to commit their funds. If the answer is at the very base of the yield curve, they can roll overnight repo indefinitely.

At times doing so can be very attractive. In early 1982, when yields were high and looking as if they might go higher, Fed funds and repo traded in the range of 14–15% while short bills were yielding only 12–13%. Thus at that time a portfolio manager who owned short bills could have picked up 200–300 basis points in yield by selling his bills and investing in the same instrument under repo. Later in 1982, as it became clear that rates had started to decline, it was more attractive for the portfolio manager to own securities outright because doing so offered an opportunity for capital appreciation.

THE OVERNIGHT REPO RATE

The overnight RP rate (see Figure 12–3) normally lies slightly below the Fed funds rate for two reasons. First, an RP transaction is in essence a secured loan, whereas the sale of Fed funds is an unsecured loan. Second, many investors—corporations, state and local governments, and others—who can invest in RP cannot sell Fed funds.[7]

An institution that can't sell Fed funds could invest short term by buying securities due to mature in a few months or even a few days. Doing so, however, is usually unattractive. The yield on the 3-month bill typically hovers around the repo rate, and on still shorter bills yield goes through (below) the repo rate. One reason is that many investors, including some state and local government bodies, can't invest in repo; they have to own the securities outright. A second reason for the thin supply of short bills is that they are often used by dealers as collateral for short positions (holding short bills for collateral exposes a dealer to no significant price risk). A third reason short bills are in thin supply is that many of them are held by investors who intend to roll them at maturity and who never consider the alternative of selling out early to pick up additional basis points. Finally there are the money funds who tend to sop up any short paper, including bills, that they can find to keep the average matu-

---

[7] Such institutions can't sell Fed funds because banks are not permitted under Reg Q to pay interest on overnight money they take domestically from nonbank sources.

FIGURE 12–3
The overnight RP rate tracks the overnight Fed funds rate closely

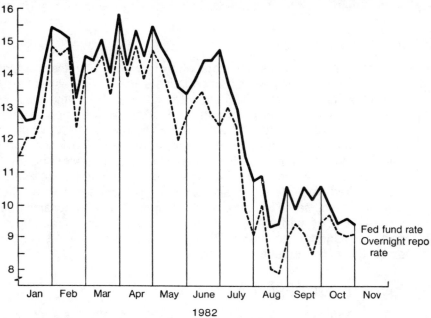

Source: Donaldson, Lufkin & Tenrette.

rity of the securities in their portfolio short. "There are," as one portfolio manager noted, "a lot of distortions in market rates because of the severe legal or self-imposed restrictions under which many portfolios are run."

The spread between the Fed funds rate and the repo rate can be anything from a full several points to just a few basis points. How wide it is depends partly on the supply of collateral available. At times when the Fed is doing a lot of adding—for example, to offset a shift in Treasury balances—the supply of collateral on the street will dry up, and the spread between the repo rate and the funds rate will widen. At other times when the Treasury has just sold a large amount of new debt that has yet to be fully distributed, dealers will have a lot of collateral, and the spread between the funds rate and the repo rate will narrow.

Most of the borrowing done in the repo market is collateralized by governments and agencies. Dealers, however, also repo CDs, BAs, and sometimes even commercial paper. The spread between the RP rate on governments and that on other securities can be negligible if there is a shortage of collateral on the street, but normally this spread is 5 to 10 basis points, and it can widen to 15 basis points.

No forward market exists in either overnight repo or term repo. However, a dealer or a bank will occasionally negotiate a forward RP deal with, for example, a government body that knows that money will be coming in on a tax date.

OPEN REPO

Under an *open* repo or *continuing contract,* a lender agrees to give a dealer some amount of funds for some period. The agreement can, however, be terminated by either side at any time. Also, the dealer typically reserves the *right of substition;* that is, he can take back securities he needs—because he has sold or wants to sell them—and give the lender other collateral.

The rate paid on an open repo, which often varies from day to day, is normally set slightly above the overnight repo rate. On an open repo a dealer incurs smaller clearing costs than when he does a series of overnight repos; he is thus willing to pay up for money obtained on an open repo.

TERM REPO

Dealers enter into term repo agreements to speculate—to create (as noted in Chapter 9) future securities they view as attractive.[8] Dealers and others also do huge amounts of term repo, when the structure of interest rates is such that cash-and-carry trades are profitable.[9] Some large banks use term RP to finance the longer governments in their portfolios to keep their book from being too short. Other large banks, however, rely strictly on overnight RP to finance their portfolios. Said one banker typical of the latter group, "We do mostly overnight RP and feel comfortable with that because the demand placed on us for collateral far exceeds the supply we have. We could repo our government portfolio two or three times over everyday."

In the repo market, as in other markets, the yield curve normally slopes upward, but at the very short end of the market, the curve frequently inverts; in particular the overnight rate is often a few basis points higher than the rate on 1- or 2-week repo. The reason is that short-period repo competes with commercial paper for investors' dollars, while the overnight repo rate relates to the frequently higher dealer loan rate that in turn keys off the Fed funds rate. Precisely what relationships exist among repo rates of differing maturities depend on the availability of financing to dealers and on the amount of collateral they have to finance.

---

[8] See pp. 298–301.

[9] For examples see Chapter 15 on futures.

In recent years there has been an extraordinary increase in the amount of funding to dates—tax dates, oil payment dates, etc.—that corporations do, and corporations as a result have become big lenders in the term repo market. The oil companies in particular have to accumulate huge dollar sums to pay the OPEC nations; these funds have to be stockpiled somewhere, and a lot of them are put into term repo. Public bodies are another big source of money in the term repo market. For the investor wanting to fund to a specific date, a big attraction of term RP is that it can usually be done in size to any date he chooses while it eliminates the need for him to scour the world for BAs or CDs maturing on that date.

Many investors, including municipalities and some financial institutions, cannot take a capital loss because of legal or self-imposed restrictions, but they can take an interest loss. Suppose such an investor has money that he thinks will be available for 6 months but that might be needed sooner. He can't invest in 6-month bills because, if he did, he might incur an accounting loss if he sold them.[10] He can, however, take the same or similar securities in on a 6-month reverse repo; that is, invest in 6-month term repo. If 3 months later the investor finds that he needs his money and the bill market is in the "chutes" (prices are down), he can repo out the collateral he has taken in. In doing so he may incur a *loss of interest* because the rate on the repo he does to borrow exceeds the rate on the term repo in which he invested (i.e., he may have negative carry on his offsetting repo transactions), *but* he won't incur a capital loss. Often municipalities can repo out securities they have obtained on a reverse but not securities they own outright. So a number of municipalities invest in term repo to get the protection and flexibility described in the example above.

Brokering of repo

It used to be that little brokering of *stock* repo was done; that is, the RP normally done by dealers and banks to finance their positions and portfolios. Banks and dealers have a customer base with which they can do such transactions directly and efficiently. Also they view RP as part of their customer line—one more thing they can show customers.

This has changed a great deal since 1978. Today dealers are using RP much more actively, not just as a financing tool but as a trading tool. Half of the multibillion-dollar matched books (discussed below) that most dealers run are necessarily RP transactions. Dealers can do that volume of trading efficiently only by relying on brokers for a lot of inter-dealer trading.

---

[10] See pp. 353–55.

Noting the change in the way RP is used by dealers today, one broker, whose volume is four to seven times what it was only four years ago, noted, "The RP traders at many dealerships now view the RP market just like any other market. They will give you bids against securities and rates at which they will offer securities based on their expectation of rates. Today our market is as actively traded as the CD or BA market."

Several major firms, Garvin GuyButler, Eurobrokers, and Tullet Riley, dominate the brokering of repo and reverses, but a number of smaller shops have also entered the business.

THE REVERSE MARKET

Many smaller banks that won't trade their portfolios will occasionally reverse out securities for various reasons: because repo money is cheaper than buying Fed funds, because—in the case of term repo— they expect the funds rate to rise and they need cash, or because they see an attractive opportunity to arbitrage.

S&Ls are also active in the reverse market. Most S&Ls do not trade their portfolios and anticipate maturing most if not all the securities they own. They will put securities out on repo but only when they are shown an opportunity to reinvest the funds they obtain at a higher yield in some other instrument—term Fed funds, BAs, or Euros. S&Ls came into the repo market in a big way after they were officially permitted to sell term Fed funds in 1970. This gave them a new attractive opportunity for arbitrage because term Fed funds yield more than bank CDs. The big West Coast S&Ls are most active in the arbitrage game. They have large portfolios and big lines to New York banks. So if the rates are there, they will do trades in size. More recently S&Ls have been given permission to invest in Euros so now they often arbitrage into higher-yielding Euros money they have raised by reversing out securities.

When the yield curve is flat, banks and S&Ls may reverse out securities as part of an arbitrage for as little as a 3/16 spread, but when the yield curve is steep they are likely to demand 1/2. Reverse agreements may or may not permit substitution. Typically they are done for a period ranging from 1 to 6 months.

For a bank or S&L that has securities a dealer wants, an alternative to reversing out these securities would be to do a straight loan—give the dealer the securities, take in other securities as collateral, and pick up a 1/2% borrowing fee. This second alternative is less attractive if the institution wants cash, which it may if it anticipates a rise in interest rates.

Most states and municipalities are strict investors of cash. They will do repos but not reverses. There are some municipalities that will lend out securities in their portfolios, but the majority either do not have the right to do so or do not understand the transaction.

Risk and liquidity

There is no liquidity in a term RP; it is not an asset that can be sold, and the underlying agreement cannot be broken. Thus one might argue, as some have, that banks and S&Ls that put securities in their liquidity portfolios out on term RP are impinging on their liquidity. In all probability, however, they are not. Most of the time they are reversing out securities that they would in almost no circumstance consider selling. Also if worse comes to worse, they can raise cash by selling or RPing the asset they have acquired as the other leg of the arbitrage.

One real risk in this game is that an unsophisticated portfolio manager might buy long bonds as a basis for arbitraging and not realize how great a price risk he was assuming. As one dealer noted, "Buying the 8s of 86 at a book yield of 10.05½ and RPing them at 7½ can look attractive to a small investor when the idea is presented to him. But should interest rates rise, he may get burned on this strategy because he loses more money selling these bonds than he has earned arbitraging against them." Note that risk arises here because the securities are purchased for the purpose of arbitraging rather than as a long-term investment.

Brokering of reverses

Reverses—other than those done by dealers as part of their matched book—are often proposed to an institution by a broker who, because his firm brokers a range of money market instruments, is in a good position to point out attractive arbitrage opportunities—to provide "one-stop shopping." A broker of such reverses is a salesman as opposed to someone who is just fast on the phone; he has to convince the customer to take in money and then to put it out elsewhere.

"We do not," commented one such broker, "just go in and say: 'Hi. 30, 60, 90 days at 30, 45, and 55. Do you want to do $25 million?' We have to show people a reason to do a reverse. To be a good reverse broker you have to know as many alternative uses as possible for money, to have a working knowledge of and a feel for more areas than in any other money market job.

"You do not just walk in and do a trade with a guy, and you do not take no for an answer. There is some rate at which a trade will go. To put together a trade on which you make money takes time and work. You have to know what your customer can do in terms of investments and what the lender is going to demand in terms of margin. Every trade that is agreed upon with respect to amount and rate is done subject to *pricing*.[11] Different accounts demand different amounts of margin. Some-

---

[11] *Pricing* refers here to the value that will be assigned to the securities reversed out. Margin is created for the lender in a reverse transaction by pricing the securities below market value plus accrued interest.

times we can't get a trade off because the two sides are half a point away on the pricing. If we get in a bind on pricing, we just start all over again."

In the brokers market for RP and in the market in general, trades are agreed upon for round-lot sums, for example, $10 million. Then the precise amount of the loan is calculated, taking into account pricing and the way the agreement is set up. Thus on a $10 million trade, the dollars lent might be more or less than $10 million.

Reverses to maturity

As noted in Chapter 5, some portfolio managers are loath to sell high-coupon securities that are trading at a premium and recommit their funds to another instrument because, if they sell these securities, they will reduce the interest income they are booking. The repo market gives the portfolio managers a way to get around his predicament.

One dealer gave an illustration, "Say a bank owns the 16¾s of 83, which have 9 months to run. If the portfolio manager sells them, he won't be able to get a comparable coupon, so he refuses to sell. What he can do, however, is to put these securities out on repo until maturity, book the interest income on them, and use the cash he has generated to invest in some other attractive instrument. That's a common transaction now. A couple of years ago no one had heard of it."

THE SPECIFIC ISSUES MARKET

Dealers go short for various reasons: as a speculation, to hedge a long position in a similar security, or to reduce their position so that they can make a big bid in a coming Treasury auction. The theory behind going into an auction short is that the new issue will, until it is distributed, yield more than outstanding issues; that, however, doesn't always occur when the Treasury is paying down its debt as it sometimes does, particularly on a seasonal basis. Whatever his motivation may be, a dealer who shorts a given issue has to obtain those securities somehow to make delivery. Normally the way he does so is by reversing them in rather than borrowing them.[12] Some widely placed issues are easy to find. Others he must hunt up on his own or with the help of a firm that brokers reverses.

The borrowers

The market for reverses to cover shorts is often referred to as the *specific issues* market because dealers shop in it for specific issues. Typically a dealer won't find another dealer who has the particular issue he needs and who also wants to finance it for some period. So dealers

---

[12] The economics of reversing in securities were discussed on p. 288.

are only a minor supplier of collateral to the specific issues market. There is also a second reason for this. Said one dealer, "I deal in specific issues only for myself. I will give them to some of my dealer friends but only because they will do the same for me. I try not to support the market for specific issues because I know that, if I give a guy $50 million year bills, he is shorting them and that is going to drive the market down. So all I am doing is hurting myself. If I can get an issue that is likely to be shorted in the future, I will hold it for myself."

The major suppliers of securities to (borrowers of money in) the specific issues and the general reverse markets are banks. This accounts for the fact that the top banks in the country, and in particular the top New York and Chicago banks, all borrow substantial sums from the dealers. Because banks reverse out so many securities to dealers, their net loans to dealers are much smaller than their total dealer loans.

S&Ls and certain other financial institutions are also large suppliers of collateral in the specific issues market. So too are a few municipalities and a few corporate portfolios. Reverses are, as noted, not well understood except by those who do them, so it is not surprising that one corporate portfolio manager commented, "I reverse out securities to dealers, but I *never* refer to it around the company as 'lending out' our valuable securities."

Reverses in the specific issues market usually have a term ranging from a week to a month. Activity in this market is greatest during a bear market because dealers increase their shorts in a declining market.

The reverse rate

When a dealer lends out money as part of a transaction in which he is reversing in securities to cover a short, the rate he gets on his money is often significantly *lower* than the going rate for financing general collateral in the RP market. "The rate on a reverse depends," as one dealer noted, "on the availability of the securities taken in. In today's market, the RP rate available to an investor willing to take in any type of collateral is 8¼. If I reversed in the year bill to cover a short, I might get only 7.60 on my money. If, alternatively, I shorted something in more plentiful supply, I might get 8%. There are no standard relationships. It is entirely a question of demand and supply."

The brokers

Dealers who want to reverse in a specific issue will often turn to a broker of RP. The brokers make it their business to know where various special issues are and at what rates they can be reversed in. The brokers are efficient in this area and can often get bonds for a dealer at as good a rate as he would if he could find the bonds. An RP broker acts in effect as a commission salesman for the dealers; if he finds bonds, he earns a commission or a spread; if he does not, he is paid nothing for his trouble.

The brokers try not to take bonds from one dealer and give them to another. The dealers talk to each other and could arrange trades of this sort themselves. As a rule, the brokers will try to pull specific issues out of regional banks, S&Ls, and other smaller portfolios. In doing so, they are using their own special knowledge and thus providing a real service to the dealers.

When they have arranged a trade, some brokers of RP will give up names to the institutions on both sides of the trade, charge both sides a commission, and leave it to them to clear the trade. Other brokers act as a principal in transactions they broker, taking securities in on one side and lending out money on the other. In doing so, a broker is acting as a credit intermediary, and he incurs risk on both sides of the transaction. Brokers who act as principals in RP and reverse trades are, like all participants in the repo market, extremely careful to deal only with institutions whose credit they know to be unimpeachable.

When a broker acts as a principal in a reverse transaction, he works for whatever spread he can get; normally it ranges from an 01 to ⅛, with the average being ¹⁄₁₆. If, however, the broker finds a firm that wants to RP stock collateral and another that wants to borrow the same collateral as a special, he might be able to earn ¼.

DEALER BOOKS IN RP

In recent years a number of major dealers in government securities have begun to *run books* in repo and reverse; they take in collateral on one side, hang it out on the other side, and seek to earn a profit by charging a lending rate slightly higher than the rate at which they borrow. Part of the impetus for this development came from the failure of Financial Corporation, which made investors extremely wary of engaging in a repo transaction with a firm whose name and credit they did not know well. Firms that had difficulties borrowing directly from retail in their own name began to borrow from the dealers.

Minor dealers supply some collateral to the dealers who run books in repo. Banks are another big source. Said one dealer, "The banks who supply the collateral are not the New York City banks. It is the superliquid regional banks like the Wilmington Trust, Seattle First, the U.S. National Bank of Oregon. Such banks have large portfolios for their size. They do not trade these portfolios actively; instead they make long-term investments which seem to suit at the time they make them. If the securities later go under or above water, it does not really matter to them because they are running a standard, old-fashioned government portfolio and they are going to hold onto these securities forever. If they have some 8s of 86, they will have them until 1986 with 90 degree probability. If the liability manager at such a bank sees an opportunity to sell 90-day Euros at 10½%, he will come into the market and ask a dealer, 'What will you lend me against $20 million 8s of 86?' Frequently such banks are able to borrow locally at below-market rates but only in small amounts. When they want big money they have to come to the street. I might offer a lend to him at 9⅜%. If he took the money, he would probably also use the offices of my firm to sell his Euros."

Aggressive corporate portfolio managers, S&L managers, and others also supply collateral to the dealers. The collateral offered here is *stock* collateral that the dealer takes in, not because he wants to short particular issues, but because he can refinance that collateral at a profitable spread.

Profit on a matched book

If a dealer repos out securities for the same period that he reverses them in (for example, hangs out on repo for 30 days any collateral he reverses in for 30 days), he is said to run a *matched book*. Spreads on such transactions are narrow, but money can be made because volume is large. "A Fed funds broker," commented one dealer, "gets 50¢ a million per trade but has no clearing costs. A dealer making a book in RP gets more but incurs clearing costs. Still, if he can make a net nickel [5 basis points] on a matched sale book, that amounts to $1.40 per million per day, which is $1,400 per billion per day, and all you need to run such a book is a kid from Queens who can add."

On a matched book, a dealer incurs no rate risk. He incurs a credit risk on both sides of the transaction, but he can control this by being extremely careful about whom he deals with. Also, dealers in RP often try to get extra protection by asking for a bigger *haircut* (more margin) on securities they take in than they give on securities they put out. "On a billion dollar book," commented one observer, "a dealer should generate an extra $35 million from the difference in haircuts if he is dealing with pros. If it is amateur hour, he would probably get an extra $60 or $70 million of cheap money." Besides reducing risk, that extra money can generate additional profits if the dealer uses it to carry some high-coupon bonds that he would have held anyway.

Profits and risks on a mismatched book

Most dealers who deal seriously in RP *mismatch* their book. They seek to profit by *lending long* and *borrowing short* if they anticipate a fall in rates or by doing the reverse if they expect rates to rise. Running a mismatched book in RP offers its own special risks and rewards. To understand them, one must visualize precisely what it means for a dealer to run a book in RP. Part A of Table 12–1 shows the flows that occur when a dealer reverses in securities on one side and RPs them on the other.

TABLE 12–1
Running a book in RP

A. Reversing in securities and RPing these securities creates a new asset and a new liability on a dealer's book

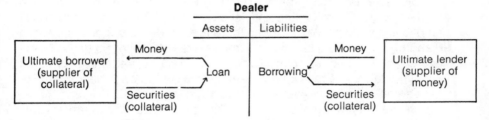

B. The dealer's book in RP

Dealer	
Assets	Liabilities
Collateralized *loans* of varying maturities	Collateralized *borrowings* of varying maturities

The essence of a repo transaction is *not* that securities are being sold; it is that secured *loans* and *borrowings* are being made. Thus the securities "sold" should be thought of simply as *collateral*. Once they are thought of that way, it becomes clear that when a dealer takes in securities, he is making a *loan* that is an *asset* to him, and when he RPs these securities, he is creating a *borrowing* that is a *liability* to him. Thus a dealer's book in RP consists of a collection of collateralized loans and borrowings (Table 12–1, part B).

In effect, in running a book in RP, a dealer is acting as a *financial intermediary* and in particular like a bank. He is taking in collateralized "deposits" on one side and lending out the money on the other. A dealer's book in RP is, moreover, much like a bank's Eurodollar book. All of the assets and liabilities that compose this book are *fixed in rate* and *fixed in term.* Thus to the extent that a dealer mismatches his book, he incurs exactly the same *rate risk* that a Euro banker does when he mismatches his book.

A dealer has *no* liquidity in his RP book. He can't sell loans he makes or otherwise liquidate them before maturity. Thus if he borrows short and lends long (e.g., finances a 30-day loan with overnight money), he incurs a *liquidity risk*. To fund his assets, he depends, like a bank, on his ability to continually buy large and highly variable amounts of money.

With that background in mind, it is interesting to hear a dealer—the quote is old but the technique has not changed—who runs a mismatched book describe how he operates: "Suppose I reverse in the 8s of 86 at par for 90 days at 5⅜. I have assumed a risk. I am now long in 90-day reverse. It is like being long in 90-day bills that you cannot sell—but the yield is higher. I might blow it out [finance the reverse] overnight for a couple of days. Or I might instantly stick it out for 30 to 60 days because I can play the yield curve. Suppose there is a major discrepancy between 90 and 60 days, and I can finance that reverse at 5⅛ for 60 days. Then I have a piece of paper coming back at me in 60 days that I can value. I look at the tail and see I will own 1-month paper [60 days hence] at 5⅞. That seems like a reasonable gamble so, bang, I do it."[13]

Because the pricing of securities RPed depends on their market value and thus on interest rates, a firm running a speculative book in reverse incurs not only a rate risk and a liquidity risk but the risk that its position will for some period of time eat up its capital. The same dealer continued, "I have built my tail. If my projection that interest rates are going to fall is correct, I benefit in two ways. First, my 30-day piece of paper comes back at me at 5⅞, and I can bang it out for the last 30 days at 4⅜. Look at the money I have made! Additionally the 8s of 86 are now worth more money. Consequently I can borrow [over the last 30 days], say, 103 against them instead of par, which never hurts when you are borrowing at the low end of the yield curve.

"The flip side of that is that there is no more stinko position in a bear market than a reverse position. Say interest rates rise. The 1-month paper I have created comes back at me at 5⅞ but I have to finance it at 6, so I lose money. Moreover, I can now borrow less money, maybe 3 points less. So hundreds of thousands of dollars of my working cash go bye-bye for 30 days. That hurts no matter who you are. You are losing in two directions at the same time. You lose on the trade, and you are out working cash. To run an unmatched book in speculative reverse, you have to be a well-capitalized firm or you will run into massive problems."

The above quote is dated in terms of rates and securities, but it still illustrates well the way the trader of a mismatched book operates. Trading a *mismatched* book in RP and reverse is a trickier game to understand and to play than trading bills, CDs, or BAs. Also, the matched book trader has the advantage that the BA trader does not have of being able

---

[13] Recall the discussion on pp. 298–301 of figuring the tail. That calculation is no different for reverses than it is for bills or other money market assets that are financed for some period.

to short the market when he is bearish by lending money short and taking in collateral long. For both of the above reasons, the profits to be gleaned from running a mismatched book are high when a trader is good at the game. Noted one such trader, "In every place I have worked, I have traded matched book like any other money market security, and my book has always been the most profitable individual item for the firm except for trading Ginnie Maes."

Trading a mismatched book started sometime in the mid-1970s. In recent years it has grown tremendously as more and more dealers have caught onto the idea of using such trades in repo and reverse—as distinct from financing their positions and covering their shorts—as a profit center.

To avoid being misleading, it should be stressed that at a lot of firms running a matched book still means just that—taking in securities for some period and putting them out for precisely or almost precisely the same period for maybe a nickle spread.

Repricing

To minimize the risk that a position in reverse will eat up capital during a bear market, many dealers running books in RP reserve the right to *reprice*. Said one such dealer, "In the reverse market there is an informal right to reprice the instrument. If I were to take in $5 million of securities for 6 months and all of a sudden the market dropped 4 points, I would be out $200,000 of my capital. In that case I have the right to call the customer [the borrower] and say it is time to reprice. There is no set time period on repricing. It can be done during any part of the life of the instrument. It is an informal but understood part of the agreement, one that reduces risk for us.

"We ask for the right to reprice because in my opinion we are paid to forecast short-term interest rates not what a 10-year government is going to be worth 5 or 6 months from now. Maybe I would feel differently if I were a government bond trader but I am not, and I will not do business with a guy who will not led me reprice. Another reason for repricing is credit risk. Say I am lending a guy 105 on an issue that is worth 101—what if he goes out of business?" While the right to reprice is reserved informally by some dealers, others make it a formal part of an RP agreement.

Note that a dealer reserving the right to reprice does not make a long-term RP borrowing unattractive to the borrower. Suppose a bank borrows 6-month money because it expects interest rates to rise and they do; then, because of repricing, the bank won't get full value for its collateral over the last part of the agreement, *but* it will still be getting cheap money.

The interdealer market

There is currently a very active and highly brokered *interdealer* market in stock-collateral RP and reverse. This market serves a purpose similar in many respects to that of the interbank market in Eurodollar deposits for banks running Eurodollar books. In it a dealer can lay off or pick up money in different maturities.

The interdealer market in RP trades actively out to 6 months. The basic run is for 1, 2, 3, and 6 months, but if the market is very active, all 6 months will be quoted. There is usually a *nickel* spread (5 basis points) between the bid and the offer.

The interdealer market trades in blocks of $5 million, but a dealer can work up that amount or he can specify that his bid or offer is for less. If the collateral is an off-the-run bond, that is generally specified; on inactive issues, the bid will be somewhat back from the market.

Margin is sometimes subject to negotiation. One trader said, "You get to know what the different dealers' margin requirements are. These come into play somewhat in the quotes you give a dealer when he asks for a run. I am generally flexible about haircut requirements when I trade with other dealers. However, I am less flexible when I deal with the few large corporations involved in the reverse market; and the amount of margin I demand from them is much more than what I demand from another dealer."

A forecast of rising interest rates will increase market activity because it brings additional collateral into the market. The appearance of attractive arbitrage opportunities does the same thing.

THE USE BY THE FED OF THE RP AND REVERSE MARKETS

The Fed uses repos and reverses extensively to make short-term changes in the level of bank reserves. The Fed used *RP* for this purpose as early as 1917, but it did not begin to use this tool regularly until after World War II. The Fed first used *reverses* to drain bank reserves in 1966; the occasion was a sudden large increase in float caused by an interruption in airline service.

Prior to 1972, when the Fed did RPs, it offered the dealers a fixed rate, usually equal to the discount rate. In 1972 it switched to asking the dealers for competitive bids when it wanted to do repo and reverses just as it does when it wants to buy or sell securities.

Not long after this change, the Fed also permitted dealers to show customer money to it when it was going reverses and customer collateral to it when it was doing repo. Many dealers' customers, however, are unaware that this possibility exists. One commercial paper issuer observed, "Sometimes on a Wednesday commercial paper issuers post attractive rates to get money, then rates start to sag in the money market, collateral dries up, and all of a sudden they get hit with money. In this sort of situation—the market falling apart—the Fed will generally come in and do repurchase agreements. A paper issuer with excess funds can at that point call a primary dealer and ask them to show, say, $20 million for him into the Fed. I do it, but I don't see many others doing it." The Fed seems to have a better handle these days on bank reserves and rarely intervenes anymore on a Wednesday afternoon. Dealers, however, can and still do show customer securities (money) into the Fed when the Fed does repo (reverses) as part of its normal daily open market operations.

When it wants to add reserves for some period, the Fed will often do term repo with the dealers; that is, give them money for several days or as long as a week. The Fed used to permit dealers who did term repo with it to break the agreement or any portion of it. "That," as one dealer commented, " made a 6-day repo something you never wanted to miss. It was fantastic in terms of moving around your RP portfolio. If the market got better, you could break the RP. If you sold something, you could take the securities you had at the Fed and use them to substitute with an RP customer. The Fed meanwhile was going crazy with the cancelations; they finally switched to fixed RPs to cut down their bookkeeping." The Fed has never permitted substitutions on repos it does with dealers.

LEGAL STATUS OF REPO

The failure of Lombard-Wall and the litigation it resulted in put the legal status of repo very much up in the air. Is RP a true sale-repurchase or a collateralized loan?

Judge Ryan's rulings in the Lombard-Wall case are that repo is a collateralized loan. His position is supported by the fact that most practices in the repo-reverse market are more consistent with repo being a collateralized loan than a true sale-resale. On a collateralized loan, everyone agrees that the lender should have margin. In contrast on an outright sale, there is no excess collateral to serve as margin, no right of substitution with respect to the securities purchased—as exists in many term repo transactions—and no passing through of coupons.

Notwithstanding the above, it was common practice pre-Lombard-Wall for participants in the repo market to take the view that, should the borrower of money in an RP transaction fail to execute repurchase (i.e., to repay the money lent), the holder of the securities had the right to sell them out to get back his money.

Any change in this implicit understanding of the ground rules of the RP game is upsetting to the market for a number of reasons. First, the risk to the lender of funds is vastly increased. As one trader noted, "We deal in highly volatile markets. It is lunacy in the case of default to have to petition some bankruptcy judge for the right to sell and then have to wait God knows how long to do so."

Also, interpretating repo as a collateralized loan could over the long-run eliminate important participants from this market. Some municipalities, for example, are empowered to buy securities but not to make collateralized loans. More importantly, the Fed, which uses repo extensively to make short-term adjustments in bank reserves, is explicitly forbidden to lend to banks in the way it currently does if its repo transactions with banks are considered to be collateralized loans.

The current limbo in which the status of repo has been thrust has created a situation in which dealers running large matched books find themselves making all sorts of assumptions whose validity is suspect. Noted one, "Can we continue to assume the right of offset? Say we have 20 million of reverses with DLJ and 20 million of RP with them and some of these trades are 500 million up and some are 400 million down. Is our total exposure 100 million because of the right of offset? Or do we really have a bundle of individual trades not one *net* mismatch with one bottom line. New York State seems to be saying that we have a lot of individual trades which makes our exposure much bigger. If we get the wrong opinion on a couple of cases like this, matched books would disappear because of credit risk. I do not think such rulings would destroy the short market because there is little risk in an overnight position, but it would destroy the 90-day trades."

Currently the street is operating on an ad hoc basis with respect to the status of repo. First, market participants are being much more circumspect about whom they deal with. So long as a repo transaction is unwound according to contracted terms, no court case will arise, and court rulings as to what repo is will have no relevance.

Second, some dealers are taking extra care to track their exposure to borrowers of money and to call for additional margin if required. Noted one, "The new bankruptcy law notwithstanding, we would feel comfortable selling out securities in the case of default. The trick is to stay on top of the market. If someone goes under, all we want is what is owed us. In that event I would sell the securities and get a difference check to the door of the defaulting party before they had time to get a stay from a bankruptcy judge."

A third tack all large dealers are taking is to rewrite their repo agreements to spell out clearly the rights and duties of both parties to the transaction. A problem here is that no lawyer familiar with the issues involved is certain that provisions of the bankruptcy law will not be interpreted by the courts as overriding any rights and obligations written into a repo agreement.

The only lasting solution to the status of repo would be for the industry to obtain legislative relief at the national level. It has petitioned Congress for a change in the 1978 bankruptcy law that would specifically exclude repo from the class of transactions normally treated as collateralized loans. A second approach would be to have Congress specifically define repo as a sale-resale agreement.

In the meanwhile the rulings arising from the Lombard-Wall case are certain to be appealed, and the status of repo will, lacking legislative action, remain in limbo.

Treasuries and agencies

Most of the collateral underlying the various repo and reverse transactions described in this chapter is governments and agencies. In Chapter 13 we turn to the markets in which these securities are bought and sold outright.

Chapter 13

Government and
federal agency securities

THE GOVERNMENT MARKET, which used to be stuffy and humdrum, has evolved over the last decade and a half into the most active, exciting, and innovative sector of the money market. The reasons are several. In 1961, Congress amended the tax law so that bank capital gains, which had been taxed at the capital gains rate, were taxed as ordinary income. "Overnight that change," one dealer noted, "converted 6,000 stodgy bankers into portfolio managers who were supposed to make a profit." At about the same time, tightening and easing by the Fed began to create wide swings in interest rates. "Back in the old days," noted the same dealer, "bonds had no sex appeal. They were not going to change much in price so you bought them, clipped the coupon, and matured them. Then suddenly, because of big fluctuations in interest rates, it became possible for portfolio managers and dealers to make money positioning and trading governments."

The huge and consistent growth of the federal debt has also contributed to the evolution of the government market by creating more supply and attracting more players into the market. So, too, did the freedom in which the government market operates. Ironically, the government market, unlike all other securities markets except the municipal market, is not regulated by the SEC. Thus, it is a market in which the street, which

425

likes to innovate, has had a free hand to do so, and it has done so repeatedly. Over the last decade, the development of the reverse market and the specific issues market has made transactions by dealers and portfolio managers, unheard of 10 years ago, now commonplace. The government market is one of the few markets in which it is possible to run large short positions—to make money on a negative attitude—and growth of the reverse market has made shorting simpler, cheaper, and more attractive. Also, introduction of trading in bill, note, and bond futures and options has opened up a host of new strategies for dealing, investing, and speculating in governments; and it has attracted many new participants to the market.

A final stimulus to the development of the government market was the decision by the SEC to force stock exchange firms to negotiate commission rates. That change effectively cut stock house commissions by 75% so they began looking for something new to do. They searched just at the time big money was being made by dealers in governments, and many decided to open government bond dealerships. A few lost a lot of money, but a number prospered and stayed.

BILLS, NOTES, AND BONDS

Bills

The Treasury currently issues bills in 3-month, 6-month, and 1-year maturities. Bills are issued in denominations of $10,000, $15,000, $50,000, $100,000, $500,000, and $1 million. A round lot in the inter-dealer market is $5 million, and a retail customer who buys bills from a dealer will get a quote somewhat off the market unless he bids for size. Trades in the bill market are normally done for cash settlement.

Bills used to be issued by the Treasury in the form of bearer certificates. The Treasury and the Fed then made it possible to hold bills in *book entry* form (described below), and since 1977 the Treasury has offered bills only in book entry form.

Notes

The Treasury currently auctions 2-, 4-, 5-, and 7-year notes on a regular cycle. It usually includes a 3- and a 10-year note during quarterly refundings. Notes are available in registered and book entry form.

When the Treasury wants to encourage individuals to invest in a new note issue, it sets the minimum denomination at $1,000. At other times it sets it at $5,000. Notes are also available in $10,000, $100,000, and $1 million denominations. In the interdealer market for notes, $1 million is a round lot, trades for $5 million occur routinely, and trades for even larger amounts are common. Money market investors typically trade notes in size. The note market is a wholesale market, except for sales to individuals and small portfolio managers who typically buy to hold to maturity. Trades in the note market are done for both regular and cash settlement.

Bonds

Because Congress has granted the Treasury only limited exemptions from the 4.25% lid it imposes on the rate the Treasury may pay on bonds, the Treasury does not rely heavily on the sale of new bond issues to fund the federal debt. It does, however, typically offer a long bond as part of each quarterly refunding. Because of past bonds sales, the number of government bond issues outstanding is large.

Treasury bonds are issued in registered and book entry form. They come in denominations of $1,000, $5,000, $10,000, $100,000, and $1 million. Interdealer trades in bonds are usually for $500,000 or more, and the bond market, like the note market, is largely a wholesale market in which institutions buy and sell. Bond trades are normally done for regular settlement.

Treasury notes are not callable, but many government bond issues outstanding are callable. Generally the call date is 5 years before maturity. On old low-coupon issues, the call provision is of small importance, but new high-coupon issues might conceivably be called someday. On dealers' quote sheets, a 14% Treasury bond maturing in November 2011 and callable in 2006 would appear as

14 B 11/15/11.06

Flower bonds. A number of old *low-coupon* government bonds that currently sell at substantial *discounts* carry a special feature. They are acceptable at par in payment of federal estate taxes when owned by the decedent at the time of death. In 1977, the capital gain realized at the time of the holder's death was made taxable. Currently, flower bonds maturing on the following dates are available: May 1985, February 1990, August 1992, February 1993, May 1994, February 1995, and November 1998. Some of the issues are callable; all are available in minimum denominations of $500.

Attraction to investors

Treasury securities offer the investor several attractive features. They expose him to zero credit risk, and while they yield less than other market instruments except for municipals, they are the most liquid instruments traded in the money market. Governments owe their liquidity to the fact that most individual issues are extremely large, and governments are thus not discrete heterogeneous instruments, like BAs or CDs. In the fall of 1982, individual bill issues outstanding ranged from $5 billion to over $15 billion; the smallest note issue was $3.5 billion, but most note issues were much larger and several were in the $6 to $9 billion range. Bond issues are not that large, but their size is still substantial, $1.5 to $4.4 billion on recent issues.

Another advantage of Treasuries is that interest income earned on them is *not* subject to state and local taxation. Also, interest earned by holding a T bill to maturity can be treated for tax purposes as having all been earned in the year the bill matures.

A final attraction of governments is the wide array of these securities available. In October 1982, the Treasury had outstanding 32 different bill issues ranging in current maturity from a few days to a year, 97 note issues, and 46 bond issues. The current maturities of these note and bond issues ranged from a few days to almost 30 years.

Ownership

Table 13–1 shows how ownership of the government debt is split between different classes of investors. The top part of the table, which refers to *marketable* Treasury debt, is of most interest for present purposes. It shows that the Fed is the biggest domestic investors in marketable governments. It is closely followed by commercial banks. State and

TABLE 13–1
Public debt of the U.S. Treasury, June 1982 ($ billions)

Type and holder		
Federal Reserve banks	127.2	
Commercial banks	117.0	
Mutual savings banks	5.7	
Insurance companies	22.2	
Other corporations	38.9	
State and local governments	98.2	
Individuals	78.8	
Foreign	141.9	
U.S. government securities dealers	11.1	
Other (including federal agencies)	177.8	
Marketable Treasury debt		764.0
U.S. government agencies and trust funds	206.0	
Individuals (savings bonds)	67.4	
Foreign (special issues)	17.6	
Other	23.4	
Nonmarketable Treasury debt		314.4
Total public debt		1,079.6

Source: *Federal Reserve Bulletin.*

local governments are also sizable investors. Among domestic investors, the next most important holders of governments are individuals and corporations.

One key entry in Table 13–1 is the $142 billion of governments held by foreigners. As this figure suggests, foreigners are at times important investors in Treasury debt. Whether they are in or out of the market can affect the rates at which the Treasury is able to sell new issues. In the period 1979–82, foreigners were big buyers of governments because rates were high, the dollar was strong, and the U.S. promised political stability.

BOOK ENTRY SECURITIES

In 1976, the Treasury announced that it would move over time to a system under which virtually the entire marketable federal debt would be represented by *book entry* securities instead of engraved pieces of paper. *Under the book entry system, banks that are members of the Federal Reserve hold securities at the Fed in accounts on which record keeping is computerized.* All marketable governments may be held in book entry form, and the bulk of the Treasury's marketable debt is now held in this form.

A bank typically has several different book entry accounts at the Fed. For example, it may have one account for securities in which it has an interest: securities in its dealer position, securities in its investment portfolio, and securities it has taken in on repo; a second account for securities it is safekeeping for corporate and other investors; and a third account for securities it holds for dealers for whom it clears.

The Fed's computer tracks the amounts and types of securities every bank has in each of its accounts. Each bank's own computer tracks for the investors and dealers for whom it holds securities what issues and amounts of these issues each such institution has placed with it.

In New York, the major banks are linked by wire to the Fed, and all securities transfers among them are made by *wire*. If Bankers Trust were, for example, to sell bills to Citibank, it would make delivery by sending a wire message to the Fed, whose computer would debit Bankers' account for *x* bills and credit Citi's account for the same number. Simultaneously, the Fed's computer would automatically transfer money equal to the purchase price of the bills out of Citi's reserve account at the Fed into Bankers' reserve account.

The movement to book entry securities and wire transfers was precipitated in 1970 by the refusal of several major insurance underwriters to underwrite government securities held by dealers. Treasury notes and bonds (but not bills) could be registered, but in fact dealers and most major investors held them, as well as bills, in bearer form. So there was a huge volume of valuable bearer paper being stored and constantly moved about on the street, thus inviting theft.

Faced with an insurance crisis, the dealers began to hold their securities in accounts at the major banks. At the same time, the Fed initiated a system that made it possible for banks to wire securities between each other during each business day. At the end of the day, however, the banks had to show up at the Fed and take physical delivery on any issues on which they had been *net* receivers over the day and to make physical delivery of issues on which they had made *net* deliveries over the day. This procedure eliminated much messenger traffic in governments, but hundreds of millions worth of them still had to be carried between the banks and the New York Fed at the end of the day to effect net settlements. The introduction of book entry securities eliminated these end-of-day movements.

Now that literally billions of dollars of governments are stored in the Fed's computers, the Fed faces a classic records protection problem. It undoubtedly has considerable backup to make its system fail-safe. Such backup can be provided in various ways; for example, by writing records out to disks or tapes and storing them in off-site locations.

The book entry system for governments was designed by the Treasury in haste and under pressure, but it has worked efficiently and has been accepted with enthusiasm by dealers, banks, and most investors.

To move to book entry, the Treasury set up an enabling regulation that had the effect of law and, to the extent that it conflicted with portions of the uniform commercial code in regard to transfers and pledges, had the effect of overriding that law.

Since the Treasury moved to book entry, all federal agencies still issuing securities to the public have come up with their own versions of the Treasury's enabling regulation. And today most agency securities, with the exception of discount paper, can be held in book entry form and are eligible for wire transfer.

Physical movements of CDs, BAs, commercial paper, and other bearer paper still occur between banks. Eliminating such movements by creating some sort of depository facility has been discussed but never implemented.

RECOGNIZED DEALERS

Any firm can commence dealing in governments and federal agency securities. The Fed, however, will deal directly only with *recognized* or *primary dealers.*

In recognizing a dealer, the Fed looks for capital, character in management, and capacity in terms of trained personnel. Specifically before the Fed will do business with a firm, it wants to ensure: (1) that the firm has adequate capital relative to the positions it assumes; (2) that the firm is doing a reasonable volume (at least 1 percent of market activity) and that it is willing to make markets at all times; and (3) that management in the firm understands the government market—particularly the risks involved—and is making a long-term commitment to the market.

When a firm expresses an interest to the Fed in becoming a primary dealer, the Fed first asks it to report its trading volume and positions on an informal basis. If the firm appears to meet the Fed's criteria, the Fed then puts it on its regular reporting list. After a time as a *reporting dealer* if the firm still appears to meet the Fed's criteria, the Fed recognizes that dealer and does business with it.

The Fed welcomes the entry of new primary dealers into the government market. Such entry increases competition in the government market. Also, the more dealers there are, the greater is the dealer community's capacity to distribute the Treasury's burgeoning debt.

While the Fed expects a primary dealer to make markets at all times, it recognizes and accepts the fact that some shops tend to specialize at either the long or the short end of market.

The big profits primary dealers make in good years (there are big losses in bad years) and the decline in brokerage income on stock trades are two reasons many firms have in recent years set up dealerships in governments. Another is that firms specializing in corporate bonds have felt it was important to get into the government market so they could have firsthand knowledge of conditions there, which they could use as a tool in marketing new corporate bonds: sell corporates, for example, by swapping customers out of governments.

Setting up a dealership in governments is time-consuming, difficult, and costly. Trained personnel, always in scarce supply on the street, must be hired and then welded into a team that works. Firms entering the government market normally expect to lose millions before they create an organization capable of producing profits.

AUCTION PROCEDURES

Bills

The Treasury offers new 3- and 6-month bills each week and a new year bill (actually a 364-day bill) every four weeks. The new 3-month bill is always a reopening of an old 6-month bill, and every fourth week the new 6-month bill is a reopening of an old year bill. Except when holidays interfere, the size of the new bill issues to be offered is announced on

Tuesday, the securities are auctioned the following Monday, and they are paid for and issued on the next Thursday.[1]

Banks and recognized dealers may submit tenders at the auction for the accounts of their customers as well as for their own account. Other bidders may submit tenders for only their own accounts. The Treasury accepts tenders from commercial banks, trust companies, and securities dealers without deposits; payment for securities purchased by these institutions must be made in immediately available funds on settlement day. All other bidders must submit the full face amount of the book entry bills for which they apply; the Treasury remits to such bidders the difference between the face value of the bills they purchase and the purchase price they pay.

Any institution bidding for bills may pay for them with maturing bills, that is, by what is called *rolling bills:* In this case the Fed pays to the bidder on settlement day the difference between the value of its maturing bills and the price at which it has purchased new bills.

Competitive bidders in the auction submit tenders stating the quantity of bills they are bidding on and the price they bid. A subscriber may enter several bids, stating the quantity of bills for which he is bidding at each price. The price bid is based on 100 and is stated to three decimal places. An investor who, for example, bids 92.485 is offering to pay $92.485 per $100 of face value on the quantity of bills for which he bids.

During the time between the day on which bills are auctioned and the day on which they are issued, the new bill issue, which has been sold but not yet delivered, is traded among investors and dealers on a *when-issued* basis. Securities traded on this basis are denoted *wi* on dealers' quote sheets.

Notes and bonds

The Treasury presently offers a mix of coupon issues at each of its regular quarterly refundings; these occur in February, May, August, and November. The Treasury's current schedule calls for the quarterly refunding to include three issues: a 3-year note, a 10-year note, and a 30-year bond. These issues are generally sold on consecutive days, with the security of longest maturity being sold last. In addition to its refundings, the Treasury also offers a 2-year note every month, and 4-, 5- and 7-year notes and a 20-year bond every quarter.

In note and bond auctions, the normal practice (see Figure 13–1) is for investors to bid yields to two decimal places.[2] As in the case of bills,

---

[1] For a description of how the auction works, see pp. 195–98.

[2] See Chapter 7.

FIGURE 13–1
Tender form for a Treasury note issue

TENDER FOR 2-YEAR TREASURY NOTES

TO FEDERAL RESERVE BANK OF NEW YORK
    Fiscal Agent of the United States
    New York, N. Y. 10045

Dated at . . . .

. . . . , 19 . . . .

    Pursuant to the provisions of the public notice issued by the Treasury Department inviting tenders for the current offering of 2-year Treasury notes, the undersigned hereby offers to purchase such currently offered Treasury notes in the amount indicated below, and agrees to make payment therefor at your Bank in accordance with the provisions of the official offering circular.

COMPETITIVE TENDER   *Do not fill in both Competitive and*   **NON COMPETITIVE TENDER**
                          Noncompetitive tenders on one form

$ . . . . (maturity value)$ . . . . (maturity value)
                                        (Not to exceed $1,000,000 for one bidder through all sources)
or any lesser amount that may be awarded.   at the average price of accepted competitive bids.

          Yield . . . .
   (Yield must be expressed with two decimal places,
           for example, 7.11)

Certification by Competitive Bidders: The Bidder's ☐ Customer's ☐ net long position in these securities (including those acquired through "when issued" trading, and futures and forward transactions) as of 12:30 pm Eastern time on the day of this auction, was —

    ☐ Not in excess of $200 million.
    ☐ In excess of $200 million, amounting to $ . . . . million.

    Subject to allotment, please issue, deliver, and accept payment for the bearer securities indicated below and/or the registered securities indicated on the reverse side *(if only registered securities are desired, please only complete schedule on reverse side):*

SCHEDULE FOR ISSUE OF BEARER SECURITIES

Pieces	Denomination	Maturity value				Payment will be made as follows:
XXX	XXXXXX	XXX	XXX	XXX	☐ Deliver over the counter to the undersigned (1) ☐ Ship to the undersigned (2)	☐ By charge to our reserve account (D) ☐ By cash or check in *immediately available funds* (F)
	$ 5,000				☐ Hold in safekeeping (for member bank only) in — ☐ Investment Account (4)	☐ By surrender of maturing securities (E) ☐ By charge to my correspondent
	$ 10,000				☐ General Account (5) ☐ Trust Account (6)	bank . . . .(D) (Name of bank)
	$ 100,000				☐ Hold as collateral for Treasury Tax and Loan Account* (7)	☐ Special instructions (3)
	$ 1,000,000					
	Totals				☐ Wire to . . . . (8) (Exact Receiving Bank Wire Address/Account)	

*The undersigned certifies that the allotted securities will be owned solely by the undersigned.
(If a commercial bank or dealer is subscribing for its own account or for account of customers, the following certifications are made a part of this tender.)

    WE HEREBY CERTIFY that we have received tenders from customers in the amounts set forth opposite their names on the list which is made a part of this tender and that we have received and are holding for the Treasury, or that we guarantee payment to the Treasury of, the payments required by the official offering circular.

    WE FURTHER CERTIFY that tenders received by us, if any from other commercial banks or primary dealers for their own account, and for the account of their customers, have been entered with us under the same conditions, agreements, and certifications set forth in this form.

Insert this tender in special envelope marked "Tender for Treasury Notes or Bonds"	NAME OF SUBSCRIBER (PLEASE PRINT OR TYPE)
	ADDRESS
	CITY STATE ZIP
	PHONE (INCLUDE AREA CODE) SIGNATURE OF SUBSCRIBER / AUTHORIZED SIGNATURE
	TITLE OF AUTHORIZED SIGNER

(Institutions submitting tenders for customer account must list customers' names on lines below or on an attached rider.)

banks and recognized dealers may submit bids for notes and bonds for the accounts of their customers as well as for their own account. Bids from commercial banks, trust companies, and securities dealers do not have to be accompanied by a deposit. Other bidders must accompany their bids with a deposit, normally 5 percent, and must pay the remaining amount due with a check that will clear on or before settlement day or with immediately available funds on settlement day. Notes and bonds bid for in an auction may also be paid for with maturing securities.

During the 1- to 2-week period between the time a new Treasury note or bond issue is auctioned and the time the securities sold are actually issued, securities that have been auctioned but not yet issued trade actively on a *when-issued* basis. They also trade *wi* during the announcement to auction period.

Secondary market

Little trading in outstanding notes and bonds occurs on organized stock exchanges. The New York Stock Exchange lists a few issues, and the American Exchange (AMEX) offers odd-lot trading in a few others, but neither exchange moves much volume.[3] The real secondary market for bills, notes, and bonds is the dealer-made market, in which huge quantities of bills, notes, and bonds are constantly traded under highly competitive conditions at small margins. Before we turn to that market, let's look at the brokers.

THE BROKERS

Dealers in government securities actively trade with retail and with each other. In recent years the volume of trading in governments has become so huge and the pace so fast that practically all interdealer trades are done through brokers.

The most important reason brokers are used in the government market is ease of communication. The number of primary dealers in governments and agencies averages about 35. Thus, no government trader can keep in touch directly with all his counterparts. Another reason that brokers are needed is that different shops split responsibility for different issues in different ways. Thus, a trader who covers 2- to 4-year notes at one shop might have to call two different traders at another shop to get quotes in his area.

---

[3] AMEX trading in odd lots of governments is primarily for the convenience of brokers. If the broker uses a dealer to execute a small buy or sell order, the dealer's fee eats up most of the commission that the broker charges the investor. In contrast, on bond trades executed on an exchange by a member firm, transaction costs to the broker are minimal.

Currently, there are five brokers who service only dealers in governments and agencies. The two largest are Garban and Fundamental Brokers, Incorporated (FBI). Garban was the first broker to replace quotes over the phone with CRTs. Now CRTs dominate brokering.

A large dealer is likely to have one or two bill traders, two or three traders of Treasury coupons, and a couple of agency traders. Smaller shops have fewer. Currently, there are over 300 traders in governments and agencies among the primary dealers and at least as many brokers to cover them. The brokers staff for peak periods because they have to service dealers adequately then to get business from them when things are slow.

Garban displays bids and offers placed with it for bills, Treasury coupons, and agencies on several different screens. When a new bid or offering comes in, the broker receiving it types it into the computer, and the new quote appears on the Garban screen in all of the dealers' trading rooms within seconds. A quote used to be good for two minutes. After that, "old" automatically appeared on the screen and the broker went back to the trader to see if he wanted to renew his bid or offer. Gradually this changed. First the brokers made bids and offers in active issues good until cancelled. Then this practice grew to encompass the whole list. Now the brokers assume that the traders pay enough attention to the screen that they can keep all bids and offers good until cancelled.

The biggest change over the last five years in bill brokering is the amount and size of trades. For bills, the pictures in the brokers' screens are all for $5 million unless otherwise indicated. That is the minimum block anyone wants to trade. Today trading a $25 million block of bills is nothing. Firms that would not have considered doing that sort of size 3 or 4 years ago now do it routinely.

When a trader wants to do a big block, what size is shown on the screen is up to the trader. Noted one bill broker, "If a trader wants to show 25, 50, or 100 million, we show that. Four years ago it was a big deal if you saw on the screen a bid for $50 million bills. That sort of bid almost told you who was bidding. Now bids of that size are commonplace. One reason is the volatility of rates which has led to much more trading."

Today on an active day $6 billion of trades might go through the bill brokers market and another $4 billion of trades through the brokers of Treasury notes and bonds. One reason for this huge volume is the futures markets which have created opportunities for traders to do all sorts of new trades: cash-and-carry trades, hedges, arbitrages of cash securities against futures, butterflies with two legs in the cash market and two in futures, and so on.

The extent to which activity of this sort has fed business into the brokers' market is suggested by a remark made by one bill trader, "It is now more efficient, for the cash-and-carry business against futures, to use the brokers when you want to buy size. Rather than call dealers to find out who has the bill I want, I can put a bid into the brokers' market and get execution almost immediately. In the old days it would take me 10 or 15 minutes to buy 100 million. These days I can do that in a second or two. The pace of this business had gotten a lot more frenetic than it was in the past."

When brokers talk to traders, they do not give advice. Brokers have inside information on what large dealers are doing, so it would be unethical for them to express opinions on what the market is likely to do.

If a trader has a bid in the market, he gets the right of first refusal on any new offering. Thus, for example, if a trader had a bid in at 6 and someone else came in with a $1 million offering at 7, a Garban broker would call the bidder and say, "6–7, a million. Your bid." The trader could then say, "I bought them," or just, "OK," the latter indicating that he has no interest. The bidder has 30 seconds to pick up his phone and take the new offering; after that, it is fair game for anyone. During the first 30 seconds a quote is on the Garban screen, it blinks to show that it is new.

The practice of giving the last seller first crack at the next bid is one reason why every trader needs to deal with several brokers. Say Merrill has a big selling job to do. They will hit a broker's bid in the issue they want to sell and every bid that comes in after it. Meanwhile nobody else can hit a bid with that broker for the issue Merrill is selling.

Whenever a trade is effected through Garban, their screen flashes "hit" or "tak" (for taken) so that the market can see what trades are done and the prices at which they are done.

Brokers do not give up names on trades done through them. The trades are cleared through the broker's clearing bank. If, for example, Salomon Brothers sold securities to Morgan through Garban, Sali would deliver these securities to Marine Midland, which clears for Garban, and Garban would redeliver to Morgan.

By acting as blind brokers, the brokers in the government market assume in effect the role of principal. However, brokers in this area think of themselves "as just rolling through a trade from, say, Sali to Merrill." This is also how dealers tend to view brokers. The principal-agent question that became such a prominent issue with respect to Chase's role in the Drysdale failure has never been a question of burning interest with respect to the brokering of governments among primary dealers because every participant thinks of the risk of nonexecution (i.e., of the credit risk) associated with brokered trades as being effectively zero.

The brokers in the government area, with the exception of Cantor Fitz, deal only with primary dealers who have already been well vetted by the

Fed. It is inconceivable that any of these firms would ever renege on a trade. In a market that operates on the principal, my word is my bond, no dealer could afford the damage that reneging on a trade would do to its reputation. This gives both brokers and dealers a high degree of comfort with respect to the huge volume of trades that are done through the brokers' market.

To a broker the major risk in his activity is that he makes a mistake. Because of tight controls, such mistakes are always marginal in size, but even one mistake can wipe out a broker's profits on a whole day's trades. To avoid errors brokers come back every two hours or so to check and make sure everyone understands the transactions that have been made the same way, that everyone knows the same trade.

Errors rarely occur when dealers talk with brokers or with other dealers on the phone because they know how to go through the reconfirm on the phone so no misunderstandings occur. Describing this process, one dealer said, "If I call on the phone and say, 'I have a par bid for $10 million on the 2-year, are you interested?' and the other guy says, 'Yes, I will sell you 10 million at the buck,' then I say, 'I buy 10 million at par.'" We have said it a few times and, when we hang up, we both write the tickets right away. Errors occur more often when salespeople talk to customers because many customers are unprofessional on the phone; so too are some junior salespeople.

Brokerage on bills generally works out to $25 per $1 million. The brokers adjust the brokerage rate charged in terms of basis points to get to this figure—they work for 1/4 of an 01 on the year bill and for 1/2 of an 01 on the 6-month bill. The fee charged on the 3-month bill is only 1/4 of an 01, which is $12.50 per $1 million.

On coupon issues, brokerage is 1/128, which equals $78.12 per $1 million. The rate on coupons used to be 1/64, but competition and increased volume in the brokers market brought it down. Brokerage is paid only by the side initiating a trade, so *locked markets,* markets in which the bid and offer are identical, can and do occur in governments. Sometimes, when there is little interest in the market—no one wants to do anything—a locked market will persist for some time.

Brokers have to be careful about the rates they quote on the phone or put on the screen because they have to stand up to those quotes. Said one, "If we put a wrong number on the screen, most traders are good about it and tell us. But there are other traders who like to hang us. When their buttons light, you almost know that there is something wrong on the screen."

The Garban screen has been in operation for almost a decade. "A lot of guys did not like the screen at the beginning," said one broker. "The Salis, Morgans, and Merrills were used to getting preferential treatment—first call from the brokers." The screen endured, however, and it has contributed to the changing way business is done in the government market. The screen gave the traders one more way to play trading games. Also, as one trader noted, "a lot of this market is psychology, and when those CRTs start blinking hit, hit, hit, it has a tremendous impact."

Going national

Cantor Fitz, the one government broker that has gone national to major retail customers, has enjoyed tremendous success and is currently the single biggest broker of governments.

Its example has naturally led other brokers to think of going national. If they did so, big customers would have access to the best prices without going through the dealers. This, in turn, would eliminate the small margin dealers get on trades with big retail customers, a margin that provides dealers with a steady profit stream that covers the cost of maintaining a sales force and of providing retail with valuable information on market conditions. As noted in Chapter 9, the philosophy of many dealers is that they are primarily a service business out to earn a little on every trade with retail. To the extent that big customers do big trades through brokers, this philosophy of operation would be threatened.

Noted one dealer, "The possibility of the brokers going national is the fear most dealers live with because there is a proprietary advantage to being part of that system. That advantage is the biggest advantage in being a recognized [by the Fed] dealer. Most everyone else trades without their headlights on.

"There is an incredible differential in the information available to an institutional investor in Okefenokee who is looking at one not very well used [by the dealers] broker's markets [Cantor Fitz's] and that available to a recognized dealer who has five brokers' TVs and is plugged in with 120 phone lines to all the other dealers and to all the exchanges where they trade futures. That information differential is how dealers outtrade their customers."

THE GOVERNMENT MARKET

So far in this chapter we have focused on background information. Let's now turn to the government market and how it is made by dealers and investors.

Bidding in the auction

The cast of bidders in a typical Treasury auction is varied. The Fed holds a huge portfolio of bills, some portion of which matures each week. The Fed replaces some or all of its maturing bills by *rolling* them in the auction; it never bids for bills in the auction to increase the size of its portolio. To add to its portfolio, the Fed buys bills in the secondary market from dealers.[4]

Retail is also a big factor in Treasury auctions. Before 1974, bill auctions were much smaller than they are today. At that time, it was common for investors to pay a dealer on 01 to make a competitive bid for them. This practice ensured the customer that he would obtain bills in the auction and at a fair price. Now Treasury auctions are so large, information on the price at which a new issue will be sold is so widely distributed, and the sophistication of retail customers is so much greater than it used to be that large portfolio managers feel either that they can price their own bids or that they can buy whatever they need in the secondary market at little or no spread over the price at which they could buy in the auction. Thus, fewer retail customers now pay dealers to bid for them, and those who do typically pay less than they used to—½ or ¼ of an 01.

The dealers are a third big factor in any auction. There are some dealers, Sali and Merrill, that can be counted on to almost always make big bids in an auction because of the huge size of their retail base. Then there are others that will sometimes bid for sizable amounts in an auction and other times bid for little or none at all.

A fourth big factor in any auction is the money funds. They are massive buyers of bills. Were it not for the Fed rule limiting any one bidder to buying 35% of a new issue at auction, a few of the biggest funds could, and at times probably would, buy up a whole new issue.

Before the auction there is a buzz of auction talk among the dealers. Dealers know the size of the issues the Treasury is offering, and they try to assess the retail interest in these issues and what amounts other dealers are likely to bid for. That is the sort of information a trader requires to hone his bid down to the last decimal point.

Much of the talk between dealers before the auction focuses on what are going to be the *top* and the *tail* in the auction; in a bill auction the top is the highest price (lowest yield) bid in the auction and the tail is the lowest bid (highest yield) accepted in the auction. Dealers bidding on bills all want to hit the tail, which takes skill. On an auction day, one dealer noted: "Today I do not want to buy much. I am just trying to bid for where I think the tail will be. I am bidding for practice, to see if my market reading is accurate. You have to keep in touch because, when you really want to buy, you need to have the confidence."

The final moment of decision for a dealer comes at about 1:25 Eastern

---

[4] To prevent the Fed from becoming a money-printing machine for the Treasury, the Fed has long been forbidden to buy—except on a rollover basis—other than small amounts of new Treasury debt directly from the Treasury. This prohibition has, under current institutional arrangements, *no* effect whatsoever on the size of the Fed's portfolio or on the amount of bank reserves it creates.

time. Then time runs out. He has to pick a price, grab a phone, and call a runner stationed near the Fed; the latter has a tender form all made out except for the bid prices, which he inks in at the last moment.

Once the Fed receives all the bids—the cutoff time is 1:30—it determines what bids it will accept; it announces the results of the auction at 6:00 in the evening.

Table 13–2 shows the results of a bill auction held on November 15, 1982. Note that on the 3-month (13-week) bill, the top and the tail were

TABLE 13–2
Results of a weekly bill auction held November 15, 1982

	13-Week	*26-Week*
Applications	$12,414,975,000	$11,794,040,000
Accepted bids	$ 5,600,275,000	$ 5,600,815,000
Accepted at low price	1%	45%
Accepted noncompetitively	$ 930,280,000	$ 799,580,000
Average price	97.865 (8.446%)	95.683 (8.539%)
High price (rate)	97.877 (8.399%)	95.706 (8.494%)
Low price (rate).	97.858 (8.474%)	95.672 (8.561%)
Coupon equivalent	8.75%	9.05%

separated by only 0.019 in price and by only 0.075% in yield. The difference between the top and the tail in auctions of Treasury notes and bonds is also usually small.

Supply in Treasury auctions varies from week to week and from month to month. At times when the Treasury is paying down the debt seasonally or extending the maturity of the debt, it will sell fewer bills than the amount maturing. At other times, it will increase the size of the regular weekly bill auctions. Supply offered also varies from one note auction to another.

Dealers act in part as distributors of the Treasury debt. How much distribution is required on a new issue depends on the relationship between the supply offered and demand by retail. When the Treasury is adding, it is likely that the new issue will sell at a fractionally higher yield than surrounding issues until it is distributed, and dealers consequently have a profit incentive to bid aggressively in the auction. When the reverse is true—for example, the Treasury is reducing the size of a bill issue—there is both less need for the dealers to act as distributors and less profit incentive for them to bid aggressively in the auction.

THE BILL MARKET

Dealers not only distribute bill issues but make a secondary market in bills by trading with each other and with retail.

Runs

Runs in the brokers' market and between dealers are for *current* issues, that is, those most recently auctioned. In 3-month and 6-month bills, an issue stays current for a week. During that period, the new issue is distributed to people who don't have it but want it and vice versa. After that activity in this issue dies down, a new issue is auctioned and becomes current, and action again picks up.

Bills are quoted in 01s. Thus, a trader's market in a given bill might be 7.10 offered and 7.12 bid. In the interdealer market, traders often refine their bids and offers to half an 01 by using pluses; a bid of 12+ means that the trader is bidding 12½ basis points. The *handle,* 7 in the above illustration, is never quoted.

A broker's run in the bill market might be: "3-month 50–49, 2 by 5. 6-month at this juncture 70 locked, 10 million up. On the year bill 96–95, 10 by 1." When a broker quotes the size of the market as "2 by 5," he means that $2 million is bid and $5 million offered. When size is "10 million *up,*" that means both the bid and the offer are good for $10 million. Sometimes dealers will make their bids and offers on an all-or-none basis. If the dealer bids for $5 million AON, no one can hit that bid for less than $5 million. Sometimes there will be a bid on an issue but no offer. In that case, the broker would quote the market, for example, as "70 bid without."

The real market

Bids in the brokers market may or may not reflect the *real market,* that is, the bid and offered prices at which size could be done. One trader commented: "I think in part of the real market as the market away from the brokers. If I were to go to a retail account who owns bills I want, what would I have to pay to buy them on a swap, what would it cost me to get them from him to me?

"At times, quotes in the brokers market are distortions of the market because they are created to be misleading. Suppose I want to buy 100 million of a particular bill. I know that everyone is looking at the brokers market. So what do I do? I make a one-man market. I make them 85 locked, 5 up on both sides. Now I go around and call the dealers and ask them for a market in that bill and they will make it 85–83 or 86–84. I will buy them at 83 or 84 and then I will take my market out [of the brokers screen] after I have bought what I needed. Then, if I want, I can put another market in, and that becomes the market. These are the games played by traders. If you want to buy or sell, you try to distort what you really want to do. Depending on the market, this can be done at times with some success.

"Of course, when I put a locked bid with the brokers I have to stand up to both sides. It might not work. I might lock the market and get myself immediately lifted. If I wanted to buy, that would ruin that act; and now I would have to buy another 5 million. You cannot lock too far from the real market. But remember, we are talking about distorting the market an 01 or half an 01. That pays because I am trading big volume.

"If a dealer does not know if the market on the broker's screen is the real market, he has to spend some money to find out—to buy or sell to find out how real the bid or offered side is in terms of size. If he spends 10 million on bills and they are reoffered, then he knows that there is a genuine seller there. If he buys 5 and that is all he can buy, then maybe that is not the real market. Maybe the market is just holding up because the bid is stronger than the offer."

Trading wi

Bills have long been traded on a when-issued (*wi*) basis between the auction and settlement dates. Some years ago the custom developed of trading bills wi after they are announced but before they are auctioned. Because of this practice, the most recently announced *and* the most recently auctioned 3-month bill will both be traded wi for several days in the middle of each week. During this period, the most recently announced 3-month bill used to be referred to as the *wiwi* bill. Now because that bill is shown on some brokers' screens as the wi bill and the most recently auctioned (but not yet settled) bill as the 3-month bill, market jargon is changing. Many traders refer to the most recently announced 3-month bill as the wi bill even if the most recently auctioned 3-month bill is still trading wi.

In bills, wi trading is very active both between dealers and between dealers and retail. For a trader who wants to short the market, selling bills trading wi is more attractive than shorting an outstanding issue, because on a wi sale delivery need not be made immediately and a wi sale is thus simpler and cheaper than an ordinary short sale. For a dealer who wants to trade 3-month bills, buying them wi is at times the only way he can do so without incurring a negative carry. Suppose, for example, that Fed funds are 8.40, the RP rate on governments at 8.20, and the 3-month bill is yielding 8 percent on a discount basis, that is, a 8.10 bond equivalent yield. A trader can't carry that bill positively, but a lot of people like to trade it so they will trade it in the wi market because buying wi is not a negative carry.

Trading on a wi basis before the auction serves other useful purposes. Noted one dealer, "A lot of regional firms are trading the wi market very actively. Before the advent of such trading, the recognized dealers with brokers wires were able to engineer auctions a lot easier than they can now because people outside the New York dealer community were not sure where the market was. So if three guys got together, they could—in the talk before the auction—push it an 01 or an 02 and buy most of the auction. Now with all this wi trading, the regionals know where the market is because the bill has been trading wi three or four days before the auction.

"Also, a lot of times people who do not like the market will build up a short going into the auction, so half the issue is really taken care of before 1:30. That really stabilizes the market when you bring in a new issue."

Weekly cycle

There tends to be something of a weekly cycle in the way the bill currently being auctioned trades. "On Monday," one trader noted, "you have the auction. Then Tuesday, right after the auction, you generally do not see too much price improvement unless it was a very aggressive auction or some extraordinary event affects the market; on Tuesday, the market performs sloppily because you have people who can sell the issue whether they have it or not. On Wednesday, there is a day to go, and people who are short start to think—shall I take my short in or not; and the market tends to behave a little better. Then Thursday you have demand. The shorters have to cover or borrow, which is expensive. Also, the previous bill matures and people who have not rolled over in the auction have to put their money to work, so they go and invest in the new bills. This is the busiest day. Then Friday it tails off a bit."

Trading games

As noted, a trader may *paint a one-man picture* in the brokers market to distort other dealer's perception of where the market is. There are also other games traders play. Whenever the Fed comes into the market, the brokers treat bids and offers as under reference until they check them. "I have a guy at Chemical," said one broker, "who tells me when the Fed is in the market. Also, the guy at Merrill tells me indirectly because he cancels all his bids and offers when the Fed is in the market. Sometimes he will cancel everything and nothing is going on. He is just creating an effect—having a lot of offers go off the screen at the same time. He is probably at the same time hitting any bids he can find at the other brokers."

The same broker described another strategy, "The traders at two top New York banks used to be good friends. They did a lot of volume through us just to show it on the screen. They paid the commission to influence the market. They might do as much as 50 million. It was advantageous for them to trade on our screen because that way the message they were trying to send got around to everyone right away."

Quotes to retail and protocols

When a good trader gives quotes to retail he will not simply *bracket* the brokers market—quote a bid slightly above that in the brokers market and an offer slightly below that in the brokers market. He will quote on the basis of his own perception as to where the real market is.[5] Also, his quotes will be influenced by the size he wants to do or retail wants to do.

One dealer commented, "Say I wanted to buy size in an issue. The bid in the brokers market is 20–18, 10 by 5. I might bid 17 to retail for 50 million. That's an 01 less than the offered rate in the brokers market, but there I can buy only 5 not 50."

If a retail customer has a lot he wants to buy or sell and he wants to get the job done properly, there are certain protocols he should follow. Say he is a big seller; he should be reasonably open with a single dealer and get that dealer to work for him—to try to retail what he is selling piece by piece to people who might be buyers. Sometimes a big seller will hit every bid around for $10 or $20 million, the market gets swamped, and the dealers all end up competing with each other to unload these securities. A customer who sells that way gets a reputation and won't get the same treatment from dealers the next time.

The dealer is also expected to be fair with retail. Said one, "A professional dealer won't move the market on a customer who tells him he's a big buyer or seller." Another dealer commented, "Say I want to sell 100 million of an issue; the World Bank comes in and wants to sell to me and the market is 84–3; I will make him 86–5. He will know right away I am not his person. He will know I am trying to sell. I will be open with him— tell him I am not in a position to help him because I too have a position to unwind."

The protocol of openness does not apply between dealers. If a dealer is trying to sell in size, he will attempt to hide that from other dealers—to try, for example, to play the games described above to distort the market and cloak his true intent.

The 90-day bill rate

The Fed directly influences a single interest rate, the Fed funds rate. In doing so, however, it strongly affects the level and pattern of other short-term interest rates. The 90-day bill rate is coupled to the Fed funds

---

[5] Recall the discussion of trading on pp. 304–5.

rate and other rates key off it; as the Fed funds rate changes, the whole structure of short-term interest rates changes.

Usually the 90-day bill trades, as Figure 13–2 shows, at or around the Fed funds rate. The two rates are coupled by arbitrage. Noted one

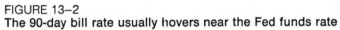

FIGURE 13–2
The 90-day bill rate usually hovers near the Fed funds rate

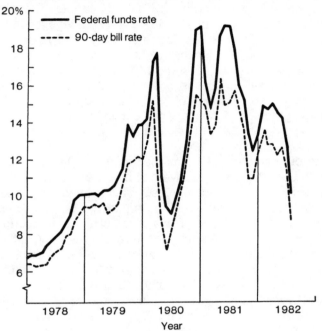

dealer, "If 90-day bills yield considerably more than the Fed funds rate, carry becomes positive, and firms like ourselves will buy 90-day bills and finance them. That puts some upside limit on the 90-day bill rate." When, in contrast, 90-day bills trade below the Fed funds rate—for example, because the Treasury is paying down in the bill area—at some point dealers' carry on 90-day bills becomes negative and dealers cease to position them; that in turn diminishes demand for the 90-day bill and sets some limit on how far through the funds rate 90-day bills can trade.

Impact of futures and money funds on bill rates. The link between the 90-day bill rate and the funds rate, while still strong, is at times altered and weakened by the activities of money funds and by futures trading.

Noted one trader, "Going back to 1974, traditionally whenever the Fed tightened, the bill curve went inverted and the 90-day bill jumped the sharpest; in the bill market, the 90-day rate was the proxy for the funds rate. Now the 90-day bill rate and the funds rate track each other less closely because money funds are constant buyers of 30- and 60-day bills.

"With over 230 billion to invest, the money funds pick clean the short bill market, which makes short bills trade chronically overpriced. Consequently when the Fed tightens, there is no clutter of short bills to force up the rate on the 90-day bill. To the contrary, traders are always trying to generate short paper for the funds by rolling existing holders of short bills out of them into the current 90-day bill. As a result short bills no longer trade as part of the normal yield curve; effectively the money funds have taken that part of the bill curve out of the market. Now when the Fed tightens and the yield curve inverts, the apex of the curve, which used to be the 90-day bill, is more often the 180-day bill." [See Figure 9–1, p. 284]."

The bill futures market has also affected the way cash bills trade. It used to be that the major buyers of bills were traditional cash investors. Futures have added another use: buying bills as part of an arbitrage against futures. As explained in Chapter 14, bill futures are used by the street in a number of different ways: to put on various sorts of hedges and as a part of complicated arbs and spread trades. By far the biggest trade the street puts on when rates make it profitable is *the cash-and-carry trade:* buy the deliverable bill for a specific futures contract; finance that bill with term RP to expiration of the futures contract, and sell the futures contract for a locked-in profit. This trade along with other arbitrages, such as rolling the current cash bill into the deliverable bill, links cash and futures prices. The trade also gets so big at times that entire 3-month issues or huge amounts of 6-month issues are committed to the futures market rather than by normal supply and demand factors to the cash market. When the cash-and-carry trade offers profits, it creates a shortage of bills, as the futures contract used approaches maturity; then because Chicago delivery is an uneconomical method of distribution, the trade creates, at settlement of the contract, supply in the cash market as arbitrageurs close out their positions and take their profits.

Relationship of the 90-day bill rate to other short rates. Whatever the forces that impinge on the 90-day bill rate, it remains true that changes in this rate are quickly transmitted to governments of other maturities. As one dealer noted, "The 6-month bill is typically a creature of the 90-day bill and technicals [prevailing supply and demand conditions]. At some spread of the 3-month bill to the 6-month bill, all the computers on the street tracking yield spreads and doing standard deviations [measuring statistically how unusual a given yield spread is in

terms of historical experience] will tell dealers and investors to buy the
6-month bill and sell the 3-month bill. Using the 6-month bill becomes an
extended part of using the 90-day bill because any trade always implies
a future trade. For example, to buy a 90-day bill and roll it, instead of
buying the 6-month bill, implies an outlook as to what the 90-day bill rate
will be 90 days from now. We know all of that. It is almost too academic.
We have it down to shorthand—we talk spreads."

Rates in other sectors of the money market key off rates in the government market. BAs, for example, carry some small credit risk and are less
liquid than bills. Thus, BAs have to trade at some spread to bills. That
spread, however, is not written in stone. If the supply of BAs increases,
the spread will widen; and if it decreases, BAs may trade almost on top
of bills.

Supply in different sectors of the money market and the search by
dealers and investors for *relative value* establish the pattern of rates
prevailing in the money market. That pattern changes constantly, but by
and large it is always a rational, explainable response to underlying
fundamentals: Fed policy, the supply and types of securities issued by
the Treasury, the state of loan demand at the banks, the demand for BA
financing, and so forth.

The reason that the Fed funds rate is coupled most directly with the
90-day bill rate and that changes in the Fed funds rate first have an
impact on the 90-day bill rate is that the 90-day bill is the shortest bill
that is auctioned weekly and has liquidity. It is thus the shortest issue in
which dealers can react to what the Fed is doing or what they anticipate
the Fed will do by going short or long in size.

The linkage—"ripple effect"—between the 90-day bill and other
short-term rates has, however, become quicker than it used to be. The
reason is the increase in sophistication at all levels—dealers, banks,
and portfolio managers. With everyone's computer tracking yields
spreads, the lags that used to occur between changes in the 90-day bill
rate and other rates have almost disappeared, and short-term rates now
move almost simultaneously in response to major developments such as
a change in the funds rate.

Short bills

The market for *short bills* (under 90 days) is a thin market that behaves
differently from the rest of the bill market. Supply is *fixed* in this part of
the market, and there is a lot of demand from money funds and from
institutions that fund to dates and that can hold only Treasuries. Consequently, short bills typically trade through the overnight repo rate.

Dealers trade short bills largely as a customer service; it is not a major
money maker for them. If a dealer positions short bills, his carry is nega-

tive. Also, a dealer has to trade short bills at a *wide* spread just to cover his clearing costs. One dealer commented, "On longer bills, I generally quote a 2-basis-point spread to retail, and I can operate at a tighter spread in the dealer and broker community. On very short bills—bills maturing within a week or two—I do not want to do trades on that basis because a couple of basis points would not cover my clearing costs." Writing a ticket is likely to cost a dealer $40, a 2-week basis point is worth less than $4; so a dealer has to pick up more than 10 basis points on both sides of a $1 million trade in 2-week bills just to cover his cost of doing the trade.

One of the reasons that CDs trade at higher yields than governments is that they are less liquid. In the 30-day area, however, CDs are often more liquid than bills. In CDs, the 30-day market is one of the best markets, and large size can normally be traded on an 05 spread. The contrast between the CD and the bill markets is due in part to the fact that a dealer's carry on a 30-day CD is not automatically negative.

In a dealership, the job of trading short bills is often given to a trainee. The market for short bills is quite stable so he can't lose much money, and trading these bills gives him an opportunity to lean the lingua franca and other fundamentals of bill trading before he goes on to trade longer bills, which is where the action is.

Due bills

A *due bill* is an IOU issued by a dealer that says the dealer owes the customer and will deliver certain securities to him at his earliest convenience. Dealers in governments had at one time, for specific short bill issues, more due bills outstanding than the Treasury had bills outstanding in these issues. Issuing due bills was in effect an attractive way for the dealers to borrow on the Treasury's credit.

Today the Fed frowns on the use of due bills; it requires that due bills outstanding for more than three days be collateralized, and the use of due bills has much diminished. Now dealers typically issue due bills as a convenience to their customers. One dealer commented, "Say we have a customer who wants to invest in a bill maturing in a few days. We can't get the bill because no one is offering it at a reasonable price, so we sell the customer a rate. Say we can repo at 7.50 and the best rate we can get the bill at is 7. We might offer the customer 7.25 on a due bill. This is a substitute from our point of view for repo financing. We do it to accommodate customers and are lucky to cover costs."

Another dealer observed, "We generally tend to 'paper bills' [give out due bills] on securities that we can't buy now and know we will be able to repurchase prior to maturity. Say a guy wants a 1-month bill I can't buy and I know he is going to sell that same bill in two weeks. I give him a due bill and then buy it back from him. This helps the customer because he gets interest income on his money and he is not forced to accept additional risk by buying something beyond the maturity range he wants."

Sometimes a dealer who gets failed to will give a due bill to a customer who he knows will take one and thus earn money on the fail.

TREASURY NOTES

The activities of a note trader closely resemble in some ways those of a bill trader but differ sharply in others, because notes trade differently from bills. In the note market yields are quoted in 32nds, but quotes can be refined to 64ths through the use of *pluses;* an 8+ bid, for example, means that the bid is eight and one-half 32nds, which is $17/64$. On dealers' runs for notes with less than a year to run, the normal spread between the bid and asked is $1/32$. On notes in the 1- to 2-year area, the spread widens to $1/16$, and on notes beyond one year, it is typically $1/8$, except on new issues that are very actively traded. Quotes on notes are normally good for $1 million, but trades much larger and smaller are also done.

Most large shops have several people trading notes. A junior trader may be responsible for trading notes with a current maturity of 0 to 18 or 21 months, an area where it is hard to lose a lot of money. A senior person will trade long notes. Often the person working with short coupons will do trades of coupons against bill futures.

Notes are traded during the morning for both cash and regular settlement. After 12:00 or 12:30, however, trading is only for regular settlement. The reason is that on trades done after this time, it is difficult for a dealer to get tickets processed quickly enough to make timely delivery. The schedule of cutoff times for securities transfers on the Fed wire was described at the end of Chapter 9.

Trading notes and bonds

Over the past few years big changes have occured in the way dealers bid for and deal in notes and bonds because of the huge increases that have occurred in the number and sizes of outstanding issues and because of the increased volatility of rates.

A fair, if oversimplified, way to describe how shops used to trade coupons would be to say that they bought notes when they were bullish, shorted them when they were bearish, and had a specialist arbitrageur who sought at all times to profit from rate anomalies.

Today talking to coupon traders, one hears them again and again speak about positioning and trading on a hedged basis where the hedge is often *generic:* The trader buys something—often a new issue at auction and sells something else so that he views his net position as zero and to boot has established an arbitrage or spread that promises to yield profits. The process is best described by quoting a few traders.

Said one, "A few years ago a major shop would easily run a billion position unhedged. Now the dealers have become arbitrageurs. For example, when the government sells 4-year notes, the street sells 2s and 6s or 2s and 5s. Then they cover their shorts in the coupon area by buying the 4-year note. Last week the Treasury sold 5 billion 5-years, and all of a sudden 2-years, 3-years, and 4-years were all over the place. The supply of these securities was created by shorts dealers put on so as to bid on the new 5-year note. Once we got done with the 5-year note auction, the 2s and 3s were still not going any place because the next auction down the pike was the year bill.

"Whereas big shops used to go long 500 or 600 of a new issue, they are now more likely to go short and long in ratio and rightly or wrongly to consider their net position zero. For example, at current interest rate levels, the yield value of 1/32nd on a 2-year note is .018 whereas on a 10-year note it is .005. If a dealer buys 4 million 2-year notes and shorts 1 million 10-year notes, he considers his net position zero.

"Actually there is a lot of risk in being long one area and short another. In 1980 Citi, for example, had a lot of 2-year notes and was short the long bond. When the note market rallied, Citi covered its short in the long bonds, let its long position in notes ride, and made 100 million." As this quote indicates, the plays dealers refer to as hedges are anything but pure hedges. Also the lines between hedging, arbitraging, and trading have become fuzzy.

Another dealer, speaking of how dealer trading has changed said, "I think you are seeing more generic hedging: 'I like the yield curve or I like the market, so I will buy the short end of the curve and sell the longer end, or 'I like the curve and the market and there is supply coming in the longer end, so I will buy the short end and short the long end.'

"Last week the year bill came and people were buying them. What were they selling? Everyone was selling the 2-years, because they expect them to come tonight. There is more of that hedge-type trading now. It is trading because there is considerable risk to this sort of thing. It is a hedge in the sense that, if the 2-year comes cheaply, the year bill will go down. What a trader is betting is that the 2-year bill will go down faster than the year bill because $6 billion of the new 2-year is coming in the auction. Consequently the 2-year should decay faster in yield than the year bill. Currently the year bill is trading 10.10–10.12; no one expects the year bill to be 10.10 and the 2-year note to be down half a point.

"On this sort of hedge you would expect to lose money on one side and to make it on the other. You hope to make more than you lose. That is not like the old game of selling the old 2-year and buying the new 2-year and letting that work out. In the past you could do that trade in considerable size; it is less easy now.

"It has also become common for dealers to use futures as a hedge, often generically. You have bought something, and you want to sell something. If it is cheaper to sell the futures market than to short the cash market, you sell futures. Which is cheaper at a given point will depend on several factors: the spread of cash to futures, transactions costs, and the cost of carrying a short [the reverse rate].

"Today it is hard to separate arbitrages and hedges. No one consciously sits down and says, 'I want to buy 2-years and sell long bonds.' They might say, 'I am going to buy the 2-year in the auction when they come, and if I have to sell something, I will sell the longer end because supply is coming there next week.' Those are not arbs. They are generic plays along the yield curve based upon supply. They may or may not work."

Hedging and arbitraging are practiced not only by coupon traders but by bill traders. Said one, "Market volatility has led people to do a lot more arbitrage trading than outright risk trading. They still do the latter when market conditions seem right. However, there are now a lot more people doing spread trades. Traders, for example, will buy a spread. Currently the spread of the year bill to the 2-year note is roughly 105 basis points. When the spread was 60 basis points, traders were buying the year bill and selling the 2-year note. They did this trade because they anticipated that the slope of the yield curve would turn positive and thought that that would widen this spread. Now that the spread has gotten to 105, traders sell the year bill and buy the 2-year. Or if they do not have the trade on, they will sell the year bill and buy the 2-year because the year bill will be auctioned next week so they expect this spread to come in at least temporarily.

"There is a lot of spread trading going on in the cash market. Traders also do spread trades between the 6-month and the year bill and between the 3- and 6-month bills."

In absorbing new supply, the street still takes risks by not taking the big naked positions it used to. By learning to hedge its bets, the street has become more efficient in distributing the debt. This explains in part how the market has managed over the last few years of highly volatile rates to smoothly absorb ever-increasing amounts of new Treasury debt in all maturity ranges.

Wi trading

Notes have always been traded wi from auction to settlement. The Treasury used to forbid the trading of coupons wi during the period between announcement of a new issue and auction of that issue. The Treasury feared that such trading would be speculative and leave room for investors to be injured. Such fears were probably always groundless. In any case the Treasury has switched its thinking. It concluded that it might save money by permitting new coupons to trade wi after announcement, so it rescinded its ban on such trading.

This was a big innovation in the coupon market. Now new coupon issues are routinely traded wi before they are auctioned. Since the Treasury auctions all its new coupons through yield auctions, traders who trade (on a yield basis) coupons wi before an auction are trading securities on which they don't know what the coupon will be. After the auction, they have to back into prices on the basis of the coupon established in the auction and then write tickets on all such trades they have done. If anyone has been inconvenienced by the new wi trading in coupons, it is the back office people who have to deal with a big new hassle every time a coupon is auctioned.

Current issues

In the note market, an issue is current from the time it is auctioned until it is replaced by another issue. Thus, the new 2-year note is current for a month, and new 4-year note for a quarter. A current issue trades much more actively than other issues until it becomes distributed or is replaced by a new issue. Although notes range in original maturity from 2 to 10 years, there are at any time only five or six current issues that are relatively new and actively traded at narrow spreads. Moreover, before the Treasury undertook its program of regularization of debt issuance, there were even fewer.

Many investors roll notes to stay in the current issue, just as they roll 3- or 6-month bills. Sometimes they will even give up coupon just to stay in a note that is active enough so that they can get a bid on size in a market that is quiet or going down. Staying in the current note allows the investor to increase yield by moving out on the yield curve while still maintaining liquidity. Dealers, too, like to position current issues. As one noted, "When I go long or short, I like to stay as current as possible because that is where most people have buying and selling interest."

In longer notes, the market used to sometimes go for months without a new issue, something that would be unimaginable in the bill market. When this occurred, trading in this market area tapered off. Where and when the Treasury chooses to issue its new debt also affect the yield curve. For example, before the 3-year note was added to the issues sold in the quarterly refunding, a trader of long notes commented, "We are going 6 months with no auction of a 3-year note. That will drive down the yield on the 3-year note relative to yields on other issues around it."

Short coupons

Coupons with a current maturity of a year or less are not actively traded. Part of the reason is that brokerage is much less on bills than on coupons. Also, the bill market naturally tends to be active because there are so many bill auctions.

Another reason short coupons trade inactively is that it is difficult for government dealers to staff all their major chairs, so they put rookie trainees on short coupons—often in a bank, it's someone who has graduated from the Fed funds desk.

Seasoning and trading

Not all issues trade strictly on the yield curve. One of the reasons is the varying reception that different issues receive in the auction.

"It takes time," one dealer noted, "for an issue to get well distributed, *seasoned.* How long depends on how well the auction went. Some auctions are sloppy and some are good. If in an auction, retail steps up and takes half or three quarters of an issue and they never intend to reoffer these securities so they are put away right off the bat, the float cleans up in a hurry. In other auctions, you have the opposite; the dealer fraternity by and large buys up the issue, it does not have anyone to sell them to, and it takes forever to get rid of them. That causes anomalies in the yield curve. You will see in the 2-year note area situations where the current 24-month and 20-month notes are trading at the same rate, and the 19-month note is trading for 10 basis points less. Why the 10-basis-point jump over one month and no jump over the next four? It is because there are dog issues out that never get as seasoned as the issues surrounding them."

How actively an issue trades over its life also depends on the reception it receives in the auction and on the volume in which it was offered to the market. One trader observed: "The 8's of '86 are a very popular 10-year note. When that issue originally came out, it was widely distributed in both individual and street hands. It is in ample supply, and it has been actively traded.

"If there is a lot of interest in an issue when it comes out, if it is large in size, and if it is widely distributed, it will continue to be actively traded. Profits can be taken, the issue becomes popular, and people buy and sell it. What counts is that there is sufficient size in trading hands—not necessarily dealers but investors who are willing to trade. It is also important that traders be able to borrow the issue. If they can't, no one will short the issue, and it won't be actively traded. It is easy to borrow the 8's of '86, and for that reason it is easier for a dealer to make a market in them than in some obscure issue."

Trading notes

A note trader is responsible for a large number of note issues, more than one person can actively follow. So the typical trader concentrates on a few issues in his area. "Once you know the issues you follow closely," commented one trader, "there are relationships. In the 2-year area, if you know where the Junes are, you know where surrounding issues should be. Even if you do not trade the Julys for a week and you have a trade a day in the Junes, you know, if you are worth your salt, where the Julys should be."

Prices are much more volatile in the coupon market than in the bill market because maturities are longer. For this reason dealers take smaller positions in coupons than in bills, and the coupon positions they assume become smaller the longer the current maturity of the securities positioned. One dealer commented, "If our bill trader is sitting there with 100 million in bills, that might be equivalent in terms of risk exposure to a 50 million position in 2-year notes and—in a normal market—to a 10 million exposure in long bonds."

Because a trader in governments is responsible for only a limited maturity spectrum, he is not in a position to arbitrage one sector of the market against another. That is a function typically carried on in a dealership in a separate arbitrage account. However, a trader can and does attempt to arbitrage temporary anomalies along the yield curve in the sector he trades. "If I see a blip in the yield curve—the Julys are out of line with the Augusts—I will short the overpriced issue and buy the other," noted one trader. "Generally, the payoff on this sort of thing is $1/32$ or $1/16$."

Technicals

A coupon trader has to be concerned about more than Fed policy and the Fed funds rate. He also has to consider any factors that might affect the yield curve, and he has to closely follow the technicals—factors affecting supply and demand—in his market.

Bill traders can and do short particular issues, but as Table 13–3 shows, net as a group they always have a substantial *long* position in bills. The same is not true for coupon traders. At times, the dealer community will go net *short* in coupons, particularly in the 1- to 5-year area. When dealers short an area, they eventually have to buy securities from retail to cover that short.

Dealers establish short positions in anticipation of a decline in coupon prices, as part of an arbitrage, for example, by shorting the 2-year note and buying the 7-year note, which is a *bull market arbitrage,* or as part of the hedge-type trades described above.

TABLE 13–3
Positions of U.S. government security dealers (par value; average of daily figures, $ millions)*

| | | | | | | | | | 1982 | |
Item	1974	1975	1976	1977	1978	1979	1980	1981	June	August
U.S. government securities	**2,580**	**5,884**	**7,592**	**5,172**	**2,656**	**3,223**	**4,306**	**9,033**	**11,075**	**4,893**
Bills	1,932	4,297	6,290	4,772	2,452	3,813	4,103	6,485	7,284	1,265
Other within 1 year	–6	265	188	99	260	–325	–1,062	–1,526	–462	–632
1–5 years	265	886	515	60	–92	–455	434	1,488	2,206	2,269
5–10 years	302	300	402	92	40	160	166	292	–254	–248
Over 10 years	88	136	198	149	–4	30	665	2,294	2,301	1,880
Federal agency securities	**1,212**	**943**	**729**	**693**	**606**	**1,471**	**797**	**2,277**	**2,976**	**3,578**

* Net amounts (in terms of par values) of securities owned by nonbank dealer firms and dealer departments of commercial banks on a commitment, that is, trade-date basis, including any such securities that have been sold under agreements to repurchase. The maturities of some repurchase agreements are sufficiently long, however, to suggest that the securities involved are not available for trading purposes. Securities owned, and hence dealer positions, do not include securities purchased under agreements to resell.

Note: Averages for positions are based on number of trading days in the period; those for financing, on the number of calendar days in the period.
Source: *Federal Reserve Bulletin.*

Whatever the reason for the short, a lack of securities on the street and a need to cover short positions can cause a *technical rally* in coupons. "Things in my part of the market," commented a trader of intermediate coupons, "can be technically bone dry in a way that never occurs in the bill market. The day before Carter killed the $50 tax rebate [April 1977] dealers were net short in my area 46 million. Carter's announcement [which caused a market rally] made the shorters uncomfortable; they wanted to cover and go long, but there were no notes around. So we had a technical rally, and the securities were dug out of customers."

One of the technicals a note trader has to constantly consider is what the arbitragers might be doing in his area of the market. Commented one note trader: "Whenever something important—an economic or political development—that affects the market occurs, I have to think as much about what the arbitragers are going to do as about where the market in general is going. If I think our arbitrage guy is sitting there getting ready to buy 3-year notes and sell 7-year notes, I sure don't want to be short the 3-year note even if I think that the market is going down."

Brokers

Traders of government notes and bonds use the brokers fully as much as bill traders do and for the same reasons. In the government market, as in other markets, one of the most important features of the brokers' market is that, whenever something occurs to cause a break in market activity, it serves as the arena in which trading is reestablished. It is part of the protocol of the dealer fraternity that whenever something big—such as a move by the Fed—has an impact on the market and causes uncertainty as to where issues should trade, dealers do *not* call each other and ask for runs. They do, however, look to the brokers market for bids and offers, and generally someone is doing something there. Gradually, as a few trades are done through the brokers, more bids and offers are put into the brokers, and a semblance of order in trading is reestablished.

Games

Traders play the same trading games in the brokers market and elsewhere that bill traders do. "Trading is much like a poker game," said one note trader. "You try to bluff, to sound like a buyer when you are really a seller. You tell the buy you are in great shape for the market to go down when you are, in fact, long and hope he will buy some of your securities. When my boss says, 'Let's get down in position,' the first thing I will do is put a bid in the brokers. The only way to get down is to find some help [create some buyers]. Sometimes my bid will be low, and sometimes it will be good; if I get hit, I have a bigger job to do.

"I have the ability to use two brokers at a time. Say the market is 11+ 12+; I have notes offered at 11+ and can't sell them. I will go out and buy them at 12+. Say I started with 30 million I bought at 10. By buying 5 million from another broker at a higher price than where I am willing to sell, I might lose 1/32 on that 5 million but I now am much more likely to be able to get the other 30 million I own off and make 2½ or 1½ 32nds on them."

BONDS

Treasury long bonds extend in maturity well past the year 2000 and are not part of the stock-in-trade of the money market.

Long bonds are much more volatile in price than short instruments, and the risks in positioning them are commensurately greater. As a result it was always typical for traders of long governments to hedge the bulk of their positions. Especially before the advent of bond futures, many bond traders, if they bought a million of long bonds from a customer and could not immediately resell them, would short a similar active issue and then wait and unwind the position when they could. In the view of other traders this sort of trading is wasted activity. Said one such trader, "You should never end up with a security you do not want. If you buy such a security, you should sell it immediately. If you can't because the issue is illiquid, you may have to sell another issue. Doing so, however, puts you in a poor position because you now have two issues that you can trade only when someone else has a need to trade them."

Spreads and active issues

In recent years spreads in the bond market have narrowed because individual issues are so much bigger these days, because the Board provides traders with so much liquidity, and because so much volume is transacted in the market. These days it is not unusual for a big shop to trade well in excess of a billion of bonds a day. Generally the volume of bonds traded has increased roughly 300% over the last years, which is roughly in line with the increase in Treasury long debt outstanding.

Because of all the volume transacted in bonds, in any active issue there is always virtually a locked market in the brokers' market. There will be a 10 lock, a 14 lock, or whatever. Locked markets occur because neither side is willing to take the initiative and pay brokerage. The widest spread that a bond trader is likely to see is half a basis point.

In 10- to 30-year coupons, virtually every issue is active because customers have positions in virtually all of them. They do a lot of swaps between securities to increase their total rate of return by 1 or 2% over a year. This is in sharp contrast to the situation in the note market. In the 10 years and under area there are only two active issues within a given area that the Treasury sells: two 10s, two 7s, two 5s, two 4s, two 3s, and two 2s. The premium placed on active note issues is phenomenal compared to that placed on more active long issues. The premium on active note issues is created by speculators who prefer to always trade the most active issues because they can get in and out of them with the greatest ease.

The end users of securities, buyers who intend to hold them to maturity or at least stay with a given security for some period, will buy off the run securities on which they can get some pick up in yield.

The distribution of bonds

Initially the Treasury and the Fed viewed the initiation of trading in bond futures with a jaundiced eye; they feared various imagined abuses and undesirable consequences to which this new market might lead. In fact the Board has been tremendously helpful in the distribution of new Treasury bond issues. If in any period there is 1 billion of open interest, in most cases the billion short is the street, the billion long is customers: dentists in Des Moines and other individuals to whom the Board offers the opportunity to speculate on interest rates. The willingness of these individuals to speculate and their preference for taking long positions has permitted the street to hedge huge positions on the board. The ability to establish such hedges enables dealers to buy a new issue when the Treasury wants to sell it and to sell the issue—sometimes at a significantly later date—when retail wants to buy it.

Investors

During the recent years of high and volatile interest rates, the Treasury has been selling record amounts of long bonds. The banks, twice-burned or worse on their bond portfolios, have let their holdings of Treasuries shrink, and the dealers have tended to hold bonds most of the time on a hedged basis. This raises the question of who have been the ultimate buyers of all the bonds sold.

Some traditional investors in long bonds, such as insurance companies and pension funds, have continued to invest in long bonds. To their ranks, especially in recent years, have been added a lot of foreign buyers. The strength of the dollar, the liquidity of the market in governments, and the credit of the U.S. government have combined to make investing in governments extremely attractive to a wide range of foreign buyers: insurance companies in Japan to cash-rich individuals in the Middle East. In long bonds as much as 1/4 of what has been sold over the last two years has been sold to international investors from the Mid East, Europe, and the Far East.

The new portfolio manager

Another source of demand that has arisen from Treasury long bonds is from the new breed of fixed-income portfolio managers who view the cash markets as their natural home and make well-timed forays into the long market. In the last few years the money under the control of such managers has gone from zero to 7 to 10 billion.

Describing their management style, one new-breed manager noted, "In the fall of 1979, the Fed radically changed the way it operates. As a result, the markets became so volatile that, whereas in the past the emphasis on constructing a bond portfolio was maturity, coupon, sector, and quality, the emphasis post fall of 1979 really should have been maturity, maturity, maturity.

"After the Fed changed its policy and after the markets started to become really volatile, the impact of choosing one sector over another— utilities over industrial bonds—was almost negligible. The impact of having a 9% versus an 8% coupon was also small compared to the impact of being short or long.

"The extremes of being long or short are cash and 30-year bonds. After the fall of 1979, the ideal strategy was to stay in cash, earn high money market rates, which became higher and higher throughout 1980 and spiraled up in 1981 and early in 1982, and to commit occasionally, when the market was right—vastly undersold, really on its hind legs—a large proportion of your cash portfolio to the long end of the market.

"As it turned out, the liquidity was mostly in governments. You could not decide to move hundreds of millions of dollars into the market and start fooling around with 10 million in telephones, 15 million in utilities, 20 million in finance company bonds, and so on. You missed that entry point into the market by trying to diversify among sectors.

"The key thing was to time market entry effectively, that is, to decide correctly when the bonds were sufficiently oversold so the long market was a low-price-risk area—i.e., high-yield area—of the market, to then put a lot of your marbles to work on those occasional forays, and to do so in the longest and most liquid end of the market, which is 30-year Treasuries. This strategy worked very well, and those folks who figured out sooner rather than later that this was a new ball game did better than those who were a little late in figuring that out.

"The new breed of portfolio managers relies more on technical indicators than on fundamental judgments as to the future level of interest rates. They are more interested in charts of price action and price momentum and in sentiment than what Kaufman of Sali is predicting about interest rates. Post 1979 the people who relied on long-term forecasts of interest rates based on fundamentals missed massive movements up and down in bond prices—10 points, even 20 points—while they sat and hung on to their long-term rate forecast.

"Price and moving averages of price are among the technical indicators watched by the new breed of portfolio manager. Another is sentiment. In bonds the way it works is the higher the bullish consensus, the
higher the euphoria, the more you should think about selling. To techni-
cians a euphoric market is a high-risk market, whereas a market in which
everyone is bearish is a low-risk market. I shoot against prevailing sentiment. When everyone is bearish and hates the market, I take money out
of cash and buy the market."

The record of the new portfolio managers is impressive. However, by
the end of 1982 the Fed seemed to be drifting back to its old policy of
controlling interest rates—if for no other reason than that it could no
longer measure money supply. This raised the question of whether the
new style of portfolio management would in the future pay the dividends
it had over the prior three years.

Some dealers advising pension and other bond accounts agreed with
this philosophy but took it a step further. They argued that a portfolio
manager should regard his natural home as cash equivalents—money
market instruments. Occasionally the right thing to do was to buy bonds;
but why bother with cash securities, they asked. A simpler approach was
to stay at all times 100% invested in cash equivalents and, when a foray
into bonds looked appropriate, to buy bond futures. A number of big
accounts adopted this approach, the logical conclusion of the philosophy of the new breed of portfolio managers.

Technical analysis

The new breed of portfolio managers are not the only people in the
money and bond market who have taken up charting. Whereas before the
advent of futures trading, street traders tended to view charting as a sort
of voodoo to be frowned upon, now a lot of them are doing it. Some
traders look at charts because they believe in charting. Others look, for
example, at head and shoulders charts because they think other people,
especially in the Chicago futures market, look at the same charts. Traders always need something to lean on. That something used to be the
funds rate, then it was money supply; now technical analysis gives traders one more thing to look at in the current markets characterized by
great uncertainty and high rate volatility.

The zoo

In recent years *zero coupons* (note and bond issues carrying a zero
coupon) have found a ready market both in the U.S. and Euromarkets. A
big attraction of zeros to buyers is that they provide a guaranteed reinvestment rate over the life of the bond. For investors buying bonds in a
high-rate environment, this guarantee significantly reduces uncertainty

over what total return a bond will yield over its life. The offset to this advantage in the U.S. is that taxable investors must pay taxes (lowered somewhat by 1982 tax law changes) on interest that accrues to them on zeros as that interest accrues whereas they actually get interest years later when the bond matures. Consequently in the U.S. zeros are most attractive to tax-exempt or low-taxed investors: pension funds and individuals investing IRA or Keogh monies.

In August of 1982, Merrill, banking on the idea that Treasuries packaged as zeros could lure into long-term government bonds many investors who would not otherwise buy them, came up with an idea of how to do this packaging: buy long bonds, put them into a bank, and issue receipts against all coupon payments and the principal repayment that the Treasury is scheduled to make. Packaging a Treasury long bond this way creates a series of zero-coupon Treasuries, one maturing on every coupon date including the final principal repayment date.

Merrill sold its Treasury Investment Growth Receipts— *TIGRS* dubbed TIGERS—at the present values of the principal amount the investor would get. Since zero coupons appealed more to long-term investors than to short-term investors, in pricing its TIGERS, Merrill, to attract shorter-term investors, offered investors buying short TIGERS a guaranteed yield to maturity slightly above the yield to maturity offered by regular Treasuries of similar maturity; on long TIGERS Merrill offered a guaranteed yield to maturity below rates on the yield curve.

On its first venture into coupon stripping, Merrill bought, cut up, and banked half a billion of the 14s of 2011; it then sold, on the basis of these securities, $2.565 billion of TIGERS. That venture—viewed with considerable trepidation by some executives at the firm—was such a success that Merrill followed it up with a new TIGER issue: $1.39 billion of TIGERS backed by $300 million of the 12¾s of 2010.

While Merrill was the first to wave its wand over interest-bearing Treasuries and create zero coupon bonds from them, Merrill's TIGERS were soon followed by Sali's CATS and Lehman Brothers' LIONS.

It is estimated that, by the end of the summer of 1982, Wall Street firms had resold nearly $14 billion of chopped-up Treasuries to an array of buyers including big tax-exempt institutions, parents looking to fund junior's college education, holders of IRA and Keogh plans, and foreign investors; the latter are estimated to have snapped up as much as ¼ of Merrill's TIGERS.

Merrill and the other firms who have transformed Treasury coupons into zeros committed themselves to make a secondary market in these securities. To the extent that they do, they have created a new attractive instrument for speculators since zeros are the most volatile in price of all bonds when interest rates change.

Whether TIGERS, CATS, and LIONS will be a lasting phenomenon— will add on a long-term basis to the demand for long-term Treasuries—is open to question. Should interest rates decline to single-digit levels, locking up a reinvestment rate at current levels would presumably be less attractive to investors; and a new issue from the zoo might be less warmly received than were past issues.

The stripping of certain long Treasuries has resulted in a scarcity of these issues, which has caused them to trade at a high premium. The amount of such issues in regular tradable form is significantly less than the amount the Treasury sold because hundreds of millions of the security have been ripped apart into the corpus and clipped coupons. This phenomenon, for example, has caused the 15¾s of 01 to trade at a premium; an educated guess is that at least half of this issue has been stripped.

DAILY TRADING VOLUME

Trading in the government market has expanded tremendously in recent years both because the government's marketable debt has grown so rapidly (see Figure 7–1) and because that debt is more actively traded than it used to be. Table 13–4 shows just how much trading in governments has expanded over the last decade and also where it is centered. By far the bulk of the action is in bills, but notes with 1- to 5-year maturities are also actively traded.

MERRY-GO-ROUND

The people trained to trade governments and agencies are all in the U.S. and mostly in New York. There are something over 300 of them. The rapid expansion in the number and size of dealers in governments has placed a tremendous premium on good traders, and there is a constant flow of people from one shop to another as dealers buy good people away from each other.

Firms don't actively recruit people to be trained as traders. They end up taking someone who was working in the back office or whatever and putting him to work trading short coupons or some other area of the market where it is safe to let a rookie try his hand. Thus it is not surprising that the head of one trading operation commented, "Staffing in some areas of the government market is horrible. A lot of traders are there simply because they grew up in the geographic area of New York. They are traders when their real natural destiny was to be a house painter."

FEDERAL AGENCY SECURITIES

The major federal agencies still issuing securities to the market have, as Table 13–5 shows, a wide range of coupon securities outstanding.

TABLE 13–4
U.S. government securities dealers transactions (par value; averages of daily figures, $ millions)

Item	1972	1973	1974	1975	1976	1977	1978	1979	1980	1981	1982 June	1982 August
U.S. government securities	**2,930**	**3,439**	**3,579**	**6,027**	**10,449**	**10,838**	**10,285**	**13,183**	**18,331**	**24,728**	**27,136**	**41,041**
By maturity												
Bills	2,259	2,643	2,550	3,889	6,676	6,746	6,173	7,915	11,413	14,768	16,831	23,655
Other within 1 year*	—	—	250	223	210	237	392	454	421	621	646	1,094
1–5 years	422	471	465	1,414	2,317	2,318	1,889	2,417	3,330	4,360	4,438	8,784
5–10 years	189	243	256	363	1,019	1,148	965	1,121	1,464	2,451	2,821	4,186
Over 10 years	63	83	58	138	229	388	867	1,276	1,704	2,528	2,400	3,323
By type of customer:												
U.S. government securities dealers†	726	665	652	885	1,360	1,267	1,135	1,448	1,484	1,640	1,693	1,997
U.S. government securities brokers†	411	795	965	1,750	3,407	3,709	3,838	5,170	7,610	11,750	13,061	19,616
Commercial banks†	998	1,092	998	1,451	2,426	2,295	1,804	1,904	2,339			
All others‡	796	886	964	1,941	3,257	3,567	3,508	4,660	6,890	11,337	12,382	19,429
Federal agency securities	**527**	**743**	**965**	**1,043**	**1,548**	**693**	**1,894**	**2,723**	**3,258**	**3,306**	**3,237**	**5,000**

Note: Averages for transactions are based on number of trading days in the period. Transactions are market purchases and sales of U.S. government securities dealers reporting to the Federal Reserve Bank of New York. The figures exclude allotments of, and exchanges for, new U.S. government securities, redemptions of call or matured securities, or purchases or sales of securities under repurchase, reverse repurchase (resale), or similar contracts.
 *Not given in earlier Federal Reserve Bulletins.
 †Included in All others beginning 1981.
 ‡Includes—among others—all other dealers and brokers in commodities and securities, foreign banking agencies, and the Federal Reserve System. In 1981 also includes commercial banks.
 Source: Federal Reserve Bulletin.

TABLE 13–5
Major federal agency securities (as of November 1982)

Agency	Security	Minimum denomination	Book entry (B) and/or registered (R)	Original maturity	Number of Issues	Volume of securities outstanding ($ billions)
Farm Credit Bank†	Consolidate systemwide discount note	50,000	B	5–270 days	4	1.4
	Consolidated sys-temwide bonds	1,000	B	6 months–15 years	75	63.1
Federal Land Bank††	Bonds	1,000	R	5–20 years	15	8.2
Federal Intermediate†† Credit Bank for	Debentures	5,000	R	10 years	2	.9
Bank for Cooperatives††	Debentures	5,000	R	10 years	1	.2
Federal Home† Loan Bank	Discount notes	100,000	B	30–360 days	16	11.8
	Bonds	1,000	B	1–20 years	74	49.1
Federal National† Mortgage Association	Debentures	10,000	B	2–25 years	89	62.6
	Notes	50,000	B	30–360 days	2	2.5
Government National Mortgage Association*	Pass-through securities	25,000	R	12-year expected life**	51,557 pools	127.2
Government National* Mortgage Association	Participation certificates	5,000	R	1–20 years	18	2.7
Federal Home Loan Mortgage Corporation	Guaranteed mortgage certificates	100,000	R	10-year expected** life	7	1.9
Federal Home Loan Mortgage Corporation	Mortgage participation certificates	25,000	R	12-year expected* life	86	17.9

* Backed by the full faith and credit of the U.S. government.
† Interest income exempted from state and local taxation.
†† These agencies now issue under the Farm Credit Bank.
‡ Smaller denominations available on some issues.
‖ These agencies are moving, except on pass-throughs, to book-entry securities.
** Expected life based on experience through the late 1970s. Expected life has been increased in recent years by the high cost and unavailability of mortgage money, which discouraged home sales and mortgage prepayments.

Most agency issues are much smaller than comparable Treasury issues. The Treasury has a few bond issues outstanding that are less than $1 billion in size, but most of its coupon issues are in the $2–$5 billion range, and a few are as large as $8 or $9 billion. In agencies, in contrast, the size of outstanding issues typically runs from $300 million up to but not above $1 billion.

Distribution

Federal agencies sell new coupon issues to the market through selling groups. The practices of the Federal Home Loan Bank system in this respect are typical. The FHLB goes to the market on a regular basis every 3 months but will go more often when its need for funds is especially high. The FHLB announces the size of a new issue to be offered on a Monday. At that time the members of its selling group—about 140 dealers—begin to distribute the issue by determining (*circling* in street jargon) customer interest in it. Small regional banks and other investors that are not rate conscious will often put in a market order for the new issue; that is, agree to buy it before it is priced. Other buyers will make a subject bid for the new paper—agree to buy some amount of the issue if the coupon is set, for example, at 10.50 or better.

Dealers are each allocated a specific share of the total issue to be sold. They attempt to presell that share, and if they are more successful in doing so than other dealers, the FHLB increases their allocation.

On the day after a new issue is announced, the FHLB starts to think about pricing. It makes its own reading on the market, talks to people at the Treasury, and talks to 30 or 40 representative dealers about how well their presales of the issue are going and precisely where they feel the coupon should be set. The FHLB seeks to price the issue so that it will trade close to par. It announces its decision on pricing on Tuesday, and the new issue begins to trade wi on Wednesday.

Dealers in a selling group get a fee, which ranges depending on the maturity of the issue from $0.50 to $3 per $1,000 on whatever securities they sell. Their function is to get the securities into the hands of a wide range of investors, not to position the new issue. However, in a sale characterized by poor retail demand, the major dealers would if necessary underwrite—buy for their own position—the new issue to get it sold.

The dealers who participate in the selling group are also market makers, and in that capacity they assume long and short positions in agencies. Sometimes after the sale of a new issue, dealers who like the issue will go back into the market as buyers and position it. This is easy to do. If an issue goes immediately to a premium of a few 32nds, some buyers will sell out and take their profit. This creates a floating supply, which the dealers must in effect distribute. How long distribution takes depends on the initial reception an issue gets in the market. If it is poor, the securities may overhang the market for a long period.

Agency securities trade wi for a week or two after they are priced and sold. The wi period used to be much longer because of the time required to print the actual certificates. Now, however, virtually all new agency issues are sold in book entry form.

The secondary market

The secondary market in agency securities, like the secondary market in governments, is made by dealers trading with retail and with each other. There are, however, significant differences between the two markets. These result in large part from the fact that agency issues are smaller than Treasury issues and are traded less actively (Table 13–4).

Several primary dealers in governments are in the market every day trading agencies, but many others are sometimes players who will position when they like a spot in the agency market and otherwise ignore it.

Dealer's positions in agencies are much smaller than those in governments (see Table 13–3). Also in agencies, as in government notes and bonds, dealers sometimes assume net short positions, so the technical condition of the agency market, like that of the government note market, can become bone dry in particular sectors.

Interdealer quotes in agencies are good for only $500,000, and a lot of trades of that size are done. A $5 million trade is a big trade in the agency market except on a new or short-term issue. A $10 million trade is a rarity.

Spreads are wider in agencies than in governments, and agencies are consequently less liquid. An agency run includes the two newest FHLB issues, the two newest Federal Land Bank issues, the most recent Federal Intermediate Credit Bank issue, and the most recent Bank for Cooperatives issue. For on-the-run agency issues, the typical spread is $1/32$ for a 1-year maturity, $1/32$ to $2/32$nds for a 2- to 3-year maturity, and as much as $4/32$nds for a 10-year bond. As issues get seasoned, these spreads widen. One reason is that currently many investors in agencies are trust accounts, state and local governments, and commercial banks that mature the securities they buy and rarely do swaps.

In recent years agencies have become, if anything, less liquid than they used to be. A problem with agency securities is that the agencies issuing them have not increased the size of their issues as the Treasury has done. On 400 and 500 million agency issues, once an issue gets distributed, it gets illiquid. Noted one trader, "I would like to see the agencies reopen issues and build up an issue to 2 or 3 billion in size. People have offered this concept to the agency fiscal agents who seem to have rejected it. There are so many agency issues that it is hard to keep track of them, and many are so small. What develops a really liquid market is the ability to short an issue because then you always have someone—an arbitrageur—there willing to buy it back at a price. But an arbitrageur has to be crazy to short agency issues. You can't borrow enough of them to do it. Whereas I can short almost any Treasury issue on the list and know I can borrow it at a price, I can't do that in agencies."

The illiquidity of agency paper is reflected in the fact that in inactive issues spreads can be virtually anything. Noted another trader, "You will even get yield bids on agency paper that trades infrequently. People will say, 'We know where the 5-year note is. These things should trade 60 basis points off the note, so if 5-year notes are trading at 10.50, we will bid 11.10 for this agency paper.' "

Agency traders use brokers just as traders of governments do but less extensively. FBI is the major broker of agencies. The market in off-the-run agencies is so thin that when a dealer wants to buy or sell such an issue, he will often be quite open about his position with other dealers to see if they can help him find securities he wants to buy or a buyer for securities he wants to sell. Said one dealer, "Look at my position. I have 940,000 of this issue, I am short 90,000 of that one, and I need 290,000 of this other issue. I am not going to go into the brokers market to clean up all that. I will go to other dealers and talk to them, to Sali and Merrill. They will help me, and I help them."

Currently there are outstanding a number of note and bond issues that were sold prior to 1974 by federal agencies, such as the Export-Import Bank and the Tennessee Valley Authority, that now borrow solely from the Federal Financing Bank. These issues are put away and rarely trade.

Agency discount notes

In addition to selling coupon securities, the FHLB, the farm credit agencies, and Fannie Mae all borrow short term by issuing non-interest-bearing discount notes, which resemble Treasury bills.

These notes are sold through dealers who get an 05 for their effort. An agency selling notes will decide what rate to offer on its notes after conferring with dealers in its selling group about market conditions. Some post rates all the time but post competitive rates only when they want to sell. Agencies invest any excess funds they raise through the sale of discount notes in RP. That's a negative carry for them so they are careful not to raise more short-term money than they need.

Agencies use funds raised through the sale of discount notes to provide bridge financing to a date when they intend to issue longer-term securities. They also issue discount notes when money is tight and they need to borrow but do not want to borrow long term at high rates. The FHLB, for example, experiences a substantial demand for loans from

S&Ls when money is tight, but this demand tapers off rapidly as interest rates fall. Thus, if the FHLB borrows long term at high rates, as it did in 1974, it is likely to find that it has locked up for a long period expensive money that neither it nor member S&Ls later want.

Outstanding agency discount paper is traded less actively than bills are, and it is somewhat less liquid than bills. When the agencies are writing a lot of new paper, the dealers will bid for old paper to get customers to swap into new paper, and activity in the secondary market for such paper picks up. At other times when the agencies are not writing, activity drys up. A dealer will always give retail a bid on old paper, but getting an offer out of a dealer may be more difficult because, to supply old paper, a dealer must go out to an account that has the paper and try to bid it away.

Agency discount notes trade at a spread over bills. This spread, which can be anything from 5 to 100 basis points, tends to rise when agencies write a lot of paper and when money tightens.

BROKERING TO RETAIL

Brokers of money market instruments typically service only dealers. There is, however, one exception—Cantor Fitzgerald. This firm, which brokers governments and agencies, has over 300 clients including most of the recognized dealers in governments, several dealers just entering the government market, and a large number of big retail accounts. All bids and offers made through Cantor Fitzgerald are displayed on three pages of the Telerate system.

When a trade is done through Cantor Fitz, names are never given up. Securities sold are delivered to Cantor's clearing bank, which redelivers them to the buyer. In effect, Cantor acts as principal on both sides of the transaction, and for this reason it checks with extreme care the financials of a retail customer before it will do business with them.

Brokerage on trades made through Cantor Fitzgerald is paid by the side that initiates the transaction. The firm charges the same brokerage rates that other brokers do, except that on trades of long coupons it charges $\frac{1}{64}$ if the trade is for less than $5 million.

Because there are primary dealers that use Cantor Fitz, the bids and offers it quotes can never be far from the inside market. Also, as one would expect, dealers are busy painting pictures on Cantor's screen just as they do on the Garban and FBI screens. And to the extent that Cantor's retail clients are less sophisticated than traders at the primary dealers, traders may play such games with slightly more success in Cantor's market than elsewhere.

Chapter 14

Treasury bills, notes, and bonds: Futures and options*

FORWARD TRANSACTIONS ARE COMMON in many areas of economic activity including the markets for commodities. *In a forward transaction a seller agrees to deliver goods to a buyer at some future date at some fixed price.* For example, a farmer growing onions might, before the harvest, sell some portion of his crop to a buyer at a fixed price for delivery at harvest. For the farmer, this transaction reduces risk. To grow onions, the farmer incurs various costs; by selling his onions forward, he guarantees the revenue he will receive for his onions at harvest, and he thus locks in a profit on his operations. That profit may be more or less than what he would have earned if he had waited to sell his crop at harvest for whatever price was then prevailing in the *cash market* (market for immediate delivery) for onions.

Forward transactions are common in the money market. Euro time deposits are sometimes sold for future delivery (a forward forward). And, as noted in Chapter 16, there is an active market in forward foreign

* All illustrative examples of different trades using 1982 quotes were put together on the basis of live quotes by James Mehling and Gerald Laurain of Merrill Lynch; the author gratefully acknowledges their help.

exchange; for example, in German marks to be delivered against dollars at some agreed-upon exchange rate at some future date. The objective of many money market participants who operate in forward markets is to reduce risk.

A *futures contract,* like a forward contract, specifies that the seller of the contract will deliver whatever item the contract is for to the buyer at some future date at some fixed price. Futures contracts differ, however, from forward contracts in several respects. First, *futures contracts are standardized agreements made and traded on exchanges that are chartered, designated, and licensed to serve as a trading arena in specific futures contracts.* Second, whereas forward contracts are normally custom-tailored contracts made with the intent that delivery shall be made, *delivery is rarely made in connection with futures contracts.* Instead, a buyer of a futures contract will typically close out his position before the contract matures by making an offsetting sale of the same contract, a seller by making an offsetting purchase.

The reason delivery is not made is that people enter into futures contracts not to buy or sell commodities, but either (1) *to offset risk on a long or short position in a commodity, that is, to hedge that position by taking an equal and offsetting position in futures,* or (2) *to speculate on a change in the price of the commodity or a change in price spreads.* The hedger attempts to put himself in a position where any losses he incurs on his cash position in the commodity (e.g., he is long and the price in the cash market drops) will be offset by an equal gain on his futures position. As shown in the examples presented below, he can accomplish this by establishing a position in futures and later closing it out. The speculator, who neither owns nor desires to own the underlying commodity, can also realize whatever gain or loss he makes on his speculation simply by closing out the position he has established in futures.

For a hedger a transaction in the futures market is a temporary substitute for a transaction in the cash or spot market. The hedger transacts in futures because, at the moment he wants to trade, the futures market offers greater liquidity than the spot market. For example a grain company that contracts to sell wheat forward to Turkey incurs a price risk, which it could cover by immediately buying grain from farmers. The spot market in wheat, however, may be thin and illiquid at the time the forward sale is made; if so, the grain company would have to offer farmers a high premium to get them to sell, and the cheapest and most efficient way for the company to cover its price risk would be to go into the more liquid futures market and buy futures contracts. Later, as grain became available in the spot market, the grain merchant would piece out its purchase of grain, buying 10,000 bushels here, 20,000 bushels there, and simultaneously selling off a comparable amount of futures contracts.

FINANCIAL FUTURES

In January 1976, the *International Monetary Market* (IMM), now part of the Chicago Mercantile Exchange (CME), opened trading in futures contracts for 3-month Treasury bills. The trading of futures contracts for financial instruments was not new. In October 1975 the Chicago Board of Trade opened trading in futures contracts for Ginnie Mae pass-throughs, and prior to that the IMM had introduced trading in futures contracts for major foreign currencies. Still, introduction of the bill futures contract was an important innovation for the money market because trading in Ginnie Mae pass-throughs and foreign exchange lies at the fringe of what could strictly be called money market activities.

In contrast, the bill market is a key sector of the money market, and as part of their normal investing or borrowing activities, every money market participant could find potential uses for sales or purchases of bill futures contracts.

The initial reception of the bill futures contract by the street was marked by uncertainty and coolness. The dealers looking at the new market all groped for the "right numbers"; they asked what the relationship between spot and futures prices should be and how they could profit from trading in the new market. Many investors were confused about the nature of the contract and uncertain as to how they might or should use it. Also, some felt that a contract traded by "commodities speculators" next to the pork belly pit was suspect.

Nonetheless, the volume of contracts traded in the bill futures market rose (Figure 14–1) rapidly and dramatically; in fact, the market in bill futures came to be used more widely and more rapidly than any futures market ever had been. Part of the reason was that dealers in governments quickly became active participants in the new market, following a pattern well established in other futures markets where dealers who position the commodity traded are big buyers and sellers of futures contracts.

By the fall of 1982, daily volume in the bill futures market averaged $25 to $28 billion; in contrast, the volume of bills traded daily in the cash market by all recognized and reporting dealers in governments averaged only $20 to $22 billion. This comparison is impressive for a futures market that is only 6 years old.

The success from the start of the Treasury bill futures contract spurred introduction by several exchanges of a host of other futures contracts on different financial instruments. Some of the new futures contracts, in particular the *Chicago Board of Trade's (CBT's)* bond futures contract, filled a real need and were highly successful. However, most new financed futures contracts quickly failed. For example, the CBT's futures

FIGURE 14–1
Average daily volume of IMM Treasury bill futures contract

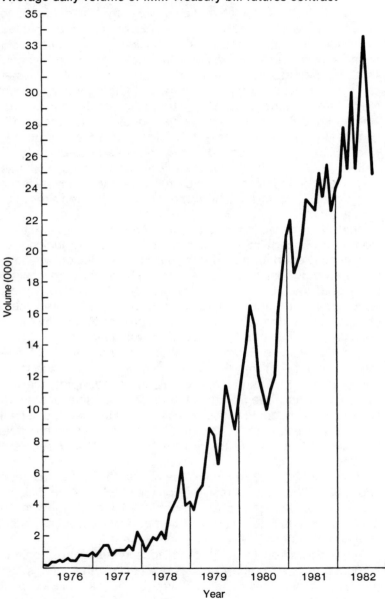

Source: Donaldson, Lufkin & Jenrette.

contract for 90-day, A-1, P-1 commercial paper never attracted much interest because the real market in commercial paper is for paper with an original maturity of 30 days or less; also, when delivery occurred at the maturity of this contract, the least attractive paper meeting delivery specifications was always delivered.

In 1981 the New York Futures Exchange (NYFE) introduced futures contracts in currencies, bills, and bonds with much fanfare and high hopes that these contracts would succeed since New York, not Chicago, is the capital of the money market and in particular the center of the cash market for money market instruments. In fact all these NYFE contracts failed partly because NYFE never had the strong locals Chicago did to build up and maintain liquidity in its contracts. Also, the initial NYFE contracts met no unfilled needs since all—with the exception of the bond contract—were me-too imitations of contracts already traded in Chicago.

Introduction of some contracts that would be obvious winners was delayed by slow moving regulators. It was not until 1981 that trading in domestic CD futures was permitted and not until 1982 that trading in Eurodollar futures was permitted. Also, introduction of the immediately successful stock index futures contracts was delayed by federal regulators until 1981.

Regulation

Currently futures trading in bills and other financial instruments is regulated by the *Commodity Futures Trading Commission* (CFTC), which first authorized trading in bill futures in November 1975. At that time the SEC, which regulates trading in most securities and in securities options, argued that contracts for the future delivery of securities were securities and that it should therefore have jurisdiction over the futures market in Treasury bills and other financial instruments. The CFTC countered that regulation of trading in such contracts fell within its purview because the law creating the CFTC gave it exclusive jurisdiction over trading in contracts for future delivery.

The dispute between the two agencies resurfaced in 1978 when the SEC recommended to Congress that it should take over the CFTC's authority to regulate futures trading in securities. The SEC's concern over futures trading in securities was heightened by the difficulties that arose in the dealer-made, off-the-board forward market for Ginnie Mae pass-throughs, when a small dealer, Winters, whose operations had been irregular, failed.

Under Chairman James Stone, the CFTC was slow to approve new futures contracts, it demanded from exchanges proposing new contracts extensive documentation that economic justification existed for these contracts. When Philip Johnson took over a chairman of the CFTC in the summer of 1981, he took a more free-market philosophy; in his view exchanges should be permitted to introduce new contracts meeting standard regulatory requirements with less a priori proof of economic justification. A posteriori the market would demonstrate whether introduction of a new contract was justified: If the new contract traded well, it fulfilled a need; if it failed, it did not.

In the summer of 1981, the CFTC finally approved a domestic CD futures contract. It also approved the first of several stock index futures contracts, which provided for *cash settlement,* an innovation that had been proposed by industry participants for a number of years.

While the CFTC began to move, its underlying jurisdictional dispute with the SEC remained; the SEC continued to argue in particular that a futures contract on an exempt security was a security and therefore should be subject to SEC jurisdiction.

Finally in the fall of 1981, Chairmen Johnson of the CFTC and Shad of the SEC reached a jurisdictional accord spelling out each agency's area of regulatory authority (Table 14–1). This agreement, passed into law in 1982, gives the industry guidance as to where jurisdiction lies and thus provides more certainty to would-be proposers and users of new contracts.

The accelerated pace at which federal regulators have begun to approve new contracts has led to a rapid expansion in the menu of securi-

TABLE 14–1
SEC/CFTC jurisdictional accord in 1981

I. SEC Jurisdiction
Options on any security including:
U.S. government and other exempt securities
Certificates of deposit
Any index of securities
Also options on Foreign currencies

II. CFTC Jurisdiction
Futures contracts including:
U.S. government and federal agency exempt securities
Broad-based indexes of securities
All currently traded futures
Also options on:
Futures contracts
Foreign currencies

III. Prohibited
Futures contracts on corporate and municipal securities
Futures contracts on narrowly based indexes of securities

ties—financial futures, options on fixed-income securities, and options on futures—being traded. The specifications of contracts, actual and proposed, as of December 1983 are outlined in Table 14–2.

BILL FUTURES

A useful way to begin our discussion of financial futures is by looking carefully at the bill contract: the basic contract terms, how the contract is quoted, the clearing function of the exchange, how margin is handled, how the market for the contract is made, and how the contract may be used for hedging and other purposes.

With respect to basics, the futures contracts for all fixed-income securities work and are traded in pretty much the same way so much of what we will say about the bill contract applies to other futures contracts as well. The peculiarities of the bond futures contract and trades that can be done using it are described at the end of this chapter along with an example of an options trade. Futures contracts for CDs, which strongly resemble bill futures, are discussed at the end of Chapter 15.

The bill contract

The basic contract traded on the IMM is for $1 million of 90-day Treasury bills. Currently a contract matures once each quarter—in those weeks of March, June, September, and December when the newly auctioned 3-month bill is a reopening of an old year bill. There are eight contracts outstanding, so when a new contract starts to trade, the furthest delivery date stretches 24 months into the future. Traders refer to the farthest out contracts as *red;* e.g., in November 1982 contracts for December 1983 bills were in pit jargon the *red Decs.*

Price quotes

Bills trade and are quoted in the *cash market* on a yield basis, and consequently because of this, the bid always exceeds the offer. Also, when yield rises, price falls, and vice versa. This seems reasonable to a person accustomed to trading money market instruments, but it confuses a person who is accustomed to trading commodities or stocks. The IMM therefore decided not to quote bill contracts directly in terms of yield. Instead it developed an *index* system in which a bill is quoted at a "price equal to 100.00 minus yield; a bill yield of 8.50 would thus be quoted on the IMM at 91.50. Note that in this system, when yield goes down, the index price rises; and the trader with a long position in futures profits. This conforms to the relationship that prevails in other commodity futures markets, where long positions profit when prices rise and short positions profit when prices fall.

TABLE 14–2
Contract specifications for financial futures and options (actual and proposed) as of December 1982

Contracts	Exchg	Symbl	Trading hours (NY time)	Trading unit	Minimum price fluctuation	Daily price limits†
Financial Futures:						
T bill 90-Day	IMM	TB	9:00–3:00	$1,000,000	.01 (1 basis pt.) = $25/contract	.60 (60 bas. pts.) = $1500/contract
T bill 180-Day*	IMM	?	9:00–3:00	500,000	.01 (1 basis pt.) = 25/contract	.60 (60 bas. pts.) = 1500/contract
T bill 1-yr.*	IMM	?	9:00–3:00	250,000	.01 (1 basis pt.) = 25/contract	.60 (60 bas. pts.) = 1500/contract
CD 90-day	IMM	DC	8:30–3:00	1,000,000	.01 (1 basis pt.) = 25/contract	.80 (80 bas. pts.) = 2000/contract
Eurodollar	IMM	ED	8:30–3:00	1,000,000	.01 (1 basis pt.) = 25/contract	1.00 (100 bas. pts.) = 2500/contract
T note 2-yr.*	CBT	SN	9:00–3:00	400,000	$1/128$ of 1% (one 128th) = 31.25/contract	$96/128$ (3/4 pts.) = 3000/contract
T note 10-yr.	CBT	TY	9:00–3:00	100,000	$1/32$ or 1% (one 32nd) = 31.25/contract	$64/32$ (2 pts.) = 2000/contract
T bond	CBT	YL	9:00–3:00	100,000	$1/32$ of 1% (one 32nd) = 31.25/contract	$64/32$ (2 pts.) = 2000/contract
Ginnie Mae (GNMA)	CBT	G	9:00–3:00	100,000	$1/32$ of 1% (one 32nd) = 31.25/contract	$64/32$ (2 pts.) = 2000/contract
Currencies:						
British pound	IMM	BP	8:30–2:24	£25,000	.0005 (5 pts.) = 12.50/contract	.0500 = 1250/contract
Deutsche mark	IMM	DM	8:30–2:20	125,000DM	.0001 (5 pts.) = 12.50/contract	.0100 = 1250/contract
Swiss franc	IMM	SF	8:30–2:16	125,000SF	.0001 (1 pt.) = 12.50/contract	.0150 = 1875/contract
Japanese yen	IMM	SY	8:30–2:26	12,500,000JY	.000001 (1 pt.) = 12.50/contract	.0001 = 1250/contract
Canadian dollar	IMM	CD	8:30–2:22	100,000CD	.001 (1 pt.) = 10.00/contract	.0075 = 750/contract
Mexican peso	IMM	MP	8:30–2:18	1,000,000MP	.000001 (1 pt.) = 10.00/contract	.00150 = 1500/contract
French franc	IMM	FF	8:30–2:28	250,000Ff	.00005 (5 pts.) = 12.50/contract	.00500 = 1250/contract
Dutch guilder	IMM	DG	8:30–2:30	125,000DG	.0001 (1 pt.) = 12.50/contract	.0100 = 1250/contract
Stock Indexes:						
Value Line	KCBT	VLIC	10:00–4:15	$500 × index	.05 (5/100 of point) = $25/contract	5.00 pts. = 2500/contract
NY Stock Exchange	HYFE	YX	10:00–4:15	500 × index	.05 (5/100 of point) = 25/contract	(None)
Standard & Poor's	IOM	SP	10:00–4:15	500 × index	.05 (5/100 of point) = 25/contract	3.00 pts. = 1500/contract
Options:						
T bond	CBOE	YAA	9:00–3:00	$20,000	$1/32$ of 1% (one 32nd) = $6.25/contract	(None)
T bond	CBOE	YBA	9:00–3:00	100,000	$1/32$ of 1% (one 32nd) = 31.25/contract	(None)
GNMA*	CBOE	GMX	9:00–3:00	100,000	$1/32$ of 1% (one 32nd) = 31.25/contract	(None)
13-Week bill	AMEX	OTB	9:00–3:00	200,000	.01% (one basis pt.) = 5.00/contract	(None)
26-Week bill*	AMEX	OTC	9:00–3:00	100,000	.01% (one basis pt.) = 5.00/contract	(None)
T note	AMEX	OOA-Z	9:00–3:00	20,000	$1/32$ of 1% (one 32nd) = 6.25/contract	(None)
T-bond futures	CBT	CG&PG	9:00–3:00	100,000	$1/64$ of 1% (one 64th) = 15.625/contract	$128/64$ (2 pts.) = 2000/contract

Last day of trading	Initial margins*	Contracts
bills { The business day preceding the first day of the contract month on which a 13-week Treasury bill is issued and a one-year bill has thirteen weeks remaining.	$2500	T bill 90-day
	2500	T bill 180-day*
	2500	T bill 1-yr*
CDs { The business day preceding the last business day of the contract month.	2500	CD 90-day
The second London business day preceding the third Wednesday of the contract month.	2500	Eurodollar
notes bonds GNMAs { The business day at least seven business days prior to the last day of the contract month.	3000	T note 10-yr.
	3000	T note 2-yr.*
	3000	T-bond
	3000	Ginnie Mae (GNMA)
	$1500	British pound
	1500	Deutsche mark
	2000	Swiss franc
all curriencies { Two business days before the 3rd Wednesday of each contract month.	1500	Japanese yen
	1500	Canadian dollar
	4000	Mexican peso
	1200	French franc
	1200	Dutch guilder
Last business day of contract month.	$6500	Value Line
Business day prior to last business day in contract month.	2500	NY Stock Exchange
Third Thursday of contract month.	6500	Standard & Poor's
Third Friday of the option month.	(All options must be paid for in cash. Option writes are margined differently.)	T bond
Third Friday of the option month.		T bond
Friday preceding the second Wednesday of contract month.		GNMA*
Third Friday of the option month.		13-Week bill
Third Friday of the option month.		26-Week bill*
Third Friday of the option month.		T note
The last Friday which precedes by five business days the futures' first notice day.		T-Bond futures

* Tenatively scheduled for 1983 approval and/or initial trading (or, in the case of the year bill futures, revitalization).
† Subject to change by the CFTC and/or Exchange.
Source: **Donaldson, Lufkin & Jenrette.** The information set forth above has been obtained from sources believed to be reliable; however, we make no representations as to its accuracy.

Price fluctuations

Price fluctuations on bill futures are in multiples of an 01, one basis point. Because the contract is for delivery of 90-day bills, each 01 is worth $25.

The maximum price fluctuation permitted in any one day is 60 basis points above or below the preceding day's settling price.[1] However, if on two successive days, a contract closes at the normal daily limit in the same direction (not necessarily the same contract month on both days), an expanded daily price limit goes into effect: On the third day the daily price limit on all contract months goes to 150% of the normal daily limit. If on that day any contract month closes at its expanded daily price limit and in the same direction as the preceding daily limit price change, the daily price limit expands to 200% of the normal daily price limit and remains there as long as any contract month closes at this expanded daily price limit.

Clearing function of the IMM

Whenever a trade occurs on the IMM, there must be a buyer and an offsetting seller. Each trader's contractual obligation, however, is not to his counterpart in the trade but to the IMM. The IMM stands between the principals in a trade; it is the opposite side of every trade effected on the exchange, even though it never itself assumes any net position long or short in bill futures. The IMM's purpose in acting as what might be called a supervisory *clearing house* is to guarantee the fiscal integrity of every trade made on the exchange.

Margin

An important part of the IMM's job is to oversee the enforcement of margin requirements and the monetary transfers they require. When a trader buys a contract on the IMM, he does not pay for it immediately, and if he sells a contract, he does not receive payment immediately. Both the buyer and the seller, however, must put up *margin*. Currently the minimum margin required by the IMM is $1,000 per bill contract on an outright position. On a special position it is less. (A brokerage house through which an individual trader deals may require more.)

When a trader assumes a long or short position, he will incur gains and losses each day thereafter as price fluctuates. The amount of each day's gain (loss) is added to (subtracted from) his margin account at the

---

[1] The *settling price* is the average of the highest and lowest prices at which trades occur during the last minute of trading.

end of the day. For example, if a trader bought a contract at 92.50 and the settling price at the end of the day on that contract were 99.20, he would have incurred a loss equal to $750 (30 basis points times $25), and that money would be subtracted by his broker from his margin account. Some other trader would necessarily have made an equal and offsetting gain, and money equal to the amount of that gain would be added to his margin account. This adding and subtracting is done through the IMM, which collects money from brokers whose clients have incurred losses and transfers it to brokers whose clients have earned profits. Because margin balances are adjusted through the IMM at the end of each business day, a trader starts each day having realized, through additions to or deductions from his margin account, the net gain or loss he has made on his position since he established it. The IMM margin system converts on a daily basis what would be *paper* gains and losses into *realized* gains and losses.

If the balance in a trader's margin account falls below the current *maintenance margin* limit, which is less than the initial margin, he must immediately deposit additional funds in this account to bring it back to $2,500. If he fails to do so, his broker is required to close out his position. If, alternatively, a trader has earned profits and his margin account has therefore risen above $2,500 he may withdraw the excess margin.

The IMM's requirements with respect to margin maintenance guarantee that a trader's losses on a given day are unlikely to significantly exceed the amount in his margin account and thus make it improbable that any investor would end up in a position of being unable to honor a contract he had made either by liquidating his position through an offsetting trade or by making or taking delivery of securities.

If a trader takes offsetting long and short positions in the two contracts closest to maturity, he is required to put up only $400 of margin, and the minimum margin he must maintain is $200. On offsetting long and short positions in contracts farther out on the maturity spectrum, the trader must maintain margin equal to any loss he has incurred on that position. If there is none, he need not put up any margin.

Collateral in the form of securities may be used as margin so that the effective cost of putting up margin can be reduced to close to zero.

End of trading

Trading in a bill futures contract terminates in the week of the delivery month on the second business day following the weekly auction of the 3-month bill, which is a reopening of the old year bill. This would normally be a Wednesday. Settlement of futures contracts outstanding at the time trading is terminated is made on the following day, Thursday. This is also the day on which settlement is made on the 3-month cash bill just auctioned. Thus there are always new 3-month bills available for delivery on the day an outstanding future contract is settled.

Buyers of futures contracts do not normally take delivery, but it can be done.[2] The buyer who wants to take delivery instructs the IMM that he wants delivery to be made at a particular Chicago bank. The IMM then instructs the seller's bank to make delivery there, and delivery is affected against payment in Fed funds.

Commissions

There used to be a minimum commission on a purchase or sale of bill futures. This was phased out with the switch to negotiated commissions, and the rates charged now vary from one brokerage house to another. Currently commissions charged are much higher on small trades than on large trades.

How the market is made

The market in cash bills, as noted in Chapter 13, is made by dealers in geographically disperse institutions who keep in contact through direct phone lines and through the brokers, and who are required to quote bid and asked prices to each other and to retail.

In bill futures, in contrast, all trades are made during regular trading hours in the bill pit on the floor of the CME in Chicago; the futures market is thus a single central market. Traders in the bill pit make their bids and offers known by crying them out. In the pit, all that is heard is the highest bid and the lowest offer. Anyone with a lower bid or higher offer remains silent until the market moves to his level. The face-to-face market in the bill pit is akin to the composite market that all the dealers in cash bills would make if they were in the same physical place.

There are three types of traders in the bill pit. First, there are employees of brokerage houses who execute trades for retail customers and for the brokerage house's own account. Many of these brokers also trade for their own accounts; a broker who does this is required to execute customer business before dealing for his own account. The second type of trader in the pit is the *"deck holder."* Deck holders sell a service to brokers; they handle limit orders (e.g., customer orders to buy at 20 when the market is at 22) and stop-loss orders (a customer orders to sell if price falls to a certain level). A deck holder files all orders given to him

---

[2] During 1981 the total open interest (contracts outstanding) in all bill futures contracts fluctuated from a single-day low of 28,001 to a single-day high of 49,065. Over the year 5,631,290 contracts were traded but delivery was made on only 5,183 contracts.

by brokers according to price and then, as the market moves, executes those orders he can. Finally, there are private persons (*locals*) in the pit who trade for their own account on an outright speculative basis or more often on a spread basis; an individual who wants to trade bill futures on the CME floor can do so by buying a seat on the exchange.

A retail customer or dealer who calls another dealer in cash bills and gets a quote 65–64 can say to the dealer, "You sold bills at 64." He can't do that in the futures market. He can call a broker on the floor and get information on the price at which the last trade occurred and on what bids and offers currently are. But if he asks the broker to execute an order at the current bid or asked price, he can't be sure that the broker will be able to. In a fast market, the five yards from the broker's phone to the pit can be a long way, and the market may have moved by the time the broker gets there. Thus a retail customer has to deal in a slightly different way with a broker in the futures market than he does with a dealer in the cash market if he wants to get orders in size executed.

Market participants

The principal participants in futures markets are speculators, hedgers, arbitrageurs, and spreaders. About speculators there is little need for explanation: These individuals buy or sell futures contracts in the hope of gain. When futures prices rise or fall sharply, to the dismay of one group or another, the blame is often placed incorrectly on speculators. Actually these much maligned individuals, who statistics show lose money more often than not, perform a function essential to any futures market; they assume risks that others—namely hedgers—seek to shed.

HEDGING

A portfolio manager who sells bill futures to limit the risk on a long position in bills and a portfolio manager who buys bill futures to lock in a rate at which he can invest an anticipated cash inflow are both managing risk by *hedging. To hedge using financial futures is to assume a position in futures equal and opposite to an existing or anticipated position, which may be short or long, in cash or cash securities.*

Delivery

An important point to note about hedging through the purchase or sale of either commodity or financial futures contracts is that delivery need not be and usually is not made or taken in connection with a hedge. Normally, hedges and speculative positions as well are closed out by making an offsetting trade in the same contract. Some newer futures contracts (Euro and stock index contracts) do away with delivery by specifying cash settlement.

The hedger attempts to put himself in a position where any loss he incurs on his cash position in the commodity (e.g., he is long and price in the cash market drops) will be offset by an equal gain on his futures position. He can do this by establishing a position in futures and later closing it out. The speculator who neither owns nor desires to own the underlying commodity can also realize whatever gain or loss he makes on his speculation simply by closing out his futures position.

If a hedger, speculator, or other futures market participant wants to make or take delivery, he is, in most markets, free to do so. A trader who maintains an open position in such a market at the expiration of a futures contract must settle by making or taking delivery.

A perfect hedge

Consider an investor who has money to invest for three months and is unwilling to assume market risk. He can (1) buy a 3-month bill and allow it to mature or (2) buy a 6-month bill and sell a bill futures contract expiring 3 months hence. If he does the latter, i.e., buys the 6-month bill and hedges his resulting future long position in a 3-month bill, he will have succeeded in eliminating *all* market risk from his position in the 6-month bill, even though he will hold it for only 3 months. A hedge established using a futures contract whose expiration date precisely fits the hedger's time horizon and on which the deliverable instrument corresponds to the instrument being hedged is a *perfect hedge*.

Imperfect hedges

In practice, *hedges are common but perfect hedges are rare*. The reason is that the standardization of futures contracts required for them to be actively traded and to have liquidity is such that the hedger is normally unable to find a futures position that will give him a perfect offset to his position in the cash market. He has to settle, if you will, for a ready-made rather than a tailor-made suit, and he willingly does so for good reasons: the ability to strike a trade, the liquidity of the position he assumes, and the protection against risk of default that the futures contract offers him.

Typically, a hedger using financial futures will find that the hedge he establishes is *imperfect* for one or both of two reasons: (1) the contract's expiration date does not precisely match the time horizon in which he anticipates dealing, e.g., he sells bill futures against a position in the deliverable bill which he intends to liquidate before the futures contract expires; or (2) he has or anticipates acquiring a position in some instrument other than the deliverable security, e.g., he sells T bill futures to hedge an intended sale of 3-month CDs or an anticipated short-term borrowing need. Hedging a cash position in one security by assuming a futures position in a different but similar security is known as a *cross hedge.*

Whenever a market participant undertakes a cross hedge to control risk in a speculative position—long or short—in cash or cash securities, the precise outcome of that hedge is uncertain. How closely his gain (loss) on his futures position will track his loss (gain) on his position in cash or the cash security will depend on how the *spread* (*basis* in commodity jargon) between the rate on the futures contract and that on the cash instrument hedged changes from the time he puts on the hedge until he takes it off.

A perfect long hedge

To illustrate hedging, we will consider a few examples. First, a *perfect long hedge.* Suppose that an investor's cash-flow projections tell him that he will have a lot of cash to invest short term in the future; that is, he is going to be *long* investable cash. He can wait to invest until he gets the cash and take the then prevailing rate, or as soon as his projections tell him how much cash he will have, he can lock in a lending rate by buying bill futures.

Table 14–2 illustrates this. We assume that our investor knows in June that he will have $10 million of 3-month money to invest in September and that when September arrives he will invest that money in bills. In June, the September bill contract is trading at 10.50. If our investor buys 10 of these contracts, he will earn 10.50 on the money he invests in September, regardless of the rate at which the cash 3-month bill is then trading.

One way he could get the 10.50 rate would be to take delivery in September of the bills he purchased at 10.50. But to see the nature of the hedge, we assume that, in September when his cash comes in, he closes out his futures position and buys cash bills.

As the September contract approaches maturity, it must trade at a yield close to and eventually equal to the rate at which the 3-month cash bill is trading. If a divergence existed between these two rates as trading in the contract terminated, potential for a profitable arbitrage would exist. For example, if, a few days before the September bill contract matured, it was trading at a much higher yield than the cash bill, traders would buy the contract, sell cash bills on a *when issued* basis (i.e., after the bill auction but before settlement), take delivery in Chicago to cover their short position in the cash bill, and profit on the transaction.[3]

In Outcome 1 (Table 14–3), we assume that, as the September contract matures, the 91-day cash bill trades at 10.20 and the futures contract consequently also trades at 10.20. At this time, our investor sells his September contracts and buys the cash 3-month bill. He purchases his futures contracts at 10.50 and sells them at 10.20, a lower rate. Since the delivery value of the contracts is higher the lower the yield at which they trade, our investor makes (Table 14–3) a $7,500 profit on his futures transaction.

When his profit on futures is deducted from the price at which he buys cash bills, he ends up paying an effective price for these bills that is $7,500 less than the actual price he pays. And this lower effective price implies that the yield he will earn on his investment is not 10.20, the rate at which he buys *cash bills,* but 10.50, the rate at which he bought bill futures.

Because the prevailing yield at which the cash 3-month bill was trading in September was lower than the rate at which our investor bought bill futures in June, he made money by engaging in a long hedge; that is, he earned a higher yield than he would have had he not hedged.

There is, however, a counterpart to this. As Outcome 2 in Table 14–2 shows, if in September the cash 3-month bill were trading at 10.80, our investor would have lost so many dollars on his hedge that he would have earned only 10.50 on the money he invested.

Calculating in basis points. It is instructive to work out a hedge example in dollars and cents. However, it is quicker to do it in terms of basis points earned and lost . In our example, the investor buys September contracts at 10.50 and, according to Outcome 1, sells them at 10.20. On this transaction, he earns on each contract for $1 million of bills 30 90-day basis points. By buying the 3-month bill at 10.20 and maturing it, he earns 1020 90-day *basis points* per $1 million of bills purchased. So *net* he earns 1050 90-day basis points per $1 million of bills purchased, a yield of 10.50 over 90 days.

Actually, the basis points earned on the cash bill are 91-day basis points, and those earned on the futures contract are 90-day basis points. This difference, however, is not reflected in the numbers in Table 14–3 because it affects yield earned only beyond the third decimal point.

The example we presented was a *perfect hedge* because our investor bought a futures contract for precisely the instrument and precisely the

---

[3] In practice, a maturing bill futures contract will trade during the last few days of its life at a yield a few basis points higher than the deliverable cash bill. The difference reflects the extra commission and other transaction costs that an investor would incur if he bought bill futures and took delivery instead of purchasing 3-month bills in the cash market.

TABLE 14–3
A long hedge in T bill futures for bills with a $10 million face value

Step 1 (Thursday, third week of June): Purchase 10 September bill contracts at 10.50.
Put up security deposit.
Pay roundturn commission.
Step 2 (Wednesday, third week of September): Sell 10 futures contracts; buy cash bills.

Outcome 1: Cash 91-day bill trading at 10.20.
Sell September contracts at 10.20.

Delivery value of futures at sale............	$ 9,745,000
−Delivery value of futures at purchase	9,737,500
Profit on futures transactions	$ 7,500
Buy 91-day cash bills at 10.20	
Purchase price of cash bills...............	$ 9,742,167
−Profit on futures transactions............	7,500
Effective price of 91-day bills.............	$ 9,734,667
Calculate effective discount at which bills are purchased:	
Face value............................	$10,000,000
−Effective purchase price	9,734,667
Discount at purchase	$ 265,333

Calculate effective discount rate, d, at which cash bills are purchased

$$d = \frac{D \times (360)}{F \times (91)} = \frac{\$265,333 \times (360)}{\$10,000,000 \times (91)}$$
$$= 0.1050$$
$$= 10.50\%$$

Outcome 2: Cash 91-day bill trading at 10.80.
Sell September contracts at 10.80.

Delivery value of futures at sale............	$ 9,730,000
−Delivery value of futures at purchase	9,737,500
Loss on futures transaction...............	$ (7,500)
Buy 91-day cash bills at 10.80.	
Purchase price of cash bills...............	$ 9,727,000
+Loss on futures transaction	7,500
Effective price of 91-day bills.............	$ 9,734,500
Calculate effective discount at which bills are purchased:	
Face value............................	$10,000,000
−Effective purchase price	9,734,500
Discount at purchase	$ 265,500

Calculate effective discount rate d at which cash bills are purchased.

$$d = \frac{D \times (360)}{F \times (91)} = \frac{\$265,500 \times (360)}{\$10,000,000 \times (91)}$$
$$= 0.1050$$
$$= 10.50\%$$

maturity in which he planned to invest. In the case of a perfect hedge, the investor eliminates *all* risk.

Speculating on spread variation. Most investors who use bill futures to hedge an anticipated long position in cash will find that the hedge they establish is *imperfect* for one or both of two reasons:

1. No futures contract or series of contracts precisely matches their projected investment period.
2. They anticipate investing in some money market instrument other than a Treasury bill, e.g., commercial paper or bankers' acceptances.

When a hedge is imperfect, the hedger does not eliminate *all* risk. Instead, he shifts the nature of his speculation from *rate level* speculation to speculation on *spread variation*. A commodities trader would call the latter *basis risk*.

To illustrate, we return to our example and now suppose that our investor's cash inflow will occur one month *before* the June contract expires and that, in closing out his hedge, he will sell the June contract one month before it expires and simultaneously buy the new cash bill. At the time our investor sells his futures contract, he will be selling the right to take delivery 1 month hence of the then 4-month bill, while he will be buying a 3-month bill. Typically, some spread exists between the rates yielded by the 3- and 4-month bills; the futures contract, because of arbitrage, should trade nearer the 4-month than the 3-month rate.

The arbitrage that causes this rate relationship is dual. If the futures contract yielded *less than* the 4-month bill 1 month before it expired, a profit could be made by buying that bill, selling a futures contract, and then unwinding this arbitrage when the futures contract expired. Note that, at that time, the rate on the futures contract and the rate on the deliverable bill must be equal because they are both prices for next-day delivery of the same cash bill. This arbitrage would tend to lower the yield on the cash bill and to raise the yield on the futures contract, thereby eliminating the discrepancy between rates on these instruments. If, alternatively, the rate on the futures contract exceeded that on the 4-month bill, it would be profitable to buy the futures contract and short the cash bill—an arbitrage that would also tend to close the divergence between these two rates. The profitability of these arbitrages depends, in the first instance, on the repo rate and, in the second, on the reverse rate. Since the relationship of these rates to bill rates varies, it is uncertain how close the futures contract 1 month from maturity will trade to the 4-month bill.

To continue our example, we assume that, at the time our investor enters his hedge, the yield curve is upward sloping and the spread between the 3- and 4-month bills is 10 basis points. Assuming that (1) there is no change in that spread and (2) the futures contract trades 1 month before expiration at a rate equal to the rate on the 4-month bill, the rate our investor will actually earn as a result of his hedge will be 10.40: the 10.50 rate at which he bought the futures contract *minus* the 10 basis point spread between the rate at which he sold it and the rate on the new 3-month bill. Also, so long as our two spread assumptions hold, this result will occur whether the investor sells his futures contract at a low yield (Outcome 1, Table 14–2) or at a high yield (Outcome 2, Table 14–2).

In practice, spreads, like rate levels, are not written in stone; they change. What our investor cares about is what happens to the spread between the rate at which he sells his futures contract and the rate on the new 3-month bill. If this spread *widens* by 10 basis points from the level assumed above, i.e., from 10 to 20 basis points, the yield our investor earns will *decrease* by a like amount from 10.50 to 10.30. If, alternatively, the spread *narrows* by 10 basis points, i.e., from 10 basis points to 0, the yield he earns will rise by a like amount, from 10.50 to 10.60.

To sum up, an investor who hedges a future long position in cash must take spread relationships into account in estimating the yield he will earn as a result of his hedge. These relationships, however, are subject to variation. Therefore, the investor cannot know with certainty what return an imperfect hedge will yield, and it is in that sense that *a hedger shifts his risk from rate level speculation to speculation on spread (or basis) variation.*

Earlier we said that a second reason a long hedge is likely to be imperfect is that the investor who hedges intends to buy an instrument other than a T bill. Suppose the investor in our example intended to buy a 3-month CD and that CDs were trading, at the time he bought his futures contract, at a 30-basis-point spread to bills. Then, in establishing a long hedge, our investor would be exchanging a natural speculative position on rate levels (generated by his anticipated cash inflow) for a speculation on the spread x months hence between either (1) the rates on cash 3-month bills and cash 3-month CDs, or (2) the rates on an unexpired bill futures contract and cash 3-month CDs.

When a short futures position in one instrument (e.g., bills) is used to hedge a long position in some *other* instrument (e.g., CDs), the hedge is called a *cross hedge.*

Short hedges

The bill futures market can also be used to hedge either a long position in money market securities or a future borrowing need. To illustrate, consider a perfect *short* hedge.

Suppose that an investor who has money to invest for 3 months is unwilling to accept any market risk. We assume that a 6-month bill yields more than a 3-month bill and that the 6-month bill 3 months hence will be the 3-month bill deliverable when the nearest futures contract expires. In the absence of a futures market, our investor would have no choice but to buy the 3-month bill and allow it to mature. However, given the futures market, he should investigate the relationship among the rates on the 3-month bill, the 6-month bill, and the nearest futures contract. This relationship may be such that, without incurring market risk, he could earn more by buying the 6-month bill and selling the nearest futures contract than by buying and "maturing" the cash 3-month bill. Note that buying the 6-month bill and selling the nearest futures contract against it converts this bill into a 3-month bill, but the return on that bill will differ from that on the 3-month cash bill.

Most short hedges are *imperfect* for one or both of the same reasons that apply to long hedges: (1) a discrepancy exists between the period over which the hedge is needed and the life of any one or series of futures contracts; and (2) the instrument or borrowing need being hedged does not correspond to the instrument traded in the futures market.

Examples of imperfect hedges are easy to find:

1. Because of rate expectations, an investor wants to swap out of a long bill into a shorter bill, but for tax or other reasons he prefers not to do the swap in the cash market. He can obtain essentially the same result by selling bill futures against the long cash bill, but there is a maturity mismatch.
2. An investor or dealer sells bill futures to hedge a long position in BAs against a rise in interest rates.
3. A corporation sells bill futures to hedge an anticipated need to borrow short term from its bank.

In each of these cases, the outcome of the hedge will depend on what happens to spread relationships. Thus, the short hedger, like the long hedger, is shifting his risk from rate level speculation to speculation on spread (basis) variation.

A cross hedge: Bill futures against prime

As an example of a cross hedge, consider a corporate treasurer who, on October 1, 1979, sold $5 million of the March bill futures contract to hedge the cost of a $5 million short-term bank loan that he expected to take down in early February 1980. At the date he puts on his hedge, the March 90-day bill contract is selling at 90.34, which corresponds to a yield of 9.66, and the prime rate is 13.25%. On February 5, 1980, he closes out his position in futures and borrows $5 million from his bank. At that time, the futures contract is selling at 87.86, which corresponds to a 12.14 yield, and prime is 15.25%.

What has the hedger accomplished? A great deal. During the time his hedge was on, the prime rate rose by 200 basis points, and the rate on the March bill futures contract rose by 262 basis points. Because it was politically difficult for the banks to raise prime to a level corresponding to their marginal cost of funds, the spread between the rate on the March contract and the prime rate actually narrowed, and the $32,750 profit the hedger made unwinding his position in futures actually *exceeded* the extra cost he incurred in borrowing $5 million for 90 days because of the 200-basis-point jump in the prime rate.[4]

A futures market participant who engages in a cross hedge *shifts* his risk from a speculation on a rate or price level to a *speculation on a spread.* He does *not* eliminate risk; instead, he *shifts* the nature of the risk he assumes. Normally he also reduces the amount of risk he assumes because *he shifts the focus of his speculation from a highly variable rate or price level to a less variable spread;* as a commodities trader would say, he assumes *basis risk.*

Many would-be hedgers do not grasp this crucial point in part because hedging is frequently described as a form of insurance, which it is not. A person buying insurance sheds a risk by paying an insurer to accept that risk; the insurer is able to do this because it pools many independent risks, e.g., the risks of Jones, Smith, etc., each dying. Reducing risk through pooling, the principle on which insurance works, has nothing to do with hedging. The hedger eliminates risk arising from a speculative position in cash or cash securities by taking an offsetting position in futures. Moreover, because the fit between his hedge and the position he is hedging is imperfect, by hedging he assumes a new risk; namely, he speculates on the rate spread between the cash and the futures instruments.

Imaginative hedging strategies

We have defined hedging as assuming a position in futures equal and opposite to an existing or anticipated position, which may be negative or positive, in cash or cash instruments. As our observation that hedging

---

[4] To state the precise before and after values of the spread on which the hedger is speculating, one must convert the bill rate, which is quoted on a discount basis, to a simple interest basis and adjust the prime rate to account for the cost of holding compensating balances. Assuming a 20 percent balance requirement, the spread between the two rates was 666 basis points at the beginning of the hedge and 648 at the end. For the calculations involved, see Marcia Stigum and John Mann, *Money Market Calculations* (Homewood, Ill.: Dow Jones-Irwin, 1981). Had the borrower negotiated a smaller and currently more typical balance requirement, the rise in the spread between the two would have been even greater.

involves speculation on a spread suggests, this definition does *not* imply that the best way to hedge a cash position is necessarily to sell (buy) a futures contract that most nearly corresponds in maturity to the long (short) position being hedged.

Consider, again, the example of a corporate treasurer who knows he must borrow several months hence. Suppose he not only fears that the Fed might tighten but believes circumstances are such that, if the Fed does, the yield curve will steepen. Given this, his best hedge would be to sell, not the futures contract maturing several months hence when he must borrow, but a longer contract, because the latter would lose more value than a nearby contract if the eventuality he feared actually occurred—namely, tightening by the Fed and a consequent steepening of the yield curve.

For a second example of imaginative hedging, consider an investor who will be long cash three months hence and wants to invest then in the 2-year maturity range. The yield curve is inverted; the investor fears that the Fed might ease shortly and believes that, if it does, the yield curve will flatten. His best hedge is not to buy a *strip* of eight consecutive futures contracts, i.e., a "synthetic 2-year note," but rather to buy eight of some long futures contract. If his fears are realized, the value of a long contract will rise more than that of shorter contracts.

Speculation on spread variation

To say that speculation on spread variation arises from "imperfect" hedges suggests that it is unfortunate that there are insufficient numbers and types of futures contracts to eliminate all risk by entering a perfect hedge. This view corresponds with the academic view of hedging, which is that the purpose of hedging is to eliminate price risk not to create an opportunity to profit from a different sort of speculation. In textbooks, hedging is viewed as a form of insurance which has a cost that, like the electric bill, is part of normal business operating expenses.

For an investor or borrower to hedge a position—negative or positive—in cash does in fact insulate his business activity from price level speculation. However, it also *retains* for him the *opportunity to speculate on spread (basis) variation*. Moreover, as our examples suggest, such speculation can become a source of profit as opposed to a cost. In this respect, two comments are important. First, speculation on spread variation did not arise in the money and bond markets after and as a result of the introduction of trading in financial futures. Quite the contrary, it has long been common. A dealer or investor who, in anticipation of a fall in rates, buys a 10-year Treasury bond and simultaneously shorts—to minimize risk—an 8-year issue is doing a *bull market arbitrage* that is nothing more or less than speculating on spread variation. Many other transactions commonly done by dealers and investors are a form of speculation on a spread. What the introduction of futures trading did was to provide a vastly more efficient and less costly mechanism for taking forward positions, long and short, and a liquid market in which such forward positions could be traded.

A second important point is that the use of hedging to minimize price level speculation while simultaneously speculating on spread variation is not an innovation fathered by money market participants. Firms that produce, process, or use commodities for which futures markets exist have long understood that speculation on spread, or basis, is a potential source of profit, and they have sought to profit from it.

Once speculation on spreads is viewed as a potential profit center, it becomes clear that hedging should not be viewed as an automatic and thoughtless operation, e.g., an investor has money coming in three months hence so he buys the most nearly corresponding futures contract. Instead, hedging is an intricate activity. To succeed at it, the participant should know what spreads have been historically and what factors cause them to change. In establishing a hedge, he should also try to predict how events are most likely to affect the spreads involved in his hedge. Finally, if the unanticipated occurs, he must be prepared to alter his hedge.

The suggestion that investors, dealers, and borrowers should consider hedging as a form of potentially profitable speculation is not inconsistent with the suggestion that hedging should be used as a tool to manage risk. Any institution that holds a portfolio or anticipates borrowing is inescapably speculating on changes in rate level, since it is impossible to be long or short cash and do otherwise. To hedge and thus speculate on spread variation is to trade one form of speculation (on a *naked* long or short position) for another, typically *less risky,* form.

Arbitrage

Controlling the risk associated with an actual or anticipated position in cash or cash securities by hedging is one use to which bond and money market participants put futures contracts. Another is as a tool for effecting *arbitrages.* Economists, who have a fixation for *certain* outcomes, long ago defined an arbitrage as a transaction in which the arbitrageur simultaneously buys something at one price in one market and resells it at a higher price in another market (or some more complicated variation on this theme). Such an arbitrage locks in a *certain* profit for the arbitrageur. It also works, through its effect on supply and demand in different markets, to bring prices in these markets into line—their being out of line is the basis for the certain profit earned by the arbitrageur on his trade.

Opportunities for highly profitable, riskless arbitrages occur only infrequently in the real world, which is characterized by instantaneous communications between different markets. Yet street people constantly talk about doing arbitrages or, as they are wont to call them, *arbs*. To a street person, an arbitrage involves taking two offsetting positions, e.g., a long and a short position in cash securities or in cash securities and futures contracts, such that, if the spread between the rates at which the securities involved trade moves in an anticipated direction, the arbitrageur will be able to close out his long and short positions at a profit.

Traders put on arbitrages because they believe that spreads are out of line with what they should be now or with what they must converge to in the future. Thus, street arbitrages are a form of speculation on a spread, one in which the street has long engaged. The use of arbitrage to describe such speculation is not wholly inappropriate, however much economists may protest. Normally, such arbitrages involve a highly favorable gamble, that is, one on which the odds strongly favor the spread moving in the direction in which the arbitrageur bets it will. Moreover, because of this, the street's "risk arbitrages," like the economists certain ones, work to pull prices into a rational pattern. The one crucial difference is that the prices being pulled into line are often prices of different instruments or different maturities of the same instrument rather than prices of the same instrument traded in different markets.

The opening of markets for financial futures created a new set of instruments whose prices could be arbitraged, and street traders now frequently arbitrage between cash instruments and futures contracts and between different futures contracts. Because of the newness of the futures markets, the constant addition of new contracts and development of new strategies, and the restrictions (external and self-imposed) on the use of futures by many potential market participants, futures markets have offered arbitrageurs substantial profit opportunities. The consequent high level of arbitrage has been productive in two senses: It has added liquidity to futures markets, and it has ensured that various prices, e.g., that between a futures contract and the corresponding deliverable security, bear a reasonable relationship to each other.

Spreading

A hedger is typically shifting his risk from a speculation on rate levels to a speculation on spread variation. A speculator with no position in cash or cash securities to hedge can also speculate on spread variation. Such speculation, which is referred to as *spreading,* calls for the trader to short one contract and go long in a neighboring contract on the expectation that the spread between the two contracts will either narrow or widen. Here's an example. In normal markets, the yield curve is steep at its base and then gradually flattens. Suppose, for illustration, that, in the futures market, the yield curve has the shape pictured in Figure 14–2. The yield spread between the two contracts nearest maturity is 40 basis points; there are 30 basis points between the second and third contracts,

FIGURE 14–2
Yields on bill futures contracts expiring in 3 to 15 months

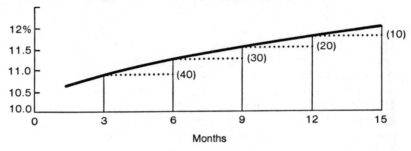

20 between the third and fourth contracts, and 10 between the fourth and fifth contracts. The spreader assumes that, as the more distant contracts approach maturity, spreads between them will widen. Given this expectation, he might short the contract maturing in 12 months and buy the contract maturing in 9 months. If, over the next 6 months, the spread between these contracts widened from 20 to 40 basis points, he would be able to close out his position at a 20-basis-point profit.

He earns a profit because, if the spread widens, the price of the futures contract in which he is long will rise in value relative to that in which he is short. Whether yields rise or fall over the holding period is immaterial to whether he profits or not. What counts is that the spread widens. His principal risk of loss is thus that the yield curve will flatten so dramatically that the spread between the contracts in which he is long and short will narrow rather than widen.

Spread traders are an important and permanent component of futures pits. A spreader who sees selling in the March contract but knows that there is a bid in the Junes will buy the Marches, sell the Junes, wait until the pressure is off the Marches, and then turn the position around. Spreaders account for over half of all trading in the longer contracts. In carrying out operations of the above sort, spreaders perform an important market function—providing liquidity to the longer contracts.

A cash-and-carry trade: The implied repo rate

Whereas when bill futures were first introduced, traders spent a lot of time scratching their heads wondering what to do with the new contracts, today there seems to be no end to the number of imaginative new strategies traders can devise for using this contract; moreover, the advent of new options contracts promises to accelerate the rate at which new strategies are devised. Since a description of every bill futures strategy that traders have pursued with success would fill a book, we limit our further examples to two; the implied-repo-rate trade, which was extremely popular several years ago when rates made it profitable, and an unlevered cash-and-carry trade, which offered cash investors a yield pickup in the fall of 1982. As these examples and our bonds futures examples suggest, the constantly changing structure of rates—among different instruments and along the yield curve—constantly alters the set of futures trades that currently offer traders profits.

A trade that is done in bill futures in huge volume when rates are right and that tends to link rates on cash and futures bills is one that has been dubbed the *cash-and-carry trade*. This trade could be done by many investors, but it is most commonly done by professional speculators and large dealers; today every dealer shop has someone who watches the relationship among cash, futures, and term RP rates and puts on this trade in size whenever that relationship makes the trade profitable.

For a levered investor, an attractive tactic is to buy a cash bill, finance it with term RP, and cover the rate risk on the resulting tail by selling that tail in the futures market.[5] Whether doing so will be profitable depends on the relationship among the term RP rate, the rate on the long cash bill, and the futures rate. There must be some term RP rate at which a dealer who does the above transaction will just break even; this breakeven rate has been dubbed the *implied repo rate*. Whenever the prevailing RP rate is less than the implied repo rate, putting on a cash-and-carry trade yields a profit.

To illustrate this trade, we use rates that prevailed in the market in the fall of 1982. On October 28, 1982, the 3/24/83 bill, which was the deliverable bill for the December 1982 bill futures contract, was trading at 8.26. On the same day the December bill contract, which expired 56 days hence, was trading at 8.28.

The repo rate is an add-on, 360-day rate. Thus to calculate the implied repo rate on a cash-and-carry trade based on the above cash and futures rates, one must calculate the holding period yield (HPY) on a 360-day basis that an investor could have earned if he had bought the 3/24/83 bill at 8.26 and simultaneously sold that bill at 8.28 for delivery 56 days hence in the futures market.

That calculation, worked out in Table 14–4, shows that holding period yield—the implied or breakeven repo rate—was 8.51.

Had the actual term repo rate for a 56-day repo been 8.25 on October

---

[5] The concept of tails and how they are created was discussed on pp. 298–301.

TABLE 14–4
Calculating the implied repo rate which equals holding period yield earned on a 360-day basis on the bill*

Step 1 On 10/28/82 purchase $1 million of the 3/24/83 bill at 8.26%.

$$\text{Purchase price} = (\$1,000,000)(.0826)\left(\frac{147}{360}\right)$$
$$= \$966,271.67$$

Step 2 On 10/28/82 simultaneously sell the December 1982 bill futures contract at 91.72, which corresponds to a yield of 8.28%.

$$\text{Sale price} = (\$1,000,000)(.0828)\left(\frac{91}{360}\right)$$
$$= \$979,070.00$$

Step 3 Calculate holding period yield (HPY), which equals the implied repo rate.

$$\text{HPY} = \text{Implied RP rate} = \left(\frac{\text{Sale price} - \text{Purchase price}}{\text{Purchase price}}\right)\left(\frac{\text{Annualization}}{\text{factor}}\right)$$

$$= \left(\frac{\$979,070.00 - \$966,271.67}{\$966,271.67}\right)\left(\frac{360}{56}\right)$$

$$= .0851 = 8.51\%$$

* For a simple formula for calculating the implied repo rate on a bill trade, see Stigum and Mann, *Money Market Calculations*, pp. 161–66.

28, 1982, then by buying the 3/24/83 bill, financing it for 56 days at 8.25, and selling the resulting tail in the futures market at 8.28, a trader could have picked up $3,908.03 per $10 million of the trade he put on (Table 14–5).

TABLE 14–5
Calculating the profit on a $10 million cash-and-carry trade if rates were those in Table 14–4 and the term repo rate was 8.25%

A: Formula

Profit = (HPY − term RP rate)(Amount invested)(Fraction of year invested)

B: Profit calculation

$$\text{Profit} = (.0851 - .0825)(\$9,662,716.70)\left(\frac{56}{360}\right)$$
$$= \$3,908.03$$

Comparing the 8.25 term RP rate with the 8.51 implied repo rate suggests that this trade offers a locked-in profit of 26 basis points on the amount invested for 56 days. In fact there are a few slips twixst the cup and the lip: a few things that might or will happen to alter the spread earned on the trade. First commissions—what commission a trader must pay on his futures trade will depend on who he is and the size in which he deals. In the worst case our trader is an investor who pays a $72 commission on his futures trade, far more than a big spec account would pay; that $72 commission would knock down his profit spread by approximately 5 basis points, from 26 to 21 basis points.

A second factor that will affect the outcome of the trade is variation margin. If bill rates rise sharply over the holding period, variation margin in the form of investable dollars will be paid into the trader's margin account, which—assuming he invests these dollars—will raise his return on the trade. Our trader's 26-basis-point profit spread would conversely be threatened by a rally in bills, which would result in margin calls that he would have to meet in cash. How much of a threat do potential margin calls pose to our trader? Relatively little. Even in the unlikely event that bills rallied 100 basis points on the day the trade was settled (10/28/82), the extra margin he would have to put up over 56 days would, assuming a 8.25 financing rate, cost him only 2¼ basis points of his profit spread.

A third factor that might marginally affect the profit earned by our trader is the price at which the 3/24/83 bills and the December bill futures contract *converge* at expiration of the futures contract. The bill futures contract is for $1 million of 90-day bills on which a basis point is worth $25. The deliverable bill is in fact a 91-day bill on which a basis point is worth $25.2777 per million. The trade thus calls for selling bills on which a basis point is worth $25 and delivering bills on which a basis point is worth $25.2777. If the convergence price on the trade is below the price level at which the trade is put on (i.e., if rates rise), the trader will have lost some of his profit because he will have lost on his cash position basis points worth $25.2777 while gaining on his futures position *a like amount* of basis points worth only $25. Much can be made of *convergence-price risk,* but in fact if the cash and futures prices converged 100 basis points above the price level at which the trade was put on, the trader would lose only 2 of his 26-basis-point profit margin on the trade. Alternatively, if cash and futures converged at a price level well below that at which the trade was put on, the trader would add a couple of basis points to his profit margin on the trade.

A final factor affecting profit on the trade will be transactions costs— back office costs or whatever. Usually these are so small that no one bothers to incorporate them into return calculations.

To sum up, a trader putting on a cash-and-carry trade does not lock in a certain rate of return. However, on a short trade of the sort illustrated, even a 20% rise in bill prices, which is big, would leave most of his profit margin intact.

We have been talking about the signal that the relationship between the implied repo rate and the actual term repo rate gives the leveraged trader. The strictly cash investor who is investing money into December also gets a signal from the relationship between these rates. If the implied repo rate exceeds the term RP rate, then the cash investor will earn more by investing in the long bill and selling December futures than he would by investing in term RP and probably more than he would by investing in the bill maturing at expiration of the futures contract. If, alternatively, the reverse is true and the levered cash-and-carry trade (Tables 14–5 and 14–6) is unprofitable, the short-bill trade offering the cash investor the highest return would probably be buying the 56-day December bill and maturing it.

An unlevered cash-and-carry trade

Above we noted that, for the cash investor wanting to invest short term, the structure of rates is at times such that his holding period yield will be greater if he does a cash-futures trade—buys a longer bill, sells the nearby futures contract, and makes delivery—than if he does a strictly cash-market trade—buys the short bill and matures it.

Table 14–6, based on market rates prevailing in late 1982, illustrates such a situation: By doing the cash-futures trade, an investor can pick up 95 basis points more in yield than he would have had he operated strictly in the cash market—bought the short bill and matured it.

Note the 95-basis-point yield pickup is not locked in stone. All the factors that we said would or might affect the outcome of the trade described in Tables 14–4 and 14–5 come into play in this example too. Futures commissions will reduce the yield pickup slightly. Also, a rally in the bill market will cost the investor a few basis points of his yield pickup both because of margin calls and because of the cost implied by the convergence of cash and futures prices at a higher level. These factors, even if they all work to lower yield pickup, are, however, too small to alter the fact that this is a productive, attractive trade for the alert cash investor to make.

TREASURY BOND FUTURES

In 1977 the *Chicago Board of Trade* (*CBT* or *Board* to street people) introduced a futures contract on Treasury bonds which was highly successful and is today by far the most heavily traded financial futures contract. Currently 60 to 80,000 bond contracts are traded daily, which is 2½ to 3 times the volume of bill contracts traded daily (Figure 14–3). That bond contract and the 10-year note contract subsequently introduced were for securities having $100,000 of face value.

In our introductory remarks about bill futures, we described the function of the clearing house, how margin is handled, and how the contract

TABLE 14–6
An unlevered cash-and-carry trade

Strategy A: Buy long bill, sell futures, and make delivery.

1. Buy, on 11/15/82 at 8.43, $1 million of the 3/24/82 bill, which matures in 128 days.

$$\text{Purchase price} = (\$1,000,000)\left(1 - \frac{.0843 \times 128}{360}\right)$$
$$= \$970,026.67$$

2. Simultaneously sell on 11/15/82, $1 million of December 82 bill futures at a price of 91.76 (8.24 yield).

3. On 12/21/82, deliver the 3/24/82 bill, the current maturity of which is now 91 days, against the December futures contract, which is assumed to settle at 91.76.

$$\text{Sale price} = (\$1,000,000)\left(1 - \frac{.0824 \times 91}{360}\right)$$
$$= \$979,171.11$$

4. Calculate rate of return on purchase and resale

$$\text{Rate of return} = \left(\frac{\text{Sale price} - \text{Purchase price}}{\text{Purchase price}}\right)\left(\begin{array}{c}\text{Annualization} \\ \text{factor}\end{array}\right)$$
$$= \left(\frac{\$979,171.11 - \$970.026.67}{\$970,026.67}\right)\left(\frac{360}{37}\right)$$
$$= .0917 = 9.17\%$$

Strategy B: Buy short cash bill and hold to maturity.

1. Buy, on 11/15/82 at 8.15, $1 million of the 12/21/82 bill which matures in 37 days. Hold the bill until maturity.

$$\text{Purchase price} = (\$1,000,000)\left(1 - \frac{.0815 \times 37}{360}\right)$$
$$= \$991,623.61$$

2. Calculate the rate of return on holding bill to maturity

$$= \left(\frac{\$1,000,000 - \$991,623.61}{\$991,623.61}\right)\left(\frac{360}{37}\right)$$
$$= .0822 = 8.22\%$$

Calculate yield pick-up by doing Strategy A, not B:

$$\left(\begin{array}{c}\text{Yield pick up from} \\ \text{doing A, not B}\end{array}\right) = 9.17 - 8.22$$
$$= .95$$
$$= 95 \text{ basis points}$$

On a $10 million trade extra return earned would be:

$$(.0095)\left(\frac{37}{365}\right)(\$10 \text{ million}) = \$9,630$$

---

*The formula for calculating the discount on a bill was given in Chapter 4. For a formula to calculate holding period yield on a bill sold before maturity, see Stigum and Mann, *Money Market Calculations*, p. 53.

FIGURE 14–3
Average daily volume of CBT Treasury bonds futures contract

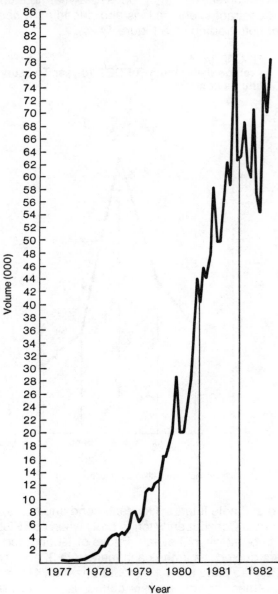

Source: Donaldson, Lufkin & Jenrette.

can be used to hedge and to do many other trades. These remarks all apply with minor variations noted below to the bond contract and to the much newer 10-year and the proposed 2-year note contracts. (For note and bond contract specifications and price limits, see Table 14–2. For volume of note trading, see Figure 14–4).

FIGURE 14–4
Average daily volume of CBT 10-year Treasury note futures contract

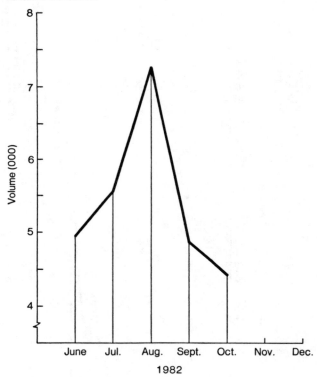

Source: Donaldson, Lufkin & Jenrette.

   T bond and note futures, like cash bond and notes, are traded on the basis of price. Consequently longs profit when bond futures rise in price, and shorts profit when they fall. Prices of T-bond and of 10-year T-note futures are quoted, as in the cash market, in 32nds. Thus on these contracts, a futures price of 74-17 should be read $74^{17}/_{32}$; and the minimum price movement or *tick*, as it is called, is $^{1}/_{32}$. In the cash market, in contrast, active bonds are commonly traded in 64ths. Addition of $^{1}/_{64}$ to a cash market price is indicated in a written quote by adding a plus sign. Thus in Table 14–7, described below, a price of 121-18+ should be read

121 plus $18/32$ plus $1/64$ or $121^{37}/64$. On the 2-year, Treasury note contract, prices are quotes in $1/128$ths (Table 14–2).

Delivery

The bond and the note contracts have one feature, *a price conversion factor,* not required on the bill contract. The 3-month bill is a homogeneous commodity of which there is, on the delivery date at expiration of a futures contract, a large supply: cash bills already trading in the market and new bills being put into the market, as the most recent bill auction is settled.

Because they carry a coupon, Treasury bonds, in contrast to bills, are necessarily heterogeneous. Once a quarter, the Treasury markets a new long bond in the refunding. It does so through a yield auction, which establishes the coupon on the new bond issue. Given the volatility of rates in recent years, this procedure has resulted in a situation in which the numerous Treasury long bonds outstanding are a heterogeneous mix: besides necessarily having varying current maturities, they have radically different coupons.

To create a successful, liquid contract for bond futures, the CBT could not design its futures contract around a single Treasury bond that would be deliverable against the contract at settlement. Instead it had to find some way to make a wide and changing array of bonds deliverable on equitable terms against its futures contract.

Delivery specifications. To do so, it set up a futures contract for a hypothetical Treasury bond with an 8% coupon and specified that deliverable-grade bonds would include any bond, whatever its coupon, that, if callable, could not be called for at least 15 years from the date of delivery or, if not callable, did not mature for at least 15 years from the date of delivery.

Factors. At any time, a basket of different bonds trading at different prices and yields to maturity and having quite different coupons and current maturities meet these delivery specifications. To make delivery equitable to both those taking and making delivery and to tie cash to futures prices, the CBT introduced *factors* for pricing each bond in the basket of those bonds deliverable against a given futures contract.

Invoice price. Each deliverable bond's factor is that number by which the settlement price on the bond contract must be multiplied to get the *invoice price* that the side taking delivery must pay for the bond delivered. At its futures-market invoice price, every deliverable bond is priced so that it will yield 8% to call or to maturity if the bond is not callable. At any point some bonds will—depending on their coupons and on rate relationships—be cheaper to buy and deliver than others, and one bond in particular will be the cheapest to deliver.

TABLE 14–7
Illustrative factors and invoice prices calculated from them for bond futures contract prices ranging from 74–13 to 74–24

CBT US Treasury Bond Futures

December 1982 Delivery

of Active Issues

69–00 to 74–31

The tables on the following pages show a range of prices for Chicago Board of Trade Treasury bond futures contracts and the equivalent invoice prices for selected deliverable Treasury issues. The invoice prices are obtained by multiplying the futures price by the delivery factor for the particular Treasury issue. Delivery factors are determined from the Financial Publishing Company's publication number 765, "Treasury Bond and Note Futures Conversion Tables". The factors for delivery of the Treasury issues against December 1982 Treasury bond futures are listed below.

			Cash bond	Factor
			14.00s 11/2011	1.6333
			13.875s 05/2011	1.6155
			12.75s 11/2010	1.4938
			11.75 02/2010	1.3853
			10.375 11/2009	1.2427
			9.125s 05/2009	1.1138
			8.75s 11/2008	1.0751
			14.25s 02/2002	1.6052
			15.75s 11/2001	1.7458

DEC 82 Us Bond	14.00s 11/2011	13.875s 05/2011	12.75s 11/2010	11.75 02/2010	10.375 11/2009	9.125s 05/2009	8.75s 11/2008	14.25s 02/2002	15.75s 11/2001
74 13	121 17	120 6+	111 4+	103 2+	92 15	82 28	79 32	119 14	129 28+
74 14	121 18+	120 8	111 6	103 4	92 16	82 29	80 1	119 15+	129 30+
74 15	121 20	120 9+	111 7+	103 5	92 17+	82 30	80 2	119 17	130 0
74 16	121 22	120 11+	111 9	103 6+	92 18+	82 31+	80 3	119 19	130 2
74 17	121 23+	120 13	111 10+	103 8	92 20	83 0+	80 4	119 20+	130 3+
74 18	121 25	120 14+	111 12	103 9+	92 21	83 1+	80 5	119 22	130 5+
74 19	121 26+	120 16	111 13+	103 10+	92 22+	83 2+	80 6+	119 23+	130 7
74 20	121 28+	120 18	111 15	103 12	92 23+	83 4	80 7+	119 25	130 9
74 21	121 30	120 19+	111 16+	103 13+	92 25	83 5	80 8+	119 27	130 10+
74 22	121 31+	120 21	111 18	103 15	92 26	83 6	80 9+	119 28+	130 12+
74 23	122 1	120 22+	111 19+	103 16+	92 27+	83 7	80 10+	119 30	130 14
74 24	122 3	120 24+	111 21	103 17+	92 28+	83 8	80 11+	119 31+	130 16

Source: Merrill Lynch, Pierce, Fenner & Smith, *Financial Futures Marketing*, September 1982.

Example. To illustrate, consider the December 1982 bond futures contract, which settled at 74–17. A trader short at expiration of this contract could elect to cover this short on any business day up to and including December 30. Among the basket of deliverable bonds were the 13⅞s of 2011 and the 7⅝s of 2007. The factor for the first bond was 1.6155 (Table 14–7), which implied an invoice price per $100 of face value of (74¹⁷⁄₃₂)(1.6155) = 120.4052. The factor on the second bond implied an invoice price of 71.8854.

Table 14–7 lists this information as well as the prices that prevailed in the cash market on 12/22/82. Assuming that a short could have bought bonds for delivery at the offered side of the market, the 13⅞s would have been much cheaper to deliver than the 7⅝s. It is typical that it is cheaper to deliver high-coupon than low-coupon bonds in settlement of a short position in futures.

Accrued interest. Note the invoice price in Table 14–8 is *for principal only*. In addition to the invoice price, the long must pay the short any accured interest on the bond delivered as of the delivery date. Receipt of accrued interest does not add to the short's net proceeds nor does it affect our calculation of the cost to deliver either bond. To buy bonds in the cash market, the short must pay the quoted price for principal plus accrued interest.

TABLE 14–8
Calculating the cost to deliver on December 22, 1982, different bonds against the December bond contract which settled at 74–17

| | | | | Cost to deliver | |
| | | Invoice | Cash market | Per $100 | Per $100,000 |
Bond	Factor	price	quotes	of face value	contract
13⅞ 5/15/11	1.6155	120.4052	120-24–121	$0.5948	$ 594.80
7⅝ 2/15/07	.9645	71.8854	74-28–75-12	$3.4896	$3,489.60

Hedging with T bond futures

Our remarks about the usefulness of bill futures as a hedging device all apply to bond and note futures, as well. The latter can be used to hedge an anticipated cash inflow or, if the portfolio manager anticipates a rise in interest rates, to hedge a long position in bonds: governments, corporates, or municipals.

Here are a few examples. A portfolio manager who anticipates an inflow of cash and fears a fall in interest rates could buy bond futures to lock in a future long-term yield. Alternatively, a portfolio manager who holds bonds and fears tightening by the Fed could liquidate his portfolio to prevent a capital loss, but a preferable course might be to hedge his position in bonds by selling bond futures. Doing the latter would protect his long position against a rise in interest rates while simultaneously permitting him to retain a portfolio of bonds, that he had carefully selected for properties such as credit risk, sector divesification, and call provisions. This obviates the need for his scrambling during a subsequent market rally to purchase securities with similar properties. The bond futures market can also be useful to the portfolio manager seeking to minimize taxes. Consider a portfolio manager who owns long bonds in which he has a short-term capital gain that will become a *long-term* gain two months hence. The portfolio manager fears interest rates will rise, but if he were to liquidate his position immediately, he would incur a tax penalty. For him, an attractive alternative would be to hedge his position by selling bond futures.

An investor who uses bond futures to hedge, like an investor who uses bill futures to hedge, is shifting his risk from speculation on rate levels to speculation on spread variation. For the hedger of long instruments, knowledge of what spreads are and what causes them to change is, if anything, more crucial than it is for the hedger of short instruments. The reason is that the hedger who uses bond futures is likely to find that deliverable bonds differ considerably in current maturity, credit risk, or other characteristics from the bonds he is hedging or from the bonds he intends to buy when an anticipated cash inflow occurs. For the portfolio manager, this imperfection in the hedge is offset by the enhanced opportunity offered to speculate profitably on spread variation.

Factors affecting spread. To evaluate the spread between the instrument being hedged and a deliverable bond and to determine how that spread is likely to change, a portfolio manager must consider several factors. The first is a possible change in the instrument that is *cheapest* to deliver. This consideration does not arise for the hedger who uses bill futures because the bills deliverable at the expiration of a bill contract are homogeneous. In the bond futures market, in contrast, a basket of bonds all trading at different prices will be deliverable at a given time. A change in the cheapest deliverable bond will necessarily affect the spread at which bond futures trade to other instruments.

A second important consideration is credit risk. When interest rates rise, yields on corporate bonds typically rise faster than yields on governments, and yields on low-grade corporates rise faster than yields on high-grade corporates.

A third consideration is the current maturity of the instrument being hedged. Normally, long-term instruments exhibit less yield volatility than do short-term instruments. However, because the yield value of $1/32$ decreases as current maturity lengthens, long-term instruments also typically exhibit more price volatility than do short-term instruments. A bond's price volatility will also depend on whether it is selling at a discount or a premium. In a bear market, discount bonds drop more rapidly in price than high-coupon bonds; also in a bull market, they rise more rapidly in price than high-coupon bonds.

Finally, the hedger should take into account possible changes in supply of and demand for both long Treasuries and the instrument being hedged.

The hedge ratio. A careful study of these factors is likely to suggest that the portfolio manager should hedge on a ratio basis; that is, he should sell or buy a number of contracts such that the face value of his position in futures equals some ratio of the face value of the bonds or anticipated cash flow he is hedging. To illustrate, consider a portfolio manager who is hedging a position in corporate bonds against a rise in interest rates. Because of the additional credit risk to which corporates expose the investor, he anticipates that they will drop faster than long governments in the face of rising interest rates. Therefore, to protect his position, he buys a number of futures contracts equal to some ratio greater than one of the value of the bonds being hedged. To determine what ratio he should use, the hedger must consider all the factors we listed as affecting spread and, in particular, the current maturity of the instrument being hedged.

The hedger who uses bond futures, like the hedger who uses bill futures, retains, through establishing his hedge, the opportunity to speculate on spread variation and should consider such speculation as a potential source of profit. If, for example, the portfolio manager believes that any change in interest rates is likely to be upward, he should consider increasing the ratio of the contracts sold to the securities hedged so that, if interest rates do rise, the profit on his short position in bond futures will exceed the mark-to-market losses on his portfolio of cash securities. For anyone who uses the bond futures contract, other useful instruments are the actively traded GNMA futures contract, which is an instrument that is essentially free of credit risk and has at issue an expected life equal to half the maturity of the longest Treasury bonds traded for future delivery.

Cash-futures arbitrages

Besides the obvious strategies of putting on hedges, bond futures can be used as one leg of a wide range of arbitrage plays, including all those illustrated in our bill futures examples. To suggest some of the less obvious arbitrages that can be put on using cash and futures, we present two examples.

Basis. One rate relationship an arbitrageur of cash against futures is always looking at is *basis, the spread of cash to futures prices.* If basis is *strong,* that is, if bond prices in the cash market are high relative to those in the futures market, an arbitrageur who owns bonds may, by selling them in the cash market, investing the proceeds in term RP, and simultaneously buying bond futures on which he plans to take delivery, be able to reduce his principal investment in the bonds.

Example when basis is strong. Table 14–9 presents an example of this trade based on rates that prevailed in early November 1982. To put it on, the arbitrageur sells $1 million of the 14s of 2011, buys December 1982 bond futures, and invests the proceeds from his bond sale in term RP. We assume that market conditions are such that the short elects to make delivery on the last delivery day for the December contract, 12/30/82, and that he delivers the 14s of 11/15/11, which were, at the time the trade was put on, the cheapest deliverable bond. We also assume that bond futures settle at the same price, 76–28, at which they were trading when the trade was put on. Using the appropriate factor, 1.633, we calculate the invoice price for $1 million of principal on the 14s of 2011. It is $9,400.62 less than the amount obtained for principal at sale of the bonds on 11/3/82. Offsetting this, however, is some net interest loss because the coupon interest forgone as a result of the trade is less than the interest earned on the term RP. Consequently, as the last calculation in Table 14–9 shows, the net gain (reduction in principal cost) realized by our arbitrageur is $6,127.69.

In this example, as in the bill example presented in Tables 14–4 and 14–5, there are several factors that will or might affect the outcome of the trade. First, commissions must be paid. Second, cash and futures might converge at a price above or below the futures price, 76–28, at which the trade was put on. If they converged at a price above 76–28 (yields fell), the arbitrageur would receive variation margin, which he could invest. He would also gain because in a rising market the price of the hypothetical 8% futures bond would rise less rapidly than the 14% coupon he has sold. Conversely if bond prices fell (yields rose), the arbitrageur would lose both because of margin calls and because the security he was long, a low-coupon futures, would rally less than the cash bond on which he anticipated taking delivery at expiration of the contract.

Since only falling bond prices threaten our arbitrageur's gain, he can easily protect that gain by hedging against that outcome. To do so, he would establish his initial position in ratio: sell a few more cash bonds than he buys futures. The amount of extra bonds he must sell will be determined by the ratio of the yield value of $\frac{1}{32}$ on the bond contract to that on the 14s of 2011. Because of the long maturity and high coupon on the 14s of 2011, the yield value of $\frac{1}{32}$ on that bond will be less than that on the bond contract.

A second less tractable difficulty with this trade is that the investor putting it on may anticipate that he will be delivered a certain bond, but

TABLE 14–9
Cash-futures bond arbitrage when basis is strong

To put on trade:

1. Sell for settlement on 11/3/82, $1 million of the 14s of 11/15/11 at 126-16.

Principal amount	$1,265,000.00
Accrued interest.	65,434.78
Total proceeds.	$1,330,434.78

2. Buy on 11/3/82 $1 million of December 82 bond futures at 76–28.

3. Invest proceeds from bond sale in term RP at 8⅞ for 57 days to 12/30/82, the last delivery day to December bond contract.

To unwind trade:

1. On 12/30/82, close out term repo:

$$\left(\begin{array}{c}\text{Interest income}\\\text{earned}\end{array}\right) = (\$1,330,434.78 \times .08875)\left(\frac{57}{360}\right)$$
$$= \$18,695.38$$

2. On 12/30/82 pay invoice price for $1 million of deliverable bonds (assuming that these are the 14s of 11/15/11 and that the settlement price is 76–28).

Factor on 14s of 11/15/11 for December 1982 delivery is 1.6333 (Table 14–7).

$$\text{Invoice price} = (76^{28}/_{32})(1.6333)$$
$$= 125.559938/100 \text{ of face value}$$

Invoice price for $1 million of principal	$1,255,599.38
+Accrued interest.	17,403.31
Amount due on delivered bonds.	$1,273,002.69

Calculate gain on trade:

Gain on principal:

Principal at sale (11/3/82).	$1,265,000.00
−Principal at repurchase (12/30/82)	1,255,599.38
Gain on principal.	$ 9,400.62

Interest loss:

Coupon interest loss*	$ 21,968.31
−RP interest earned.	18,695.38
Interest loss	$ 3,272.93

Net gain:

Gain on principal.	$ 9,400.62
−Interest loss	3,272.93
Net gain.	$ 6,127.69

* Accrued interest calculated from Merrill Lynch's yield book table; trade covered a coupon date. For accrued interest calculation on governments, see Stigum and Mann, *Money Market Calculations*, pp. 87–88.

he can never be sure that he will get that bond. There is always the danger that market conditions will change so that some other bond becomes the cheapest bond to deliver.

Example when basis is weak. When the basis of cash to futures is *weak*—cash prices are weak relative to futures prices—a different arbitrage opportunity is presented to the investor who wants to make a short-term investment. He can (Table 14–10) make a short-term investment by buying bonds, selling bond futures, and delivering the bonds he has bought at settlement of the futures contract. This trade, when the basis is

TABLE 14–10
Cash-Futures bond arbitrage when basis is weak

To put on trade: 1. Buy for settlement 7/6/82, $1 million of the 8¾s of 11/15/08 at 69¹²⁄₃₂.

Principal amount	$693,750.00
Accrued interest	12,364,13
Total amount paid	$706,114.13

2. Sell on 7/6/82 $1 million of September 82 bond futures at 64–28.

To unwind trade: Deliver on 9/1/82 $1 million of the 8¾s of 11/15/08 and receive invoice price (assuming settlement price is 64–28).

Factor on the 8¾s of 11/15/08 for September 1982 delivery is 1.0757 (Table 14–5)

$$\text{Invoice price} = (64^{28}\!/_{32})(1.0757)$$
$$= 69.786038/100 \text{ of face value}$$

Invoice price for $1 million of principal	$697,860.38
Accrued interest	25,917.12
Amount due on delivered bonds	$723,777.50

Calculate return on trade: **Calculate net gain:**

Invoice price at sale.	$723,777.50
− Invoice price at purchase	706,114.13
Net gain	$ 17,663.37

Calculate rate of return:

$$\text{Rate of return} = \left(\frac{\text{Net gain}}{\text{Amount invested}}\right)\left(\begin{array}{c}\text{Annualization}\\ \text{factor}\end{array}\right)$$
$$= \left(\frac{17,663.37}{706,114.13}\right)\left(\frac{365}{57}\right)$$
$$= .1602$$
$$= 16.02\% \text{ bond equivalent yield}$$

Compare this rate to rates available on other 2-month investments, e.g., 2-month commercial paper, CDs, Euros, and term repo.

weak, will yield some positive return, 16.02, over a 57-day period in our example.

If this—slightly exotic compared to buying 57-day commercial paper—trade produces a yield higher than those available on other short-term investments, a portfolio manager with 2-month money to go should do the trade.

Our example illustrates just two of many different cash-futures arbs a trader might put on. Here is another. Said one arbitrageur, "If I like the 10-year versus the long bond, instead of buying the cash 10-year and shorting the bond, I might buy the *NOB,* which is the note-bond spread. Having done that, I might, if I thought the 10-year note was too cheap, buy it in the cash market and short the cash 5-year note creating a butterfly."

Spread trades

Arbitrageurs using bond futures, like those using bill futures, have various spread trades they will—depending on rates—put on. Noted the same arbitrageur, "Another way to use bond futures is to play the spread between two bond contracts against another instrument. We have been looking at the Dec [pronounced dees] bond futures against the next Dec contract [the red Dec]; that spread, the Dec-red-Dec, is an implied 1-year financing rate that ought to have some relationship to the rate on the year bill. If you think that the spread is cheap relative to the year bill, you can buy the Dec-red-Dec and short the year bill; alternatively, if you think that the spread is too expensive relative to the year bill, you go the other way."

Market liquidity

Some portfolio managers, eyeing the futures market, are anxious to get permission to use it, not so they can do long hedges, i.e., buy, but so that they can sell futures. Said one big portfolio manager, "The reason I want the right to use futures is so that I can sell. I can always buy 100 million of bonds. It is 10 times as hard to sell that amount."

This portfolio manager obviously thinks that the futures market is more liquid than the cash market. A large trader of bonds disputed this view. He observed, "In most instances futures market liquidity is feigned liquidity. When it really doesn't matter—you can buy or sell 100 million off a 4-locked cash market—futures are very liquid. But if it is difficult to buy or sell in the cash market, you will find that condition exacerbated by the Board. Margins do not allow people to make the level of mistakes they can in the cash market. If your futures position goes to a loss, you will immediately get margin calls, and consequently you will tend to close out your futures position almost immediately. That sort of system exacerbates price movements, especially on volatile days; it also makes the futures market less liquid than the cash market when rates are moving strongly up or down. At such times needs to buy or sell dominate the situation completely. A guy has got to liquidate his position, and price becomes pretty much irrelevant."

WHO USES FINANCIAL FUTURES?

As noted, the futures contracts introduced for bills and bonds have been among the most successful commodity futures contracts ever launched. An interesting question is who are the players who have entered this increasingly popular new game?

The not surprising answer is that money and bond market dealers were among the first to enter and use the market actively. They were quick to understand the market and had back offices equipped to clear and track futures trades. Also, and more importantly, they had a need to be *nimble* in the volatile markets that prevailed after the inception of trading in financial futures, and futures contracts gave them a new and extremely useful tool for moving their positions quickly and with facility.

Dealers, particularly of long bonds, quickly saw that the sale of futures contracts was an attractive alternative to short sales as a hedging device. The use of futures to hedge has increased dealers' ability to bid for and position securities during difficult markets, and that in turn, has contributed to liquidity in the cash market.

Arbitrageurs, often ex-traders for major shops, who assembled capital and set up their own shops, have also been important participants in the market. The newness of financial futures has given them many opportunities to put on profitable arbitrages between cash instruments and futures contracts and between different futures contracts. Their activities are a strong force in pulling rates in the cash and futures markets into line with each other.

Another important set of participants in the markets for financial futures, as in all futures markets, has been speculators. Without the liquidity they give the market, there would be no market.

We have said much about the potential usefulness of futures to end users as a means of controlling risk through hedging Some end users have already perceived the market's usefulness in this respect and have begun to use it in the ways described above—to hedge long positions in securities and to lock in future lending rates.

The majority, however, have yet to enter the market. Some have still to understand how positions in futures may be used to control risk. Many more have understood this and are now seeking to overcome other problems that must be dealt with before they can trade futures. All sorts of potential end users of financial futures—corporations, banks, bank trust departments, and other financial institutions—have set up task forces to investigate the legal steps they must take and the accounting, clearing, and control procedures they must set up to use futures. This takes time and effort. However, the market volatility over the period 1979–82 drove home to a wide range of potential end users the message that futures were *a valuable tool to control risk, one they needed to be able to use.* The Fed's Saturday night special in October 1979 and the subsequent shocks the Fed has given the market have been a great advertisement for futures.

Having said that, we should hasten to add that many institutions and portfolio managers are discouraged or outright prevented from using futures by external factors over which they have no control. For example, it makes a lot of sense to say bond portfolio managers who anticipate both a sharp break in rates and a predictable inflow of investable funds ought to lock in current rates for future investment by buying bond futures. However, New York state regulators have yet to permit insurance companies to deal in futures. Also, many pension funds and other institutional portfolios may not do so. The rare portfolio manager who has the freedom to use futures finds that a long bond hedge works out less smoothly than he would like it to. When rates are 14 and he anticipates they will drop to 10, what he would like to buy for future delivery is 14% bonds. What he will get, if he buys bond futures and rates do go to 10, is a big taxable capital gain and low-coupon bonds.

Outside the dealer community, the number of people who will use futures to arbitrage is even smaller than the number who will use them to hedge. As one dealer noted, "The percentage of short- and long-term portfolio managers who use futures to arbitrage is small but growing. Right now [fall of 1982] the levered cash-and-carry trade does not pay. People who will do the reverse [sell bonds] are even fewer. Almost no portfolio manager will sell bonds if it means taking a loss. Another problem for a portfolio manager who sells bonds and buys futures is that he does not know what he is going to get. A portfolio manager may say, 'I have the 8¾s and I don't want to risk getting the 14s,' or 'I have the 14s and I don't want to risk getting the 8¾s because I want high current yield.' An investor can't tell what the final result of an arbitrage will be because things can change a lot during the period the trade is on. The uncertainty that surrounds delivery makes people reluctant to be long futures; consequently more and more people want to sell futures and fewer and fewer want to buy them. Government bond traders, muni bond traders, corporate bond traders, arbitrageurs, and preferred stock traders all prefer to be on the selling side controlling delivery rather than on the long side not knowing what they are going to get. As a result futures have gotten over time cheaper and cheaper relative to the cash market.

"Futures are used most often by money managers who have gone to a corporation and said 'I will manage your money for you.' They say, 'These are the things I will do: buy governments, buy Euros, . . . ,' and they bury in this list using futures. The corporation says, 'Fine;' they don't mind because this guy has demonstrated expertise. An outside manager can get authority to utilize the futures markets—do futures arbitrages and use other futures strategies—whereas an in-house guy cannot.

"A corporation may have an MBA out of Harvard running the portfolio, managing the firm's international float and foreign exchange exposure, and trying to make sure he has written all his memos for the day. He can't simultaneously trade secuities well. In particular he has neither the time to initiate a hedge or other futures trade properly nor the time to monitor it. But a professional money manager can go in and say, 'Give me 10 million and let me do for you just what I am already doing for others.' He, justly so, has credibility with the corporation."

OPTIONS

The trading of puts and calls on governments and federal agency securities is not new. A number of dealers, bank and nonbank, have offered them for years. The over-the-counter business done in such puts and calls, however, has always been small and so low in visibility that most money market participants are unaware that it occurs. The one exception is the wide spread and well-publicized sales made by dealers to thrifts and other investors of *standbys* (*put* options) on Ginnie Mae pass-throughs.[6]

The success with which futures contracts on GNMAs, T bills, and T bonds were introduced led futures exchanges—always on the lookout for a promising new contract to trade—to propose that they also be permitted to trade options both on the securities underlying the futures contracts they traded and on the futures contracts themselves. The CBT, home of the T bond and GNMA futures contracts, was particularly eager to snare for itself the right to trade options on T bonds and GNMAs. It faced competition, however. Both the American Stock Exchange (AMEX) and the Chicago Board Options Exchange (CBOE) also wanted to trade options on Treasuries and on GNMAs.

The CBT applied to the CFTC for permission to trade options on

---

[6] Ginnie Mae pass-throughs, as noted in Chapter 13, are a government-guaranteed, mortgage-backed security. Prior to the steep rise in interest rates in the late 1970s, it was common for dealers to sell GNMA standbys to thrifts and others. As rates rose from 1977 on, some regional dealers and a lot of unsophisticated investors got into trouble—many went bankrupt—doing trades in GNMAs: standbys, forwards, and reverses. The problems in many cases arose because minimally trained sales people proposed trades and tactics to unsophisticated portfolio managers who had no idea of the high risks to which such trades and tactics would expose them.

GNMAs and Treasuries, while the AMEX and the CBOE applied to the SEC for the same permission. These competing applications naturally raised the question of which commission was to regulate these new options—whose OK would count. As noted, the CFTC and the SEC, having sparred over turf for years, finally reached the accord outlined in Table 14–1 in the fall of 1981. This accord gave the SEC jurisdiction over options on U.S. governments and other exempt securities, including agencies, while reserving for the CFTC jurisdiction over options on futures contracts for securities, commodities, and foreign exchange.

It was not until September 1982 that Congress officially ratified the SEC's jurisdiction over options on governments and agencies. During the intervening year, the CBT fought, through repeated court actions, the SEC's authorizing of options exchanges to commence trading options on governments and GNMAs. It was thus not until October 1983 that the AMEX, with the blessings of the SEC and the courts, began to trade options on Treasury notes and bills and the CBOE options on Treasury bonds. While unsuccessful in its attempt to gain the right to trade options on Treasuries and GNMAs, in October 1982 and with CFTC approval, the CBT did initiate trading in options on its T bond futures contract.

Options: The instrument

An *option* is the right either to buy or to sell a specific security or commodity at a specified price during a specified period. An option is referred to as a *call option* if it gives the holder the right to buy; as a *put option* if it gives the holder the right to sell.

In the U.S., stock options have been widely traded for years and are commonly used by a broad range of stock market participants. Stock options used to be traded in the over-the-counter market for puts and calls. This market, like over-the-counter forward markets, had several disadvantages. First every trade struck in it was necessarily a contract between a single buyer and a single seller, and as such, it exposed both sides to a credit risk—the risk that the other side would fail to fulfill its obligation under the contract. Also, like forward contracts, puts and calls traded over the counter were heterogeneous; consequently they were difficult to trade, and they lacked good liquidity.

To overcome these two difficulties, the Chicago Board Options Exchange proposed to and was permitted by the SEC to establish a market in listed stock options. In this market the heterogeneity of options was substantially reduced because only a limited number of well-defined options were traded on each listed stock. Also, a new institution, the *Options Clearing Corporation (OCC),* was created to interpose itself between buyers and sellers of options; the OCC, functioning much like a clearing corporation on a futures exchange, assumes the other side of every buy and sell transaction in options and, by doing so, gives its guarantee to the trade.

These two innovations, limiting the number of options traded on any one stock and creating the OCC, made it possible for greater liquidity to develop in the new standardized options and thereby set the stage for an explosion in the trading of stock options. The example of the CBOE was imitated by the AMEX and by various regional exchanges, which were also permitted by the SEC to list and trade stock options.

Until recently neither options on commodities nor on exempt, fixed-income securities were listed and traded on U.S. exchanges. Commodity options got a bad name in the U.S. because London and other commodity options were peddled by bucket shops to U.S. investors, many of whom lost a lot of money due to the improper practices these shops employed; these included charging inflated prices, failing to execute buy and sell orders, and manipulating markets. In 1978 Congress reacted to these abuses by outlawing for a time the sale of commodity options in the U.S. Not until the fall of 1982 did the CFTC partially remove this ban by introducing a pilot program under which it authorized commodity exchanges to trade options on a limited number of commodities beginning with gold and sugar.

As noted, the arrival of options on exempt, fixed-income securities was stalled by a jurisdictional dispute between the SEC and the CFTC. Under terms of the accord that settled this dispute, the futures exchanges were clear losers; the accord gave the SEC the right to approve proposals to trade options on exempt, fixed-income securities, whereas it gave the CFTC the right to approve only proposals to trade options on futures contracts on these instruments; this meant that it was options exchanges, regulated by the SEC, not futures exchanges, regulated by the CFTC, that would and did get approved to trade options on GNMAs and Treasuries.

Option characteristics

We begin with some jargon. As noted, an option gives the holder the right either to buy or to sell a specific security or commodity at a specified price during a specified period. The price at which a listed option, put or call, may be exercised is called its *striking price* or *exercise price*. The last day of the period during which an option may be exercised is known as its *expiration date*.

Any option contract is uniquely defined by four specifications: (1) whether it is a put or a call, (2) what the underlying security or commodity is, (3) the date on which it expires, and (4) the striking price at which it may be exercised.

For example, the first option quoted in Table 14–11, which lists all

TABLE 14–11
Daily quotes on interest rate options

Interest Rate Options

Friday, January 7, 1983
For Notes and Bonds, decimals in closing prices represent 32nds; 1.1 means 1 1/32. For Bills, decimals in closing
prices represent basis points; $5 per .01

American Exchange

U.S. TREASURY NOTE–$20,000 principal value

Underlying Issue	Strike Price	Calls–Last			Puts–Last		
		Mar	June	Sept	Mar	June	Sept
13¾ note	112	....	....	....	0.10	....	....
due 5/15/92	116	2.5	2.22	....	....	....	....
		Mar	June	Sept	Mar	June	Sept
10½ note	100	1.28	....	....	1.15	....	....
due 11/15/92	104	0.16	....	....	....	4.25	....

13-WEEK U.S. TREASURY BILL–$200,000 principal value

	Strike Price	Calls–Last			Puts–Last		
		Mar	June	Sept	Mar	June	Sept
	92	.62	....	....	....	....	....

Total call vol. 339   Call open int. 3842
Total put vol. 14   Put open int. 1380

Chicago Board Options Exchange

U.S. TREASURY BOND–$100,000 principal value

Underlying Issue	Strike Price	Calls–Last			Puts–Last		
		Mar	June	Sept	Mar	June	Sept
14% bond	122	5.4	....	....	1.22	....	....
due 11/11	124	3.20	....	....	....	....	....
	126	2.16	3.16	....	....	5.16	....
		Mar	June	Sept	Mar	June	Sept
10⅜% bond	100	1.19	....	....	....	....	....
due 11/12	104	0.18	....	....	....	....	....

U.S. TREASURY BOND–$20,000 principal value

Underlying Issue	Strike Price	Calls–Last			Puts–Last		
		Mar	June	Sept	Mar	June	Sept
10⅜% bond	100	1.31	....	....	2.28	....	....
due 11/12	104	0.19	....	....	....	....	....

Total call vol. 179   Call open int. 2031
Total put vol. 20   Put open int. 942

Futures Options

Friday, January 7, 1983

Chicago Board of Trade

TREASURY BONDS–$100,000; points and 64ths of 100%

Strike Price	Calls–Last			Puts–Last		
	Mar	Jun	Sep	Mar	Jun	Sep
64	....	....	....	0-01	....	....
66	....	....	....	....	....	....
68	8-39	8-21	...	0-01	....	....
70	6-41	6-46	...	0-03	0-45	....
72	4-45	5-15	....	0-12	1-07	....
74	3-06	3-60	....	0-30	1-44	....
76	1-50	2-55	....	1-12	2-33	....
78	0-56	2-00	....	2-16	3-40	....
80	0-26	1-24	....	3-50	4-63	....

Est. total vol. 2,000
Calls: Thurs. vol. 1,154; open int. 7,845
Puts: Thurs. vol. 535; open int. 6,166

Source: *The Wall Street Journal*, January 7, 1983.

interest rate options that were traded as of January 7, 1983, is an option for $200,000 of the 13¾s Treasury notes of 5/15/92. The strike price is 116, and calls and puts on this security expired on three quarterly dates in March, June, and September.

It is common in a market for listed stock options to trade a *class* of options on a single stock; this class consists of options that expire on a number of different quarterly dates and that have a number of different strike prices. The new interest rate options began with smaller classes than those of stock options. The widest range of strike prices was for options on T bond futures (Table 14–11); options on one bond deliverable under this contract, the 14s of 2011, were traded for only three strike prices.

In an options market, the more interest investors have in an option, the more options with different strike prices can be traded without impairing liquidity in this option. When options on a security are traded at different strike prices, the width of the bands set between these different prices will depend partly on the volatility of the price of the underlying security; the more volatile it is, the wider the bands will be set. If the price of a security underlying a class of options moves sharply, the exchange on which this security's options are traded will normally respond by introducing new options having strike prices that bracket the security's current market price.

Value of an option

The strike price of an option on a security may exceed, equal, or be less than the current price of the security. A *call* option is said to be *in-the-money* if the price of the underlying security exceeds the strike price. In street jargon, the term, in-the-money, denotes a call that has an *intrinsic value;* this value equals the price of the security minus the striking price on the options. A call has no intrinsic value if its strike price equals or exceeds the price of the underlying security; in the latter case—strike price exceeds market price—the option is said to be *out-of-the-money*.

A *put* option is said to be *in-the-money* if the strike price of the underlying security is less than the security's price. In that case the intrinsic value of the put equals the strike price minus the price of the security. A put has no intrinsic value if the strike price equals or is less than the price at which the underlying security is trading; in the latter case—strike price is less than market price—the option is said to be *out-of-the-money*.

The price, *premium* in options jargon, at which a put or call option trades consists of two parts: intrinsic value, which may be positive or zero, and a *time value premium*. If an option has no intrinsic value, its price (premium) equals the time value premium. Alternatively, if an option commands no time value premium, i.e., trades at a price equal to its intrinsic value, it is said to trade at *parity*.

The price at which an option trades will depend on several factors, the most important of which are the price of the underlying security, the volatility of that price, the striking price of the option, the time remaining until the option expires, and the tone—bullish or bearish—of the market for the underlying security.

The intrinsic value of a put or call option is a simple, straightforward function of the relationship between the price of the underlying security and the striking price on the option (Figures 14–5 and 14–6). As noted the price at which an option trades equals its intrinsic value, if any, plus the time value premium accorded it by the market. Normally the time

FIGURE 14–5
Intrinsic value of a call option

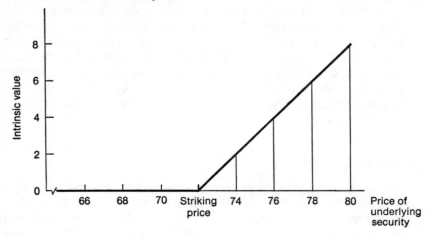

FIGURE 14–6
Intrinsic value of a put option

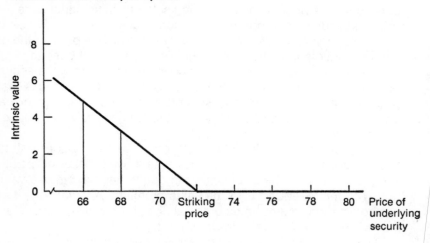

value premium accorded an option will be greatest when the underlying security is trading at a price at or near the strike price of the option. Also, since an option is a wasting asset—its value declines as time passes and its expiration approaches—the time value premium assigned by the market to an option will be greater the farther the option is from expiration. The impact of these two factors on the time value premium commanded by an option is illustrated in Figure 14–7.

FIGURE 14–7
The time value premium—price minus intrinsic value—on an option is greater the closer to zero its intrinsic value and the longer its time to expiration

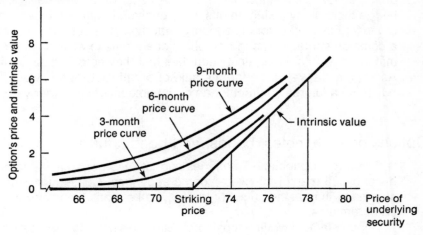

As an option approaches expiration, its time value premium is said to decay. Normally the rate at which an option's time value premium decays will constantly increase as time passes and the option's time to expiration decreases.

Risk

For a *buyer,* options offer one big advantage over futures: *limited downside risk.* A buyer of a put or call option can lose no more than the price he paid for his option, which is precisely what he will lose if he holds the option to expiration and if, at expiration, the option has no intrinsic value and is therefore worthless. A buyer of futures, in contrast to a buyer of options, has unlimited downside risk; should the price of the underlying security drop sharply, he will lose through margin calls an amount equal to the total decline in the market value of the securities he has contracted—by buying a futures contract—to purchase. As disciples of the dismal science, economics, are wont to point out, there is no free lunch. In a bull market the buyer of a futures contract participates fully in any rise in the value of the underlying security, whereas a buyer of an option profits only to the extent that the price of the underlying security rises more than the time value premium he has paid for his option. The amount by which payment of a time value premium for an option reduces the profit earned by the option buyer in a rising market is the price the buyer pays for the limited downside risk to which the option exposes him.

Selling a call or put option, as opposed to buying one, exposes the option seller to *unlimited risk* of loss. A seller of options can, however, hedge that risk by taking an offsetting position in either the cash market or the futures market for the security underlying the option. For example, a common strategy among portfolio managers is to *write covered calls;* that is, to write calls against securities that they hold in their portfolios. An alternative way to hedge the sale of a call (put) option would be to buy (sell) a futures contract for an equal amount of the underlying security.

Options on bills, notes, bonds, and bond futures

Trading in options on Treasuries and GMNAs began in the midst of a historic bull market for fixed-income securities. Consequently it is not surprising that, at the outset of trading, call options commanded generous premiums.

Another factor swelling these premiums was models. For years economists and econometricians have been building and refining option-pricing models, the first and most reknowned of which was the Black-Scholes model.[7] Since having a model that spits out the price at which an option should trade ought to give an advantage to an options trader privy to that information, dealers in fixed-income securities (before trading in options on fixed-income securities commenced) all hired Ph.D.s to develop proprietary models to tell them what the premium on such options should be.

During the initial months of trading, the models all said that call option premiums on interest-rate options should be high; and high they were. Generous premiums on call options on Treasuries permitted big portfolio managers to make a lot of money writing covered calls, while dealers who were smart enough to do so generally found they could make money by selling calls *naked* (unhedged) even when the cash market was rallying.

Speaking of this, one trader noted, "The mathematical models on the street have produced incredible premiums on bonds. In late 82 an investor could buy bonds, sell a call at a price slightly above the purchase price, and earn a *stand-still rate of return* [the return earned if the price of the bond moves not one iota and the call expires worthless] of 20 to 25% over the 4 or 5 months that remained before expiration of the March [1983] options. Moreover, if the market were to rally to the point where

---

[7] For a description of this model, see Lawrence McMillan, *Options as a Strategic Investment* (New York: Institute of Finance, 1980), pp. 392–99.

the customer was forced to give up his bonds in March, his return on the trade would run 30 to 35%. Because of these incredible rates, we have had aggressive call writing. The mathematical models that produced the premiums that made these rates of return possible have been the greatest sales tool we have ever had to sell covered call writing. In bills, the return on covered call writing has been positive but nowhere near what it has been on bonds."

A covered call write

Stock options have long been used as part of a host of often complicated strategies for speculating, arbitraging, and hedging. Traders of fixed-income securities will undoubtedly think of all sorts of strategies they can implement that will involve the use of options. By late 1982, street traders and portfolio managers had just begun to explore the possibilities that options on fixed-income securities offered them.

To illustrate one of the many ways in which an investor might profit through the use of options, we have chosen the example of a covered call write described in Table 14–12. We assume that in early December 1982 our investor had money he wanted to invest until mid-March 1983. If he had bought the cash bill maturing on 3/24/83, he would have earned a return on a simple interest rate, 360-day basis of 8.48 (Choice A, Table 14–12). Alternatively, if he had been bullish, which people were in early December 1982, he could have bought the 6/23/83 bill at 8.50 and sold against it the out-of-the-money call that was closest to the cash market; this was a call option having a strike price of 92 and selling at a 38 basis-point premium. As the calculations under Choice B in Table 14–12 show, if the market had in fact traded up and if our investor's bills were consequently called from him at expiration of the option, he would have earned, over the 105-day holding period, 9.72; that is, 124 more basis points than he would have earned by buying and maturing the 3/24/83 bill.

To get return rate, 9.76, we had to make several assumptions. One was that the bills were not called from our investor until expiration of the option. In fact an option, put or call, may be exercised *at any time* during its life. Our second assumption was that the market rallied sufficiently so that the bills were called from the investor. Had the market instead declined, the investor would have had on his trade a substantial built-in margin of protection against a market decline because the option sale generated a premium and because the 6/23/83 bill was trading two basis points above the 3/24/83 bill. Specifically he could have sold the 6/23/83 bill on 3/24/83 at a rate as high as 9.46 and still have earned over the holding period the 8.48 return that Choice A would have yielded him.

TABLE 14–12
A covered option write on a T bill

Choice A:	Buy for settlement on 12/9/82, $1 million of the 3/24/83 bill at 8.28 and hold 105 days to maturity. Earn rate of return, i, on a simple interest, 360-day basis of:

$$i = \frac{(.0828)(360)}{360 - (.0828)(105)}(100) = 8.48$$

Choice B:	Do a covered option write with the bullish expectation that the call sold will be exercised.

Trade put on:

1. Buy, for settlement on 12/9/82, $1 million of T bills maturing on 6/23/83 at 8.50.

$$\text{Gross purchase price} = (\$1,000,000)(.0850)(^{196}\!/_{360})$$
$$= \$953,722.30$$

2. Sell five March 92 calls, each for $200,000 of bills at a 38 basis-point premium. Since a basis point on $1 million of bills is worth $25, a basis point on an option for $200,000 of 90-day bills is worth one fifth of that amount, or $5. Therefore,

$$\text{Proceeds from call sale} = (38)(\$5)(5)$$
$$= \$950.00$$

3. The call sale reduces the net purchase price to:

$$\text{Net purchase price} = \$953,722.30 - \$950.00$$
$$= \$952,772.50$$

Call exercised at option expiration:

1. Deliver 6/23/83 bill on 3/24/83 at a price of 92, i.e., at a yield of 8.00.

$$\text{Sale price} = (\$1,000,000)(.0800)(^{91}\!/_{360})$$
$$= \$979,777.80$$

Compute return earned:

$$\left(\begin{array}{c}\text{Rate of return,}\\ \text{a 360-day basis}\end{array}\right) = \left(\frac{\text{Sale price} - \text{Net purchase price}}{\text{Net purchase price}}\right)\left(\frac{360}{105}\right)(100)$$

$$= \left(\frac{\$979,777.80 - \$952,772.30}{\$952,772.30}\right)\left(\frac{360}{105}\right)(100)$$

$$= 9.72$$

WHEN COVERED TURNS OUT TO BE NAKED

As the bill option contract is now written, the example we have just worked out turns out to be not a covered write, but a naked write. The bill option contract, unlike either the note or bond option contracts, is not for a specific underlying security but rather for the 91-day bill that is current upon exercise of the option. Thus an investor who, as in our example, bought in December 82 a June 83 bill and sold March 83 calls against that bill would in effect be writing—until the call had almost expired—a *naked* option against which he would have to put up *margin*.

Few institutions are permitted to have margin accounts. Consequently from the start of trading in options on Treasuries, covered writes and thus activity in options was much greater in note and bond options than in bill options.

Street traders have suggested to the AMEX that it remedy what they view as a defect in the bill options contract by having the contract rewritten so that it represents a call on a specific bill. The exchange is concerned about the mathematics of such a change: What is a bill is called on a date when it is not a 90-day bill? A possible solution is to go to the European system of option trading which does not permit early exercise of an option.

Other strategies

An attractive feature of options on Treasuries, one guaranteed to encourage traders to use them, is that they are one of three ways a trader can take a position in the underlying cash security; the other two ways are by doing a cash trade or a futures trade. The existence of so many ways to take a position in Treasury bills, notes, and bonds means that a trader who uses options can put on an array of speculative, hedge, and arbitrage positions; also, he can easily hedge or reverse any options position he takes should the market appear to be going against him.

As one trader noted, "If you can trade cash, futures, and options, there are a lot of strategies that will produce quite acceptable rates of return with small amounts of risk and small amounts of capital as well. Also, you can set a strategy in one market that looks good to you at the time you set it, and before it has gone against you to the point where you are losing money, you can reverse the strategy by taking a position in one of the other two markets without disturbing your original position in the third market."

Chapter 15

Certificates of deposit: Domestic, Euro, and Yankee

AMONG THE CASH SECURITIES traded in the money market, the certificate of deposit is the youngest; the first domestic negotiable CDs backed with a dealer commitment to make a secondary market in them were issued in 1961. Since then CDs have become a major money market instrument, and money market banks have come to rely so heavily on the sale of CDs as a source of funding that it is impossible to imagine how they could manage their liability positions without them.

DOMESTIC CDS

Major U.S. banks get some large time deposits from domestic individuals, partnerships, and smaller corporations and from overseas customers who do not want the headache of safekeeping a CD even though the selling bank would do it for them. The total of such deposits is, however, small relative to the banks' need for longer-term deposits. To fill the resulting gap, the banks turn to the one sector of the money market where they can buy longer-term funds in volume, the CD market.

A certificate of deposit is a negotiable instrument evidencing a time deposit made with a bank at a fixed rate of interest for a fixed period

FIGURE 15–1
A specimen CD

NEGOTIABLE TIME CERTIFICATE OF DEPOSIT

BC 000015

CONTINENTAL BANK
CONTINENTAL ILLINOIS NATIONAL BANK AND TRUST COMPANY OF CHICAGO
231 SOUTH LA SALLE STREET CHICAGO ILLINOIS 60693

CHICAGO_____19____

THERE HAS BEEN DEPOSITED IN THIS BANK THE SUM OF $_____

_____DOLLARS

PAYABLE TO
THE ORDER OF_____

ON_____WITH INTEREST FROM THE DATE HEREOF TO MATURITY AT THE RATE OF_____PERCENT PER ANNUM

CANCELLED

INTEREST COMPUTED ON ACTUAL NUMBER OF DAYS ON 360 DAY BASIS. NO INTEREST WILL BE PAID ON THE DEPOSIT AFTER MATURITY DATE.

AUTHORIZED SIGNATURE

⑈000015⑈ ⑆0710⑈0003⑉ 47⑈02379⑈

(Figure 15–1).[1] CDs bear interest, and CD rates are quoted on an interest-bearing rather than a discount basis.[2] Normally interest on a CD, which is calculated for actual days on a 360-day-year basis, is paid at maturity. However, on CDs issued with a maturity beyond one year, interest is paid semiannually. CDs trade in the secondary market most often for regular settlement, but cash trades can also be made.

CDs are normally issued in $1 million pieces.[3] Smaller pieces, while technically negotiable, have poor marketability and trade at a concession to the market. Most CDs, regardless of where the issuer is located, are payable in New York. Thus, there is no need to ship the security out of New York to be presented to the issuing bank for payment at maturity.

CDs were introduced in 1961 by New York banks attempting to tap the national market for deposits; their example was soon followed by banks elsewhere. Since that time the volume of CDs outstanding has risen dramatically albeit in a sharply fluctuating pattern (Figure 15–2).

When first issued, CDs were subject to a rate lid under Regulation Q. In 1969 this lid became binding as money market rates pushed through the Reg Q ceiling. As a result money moved from domestic time deposits into Eurodeposits, and U.S. banks lost $14 billion of CD money. In response they promptly borrowed the $14 billion back from the Euromarket; and the Fed's ill-conceived attempt to limit bank lending by cutting off the banks' access to bought money failed. Since 1973 the Fed has imposed no lid on the rate that banks may pay on time deposits of

---

[1] Variable-rate CDs, mentioned below, are an exception of recent origin.

[2] As noted in Chapter 3, the attempt made by dealers in the late 1970s to launch discount CDs failed.

[3] An exception mentioned later in this chapter is the smaller-denomination CDs sold by some wire houses through their branch offices.

FIGURE 15–2
Domestic CDs outstanding

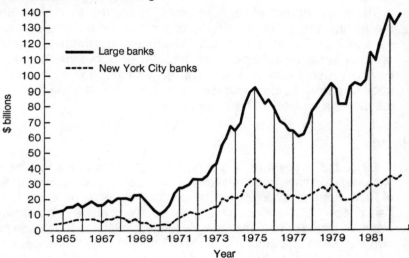

Source: *Federal Reserve Bulletin.*

$100,000 or more. While the Fed could reimpose a rate lid on large-denomination time deposits, the unproductive outcome of its last sortie in this direction and the current trend toward rate deregulation suggest that it is unlikely to do so.

Variable-rate CDs

Traditionally banks issued CDs at par with a fixed maturity and carrying a fixed coupon. In the late 1970s, largely in response to demand from dealers who sold CDs to money funds, banks began to sell a new type of negotiable CD, *variable-rate CDs*. The two most prevalent types are 6-month CDs with a 30-day *roll* (on each roll date, accrued interest is paid and a new coupon is set) and 1-year paper with a 3-month roll.

The coupon established on a variable-rate CD at issue and on subsequent roll dates is set at some amount (12.5 to 30 basis points depending on the name of the issuer and the maturity) above the average rate (as indicated by the *composite* rate published by the Fed) that banks are paying on new CDs with an original maturity equal to the length of the roll period.

Variable-rate CDs give the issuing bank an opportunity to make a rate play. They offer some rate protection to customers, but they have the offsetting disadvantage of illiquidity because they trade at a concession to the market on other than roll dates. During their last *leg* (roll period) variable-rate CDs trade like regular CDs of similar bank name and maturity.

The major buyers of variable-rate CDs are money market funds. In calculating the average maturity of their portfolios, these funds treat variable-rate CDs as if they matured on their next roll date, a justifiable practice since such paper must trade at or above par on roll dates. Buying variable-rate CDs enables money funds to get a rate slightly above the prevailing rate for the relevant roll period while holding down the average maturity of their portfolios.

Volume

Since the removal of Reg Q on CDs, changes in the volume of outstanding CDs have occurred largely in response to variations in the level of loan demand experienced by banks. This is to be expected since banks view CD money as a marginal source of funds to be drawn upon when an increase in loans must be funded. In this respect, one particularly desirable characteristic of the CD market is its tremendous elasticity. CDs outstanding can and do fluctuate by tens of billions of dollars in response to changes in the banks' needs for CD money.

In addition to the cyclical ups and downs in the amounts of CDs outstanding, there are also seasonal changes. While any bank analyst worth his salt views CD money as bought money, banks still try to pick up "deposits" through the sale of CDs around statement dates. Because this quarterly phenomenon is particularly pronounced in December and because bank loans tend to run off in January, CD rates posted by banks often drop noticeably at the beginning of the year as banks withdraw from the market.

Another factor influencing the volume of CDs outstanding is the need that issuing banks feel to have a continuing presence in the market. As a funding officer of one large bank said, "It would be unthinkable for us, whatever our needs might be, to be totally out of the market." For regional and foreign banks, the need to be in the market on an ongoing basis is especially acute. These banks have to keep selling to establish and maintain their names on investors' approved lists. Such banks must walk a fine line; they can't stay away from the market too long, but they also must be careful not to flood the market, since many investors can take only small amounts of regional and foreign names.

Risk and return

Because FDIC insurance offers a depositor protection on only the first $100,000 of deposits with a bank, it is meaningless for corporate and other large depositors. Thus the investor who puts one or many millions into bank CDs assumes some small credit risk. One would therefore expect CDs to yield, as Figure 15–3 shows they do, more than bills of the same maturity. Another reason for the greater yield on CDs is that they are significantly less liquid than bills.

FIGURE 15–3
CD rates track but consistently exceed the yield on Treasury bills

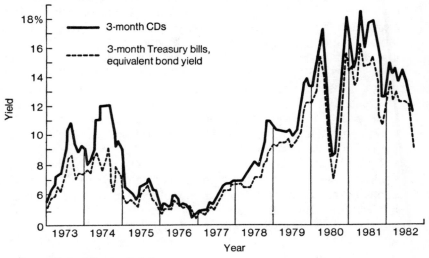

Source: *Federal Reserve Bulletin.*

Spreads between yields on bills and CDs widen when money tightens for several reasons. First, there is the familiar, if irrational, tendency of investors to back away, when money market rates rise, from risks that, when rates are low, they willingly assume to raise return on their investments. Second, the condition of the banking system appears to worsen when the nation's financial system is under strain; thus the risks associated in the eyes of many investors with holding bank CDs tend to be positively correlated with the rate yielded by such instruments. Finally, tight money tends to adversely affect the liquidity of CDs.

Today money funds are the major buyers of CDs; these funds buy as much as 60% of the CDs issued by money market banks with a good name. This represents a sharp break from the past when corporations were the major buyers of CDs. Over the last few years corporations have gone from a position where many of them were cash rich to a position where most of them are heavy borrowers of short-term money; if long rates come down and stay down, and if corporations respond by issuing more long bonds and in particular by prefunding their long-term needs for capital when they think long rates are attractive, this situation may change. However, money funds seem destined to remain the dominant buyers of CDs because these funds are so attractive to such a wide range of investors—institutional and retail—that, until the recent introduction of MMDAs and of super-NOW accounts, they continued to garner more and more funds whether rates rose or fell.

CDs are also bought by state and local governments and by other financial institutions. Generally banks do not invest actively in CDs other than when they position them as a part of their dealer operation. The exception might be if rates were expected to drop sharply. There are two factors that discourage a bank from buying another bank's CDs. One is that a bank's holdings of CDs are not deductible from its reservable deposits as are its demand deposits with other banks. Second, a bank incurs a reserve requirement if it RPs CDs except with another bank. In this respect it should also be noted that a bank may not invest in or buy back one of its own CDs. The Fed would view this as violating the condition that legally permitted the bank to issue the instrument, namely the receipt of a fixed-maturity time deposit.[4]

Because CDs expose the holder to a credit risk, large investors in CDs seek to assess the creditworthiness of different banks. On the basis of such assessments, each investor establishes a list of banks whose CDs it is willing to buy and sets limits, *undisclosed lines* in street jargon, on the amounts it will deposit with individual banks on its approved list. The analysis investors put into deciding which banks they will invest with and in what amounts ranges from casual to elaborate. An average-sized S&L might check out the credit of a bank whose CD it was thinking of buying by asking its own bank whether it would sell Fed funds to the issuing bank. If the answer was yes, it would buy the CD. Such analysis, while unsophisticated, is cheap and quick. At the other extreme are investors who pour over the reams of detailed information on the financial condition of individual banks that is provided in publications put out by Sheshunoff & Co.; Keefe, Bruyette & Woods, Inc.; the Chase Manhattan Bank; and other bank analysts. Not surprisingly the sale of such publications rose dramatically after the Franklin National Bank got into trouble in 1974 and again after Penn Square, Chase, and Continental all made headlines in 1982 (see end of Chapter 5).

While many investors worry seriously about the possibility that a major bank issuing CDs might fail, other investors, including some of the most sophisticated, completely discount that possibility. In the words of

---

[4] A few money market banks, including Citi, trade their own paper in their role as *dealers* in CDs. The Fed has never challenged their doing so. No one wants to open the issue because it would get the banks and the Fed back to discussing whether a CD is a security or a deposit; and reopening that discussion would again raise the question of state blue sky laws and other issues that were considered 20 years ago when Citi first began issuing negotiable CDs.

one investor typical of this latter group, "Money market banks are agents of the central bank. The Fed knows it and they know it, and the Fed is not going to let one of them fail so long as they play ball. A bank that doesn't may end up closing or being merged with another bank, but depositors are not going to lose money. I do not worry about problems at the Chase versus those at the Morgan because the truth is that the Chase has no more chance of failing than the Morgan. Moreover, if either were to fail, conditions would be such that other worries would preempt my concern over lost CD dollars."

To such an investor the main reason for tracking the problems of individual banks closely is that other investors' reactions to these problems create market premiums and discounts, which in turn create opportunities and risks for all investors. The same individual went on to say, "If bad news comes out about the Chase, I know that the market is going to overreact. So I check with the dealers on the spreads at which Chase CDs are trading. If liquidity is still there, I dump my Citis and buy Chase CDs. Experience has proved me right."

Tiering

Prior to 1974 tiering in the CD market was modest, and CDs of all the top banks traded at roughly the same level. Then problems emerged at the Franklin and elsewhere in the banking industry, and things changed.

Investors began to look more closely at the condition of individual banks issuing CDs, and tiering became pronounced. It's difficult to generalize about tiering in top names other than to say that it appears to have become a permanent phenomenon. Who has to pay up changes constantly as investors' perceptions of the financial strengths and weaknesses of individual banks change. For example, when New York City appeared to be on the verge of bankruptcy, the top New York banks, all of which had substantial holdings of New York City securities, had to pay higher rates than top Chicago banks to issue CDs. Several years later the situation had reversed. The size of the spreads that exist between CDs issued by top banks is highly variable. They widen as money tightens; also, whether money is easy or tight, the spreads are greater the longer the maturity of the securities compared.

The year 1974 was particularly hard on regional banks. At that time many CD investors reacted to the troubled state of the banking industry by paring regional banks from their lists of acceptable names. This forced regional banks out of the New York market and caused others to pay high rates. As money eased, the situation reversed somewhat. Customers began looking at a wider range of names and found that some regional banks were strong credits compared with some of their big New

York sisters. Gradually more regional names became acceptable to investors in the national market, and spreads narrowed between the rates at which prime regional names could issue CDs and those at which the nation's top banks could write. However, no matter how good they may be as credits, regional banks will never be able to sell their paper at the same rates top banks do because they have so little paper outstanding that it does not trade actively in the secondary market and it is thus illiquid.

Small banks often sell limited amounts of CDs to local customers at the rates posted by top banks. They can do so because local firms tend to place their liquidity with local banks. Access to the New York market, however, is closed to a small bank. As one investor noted, "A guy from Springfield can tell me he's better than Morgan and maybe he's right. But how could I resell his CD without my making the same case to the market? I can't, so I would not buy his CD."

The tiering that developed in the mid-1970s among the CDs issued by the top banks gradually worked itself off. As this occurred, management in certain top banks came to the dealers and reminded them that their banks provided the dealers with a lot of financing and other business. They then added that they saw no reason why their CDs should not trade as well as those of any of the other top 10 banks. The dealers said, "OK, we will trade the top 10 names on a no-name basis." This meant that a dealer's bid or offer to another dealer would be good for any of the top (by asset size) 10 banks.

Initially this change tended, if anything, to improve trading in CDs. By making heterogeneous paper more nearly homogeneous, it increased the ease with which CDs could be traded, and that in turn increased the attractiveness of CDs as a trading vehicle and thereby liquidity in the CD market.

However, no dealer agreement—written or in this case understood—can make paper trade for long at a level other than that at which the forces of supply and demand determine it shall trade. The events of 1982 clearly demonstrated this. As noted in Chapter 5, both Chase and Continental got into some severe, well-publicized difficulties in 1982. No dealer or sophisticated investor for that matter thought either bank was in any danger of failing. Nonetheless, suddenly a lot of investors did not want to touch either Chase or Continental paper. They feared that the paper of both banks would become less liquid. Also, a corporate portfolio manager might want to get out of Chase paper because he did not want to have to defend holding it to his board; money funds, with thousands of investors to whom they are answerable, did not want to have, say, some lady in Des Moines with $5,000 in their fund call up—and investors do call—asking why *her* fund was holding paper issued either by a bank that had made tons of bad loans or by a bank that had just dropped a quarter of a billion in connection with the failure of a New York dealer (Drysdale).[5]

Chase recognized the problem, bought back a lot of its paper through its holding company, and thus prevented its paper from trading at a significant concession to the market. It also took special care to ensure that Chase paper meeting the delivery specifications on the next-to-mature CD futures contract on the IMM was *very* scarce. As a result of these moves, there was never any reason for Chase's name to be deleted from the IMM's list of deliverable names.[6]

Continental, unlike Chase, was willing to pay up to issue CDs and at times was hitting bids in the 2- or 3-month area as much as 75 to 80 points above prevailing rates on top name paper. To avoid being asked to remove its name from the IMM's list of deliverable names, Continental, which had previously delivered a lot of paper at the expiration of CD futures contracts, asked the IMM to take its name off the list of deliverable names until it got its house in order.

For banks like Chase and Continental that are temporarily experiencing difficulties and don't want to add to them by being seen in highly visible markets as having to pay up by a wide margin to get funds, a question arises: Where do such banks go to pick up funds? One possibility is retail.

All money market banks post a scale of rates they will pay on small-denomination CDs. Normally these rates are anywhere from 20 to 50 basis points below the rates these same banks post for million-dollar CDs. By posting an aggressive rate on small CDs—the market rate or 1/8 above it, a bank, especially one like Chase with many branches and good access to retail, could and perhaps did raise a lot of money selling $100 and $200,000 CDs to retail. Those CDs would never see the light of day on the street because they are much too small to trade in the normal secondary market.

Maturities

Most CDs issued in the U.S. market are in the 1- to 3-month area. There is a market in 6-month paper, but beyond that no issuing is done in real size. There are several reasons for the short maturities in the CD market. One is demand. Money funds (see Chapter 20) are required to maintain a short average maturity on the securities they hold. Many other investors buying CDs are corporations funding tax and dividend dates that are at most 90 days in the future. These investors need liquidity, and many prefer to obtain it by buying short paper that they can hold to

---

[5] For the Drysdale story, see pp. 323–27.

[6] The IMM futures contracts for domestic CDs and for Eurodollar time deposits are discussed at the end of this chapter.

maturity rather than by buying long paper whose liquidity is inherent in its marketability.

A second reason for the thin market in CDs with a maturity at issue of 6 months or longer is that, in normal times when the yield curve is upward sloping, it's cheaper for banks to buy longer-term money by rolling 3-month CDs. As one banker noted, "Six-month money is high-cost money. So you have to believe that the Fed is going to move dramatically to justify buying it on rate considerations alone. If you buy it at all, it's likely to be to improve—at an acknowledged cost—your liquidity."

The market for CDs with a maturity of 6 months or longer is referred to as a *professional investors' market*. There are some trading accounts and speculative players who buy these CDs, but most are sold initially to dealers. A dealer who buys such CDs often finances them for some period with term RP, thereby creating a future security with some built-in yield (recall Chapter 9's discussion of figuring the tail).[7] For a dealer to profit from this strategy, that is, to be able to sell out the future security he is creating at a profit, interest rates over the holding period must fall, remain stable, or at least not rise sharply. This raises an interesting point. The dealer and the banker are both attempting to make sophisticated predictions as to where interest rates are going. If the dealer is right in believing that he can make money positioning longer-term paper, then the banker is wrong in thinking that he can reduce funding costs by issuing it. A bank funding officer put this succinctly, "When dealers ask me why we don't do more business with them, my answer is that, if they are making money, I'm doing a lousy job. For us to do business, one of us has to be making a bad mistake."

The all-in cost of CD money

When a bank evaluates the cost of CD money, it thinks in terms not of the rate it posts but of its *all-in cost*—reserve requirements and FDIC insurance included. This number is of particular interest to a bank when it is choosing between issuing CDs and buying term Fed funds or when it is considering buying domestic CD money to do an arbitrage into the Euromarket.

The Fed used to be concerned over the short average maturity of bank CDs outstanding. To induce banks to issue longer-term CDs, the Fed first raised Reg Q ceilings on CDs of longer maturity and then cut reserve requirements on them.[8] However, when money tightens and interest rates rise—precisely the time when the Fed would like to see the banks buying some longer-term money, the average maturity of CDs outstand-

---

[7] See pp. 298–301.

[8] The Fed currently imposes no rate ceiling on CDs with denominations of $100,000 or more.

ing falls noticeably. During such times the banks would like to issue longer-term CDs, but as a practical matter investors refuse to buy them. When money rates rise toward a peak, investors want to keep their options open. They will give banks money for only a month to ensure that they will be in a position to extend into longer maturities when rates peak. Investors, of course, are happy to buy longer-term CDs when rates are falling, but that's precisely when banks have no incentive to issue them.

The Fed's old structure of reserve requirements—lower requirements on longer CDs—probably had little impact on CD maturities because it was outweighed by the impact of investors' preferences with respect to maturities. In any case, under the Banking Act of 1980, reserve requirements on time deposits of *all* maturities are being phased by 1984 to a single level, 3%. Thus by 1984 the all-in cost to a bank of CD money will be the same whether the bank buys 1-month or 1-year money. Formerly the longer the maturity at issue, the lower the all-in cost.

What reserves a bank must now hold on time deposits depends on the maturity structure of the CDs it had outstanding in September 1980 when the phase-in period began. Most big banks seemed by late 1982 to be already at or near the 3% level. For such a bank the all-in cost of CD money is 103.09% of their posted rate plus 8 basis points for FDIC insurance, which totals 103.17% of the posted rate.[9] To illustrate, if a bank is posting a rate of 9.15 on 3-month CDs, its all-in cost on that money will be:

$$1.031 \times 0.0915 = 0.0944$$
$$= 9.44\%$$

THE NEW ISSUE MARKET

Most banks issuing CDs prefer to place as many as possible directly with customers. A bank feels that the less visible borrowing it does through brokers and dealers, the better its credit will appear. Also a bank fears that CDs it issues through dealers may end up back on the street at

---

[9] Calculating the all-in cost of CD money to a bank that must hold non-interest-bearing reserves at the Fed is simple. Let

r = the quoted rate paid on the CD
r^* = the all-in rate paid when required reserves are taken into account

If a bank must keep 3% reserves against time deposits, then the amount of money available to it will be, per dollar taken in, only $1.00 - \$0.03$; and the all-in cost of this money will be r^* in the expression

$$r^*(1.00 - 0.03) = r$$

which simplifies to

$$r^* = \frac{r}{0.97}$$

just the time when it wants to borrow additional funds, thereby creating a situation in which it must compete with itself to write new CDs.

Despite their predilection for writing direct to customers, banks do issue a lot of CDs through dealers. As a funding officer whose attitude is typical noted, "All things being equal, we would rather place the deposit ourselves. But if a dealer is willing to take our CDs at a competitive rate and it fits our needs, we sell to them."

Every morning a bank will talk with 10 or 15 major dealers who quote the bank their runs; this gives a bank some idea of where the market is and of the conditions under which it could write. The inter-dealer run, which (as noted below) is now good for the top 7 names, often comes from a dealer with some editorializing, "If you are interested, this is what I will pay you for your name." In giving a bank a run, the dealer is also trying to find out at what rates in different maturities that bank would be interested in writing. If a dealer has an interest from a customer in a particular area of the market, he shows the bank a bid for a specific amount and maturity. Since the customer wants his instrument at par, if the bank accepts the bid, it issues the CD at par and pays a commission to the dealer by check.

Alternatively a dealer might be looking for CDs to position because he knows where he could sell them or because he thinks rates are going down. In that case he might call a bank and say, "We can use some 180-day CDs and our bid is 9.50." Should the bank reply, "Sorry we're at 9.45," the dealer might respond, "Too low," or "Oh, what the hell, we'll take them."

The initiative might also come from the bank's side. In CDs the floating supply is smaller than that in bills, and a CD dealer can at times move the market by ¼ with as little as a $50 million deal. For that reason a bank with a big program, say, raising $200 million, might come to a dealer and ask, "What do you think we can get it at?" or "Do you have any interest?" The dealer would spend five minutes calling customers to survey their needs, and even if retail interest was thin, he might, depending on his view of the market, bid on and position the securities with just a few presales.

A bank with a big program might also call a dealer and say, "We want you to know that we're writing in 180 days, our rate is 9.5, and we'll give you an 05 on what you sell." In that case the bank in effect hires a large sales force for a day for a small commission. The pressure on dealers to help banks by either positioning their paper or providing them with a sales force becomes particularly acute when money is tight and banks need to write a lot of paper to fund burgeoning loan demand.

Another advantage to a bank in using a dealer is that, when a bank writes a big program on its own, talk about what it's doing gets around. An investor who knows that a bank is writing big amounts at, say, 9.5 is likely to reason, "If the bank has that sort of appetite, I ought to demand ⅝." And pretty soon the bank finds it has to start stepping up its offering rate by 05s. If, in contrast, the bank operates through a dealer, it is often able to get in and out of the market at a single price.

While the dealers still play an important role—depending on the time and market conditions—in helping banks distribute new paper, two developments have occurred in recent years that have somewhat diminished their role. One is that many banks, especially those having dealer departments, have beefed up their own sales force and are thus able to locate retail interest more readily on their own. A second and more important development is the big share of the total CDs issued by top banks that are taken by money funds.

Said one bank officer, "The money funds just sop up enormous amounts of paper. Every time we post a rate, the money funds are the first buyers we see. Much of that money comes direct because the funds figure that the dealer, if he does the trade, will have his 02 or 05, whereas if they come direct, they can get the full rate." Having said that, the same dealer went on to note, "Dealers willing to work at it are still able to distribute quite well. I see less of the small firms coming into us and bidding aggressively, but I sure see the Salis and Merrills."

The funding officer

The role of the bank officer who decides what CD money to buy and at what rate to buy it differs vastly from what it was and is vastly more hectic than it was. Noted one, "We are not just funding the bank any more. We are asset and liability managers. We are giving rates to the lending side off which they price loans to domestic borrowers and to our branches; then we have to decide how to fund those loans. If we make a 6-month, fixed-rate loan, do we match fund or buy 3s against it?

"We run daily position sheets now—unheard of in the past—to measure our exposure in all maturity categories in each of our books: our fixed-rate book, our CD loan book, our foreign branch exposure, and so on. We are running a more European-type book than was done historically in the U.S. Years ago the S&U committee got together and came up with a total, decided where rates were going, and told me to buy half a billion in X maturities over the next couple of weeks. Now it is a constant funding decision."

Regional banks

Regional banks are not linked into the national market the way money center banks are. However, many of them do a good job selling their CDs by relying on local money. As one dealer noted, "Local investors feel more comfortable putting money into a bank where they can talk to the bank's officers and get some scuttlebutt on the quality of its loans. Some regional banks have gotten super cheap money because local investors feel they know more about them than they can about the national banks. It is basically the New York money center banks, the Chicago banks, and the Texas banks—anyone perceived as being impacted by the low cost of oil—that are getting slightly cut back by the regional investor. The exception is Morgan, which has held up best in the top 10 and is perceived as untarnished in the eyes of investors."

Selling to the small investor

Basically the CD market is a market for million-dollar pieces of paper. However, a few dealers who possess extensive branch networks have made a big business out of selling CDs and BAs to retail accounts with $100 or $200,000 to go. A bank like Morgan prefers not to write that sort of paper on its own but is perfectly happy to sell Merrill a large block and then have its computer knock down that block (which is from the vantage point of Morgan's funding desk just one ticket) into many small pieces. For a big bank selling in small pieces through Merrill is a good deal because at least the stuff is away; it is not going to come back into the market and compete with new paper the bank may later want to write.

In conversations with bankers, dealers, and brokers, Merrill, with its vast network of offices and its 6,000 account executives (AEs), is always mentioned as the first dealer that was out there selling BAs, CDs, and commercial paper in small pieces to small retail accounts. Merrill wisely chose not to offer just small pieces of top name bank paper to regional investors. Unlike many other dealers, Merrill buys paper from a huge number of what it considers to be creditworthy regional banks that need help in funding. This gives AEs in every one of Merrill's branch offices a product to sell that has local recognition: Investors in New York may not have heard of a Des Moines bank, but Des Moines investors have. In selling $100,000 CDs of regional banks, Merrill heavily promotes the FDIC (FSLIC in the case of S&L paper) to its customers. These include municipalities, bank trust departments, wealthy individuals, and smaller institutional investors. Other firms with national distribution networks, such as Hutton and Paine Webber, are doing much the same thing Merrill is.

Yankee CDs

Foreign banks open branches in the U.S., the natural home of the dollar, to expand their liability base in dollars for several reasons: to finance and to be better able to fine tune the maturity structure of their overall Euro book, to finance loans made to U.S. and foreign corporations operating in the U.S., and to be able to arbitrage dollars out of the U.S. market into the Euromarket. Like U.S. banks, most foreign banks also run Cayman and Nassau branches out of New York.

A foreign bank that makes a reasonable attempt to cultivate relationships with domestic banks can easily gain access to money in the Federal funds market. However, since this market deals primarily in overnight funds, foreign banks wanting to obtain financing for longer periods must rely on the sale in the New York market of either their CDs or their BAs.

While dealers can be helpful to U.S. banks in writing CDs, particularly second-tier banks, they are a necessity to U.S. branches of foreign banks. A foreign bank branch trying to sell CDs in the U.S. market faces several problems. To many investors its name is not well known. Second, even investors who have heard of a particular foreign bank often fail to perceive that, say, Barclays or Crédit Lyonnais is a giant on the world banking scene just as is Citi or Chase. Third, many sophisticated investors feel that they don't know enough about French, Japanese, or other foreign accounting practices to read intelligently the financial statements of foreign banks. Fourth, investors tend only to hear and know about the problem loans on a foreign bank's balance sheet; they do not, for example, know that Barclay's sovereign risk exposure is half of Citi's exposure to Brazil.

In issuing CDs in the U.S. market, a foreign bank branch starts with a few U.S. commercial customers who, because they have dealt with that bank abroad, know it and are willing to buy its CDs. To sell beyond this limited customer base, a foreign bank branch must turn to a dealer, who for an 05 will push that bank's paper by acquainting other investors with its name and credit. The resulting education takes time, so a foreign bank branch normally starts out having to pay substantially more than domestic issuers, a condition that gradually diminishes as its name grows in acceptability.

An alternative some foreign banks, including a few Japanese banks, have used is to post a low rate with dealers and then pay up to retail customers. One danger in this approach is that once customers get accustomed to earning a premium, they will expect to continue to get it. Another is that a bank that pays a large premium to the street may cheapen its name, a situation that takes time and effort to reverse.

U.S. dealers, who are always looking for a new product to peddle, would like to sell foreign bank CDs to domestic investors but are leery of positioning much of this paper since they know it is difficult to sell to investors. The reluctance of dealers to position foreign paper, in turn, decreases the willingness of investors to buy it because paper that dealers won't position is, by definition, illiquid, and most investors place a high value on liquidity.

This is not to say that foreign banks can't and don't sell CDs in New York. They do, and a goodly bit of such paper passes through the hands of and is traded by dealers. However, the quantity of paper foreign banks can sell in New York is small relative to that which U.S. banks of similar size and credit worthiness sell in the same market. Over time, the acceptance of foreign bank CDs has grown among U.S. investors, but the recent switch in Fed policy toward permitting short-term rates to be more volatile has hurt the sale of such paper; volatile rates encourage dealers to seek profits on turnover rather than on positioning, a development which, in recent years, has strengthened the preference of dealers for paper that is readily salable to a wide range of investors.

Lack of familiarity with foreign names is not the only problem foreign banks face in selling their paper in the U.S. As the manager of the New York branch of a big French bank noted, "Foreign banks, in bidding for dollars, face two limits: One is set by investors on the basis of the institution's financials; the other is set by dollar holders on the country risk they are willing to accept." With respect to the second limit, French banks compete with each other and with corporate bidders for dollars, such as Gaz de France, which is a big issuer of commercial paper through Goldman Sachs. Finally it should be mentioned that the growing number of foreign banks that are issuing commercial paper through a holding company in the U.S. may be raising cheap dollars this way, but such paper competes with the bank's CDs for an investor's limit on the name.

A continuing problem with Yankee CDs is their lack of liquidity. In 1982 the volume of secondary trading in Yankees actually dropped. The sources of the illiquidity of Yankee paper are several. Dealers are loath to actively position and trade such paper. Also, in Yankees there is no established interdealer run as there is in domestic and Euro CDs. Each country trades differently, and each bank within that country trades differently. In the absence of a top bank, no-name run, a dealer calling another has to say, "I am offering X, Y, and Z at these levels. Could you use them?" Said one broker of Yankee CDs, "The dealers could not trade domestics and Euros with the ease they do without an established run, and that ease creates liquidity."

Because dealers take small positions in Yankee CDs, they will not give the same support to the Yankee CDs in a down market that they will, to protect their positions, to domestic CDs. Noted one dealer, "You can sell Yankees till the cows come home during a bull market. In a bear market no one wants to touch them. Yankees are the least liquid paper we trade on the desk."

The liquidity of Yankee CDs contrasts sharply with the liquidity of Japanese BAs (Chapter 17). Both are foreign-name paper handled by U.S. dealers and brokered by several U.S. shops. Japanese BAs, of which there are a lot more outstanding than there are of Yankee CDs, have a top bank, no-name run, and a lot of names trade on this run. Currently the liquidity of Japanese BAs makes them an excellent trading vehicle, better than domestic BAs and at times possibly as good as domestic CDs. Having a foreign name does not guarantee that paper will be illiquid.

The typical buyer of a CD issued by a foreign bank is a *yield buyer*. To get that yield, he incurs what he perceives as some extra risk, and he accepts limited liquidity. Since many foreign banks issuing CDs in the U.S. market work through an exclusive dealer, the primary if not the only place where the holder of such a CD can get a bid on it is from the selling dealer. The latter may—given the state of the market—offer the CD holder a good bid, but still that holder is not in the comforting position of being able to shop the street for bids as he would be if he held a Citi or Morgan CD. Also, spreads between bid and ask quotes on Yankee CDs are greater than those on top-grade U.S. paper.

We've said something about the tiering in the U.S. market between different U.S. names. If we look at the overall picture, the tiering becomes more complex. Some investors prefer a foreign bank CD issued out of New York to a CD issued out of London because they feel the latter exposes them to sovereign risk. More typical these days is the investor who asks: Why should I buy a Yankee if I can get a top U.S. name Euro at the same price? Thus tiering in the overall CD market is roughly as follows. The lowest rates are paid by the top 25 U.S. banks (excepting those with temporary name problems—Chase and Continental in 1982) on CDs issued in the U.S. market. The next lowest rates are paid on CDs issued by very top U.S. names in London. These are followed by CDs issued by good foreign names in New York. Finally, at the top of the yield scale are CDs issued by good continental names in London.

Shills and backdooring

Domestic banks have a sort of love-hate feeling for dealers. They realize that dealers can be useful to them in writing and that dealers make their paper salable by creating a secondary market for it. However, the banks don't like to pay the dealers at 05, and they don't want the dealers holding paper that could be dumped at an unpropitious moment on the street. Because of this ambivalent attitude, the banks and the dealers have at times played interesting games with each other.

A few banks absolutely refuse to sell to or through dealers. The dealers, not to be outwitted in their search for inventory, respond by finding corporations that are willing to act as "shills" for them. These corporations go to a bank, take down a big block of CDs on which they are sometimes offered a rate concession by the bank, and then turn around and sell this paper to the dealer for an 02, a practice known as *backdooring*.

The hoaxed bank often finds out. As one funding officer noted, "The dealers like nothing better than to call and say, 'Hey, we just got 50 million of your CDs at $10.60. You could have sold them to us direct and saved the hassle.' Still, when we started to use the dealers, I was amazed at how many of our 'customers' had been fronting for dealers."

Sometimes when a bank has a big program to do, it practices price discrimination. It sells to big corporations through the bid side of the CD market to entice them into taking down a couple hundred million dollars of new CDs. Then, when the bank thinks these securities are put away at retail and will not come back to haunt it on the street, the bank offers the dealers maybe the last $50 million of the program at the true bid side of the market; by that time the bank has offered many big customers, whom the dealers might call, the same securities at a better rate.

The idea, of course, is not to ruffle the market, but the strategy frequently fails. The customers who buy the new CDs hit the dealers' bids with old CDs, and the market backs up, which is exactly what the bank was trying to avoid. Meanwhile the corporations buying the new CDs and kicking out old ones take out a "nickel" or a "dime" (5 or 10 basis points) on the transaction.

As one ex-corporate money runner noted, "I never thought this practice did the banks any long-run good, and I never encouraged it. But if a bank offered me the opportunity to earn money, I was *not* there to turn it down. If they said they did not want the new CDs flogged on the street for a week, I would honor that. I would not backdoor the securities for an 02, but I would kick out some old CDs. In came some new Citis and out went some old Citis or Morgans or what have you. It was just a transfer on which I could take out ⅛ on the banks."

Practices of this sort are less prevalent than in the past. The dealers are careful to monitor what is going on "away." Also, many banks realize that the dealers are more useful to them than they had thought and that the kind of aftertaste the market has for a bank's CDs depends partly on how fairly the bank treats investors and dealers when it issues.

Today many banks believe that it is not in their interest to offer similar institutions CDs of the same maturity at different rates or to sell a dealer a block of CDs and then raise rates five minutes later, leaving the dealer "hanging there" with paper at a loss. As one CD writer noted, "When I do a big block with a dealer and think that's it for awhile, I tell him. Naturally top management may suddenly change strategy and start selling again, but at least the dealer knows I tried to be honest. Dealers like this and regard banks who operate this way as 'professionals.'"

DEALER OPERATIONS

There are currently about 35 dealers in CDs, about ⅖ths of whom are banks that have wires into the brokers and do trades through them. The number of dealers who are big players and active market makers in both good and bad markets is much smaller. Many dealers are relatively new at the game, being stock firms that entered the money market after negotiated commissions cut their brokerage income. There is a lot of variability in size and importance among dealers, and the key ones are the firms that were there originally: Salomon Brothers, Goldman Sachs, Discount Corp., A. G. Becker, First Boston, Lehman Brothers, and Merrill.

A bank incurs a reserve cost, which a nonbank dealer does not, if it finances its CD position with RP money, as nonbank dealers typically do; but a bank can buy Fed funds which nonbank dealers cannot. A bank dealership has the advantage that its CD trader knows at least what his own bank plans in terms of writing CDs. One benefit to a bank of dealing in CDs is that the bank's CD trader, who is in constant contact with the market, can provide the bank's funding officers with useful, up-to-the-minute information on rates.

Part of a dealer's job is distribution, getting new CDs that banks want to write out into investors' hands for an 05. Since many sales of this sort are generated by inducing investors to swap out of old CDs into new ones, such sales often create the basis for an additional string of transactions.

A second and more important part of the dealers' job is creating a secondary market for CDs. Dealers do this by standing ready at all times to quote bids and offers both to retail and to other dealers. Because of the diversity of names and maturities in the CD market, dealers cannot short CDs, but in their role as market makers, they do position them, sometimes in large amounts.

Because bank CDs vary, depending on who the issuer is, with respect to both credit risk and liquidity, CD dealers, like investors, establish lists of banks whose CDs they will buy and limits on the amounts they will position of each of these names. As might be expected, dealers specialize somewhat. Some, for example, have made an effort to develop a market in foreign bank CDs, whereas others shy away from non-U.S. names. Also, some dealers are stronger in regional names than others. All deal actively in major names.

The inside market

Dealers operate in two markets, the *retail market* in which they do business with customers and the *inside market* in which they trade with each other.

In the interdealer market, bids and offers are good for $5 million with the understanding that good delivery is 5 by 1: five pieces for 1 million each. Some dealers will trade variable-rate CDs on their last leg on the run; others will not. Also, old 1-years with a lot of accrued interest will not trade on the run.

It used to be that a dealer's bids and offers, whether made on a run to another dealer or put into a broker, were good for paper issued by the top 10 banks. Dealers make no official pronouncement as to what banks are on the run; they agree informally among themselves.

Trading top domestic CDs on a no-name basis worked reasonably well until some of these banks started to get into sufficient trouble that the normal forces of supply and demand in the market caused their paper to trade back from paper issued by the top credits among the 10 largest banks. By fall 1982, the number of banks whose paper was traded on a no-name basis among the dealers had dropped from 10 to 7—First of Chicago, Chase, and Continental having been taken off the list. Even among the banks whose names were left on the list, some tiering continued to exist which made it difficult for the market to function smoothly. Whenever tiering exists among on-the-run names, say, Morgans trade better than Mannys, a dealer can be sure that, if his bid is hit, he will get Mannys not Morgans.

The interdealer market is supposed to trade at a 10-basis-point spread but in reality trades at a much wider spread if there is tiering among on-the-run names. For example, one dealer noted in August 1982, "If the market is quoted 11 to 10.90, you know that, if you hit the bid, you will get Mannys, whereas, if you held Morgans and a retail order came in, you could lose them at 85. Alternatively, if you had 50 million Mannys and called up Sali and said, 'What would you pay for them?' his answer would probably be '11.10.'"

On a dealer run, maturities from a month out to a year are quoted, but specific dates are not mentioned. Instead a dealer will give bid and asked prices for, say, "late Novembers" and "early Decembers."

When a dealer takes a $5 million offering from another dealer, he would naturally like to know if there's another big block behind that offering or if $5 million is it. That is exactly the sort of information the other dealer will not divulge, especially if he is a big seller.

The brokers

In January 1976 one firm started brokering dealer trades in CDs, and since then a number of other firms have entered the business. Brokers are actively used by CD traders for the same reasons they are used by traders in governments—they provide anonymity and speedy communication with other dealers. Also, a dealer may be able to do a large volume in the brokers market, which would be difficult to do direct. In the dealer-to-dealer market a $10 million trade is considered big, except between the largest shops, but sales of $50 million blocks have been done in one shot through a broker with a number of bids on his pad.

When a dealer puts a bid or an offering into a broker, he is expected to let it stand for two or three minutes. During that time the broker pounds his phone board, getting the information out to other dealers. The "pictures" quoted by brokers are in the actively traded areas, 3 to 6 months, and usually there is a two-way market. In CDs, as in bills, dealers play trading games, and the bid and ask quotes given by a broker in a particular maturity may be a "one-man picture." Whether they are is something no broker is supposed to divulge.

Normally bids and offers are for $5 million blocks. If they are for more, the broker will specify by saying that the market is, for example, "10 by 5." In the CD market brokerage equal to an 01 is paid by the dealer that initiates a trade. Because brokerage is paid by only one side in each transaction, *locked markets* can occur. CD trades made between dealers, whether direct or through a broker, are cleared through one of the New York clearing banks.

CDs, domestic and Euro, and BAs, domestic and Japanese, were the last areas of the money market to be invaded by screens, which are now used by all but one of the brokers. So far the existence of brokers' screens in the CD and BA markets has not cut down on dealers speaking directly with one another. Whereas almost all trades in governments are done through brokers, the bulk of trades in CDs and BAs are done direct. Some dealers think brokers' screens actually impair market liquidity, at least when there is tiering among banks on the no-name list, because at such times big dealers deal in blocks at prices quite different from those on the CRTs. The more tiering there is in the market, the more dealers prefer to trade direct.

Also, the failures of Drysdale and Lombard-Wall have raised some concern among dealers about doing trades through brokers who do not give up the name of the other side, which most don't on domestic CDs. Normally CDs and BAs trade for next day settlement. A dealer who sells blind through a broker, especially on a Friday, may worry about what happens if rates go up before the trade settles and the other side turns out to be a small dealer who has gone bust.

CD brokers also handle regional names: Crocker, Harris, Mellon, First Minnie, Texas Commerce, Rep Dallas, First Interstate, and First Atlanta to name a few. Normally regionals are done verbally by the brokers, but FBI has the capacity to type offerings of regionals onto a page that can be brought up by the dealers; other brokers are working on similar systems.

Dealers that are banks are not supposed to deliver new paper they are writing when their bid is hit in the brokers' market. However, there are ways this rule can be gotten around; one is washing new paper through another dealer for an 01.

Financing

Dealer inventories in CDs, with the exception of those held by bank dealers, are normally financed in the RP market. A dealer who wants to hold CDs available for immediate sale to customers will do overnight or short-term RPs. If, alternatively, he wants to hold CDs for some time as a speculation, he will probably do term RPs for 30, 60, or even 90 days.

Since some credit risk attaches to CDs as opposed to governments, the rate on RPs backed with CDs is often slightly greater than that on RPs collateralized with governments. How much a dealer has to pay up to RP nongovernment paper depends in part on market conditions and on the kind of paper he's financing—spreads are wider the tighter money is and the poorer the credit of the issuer. Cost also depends on how clever the dealer is. As one noted: "RP financing is an art. There's tiering in the RP market, but a dealer who knows his retail outlets—who they are and what they will take in terms of names and maturities—can finance CDs and BAs with RP money at or only slightly above the RP rate on governments."

That statement, made several years ago, probably did not hold true in late 1982 when the failures of Drysdale and Lombard-Wall were still on everyone's mind and investors were viewing banks with a jaundiced eye because of all their problem loans, country—Poland, Mexico—and company—Dome Petroleum, International Harvester. One nonbank dealer noted, "We can get money but tiering is terrific. Today government RP was going at 5.75, BAs and CDs at 8.70. One of the problems is that a lot of money funds can do RP only against governments. Also, banks have gotten more conservative in terms of what size loans they will give dealers. Whereas before a bank might have been willing to give a dealer 100 million against collateral, it might now apply its legal lending limit, a much smaller figure, even to overnight loans."

In the RP market transactions from overnight out to 30 days are easy to do. RPs for 60 or 90 days are tougher because so many investors want liquidity. To get around this difficulty, some dealers permit customers to put an RP back to them at the bid side of the RP market. That gives the investor the opportunity to enjoy both liquidity and the higher yield of a term RP.

When a dealer finances CDs in the RP market, he encounters a problem that he does not find when he finances discount securities such as bills or BAs; namely, that financing CDs eats up dealer capital. CDs bear interest, and the normal practice in the RP market is for a loan against such instruments to be made for only face value *not* for face value plus accrued interest. Thus the dealer who buys a CD has to put up his own capital to finance any accrued interest. The problem of capital attrition becomes even more acute if the CD happens to be selling at a premium. Because accrued interest on a CD cannot be financed in the RP market, dealers are loath to take in old paper, especially if it carries a high coupon. For that reason a dealer offering "stale dated paper" in the interdealer market is expected to specify that it is such.

Dealer philosophy and position

Some of the profits a CD dealer earns arise from the 05s he picks up distributing new paper and from the chain of swaps that such distribution frequently sets off. In many areas of the money market, day trading is another important source of profit. This tends not to be so in CD trading because the CD market does not have liquidity in size.

To win big, a CD trader has to position. The extent to which shops active in the CD market are willing to position and the fashion in which they do so vary considerably. In some shops the primary focus is on keeping retail happy, and most of the inventory on the dealer's shelf is for sale, the occasional exception being when the dealer really likes the market and decides to bet big. At the other extreme are *spectail* shops: shops that specialize in speculation but also do some business with retail.

Since a trader can't short cash CDs, the only position he can take in the cash market is a long one. As noted, a firm that assumes a speculative long position in CDs often does so by buying longer-term CDs and putting them out on term RP. This is the riskiest form such speculation can take but the one that pays off most when the dealer is right.

In evaluating the merits of going long, a CD trader, like any other money market trader, watches the Fed's every move and every other indicator that might tell him something about future trends in interest rates. The main threats to the trader are (1) that interest rates in general might rise, (2) that short-term interest rates alone might rise due to a shift in the yield curve, and (3) that yields on CDs might rise relative to yields on other short-term instruments. With respect to this final risk, every CD trader constantly bears in mind that "any clown with a pencil [bank liability manager] can create as many CDs as he wants to"; thus predicting future spreads between CDs and bills is extremely difficult. Another special factor the CD trader faces is that liquidity is poorer in the CD market than in the bill market. Thus an ill-conceived long position in CDs will be harder and more costly to liquidate than one in bills.

The increased volatility that has characterized interest rates in recent years has magnified the risk to a dealer of holding positions. Recognizing this, position managers in every dealership have set new, smaller limits on the positions they will take in different instruments and maturity ranges. As one position manager noted, "Whereas rates could go 50 basis points in 1977 and that would be a disaster, today they can go 250. Simple arithmetic says, if before you took positions of 800 million, you should now play with only 100, 200, or 300 million positions. If you don't, you risk losing the shop."

The decreasing willingness of dealers to position appears to have had no noticeable impact on the ability of banks to get new paper sold, perhaps because so many new dealers have entered the CD market and also because banks sell an increasing proportion of the CDs they issue directly to retail. One funding officer, speaking of recent experience at his bank, noted, "Once in awhile we have done some enormous issuing that we could never have done historically, and the market does not even realize it is out there. It may be that individual dealers have cut back on the positions they are willing to take, but the market now is just so large that it seems to me that we can issue an enormous amount of paper compared to what we could have done four or five years ago. One day in 76 or 77, we hit *The Wall Street Journal* by doing 400 million of CDs in a day. Now I can do over half a billion, and no one knows I have done it."

One area of the CD market that has been hurt by the dealers' decreased willingness to position CDs is variable-rate CDs. Such CDs are normally issued with a *put letter* from the selling dealer saying that the buyer can put these securities back to that dealer at par on a roll date. This put right, which is given by the dealer to the investor with the tacit understanding that the put will never be exercised, hinges on the ability of the dealer to take back CDs in an adverse environment and, if necessary, finance them to maturity. In the economic environment prevailing in 1982, dealers began to worry that, if a put were exercised, it would be on paper of a poor credit, paper that the dealer might be unable to finance. Consequently dealers became less willing to write put letters.

Whatever his appetite for positioning may be, every dealer takes his relations with retail seriously. He earns from retail when he helps banks distribute. Also, retail is the only place he can unload regional and foreign bank CDs that end up in his position. And in bad markets retail may be the only place he can sell even the best-quality CDs he has in inventory. Finally, to every dealer retail is of crucial importance because a dealer looks to his retail customers as a source of RP money for financing his position.

LIQUIDITY

Since different dealers handle different names, an investor cannot count on getting a bid from every dealer on paper he holds unless it's top name paper. He can, however, be sure that a dealer who has sold him paper will always make him a bid on that paper.

How far back a dealer's bid to retail will be from his offering rate depends both on the name on the paper and on market conditions. In a stable market the dealer might bid back an 02 to an 05 for major-name paper, whereas in foreign and other more difficult names, he might bid back 10 basis points or more. When the market is backing up, dealers' bids get more defensive, especially for regional and foreign names.

While liquidity in the CD market, measured in terms of spreads between bid and asked prices, is good in reasonably stable markets, the CD market reacts more violently to an upward nudge in interest rates than does the bill market. There are several reasons. First, when interest rates start rising, there is concern on the part of both dealers and investors that banks will respond by writing more CDs; the specter of rising interest rates, which makes dealers and investors want to get out of CDs, gives banks an equally rational incentive for creating more of them. Thus as money tightens, supply becomes more uncertain in the CD market than in the bill market; and as a result the CD market backs up faster.

Another difference between the CD and the bill markets is that many buyers of bills are required by law, charter, or management-set parameters to limit their investments to governments or to governments and RP collateralized by governments. To the extent that these investors have funds to invest, they provide automatic support for the bill market. No such institutionally created support exists in the CD market.

During credit crunches prior to 1974, the problem of liquidity in the CD market was particularly acute. Dealers permitted themselves to get trapped with large positions and in self-defense simply ceased to bid. Once that occurred, the secondary market disappeared by definition; CDs did not trade, and they had to be bought as an investment.

While the CD market was not without its problems in 1974, it did give a better account of itself. Dealers had learned how to react to rising rates; they did not permit themselves to get trapped with big positions, and CDs continued to trade during the crunch. The same held true during the 1979–82 period of high and highly volatile rates. Also, starting in 1981, CD dealers could lay off risk in the CD futures market.[10]

Term CDs

The improvement that has occurred in the behavior of the short-term CD market during crunches bodes well for the future of the market for term CDs; that is, CDs with maturities ranging from 2 to 5 years. There is no way that banks can sell CDs in any maturity range without a viable

---

[10] See discussion of CD futures at the end of this chapter.

secondary market because investors demand liquidity, which can be provided only through active market making and positioning by dealers. Positioning CDs eats up capital, and the capital attrition becomes larger the longer the maturity of the CDs involved. Thus dealers were slow to make a market in term CDs.

In the fall of 1976, however, dealers started to take a serious look at this market—to work for spreads and to establish lines in bank names. They also retailed fair-sized term issues for Citibank and for Chase. These issues were anything but successful, partly because of pricing and market conditions, and dealers were left holding at a loss big positions in a thin market. Thus for a time it looked as if the term CD market might die at birth, but in retrospect it was probably only going through the same birth pangs that the original CD market did. The market for term CDs did come back, and over time it seems likely to grow and develop as more dealers make a commitment to it.

The high interest rates that prevailed in the late 1970s and early 1980s discouraged banks from issuing term CDs. However, as rates began to decline steeply in the fall of 1982, many banks displayed renewed interest in doing term issues. For a bank, even one that is a big dealer in CDs, it is crucial to get one or more other dealers involved in the underwriting of any term issue it does because the bank doing the issuing cannot create a secondary market in its own paper; it needs other interested dealers to trade the issue and give it liquidity throughout its life.

Savings and loan association CDs

Savings and loan associations, like banks, are permitted to issue large-denomination negotiable CDs free from any rate lid. A few do so through New York dealers, but the volume outstanding is small and likely to remain so. In the market for bank CDs, only paper issued by relatively large banks is traded actively enough to have real liquidity and thus to be attractive to investors in the national market. Since the country's largest S&Ls, even after the numerous consolidations that have occurred in recent years, are no larger than a respectable-sized regional bank, it's hard to envision how a large and active market for S&L paper could develop.

EURODOLLAR CDs

Eurodollar CDs were first issued in the London market in 1966 by Citibank. The new instrument was quickly and readily accepted by the market, and as Figure 15–4 shows, the volume outstanding rose rapidly. In early 1982, there were $78 billion of Eurodollar CDs outstanding. While this figure seems impressive, it is small compared to the $140

FIGURE 15–4
Eurodollar CDs outstanding (U.S. $ billions)

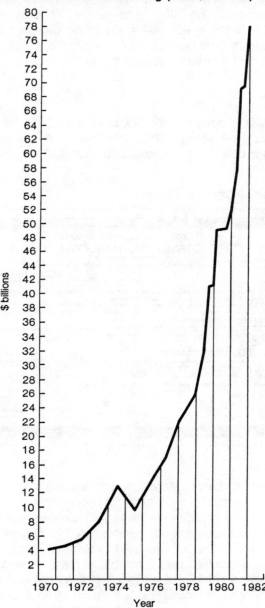

Source: Bank of England.

billion of CDs outstanding in the domestic market. Part of the reason for the contrast lies in the smaller size of the Euromarket. A more important factor, however, is the differing roles that CDs play in the two markets. Selling CDs is *the* major way a domestic banker obtains longer-term funds, but for a Euro banker the CD market is merely an adjunct to the more important interbank deposit market.

Characteristics

A Euro CD, like a domestic CD, is a negotiable instrument evidencing a time deposit made with a bank at a fixed rate for a fixed period (Figure 15–5). Euro CDs bear interest, and Euro CD rates are quoted on an

FIGURE 15–5
A Euro CD issued by Chase in London

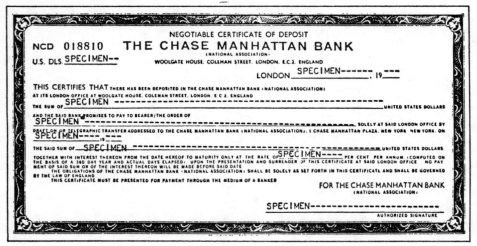

interest-bearing basis. Interest, which is calculated for actual days on a 360-day-year basis, is paid at maturity on Euro CDs with a maturity of 1 year or less and annually on those with a maturity of more than 1 year.

All Euro CDs are currently denominated in dollars. There is demand by investors for CDs denominated in German marks and Swiss francs, but the German and Swiss central banks have requested that the Bank of England not permit the issuance in London of CDs denominated in their currencies. Their objective has been to discourage any innovation that in their view might create additional opportunities for speculation in their currency or encourage the use of their currency as a reserve currency. The Bundesbank has also discouraged the issuance of Euromark CDs outside London.

For all intents and purposes the market in Euro CDs is a London market. Eurodollar CDs are issued in centers outside London, but their numbers are small, and the liquidity and marketability of non-London CDs are limited. The major issuers of Eurodollar CDs in the London market are the branches of top U.S. banks. Eurodollar CDs, however, are also issued in London by the British clearing banks, the British overseas banks, Canadian bank branches, continental bank branches, Japanese bank branches, and regional U.S. bank branches.[11]

Sales of Euro CDs are normally made for settlement two days forward, although settlement on a same day basis can be arranged. Settlement is made by payment of funds in New York, but the actual securities are issued and safekept in London.

Eurodollar CDs issued in London are subject to British regulations. These specify that payment at maturity must be authorized by the issuing bank in London, but actual payment is made in New York for value the same day the CD is presented in London for payment.

One problem both for banks issuing Euro CDs and for investors in these instruments is that, because of the difference in time zones between New York and London, it is impossible to synchronize—as is normally done in money market transactions—delivery of and payment for Euro CDs. To cope with this difficulty and to minimize the physical movement of securities, the First National Bank of Chicago has set up in London a *CD Clearing Centre,* which assures participants payment and delivery on any transaction they make with another member of the Centre.

Euro CDs, like domestic CDs, are normally issued in $1 million pieces. However, Euro CDs of $500,000 trade at less of a concession to the market than do domestic CDs of similar size. Because most Euro loans are rolled every 3 or 6 months, the bulk of Euro CDs issued are in the 3- to 6-month maturity range. However, Euro CDs with maturities as long as 5 years are common; the proceeds of such term CDs are used to match fund assets of similar maturity.

Rates

The Fed has ruled that Euro CDs issued by foreign branches of U.S. banks are exempt from Reg Q because they are liabilities of the branch. Thus U.S. bank branches in London have always been free to pay the going market rate for CD money, a situation that led in 1969 to substantial gaps between the rates paid on CDs in New York and London. Today,

---

[11] Deposit taking and short-term lending in the domestic sterling market are dominated in Great Britain by a few large institutions that are referred to as *clearing banks* because they are members of the London Clearing House. The British *overseas banks,* which have branches around the globe, are a relic of the British Empire, whose specific financial needs they developed to serve.

with Reg Q in abeyance on all large-denomination CDs, rates on Euro CDs track domestic CD rates closely, as Figure 15–6 shows. Normally Euro rates are higher than U.S. rates, with the spread between the two being wider the tighter money is and the longer the maturity of the securities compared is.

FIGURE 15–6
Yields on 3-month CDs, Euro and domestic

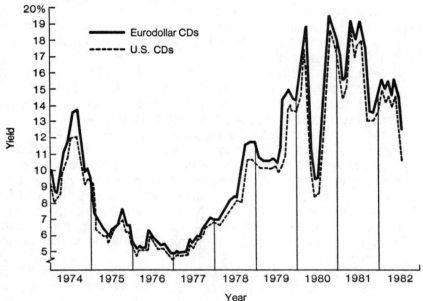

Source: *An Analytic Record of Yields and Spreads,* Salomon Brothers.

The gap between yields on domestic and Euro CDs is due to two factors. First, Euro CDs are less liquid than domestic CDs, for which investors demand a rate premium. Second, many U.S. investors view Eurodollar CDs as a riskier investment than domestic CDs either because they are worried about the loans that the London branches of U.S. banks have granted to places like Poland or because they are concerned about the possibility that the British might act against the Euro operations of London banks. In this respect it should be noted that any Eurodollar CD issued by the London branch of a U.S. bank is a direct obligation of that bank, and *the credit is thus that of the parent.* Therefore an investor who is worried about, say, Citi London's loans to Poland will expose himself to no less risk if he buys a Citi New York CD in preference to a Citi London CD. With respect to sovereign risk, it is true that some sticky legal questions would arise should the British stop payment on Eurodollar CDs issued in London. However, as noted in Chapter 6, the likelihood of their doing so is close to, if not, zero.

The investors

Knowledgeable people in the London market estimate that as much as 50 percent of all Euro CDs are *lock-up CDs*. As noted in Chapter 6, a lock-up CD is really a Euro time deposit masquerading as a CD. Lock-up CDs are issued with the understanding that they will not be traded, and typically they are safekept by the issuing bank. Usually they yield a rate close to that paid on time deposits of similar maturity. Lock-up CDs are bought primarily by foreign banks and bank branches in London and on the Continent; some, however, are purchased by U.S. bank branches in London. The motivation of the buyer is always to improve the cosmetics of his dollar book by giving his dollar assets the appearance of greater liquidity.

Another big chunk of money invested in Euro CDs comes from banks in the expatriate money belt of Switzerland: Geneva, Lausanne, and Lugarno. The money invested is customer money, and the Euro CDs acquired are almost never traded because the customers for whom Swiss banks invest are interested in avoiding taxes and obtaining safety, not in earning 16ths or 8ths through trading. Sometimes, such a customer needs cash; if he does, the Swiss bank simply lends to him against his CD rather than selling the instrument.

A large fraction of the remaining Eurodollar CDs issued are sold to investors in the United States, often by U.S. dealers active in the London market. Some large and sophisticated U.S. corporate portfolio managers invest actively in Euro CDs and will readily swap back and forth between Eurodollar CDs and domestic CDs in response to changes in yield spreads. In general, however, sellers of Euro CDs, until recently when attitudes began to change, experienced only limited success with U.S. corporate portfolio managers. Many of the latter are either unfamiliar with the instrument or concerned about sovereign risk. Also, even the portfolio manager who views Euro CDs as an attractive investment vehicle may end up asking himself: Is explaining the instrument and the risk to the board worth an extra 30 basis points? Many of the Euro CDs placed in the United States are sold to smaller banks that view the instrument as giving them the opportunity to earn extra yield while still maintaining reasonable liquidity.

A recent and rapidly growing entrant to the ranks of Euro CD buyers is U.S. money funds. Most money funds are precluded by restrictions in their prospectuses from investing in Europaper. Nonetheless in 1982 there were eight funds (six retail and two institutional), each with assets in excess of a billion dollars, that held a proportion, sometimes sizable, of their total assets in Euro CDs or Euro time deposits.

Tiering

In the London market a wide range of names is accepted in both the new issue and secondary markets. However, few CDs other than those issued by top U.S. names are sold in the U.S. because that is all U.S. investors are currently willing to buy.[12] The narrow range of names acceptable in the U.S. market is a source of amazement to some British participants in the Euro CD market. As the head of a British discount house observed, "If you try to trade with a New York dealer, his idea of top American is seven names. God knows how he does a business. It is inconceivable to me that you can claim to be a market maker and trade only half a dozen names. There must be different levels at which and different volumes in which different names will trade."

And in London just these conditions prevail. Banks with better names can write more paper and pay less to issue than banks with lesser names; moreover the tiering between different names, which first became pronounced in 1974, is quite complex. At the top of the pile paying the lowest rates are the four to six largest U.S. banks. Tier two contains the next largest U.S. banks. They are followed by the next 10 U.S. names plus the British clearers. Japanese banks and top continental names fall below that tier. Finally, at the bottom of the pile paying the most are merchant banks and some other lesser names.

Tiering always reflects very much the problems that a particular bank or banks in a particular country have encountered recently. This was particularly true in 1982. Among top U.S. banks, Chase and Continental were out of favor. To prevent this from being reflected in the yields at which outstanding Chase Euros traded, Chase London was reported to have brought up a lot of its paper that found its way to the market. Canadian banks were viewed as a problem because of their big and souring energy-related loans. German banks were viewed with concern because of their large exposure to Eastern European countries. One point that should be made about tiering is that investors are a skittish group. They react rapidly to news and often they overreact. As a result patterns of tiering change constantly: Today's top name is tomorrow's dog, and visa versa.

Tiering among top U.S. names in London is more strongly influenced by size than it is in New York; in 1974 when bad earnings caused Chase to pay up in New York, its need to do so was less pronounced in London.

---

[12] The exception that proves the rule: West Coast banks will buy Japanese paper because they know the credits.

The Euro CD market, however, is more susceptible to temporary indigestion due to large volume than is the domestic CD market. Therefore rate tiering may reflect concern over a bank's issuing habits.

The new issue and secondary markets

Banks issuing Euro CDs in London prefer to sell directly to investors for the same reasons they prefer to do so in issuing domestic CDs. However, they also issue through dealers and brokers.

The presence in London of U.S. dealers such as Salomon Brothers, Goldman Sachs, Lehman Brothers, First Boston, Merrill Lynch, and A. G. Becker dates from the mid-1970s. Becker, the first to arrive, came in 1972. Before that, the banks relied on *brokers* and the *discount houses* for any help they needed in selling CDs.[13]

The firms that took up brokering Euro CDs were London houses that already actively brokered Euro time deposits, foreign exchange, and sterling deposits. These brokers were not then permitted to talk to corporate retail, so primarily they brokered CDs between issuing and buying banks. Brokerage, paid by both sides, was initially 1/32, but as volume increased, the banks beat down the rate first to 1/40 and then to 1/50. Discount houses, which do buy from and sell to retail, participated in the market in two ways. They bought CDs for position and to sell to retail. In the early days of the market, the discount houses received a *placing fee* (equal to brokerage due from the seller) on every CD they bought regardless of whether they held it or sold it to a customer.

With the arrival of the U.S. dealers in London, things changed. The dealers, who bought CDs initially through the brokers, eventually managed to go around them and deal directly with the banks. In doing so, moreover, they operated as they did back home, taking a commission when it was the bank that wanted the dealer to work for it and buying on a net basis when it was the dealer that wanted to position the bank's CDs. This practice spelled an end to the placing fee the discount houses had been receiving.

Today the discount houses have largely retreated from the distribution of CDs to retail. Some, however, do supply Euro CDs to New York dealers that have no London office. The U.S. dealers that come to London enjoy several commanding advantages over the discount houses in trading and distributing CDs. First, the discount houses do not have and cannot get the retail outlets in the U.S. that the U.S. dealers have. Geography also puts the discount houses at a disadvantage with respect to market

---

[13] The *discount houses,* an institution peculiar to Britain, use call and overnight money obtained largely from banks to invest in and to trade short-dated governments, local authority bonds, U.K. Treasury bills, and commercial bills. In effect these institutions hold and invest a large portion of the British banking system's reserves.

feel and information. As one discount house official put it, "We are operating in what is basically one facet of the New York market. But we are
3,000 miles away, so we can't expose ourselves to the risks we would if
we were sitting in New York."

Today the activities of the discount houses in the Euro CD market are
confined largely to holding such CDs for carry profits. The houses buy
CDs, finance them with short-dated funds at a positive spread, and stand
prepared to run down their CD books smartly if that positive carry disappears. Discount houses still do some trading in CDs, but by U.S. standards they are not active traders.

In recent years the number of firms that actively broker Euro CDs has
increased. Also, the nature of such firms has changed. For reasons noted
in Chapter 16, it made a lot of sense for brokers of foreign exchange and
time deposits in London and in New York to engage in various trans-
Atlantic mergers and affiliations that permitted them to be truely international, full service shops. Most of these brokering firms now also broker Euro CDs. Brokering operations have grown because of growth in the
markets they serve and because of the amalgamation among the brokers. It is now common in a large brokering operation to find a number of
desks, one brokering Euro time deposits, another Euro CDs, another Fed
funds, another foreign exchange, and so on.

The techniques used in brokering Euro CDs are much like those used
in brokering Euro time deposits, which we describe in the next chapter.
One exception is that CDs issued by those U.S. banks currently considered to be in the top American category trade on a *no-name* basis. The
broker quotes both bid and asked prices, and in doing so he is always
careful to specify what category of paper he is talking about; for example, on-the-run American, Canadian, British clearer, regional American,
or top continental.

A bank that wants to write CDs will sometimes call a broker to get a
feel for the support price in a given tenor. If the bank likes the level, it
may ask the broker to sell what he can at that level or it may ask him to do
some fixed amount. A broker who quotes bids and offers as firm is
supposed to *substantiate* these quotes, for example, provide a would-be
seller with a buyer at the bid price he has quoted unless line problems
arise; that is, unless the buyer can't take the name the seller is offering.
The brokers' primary customers are banks, the discount houses, U.S.
dealers, and in some cases big retail accounts such as the oil companies; the bank customers include some London banks that run a dealer
operation in other banks' Euro CDs.

The U.S. dealers operate in the Euro CD market much as they do in the
domestic CD market. If a bank that wants to write comes to a dealer, the
dealer will take an 02, which equals the brokerage (1/50) that the selling

bank would have to pay if it sold through a broker. A dealer does not get brokerage from the customer to whom he sells the CD, but he does have profit opportunities that a broker, who never positions, lacks; he can profit from positive carry and from favorable movements in the market.

The dealers all regularly call the major issuing banks to give them runs. Generally their bids are good for $5 million, and they buy at a net price if their bid is hit. A few banks, when they want to do a sizable piece, will be quite open with a dealer they trust. They might, for example, ask the dealer, "If I wanted to do 50 million, what kind of a job could you do for me?" At that point the dealer would call New York to see how much and at what levels his firm could generate retail demand by bidding on securities in customers' portfolios, swapping, for example, customers out of bills into Euro CDs for a yield pickup. Then the dealer would call back the bank, giving it his firm's assessment of the market and a bid on the CDs the bank wanted to write. If word gets around that a large bank is writing a lot of CDs, this will move the market. Thus a bank will talk to a dealer in confidence about what it wants to do only if it is sure this confidence will not be betrayed.

For a bank that wants to write a lot of paper, dealers tend to be a more attractive outlet than brokers. The brokers, who can't position, sell mostly to other banks. They can place $2 million here and $5 or $10 million there, but unless a broker has a lot of bids on his pad, he won't be able to do a $25 or $50 million piece other than in bits and dribbles, a process that gives the market time to learn what the issuing bank is doing and to react to it. In contrast, a U.S. dealer, who is sourcing the huge domestic market, can and will bid on and buy in a single shot large blocks of new CDs. An additional advantage to an issuing bank of using a U.S. dealer is that securities sold to such a firm tend to move out of the London market into the U.S. market, which gets them out of the way of any additional CDs this bank might later want to write.

Any dealer who sells a Euro CD to retail will always bid at market for that CD if the customer later wants to sell it. In addition, the dealers and discount houses trade CDs among themselves. There is thus an active secondary market in Euro CDs. In this market the normal spread between bid and asked prices is 10 basis points, but it may narrow to 5 in active markets. The dealers trade with each other not only directly but through the brokers, who offer them both information on where the market is and anonymity.

In recent years the liquidity of the secondary market for Euro CDs has increased for several reasons. Introduction of a no-name run for top American paper has made interdealer trading and brokering of Euro CDs easier for the same reason it did so in the domestic CD market: It increased the homogeneity of top-grade paper traded there. A second reason for the growth of liquidity in the Euro CD market is that the market has grown rapidly as more and more investors have become familiar with and are willing to invest in Euro CDs.

Liquidity

While there is an active secondary market in Euro CDs, their liquidity—measured in terms of spreads between bid and asked quotes and volume that can be done at these quotes—is less than that of domestic CDs. The reason is that the volume of Euro CDs outstanding is smaller and much of it is lock-up paper. In the Euro CD market, liquidity also depends on name. A seller will get a better quote on top name paper that is traded among the dealers and can be sold through the brokers than on lesser name paper that can be resold only to retail.

Communications

The Euro CD market is very much a two-continent market, with active trading in both London and New York. That such a market can exist is a tribute to modern communications techniques. Dealers show markets into Europe and the United States on both Reuters and Telerate. To communicate across the Atlantic they use open telephone lines and dedicated Telex machines.

CDs versus time deposits

Most lending by banks in the Euromarket to other banks is currently done through the placing of time deposits rather than the purchase of CDs. For the lending bank, time deposits have two disadvantages: They are illiquid and they tie up the lines that each bank sets up to limit its exposure by country and by bank. Because of these disadvantages, some market participants feel that CD purchases will eventually displace deposit placements in the interbank market. If this were to happen, however, the discount at which banks can currently buy money in the Euro CD market would be eliminated, a development the banks are not yet prepared to accept.

CD FUTURES

The great success with which futures contracts for bills and bonds were introduced naturally led futures exchanges and dealers who acted as *futures commission merchants* (*FCMs*) to search for other contracts on fixed-income securities that would meet a genuine need and thus turn into yet another success story. Many thought that a CD futures contract would be a natural winner. Banks were becoming ever more sophisticated in asset and liability management; and CD futures, it was argued, would give them an extremely useful tool for hedging fixed-rate loans and for adjusting their interest rate exposure without ballooning their balance sheet.[10] It was also argued that, to corporations and other borrowers, CD futures would provide a better means than bill futures to hedge future borrowing costs and that, to CD dealers, CD futures would provide a useful tool both for hedging CD positions and for doing new CD trades.

Despite the enthusiasm of the exchanges and the street for introduction of both a domestic CD and a Euro time deposit contract, the CFTC, which, as noted in Chapter 14, moved slowly under Chairman Stone, did not approve trading in domestic CD futures until Philip Johnson became chairman. At that time the CBT, NYFE, and the IMM had all applied to the CFTC for permission to trade a domestic CD futures contract; in spring 1981, the proposals of all three exchanges, starting with the NYFE contract, were approved by the CFTC. The IMM contract, which began to be traded in early summer 1981, turned out to be the one that succeeded among the three contracts approved. The IMM had the locals to provide liquidity, which NYFE did not. The IMM also had the advantage over the CBT of being the exchange where the bill contract was traded; this meant that its CD futures contract could be traded with greater ease and lower margin requirements at a spread to the bill contract than could the CD futures contracts traded on other exchanges. This advantage was crucial because the spread trade between CD futures and bill futures was popular from the start of trading in CD futures and a key source of liquidity in the IMM CD futures contract.

For the many banks, domestic and foreign, that operate in the Euromarket, LIBOR for any period is the marginal cost of funds bought for that period. This led many to think that either a Euro time deposit or Euro CD futures contract (the latter would normally trade at a small spread below LIBOR) had the potential for being the most widely used and traded of all financial futures contracts; and futures exchanges were consequently eager to introduce a Euro contract. In the spring of 1982, the IMM was finally authorized by the CFTC to begin trading a futures contract for 3-month Euro time deposits. The *London International Financial Futures Exchange* (LIFFE), when it opened in September 1982, introduced a similar contract for 3-month Eurodollar time deposits.

The contracts: Domestic and Euro

The domestic CD and Euro time deposit contracts that have been introduced resemble the bill contract in certain respects. Like it, they are

---

[10] See Marcia Stigum and Rene Branch, *Managing Bank Assets and Liabilities: Strategies for Risk Control and Profit* (Homewood, Ill.: Dow Jones-Irwin, 1983), pp. 324–32.

contracts for $1 million of a 90-day instrument and they can be used to put on a wide array of trades: long and short hedges, cash-and-carry trades, creation of synthetic securities, and spread trades—futures to the underlying cash instrument or to some other futures contract.

One big difference exists, however, between CD and Euro futures and bill futures. It stems from a crucial difference between CDs and bills: Whereas 3-month bills are a homogeneous instrument, both domestic CDs and Euros are not. For both domestic CDs and Euro time deposits, a contract allowing for delivery must—to ensure that a sufficient supply of deliverable paper is available and that delivery does not disrupt the cash market—specify first that paper written by (deposits at) a number of banks be deliverable at expiration of the contract and second that delivery may be made on any day over some time period.

The IMM domestic CD contract allows for delivery over roughly two weeks with the acceptable names being basically those banks whose paper trades on a no-name basis in the interdealer market. If the top 10 banks never experienced any difficulties, this list would never change; in fact it does. As noted earlier, the difficulties the Continental Bank experienced in the summer of 1982 caused its CDs to trade, temporarily at least, at levels above those of other top banks; this led the Continental to ask the IMM to remove its name from the list of names deliverable against the CD futures contract, a step the IMM would otherwise have taken on its own. Chase, which also had troubles in the summer of 1982, took a different tack: It sought to keep yields on its paper as much in line as possible with those on other top-bank paper by making its paper scarce, particularly Chase paper deliverable against IMM CD contracts. Consequently the IMM felt no need to delete Chase's name from its list of deliverable bank names.

Given the heterogeneity of bank paper and the tendency of investors to overreact to any problems, however temporary, a bank may experience, a futures contract for money that banks buy is bound to trade and settle more smoothly if, at expiration of the contract, outstanding positions are settled by cash payments only rather than by payments of cash against paper.

The idea of cash settlement on a futures contract has been around for a long time, but until the introduction of the IMM Euro contract, it was never incorporated in any futures contract. Those opposed to cash settlement of a futures contract argued either that such a contract was suspiciously close to gambling or that a mechanism for delivery of the commodity or instrument underlying the futures contract was required to assure convergence of cash and futures prices. Those favoring cash settlement saw it as a means to create a viable futures contract in an instrument on which delivery would be difficult or impossible to effect smoothly because of the heterogeneity of the underlying instrument. They also saw cash settlement as the simplest of innovations to effect.

Effecting delivery in London on a Euro CD futures contract traded in the U.S. would be, if anything, less smooth than effecting delivery of domestic CDs. Therefore the IMM proposed and the CFTC accepted a futures contract for a 3-month Euro time deposit with the settlement price (100 minus yield) being established off 3-month LIBOR quotes prevailing in London on the day of settlement. By authorizing cash settlement on the IMM Euro contract, the CFTC, in its role as federal regulator of futures markets, overcame a practical barrier that had existed to cash settlement of futures contracts; by its action, it preempted state gaming laws under which a futures contract providing for cash settlement might have been judged to be an unenforceable gaming contract.

Gaming laws also exist in the U.K. and other countries. Because of them, LIFFE opted for a Euro time deposit contract with provisions for delivery at settlement of the contract or optional cash settlement. In doing so, LIFFE had little choice. U.K. futures markets are regulated informally by the Bank of England, which lacked the power, even if it had chosen to do so, to take any action that would have insulated a futures contract providing for cash settlement from U.K. gaming laws.

Trading in domestic CD and Euro futures

While it is easy to make a strong case that the domestic CD contract, because it meets so many needs of banks, dealers, and bank borrowers, should be enormously successful and while it is possible to make an even stronger case that a Euro time deposit contract—a contract on the cost of money in the international capital market—should be enormously successful, in fact trading in these contracts got off to a slow start (Figures 15–7 and 15–8). As with the bill and bond contracts, the entry of natural end users into these futures markets has been slowed—in some cases temporarily precluded—by various constraints: regulatory dictates on what different classes of institutions—banks, thrifts, insurance companies, and others—could and could not do, accounting practices that caused successful hedges to threaten desired earnings stability, and lack of expertise. The last of these factors was a particular problem for the LIFFE Euro contract. When domestic CD and Euro futures were introduced in the U.S., numerous money market participants, both inside and outside the banks, had been trading financial futures in Chicago for years. In contrast when LIFFE opened trading in financial futures, almost every potential market participant, except the U.S. dealers who bought seats on LIFFE, found themselves playing a brand new ball game. London traders, while they had watched the Chicago markets with interest,

FIGURE 15–7
Average daily volume in the IMM domestic CDs futures contract

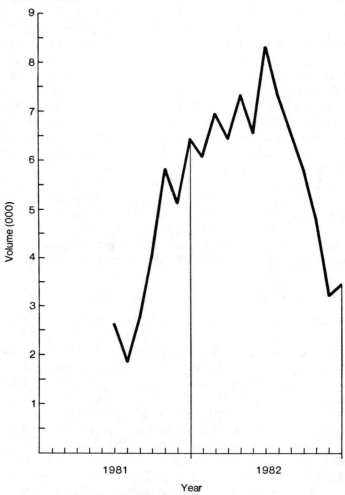

Source: Donaldson, Lufkin & Jenrette.

had never traded them. LIFFE also opened with the disadvantage that it had no existing population of floor traders who could be counted on to at least take a shot at trading its new contracts and thereby guarantee these contracts some initial liquidity.

Locals. In U.S. futures markets, local floor traders account for a significant part of total trading volume and make an important contribu-

FIGURE 15–8
Average daily volume in the IMM Euro futures contract

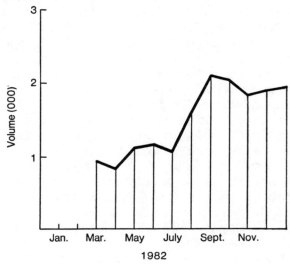

Source: Donaldson, Lufkin, & Jenrette.

tion to market liquidity. When the IMM CD contract was introduced, the locals had no notion of how to trade it relative to the cash market. They began and have continued to trade CD futures at a spread to bill futures; by spreading CD futures off bill futures, locals can trade the new contract with much less risk than they would incur if they traded it outright on the basis of where the contract should trade relative to cash CDs. Unfortunately the tendency of locals to take only spread positions in CD futures has meant that trading by locals contributes much less liquidity to the CD contract than it does to the bill contract.

Dealers. The introduction of CD and Euro futures has added liquidity to the cash markets for domestic and Euro CDs. Prior to introduction of these contracts, a CD trader, since it is impossible to short cash CDs, could go only one way: *long*. Also a CD trader had only one way to hedge a long position—by selling bill futures. For a CD trader who was long CDs and did not like the market overall, shorting bills was at times a poor to nil hedge. The late summer and fall of 1982 provided an example of this. Problems ranging from Chase's role in the Drysdale debacle to jitters over banks' souring Euro country loans set off a flight to quality by investors that caused CD yields to rise by 100 basis points in September 1982, while bill yields stayed the same or dropped. This flight to quality and the consequent decrease in CD trading was largely responsible for the steep drop in CD futures trading that began in September 1982 (Figure 15–7).

Volume in CD futures, while small compared to that in bill futures, far outstrips the volume of interdealer trading in cash CDs. Noted one CD trader in August 1982, "Chicago is doing 7 billion [7 thousand contracts] a day, while the cash market is trading tops a billion a day. Most of the Chicago trading in CD futures, however, is spread trading: CD futures against bill futures or Euro futures. Also a bunch of guys are doing CD spreads against an outright position in bill futures."

While useful for position hedging, CD futures have offered dealers less opportunity for doing profitable spread trading between cash and futures than bill futures have. Depending on whether a bill trader thinks cash bills are cheap relative to bill futures or vice versa, he can buy the cash bill and short futures or do the reverse trade. On either trade, transactions costs are low; in fact to go long a wi bill, a dealer incurs only the cost of writing a ticket. In CDs there is no such thing as a wi CD. Also, when cash CDs are cheap to futures, only issuing banks can in effect short cash CDs by issuing their own paper. Doing so, however, is not costless to a bank because a bank that writes CDs incurs the cost of reserve requirements and FDIC insurance. This means that, if CDs are trading at, say, 10%, there is a 45 basis-point window where it is difficult even for an issuing bank to make money by reserving a cash-futures, spread trade in CDs. This window, together with name problems, has caused cash CDs to trade less cleanly to CD futures than cash bills trade to bill futures. In both bills and CDs, there is synchronization between the movement of cash and futures prices, but in CDs that synchronization is sloppy.

Banks.   While the potential use by banks of domestic CD and Euro futures to hedge loans and manage the maturity structure of their assets and liabilities is larger, banks initially made small use of these instruments. They hedged some term loans, but accounting practices prevailing in 1982 discouraged banks that wanted stable earnings from hedging term loans unless they were willing to go to the expense of keeping two sets of books.[11]

In managing their asset/liability structures, banks have only begun to use—in marginal ways at best—both CD and other futures contracts. As noted, banks have been constrained in their use of futures by regulatory fiats, accounting practices, and other factors. To this list we should add one additional constraint: the limited depth and liquidity, at least at their inception, of the markets for domestic CD and Euro futures.

Examples of marginal, tentative trades banks have put on as part of their asset/liability management are easy to find. A banker, describing

---

[11] Stigum and Branch, *Managing Bank Assets and Liabilities,* pp. 336–37.

one that predated the introduction of trading in CD futures, said, "A few weeks ago we feared interest rates might rise in the short run. Finally, at 11 o'clock on a Tuesday, we decided we should do a half billion of 90-day CDs. You can't write much in the way of new CDs after 1 o'clock, so we figured we could do no more than $200 million of cash CDs that day, which is what we, in fact, managed. To go long $500 million of 90-day money, we sold—starting the moment we decided to move—$300 million of 90-day bill futures. When the market opened on Wednesday, rates in both the cash CD market and the bill futures market were up 40 basis points. We wrote the other $300 million of CDs we wanted at the new, higher rate and made up the extra cost by covering our short position in bill futures at a profit. Effectively doing the hedge was the same thing as having written $500 million of CDs on Tuesday at Tuesday's rate.

After the startup of trading in CD futures, a bank wanting to lock up future CD funding costs no longer needed to do a cross hedge. Describing the possibilities offered by this new market, one bank funding officer noted, "June [1982] was a horror story. Rates moved up to 15 again, and everyone was nervous that the whole thing was coming apart and that we were going to be back where we were. In that atmosphere, you could not do any retail other than 1-month paper. I wanted to match our book by doing 50 or 60 million of 3-month CDs. I noted that CD futures were about 15 basis points out of line with the cash market in which we could not do size anyway. So I sold CD futures and delivered; that threw everyone into a tizzy on the IMM, but we had experimented and it worked; they took delivery even if they did not want to."

A trader who closely watches the CD futures market suggested one common use big banks make of CD futures, "In my experience the majority of end users of CD futures are issuing banks. Many domestic CDs are issued to corporations that fund date, normally to the end of the calender quarter. Consequently a lot of CDs run out in the last week of each quarter, and banks have big rollovers to do at this time. To lock in an issuing rate, banks collectively sell CD futures toward the end of each quarter, then as they write a pile of new CDs, they gradually buy back the CD contracts they had previously sold."

CD futures trades

In discussing bill, note, and bond futures, we gave examples of various trades for which these contracts may be used—depending on the structure of market rates: long and short hedges, cross hedges, spread trades, and cash-and-carry trades in which the arbitrageur buys, finances, and sells for future delivery deliverable-grade securities. CD futures can be used for all of these purposes.

Examples of hedges and of cash-and-carry trades put on using CD

TABLE 15–1
Creating a synthetic CD using CD futures

Creating a syn-thetic CD:	For settlement 11/3/82, buy late December (50-day) cash CDs at 8.90. Simultaneously buy December CD futures at 9.10.
Figuring yield on synthetic CD:	Calculate rate of return on synthetic 140-day (50 days + 90 days) CD created if the long position in futures is settled by taking delivery and if the interest earned on the cash CD is reinvested.

1. Calculate interest earned, i, on the 50-day cash CD:

$$i = (\$1,000,000)(.0890)(50/360) = \$12,361.11$$

2. Calculate interest earned, i, on future CD, assuming reinvestment of accrued interest:

$$i = (\$1,012,361.11)(.0911)(90/360) = \$23,031.22$$

3. Calculate total rate of return, r, earned on \$1 million over the 140-day investment period:

$$r = \left(\frac{\$1,035,392.33 - \$1,000,000}{\$1,000,000}\right)\left(\frac{360}{140}\right)(100)$$
$$= 9.10$$

The choice:	On 11/3/82, 140-day cash CDs were offered at 9.05. By choosing synthetic CD over cash CDs, investor picks up 5 basis points, which on a \$10 million trade is worth \$1,944 of extra interest.

$$(\$10\text{ million})(.0910 - .0905)(140/360) = \$1,944$$

Comments:	1. The investor is able to earn, on the synthetic CD, a rate of 9.10—not a lower, weighted average of the 8.90 and 9.10 rate—because, due to reinvestment of interest earned, he earns a compound rate of return.
	2. As in our bill futures examples (Chapter 14), factors such as transactions costs and the operation of maintenance margining will or may affect the return yielded by a synthetic CD.
	3. Some imprecision is introduced in the calculation of return on this and certain other CD futures trades because delivery may be made by the short on any business day from December 16 to 31. We assume in our example that delivery is made midway between the 16th and the 31st.
	4. We also assume that the investor reinvests accrued interest at the rate locked in through the futures trade. Normally, he would be able to do so only if the trade were done in size and in a ratio designed to permit such reinvestment.

futures are easy to work out. We therefore present, as an example of profitable trade using CD futures, a trade we have yet to illustrate—the purchase by an investor of an *synthetic security,* specifically of a long CD composed of a short cash CD *plus* a CD futures contract maturing at or near the maturity date of the cash CD. In late 1982, when our example (Table 15–1) was constructed, rates were such that an investor could get a better rate on 140-day paper by buying 50-day cash CDs at 8.90 and 90-day CD futures at 9.10 than by buying cash 140-day CDs. As Table 15-1 shows, by buying a synthetic CD, an investor doing a $10 million trade could have earned $1,955 more interest than he would have earned by buying a cash CD.

Depending again on rate relationships, the sale of synthetic, as opposed to long cash, CDs may enable a bank to pick up funds more cheaply than it could by writing long cash CDs. The Continental, before its name was removed from the IMM list, is said to have used this tactic successfully.

Euro futures

The Euro futures contract, despite its enormous potential, is thinly traded. Locals trade it only on the basis of spreads to either CD or bill futures: the popular T bill to Euro futures spread has been dubbed the *TED spread.*

Some banks have used Euro futures to arbitrage against forward forward positions in the interbank Eurodeposit market. In 1982, when the Euro contract was new and few people were watching this trade, bank traders who did it were at times able to take out a 50 to 100 basis-point profit. Presumably as volume in Euro futures grows, rates in this market and rates on forward forwards in the interbank market will move into closer synchronization.

Rates on the LIFFE and IMM Euro contracts move in tandem. In the fall of 1982, the IMM contract consistently opened about 17 basis point under the LIFFE contract. This spread reflected several factors: the specs of the LIFFE contract are such that it settles 25 basis points above the IMM contract; however, the LIFFE contract also settles a week earlier than the IMM contract, so a positively sloped yield curve tends to narrow the spread between the rates at which the two contracts trade.

The LIFFE Euro contract, despite the fact that it was introduced in London, the birthplace of the Eurodollar market and still the largest single Eurocenter, got off to a respectable but less-than-impressive start; in early 1983 daily volume in the contract had grown to roughly 4,000 contracts a day.

Chapter 16

The Euro time deposit market

Broker: I'm ⅞–¾ in the one month. Do you do anything?
Dealer: I'll support you at ⅞, and I'm in there for size.

Such is the chatter that fills the phone lines over which Euro time deposits are traded.

ROUND THE GLOBE MARKET

The market for Eurocurrency deposits follows the sun around the globe. Due to the position of the international date line down the middle of the Pacific, the market starts at 9:00 A.M. local time in Singapore. Singapore is the major but not the only Southeast Asian center for trading in Eurocurrencies. Hong Kong is also an important center, and some trading occurs in Kuala Lumpur. The banks that are active in the Singapore market, mostly foreign banks and in particular the big U.S. banks, do some trading there that is "a natural" against business in Southeast Asia: funding loans to finance and accepting deposits generated by economic activity in that area. Such activity, while growing, is still small compared with that in Europe and the United States, so less natural business is done in Singapore than in London or New York.

Much of the trading by banks in Singapore involves position taking against what will happen later in the day. In such trading, Singapore owes its importance to its strategic geographic position and to the favorable access and tax treatment accorded foreign bank branches beginning in 1976. It now has 90 foreign bank branches opposed to the 5 it had before it changed its banking and tax laws with the aim to become the Zurich of the Far East. Singapore is instrumental in starting off each trading day because it is the first center in which the banks can react in volume to anything that might have happened after the New York close—a late economic announcement in the U.S. or an international incident such as war in the Mid East.

After the Euromarket opens in Southeast Asia, the next important centers to enter the market are those in the Mid East, Bahrain in particular. Here again natural activity is limited. Arab money is placed in the Euromarket largely through banks in Paris, London, and elsewhere in Europe; and Bahrain's importance is primarily as a booking center.[1]

London and other European centers, which are the next to open, do so early to catch the Singapore close. Singapore tends to be a net taker of funds, and as a result the London market often opens on the firm side due to buying interest from Singapore.

Because of the huge volume of natural activity in Eurocurrencies in London and other European centers, the New York market still leans, though less than it used to, on these markets. New York opens early—some banks have traders at their desks as early as 5:00 A.M.—but whereas it used to normally close at noon as London closed, the New York market now works until late afternoon because of all the natural business generated in New York due to its growing importance as a Eurocenter.

From the time New York closes until Singapore opens, the Euromarket goes through its "dark hours." Some trading occurs in San Francisco, the Philippines, and other centers, but the volume is so small that the banks cannot react in size to any major development until Singapore opens.

THE BROKERS

The major banks in the London market post rates at which they are willing to take Eurodollar deposits of different maturities, and they do pick up some money directly, particularly from banks on the Continent. Much interbank trading in Euros however, is done through brokers. Bro-

---

[1] Bahrain replaced Beruit as the financial center of the Mid East after civil war in 1974 destroyed Beruit and the then flourishing Lebanese economy. Beruit, because it was a prosperous business center and had an indigenous supply of traders, had a natural and better base for becoming a major financial center than Bahrain has or is ever likely to have.

kers are a necessity in the Euromarket because there are so many participants in this market and because they are scattered around the globe.

The brokering of Eurocurrency deposits used to be dominated by
several British firms that had offices in London and other Eurocenters.
Most of these firms also brokered foreign exchange, Euro CDs, and
sterling; and each was a substantial operation. The domination of Euro
brokering by British firms ended as a result of a series of mergers, begun
in 1974, between New York and London brokers. Because of geography,
London brokers had an edge in the deposit market; because of the
strength of the U.S. banks in foreign exchange trading, U.S. brokers
had an edge in foreign exchange. Since the Eurodeposit and foreign
exchange markets are closely linked, every broker wanted to be a full
service shop that handled both deposits and foreign exchange. Hence
trans-Atlantic mergers made sense. Now the major brokers of foreign
exchange and Eurodeposits are all international firms that have offices
or affiliates in New York, London, Paris, Singapore, and other centers. If
the present trend toward amalgamation among brokers in these rapidly
expanding markets continues, in a few years there are likely to be less
than a dozen shops—each employing a minimum of 250 to 300 brokers
doing the business.

Each brokerage firm is selling to its client banks a vast, fast-operating
information network, which no bank could duplicate with its own resources. In this respect it's interesting to note that the British, perceiving
the importance of good communications to London as a financial center,
have created excellent and relatively cheap phone and Telex facilities to
link London with the rest of the world. Domestic communications are
another matter. As one market participant noted, "I can always get
Singapore or New York in seconds on the phone or the Telex, but if my
house caught fire, it might burn down before I could get through to the
local fire department."

Brokering Euros, like Fed funds, is a rapid-fire, bang bang game. It
requires total concentration on the part of the broker and an ability to
simultaneously listen to the phone with the right ear and keep track with
the left of any changes in quotes other brokers in the room shout out.
Brokering requires thinking but only of the quickest sort. "The thing that
comes closest to it in the United Kingdom," said the director of a big
brokerage outfit, "is a British turf accountant [bookie] calling rates
across the wire."

In London and many other centers as well, most of the Euro brokers
and bank dealers as well turn out to be British and more specifically to
be cockneys. For some reason the east end of London, an ordinary
working-class area, seems, like similar areas in many big cities, to breed
the sort of person that brokering and dealing require—one who is quick-

witted and has a sense of humor that keeps him from going balmy at the end of a day of pressure. Perhaps another reason for the ubiquitous presence of the cockneys in the market (there's even a cockney dealer in the trading room of the Moscow Narodny Bank's London branch) is the fact that it takes one cockney to understand what another one is saying.

Brokering in the Euro time deposit market is an extremely professional operation. As noted in our discussion of a bank's Euro activities, one of the advantages to a bank of using a broker is anonymity. A big bank can bid for large sums of money in this market without pushing up price, something it could not do if it went direct.

To preserve anonymity, it is a cardinal rule among brokers that they never give up the name of a bank bidding for or offering funds until one bank actually initiates a transaction. At that point the broker tells the lender the borrower's name so that the lender can check that his line to the borrower is not full. If it is not, the ethics of the game are that the lender must sell the funds he has offered to the bidding bank; in particular he is not to go around the broker and sell directly to the bidding bank.

Because Euro brokers have a reputation (one not shared by some continental brokers of foreign exchange) for not "blowing around" information on who is bidding and offering in their market, some large banks are willing to be quite open with their broker about what they want to do. A bank dealer, for example, might say to a broker, "In the 6s I want to do a really lumpy piece. What's that market really like? If I took 500 million, would it move against me?" Since a broker monitors the market minute by minute, that's a question to which he can give an informed reply. Thus in the eyes of many bankers and brokers, an open relationship should exist between a good bank and a good broker. That opinion is, however, not universally shared. Many banks never tell their broker what they really want to do.

As we've said, a big part of the broker's job is to provide the banks with an information network. This is a vital service to the banks, and no large bank would start dealing in the morning without first calling the brokers to get a feel for levels and tone in the market. A good broker does more, however, than just quote prices. He works to narrow spreads and create trades by persistence, cajolery, pleading, humor, and any ploy he can come up with.

If, for example, the 1-month were quoted at $11\frac{7}{8}$ to $\frac{3}{4}$, the broker might call a bank and say, "Can you close that price for me?" If the bank dealer answered, "I'll pay 13," the market would be at $\frac{7}{8}$–$13\frac{3}{16}$, and the broker would start calling around to find a bank that would offer below $\frac{7}{8}$. Suppose he found an offer at $27\frac{7}{32}$. Now the bid and the offer would be only $\frac{1}{32}$ apart. At that point the broker and his colleagues, each of whom might have direct phone lines to a dozen banks, would start "banging around the board" (punching those direct phone line buttons) saying, "Anything in the 1s? Nice close price." Eventually some bank would probably bite, and a trade would have been created and done.

Not every brokerage firm covers every bank. The typical brokerage firm may have 30 to 50 big banks that are very important customers and three to four times as many smaller customers who, even though they may deal only a few times a week, are useful because they give the market dealing ability and depth. As one broker noted, "Sometimes when the market seems stuck, a small- or medium-size bank will come up with a bit of natural to do. The resulting trade will set a mood for the market again, and suddenly we have a chain reaction of trades. If we had just a few big banks as customers, we might at times, particularly when the market is moving, be unable to get anything done because the customers would all be facing in the same direction, all be bidders or sellers. The beauty of having so many banks in the market is that their presence guarantees diversity of position and opinion, a condition that ensures a market will function and trade."

When a bank puts a bid or an offer into a broker, it is understood in London, where the primary participants in the market are international banks with traders who do at most deposits and foreign exchange, that the quote is good until a trade is made or the bank calls back to say, "I'm off." In the U.S. a trader at a regional bank may be responsible for not only Euros and foreign exchange but for a number of domestic instruments as well; for that reason a broker, depending on the customer, may feel the need to call him back if some time (a half hour or more) has passed to reconfirm his bid or offer. The broker for his part can be held to any price he quotes as firm provided that a line problem does not tie up a trade. If, for example, Chase London offered to sell 6-month money at the bid rate quoted by a broker and the bidding bank then told the broker he was off and had forgotten to call, the broker would be committed to *substantiate* his bid by finding Chase a buyer at that price or by selling Chase's money at a lower rate and paying a *difference* equal to the dollar amount Chase would lose by selling at that rate. Because activity in the Euromarket is hectic, mistakes of this sort do occur, and they can be expensive: On $5 million for 6 months, even $1/16$ of 1% works out to $1,562.50. Since brokers operate on thin margins, a broker wouldn't be around long if he got "stuffed" often; so good brokers take a lot of care to avoid errors.

It used to be that whenever some important news hit the market—Citi raised its prime or whatever—the banks would call the brokers to shout "Off, Off!" on their bids and offers, and a broker would quote rate on an "I suggest," "I think," or "I call" basis, which meant that a bank could not hold him to these quotes. A sharp break in market activity put a broker back in the position in which he started the day, with a blank pad. To get trading started again, he had to call around to the bank dealers to find out where they anticipated money would now trade and then try to find some banks that would substantiate these new levels by making even small firm bids and offers. Today with the large presence of U.S. banks—there are over 200—this is less true. Americans tend to keep trading with other Americans pretty much regardless of what news hits the market.

QUOTES AND MATURITIES

In the market for overnight Federal funds, money normally trades for immediate delivery. In the Euromarket, in contrast, the delivery data, or *value date* as it is called, is two days hence unless otherwise specified. The reason is that foreign exchange settles two days forward. If a Euro spot transaction is consummated on, say, a Tuesday it results in funds being delivered on Thursday. The Euromarket, however, also deals in overnight funds for immediate delivery and for delivery the next day. The former sort of transaction is referred to as a deal in *overnight* funds *dealing over today;* the latter is referred to as a *tom next* (for tomorrow next) transaction in London and as a *rollover* or as *dealing over tomorrow* in the U.S.

Eurodollar deposits are quoted in the interbank market in a wide range of maturities: overnight, tom next, spot, the week, 1 to 6 months, 12 months, and 1 to 5 years. The Euromarket is a short-term market; depending on rate expectations, 50% or more of trading volume occurs in the 3-months-and-under range. Most of the rest occurs in the 3-months-to-1-year range. Trades of 2- to 5-year money occur but are uncommon.

While the Euromarket actively trades 1-, 2-, 3-, 6-, and 12-month deposits, it is, like the RP market, a flexible-date market in which participants may do any number of days they need. Odd-day, off-the-run deposits (e.g., for 26 days) are referred to as *broken* or *cock dates*. Brokers quote them by saying, for example, "We want early 2s out to the 15th [a deposit for less than 2 months that ends on the 15th]" or "We have 1 week short of 2s to go." Depending on the time a call is put into a broker, dealing over today may be a hassle, but dealing over tomorrow is not.

It is possible to carry out Eurodollar transactions over the Fed wire when both sides of the transaction have a Fed account. Such transactions, referred to as *Euro Feds,* are the exception rather than the rule. Most Euro transactions are settled through the New York Clearing House Payments System (CHIPS), which is described below. It used to be that clearing house funds differed from Fed funds in that they turned into immediately available funds, that is, Fed funds, only on the day after the delivery or value date. The distinction that existed in the Eurodollar market between the value date and the day on which good funds were available to the recipient created the basis for some very actively pursued technical arbitrages between Fed funds and short-dated Euros.[2] All this ended in 1981 when CHIPS moved to same day settlement, a procedure described later in this chapter.

Euros are quoted in 32nds, and spreads between the bid and the asked can range anywhere from 1/32 in short-dated funds to 1/4 or more in the longer dates. London quotes the rates "tops and bottoms;" that is, the offered rate and then the bid rate. New York does the reverse for reasons now shrouded in history.

Euro brokers work for small commissions, which are paid by both sides in a transaction and are calculated as a percentage per day of the amount traded. Brokerage rates range from 2 to 2 1/2 basis points on an annual basis, which is roughly 62 1/2 cents per $1 million per day. At those rates brokers have to do many hundreds of millions of dollars of business a day to survive. Brokerage is higher in New York than in London because the New York market is less active than the London market. Presumably as activity increases in New York, brokerage there will fall to the London rate.

On occasion in the Euromarket, one encounters a situation in which the bid and asked rates are identical—what a Euro broker would call an *either-way market.* Since brokerage is paid by both the buyer and the seller in the Euromarket, an either-way market can occur only when the market in a given tenor gets "hung up on lines." Suppose Dresdner were offering $5 million of 1-month money through a broker and that Toronto Dominion decided to take this money. The broker would call Dresdner and say, "OK, we will pay at your price." Dresdner would then ask, "Who is it?" and the broker would say, "Toronto Dominion." At that point Dresdner might say, "Done for 5," or "I'm full on that name," or "All I can do for him is two." In either of the last two cases, Dresdner would still have dollars to sell, Toronto Dominion would still have dollars to buy, and the two might end up quoting identical bid and offer rates.

The minimum size in which brokers of Eurodollars will deal is $1 million, but most trades are larger. In the market for overnight and short-dated funds, trades of $10, $20, $50, and even $100 million are common. In the fixed dates, trades of $20 million are considered good size with the average being more like $5 or $10 million.

Normally activity in the Euromarket is heaviest in the 6-month-and-under maturity range, since most of the assets Eurobankers are funding are either short in tenor or roll every 3 to 6 months. When borrowers anticipate that rates might rise and the yield curve is not too steep, activity will be centered in the 6-month area because borrowers will opt

---

[2] For a description of the technical arbitrages that occurred between Fed funds and overnight Euros before CHIPS moved to same day settlement, see Chapter 17 of the first edition of this book.

for a 6-month roll. Alternatively, if rates are expected to drop or remain stable, activity will be strong in the 3-month area. Trades of long-dated funds, up to 5 years, occur in the interbank market, but normally they are done direct because brokerage is high on a big trade of long-dated funds.

Naturally brokers prefer trades in the long dates to those in the short dates. But they try to give all their customers, including heavy traders of overnight funds, good service on the theory that if they support a bank in the short dates, they will occasionally get in on the gravy train when the bank trades long-dated funds in the brokers' market.

Tiering

Eurodollar deposits are a heterogeneous commodity. They differ with respect not only to maturity but to the credit risk associated with the name of the buying bank. Thus there is a tiering of quotes according not only to maturity but to which bank is buying. In particular, for any maturity it is understood that bids in the brokers market are those of top name banks unless otherwise specified.

Five years ago the top British, Canadian, French, and German banks could buy funds at the same rates at which the top U.S. banks could, but occasionally they had to pay an extra $1/16$ or so. Banks outside this elite group consistently had to pay up, the amount being a function of their name and market conditions. Also, branches of even the best-regarded banks, if they were located in centers to which the market attached greater sovereign risk than it did to London, had to pay a $1/16$ or so more than their London sister did.

The pattern of tiering in any market where rates paid depend both on the name of the borrowing institution and on its country of origin is bound to shift continually as individual borrowing institutions experience difficulties or recover from them and as investors' perceptions of country risk change for one reason or another. The Eurodeposit market is no exception. Today there is probably more tiering in this market than there was 5 years ago, and the pattern of tiering has changed.

The top American banks still pay the lowest rates. However, a top American bank that has serious and highly visible problems, as did Chase and Continental in the summer of 1982, can find itself being forced to buy at the offered side of the market. The top American banks that are still regarded as solid credits are followed by the U.K. clearers, then the Japanese banks, and maybe with them the Mid East banks. Because of their big exposure to Eastern European countries, the top German banks with the exception of Deutsche Bank, are no longer treated as prime names. Also, French names, once considered prime, are out for a lot of investors because they don't like the fact that the

French banks have been nationalized, that their capital ratios are so low, and that there are communists in the French government.

Some of this tiering reflects the attitudes—somewhat provincial at times—of U.S. regional banks. In recent years U.S. regionals have become a lot more active in the Euromarket and particularly in the brokers' market both as takers and givers of funds. It is regionals who are more likely than New Yorkers to cut back their lines to, say, a German bank because they hear it has a big exposure to Eastern Europe or perhaps to a French bank, like the Credit Lyonnais, which has been government owned for years, because they have read that French banks have been nationalized.

Japanese banks have always been strong banks, operating in a strong economy, under strong guidance from the Japanese Ministry of Finance. Yet in past years, Japanese banks often had to pay up perceptibly, perhaps because of the unfamiliar ring of their names and also because they were consistently big takers of funds. Today they are a bigger force than ever in the market and are exceedingly active both as takers and givers of funds. The growing acceptance of Japanese banks by investors probably reflects the increasing familiarity of their names to non-Japanese investors. Also, the Japanese banks seem to have been conspicuous by their absence whenever the list of lenders to a big problem credit—be it private like Dome Petroleum or a country such as Poland or Mexico—was published.

Tiering among centers in different geographic areas still exists for several reasons. Investors perceive some political risk associated with Mid East banks. Consequently branches of such banks have to pay up in both New York and London. So too do branches of U.S. banks in Bahrain. Singapore must pay up slightly.

A second reason these centers pay up has to do with time zones. Singapore comes in first and then Bahrain. Both tend to be net takers of funds, and to get them, they shove rates up slightly. The Euromarket looks to New York to be the lender. That is the pattern that has been established. Singapore normally opens the market with an up bid. Later London will come in and may sit on the fence for a bit waiting for New York to work. If New York comes in and they are not lenders, then some arbitrage of funds out of the New York market into the Euromarket may occur.

The New York Euromarket has the ability to arbitrage. If the domestic market starts to look easy, the Citis and the Chases will issue CDs, switch them into their Eurodollar book, and lend them out at maybe a 50- or 60-basis-point profit.

One reason that the foreign banks must now be in New York is that it is the first market in which there is an opportunity to arbitrage back into the Euromarket. If the domestic money market starts to look a little easier, foreign banks can start to play the same games domestic banks do; however, their access, relative to their size, to domestic dollars is much more limited than that of top U.S. banks.

As we've said, brokers never divulge the names of the banks that have placed bids and offers with them, but to cope with the problems posed by lines, names, and locations, they sprinkle their runs with bits of information that can be helpful to the bank to whom they are quoting a run. For example, a broker might note that the bid in a given tenor was by a "prime name out of Hong Kong" or that the offer in some other tenor was from a "rather difficult lender," that is, one with lines to only a few banks.

To be as informative as possible, the brokers also throw in with their regular quotes some hints as to what is being done or could be done in the market. For example, a broker might note, "The 3s are 10³⁄₁₆–⁵⁄₁₆ but may come at ¼," or "Wednesday/Thursday funds are bid ⁷⁄₁₆ out of London and Bahrain and come OK at ½. The variations are endless, but the point is that a good broker does more than just quote rates. He tries to give his client banks at a rapid-fire pace all the useful information he can.

SETTLING THROUGH CHIPS

In Chapter 6, to keep things simple we ignored the fact that most Eurodollar transactions clear not over the Fed wire but through the New York Clearing House. The New York Clearing House, one of the oldest and most prominent clearing houses in the country, was set up to provide a mechanism for clearing both customer checks and bank official checks. Since the institution of the Fed wire, the bulk of the funds New York banks exchange among themselves now go over that wire, but the Clearing House has assumed a vastly more important function, *clearing Eurodollar payments* between domestic and foreign banks.

Almost every Euro transaction creates the need for an interbank payment. In the old days New York banks made such payments by issuing official checks, which were cleared through the New York Clearing House. A big New York bank might both issue and receive 1,500 or more official checks a day. Thus clearing was tedious, expensive, and involved a huge amount of paperwork. Despite the enormity of the job to be done, checks received by the Clearing House were normally *cleared* on the same day so that *settlement* in Fed funds could be made between the banks on a timely basis the next day. Sometimes, however, checks got lost, and clearing them took three or even four days.

To reduce the unnecessary float such delays caused, the Fed strongly urged the New York Clearing House banks to set up a computerized communications network to handle interbank money transfers. This system, *CHIPS,* an acronym for *Clearing House Interbank Payments System,* went on-line with live transactions in April 1970. Participants in the CHIPS system include the 12 New York Clearing House banks and about 100 other New York banking institutions, two thirds of whom are foreign, who participate in CHIPS; the ranks of the latter include foreign bank branches and agencies and Edge Act corporations set up by domestic banks. Another 60 banks, mostly foreign, have applied to join the system.

Every participant in CHIPS has a terminal computer, linked by leased telephone lines to the central CHIPS computer, through which it can directly send and receive payment messages. The central CHIPS computer immediately processes all such messages. Then, at 4:30 P.M., it produces for each participating bank item-by-item detailed reports of payments made to and received by it and by institutions holding accounts with it; the printout also indicates the bank's gross position with CHIPS, the gross and net positions of any banks for whom the bank settles, and finally, if the bank is a *settling bank*, its *net net*—the dollars it must send out or will receive due to CHIPS settlement. Also, by netting debits and credits, CHIPS figures each participating bank's net position vis-à-vis every other participating bank and the system as a whole.

The settlement system from there on is both efficient and swift. Of the roughly 110 banks that participate in CHIPS, 22, with the Fed's permission, have become *settling banks*.[3] After the CHIPS figures come out at 4:30, CHIPS participants who are not settling banks settle their account at one of the settling banks. Each settling bank that, on a net-net basis, has a debit balance with CHIPS sends over the Fed wire to the account that CHIPS maintains at the Fed the sum required for it to settle. After CHIPS has received these monies, it in turn wires out, again over the Fed wire, all monies it owes settling banks who have ended the day on a net-net basis with a credit balance at CHIPS. Monies are supposed to flow into CHIPS' account from settling banks with a net-net debit balance by 5:30 and to go out to settling banks with a net-net credit balance by 6 P.M.; at that time the balance in CHIPS' account at the Fed should return to *zero*.

CHIPS strives mightily to stick to the above time schedule, but sometimes it doesn't make it. Occasionally its own computer system goes down causing delays. More commonly the computer of a participant goes down making it impossible for that bank to get out all its payments due to CHIPS participants by the 4:30 deadline. In such a situation CHIPS no longer grants extensions except in extraordinary situations. An extraordinary situation would be if the bank having a computer problem were, say, Morgan and if Morgan owed another settling bank so much money that the other bank could not settle with CHIPS without getting its

---

[3] The Fed permits banks to become settling banks if, in its view, they have the size and financial strength to handle huge payment volumes.

money from Morgan; in that case, so as not to jeopardize settlement, CHIPS would remain open until Morgan got its computer up and its payments out.

Volume through CHIPS

The volume of funds flowing through CHIPS each day is staggering. On an average day, CHIPS handles between 70 and 80,000 transactions (Figure 16–1). The average amount per transaction (Figure 16–2) is

FIGURE 16–1
Average daily number of transactions on CHIPS

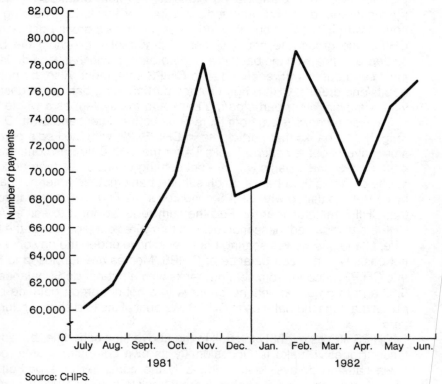

Source: CHIPS.

nearing $3 million. In total CHIPS clears payments whose value is rapidly approaching $5 trillion a month (Figure 16–3).

Why CHIPS is still with us

Since CHIPS moved to same day settlement, Fed funds and what used to be called clearing house funds have become fungible in the sense

FIGURE 16–2
Average dollar amount per transaction on CHIPS ($ millions)

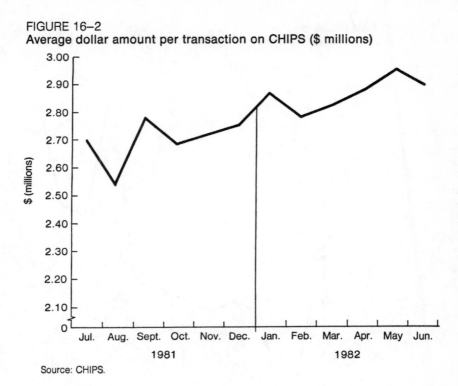

Source: CHIPS.

that a payment made through either system results in the receipt of good funds on the day the payment is made. To the outsider this raises the question of why CHIPS continues to be used. There are several compelling reasons.

All payments mechanisms are bound by the payer's technical capability to execute payments which in turn depends on how execution has traditionally been done. Originally money markets participants in New York made payments to each other by check. Messengers delivered these checks to the New York Clearing House, where they were cleared and settled on the next day. Then the Clearing House switched to a computerized system, which automated the settlement procedure, but by tradition these checks were next-day money. So there was in place a next-day settlement system with which everyone was happy. Also, and more importantly, there was an infrastructure in place for using this system; participants had both a computer link up to CHIPS and people trained to use it; the system worked; and everyone used it.

Then participants in CHIPS gradually became uncomfortable with the huge overnight or worse still over-the-weekend risk to which next day settlement exposed them. CHIPS solved this by moving to same day settlement. Now the value date of the funds paid over both CHIPS and

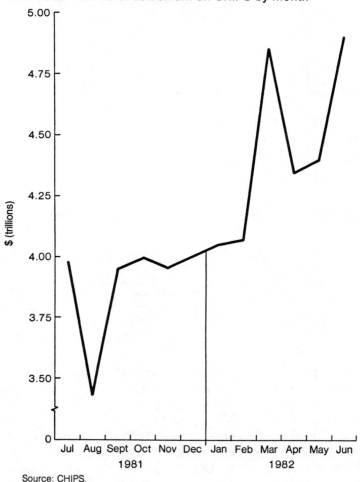

FIGURE 16–3
Total dollar volume of settlement on CHIPS by month

Source: CHIPS.

the Fed wire are the same. In this respect they are fungible, and in theory participants could use either network to transfer funds.

In practice foreign banks make and receive the bulk of their payment through CHIPS because their pattern of making and receiving payments tends to create huge daylight overdrafts in the accounts that they keep with settling banks. The Fed will not permit foreign banks to run daylight overdrafts with it. It reasons: Why should we take the risk? The big New York banks are willing to take this risk for foreign banks who are their customers because they feel that they are compensated for assuming it through customer relationships.

Domestic banks are also heavy users of CHIPS. A typical money center bank probably makes about 40% of its transfers over the Fed wire, 40% through CHIPS, and another 20% through book transfers; (a book transfer, which is a transfer of funds from the account of one depositor at a bank into the account of another, can be done through internal book-keeping entries).

Given his choice, an operating man will always use a more efficient and cheaper system. "Right now," noted one banker, "CHIPS is a better system than the Fed wire. It has a formatted transaction type which means that on two out of three transactions, no clerical labor is required to post to a customer's account items received over CHIPS. The comparable figure for incoming Feds is 1 to 2%. Also, CHIPS is less expensive than the Fed wire (about 31 cents against 65 cents per transaction per party), but it is the labor saving permitted by CHIPS that creates a real cost savings!"

The Fed is preparing to institute a transactions format that will enable the Fed wire to do the same sorts of things CHIPS can already do. However, since CHIPS is run by 12 member banks it is more nimble at making decisions than the Fed; therefore, it is reasonable to assume that CHIPS will always stay technologically a step ahead of the Fed wire.

Daylight overdrafts

Currently there are huge *daylight overdrafts* at three levels in the payments system: in the accounts of major domestic banks at the Fed, in the accounts of some participants in CHIPS, and in the accounts of correspondent banks, particularly foreign banks, at their domestic correspondent bank.

These overdrafts are, under the current system, operationally unavoidable because banks and bank customers are making and receiving huge payments leveraged on the basis of small balances. The average demand deposit at one major New York bank turns over 7,000 times a year! Noted an officer of this bank, which has an institutional—as opposed to retail—client base, "I pay and receive on an average day $145 billion. The assets of my institution are $55 billion. I roll those assets every 2½ hours, and I roll the bank's capital 70 times a day—roughly every 10 minutes. Operations of this size mean that I must at times experience large extremes in my net debit or credit positions at CHIPS and at the Fed. There is no way we can regulate the flow of these payments so everyone stays in balance so long as so many payments are made on the basis of such small balances."

One of the problems facing this bank and others is that in real terms demand deposits at U.S. banks declined by 50% between 1971 and 1981 while the volume of payments being made by bank depositors mushroomed.

Every morning someone has to start making payments to get the system going, and the people who do will probably end up OD for a time. These people will either be those who have to borrow the most because they owe the most (e.g., a bank returning Fed funds bought overnight) or those banks with the most efficient system who can execute payments the fastest.

Daylight overdrafts create credit risk for the Fed, for settlement of CHIPS, and for banks at which other banks run them. All of these institutions are concerned about this risk. However, it is impossible to impose the simplistic solution of banning daylight overdrafts. Solving the credit problem they create by imposing a credit control system that would shut down payments in progress if they would result in an overdraft would put the system into *gridlock*—Bank X could not pay Bank Y because it had not received payment from Bank Z and so on.

A payments system and a credit control system are in direct conflict. This reality notwithstanding, the Fed is campaigning to limit daylight overdrafts. They have told the big banks that, if they go OD at the Fed by more than 50% of their capital on so many days for so many hours, they will get a strong letter of protest from the Fed. Currently it is almost imperative that the major money center banks violate the Fed's rule daily.

If the Fed is serious and constricts ODs at the Fed, they will bulge out somewhere else, presumably on CHIPS. If the Fed also constricts ODs on CHIPS, the bulge will occur elsewhere, perhaps at a new CHIPS in Zurich.

Failure of CHIPS to settle

CHIPS functions on confidence. When the German authorities closed Herstatt, confidence drained out of the system even though Herstatt was not a participant in CHIPS, only an account number at a participating bank. The loss of confidence in CHIPS caused *gridlock*; Bank X would not make a payment to Y until it got cover which deprived another bank of cover with the result that everything froze in the system. Fortunately a fast meeting and some fast decision making sufficed to restart the system.

This illustrates an important point. It is crucial for CHIPS to limit access to the system to New York-based entities because when a problem—real or potential—arises, proximity of the major participants is required for a quick solution to be reached and for the market, which is easily disturbed by rumors, to be calmed. While regional banks would like CHIPS to provide nationwide access to CHIPS, CHIPS is and will remain a New York institution because both the markets and the key players in them are there.

While CHIPS has always settled, the possibility exists that it could not, and rules have been designed to cope with this contingency. If a settling bank informs CHIPS that it will not settle for a participant because that bank does not have, say, $50 million to settle and the settling bank will not lend the money, the clearing house has authority to take one of several actions. It can settle on the positions that exist, which means that some bank will go unpaid. It can come up collectively with a loan for the bank that cannot settle. Or it can rerun the day's transactions as if the nonsettling bank had never existed. This will produce new settlement figures that could conceivably put some other bank—for example, one supposed to receive the bulk of the $50 million that now will not be paid—in the position where it cannot settle, which would put CHIPS again in the position of being unable to settle.

CHIPS has never failed to settle. Said one officer who oversees his bank's operations on CHIPS, "If CHIPS fails to settle, I jump out of my [14th-story] window. CHIPS cannot not settle because, if it were to do so, it would destroy confidence in the money market internationally—create a worldwide financial panic, perhaps worldwide depression."

So long as huge deposits are leveraged on a small deposit base, big daylight overdrafts will continue to put at risk a system that cannot be permitted to fail. Senior people at the Fed want to eliminate this risk by eliminating the daylight overdrafts. Knowledgeable and responsible bank officers who understand the system at an operational level—as well as operational people at the Fed—know that this cannot be done. They agree that ". . . the only solution is that, if there is a bad guy in the system, you have to identify him and get him off the system before he has an opportunity to create trouble."

An intraday funds market

Money center banks are not charitable institutions, and the idea is growing among them that, if they are going to permit correspondent banks to run huge daylight overdrafts with them, these banks ought to pay some fee for exercising that privilege. One possibility is creation of a intraday market in funds, say, a market for 4-hour funds with multiple settlements. Such a system would impact banks that are very active players in the market relative to their deposit base. An example would be certain Japanese banks that have total money payments through their accounts of $3 or $4 billion a day. Such a bank may be a billion OD during the day, and its correspondent who is supporting that position may justly feel it should be compensated for assuming the risk of doing so.

One method would be to set a charge schedule for intraday line usage. The charge might be on the order of 1 or 2%, nothing as high as the Fed funds rate. It would be easy for major banks to institute such a system; they already have a computer routing such that, if a foreign bank asks them to make a payment, first the balance of the sending bank is checked, and if it is negative, it is then checked against the approved credit line for that bank. If the sum to be paid out exceeds the line limit, a credit officer must approve before the payment goes out. The Fed will have a similar system as part of its new wire system.

SWIFT

It used to be common for banks to use Telex and other common carrier systems to transmit among each other payments instructions for international transactions that were eventually cleared through CHIPS. In 1973 the leading international banks began planning a *private* bank communications network called SWIFT, an acronym for Society for Worldwide Interbank Financial Telecommunications. SWIFT, a computerized message switch, is owned by the hundreds of banks—located in Europe, the U.K., the U.S., Canada, and the Far East—that currently subscribe to the system. SWIFT first went live on a limited basis in Europe in 1977. It was then extended to North America and after that to the Far East. It is scheduled to extended to the Mid East in 1984.

The major advantage of SWIFT is that it has a strict format requirement for messages. This enables subscribing banks to construct a computerized interface that keys messages transmitted via SWIFT directly into the CHIPS system. Doing so eliminates clerical processing of Telex messages and thus streamlines for subscribing banks the making and receiving of payments through CHIPS.

SWAPS—THE MECHANICS

A substantial part of the total Eurocurrency market represents deposits of nondollar currencies (see Table 6–5). Eurodeposits denominated in currencies other than the dollar are actively traded in the interbank market in the same way that dollars are. The only significant difference is that trading volume in them is much smaller than in dollars.

Some trading in Eurocurrency deposits is generated by swaps, which, as noted in Chapter 6, are extensively used by banks to match assets and liabilities in their Euro books by currency and to create deposits in a desired currency as cheaply as possible. Not surprisingly the movement from fixed to floating exchange rates has somewhat changed the environment in which swaps occur. The increased volume of hedging improved forward markets, and bid-asked spreads in the foreign exchange market diminished. These developments favor the use of swaps. However, floating rates have also created a situation in which adjustments occur more rapidly. If a rate gets out of line, creating a possibility for profitable arbitrage, someone will hit it quickly and put it back in line. Thus the opportunities available to a bank to cut funding costs by using swaps to create currency deposits are more evanescent than they once were, and where they are varies tremendously.

In Chapter 6 we described how a swap (*switch* to the British) operates in intuitive items, but we did not derive a formula for calculating the all-in interest cost of funds generated through a swap. The easiest way to do that is by working an example.

Swap: Dollars into DM

Suppose a bank that has committed itself to lend 6-month Euro DM must now fund this loan. It could take in the funds *natural,* that is, take a 6-month DM deposit, or it could take 6-month dollars and swap them into DM. To determine which is cheaper, the bank dealer has to calculate the *all-in* rate of interest the bank would have to pay on DM obtained through a swap and compare that with the interest cost on a natural DM deposit.

The all-in interest cost on a currency deposit obtained by swapping another currency into that currency is the interest cost on the original deposit *minus* the gain (*plus* the loss) on the swap calculated as an annualized percentage rate. A swap is a sell-now-buy-back-later transaction, for example, like shorting Ford stock in February and covering in June. On swap transactions the percentage rate of gain or loss is calculated as:

$$\frac{\text{Selling price} - \text{Buying price}}{\text{Selling price}}$$

Since in the swap at hand (dollars into DM) the bank is going to sell dollars spot and buy them back forward, the percentage rate of gain or loss on the swap can be expressed as follows:

$$\frac{\left(\substack{\text{Selling price of \$s}\\ \text{in the spot market}}\right) - \left(\substack{\text{Buying price of \$s}\\ \text{in the forward market}}\right)}{\left(\substack{\text{Selling price of \$s}\\ \text{in the spot market}}\right)}$$

The rate given by this expression is the percentage rate of gain (loss) on the swap over the life of the swap. If the swap is for a period less than a year, as in our example, this figure will understate the annualized rate of gain or loss. To see why, note that if it were possible to earn a 2% gain on a 6-month swap, then repeating that swap twice during the year would result in a total gain of 4% over the year. To calculate the *annualized* rate of gain (loss) on a swap that extends less than a year, we have to divide the expression for the actual percentage gain (loss) on the swap by the fraction of the year that the swap is outstanding.

Let

$$t = \text{days the swap is outstanding}$$

Then with rates quoted on a 360-day-year basis,

$$\begin{array}{l}\text{Annualized \% gain (loss)} \\ \text{on a swap of \$s into DM}\end{array} = \frac{\text{Selling price of \$s} - \text{Buying price of \$s}}{\text{Selling price of \$s}} \div \frac{t}{360}$$

If the spot rate for DM is quoted in the U.S. as 0.3886, that means it takes \$0.3886 to buy a deutsche mark.[4] Since the spot rate for DM is expressed in units of dollars per DM, it is the buying price of DM. To get the selling price of dollars, which we need to calculate the cost of the swap in our example, we have to invert the spot rate. For example, with the spot rate at 0.4375, the selling price of dollars is

$$\frac{1}{\$0.3886/\text{DM}} = 2.5735 \text{ DM/\$}$$

Let

$$S = \textit{spot rate} \text{ for DM quoted in U.S. terms}$$
$$F = \textit{forward rate} \text{ for DM quoted in U.S. terms}$$

Then in a swap of dollars for DM,

$$\text{Selling price of \$s} = \frac{1}{S}$$

$$\text{Buying price of \$s} = \frac{1}{F}$$

Substituting these values into the formula derived above, we get

$$\begin{bmatrix}\text{Annualized \% gain (loss)} \\ \text{on a swap of \$s into DM}\end{bmatrix} = \begin{bmatrix}\dfrac{\dfrac{1}{S} - \dfrac{1}{F}}{\dfrac{1}{S}} \div \dfrac{t}{360}\end{bmatrix}$$

$$= \left(1 - \frac{S}{F}\right)\left(\frac{360}{t}\right)$$

---

[4] When a foreign currency is quoted in terms of the amount of local currency required to buy a unit of foreign currency, this is called a *direct quote*. In our example, the rate 0.3886 is the U.S. direct quote for DM. The German direct quote for the dollar would be inverse of this rate, i.e.,

$$\text{German direct quote for \$s} = \frac{1}{0.3886 \text{ \$/DM}} = 2.5735 \text{ DM/\$}$$

In most countries, foreign exchange rates are quoted the direct way. The U.K. is, however, an exception. There rates are quoted the *indirect* way, which means that a British foreign exchange trader, for example, would quote the exchange rate between dollars and pounds in terms of the number of dollars required to buy a pound sterling. Note that this corresponds to the U.S. direct quote on pounds.

Above we said that the all-in interest cost of DM obtained through a swap equals the interest paid on the dollars borrowed *minus* the annualized rate of gain on the swap. Let

i_{DM} = all-in interest cost of the DM generated through a swap out of dollars

$r_\$$ = interest rate paid on the dollars swapped into DM

Then in symbols[5]

$$i_{DM} = r_\$ - \left(1 - \frac{S}{F}\right)\left(\frac{360}{t}\right) = r_\$ + \left(\frac{S}{F} - 1\right)\left(\frac{360}{t}\right)$$

To illustrate how this formula is used, let's work through a numerical example in which 6-month dollars are swapped into 6-month DM. Assume that the spot rate is 0.3886, the forward rate is 0.3942 (the forward mark is at a premium), the interest cost of 6-month Eurodollars is $9^{13}/_{16}\%$, and the bid-asked quotes on 6-month Euro DM are $6^7/_8$–7%. Plugging the first three of these numbers (they are all quotes that prevailed one noon in the market) into our formula for i_{DM}, we get:

$$i_{DM} = 0.98125 + \left(\frac{0.3886}{0.3942} - 1\right)\left(\frac{360}{180}\right)$$
$$= 0.098125 - 0.02841$$
$$= 0.02412$$
$$= 6.971\%$$

In following this calculation, note that because the forward DM was selling at a premium, the swap results in a gain. The annualized cost of the swap is thus negative, and adding it to $r_\$$ reduces i_{DM} below $r_\$$, so far below $r_\$$ that borrowing expensive dollars and swapping them into DM turns out to be slightly less expensive than buying 6-month DM at the offered rate of 7%. Often in actively· traded currencies, the cost of a Eurocurrency deposit obtained through a swap lies in the mid-range of bid and offer quotes in the interbank market for deposits of that currency in that tenor.

Swap: DM into dollars

Swaps, of course, are done not only out of dollars into a foreign currency but also out of foreign currencies into dollars. For example, had the swap been DM into dollars, then we would have been interested in the all-in interest cost of the dollars obtained through the swap. That rate can be calculated as follows. Let

$i_\$$ = all-in interest cost of the dollars generated by a swap out of DM

r_{DM} = interest rate paid on the DM swapped into dollars

[5] This formula does not take into account the impact of hedging interest which is earned in DM and paid out in dollars.

Then

$$i_{\$} = r_{DM} + \left(\frac{F}{S} - 1\right)\left(\frac{360}{t}\right)$$

In this discussion of swaps we have consistently assumed that the mark was the foreign currency involved in the swap. The formulas we have derived, however, are naturally valid for a swap between dollars and any other Eurocurrency.

Arbitrage

Arbitrage strictly defined involves buying at a low price in one market and selling simultaneously at a higher price in a second market. Swaps in the Eurocurrency deposit market are nothing but a form of arbitrage, one that is so widely practiced that it creates, except under unusual conditions, a very consistent relationship in each maturity range between (1) the interest differential at which deposits of a given currency trade relative to Eurodollar deposits and (2) the premium or discount at which that currency trades relative to the dollar in the forward market for foreign exchange.[6]

While it is true that a dollar is a dollar, there are, as noted in Chapters 5 and 6, subtle differences to U.S. banks between Eurodollars and domestic dollars because of reserve requirements and other institutional factors. Thus to some degree the Eurodollar market is separate from the domestic money market, a situation that creates the possibility for arbitrages between the two.

ARBITRAGES BETWEEN THE U.S. AND EUROMARKETS

Figures 16–1 to 16–3, which plot U.S. and Euro rates in different maturity ranges, show that, with the exception of overnight funds, Euro rates tend to be higher than U.S. rates most of the time.

---

[6] The difference between the spot and forward rates at which a currency trades ($S - F$) is called the *swap rate*. Whenever short-term interest rates are lower on deposits of a nondollar Eurocurrency than they are on Eurodollar deposits, the swap rate on that currency quoted in U.S. terms will be *negative;* i.e., that currency will trade at a forward premium. Moreover, because of the activities of arbitragers—institutions seeking to borrow at one rate and lend at a higher one—the size of the premium will be such that the cost of borrowing that currency and swapping it into dollars will equal or nearly equal the cost of borrowing dollars. Note that in our example of swapping dollars into DM, the interest rate on 6-month DM was lower than that on 6-month dollars, and the swap rate was accordingly negative

$$0.3886 - 0.3942 = -0.0056$$

Because the swap rate is the difference between the spot rate and a specific forward rate, its size depends on the tenor of the swap transaction.

Whenever short-term interest rates are higher on deposits of a nondollar Eurocurrency than on Eurodollar deposits, the arbitrage will work the opposite way, making the all-in cost of borrowing dollars and swapping them into that Eurocurrency approximately equal to the cost of borrowing that currency directly.

The explanation is simple. At any time there is a certain worldwide supply of dollars available to banks. A portion of these are held by foreign institutions and other foreign investors, some of whom prefer to deposit their dollars outside the U.S. The majority, however, are held by U.S. investors. Many of the latter feel that placing dollars in the Euromarket exposes them to a significant sovereign risk, and they can therefore be induced to do so only if they are offered a premium rate on Eurodeposits.

U.S. banks operating in both markets could attempt to get around the higher cost of Eurodollars by taking deposits in the domestic market and using them to fund their Euro operations, and at times they do. However, the full cost of the deposits they purchase in the domestic market exceeds the nominal interest rate they pay because of FDIC insurance and reserve costs.[7] Thus nominal Euro rates have to rise above domestic rates before the all-in cost of Eurodeposits exceeds that of domestic deposits to U.S. banks. Foreign banks incur no FDIC and reserve costs on funds they source in the U.S. money market, but they must pay up in the U.S. market; also, their ability to buy funds in this market is limited.

A second interesting feature shown in Figures 16–4 to 16–6 is the startling way in which U.S. and Eurodollar rates in differing maturity

FIGURE 16–4
Overnight rates, Euros, and Fed funds

Money market rates (weekly averages)

Source: Donaldson, Lufkin & Jenrette.

---

[7] See Chapter 15 for the calculation of the all-in cost of domestic CD money to a bank.

FIGURE 16–5
Yields on 3-month CDs, Euro and U.S.

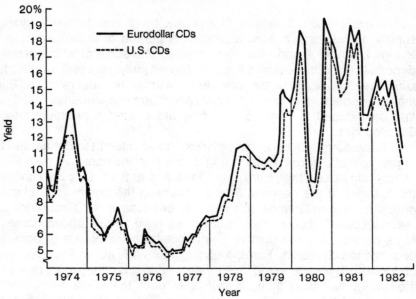

Source: Donaldson, Lufkin & Jenrette.

FIGURE 16–6
Yields on 6-month CDs, Euro and U.S.

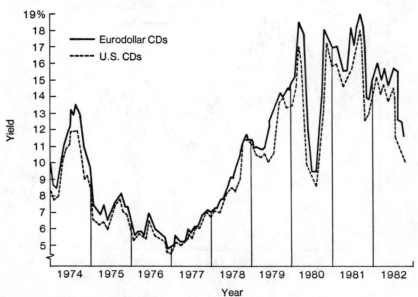

Source: Donaldson, Lufkin & Jenrette.

ranges track each other over time. Spreads widen and narrow and sometimes rates cross, but the main trends up and down are the same in both markets. There's no doubt that this consistency in rates is the work of arbitrage, but that still leaves open the question of where the major impetus for rate changes typically comes from. Are changes in U.S. rates pushing Euro rates up and down, or vice versa? A British Eurobanker succinctly answered that question: "The U.S. money market is the dog, the Euromarket the tail. Rarely does the tail wag the dog."

The truth of this statement has created a whole new set of Fed watchers—bankers in London, Paris, Singapore, and other Eurocenters. Much as some of these bankers, especially foreign ones, would like to think of the Euromarket as an international market that responds largely to developments external to the U.S. economy, experience has taught them that whenever the Fed moves, its actions immediately affect the Euromarket. Consequently to be successful, Eurobankers have to understand the workings of the U.S. money market and follow closely developments there.

Two sorts of arbitrages, used to link U.S. and Euro rates, *technical* and *transitory*. Technical arbitrages were most important at the short end of the market, and opportunities for them occured because of the way Euro transactions affected, due to institutional arrangements, the reservable deposits of U.S. banks buying and selling Eurodollars. Opportunities for technical arbitrage vanished with the movement of CHIPS to same day settlement.

Transitory arbitrages, in contrast, are money flows that occur in response to temporary discrepancies that arise between U.S. and Euro rates because rates in the two markets are being affected by differing supply and demand pressures. Much transitory arbitrage is carried on by banks that actively borrow and lend funds in both markets. An example of such *intrabank arbitrage* would be a bank that responded to a relatively high rate on 6-month Euros by buying money of that tenor in the U.S. market and lending it in the Euromarket. Another group whose activities tend to pull together U.S. and Euro rates are investors who shift from domestic to Euro CDs and back in response to changing yield spreads. Finally, there is a small but growing number of borrowers who shift between the domestic and the Euromarkets in response to changes in the relationship between lending rates in the two markets. Their activities too hold rates together.

RESERVE EFFECTS OF EURO TRANSACTIONS

When a domestic bank arbitrages between the domestic and the Euromarkets, it is always concerned with all-in cost and total return. An important element in the calculation of both is the effect that Euro lendings and borrowings have on the reserves that a domestic bank must maintain with the Fed.

As noted in Chapter 15, during 1969 U.S. money market rates rose above the Reg Q ceiling on the rate that U.S. banks could pay on large-denomination CDs. As a result money flowed out of the U.S. market into the Euromarket, and U.S. banks were forced to buy back that money from the Euromarket to fund their domestic operations. To thwart the backflow of funds from the Euromarket to the U.S. market, the Fed imposed under *Regulation D* a requirement that member banks hold reserves against Eurodollars borrowed by head office either from their own foreign branches or from foreign banks. Currently, Reg D, which has been changed considerably over time, requires U.S. banks to hold reserves equal to 4% of their *net borrowings* from the Euromarket calculated over a 7-day averaging period. Generally money market banks have so much flexibility that they can offset their borrowings (takings) from the Euromarket with lendings (placements) there, so net under Reg D they incur no required reserves on such borrowings.

ARBITRAGES IN THE LONGER DATES

Supply and demand pressures in the U.S. and Euromarkets are constantly changing, and rates in both markets constantly adjust up and down in response. They do not, however, adjust independently because there are strong forces pulling these rates together. Many investors will readily switch back and forth between Euro and domestic CDs depending on rate spreads and where they perceive greater relative value to be. Borrowers too are becoming increasingly sophisticated, seeking to borrow in the market in which all-in lending rates are least. Finally, the big banks are ever alert to any opportunities for profitable arbitrage created by rate discrepancies between the two markets.

Still, as Figures 16–5 and 16–6 show, in the longer dates Euro rates are almost always higher than comparable domestic rates. There are several reasons, some obvious and some not so obvious, why these rate discrepancies are not arbitraged out.

First, the fact that for a U.S. bank the all-in cost of domestic CD money exceeds the nominal rate paid permits some fairly large rate discrepancies to persist. As one U.S. banker noted, "Today 6-month Euros are at 6⅛. I could buy 6-month money in New York at 5¾, but the all-in cost would be 6.03. That sort of arbitrage [buy at 6.03 and sell at 6.18] is probably not worth the bookkeeping. But if the domestic all-in rate fell to 5.70, I might do the arbitrage in size."

The "might" arises because of a second problem a bank faces in such arbitrage—whether it can use the money. The same banker went on to say, "It's pretty tough to just go out and buy domestic money and relend it in the Euromarket because you've got to have the credit lines to sell it. Chances are that you are already using your lines to the fullest, so you can't just say—hey, let's do 2 billion."

The "2 billion" was clearly hyperbole because a third and crucial problem U.S. banks face when they arbitrage the domestic and Euro-markets in the longer dates is the limit that market depth imposes on the size in which such arbitrages can be done. The U.S. and Euromarkets differ sharply in structure. In the Euromarket it's easy for a bank to borrow 6-month, 1-year, or longer-maturity money in size. In the United States, in contrast, it's difficult for a bank to do so; the domestic CD market has great depth in the 3-month area, but beyond that it becomes increasingly thin. The sharpness of the contrast between the two markets is illustrated by one banker's remarks, "Currently domestic 6-month CDs are 6⅞. If we took the view that rates were going to rise steeply, we might well take 6-month Euros to fund our domestic book because, whereas we could do only 50 million at the domestic 6-month rate, we could do 250 million at the Euro 6-month rate."

The thinness of the U.S. market in longer-term funds means that when Euro rates in the longer dates rise to a substantial premium above U.S. rates, it is difficult for U.S. banks to arbitrage that rate differential in size. This is not, however, to say that such arbitrage doesn't occur. If, for example, a bunching of 6-month rollovers in the Euromarket causes the spread between domestic and Euro 6-month rates to widen, banks will pull money out of the domestic market and place it in the Euromarket. But because of the thinness of the domestic market in 6-month money, the volume of such arbitrage may be insufficient to arbitrage out the rate differential.

Any arbitrage that calls for a bank to lend term funds into the Euro-market will also permit that bank to pull back Euros in some other tenor reserve free. Usually the funds pulled back are short dated, so a bank considering such an arbitrage will be concerned with the relationship between U.S. and Euro rates not only in longer dates, but also at the short end of the market.

A final factor that probably bears some responsibility for discrepancies between long U.S. and Euro rates is the difference in bank lending practices between the domestic and Euromarkets. A domestic banker uses the bulk of the funds he buys to finance floating-rate loans, and he can therefore continually roll relatively short-term liabilities without experiencing any real interest rate exposure. The Euro banker in contrast has to finance fixed-rate assets, many of which have a 6-month life; thus he must constantly take a view on interest rates, asking whether he should borrow long money. That is something the domestic banker does less often. Lending practices can at times create in the Euromarket a demand for long money and a willingness to pay up for it that do not exist in the same degree in the U.S. market because a domestic banker in borrowing long is more likely to be assuming than cutting interest rate risk.

Arbitrage and proper profit center analysis

In Chapter 6 we stressed the importance, in controlling interest rate risk, to a bank with international operations of running a global book. Once a bank does this, many benefits will accrue to it. One is that it will be more easily able to rationally arbitrage the Euro and domestic money markets and thereby reduce its worldwide funding costs.

To successfully run a global book, a bank must correctly organize its profit center accounting. Most banks analyze their sources of profits at a fine level of detail. Doing so is part of a bank's overall planning and budgeting process. In seeking to maximize earnings, a bank tries to determine how profitable each activity is. If the bank then runs up against a balance-sheet constraint that forces it to curtail activity in some area, it can do so rationally.

The way most major banks have grown up is that their international business has been tacked on to their domestic banking activity almost as an adjunct. What these banks went through since 1960, regional banks are going through now.

When a bank that already has a profit center analysis enters the international business, it is natural for it to treat this new business as a separate profit center. Doing so, however, is a big mistake because it impedes the free flow of funds between head office and the branches. Narrow profit center definitions, for example, will prevent a bank from taking advantage of opportunities for arbitrage that require the use of domestic funds in the Euromarket or vice versa. If the domestic and international treasuries are separate profit centers, such arbitrages can be carried out only if a transfer price can be agreed upon that will make both sides happy. This will rarely occur because spreads are often thin.

In a bank that does international business, profit center accounting should be based on two broad profit centers: the worldwide lending and worldwide treasury divisions. Note that lending and funding are basically all a bank does.

To separate lending profits from funding profits, a bank must treat loans funded by the treasury as income-producing assets to that division and liabilities incurred to fund loans as a cost to the lending division. Under this approach, the lending division's profits will equal the spread between the rate at which it puts on loans and the bank's marginal cost of funds. The treasury's profit will be any savings it can realize on funding—for example, by mismatching.

A decade ago, when the major banks treated the domestic treasury division as one profit center and their international treasury—which was part of their international banking division—as a separate profit center, they created an incentive for head office and London office to each maximize its own profits. There was no provision for having the domestic treasury work hand in glove with London office to maximize the bank's total profits by, for example, using domestic funds to support assets which London office would acquire. Creating a profit center apparatus that fosters such cooperation enables head office and London office to earn a combined profit that exceeds the total the two could earn acting independently.

To illustrate, suppose that 3-month Euros are trading at 15⅞ while domestic CD money can be bought at 14¾. After 3% reserves, a bank issuing 3-month CDs has an all-in cost of about 15.20; consequently, by buying money in the domestic CD market and relending it in the Euro market, the bank can pick up over 65 basis points. There is no question that a bank should do such profitable arbitrages if the bank has a foreign branch that needs 3-month money and would, if it did not receive that money from head office, have to bid for it in the Euro market. The situation is different if none of the bank's foreign branches need 3-month money. In that case, the bank, to take advantage of the arbitrage, will have to have one of its foreign branches redeposit the money it has bought in the domestic market with some other bank operating in the Euromarket. That tack, while profitable, has the disadvantage that it will balloon the bank's balance sheet and deteriorate its capital ratio.

Today, arbitrages of the sort just described must be looked for carefully. This was not so as late as the end of the 1970s. At that time, the domestic and international treasuries in most large banks were still operating as independent profit centers: Therefore, they were not set up to take advantage of the arbitrage, and for that reason, U.S. and Euro rates sometimes widened to the point where such arbitrages offered a 300- or even 400-basis-point profit.

Making the global treasury function as a profit center still leaves a problem with respect to interbranch transfers of funds. If the treasurer of Paris office says to London office, "How do you lend me the 3s?" he is not going to get a break from London office, which will want to make something on the trade. Head office, in contrast, would be willing to give Paris office a break in the form of money at cost to improve not its profits, but the total bank's aftertax return. With respect to maximizing the latter, the terms on which interbranch transactions occur are unimportant. The whole concept of a global treasury function is that it does not matter—except for tax purposes—whether profits are booked in London or Paris.

What matters is not having the domestic side maximizing its profits against the international side. If this occurs, each branch is forced to do its own funding, which is undesirable because the London treasurer cannot borrow money from other banks in the domestic market as he can in the Euromarket. If domestic money is cheaper than Euro money, the *only* way a money market bank can take advantage of this in a global sense is by having head office borrow domestic money and give it to the offshore branches.

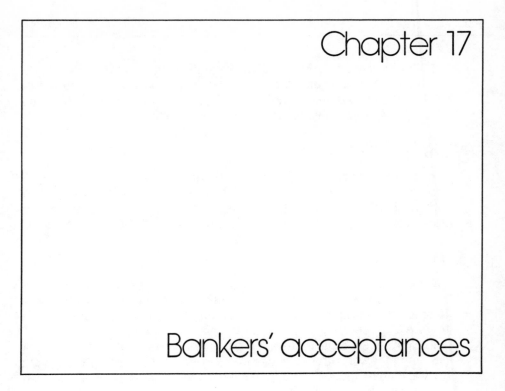

Chapter 17

Bankers' acceptances

BANKERS' ACCEPTANCES OR BILLS OF EXCHANGE, as they are also called, are an old financial instrument dating back to the 12th century when early forms of this instrument were used to finance international trade. For the two centuries prior to creation of the Fed, world trade was denominated and financed primarily in sterling, and a market in sterling bankers' acceptances flourished in London.

The founders of the Federal Reserve System, created in 1913, felt that a domestic bankers' acceptance market patterned after the London market should be developed to enhance New York's role as a center of international trade and finance, to promote U.S. foreign trade, and to improve the competitive position of domestic banks. The Fed's founders thus empowered national banks to accept time drafts, which these banks were previously unauthorized to do. They also took other actions to support the growth of this infant market, including permitting the Federal Reserve to rediscount and purchase eligible acceptances.

By the late 1920s, with the Fed's help, a domestic market in bankers' acceptances had become well established, and more than $1.7 billion of acceptances were outstanding. Then due first to the Depression and then to World War II, acceptances outstanding declined sharply. In May

1945, they totaled only $104 million. After the war, as international trade revived, acceptance financing again became popular; and by the end of 1973, the total volume outstanding was $8.9 billion. Since that time, as Figure 17–1 shows, this volume has grown exponentially.

THE INSTRUMENT

A bankers' acceptance is a time draft; that is, an order to pay a specified amount of money to the acceptance holder on a specified date. BAs are drawn on and accepted by a bank that, by accepting the draft, assumes responsibility to make payment on the draft at maturity.

Creation

Under current Fed regulations BAs may be created by accepting banks to finance foreign trade, the domestic shipment of goods, domestic or foreign storage of readily marketable staples, and the provision of dollar exchange credits to banks in certain countries.

In Chapter 3 we gave one example of how a BA might be created. A U.S. importer wants to buy shoes from a foreign seller and pay for them several months later. To obtain the necessary financing, he has his own bank write a letter of credit for the amount of the sale, which it sends to the foreign exporter. When the shoes are exported, the foreign firm, using this letter of credit, draws a time draft on the importer's U.S. bank and discounts the draft at a local bank, thereby obtaining immediate payment for its goods. The exporter's bank in turn sends the time draft along with proper shipping documents to the importer's U.S. bank. This bank accepts the draft—at which point it becomes an irrevocable obligation of the accepting bank—and pays out the proceeds of the draft to the exporter's bank. The accepting bank may then hold the accepted draft as an investment, or it may sell it in the open market. When the draft matures, the drawer is responsible for paying the accepting bank the face amount of the draft.

If a U.S. firm uses BAs to finance exports, the process is the reverse. For example, a Japanese firm that wanted to purchase U.S. goods on credit might arrange for a letter of credit from a New York bank under which this bank would agree to accept dollar drafts drawn by a U.S. exporter to cover specified shipments to the Japanese importer.

While the drawing of BAs is frequently preauthorized by a letter of credit, in many instances BAs also arise out of contractual arrangements that are less formal than a letter of credit and are later supported by appropriate documentation. In effect BAs can be created in a myriad of ways. Precisely how a given BA is created depends on who the participants in a transaction are and on the nature of that transaction.

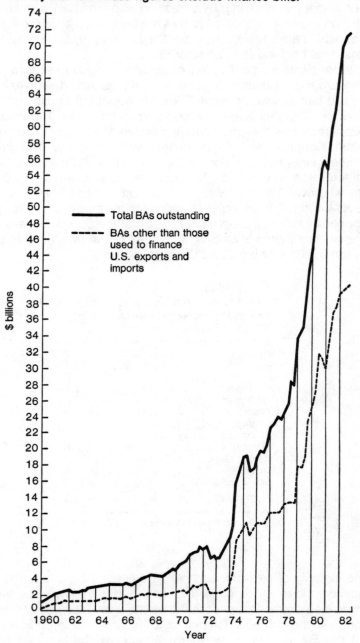

FIGURE 17–1
In recent years the volume of BAs outstanding has expanded at an extremely rapid pace. The big growth of BAs other than those used to finance U.S. exports and imports reflects in large part the financing of foreign oil imports in the U.S. money market. These figures exclude finance bills.

Total BAs outstanding

BAs other than those used to finance U.S. exports and imports

$ billions

Year

Source: *Federal Reserve Bulletin.*

Creating BAs requires much specialized knowledge on the part of the accepting bank. Consequently it is done only by banks that have foreign departments staffed by personnel who are knowledgeable about the market. A large proportion of BAs are originated by Edge Act corporations, which are specialized subsidiaries set up by banks to engage in international banking (see Chapter 5).

Top money market banks have established Edge Act subs in financial centers around the country to service local business. It used to be that a bank, like Morgan, would issue Edge Act paper out of each of its subs: its Houston Edge, its San Francisco Edge, and so on. The trouble with this approach was that each sub had only limited capital. To solve this problem, Congress in 1982 permitted banks to merge their Edge Act subs into a single corporation; one sub took over the role of head office, the others became branches. Now U.S. banks issue all of their Edge Act paper, wherever it is originated, out of a single head office—Miami in the case of Morgan. This change has enhanced the creditworthiness of Edge Act paper by enlarging the capitalization of the corporations issuing it. Currently the majority of all BAs, as Table 17–1 shows, are originated in New York, San Francisco, and Chicago.

TABLE 17–1
Bankers' acceptances outstanding by Federal Reserve district, July 31, 1981 ($ billions)

Boston	1.9
New York	32.2
Philadelphia	.6
Cleveland	3.1
Richmond	1.5
Atlanta	.9
Chicago	4.7
St. Louis	.5
Minneapolis	.6
Kansas City	.1
Dallas	2.4
San Francisco	15.1
Total	63.6

Source: Federal Reserve Bank of New York.

The majority of bankers' acceptances used to be created to finance domestic exports and imports. This changed in 1974 when the price of oil increased dramatically. At that time the Japanese and others began to borrow in the domestic BA market to finance their imports of oil. As a result the BA market grew sharply. Also, as Table 17–2 shows, it

TABLE 17-2
Bankers' acceptances outstanding according to the nature of
the transaction financed, July 31, 1981 ($ billions)

Imports	13.1
Exports	13.3
Goods stored in or shipped between foreign countries	35.7
Domestic shipments	.2
Domestic storage	1.3
Total	63.6

Source: Federal Reserve Bank of New York.

changed in character. Currently more than half of all BAs outstanding are created to finance the storage or shipment of goods between foreign countries; and most of these BAs represent financing of *third-country trade;* that is, transactions in which neither the exporter nor the importer is a U.S. firm.

The prominence of third-country financing in the U.S. acceptance market reflects the fact that the U.S. market is the only world financial center in which there is a wide market for dollar-denominated acceptances. There was talk in London of starting a market there in Eurodollar bankers' acceptances, but nothing ever came of it. The biggest items in the mix of commodities financed in the BA market have not changed much in the last few years. "Grains," which in bankers' lingo covers wheat, corn, soybeans, and sorghum, are by far the largest single item. Other big items are cotton and oil.

Characteristics

BAs are a discount instrument, and yields on them are quoted on a discount basis. Most BAs are backed by documentation such as invoices, bills of lading, or independent terminal or warehouse receipts. This documentation is held by the accepting bank, so the instrument sold to investors is, as Figure 17-2 shows, a simply drawn note. This note describes the nature of the transaction being financed and has been stamped "accepted" by the accepting bank. BAs are generally issued in bearer form. They may be drawn for varying maturities, but the largest volume of BAs traded in the market is in the 3-month area.

The amount of BA financing required by a borrower depends on the transaction he is financing; often it is quite large. In the interdealer market, $5 million is a round lot, and bids and offers are quoted on the understanding that, if a deal is struck, the paper delivered will—unless otherwise specified—be 5 by 1, that is, 5 pieces for a million each. Thus for BAs $1 million is a good trading amount, and usually a bank's clients

FIGURE 17–2
Specimen bankers' acceptance, Harris Bank

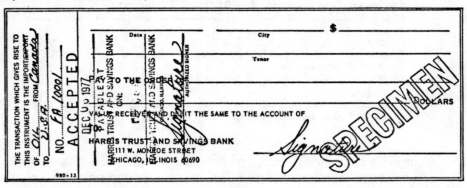

will structure their paper so that it comes in $1 million lots. Sometimes a bank will break up $1 million BA into $500,000 or even $100,000 pieces for sale to its retail clients: small money funds, bank trust departments, foreign bank branches, and wealthy individuals.

The credit risk to an investor of holding a BA is minimal. The instrument not only constitutes an irrevocable primary obligation of the accepting bank but is typically a contingent obligation of the drawer; it is also an obligation of any other institutions that have endorsed it. During the 65 years that BAs have been traded in the U.S., no investor in BAs has suffered a loss of principal.

There are currently about 30 dealers in BAs who make an ongoing market in this instrument. The volume of trading in the secondary market for BAs is such that BAs are at least as liquid as CDs in terms of the spreads at which they trade.

As Figure 17–3 indicates, BA rates closely track bill rates. In the 3-month area, the traditional spread is 15 to 25 basis points, but when money is easy, BAs may—depending on the supply in the market—trade just a few basis points about the bill rate; conversely when rates are high or volatile, the spread may widen to a full point or more.

ELIGIBILITY REQUIREMENTS

A high official of the New York Fed recalls that, when he first came to the bank, one of the first questions he had to answer was: Are yak tails readily marketable? That's not common knowledge, but fortunately he was able to come up with a quick answer—yes they are—because he had just read that yak tails were used in the United States to make high-quality Santa Claus beards. And why, one might wonder, did the New

FIGURE 17–3
The bankers' acceptance rate tracks the T bill rate, with the spread
between the two widening when money is tight

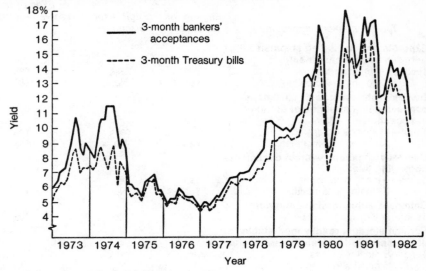

Source: *Federal Reserve Bulletin.*

York Fed care about the marketability of yak tails? The answer is that it
determined whether a particular BA was or was not eligible.

To understand the BA market, one has to know something about eligibility requirements. The initial Federal Reserve Act specified that BAs
eligible for discount at or purchase by the Fed had to meet certain
requirements. These, as noted in the second column of Table 17–3, are
complex. Generally their spirit is that, for a BA to be eligible, it should
finance a short-term (no longer than 6 months), self-liquidating commercial transaction of one of several specified types.

The implications of this set of criteria for eligibility have changed
considerably over time. The initial intent and practice were that banks
experiencing a temporary need for funds would sell to the Fed (that is,
rediscount at the discount window) BAs and other eligible paper. Later
open-market operations replaced the discount window as the Fed's
primary tool for creating bank reserves, and the Fed's view as to what
was an appropriate use of the discount window changed. Now no bank
would ask the Fed to rediscount a BA to maturity to raise funds because
doing so would violate the spirit in which loans are currently extended at
the discount window.

The key importance today of the eligibility requirements stated in the
original Federal Reserve Act (see the third column of Table 17–3) is that

TABLE 17–3
Bankers' acceptances: Eligibility and reservability

Type of bankers' acceptance	Eligible for purchase*	Eligible for discount†	Exempt from reserve requirements if sold‡
Export-import, including shipments between foreign countries:			
Tenor—6 months or less..................	Yes	Yes§	Yes
6 months to 9 months.............	Yes	No	No
Domestic shipment, with documents conveying title attached at the time of acceptance:			
Tenor—6 months or less	Yes	Yes§	Yes
6 months to 9 months.............	Yes	No	No
Domestic shipment, without documents conveying title:			
Tenor—6 months or less.................	Yes	No	No
6 months to 9 months.............	Yes	No	No
Shipment within foreign countries:			
Tenor—any maturity	No	No	No
Foreign storage, readily marketable staples secured by warehouse receipt:			
Tenor—6 months or less	No	Yes§	Yes
6 months to 9 months	No	No	No
Domestic storage, readily marketable staples secured by warehouse receipt:			
Tenor—6 months or less.................	Yes	Yes§	Yes
6 months to 9 months.............	Yes	No	No
Domestic storage, any goods in the United States under contract of sale or going into channels of trade and secured throughout its life by warehouse receipt:			
Tenor—6 months or less.................	Yes	No	No
6 months to 9 months.............	Yes	No	No
Dollar exchange, required by usages of trade, only in approved countries:			
Tenor—3 months or less	No	Yes	No‖
3 months to 9 months	No	No	No
Finance or working capital, not related to any specific transaction:			
Tenor—any maturity	No	No	No

Tenor refers to the full length of time of the acceptance from date of inception to maturity. To be eligible for discount, a bankers' acceptance must be endorsed by at least one member bank, as provided in Section 13(6) of the Federal Reserve Act.

* Authorizations announced by the Federal Open Market Committee on April 1, 1974.

† In accordance with Regulation A of the Federal Reserve Act.

‡ In accordance with Regulation D of the Federal Reserve Act.

§ Providing that the maturity of nonagricultural bills at the time of discount is not more than 90 days.

‖ According to revised Regulation D, these acceptances are reservable, but the Federal Reserve Board's legal staff has expressed an opinion that the exemption from reserve requirements is also applicable to dollar exchange acceptances.

Source: Jean M. Mahr and William C. Melton, "Bankers' Acceptances," *Quarterly Review,* Federal Reserve Bank of New York, Summer 1981, p. 53. In constructing this table the authors relied on an unpublished paper by Arthur Bardenhagen.

only acceptances that are deemed eligible according to these requirements may be sold by member banks without incurring a *reserve requirement.*

Currently banks can and do create large amounts of ineligible acceptances. If they sell such acceptances in the market, they incur a reserve requirement. The resulting reserve cost is passed on by the bank to the borrower. Thus a borrower who requires ineligible as opposed to eligible BA financing pays a higher rate.

Eligibility for purchase

In the early 1970s the Fed was active in the BA market in four ways: It bought BAs for its own portfolio and did RP with BA dealers as part of its normal open-market operations; in addition it lent to banks at the discount window against BAs as collateral, and it bought—adding its own guarantee to them—BAs in the open market for the account of foreign central banks.

Buying BAs for its own portfolio on its own initiative was nothing new for the Fed. It did this continually from the inception of the BA market to encourage the market's growth. By 1974 a big change had occurred in the composition of the BAs that were being created by the banks. At this time the Fed decided to modernize its rules on what BAs it could purchase as part of its open-market operations; responsibility for setting eligibility requirements for purchase was passed from the Board of Governors to the Federal Open Market Committee. The new eligibility requirements relative to purchases issued by the FOMC are summarized in the first column of Table 17–3. One major change was that BAs with a maturity of up to 9 months, provided they met other eligibility requirements, became eligible for purchase even though they were ineligible for discount.

At this time, when the Fed bought BAs, it did not usually ask a dealer to tell it in advance which banks' paper the dealer was offering; the Fed made no attempt to distinguish gradations in quality among different banks' paper. Instead it asked the dealers only that they offer it *prime* paper. The Fed's main criterion for determining that a bank's paper was prime was that it be traded in reasonable volume and with reasonable frequency in the secondary market: that the paper was acceptable to the market.

In the market's view, however, there were and still are quality gradations in paper, and tiering exists in the rates paid by different institutions. To avoid acquiring undue amounts of paper considered by the market to be less attractive, the Fed instructed dealers to offer and deliver to it a reasonable mix of acceptances created by prime banks. If the Fed's holdings of any one bank's paper became unduly large, it would temporarily refuse to accept that name until its holding was reduced to an acceptable percentage.

The Federal Reserve Bank of New York has for years purchased for foreign correspondents (mainly other central banks) government securities, agency securities, and bankers' acceptances.

Prior to November 8, 1974, the Federal Reserve guaranteed the acceptances it purchased for its foreign correspondents. The policy of guaranteeing acceptances held by foreign correspondents was developed in the process of working out reciprocal correspondent relationships with other central banks during the early years of the Federal Reserve System. Such guarantees were at that time considered useful in encouraging the development of the bankers' acceptance market. In part, due to the favorable rate spread between acceptances and Treasury bills, foreign correspondent holdings of bankers' acceptances guaranteed by the Federal Reserve increased rapidly during 1974 to a level of about $2 billion. Against this background, officials of the Federal Reserve concluded that there was no longer justification for extending a guarantee favoring a particular private market instrument or a particular group of investors.[1]

Because of the Fed's decision to stop guaranteeing BAs, the number of foreign banks buying these instruments dropped by about two thirds, and the holdings of the remaining foreign customers fell to about $300 million in 1975. To cushion the effect on the BA market of this large drop in foreign purchases, the Fed temporarily increased its own purchases of BAs by a like amount.

Then gradually the Fed let its own BA holdings drop. Finally, in March 1977, when the Fed was buying for its own portfolio only an insignificant amount of BAs—$1 or $2 million daily—it determined that the BA market was mature enough to no longer need federal support, and it stopped buying BAs for its own portfolio.

Eligibility requirements with respect to purchases still have significance, however. BAs that are eligible for purchase are eligible for RP, and the Fed continues to do RP with BA dealers (it never does reverses with them).

The ability to do RP with BA dealers gives the Fed one more useful way to make temporary injections of reserves into the banking system. It also gives the Fed's BA staff a chance to spot check the acceptances RPed by the dealers to the Fed to determine that eligibility requirements are being met. It is market practice for a bank that issues paper ineligible for discount to stamp "ineligible" on that paper.

Currently banks may use as collateral for loans at the discount window any BAs that are eligible for purchase by the Fed and any other

---

[1] Ralph T. Helfrich, "Trading in Bankers' Acceptances: A View from the Acceptance Desk of the Federal Reserve Bank of New York," *Monthly Review*, Federal Reserve Bank of New York, February 1976, p. 53.

paper that meets the general eligibility standards established by the window.

DOLLAR EXCHANGE ACCEPTANCES

Most bankers' acceptances are based on specific merchandise trade or storage transactions. *Dollar exchange acceptances* are an exception. They are time drafts drawn by foreign banks—usually central banks—on U.S. banks that accept these drafts. Countries, mostly Latin American, have issued dollar exchange bills to obtain dollars to satisfy temporary, and often seasonal, needs. A one-crop country, for example, might issue dollar exchange bills to pay for imports of seed and other raw materials it needs to grow a crop whose sale at maturity produces dollars.

Dollar exchange bills have never been a large item in the BA market; outstandings have ranged between $50 and $200 million. Countries that issue this paper have the perhaps cheaper alternative of borrowing in the Euromarket.

FINANCE BILLS

In the Fed's traditional view, BAs should be used to finance only a specified set of self-liquidating, commercial transactions not to provide working capital. Precisely how a line can be drawn between the two is something that occasionally calls for bankers to apply the wisdom of Solomon. Grain stored in an elevator may be financed by a BA, since it is going to be sold, which makes the elevator operator's investment in inventory self-liquidating. But if cotton is stored at a mill, funds used to finance it are considered to be working capital even if the cotton is still owned by a broker rather than by the mill. One of many gray areas is the financing of tobacco because the storage process includes curing, a manipulation of the commodity stored. For bankers, a real problem in this area is that they are working with regulations that are subject to interpretation, often after the fact.

During the late 1960s when the Fed tightened money severely on several occasions and made it difficult for banks to meet loan demand, the banks conceived the idea of selling *working capital* BAs; that is, they would issue normal commercial loans in the form of BAs—also called *finance bills*—and sell them in the open market. This technique permitted banks to continue to make loans at a time when their reserve positions were so tight that they could not otherwise have done so.

By mid-1973 the amount of working capital BAs outstanding had reached a record $1.5 billion. At that point the Fed imposed reserve requirements on the sale of such acceptances; this action caused a rapid and sharp contraction in their use. Noted one banker of the Fed's ruling, "It was a dictatorial act of fiat. There is no way that the sale of such BAs should be considered reservable deposits. They are sales of assets."

The Fed's ruling raises an interesting issue. If banks were permitted to sell working capital BAs free from reserve requirements, their loan portfolios would have some liquidity. Also, during a monetary crunch, it would permit banks to go on lending no matter how much the Fed tightened, since at some rate it is always possible for banks to sell BAs to the market. Permitting banks to operate this way would, of course, eventually drive open-market interest rates high enough so that it would become economically infeasible for certain corporations to borrow; thus the effect of the Fed's tightening would be felt in time because gradually some firms would be rationed by *price* out of the loan market.

Rationing loan demand by price would presumably cause loans to flow to those firms that could use borrowed funds most productively. But the Fed, although it never said so publicly, used to feel that it would be politically infeasible to permit interest rates to rise to market-clearing levels. Therefore it preferred to maintain a system in which it could periodically induce crunches that forced banks to curtail lending. During such crunches the major commercial paper issuers are in no way inhibited from borrowing, since they could always sell their paper no matter how tight money got. Thus the effect of the system was to place the major burden of a credit crunch on firms that for one reason or another lacked access to the commercial paper market and therefore had to rely on bank credit. Both the justice and economic rationality of such a system seemed questionable at best. Since its 1979 switch to monetarism, the Fed has permitted money market rates to soar to historically high, market-clearing levels.

BANK PRICING AND SALE

When a bank creates an acceptance, it prices it as follows. First, it checks the rate at which paper of the maturity it is creating and carrying its name is trading in the dealer market; that is, the rate at which it could sell the acceptance in the market. To this rate it adds on any reserve cost it would incur in selling the acceptance. Reserve requirements on ineligible acceptances and finance bills are frequently altered by the Fed and have ranged from 2.5 to 8%. They also depend on the tenor of the instrument created.

To the sum of these two costs, the bank adds on a commission for its services. The standard acceptance fee used to be 1.5%, and this figure is still often quoted as a standard. However, in practice the acceptance fee charged by a bank may range anywhere from 25 basis points to 2%. It is less for prime than for non-prime customers. Also, when money is easy and loan demand is slack, many banks will cut their acceptance fee—sometimes by quoting a low all-in rate—to compete for additional BA business.

The acceptance fee charged also depends on the amount borrowed. On odd-lot acceptances, certainly on those less than $100,000, a bank will charge an extra 10 or 20 basis points because such acceptances can be sold only at a concession to the market.

Selling versus holding

Once a bank creates a BA, it can either hold the paper as part of its loan portfolio, that is, as an investment, or sell it to the market. Bank attitudes on this point vary considerably. When the Fed is tightening and banks are short on reserves, they will normally choose to sell out BAs to be able to fund more straight loans.

When money is easy, there is more variability in bank behavior. Some banks consistently sell a large proportion of the BAs they create to correspondents and foreign customers who demand them as a means of accommodating these customers and improving their relationship with them. For other banks, the decision whether to sell BAs is strictly an investment decision.

Noted one such banker, "We will hold BAs if we think that rates are coming down and will sell them if we think that rates are going up. However, our decision on BAs is usually weighted toward selling them out rather quickly because, if you have a profit in them and you sell them out fast, you get the profit for sure and right away for the whole maturity of the BA. If you wait, you are speculating on what will happen to the cost of funding. BAs are a relatively low-yield instrument, and your spreads are narrow. So it does not take much of a rise in rates to take you from a profitable to an unprofitable position in BAs. Also the cost of funding BAs is not as low for a bank as for a dealer because a bank incurs a reserve requirement when it RPs acceptances unless it does the RP with another bank. Because of this, the cheapest way for us to fund BAs is usually with Fed funds."

Another banker made the same point more succinctly, "Whenever we position BAs, it is a rate decision. I tell our trader, any time we think it is a good idea to buy 90-day money, he had better not build up any assets— just sell the BAs we create out to the market."

A funding officer at still another larger bank took a slightly different view, "We turn out BAs whether money is easy or tight. We can make short-term investments in bills, and we think we can manage a bill portfolio in a way to maximize return better than we can manage a BA portfolio. We notice we differ from other banks in this respect, but we have tested our policy and think it permits us to make more money."

Finally, it should be noted that some banks will build up their BA holdings when loan demand is slack to show a stronger loan position on their balance sheet. BAs held as an investment are recorded on a bank's balance sheet as loans.

Borrowing via the BA route

Five years ago when rates were much lower and much less volatile, a firm with a financing need that could be covered in the BA market faced a relatively simple choice: go the BA route or borrow at a floating-rate prime. The advantage of BA financing was that it was cheaper, and a firm's decision to use BA financing was typically a rate decision.

As rates rose and became more volatile, the spread of prime over the lower commercial paper rate got as wide as 350 basis points, and borrowers began to view prime as a punitive rate. To retain borrowers, banks changed their lending terms dramatically (Chapter 5). Today a firm financing a commodity transaction will—depending on its size, credit, and relationship to its bank—have a menu of borrowing alternatives from which to choose: a loan at a floating prime, a Euro loan, a fixed-rate advance, or BA financing.

A firm with a financing need will seek to borrow as cheaply as possible. Thus today, as before, a borrower's choice as to which financing method to use is typically a rate decision. Table 17–4 illustrates the

TABLE 17–4
Comparing the cost of BA financing with other forms of bank financing

Acceptance		Bank loan at prime	
Discount rate for a 6-month acceptance	9.05%	Estimated average floating "prime" rate	12.00%
Acceptance commission	.50%	Implicit cost of holding 20% compensating balances†	3.00%
Total cost to borrower on a discount basis	10.55%	Total cost to borrower on a simple interest basis	15.00%
Total cost to borrower on a simple interest basis*	10.84%		
Euro loan		Fixed-rate bank advance	
LIBOR on 3-month money	10.25%	All-in cost of 3-month CD money	10.38%
Spread	.50%	Spread	.50%
Cost to borrower	10.75%	Cost to borrower	10.88%

* Recall the formula on page 49. Because the prime rate is quoted on a 360-day-year basis, the appropriate conversion formula here is:

$$r = \frac{d \times 360}{360 - d \times t}$$

† If a borrower has to hold 20% of the amount borrowed as compensating balances, he must borrow a sum equal to 125% of the amount he actually needs, and consequently the effective loan rate he pays is 125% of the nominal rate. Note: 125% of 7% is 8.75%.

comparative cost calculations; the numbers used reflect prevailing market rates and spreads in early October 1982. Note in the example that borrowing for 3 months at prime is the most expensive alternative, even if compensating balances—the imposition of which is falling into disuess— are not imposed; borrowing via the BA route costs slightly more than a Euro loan priced off LIBOR, slightly less than a fixed-rate advance priced off the all-in cost of domestic CD money.

The unrealistically high levels at which banks have at times quoted prime in recent years has led borrowers to maximize, to the extent possible, their use of the BA market. On the other hand, the introduction by banks of fixed-rate advances priced off money market rates has led to some decline in the amount of ineligible paper issued. In the past, the rate on ineligible paper was less than prime; this is still true, but now the rate on a fixed-rate advance is likely to be still cheaper. Certainly advances compete in rate with ineligible paper.

The volatility of interest rates, the increased sensitivity of borrowers to relative borrowing costs, and the switch by banks to pricing loans off their marginal cost of funds have made lending officers in a bank's BA department conscious as never before of where rates are, not just for the day but at the very moment they are trying to set up a BA deal with a prospective borrower and a base rate for that deal is being quoted to them by the bank's money desk. Noted one banker, while scanning his Reuters screen, "I have never been so sensitive to rates and to how government actions affect rates on a day-to-day basis. Now if the government comes in for $38 billion, I am concerned about how that is going to impact money market rates and in particular the rates I must charge my customers."

Rate volatility has also rendered the life of a BA lending office more difficult in other ways. Said one, "Now if the bank takes the view that rates are going up, they may quote me a base rate that puts me out of the market. If that happens, then I have to reenergize my whole client base; that never used to happen. If one day our rate is 50 basis points too high, the next day the clients who got that rate are not going to call us back. To get back into the picture, we must call them."

The commercial paper market is the cheapest source of short-term financing available to firms. Borrowing via the BA route is a way for a firm that lacks direct access to the open market—because it cannot sell commercial paper—to obtain indirect access to this market; the access is more expensive because the firm must pay the accepting bank a fee for opening the door for it to this market.

Many domestic firms that use the BA market are financing commodity imports and exports—grains—frequently huge amounts. These firms have tremendous financing needs. Also due to the extreme variability of commodity prices, their financing needs are equally variable and also unpredictable. Because of this, such firms, in addition to trying to minimize their borrowing costs, feel the need to maintain as many sources of financing open to them as possible. Thus some top firms finance part of their needs in the commercial paper market, part in the BA market, and part with bank loans.

Bank loans become an attractive alternative to BA financing when spreads are reasonable and the borrower is unsure how long he will need financing. If a borrower repays a BA early (as Fed regulations require him to do if the underlying transaction is terminated early), no proportion of the bank commission on the BA is repaid to him. He does get a prorated rebate on the discount fee but minus ¼ or so.

The Japanese are such large users of the domestic BA market in part because their access to the commercial paper market is limited. Some Japanese BAs are created by U.S. banks, but the U.S. branches of Japanese banks also create huge amounts of acceptances in their own name. Only a few non-Japanese, foreign bank branches have entered the acceptance business.

MARKET GROWTH

In recent years BAs outstanding have grown phenomenally, and all signs indicate that this trend will continue. More cost-conscious firms want to use the BA market to shave their borrowing costs, and bankers—always inventive—are looking for new ways in which BA financing may be used.

One impediment to continued growth of the BA market was an antiquated and economically hard-to-defend rule incorporated in the Federal Reserve Act. This rule limited the amount of BAs a bank could have outstanding to 100% of its capital and surplus. With Fed permission, granted semiautomatically, this limit could be extended to 125%. In mid-1982, the 125% rule, which never had been a binding constraint on BA creation, became so for many major banks, some of whom sought to get around the rule by issuing more Edge Act paper. In the fall of 1982, Congress passed legislation permitting banks to issue eligible acceptances equal to 150% of their capital and surplus. Congress also made it easier for banks to use acceptances to finance domestic trade. Both changes are likely to stimulate BA creation by the major domestic banks.

While the top banks and their Edge Act subs create a lot of BAs, the big increase in BAs outstanding is not their work alone. In recent years, many more regional banks have gotten into the business of creating BAs. Also, the Japanese banks, whose number and presence in the U.S. markets have grown constantly, have been writing more and more BAs.

In BAs there are nine banks whose paper trades on a no-name basis on the interdealer run. These names are the top 10 banks excluding Continental, which asked that it be taken off the run when it experienced difficulties throughout 1982. In BAs the bid remained definitely good for Chase paper throughout 1982 despite Chase's well-publicized losses; Chase managed this by offering to buy any and all Chase BAs presented to it at the offered side of the market. It was a gift to a dealer to get hit on the bid side with a Chase BA because he could put it right back to Chase at the offered side of the market and make the spread.

Some dealers will informally slip in a few other names than the top nine: Rep Dallas, Mellon, Crocker, Wells Fargo. The bids of these dealers are generally good for those names, and these dealers will not sell those names any cheaper than they would the top nine. Depending on a dealer's retail base, they will bid more or less aggressively for second-tier names.

All in all there are about 13 names that exchange in a quite liquid way in the interdealer market. There are about 15 other banks that have access to the national market in the sense that there are a couple of places they can go for bids. Two hundred and fifty banks can go to Merrill Lynch and get bids; getting a bid from one place, however, is not access to the national market.

THE DEALER MARKET

In recent years, as the volume of BAs outstanding has soared, the number of firms dealing in BAs has also increased. Today there are about 30 firms that have access to the brokers' market in BAs. Most of the recognized government dealers also trade BAs and CDs, although some don't. A lot of nonrecognized dealers, including regional banks—Wells Fargo and Crocker to name two—also trade BAs and CDs. One reason for the entry of more dealers into the BA and CD markets is demand by their customers for this paper; dealers, if they do retail business, want to offer a full menu of securities. A second reason for the entry of more dealers into BAs is that trading BAs can be highly profitable for a shop that positions correctly more often than not.

The style and approach of different BA dealers differ sharply. At one extreme are big *trading* shops like Sali that look to successful positions to make big profits. At the other extreme is Merrill Lynch, which focuses on profiting from *distribution to retail*. Merrill has been described by one broker as ". . . a breed apart. They are complete buyers. Their BA 'traders' do nothing but buy BAs and put them up on their screen. They buy the top 250 banks because they have regional sales offices everywhere and can sell those names. A Hartford National Bank and Trust Co. BA means something to someone who is controlling, say, the funds for a local private school and has $100,000 to invest. Merrill shows Hartford paper in Hartford, Oklahoma paper in Oklahoma."

Other shops fall between these extremes. Discount and Becker are trading shops with fabulous retail appetites for regional BAs. They will take big positions in such names in anticipation of a market move and then sell them out; they are not concerned about the liquidity of regional names because they have a good sales force that can move those names. First Boston is another shop that has good retail demand in regional names. Traders at banks that actively trade BAs, such as Morgan and the B of A, have a twofold job: selling out paper created by their own bank and trading paper created by other banks.

In 1970 there were only half a dozen BA dealers who were recognized by the Fed; today there are around 20. The Fed buys BAs for foreign accounts and does RPs against BAs with firms that it recognizes as BA dealers. Its criteria for recognizing BA dealers are similar to those for recognizing dealers in governments. To become a recognized dealer in BAs, a firm must be in the market on a daily basis, trade in significant volume, maintain a portfolio of satisfactory size, be reputable and financially sound, and have competent management and staff.

Most nonbank dealers in BAs rely heavily for financing on RPs that they do with corporations, state and local governments, and other investors. For odd pieces and regional names that are hard to RP, they finance with dealer loans. When money is easy, BAs can be RPed at rates equal to or only slightly above the rates at which governments can be RPed. When money tightens, the spread widens.

THE NEW ISSUE MARKET

In the early 1970s, when the BA market was small—$6–8 billion of outstandings—dealers did not position much, and activity in the market was light. At that time it was a tradition, respected by all dealers, that the spread between their bid to the banks and their offer to retail was ¼. Thus, if the banks were creating BAs at 5, the dealers would automatically resell them to retail at 4¾. With all the dealers posting and bidding the same rates to the banks, which dealers got what was strictly a function of their relationships with particular banks. To break this pattern, Merrill and Sali in 1970 began quoting competitive rates; and once they did, all the other dealers followed.

Now BAs are issued to the market much as CDs are. The dealers call the banks with bids, and issuing banks call the dealers asking for bids. When some major banks want to sell, they will shop all the dealers; others use a selected few whose style they like.

In BAs, as in CDs, the banks prefer to sell their BAs directly to retail to the extent possible in order to keep the floating supply of their paper on the street at a minimum. As one dealer noted, "Banks still bow down to the idol of retail. I see it all the time. I will call a bank and bid him a 8.35, and he will say, 'I have nothing.' Then two minutes later a retail customer will call and offer us, at ⅜, 25 million of that bank's BAs which he has just bought at 40. Here I am buying the same 25 million I wanted from one of the bank's 'retail' customers at 2½ basis points less than I bid the bank. Banks that sell cheaper to retail than to dealers are not optimizing. Banks recognize this and now write to dealers more than they used to."

In bidding for paper from the banks and reselling it to retail, the dealers try to take out an 05, but in competitive markets for top names they often work for as little as an 03 or an 02.

Some dealers won't take less than a $5 million block from a bank, but others will take smaller amounts, recognizing that for the sake of relationships, they have to help the banks get rid of their smaller blocks.

Regional names

Prior to 1974 the Fed supported the market for regional bankers' acceptances by buying such paper for the account of foreign buyers and adding its guarantee to it. When the Fed stopped this practice, some of the regional banks took a beating. The year 1974 was characterized by tight money and well-publicized difficulties in the banking industry. Investors then became very credit conscious. Prior to that time most big investors would buy the paper of any $1 billion bank. But in 1974 some investors began to revise their criteria and decided that size was equal to quality With a number of them saying they would take only the top 10 or 15 banks' paper, the regionals were forced to pay up, and tiering developed. Later the acceptability of regional bank BAs, like that of regional bank CDs, improved; and today, as noted, there is a good market for regional bank BAs.

However, the regionals are in a different position from the top banks. To develop a market in New York for their paper, and in particular to get it classified as *prime* by the New York Fed (which now means eligible for repo with the Fed), such a bank must find two or three dealers who will bid on and make a market in their paper. No dealers make markets in all banks' BAs, and different dealers specialize in different regional names. To sell regional names, a dealer has to look to retail, since the interdealer market in BAs, as in CDs, is largely in top-name paper.

Foreign banks are in much the same position as regional banks. They have to develop a relationship with several dealers who will promote their names and establish a market in their BAs. Japanese and other foreign banks that have done this have gotten on the Fed's list of prime names.

Three-name paper

A certain amount of what is known as *three-name paper* trades in the BA market, although such paper is less common now than it once was. Some investors, often foreign, will ask a bank to purchase an acceptance of another bank, endorse it, and sell it to them. The demand for such three-name paper comes from several sources—investors who are incredibly conservative and others who simply want a particular bank's paper but cannot find it in the market. Some Japanese banks still ask top domestic banks to endorse their paper before they sell it.

Tiering

Since 1974 tiering has been a continuing phenomenon in the BA market. It is difficult to generalize about the structure of this tiering because it changes depending on supply conditions, on how tight money is, about what news—good or bad—has hit the street about a bank or group of banks. Normally the top 10 to 13 banks sell their paper at the lowest rates. Then there is another tier that extends out to the 25th or 30th bank. Weaker banks in both tiers pay up, especially when money is tight. Somewhere around perhaps the 40th largest bank tiering fades, and banks beyond that size all pay pretty much the same rates.

Japanese paper trades at varying spreads off the New York market. The size of the spread is a function of what quantity of paper these banks are supplying to the market and of how tight money is.

Most banks give their Edge Act subs names such as Bank X International, so that the name of the parent bank is obvious to the investor. Currently there is a tendency for Edge Act BAs to trade at 1/8 or so above the rate at which the parent bank's BAs trade. This spread, however, tends to be less for the Edge Acts of top banks that issue large amounts of paper to the market.

To narrow the spread between the rates at which parent bank and Edge Act BAs trade, many banks are currently stamping the paper accepted by their Edge Act subs as "accepted" by the parent, thereby creating a sort of hybrid variety of three-name paper.

Many investors know that there is a distinction between eligible and ineligible BAs, and they want only eligible paper. This makes little sense, since from their point of view this distinction is of no importance. Said one dealer," Many investors seem to think that the Fed will act as some sort of lender of last resort on eligible BAs. They simply don't understand what eligibility is all about." In any case, only eligible paper trades on the run.

THE SECONDARY MARKET

In BAs, dealers quote runs to each other; the maturities quoted on the run are for 1- to 6-month paper. As in CDs, quotes might be for early Junes or late Septembers. All bids and offers are good for $5 million, and it is understood that drafts delivered will be in denominations no larger that $1 million. Typically a dealer whose bid is hit will get 5-by-1 delivery [five $1 million drafts], but 10-by-5 deliveries [10 drafts for $500,000 each] are not uncommon.

If a dealer hits another dealer's bid or takes his offer and then wants to do more business, he will ask the other dealer, "Where are you now?" and the other dealer, having just done a trade, is free to adjust his quotes.

There is no obligation, as in the government market, for one BA dealer to make a run to another recognized dealer, and many dealers actively trade with only a few dealers directly.

The normal spread on a run given by one dealer to another is 10 basis points. On a slow day or on a day when a trader has a strong opinion, he might tighten that up to an 05 or an 02. If the market is, say, 98–95 on the broker's screen and a trader is a seller (buyer), it makes no sense for him to put his offer (bid) outside those pictures.

THE BROKERS

In 1977 one broker entered the BA market. Now a number of firms broker BAs, the biggest being Garvin, FBI, RMJ, GMS, and Hill Farber. The market for BAs, like that for CDs, was one of the last areas of the money market to be penetrated by live screens. Garvin was the firm that first brought them there. Whereas in the government market, 99+% of all interdealer trades go through the brokers, in BAs the bulk of such trades are still done direct despite the lively volume that has developed in the brokers' market. In the BA market it is still common for one dealer to call another four or five times a day to exchange runs.

Brokerage in the BA market is currently an 01 charged to the firm that hits a bid or lifts an offering.

Several of the top BA dealers—the B of A, Citi, Morgan, and Chemical—are banks that create and sell into their market their own BAs. The dealers have agreed that they will not permit primaries (newly created BAs) to trade in the brokers' market. As in CDs, this rule is easy to circumvent; a dealing bank that wants to sell new paper can offer some other dealer an 01 to wash the paper through the broker's market for him.

Brokers' quotes are good for BAs that trade on a no-name basis. Brokers also do regionals, but most of them have to do such names verbally. FBI has the capacity to type regional offerings onto a CRT page, and Garvin will soon have something similar.

JAPANESE PAPER

Japanese banks, as noted, are active issuers of BAs. The same cannot be said of any other foreign banks with U.S. branches. Four or five non-Japanese, foreign names—Crédit Lyonnais, a couple of Canadian banks, Algemene—are sporadic issuers of BAs; their paper is very illiquid.

Japanese BAs are traded and brokered—half of Garvin's BA screen is devoted to bids and offers for Japanese paper—in much the same way that top domestic BAs are traded and brokered. There is a no-name run for Japanese banks, and the names of 13 banks are on it. In addition to these banks, a number of other Japanese trusts and regionals issue from time to time.

One peculiarity of the Japanese BA market is that odd lots are often traded. A Japanese bank will break up a big block of BAs, say 10 million, if a customer wants 2½ million, whereas a domestic bank tries to keep pieces in 5 million lots. Garvin indicates odd lots—$6,180,000—on its screen. Odd lots don't seem to impede the trading or liquidity of Japanese BAs in any way.

Japanese BAs trade at a spread over top domestic BAs. That spread can range from 90 basis points in bad markets to almost zero in good markets. The Japanese banks are regarded, especially these days, as prime credits. They have been unscathed by the many and various problems that have troubled other top banks around the world; the Japanese economy is in good condition; and the Bank of Japan is regarded as a strong regulator that can be counted on to stand behind the Japanese banks. The Japanese banks pay up for one principal reason: They are *huge* takers of dollars.

After Chase and Continental had their well-publicized difficulties in the summer of 1982 and a lot of dealers and retail customers started saying, "I won't buy this name or that," the big traders—day traders and positions takers—moved from top name domestic paper into Japanese paper. There were no name problems in Japanese paper so trading it was cleaner than trading domestic paper, and volume in the brokers' market for top Japanese names outran that for top domestic names. For a time, at least, Japanese BAs were regarded by money market traders as, next to bills, the most liquid, short-term instrument for pure trading purposes. How long that ironic condition would prevail was difficult to predict.

INVESTORS IN BAs

BAs have many attractive characteristics to investors. Risk is minimal; also, the instrument is quite liquid. Any of the dealers will give retail a bid on top name paper, usually no more than an 05 off the inside market. In regional BAs, as in regional CDs, an investor can always get a bid from the dealer from whom he bought the paper, but that may be the only dealer to give a bid. Thus liquidity, in the sense of being able to shop around for bids, is less for regional paper than for top name paper. How attractive the return on BAs is relative to that on bills, which are definitely more liquid, varies, as Figure 17–3 shows. At times the spread of BAs to bills can be very attractive, so BAs possess relative value.

One advantage of the BA market over the CD market is that rates do not tend to back up quite so fast as they sometimes do in the CD market. As one dealer noted, "In BAs there is some sort of governor on the total supply that can come out. If banks put out 100 million of December BAs, you can be sure that that will be it. But you can buy 100 million of December CDs at 9:00 A.M. and then at 10:00 A.M. have another four banks in there selling a billion more CDs at a higher price."

As the size of the BA market has expanded, so too have the number and variety of investors in the market. Corporations, bank trust departments, savings banks, and foreign banks have been in the market for a long time. One banker noted, "The Swiss investment banks are heavy buyers of acceptances from us and from the dealers, mostly for their customers. They like the instrument: It yields more than T bills, it's marketable, and it's short in tenor; also they have told us they think it's a safer investment than CDs because a goods transaction underlies it."

In 1974 the amount of BAs outstanding jumped from $9 to $18 billion in one fell swoop. With oil imports being financed in the BA market, it is now common to get $25 or $50 million blocks. This has attracted a lot of new investors to the market. Municipalities, which like the safety of the instrument, and federal agencies were the biggest new entrants to the market in the mid-1970s. Also, banks became more aggressive buyers of other banks' BAs. As one dealer noted, "You can find even small banks taking down big—250 million—positions in BAs and playing them against the funds rate. They get a better rate that way than by selling Fed funds."

The latest, biggest, and most aggressive investor group to enter the BA market has been the money funds. The funds, which like the short maturity and low risk of BAs, have been big buyers of BAs, especially of those in the 3-months-and-under maturity range. Money funds have also been moving into regional BAs for which they demand and receive higher yields. While investors all over the country buy Japanese BAs, by far the big investors in such paper are West Coast accounts: banks, bank trust departments, county funds, and money funds run from the Coast.

Chapter 18

Commercial paper

COMMERCIAL PAPER is an unsecured promissory note with a fixed maturity. The issuer promises to pay the buyer some fixed amount on some future date but pledges no assets, only his liquidity and established earning power, to guarantee that promise. Public offerings of commercial paper are exempt from SEC registration and prospectus requirements if the issuer uses the proceeds to finance current transactions and the maturity of the paper sold is no longer than 270 days.

Commercial paper is typically issued in bearer form (see Figure 18–1) but can be issued in registered form. Rates on commercial paper, like those on bills, are quoted on a discount basis. It used to be that all commercial paper was issued as discount notes, but some paper is now issued in interest-bearing form; the reason for the switch is that it simplifies calculations for an investor who wants to invest a fixed-dollar sum, say, $250,000.[1]

The commercial paper market is almost solely a wholesale market. A few issuers sell paper in amounts as small as $25,000 and $50,000 to

---

[1] All commercial paper rates are quoted on a discount basis. When an issuer sells interest-bearing paper he converts the rate paid from a discount rate to an equivalent simple interest rate so that the investor gets the same effective rate of return whether he buys discount or interest-bearing paper.

FIGURE 18–1
A commercial paper specimen, Haverty Furniture Companies

individuals and small firms but most set a minimum denomination of $100,000, and multimillion-dollar sales are common.

The major investors in commercial paper are large institutions: money market funds, insurance companies, corporations, bank trust departments, and state pension funds. Banks, once large buyers of commercial paper, now buy little paper for their own accounts. S&Ls are permitted to buy commercial paper but do not because they may not count such paper as part of their liquidity reserves.

ISSUERS OF PAPER

The large market for commercial paper in the United States is unique to the U.S. Its origins trace back to the early 19th century when firms needing working capital began to use the sale of open-market paper as a substitute for bank loans. Their need to do so resulted largely from the U.S.'s unit banking system. Elsewhere, it was common for banks to operate branches nationwide, which meant that seasonal demands for credit in one part of the country, perhaps due to the movement of a crop to market, could be met by a transfer of surplus funds from other areas. In the U.S., where banks were restricted to a single state and more often to a single location, this was difficult. Thus, firms in credit-scarce, high-interest-rate areas started raising funds by selling commercial paper in New York and other distant financial centers.

For the first 100 years or so, borrowers in the commercial paper market were all nonfinancial business firms: textile mills, wholesale jobbers, railroads, and tobacco companies, to name a few. Most of their paper was placed for a small fee by dealers; the principal buyers were banks. Then in the 1920s the market began to change. The introduction of autos and other consumer durables vastly increased consumers' demands for short-term credit, which in turn led to the creation and rapid growth of consumer finance companies.

One of the first consumer finance companies was the General Motors Acceptance Corporation (GMAC), which financed consumer purchases of General Motors cars. To obtain funds, GMAC (*Gee Mack* in street argot) began borrowing in the paper market, a practice that other finance companies followed. Another innovation by GMAC was to short-circuit paper dealers and place paper directly with investors; this made sense because GMAC borrowed such large amounts that it could save money by setting up in-house facilities to sell its paper.

Despite the advent of finance company paper, the paper market shrank during the 1920s, stagnated during the 1930s, and then slumped again during World War II; by 1945 commercial paper was a relatively unimportant instrument. Since then the volume of commercial paper outstanding has grown steadily and rapidly. One reason is the continuing growth that has occurred since World War II in the sale of consumer durables and consumers' increasing propensity to buy on credit.

A second factor was the Fed's decision to pursue tight money with a vengeance on a number of occasions starting in the mid-1960s. In 1966 and again in 1969, firms that were accustomed to meeting their short-term borrowing needs at their banks found bank loans increasingly difficult to obtain. On both occasions money market rates rose above the rates banks were permitted to pay on CDs under Reg Q, and banks therefore had difficulty funding new loans. Once firms that had previously borrowed at banks short term were introduced to the paper market, they found that most of the time it paid them to borrow there because money obtained in the open market was cheaper than bank financing, except when the prime rate was being held down by political pressure.

As Figure 18–2 shows, from the end of 1977 to the middle of 1982, the amount of commercial paper outstanding increased from $64.6 billion to $180.7 billion—an increase of 280%.

Today nonfinancial firms—everything from public utilities to manufacturers to retailers—still issue paper, and their paper, which is referred to as *industrial paper,* accounts for about 32% of all paper outstanding (Table 18–1). Such paper is issued, as in the past, to meet seasonal needs for funds and as a means of interim financing; that is, to fund the start-up of investment projects that are later permanently funded through a long-term bond issue. In contrast to industrial borrowers, finance companies have a continuing need for short-term funds throughout the year; they are now the biggest borrowers in the commercial paper market, accounting for 48% of all paper sold.

In the recent years of tight money, bank holding companies have also joined finance companies as borrowers in the commercial paper market.

FIGURE 18–2
Commercial paper outstanding has risen dramatically

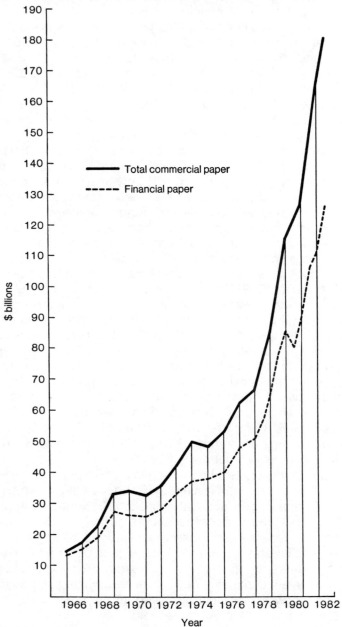

TABLE 18–1
Commercial paper outstanding in July
1982 ($ billions)

All issuers	180.7
Financial companies*	
Dealer-placed paper†	
Total	38.0
Bank-related	6.4
Directly placed paper‡	
Total	85.7
Bank-related	31.1
Nonfinancial companies§	57.0

* Institutions engaged primarily in activities such as, but not limited to, commercial, savings, and mortgage banking; sales, personal, and mortgage financing; factoring, finance leasing, and other business lending; insurance underwriting; and other investment activities.
† Includes all financial company paper sold by dealers in the open market.
‡ As reported by financial companies that place their paper directly with investors.
§ Includes public utilities and firms engaged primarily in activities such as communications, construction, manufacturing, mining, wholesale and retail trade, transportation, and services.
Source: *Federal Reserve Bulletin.*

Many banks are owned by a holding company—an arrangement offering the advantage that the holding company can engage in activities in which the bank itself may not. Initially bank holding companies borrowed in the commercial paper market partly to fund bank operations by purchasing a portion of the bank's loan portfolio. In August 1970 the Fed ruled that funds channeled to a member bank that were raised through the sale of commercial paper by the bank's holding company or any of its affiliates or subsidiaries were subject to a reserve requirement. This ruling eliminated the sale of bank holding company paper for such purposes. Today bank holding companies, which are, as Table 18–1 shows, still active issuers of commercial paper, use the money obtained from the sale of such paper to fund nonbank activities in areas such as leasing and credit cards.

New borrowers

Commercial paper dealers are always seeking new business: cultivating new classes of issuers they can put into the market. In the last several years, they have met success on several fronts.

Muni commercial paper. It was not until several years after taxable money funds had been successfully launched that *tax-exempt money* *funds* were begun. One reason for the slow start of the latter was the scarcity in the market of short-term, tax-exempt paper. Once tax-exempt money funds opened shop, they grew rapidly; and their growth created a demand for the invention of new short-term instruments that would be attractive to municipal borrowers. One such instrument was muni commercial paper; another was muni 7-day demand notes (Chapter 20).

Muni borrowers were attracted to the idea of issuing commercial paper because it permits them, when the yield curve is upward sloping, to borrow at cheaper rates than they could if they sold muni notes, which usually have an original maturity of 6, 9, or even 12 months. The first muni commercial paper was issued by the same types of borrowers who issue revenue bonds: A power authority might use commercial paper to finance an inventory of fuel, a corporation to finance construction that it would later fund long-term by issuing industrial revenue bonds. Later general obligation (GO) issuers—Connecticut, Massachusetts, Oregon, Big Mack, and Columbus, Ohio, to name a few—came into the market and began issuing commercial paper as a permanent alternative to other financing sources.

It is difficult to assess how far and how fast the volume of outstanding municipal commercial paper will grow. A number of states and municipalities within them may not issue such paper until and unless state legislation is passed permitting its sale by the state and municipal issuers.

All muni commercial paper is top rated. Most issuers back their paper with revolving credits, some with straight bank lines, a few—the minority—with letters of credit, and one with a guarantee from a group that sells insurance to issuers of municipal bonds.

Currently Goldman, Lehman, First Boston, and Sali—all big dealers in commercial paper—have a lock on the municipal paper market.

Foreign bank holding company paper.   In recent years a large number of foreign banks have opened branches in New York. One prime motive for their doing so was to expand their dollar liability base. Some of these foreign banks have formed U.S. holding companies that issue commercial paper guaranteed by the parent bank. Doing so enables the bank to buy short-term money at rates lower than those they would have to pay to take deposits of equal maturity in the Eudodollar market. Commercial paper issued by foreign bank holding companies is getting to be big time; at least one French bank holding company has a billion of commercial paper outstanding.

One problem for a foreign bank holding company issuing commercial paper in the U.S. is that such paper necessarily competes with the Yankee CDs that the bank's U.S. branch is trying to sell to investors. If an investor has a line of only X dollars to a particular bank or, if he views the bank as part of a country risk and has a line of only x dollars to that country, the more of the bank's holding company paper the investor buys, the less room he will have for the bank's CDs.

Foreign bank holding company paper is issued through big U.S. commercial paper dealers such as Goldman.

Paper sold to garner foreign exchange. As the money market constantly grows in sophistication, new twists are always being added. Here is one. Foreign companies in the U.K., Germany, and other countries have at times found that the cheapest way to raise local currency— sterling for a U.K. company, DM for a Germany company—was to borrow Eurodollars and swap them into local currency.[2]

Goldman led several such borrowers into the U.S. paper market by showing them that they could shave their borrowing costs 50 to 150 basis points by selling commercial paper for dollars that Goldman would then swap into the borrower's local currency. A private British company began the parade of new foreign borrowers into the U.S. commercial paper market. It was followed by several French companies whose paper carries a government guarantee.

The changing mix of investors

Five years ago cash-rich corporations used to be important buyers of commercial paper. Some of these corporations were cash rich because they prefunded their long-term debt; when they anticipated running out of cash *or* when long rates looked particularly attractive to them, they would do a big bond offering and then park the proceeds in short-term instruments, including commercial paper. This practice became less common after 1979 as rates reached historic highs. These highs discouraged many top corporations not only from prefunding but from selling any long bonds at all. During the period 1979–82, corporations by and large tapped the short-term market for any extra funds they needed, and while watching their short-term debt build up—commercial paper IOUs included—they prayed that long rates would eventually fall. The dry up in corporate liquidity has diminished the amount of funds corporations had to invest in the paper market.

The slack left by corporations in this market has been more than taken up by money funds who have become huge investors in commercial paper. For these funds, such paper is a natural; it is short in maturity and low in credit risk, and because the number of companies issuing paper is so large, it permits further reduction of credit risk through diversification.

---

[2] For foreign exchange swaps, see Chapter 16.

BANK LINES

While commercial paper may have an initial maturity as long as 270 days, the average maturity of paper issued has declined sharply over time; today it is less than 30 days. By issuing the bulk of their paper in the under-30-days maturity range, paper issuers are able to pay low rates because they are borrowing at the base of the yield curve; also, they escape competition from bank CDs, which may not be written with an initial maturity of less than 30 days.

Because of the short average maturity of commercial paper outstanding, issuers must currently pay off billions of dollars of maturing paper each month. An individual issuer is sometimes able to pay off maturing paper on a seasonal basis with funds generated from his operations, and sometimes he pays it off with funds generated by the sale of long-term debt. But by far the bulk of all maturing commercial paper is paid off by *rolling* that paper: the issuer sells new paper to get funds to pay off maturing paper.

This creates a risk for both the issuer and the investor; namely, that an adverse turn in events—say, the failure of a big issuer—might make it extremely expensive, even impossible, for the issuer to sell new paper to pay off maturing paper. To obviate this risk, all issuers back their outstanding paper with *bank lines of credit.*

An issuer who did not pay the insurance premium, which the cost of bank lines really is, might at some point find himself in a position where difficulties in marketing new paper forced him to sell off assets at fire sale prices or to cut back on the volume of his business. Issuers' concern over this eventuality has a basis in fact. When the Penn Central went bankrupt with $82 million in commercial paper outstanding, this created difficulties for all issuers, particularly those in weak financial condition. Tight money, as in 1974, also creates difficulties for issuers who lack a top credit rating.

A second reason commercial paper issuers pay to acquire bank lines, whether they think they need them or not, is that investors will buy only paper backed by bank lines.

Amount of lines

Most issuers attempt to maintain 100% line backing for their paper or a figure close to that. There is, however, much variability among issuers and even for individual issuers over time.

An issuer who has a big seasonal need to borrow, say, at Christmas, will allow his percentage of line backing to fall temporarily during his peak borrowing period. Also, an issuer who pays down the amount of commercial paper he has outstanding because he had funded some of his debt with a new long-term issue may go *overlined* for a period; that is, have line backing in excess of 100%. Banks that grant a firm a line do not like to have that firm terminate the line after one month and ask to have it extended again six months later; so going overlined at times is a price issuers pay to maintain good relations with their banks.

The biggest single issuer of commercial paper, the General Motors Acceptance Corporation, has less than 60% line backing for its paper because it borrows so much that it would have difficulty getting 100% line backing even if it used every bank in the country. Also, some of the other huge top-grade issuers have line backing well below 100%.

How much line backing is really needed by an issuer as insurance depends on its position. Top issuers have had to pay up at times for money, but they never experienced real difficulty in selling their paper even during periods of crisis (Penn Central) or when money was tight.

Types and cost of lines

Commercial paper issuers use different types of lines to back their paper. Under a standard line agreement, if the issuer activates his line, his borrowing automatically turns into a 90-day note. Issuers also use *swing* lines which permit the issuer to borrow one day and repay the next if he chooses. Swing lines are attractive to issuers because issuers occasionally experience short, unanticipated needs for cash; on a given day an issuer may not sell as much paper as he expected to, but he may be able to cover this deficiency on the next day.

It used to be normal practice for issuers to pay for lines with compensating balances; and the standard formula was a 10% balance against the unused portion of the line and 20% balance against any monies taken down under the line. Today these standard figures are more honored in the breach than in the observance. What an issuer pays a bank for a line is a matter of negotiation. The strongest issuers pay much smaller compensating balances than the standard figures. Also, banks sometimes permit double counting; that is, they will permit balances to be counted as compensation both for normal activity in the issuer's bank account (check writing, wire transfers, etc.) and as payment for a line of credit.

In recent years it has become increasingly common for issuers to pay a fee instead of balances for lines, or a fee plus reduced balances. Banks initially resisted the trend toward fee lines but have gradually given in on that point. Except when money is very easy, it is cheaper for an issuer to pay a straight fee of 3/8 or 3/4% for a line than it is for him to hold compensating balances with his bank. Foreign banks entering the U.S. encouraged the trend toward fee lines by offering U.S. companies cheap fee lines as a sort of loss leader—to obtain some business and to justify their existence here. The cost of fee lines varies, being greatest when money is tight.

A number of commercial paper issuers back some small portion of their outstanding paper with *revolving lines of credit*. Under a revolver, the bank customer pays a commitment fee of ¼% on top of the normal compensation he pays the bank for the line. In exchange for that extra commitment fee, the bank guarantees that it will honor the line for some number of years. The big advantage such a line offers the customer is that it guarantees that, no matter how tight money gets or what happens to his position, he can borrow from his bank. As icing on the cake, the issuer obtains a second advantage—because he can turn any borrowing under the line into a term loan, he may treat commercial paper backed with a revolver as long-term debt for statement purposes.[3]

Most firms that take out revolvers do not have a top rating and want to ensure that money will be available to them from their banks under any circumstances. Several years ago one such issuer noted, "In the latest period of market tightness, the commercial paper market had problems. There was the failure of W. T. Grant and the difficulties of the REITs [real estate investment trusts], and the banking community itself was experiencing shock waves. Because of all that, there were questions within and without the banking industry as to how good bank lines were, particularly annual credit lines. Some companies attempted to activate credit lines without success. They got either a direct refusal or a refusal on the basis that a material adverse change had occurred in their condition. So being an A company [A bond rating] in a market dominated by AA and AAA companies, we felt it was prudent to strengthen ourselves in the minds of investors and one way to do this was to put together a multiyear credit, which we did."

Testing lines

A number of issuers make it a practice to test their lines of credit: to borrow on a rotating basis, whether they need to or not, small amounts from each of the banks that have granted them lines. One reason for doing so even when money is easy is to build goodwill with banks, which are glad at such times to get a new loan on their books.

Other issuers never test their lines. One such issuer observed; "Testing lines is expensive and time consuming. Also it means little because you can't test lines against the set of circumstances that might cause you to really want to use them. We don't borrow against our lines when money is easy to build our banking relationships; the counterpart to that is that,

---

[3] Some multiyear credit lines give the lender a chance to take a second look at a company before permitting them to take down funds under their line. If a multiyear line agreement contains a "no change in material circumstances" clause, borrowing under it may not be treated as long-term debt.

when money is tight and banks don't want loans, we stay out of the banks even when there would be a cost advantage in borrowing from them."

A few issuers of commercial paper have used Eurodollar revolving lines of credit to back some portion of their outstanding paper. The REITs in particular established a number of such lines in London with the understanding that they would never be used, but when the REITs fell upon hard times some of these lines were used. A few U.S. utility companies also have used Euro lines to back their commercial paper.

RISK AND RATINGS

Since the early 1930s few issuers of commercial paper have defaulted on their paper. In the case of dealer paper, one reason is that, after the 1920s, the many little borrowers that had populated the paper market were replaced by a much smaller number of large, well-established firms. This gave dealers, who were naturally careful about whose paper they handled, the opportunity to examine more thoroughly the financial condition of each issuer they dealt with.

Since 1965 the number of firms issuing at any time a significant quantity of paper to a wide market has increased from 450 to 1,200; of these about 130 are currently non-U.S. borrowers.

Only five issuers of commercial paper have failed over the last decade. Three of these five were small domestic finance companies that got caught by tight money; in each case the losses to paper buyers were small, $2–$4 million. The fourth firm that failed was a Canadian finance company that had sold paper in the U.S. market; losses on its paper totaled $35 million. The fifth failure, one that shook the market, was that of the Penn Central, which at the time it went under had $82 million of paper outstanding.

One positive result of the Penn Central's failure is that rating of paper became more widespread and rating standards were tightened. Today a large proportion of dealer and direct paper is rated by one or more of three companies: Standard & Poor, Moody, and Fitch.

Paper issuers willingly pay the rating services to examine them and rate their paper, since a good rating makes it easier and cheaper for them to sell paper. The rating companies, despite the fact that they get fee income from issuers, have the interests of the investor at heart because the value of their ratings to investors, and thereby their ability to sell their rating services to issuers, depend on the accuracy of their ratings. The worth to an issuer of a top rating depends on the track record of borrowers who have held that rating.

Each rating company sets its own standards, but their approaches are similar. Every rating is based on an evaluation of the borrower's management, earnings, and balance sheet. Just what a rating company looks for depends partly on the borrower's line of business; the optimal balance sheet for a publishing company differs from that of a finance company. Nonetheless, one can say in general that the criteria for a top rating are strong management, a good position in a well-established industry, an upward trend in earnings, adequate liquidity, and the ability to borrow to meet both expected and unexpected cash needs.

Since companies seeking a paper rating are rarely in imminent danger of insolvency, the rating agencies' main focus is on *liquidity*—can the borrower come up with cash to pay off its maturing paper? Here the rating company looks for ability to borrow elsewhere than in the paper market and especially the ability to borrow short-term from banks. Today for a company to get a paper rating, its paper must be backed by bank lines.

Different rating firms use different classifications to grade borrowers. Standard & Poor rates companies from A for highest quality to D for lowest. Also, it subdivides A-rated companies into three groups according to relative strength, A-1 down to A-3. Fitch rates firms F-1 for highest grade to F-4 for lowest grade. Moody uses P-1, P-2, and P-3.

What factors separate differently rated borrowers? The answer is suggested by the following requirements a company must meet to get Standard & Poor's ratings

A rating
1. Liquidity ratios are adequate to meet cash requirements.
2. Long-term senior debt rating is A or better; in some instances BBB credits may be allowed if other factors outweigh the BBB.
3. The issuer has access to at least two additional channels of borrowing.
4. Basic earnings and cash flow have an upward trend with allowances made for unusual circumstances.
5. Typically, the issuer's industry is well established, and the issuer should have a strong position within its industry.
6. The reliability and quality of management are unquestioned.

B rating
1. Liquidity ratios are good but not necessarily as high as in the A category.
2. Long-term senior debt rating is no less than BB.

C rating
1. There would be wide swings in liquidity ratios from year to year.
2. Long-term senior debt rating would not be of investment quality.

D rating
Every indication is that the company will shortly be in default.[4]

---

[4] "Corporate Bonds, Commercial Paper, and S&P's Ratings," a talk given by Brenton W. Harries, President, Standard & Poor's Corporation, on May 6, 1971, in Philadelphia, Pennsylvania.

Standard & Poor's has phrased the meanings of its ratings in less formal terms as follows:

"A-1" to us means a company that is overwhelming—a Sears, a Shell Oil, a Union Carbide, GMAC, or an IAC. . . . An "A-2" is a very good credit and basically has no weaknesses. It has a good operating record and is a long-time company, however, it just isn't overwhelming. . . . An "A-3" to us and our department of professional skeptics is a good credit, but generally has one weakness which can range from a company that is growing too fast and constantly needs money to a company that has temporary earnings problems. . . . Our "B" rating . . . is reserved for companies who are relatively young or old and are mediocre to fair credit risks and should use the commercial paper market only during periods of relative easy money. Our "C" rating is reserved for companies who are in serious financial difficulties.[5]

From the above quotes it is clear that a company has to be in top financial shape to get any sort of A rating from Standard & Poor and the same is true of a P (for prime) rating from Moody. Commercial paper investors are, however, a conservative lot—disinclined to take extra risk to earn an extra ⅛; many of them will buy only A-1 and P-1 paper. Paper rated A-3 and P-3 is salable only to a very few investors. These include some insurance companies that, because they hold large bond portfolios, track on an ongoing basis the earnings and condition of a wide range of firms.

RATES AND TIERING

In the early 1960s when the commercial paper market was small, all issuers paid similar rates to borrow there. Then, after the Penn Central's failure and periods of extremely tight money, investors became very credit conscious; they wanted top names, and rate tiering developed in the market. That tiering today is a function not only of issuers' commercial paper ratings but of their long-term bond ratings. The market distinguishes between A-1 issuers with a triple-A bond rating and those with only a double-A bond rating. Many investors want to buy only unimpeachable credits; looking up an issuer's bond rating is a quick way for an investor to check the credit of an issuer with whom he is unfamiliar.

The spread at which A-1, P-1 paper trades to A-2, P-2 paper varies depending on economic conditions. When money is tight and people are more concerned than normal about risk in general and credit risk in particular, they may drive the yield on A-2 paper 200 point basis points above that on A-1 paper; this occurred in the summer of 1982. When—after a period of tight money—rates begin to fall, investors, seeking to

---

[5] Speech by Brenton W. Harries, President of Standard & Poor.

maintain past portfolios yields, tend to become yield buyers; they switch out of lower yielding, top-rated paper into higher yielding, second-tier paper. As they do, they drive down the spread between A-1 and A-2 paper so that, by the time money eases, it may be only ⅜ or even ¼. Whether money is easy or tight, no institutional investors will buy P-3 paper from dealers.

Commercial paper, as Figure 18–3 shows, yields slightly more than Treasury bills of comparable maturity, the spread being widest when

FIGURE 18–3
Commercial paper consistently yields a somewhat higher rate than Treasury bills of the same maturity

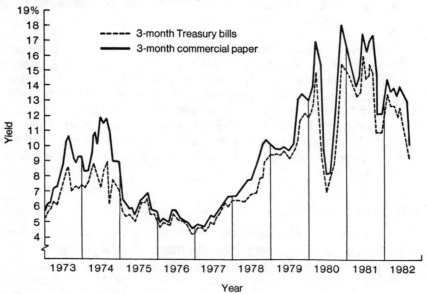

Source: *Federal Reserve Bulletin.*

money is tight. There are two reasons. First, paper exposes the investor to a small credit risk. Second, commercial paper is much less liquid than bills because there is no active secondary market in it.

DEALER PAPER

As Figure 18–4 shows, close to 40% of all commercial paper is issued through dealers. Most of the paper placed through dealers is industrial paper, but some of it is issued by smaller finance companies, bank holding companies, and muni borrowers.

FIGURE 18–4
Percentage of commercial paper issued through dealers

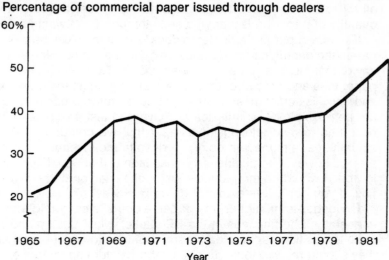

The two largest dealers in commercial paper are Goldman Sachs and A. G. Becker. Lehman Brothers, Salomon Brothers, First Boston Corporation, and Merrill Lynch are also important; in addition there are a number of fringe dealers.

Issuers who sell through dealers tell the dealer each day how much they want to sell and in what maturities. The dealer's sales force, in turn, tells the firm's retail customers what names and maturities are available and what rates are.

The standard fee dealers charge issuers of commercial paper who sell through them is ⅛ of 1%, which works out to $3.47 per 1 million per day. In exchange for this fee, the dealer assumes several responsibilities vis à vis both issuers and investors. First, every dealer carefully checks the credit of each firm that sells paper through him. The dealer has a fiduciary responsibility to do this. He also wants to ensure that he does not tarnish his own good name in the eyes of either issuers or investors by selling paper of an issuer who goes bankrupt. A second responsibility of a dealer is to introduce the name of a new issuer to investors. He does this by having his sales force constantly show the name to investors and explain to them who the issuer is and what his credit is.

Some sophisticated issuers will themselves set the scale of rates to be offered on their paper in different maturities ranges. And if they do not want money badly, they may post rates slightly off the market in an attempt to pick up some cheap money. Most issuers, however, rely on the dealer to determine what rates should be posted on their paper.

Dealers all compete with each other for issuers, and for this reason they all try to post the lowest rates at which it is possible to sell whatever quantity of paper an issuer who sells through them wants sold.

If an issuer permits a dealer to decide what rates will be offered on his paper, the dealer in turn assumes an obligation to position at these rates any of that issuer's paper that goes unsold. Normally a dealer finances paper thus acquired through dealer loans. Such financing is expensive, and carry is sometimes negative; dealers prefer to position as little paper as possible. Said one dealer, "Over the last 4 or 5 years, when we have had to take into position paper that we could not sell, we have actually made money on doing so despite the inverted yield curve. We are not, however, in business to make money that way. Every day I come to work, I would be thrilled if we just broke even on carry. If you make it, fine. If you don't, it is a cost of doing business.

On longer-term, higher-rate paper, a dealer's carry might be positive, especially if he finances in the RP market. Most dealers, however, are loath to position paper to earn carry profits or to speculate; they believe they should reserve their capacity to borrow for financing the paper—in amounts that cannot be predicted—that they might have to position as an obligation to their issuers. Also, some dealers think that, if positioning long paper that an issuer wants to sell seems an attractive speculation because they expect rates to fall, it is their responsibility to advise the issuer that he would be better off issuing short paper.

Dealers don't like to sell very short-dated paper because their transactions costs can easily exceed the fee they earn selling such paper. But to avoid positioning paper, they will occasionally sell even 1-day paper. Also, at times they will, if necessary, *break rates* to get paper sold; that is, offer rates above those they have posted.

On some dates, such as a tax date, it is more difficult and thus more expensive to sell paper. To help a customer who needs to borrow on such a date, a dealer may suggest that the issuer borrow a day or two early to get a lower rate and then put the money back to the dealer on repo. If the issuer has a good name, it is often possible for him to earn on such a *bridge repo* a rate no lower than the rate at which he borrowed so that borrowing for an extra few days costs him nothing.

Because they are assuming responsibilities—sometimes costly ones—to issuers, dealers try to get an exclusive relationship with each issuer who uses them. Such relationships are common, but some issuers use more than one dealer. This is true in particular of utilities, who are accustomed to issuing bonds through competitive bidding.

Secondary market

Every dealer who sells commercial paper stands ready to buy back paper sold through them at the going market rate for paper of that grade and current maturity plus ⅛ or so. Also, if an investor wants paper of an issuer who is not selling on a particular day, a dealer will attempt to find an investor who holds that issuer's paper and swap him out of it to generate supply.

Thus there is some secondary trading in dealer-issued commercial paper; such paper is, however, nowhere near as liquid as other money market instruments. An investor who holds commercial paper cannot really count on getting a bid on it from more than one dealer, and an ⅛ bid above the market is a wide spread.

The failure for an active secondary market to develop in commercial paper has several causes. Commercial paper outstanding is even more heterogeneous than bank CDs outstanding and thus more difficult to trade actively in the secondary market. Also, many buyers of commercial paper are hold-to-maturity investors, so the demands made on dealers to take back paper are minimal. One major dealer estimated that "buy backs" at his shop run to only 1 to 1½% of the paper they place.

Opportunities for growth: Foreign issuers

While the commercial paper market is primarily a domestic market, an increasing number of foreign companies borrow large sums in it. The first to do so was Electricité de France, the nationalized French electric company, which began in 1974 to issue commercial paper through Goldman Sachs to finance oil imports that it pays for with dollars. EDFs' commercial paper borrowings are now approaching $2 billion.

Most of the Fortune 500 are either cash-rich firms, such as IBM, or firms that already issue commercial paper through dealers or directly. Thus the richest potential source of growth for dealers lies in introducing more foreign borrowers to the U.S. commercial paper market—to sell for example, commercial paper issued by multinational corporations that could profit by taking advantage of the lower short-term rates prevailing in the U.S. paper market. Some such companies already borrow long-term in the U.S. market; for others who do not, starting a paper program can provide an entrée to managers of insurance company, pension fund, and bank trust department portfolios. These investors can later be approached—once a relationship is established—to buy the foreign issuer's bonds and equities.

Initially domestic investors were leery, to say the least, about taking foreign names. This, however, is changing rapidly. In 1978 foreign issuers had to pay a rate 20 to 35 basis points above the 7% rate top domestic issuers were paying. Four years later when these same U.S. issuers were paying 14%, the premium commanded for foreign paper had dropped to 20 to 30 points.

LOC paper

Some smaller or less well-known domestic firms and a number of foreign firms borrow in the commercial paper market by issuing LOC (line of credit) paper. This paper is backed by normal bank lines *plus* a letter of credit from a bank stating that the bank will pay off the paper at maturity if the borrower does not. Such paper is also referred to as *documented discount notes.*

Obtaining a letter of credit to back its paper may permit an issuer to get a P-1 rating on LOC paper, whereas on its own paper it would get only a P-3 rating or no rating. Documented discount notes, which represent only a small fraction of commercial paper outstanding, have been issued by firms that sell nuclear fuel or energy derived from it, leasing companies, REITs, mortgage companies, U.S. subsidiaries of Japanese trading companies, and a number of foreign companies.

Borrowers who get a LOC could not get into the market without it. It is not that they are not creditworthy. Some are foreign companies who do not care to disclose all their financials to the general public but do not mind disclosing them to their dealer or to the rating agencies. Other LOC borrowers are just not large enough to get a rating. U.S. subs of Japanese companies make extensive use of LOC paper because these subs are not sufficiently big and self-sufficient to get a rating: Their parent company could guarantee the sub's paper but prefers to have the sub get a LOC to back it. The cost of a letter of credit runs anywhere from $\frac{1}{2}$ to $\frac{3}{4}$, whereas the cost of normal lines is more like $\frac{1}{4}$.

Picking a dealer

In selecting a dealer, issuers look for one who will get them the lowest borrowing rates possible and who also stands ready to position their paper. Most feel that differences among the major dealers are small.

Some issuers prefer to deal with the firm that acts as their investment banker. Others prefer to split their business. One advantage to issuers of selling commercial paper is that doing so acquaints a wide range of investors with their name and credit, something that helps when they market new bonds or equity issues.

DIRECT ISSUE PAPER

About 50% of all commercial paper outstanding is placed directly by the issuer with investors. Firms issuing their paper direct—less than 80 do so—are mostly large finance companies and bank holding companies. Some of these finance companies, such as GMAC, Sears Roebuck Acceptance Corporation, and Ford Motor Credit, are captive finance companies that borrow primarily to finance the credit sales of the parent industrial company. Others, such as Household Finance, Beneficial Finance, and Associates Corporation of North America, are independent finance companies.

The major incentive for an issuer to go direct is that, by doing so, he escapes the dealer's ⅛ commission. For a firm with $200 million of commercial paper outstanding, this would amount to a savings of $250,000 a year. However, the direct issuer has to set up its own sales organization. A firm with a top credit rating can sell a huge amount of commercial paper through a small sales force—three to six people. Thus, for such a firm, it pays to go direct when the average amount of paper it has outstanding climbs to around $200 to $250 million. A few issuers who are big borrowers in the paper market continue to use a dealer either because they anticipate selling long-term debt to reduce their short-term borrowing or because the amount of paper they have outstanding varies sharply during the year.

Direct issuers determine each day how much they need to borrow, what maturities they want, and what rates they will post. Then they communicate their offerings to investors in three ways. All of the big directs post their rates on Telerate. In addition, their sales representatives call various investors. As one such representative noted, "There are a large number of A-1, P-1 issuers who are posting the same rates. So the sales representative's job is partly to develop personal relationships that will distinguish his firm in investors' eyes from the crowd."

The third way that the top direct issuers sell their paper is by posting their rates on bank money desks. Banks are forbidden by Glass-Steagall from acting as dealers in commercial paper, but they can and do post rates for issuers and arrange sales of their paper to investors.[6] The banks do this partly to service clients who use them to invest surplus funds. By posting paper rates, the banks can offer such clients a full menu of money market instruments. Also, direct issuers typically purchase large backup lines from banks that post their paper rates.

The rates that a direct issuer has to pay are a function of its name, credit rating, and use of the market. A non-prime borrower that uses the market extensively will have to pay up.

Once a direct issuer posts rates, he carefully monitors sales throughout the day by his own sales force and on bank money desks. When money market conditions are volatile, an issuer may change his posted rates several times a day to ensure that he gets whatever amount he set out to borrow. Also, if he achieves that goal early in the day, he will typically lower his rates to make his paper unattractive to investors and thereby stem any further inflow of funds.

Most issuers will break rates for a large investor if they want money. Some, when they are just entering the market, will also consistently offer

---

[6] Glass-Steagall does not preclude banks from dealing in muni commercial paper, but so far at least, it is nonbank dealers who have developed this market and have a lock on it.

selected large investors rates slightly above their posted rates. The prevalence of rate breaking tends to increase when money is tight and to decrease when it is easy.

An issuer who fails to borrow as much as he had intended to can always fall back on his bank lines. Also, when money is easy and the demand for bank loans is slack, some banks will position short-term paper at a rate equal to the Fed funds rate plus a small markup; this is a way of giving the issuer a cut-rate loan.

A more recent development is the offering by banks to commercial paper issuers and other borrowers of short-term money, fixed-rate advances priced off money market rates (see Chapter 5). The availability of such loans is likely to be particularly helpful to big direct issuers who on a given day may find themselves $100 or 200 million short.

Prepayments

The big direct issuers of commercial paper will all prepay on paper they have issued if the investor needs money before the paper he has purchased matures. Some issuers do this at no penalty. Others will give the investor who requests prepayment the rate that he would have gotten on the day he purchased his paper if he had bought paper for the period he actually held it. The no-penalty system would seem to invite abuse—to encourage investors to buy, whenever the yield curve is upward sloping, paper of a longer maturity than that for which they intend to invest in order to get a higher rate. Issuers, however, figure that game out quickly and don't let an investor get away with it for long.

One reason issuers are so willing to prepay is that most do not want investors to sell their paper to a dealer for fear that the dealer's later resale of that paper might interfere with their own sales. Still a few of the largest issuers, GMAC in particular, will occasionally sell longer-term paper to dealers who position it for carry profits and as a speculation.

Master notes

Bank trust departments have many small sums to invest short term. To provide them with a convenient way to do so, the major direct issuers of commercial paper offer bank trust departments what are called *master notes*. A master note is a variable-rate demand note on which the issuer typically pays the rate he is posting for 180-day money, that rate plus 1/4, or some similar formula rate.

A bank trust department with whom an issuer has opened a master note invests monies from various trust accounts in it. Then each day the bank advises the issuer what change, if any, has occurred in the total amount invested in the note. From a trust department's point of view, a master note provides such a convenient way for investing small sums to any date that it typically keeps the balance in any note issued to it close to the limit imposed by the issuer on the size of the note; daily variations in the size of a large master note—say, one for $15 million—might be no more than $100,000.

For the issuer, master notes provide a dependable source of funds and reduce bookkeeping costs. Money obtained through a master note, however, is expensive for the issuer because the rate paid is based on the 180-day rate; most issuers limit the amount of master notes they issue to some percentage—typically well below half—of their total outstandings.

A and B notes. Because bank trust departments keep master notes filled up most of the time, some direct issuers said to them, "Look, you have a master note for *x* million, and most of the time you have it 90 percent full. Let's call the top half of that note an *A note;* you can take money out of it on demand. The bottom half of the note we will call a *B note;* on that part you have to give us a 13-month notice to withdraw funds."

The advantage to the issuer of this arrangement, which is now common among direct issuers, is that the issuer gets cheap money that he can record on his balance sheet as *long-term* debt. From the trust department's point of view, the arrangement provides a high rate on what is really short-term money because different monies are constantly being shifted into and out of the overall note.

Issuers of B notes argue that such debt is not commercial paper but rather a private placement. Still such debt is recorded in money market statistics as commercial paper. A few issuers who do not offer B notes fear that by doing so they would be making an offering that, due to its term and the lack of a prospectus, would not comply with SEC regulations. Because of the attraction of B notes to the issuer, many issuers who offer master notes to bank trust departments will not issue an A note unless they also get a B note.

Prior to its getting into serious financial difficulties, W. T. Grant had a number of master notes outstanding with bank trust departments. While it had closed out these before its bankruptcy, that event did cause a number of bank trust departments to question whether they should not invest cash balances in trust accounts in an institutional money fund rather than in a master note. An institutional money fund offers a bank trust department the same convenient subaccounting that a master note does and a comparable yield. In addition an institutional money fund has the advantage over a master note that it offers, instead of exposure to a single credit risk, *diversity of credit risk.*

Laying off money

It is difficult for the big direct issuers to borrow on a given day precisely the quantity of money they need. Typically they borrow slightly more; and at times, if they are not quick in cutting rates, they may be hit with a lot of unwanted funds because rates elsewhere in the market are falling. Direct issuers all run a short-term portfolio to lay off excess funds. Their investments include a wide range of money market instruments and are made with varying degrees of sophistication.

Because they can borrow short-term at very low rates, the big directs with prime names could arbitrage—buy short-term money in the commercial paper market and lay it off at a positive spread elsewhere. They do not do so, however, out of concern for the aesthetics of their balance sheet. One individual responsible for investing excess funds raised by a large direct issuer observed, "We would not take on money to lay it off at a profit. But as a matter of policy we stood on a posted rate, and sometimes we got hosed with excess money. Then we'd lay that off. I wanted to look at it differently: We can raise money at 8 and lay it off at 9, let's make a million. But management wanted the ratios of the credit company to conform to what people analyzing the company's credit wanted. Maybe they were overly conservative, but we never borrowed as an arbitrage."

Secondary market

Secondary market trading, uncommon in dealer-issued paper, occurs with increasing frequency in direct-issue paper. Big finance companies, such as GMAC, and big bank holding companies, such as Citicorp, have huge amounts of paper outstanding, some of which has been issued in large blocks that mature on a given day.[7] Money market dealers, who trade BAs and CDs, sometimes position such paper as a rate play.

This practice has become so common that at least one broker of money markets, Garvin, has started to broker blocks of commercial paper among dealers.

Shelf paper

A number of the big direct issuers are now offering medium-term notes in the 2- to 5-year area. There are two possible approaches to selling such notes. One is for the issuer to go to a dealer who is a pro and have him sell a single large issue. The other approach is for the issuer to

---

[7] Taking its cue from the Treasury, Citi's holding company auctions $150 million of its commercial paper every Wednesday.

sell himself what is called *shelf paper.* The issuer registers a note issue with the SEC and then posts a scale of rates each day on notes of varying maturities; that scale is simply an extension of the yield curve of rates he is offering on short-term commercial paper. Money pulled in by selling notes this way is cheaper than money obtained by making a single large note placement through a dealer. Another advantage to an issuer of offering shelf paper is that it makes him more interesting to investors; he is no longer just a source of commercial paper—he can now offer the investor instruments that range in maturity from 1 day to 5 years. Some direct issuers anticipate a big expansion of borrowing in the intermediate-note area.

PRIVATELY PLACED PAPER

Commercial paper, to be exempt from registration with the SEC, is supposed to be used to finance short-term commercial operations. Paper can, however, also be used to finance long-term assets if it is sold through a restricted offering; that is, offered directly by the issuer or through a dealer to only a limited number of investors. Such private placements of paper are not uncommon. They have been used, for example, by oil companies to finance the Alaskan pipeline during its construction, by bank holding companies to partially finance their leasing operations, and by others to finance the acquisition of various long-term assets.

The SEC has also begun to allow firms to issue, through restricted offering programs, commercial paper with an initial maturity of more than 270 days. The issuer of such paper must make full disclosure to prospective investors of what the paper proceeds are to be used for. He must also give a list (up to 100 names are permitted) of the investors from whom funds will be solicited to the SEC, which must approve of this list. Long-term paper offered on a restricted basis has been used by utilities to fund construction payments.

CANADIAN PAPER

Many of the big domestic finance companies also have big Canadian operations that they finance partly with commercial paper. Also, some U.S. industrial firms operating in Canada issue commercial paper.

When interest rates are significantly higher in Canada than in the U.S., much Canadian paper is sold in the States. The investors who buy such paper do not want to assume a foreign exchange risk by holding on an unhedged basis commercial paper denominated in Canadian dollars, so they hedge typically in one of two ways. A few large investors will arrange their own hedge: buy Canadian dollars spot, invest in Canadian dollar paper, and sell the proceeds forward.[8] The other approach is for issuers or dealers to hedge large amounts of Canadian paper and sell it to investors for U.S. dollars. Such paper is referred to as *dollar pay paper*.

When Canadian rates are higher than U.S. rates, covered interest arbitrage forces the Canadian dollar to a discount in the forward market and the U.S. investor loses on his swap; as a result, the rate he earns on hedged Canadian paper will typically exceed by only a small margin the rate offered on U.S. paper of similar maturity.

EUROPAPER

Beginning in the mid-1960s, when exports of capital from the U.S. were restricted by taxes and other measures, several corporations began to issue dollar-denominated commercial paper through U.S. dealers in London. The market for Europaper, which offered investors an opportunity to diversify out of Eurodollar time deposits, started small but showed signs of promise. Then, when it had grown to about $100 million in outstandings, the U.S. eliminated the Interest Equalization Tax. This change made it cheaper for corporations to borrow in the U.S., and the market in Europaper dried up. Since Euro rates are unlikely to ever be less than domestic rates, the market in Europaper will probably never revive unless the U.S. again imposes restraints on the outflow of capital.

---

[8] Recall the discussion of swaps and hedges in Chapter 16.

Chapter 19

Municipal notes

THE TERM *MUNICIPAL SECURITIES* is used in blanket fashion by the street to denote all debt securities issued by state and local governments and their agencies. The latter includes school districts, housing authorities, sewer districts, municipally-owned utilities, and authorities running toll roads, bridges, and other transportation facilities.

Municipal securities are issued for various purposes. Short-term notes are typically sold in anticipation of the receipt of other funds, such as taxes or proceeds from a bond issue. Their sale permits the issuer to cover seasonal and other temporary imbalances between expenditure outflows and tax inflows. In contrast, the sale of long-term bonds is the main way that state and local governments finance the construction of schools, housing, pollution-control facilities, roads, bridges, and other capital projects. Bond issues are also used to fund long-term budget deficits arising from current operations.

In recent years the amount of municipal securities outstanding has grown rapidly, more rapidly in fact than the Treasury's outstanding debt. The latter, however, is still larger; at the beginning of 1982, there were $720 billion marketable Treasury issues outstanding and approximately $411 billion of municipals. The bulk of outstanding municipals, over 95%, is accounted for by long-term bonds. The remainder represents short-term borrowings via the sale of tax, bond, and revenue anticipation notes.

Municipal securities are lumped into two broad categories: general obligation securities and revenue securities. On *general obligation securities* (GOs), payment of principal and interest is secured by the issuer's pledge of its full faith, credit, and taxing power. Usually this means that the securities are backed by all of the issuer's resources plus its pledge to levy taxes without limits on rate or amount. In some states and localities such a pledge can be made only on a qualified basis because the issuer's taxing power is limited to some maximum rate. GOs of such issuers are called *limited-tax securities*.

On *revenue securities* payments of interest and principal are made from revenues derived from tolls, user charges, or rents paid by those who use the facilities financed with the proceeds of the security issue. An example would be bonds used to finance construction of a toll bridge and secured by toll collections.

TYPES OF MUNI NOTES

In a discussion of the money market, the focus with respect to the municipal market must be on the note market. Investors who buy municipal bonds frequently hold them to maturity, and for this reason these securities are not actively traded as they approach maturity.

Municipal notes fall into four categories: tax, bond, and revenue anticipation notes, plus a special class of federally backed notes called *project notes*.

Tax anticipation notes. *TANs* are issued by municipalities to finance their current operations in anticipation of future tax receipts. Usually they are general obligation securities.

Revenue anticipation notes. *RANs* are offered periodically for much the same purpose except that the revenues anticipated are not general tax receipts. RANs, like TANs, are usually GO securities.

Bond anticipation notes. *BANs* are sold to get interim financing for projects that will later be funded long-term through the sale of bonds. Normally, payment on BANs is made from the proceeds of the anticipated bond issue. BANs are usually GOs.

Project notes. *PNs* are issued through bimonthly auctions by the U.S. Department of Housing and Urban Development (HUD) on behalf of local authorities. The funds obtained are used by these authorities to finance federally sponsored programs for urban renewal, neighborhood development, and low-cost housing. Payment on PNs is made by rolling these securities or by issuing bonds whose proceeds are used to provide long-term funding. PNs are backed by the full faith and credit of the federal government. HUD creates this backing by entering into an agreement with PN issuers guaranteeing that the federal government will, if necessary, lend the issuer an amount sufficient to pay the principal and interest on its notes.

Construction loan notes. *CLNs* stretch slightly our definition of muni notes, since they are issued with an original maturity from 18 months to 3 years. Like PNs, CLNs are used by housing authorities to finance construction. CLNs are insured by the FHA and have an assured mortgage take out from one of three sources: Ginnie Mae, a state housing authority, or a bond issue done simultaneously with the CLN issue. In the case of the bond-issue take out, the issuer invests the proceeds of the bonds sold in governments of the same maturity as the CLNs. Once construction is completed, the issuer uses the bond proceeds—temporarily invested in governments—to pay off the CLNs; by simultaneously selling CLNs and bonds, the housing authority locks in a long-term mortgage take out before beginning construction.

Short muni coupons. In recent years of very high interest rates, many traditional issuers of long bonds decided the cost of borrowing long was just too high; they began issuing 2- and 3-year paper. This fitted nicely a tremendous demand for paper in the 3-year area; investors who saw bonds they had bought selling at 57 cents on the dollar had a much diminished appetite for long bonds.

7-day demand notes. A new and now important class of investors in short-term, tax-exempt paper is tax-free money funds. Rapid acceptance by investors of these funds—now estimated to own $10 billion of tax-exempt securities—created a problem: The funds' appetite for short-term, high-quality muni paper exceeded available supply.

Initially, to hold down the average maturity of their portfolios, the funds were all rushing out to buy the same short-term muni paper; this drove its price up, drove its yield down, and thereby decreased the desirability of the funds to investors. In response to the demand by tax-exempt money funds for high-quality, short-term paper, issuers and dealers—always innovative—came up with several new instruments: One, muni commercial paper, was described in Chapter 18; another is what muni note dealers call *7-day demand notes.*

On a 7-day demand note, the issuer sells through a private placement a security which might have an original maturity as long as 40 years. This security is distinguished from a standard muni bond by two features: First, it pays a floating rate usually linked to the prime rate; second, it contains a contractual arrangement whereby either side may terminate its participation in the arrangement by giving 5-business-day notice.

The new 7-day demand notes are advantageous both to the money funds who buy them and to the borrowers who issue them. The money funds get paper that both pays a good yield and can be counted as 7-day paper when a fund calculates the average maturity of its portfolio.

Having such paper on their book permits the funds to take a new tack: Instead of just 3- and 4-month PNs, they can extend—buy some high-yielding 9-month paper, the impact of whose long maturity on the average maturity of their portfolio is offset by their 7-day demand notes.

For borrowers, whose ranks include municipal power authorities and corporations installing pollution control devices, 7-day demand notes are also a good deal. Borrowers get what is in effect long-term money at rates below what they would have to pay if they issued muni bonds; they face the risk, however, that rates might shoot back up again. The issuance of 7-day demand notes, which has been going on since 1980, has so far been for ever increasing amounts. The real test of the future of the instrument will occur when long-term rates get down, if they do, to 8 or 9%. Will borrowers, recalling that rates were once in the teens, then prefer to lock in what appear to be attractive long-term rates?[1]

While no money fund has yet exercised the put option that 7-day demand notes offer, issuers of such paper could not have sold it without being able to give solid assurance to buyers that they could honor this put. To provide such assurance, each issuer obtained from a major bank a binding commitment to provide the issuer with interim financing if he needed it in the event of a put being exercised. In essence the put is to a bank, but legally the notes are worded so the put is to the issuer.

CHARACTERISTICS

Technically municipal notes are securities with a maturity at issue ranging from a month to a year. However, municipal securities with maturities at issue as long as 3 years are also often referred to as muni notes.

Most municipal notes are issued in *bearer* form (Figure 19–1). For securities of such short duration, registration would not be worth the trouble involved and as a practical matter does not occur.

Under the 1982 tax law, interest income on municipal securities issued after 1982 will be subject to federal taxation unless those securities are issued in registered form. This provision will force muni bonds to henceforth be issued in registered form. However, since muni notes with a maturity at issue out to 14 months are exempt from this provision, such securities will presumably continue to be issued in bearer form.

The minimum denominations in which municipal notes are issued range from $5,000 to $5 million. The choice depends on whether the market for the issuer's securities is likely to be composed of partly individuals, only institutions, or only very large institutions. Thus part of a

---

[1] A parallel to 7-day demand notes is master notes sold by finance companies who issue both commercial paper—of which master notes are a variant—and long-term notes and bonds (see pp. 644–45). The continued growth of master notes, which have been around for a long time, suggests that 7-day demand notes are here to stay.

FIGURE 19–1
A municipal note

dealer's job is to advise an issuer as to where the market for his securities is and what minimum denomination he should set. When New York City experienced difficulty selling its notes, dealers suggested that the city lower the minimum denomination on its notes so they would appeal to a new class of investors, individuals. That was good advice from dealer to client, but in retrospect it looked like a conspiracy to defraud the little guy. Dealers shy away from suggesting that a borrower with a credit problem issue in small pieces.

Most municipal notes are *interest-bearing*, but they may also be issued in *discount* form. At times discount notes can be sold at a lower interest rate than interest-bearing notes, but usually the difference is small. One reason for the declining popularity of discount issues is the public's lack of sophistication. If a municipality authorized to borrow $400 million gets $394 million by selling discount notes, the public will think that the municipality has not exhausted its borrowing authorization; that can pose problems if the municipality needs to borrow more money. A second reason why muni notes are not sold in discount form is that the price of a muni discount note would be more volatile than that of an interest-bearing note.[2] A third reason muni issuers have resisted issuing zero-coupon notes is that it might create tax complications for investors; the maximum tax-exempt income an investor in a muni discount note may earn is the discount at issue.

Interest on municipal notes that bear interest is normally paid at maturity. Whereas, muni bonds all accrue interest on a 30-360 day basis, issuers of muni notes use different bases: 30-360, actual-360, and actual-365.[3] Muni discount notes are redeemed at face value at maturity.

Measured in terms of participating issuers, the muni note market is broad—something like 18,000 communities finance in it. The CD market, in contrast, is open in volume to perhaps 25 banks. A community's access to the muni note market depends on its credit rather than on its size or the size of its issues. Most municipalities are not New York Cities that borrow tomorrow what they spent yesterday; and those that are not have easy access to the municipal market.

The amounts and types of short-term borrowing in which a municipality may engage are controlled by state law. California sets the rules for how Los Angeles County may borrow, and New York State law enfranchised New York City to accumulate a huge volume of short-term debt. Some states' laws on local borrowing are more liberal than others; in the case of New York State, hindsight suggests that its control was too liberal.

---

[2] See last section of this chapter.

[3] Different bases for accruing interest are described in Marcia Stigum's *Money Market Calculations* (Homewood, Ill.: Dow Jones-Irwin, 1981), Chap. 8. The method of accrual can significantly affect true yield on short notes carrying a high coupon.

Taxation

The most important advantage of municipal securities to the investor is that interest income on them is exempt from federal income taxes and usually from state and local taxes within the state in which they are issued. Interest income on municipal securities issued within territories of the United States and securities issued by certain local housing and urban renewal agencies operating under HUD are exempt not only from federal taxes but from state taxes in *all* states. The federal tax exemption has a constitutional foundation; the courts have ruled that the constitution bars the federal government from imposing on the states without their consent any taxes that would interfere with the latter's governmental functions. Whether federal taxation of interest paid on municipal securities would in fact constitute such interference is unclear. The issue has never been tested in the courts because in every revenue act passed since the original one in 1913, Congress has excluded income on municipal securities from taxable income.[4] As noted, the states reciprocate by exempting income on federal securities from state taxation. Thus, state and federal taxation of interest income on each other's securities is characterized by *reciprocal immunity*.

To compare yield on a municipal security with that on a taxable security, an investor must compute the *equivalent taxable yield* on the municipal security; that is, the *taxable* return that would leave the investor with an *after-tax* return equal to the return paid on the municipal security. For example, for a corporation taxed at a 50% marginal rate, the equivalent taxable yield on a new muni note offered at 6% would be 12%.

The exemption from federal taxation granted on income from municipal securities applies only to interest income paid by the issuer either directly or indirectly in the case of discount notes. If, due to the rise in interest rates, a municipal security trades below its issue price, the buyer of this security will receive not only tax-free interest income but a taxable capital gain. Because of this, equivalent taxable yield on a municipal is lower, relative to its quoted yield to maturity, if that security is selling at a discount than if it is selling at par. In contrast, a taxable bond selling at a discount yields more aftertax income than one selling at par that offers the same yield to maturity.

Table 19–1 shows the relationship between yield on a tax-exempt municipal and equivalent taxable yield for investors in selected federal tax brackets. The figures in the table are based on the assumption that the securities are trading at par; also, no account is taken of possible state taxes. As the figures show, the value of the tax exemption granted on income from municipal securities is greater the higher the investor's

---

[4] The 1982 tax act only limited this exemption on new bond issues to bonds issued in registered form.

TABLE 19–1
Equivalent taxable yields for selected marginal tax rates

Municipal coupon (*percent*)	Investor's federal tax bracket (*marginal tax rate*)			
	15%	*25%*	*50%*	*70%*
5.0	5.88	6.67	10.00	16.67
5.5	6.47	7.33	11.00	18.33
6.0	7.05	8.00	12.00	20.00
6.5	7.64	8.67	13.00	21.67
7.0	8.23	9.33	14.00	23.33
7.5	8.82	10.00	15.00	25.00
8.0	9.41	10.67	16.00	26.67
8.5	10.00	11.33	17.00	28.33
9.0	10.59	12.00	18.00	30.00
9.5	11.18	12.67	19.00	31.67
10.0	11.76	13.33	20.00	33.33
10.5	12.35	14.00	21.00	35.00
11.0*	12.94	15.33	22.00	36.67

* One issue of Big Mac (Municipal Assistance Corporation for the City of New York) offered this coupon. As indicated by both foresight and hindsight, it was a risky issue.

tax bracket. For example, the equivalent taxable yield on a municipal security paying 6% is only 7.05% for an investor whose marginal tax rate is 15%, but it is 20% for an investor whose marginal tax rate is 70%. Thus the muni market attracts highly taxed investors.

An interesting feature of the muni market is that individual issues tend to have *regional* markets in which they sell best. One reason is the state and local taxation of income. A municipal security issued by New York City offers a much higher equivalent taxable yield to an investor who lives there and has to pay high city and state income taxes than it would to an out-of-state investor. A second factor creating regional markets for municipal securities is the tax on intangibles that many states levy. Normally this tax is not applied to local issues. Thus to a resident of a state such as Ohio, which has a low tax on income but a high tax on wealth, ownership of local municipal securities offers a double-barreled tax advantage.

Tax reform. Because interest income on municipals is tax exempt, a wealthy individual can earn a huge tax-free income by investing in municipals, and many wealthy individuals do just that. Periodically, this practice leads to calls for tax reform, in particular for ending the tax exemption on municipal securities. These calls are countered by pressure from state and local governments to maintain the present system, which permits municipal issuers to borrow more cheaply than they otherwise could.

The current system of reciprocal tax immunity amounts to an expensive, inefficient federal subsidy of state and local borrowing. It has been estimated that every $1 saved in borrowing costs by municipal issuers costs the federal government $2 to $3 in lost tax revenue. The current system also *narrows* the market for municipals because only investors taxed at high marginal rates—and that leaves out many institutional investors—have an incentive to invest in municipals. To make matters worse, the rapid post-World War II growth in municipal issues has required that investors in progressively lower marginal tax brackets be drawn into the municipal market. As a result the differential between taxable and nontaxable rates has narrowed, and the value to municipal issuers of the federal tax exemption has diminished. Recent high inflation rates, however, have tended to offset this trend by pushing investors into constantly higher marginal tax brackets.

A possible alternative to the present system would be for Congress to end the federal tax exemption for municipal securities and provide a federal subsidy for municipal issues, perhaps couped with a federal corporation to insure municipal issues for a fee. Proposals of this sort have often been made but never acted upon.

Credit risk

Municipal securities unlike governments, expose the investor to a credit risk. Consequently for a municipal issue to sell in the national market, it must, like commercial paper, be rated. The major rating services providing this service are Moody and Standard & Poor. Some smaller firms also rate issues within individual states.

In establishing a rating, the rating services's main concern is whether the issuer will be able to make promised payments of interest and principal. The first thing the rating services look at is the pledge behind the issue; it may be a general obligation pledge, a limited tax pledge, a revenue pledge, or a mix of these.[5] In the case of GO issues, the relationship between the issuer's total debt burden and its tax base is crucial. In the case of municipal bonds, projections into the future necessarily play a major role in any rating; the rating service must ask how the community issuing the security is likely to fare over time: Is it growing? Does it have a diversified economy? Is local government well managed? In the case of revenue bonds, the main focus is on whether the facility being financed—be it a toll bridge or a college dorm—provides a service that

---

[5] Issues guaranteed by the federal government need no credit rating as they are considered credit-risk free.

the public will purchase in sufficient quantity to permit the issuer to service its debt.

The information and analysis that go into rating a municipal bond are summarized in a shorthand way by assigning to the issue one of several possible ratings; those given by the national rating services are listed in Table 19–2.

TABLE 19–2
Ratings given by Moody and Standard & Poor on municipal bonds

Rating interpretation	Moody*	Standard & Poor†
Best-quality grade	Aaa	AAA
High-quality grade	Aa	AA
Upper medium grade	A	A
Medium grade	Baa	BBB
Speculative grade	Ba	BB
Low grade	B	B
Poor grade to default	Caa	CCC
Highly speculative default	Ca	CC
Lowest-rated grade	C	C

* Bonds of the highest quality within a grade are designated by A-1 and Baa-1.
† For rating categories AA to BB, a plus sign is added to show high relative standing, a minus sign to show low relative standing.

Municipal *notes* are rated separate by Moody in order of declining credit worthiness: MIG 1, MIG 2, MIG 3, and MIG 4. S&P rates muni notes P-1 to P-3.

Investors view the ratings assigned to municipal securities as important indicators of quality and risk, and ratings affect the yields at which notes trade. Direct comparisons are however, difficult because the yield on a muni note depends on so many things: what type of note it is (TAN, BAN or RAN), how much paper the issue has in the market, and whether the paper is "double tax exempt," that is, offers local investors exemption from high state and local taxes.

While it is difficult to generalize about quality spreads, they do exist. In October 1982, June 83 PNs were trading around 5.50, while June 83 NYC notes were trading at 7.50. New York City issues both TANs and RANs. The TANs are considered a better credit and, reflecting this, out trade the RANs.

In recent years investors have demanded quality and have been willing to give up yield to get it. On muni notes, the MIG 1 rating means a lot; and issuers, working closely with Moody, have done some imaginative things to get it. Michigan, for example, got a MIG 1 rating for a note issue by backing it with letters of credit from five Japanese banks. When the concern of the rating agency is not over the issuer's credit but over its ability to roll or refund the notes being rated, a committed facility from a bank may suffice for an issuer to get a MIG 1 rating on its paper. Such a facility takes away market risk—the bond market is terrible when the notes mature; it does not eliminate credit risk because no bank is going to honor a committed line to a bankrupt borrower. Committed facilities have been used by many muni note issuers in recent years because the cost of a back stop from a bank was less than the difference in yield between MIG 1 and MIG 2 paper.

A rating is not a once-and-for-all affair. Ratings on individual issues are constantly upgraded or downgraded in light of changes in the position of the issuer. Sometimes, instead of changing the rating of a given issue, the rating services will withdraw their rating altogether, as they did in the case of several New York issues. Generally, what this means is that circumstances surrounding the issue have become so uncertain that a meaningful rating cannot be given. It may also reflect the rating services' belief that adverse factors creating the uncertainty may be temporary.

Municipal security insurance. To increase the marketability of their bonds, some municipal issuers have payment on new bond issues insured for a fee by one of several consortia of insurance companies: MGIC, MBIA, and AMBAC. From the issuer's point of view, such insurance is worth the premium charged if the insurance reduces the coupon interest they must pay by an even larger amount. While insurance of muni bonds has been around for a decade, only recently has one of the insurers, MBIA, began offering insurance on muni notes.

Investors

The distribution of outstanding municipal securities among investor groups differs sharply from that of federal and federal agency securities. Since the single most important advantage of municipals to the investor is the federal tax exemption, the groups holding these securities are those to whom this exemption is worth most.

Commercial banks, whose interest income is not shielded from federal taxation, hold close to 38% of total outstanding municipals. Individuals hold another 31%. Most of the remainder is held by casualty insurance companies and other nonbank financial institutions that pay a high tax rate on interest income. Life insurance companies and pension funds, to which the exemption is of small benefit because of the low rates at which their income is taxed, hold few municipals.

Whether municipals are attractive to nonfinancial corporations depends on the amount and type of borrowing they do. Except for specifically exempted institutions such as banks, the Internal Revenue Service (IRS) Code prohibits the expensing of interest on funds borrowed for the purchase or carry of tax-exempt securities. The precise meaning of this prohibition is a gray area because the IRS has issued few definitive rulings despite the many requests investors have made for such rulings.

Borrowing money to directly fund holdings of municipal securities and expensing the interest paid on the borrowing is clearly a prohibited arbitrage. Many corporations take the position, however, that if they have borrowed money long term to, say, fund construction and don't spend all of the money right away, expensing the interest on the bond issue and simultaneously investing surplus funds in tax exempts is OK.

Also, some corporations with debt outstanding will invest in muni notes funds earmarked for a specific purpose such as funding dividends. The view here is that holding munis is permissible because the investment bridges a gap between an inflow of funds and a specific outflow that must be met. Despite these practices, some hardnosed corporate lawyers advise a firm against buying munis if it has any debt outstanding.

In this respect it should also be noted that there is also an IRS guideline that states that a corporation's holdings of municipal securities should not exceed 2 percent of its total assets. Investors are careful to comply with this ruling.

With the exception of casualty insurance companies, the major investors in the muni note market are largely the same as those that are important in the muni market overall—commercial banks, cash-rich corporations, and wealthy individuals. To their ranks has recently been added a big and growing group of investors—tax-exempt money funds.

In several respects, the muni note market differs significantly from other sectors of the money market. First, it is more of an investors' market; that is, people who buy notes generally have a bona fide need for tax-free income, and they need it to the maturity date. Moreover, on the maturity date they will probably roll their old notes into new "tax frees." That is not to say that investors who expect interest rates to rise won't sell muni notes, but generally they don't play the yield curve game or otherwise trade these securities. In the muni note business, most sales are to investors who hold to maturity.

A second distinctive feature of the muni note market is that individuals become a *huge* factor in this market when rates are attractive. The moment good credits start paying tax-free rates that exceed rates on passbook savings accounts at a bank or S&L, the public moves funds in volume into the note market.

Institutional investors and tax-exempt money funds, some of which are limited by their prospectuses to buy MIG 1, P-1 paper, will almost without exception buy only high-quality muni notes. The principal buyers of lower-rated paper are individuals—doctors, lawyers, and Indian chiefs—to whom such paper is peddled in small blocks by Merrill and other wire houses. There are probably one or two institutional buyers who will buy NYC notes. The rest have to be sold to individuals. That is the difference between the MIG 1 market and the rest.

Yield

The yield on any particular muni note issue depends on the credit of the issuer, the maturity of the issue, the general level of interest rates, and the value of the tax exemption to investors.

Given that the tax rate on profits is 46%, it seems reasonable to assume that the average marginal tax rate of investors in the municipal market is around 50%. If so, then when taxable Bell (AT&T) bonds trade at 10%, a good muni credit ought to be able to borrow long term at 5%. In practice, however, muni bonds have never traded at their full taxable equivalent; the good muni credit would probably have to pay at least 6% if Bells were yielding 10%. The reason is that Congress keeps discussing possible "tax reform" in the municipal area—reform could leave an investor in munis holding low-coupon securities worth much less after reform than before.

Because muni notes have short maturities, this uncertainty effect does not spill over into the muni note market. PNs, which are really backdoor Treasuries, trade much of the time at or near half the yield on Treasury bills of equivalent maturity. Sometimes, when supply is limited and a lot of high-tax-bracket (60+%) investors are in the market, they will even trade through this level.

Volume outstanding

As Figure 19–2 shows, the muni note market, which is currently a $21.6 billion a year market, grew steadily until 1975, after which it took a noticeable dip. Prior to 1974, the typical municipal officer in charge of debt issuance, usually a senior civil servant who had been around forever, operated on the principle that you don't sell long-term munis except when they yield around 3%. Also, in some states, the rate a municipality could pay on bonds was limited by law. Massachusetts, for example, would not permit municipalities to pay more than 2.5% on bonds. The upshot was that by 1974 a lot of municipal funding officers were rolling large quantities of notes, waiting for low rates that never came.

The dip that began in 1975 in municipal notes outstanding was largely the result of New York City's well-publicized difficulties. These forced the city, which had been a huge issuer of notes, and some other poorer credits out of the note market. New York City's difficulties also caused banks and dealers to take a closer look at the note issues they were underwriting. Before, no one had been concerned about or even

FIGURE 19–2
Volume of municipal notes outstanding

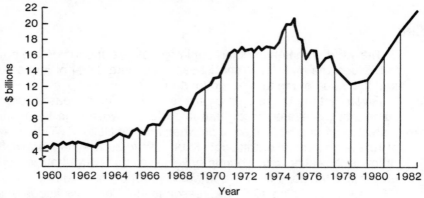

Source: Board of Governors of the Federal Reserve System.

knew if the anticipated tax revenues of a municipality selling TANs would suffice to cover these securities. After New York's problems, however, the banks and dealers started to ask such questions and to say to municipalities, "You can't continually roll notes you can't pay off; you have to fund such accumulated debt long term." As a result some municipalities were forced to refund note issues with bonds at the worst possible moment. The dealers, having turned cautious, saddled some communities that could have borrowed at 5 or 6% in normal times with 20-year problems in the form of bonds carrying a 9 or 10% coupon; on $10 million that works out to an extra $400,000 of interest a year.

THE NEW ISSUES MARKET

State and local governments and the authorities they create run into short-term needs for cash that are totally separate from their long-term capital needs; when they do, they borrow just like any other spending unit. Because state and municipal borrowers differ sharply in size and character, the ways in which they issue notes vary widely, a situation having no parallel elsewhere in the money market.

At one extreme is the situation where a town needs $50,000 to pay for a fire engine and tax receipts are not coming in until later. It goes to its local bank and signs a $50,000 note, which the bank calls a TAN and sticks in its portfolio. Deals of this sort, which represent perhaps 99 percent of all muni note deals, are not made on a competitive basis. The rate on the note is not a market rate but often something related to prime.

At the other extreme is a situation where the amount of money to be borrowed is huge, and the loan may not be in the strict sense a *bridge financing*—one that tides the borrower over until some identifiable receipt comes in. Often state or local governments are doing just what the federal government does: They have gotten themselves operating on a perpetual cash-deficit basis, and they are always in arrears because they spend future taxes before they collect them.

At this end of the spectrum, one might, for example, find Los Angeles County going to the Bank of America to borrow, just as the small town in the example above went to its local bank to get money. Only Los Angeles County needs $400 million instead of $50,000. This is more exposure than the B of A wants to one borrower, so—and this is where the analogy between the little borrower paying for a fire engine and the big borrower breaks down—the big borrower's bank says, "OK, we'll get you the money, but we have to do a public offering."

On small-sized muni borrowings, it is common for the banker and the borrower to work out a sweetheart deal. The borrower sells the bank a note to finance a cash need that won't occur for 60 or 90 days. It then places the funds borrowed in a CD issued by the lending bank. If that bank has a high effective tax rate, there is an automatic arbitrage for both sides. The municipality earns a higher rate on the CD than it is pays on its note; the bank profits because the interest it pays to the municipality is a deductible expense, whereas the income it earns on the muni note is tax exempt.

Not all anticipatory borrowing by state and local governments involves an attempt to cash in on an arbitrage created by federal tax laws. A big borrower like New York State might, for example, borrow several billion dollars it does not need for a month or two simply because the current market is attractive. However, any municipal borrower that takes down short-term funds before it needs them creates, whatever its motivation, a profitable arbitrage because it can always invest the loan proceeds in RP or other money market paper at a spread above its borrowing rate.

Prior to 1969 some municipalities issued *arbitrage bonds;* that is, they borrowed money specifically to reinvest it in higher-yielding taxable securities. The Tax Reform Act of 1969 ended the exemption from federal taxation of interest income on arbitrage bonds. The act, however, also stated that a municipal security would not be treated for tax purposes as an arbitrage bond simply because the proceeds of the issue were invested temporarily until needed in taxable securities.

Despite the 1969 tax act and subsequent Treasury rulings designed to narrow the opportunity for states and municipalities to profit from arbitraging between the tax-exempt and taxable markets, muni note issuers can still get away with borrowing for as long as a year an amount equal to their peak borrowing needs during the year. For issuers whose short-term borrowing needs are highly variable, this creates a loophole as wide as a barn door, and many such issuers go right through it. For example, if November is a really bad month for a municipality—it needs 50 million most months but 80 million that month, it can probably get away with borrowing 100 million for the year. Even that is not extreme; there are muni note issuers who can show that they need 80 million for 4 days of the year and use that need to justify borrowing 105 million for a whole year. By playing the arbitrage game to the hilt, some muni note issuers are able to reduce the cost of their short-term borrowing to zero—others even profit from the deal.

Disclosure

Issuers of municipal bonds obtain their authority to issue such securities from the state constitution or statutes. In some cases this authority is limited, and a favorable vote by the electorate may be necessary before bonds can be issued.

The legality of every municipal bond issue must be approved by an attorney. Such opinions are obtained from bond attorneys who specialize in municipal law. The legal opinion on a bond issue is either printed on the back of the bond or attached to the security.

Municipal securities are specifically exempt from the registration requirements of the 1933 Federal Securities Act. The only exception is industrial development issues that do not qualify for tax exemption. However, every issuer of new municipal bonds—to make their issue salable—must prepare a detailed prospectus describing the issue and giving comprehensive data on which investors may judge the credit behind the issue.

In the muni note market, as opposed to the muni bond market, disclosure on publicly issued securities used to be rather casual. The issuer would put together a one-page statement of condition, a balance sheet, and a flowchart (the municipal equivalent of a cash flow or income statement). This would be certified and possibly, but not necessarily, audited. And that was it.

In the wake of New York City's difficulties, pressure arose for change. Politicians in Washington thought investors in municipal securities deserved more information on the issuer's condition. Also, dealers became concerned over their liability if disclosure on securities they underwrote proved inadequate, so they refused to bid on note issues on which disclosure was incomplete. As a result, issuers of muni notes began to provide detailed information on their condition, often by updating their latest bond prospectus.

Before dealers bid on a muni note issue or negotiate the sale of such an issue, they often do their own research on the quality of the issue.

They look at the community selling the notes: its tax collections and tax base, who lives there, and the profitability of local industry. Research of this sort protects the dealer. It also gives him a selling point when he approaches retail. Finally it may permit a dealer to expand his business by finding borrowers with good credit who through no fault of their own find access to the public market difficult. This happened to some New York communities when the difficulties of New York City and New York State cast a pall over all municipal securities issued within the state.

An interesting question with respect to disclosure is why, as New York City slipped deeper and deeper into trouble, Moody did not react faster in downgrading the city's securities and why the banks that were underwriting the city's issues did not sense trouble sooner.[6] The view of one person close to the scene is that, when the rating services and the bankers looked at the city's statement of condition, they simply could not believe that things were as bad as the numbers indicated. In their guts they thought there must be a mistake somewhere, that the city must have revenues or something it was not disclosing. No one could really believe that city officials thought that ever-increasing borrowing was a way to balance the city's budget. Unfortunately, the numbers were not lying; the unthinkable was not only thinkable but fact.

Sale of a public issue

Municipal notes issued through a public offering are sold by dealers who also make a secondary market in these securities. About 10 firms, 7 banks and 3 nonbank dealers, have made a strong commitment to the muni note market and participate in it on a steady basis. Another 10 dealers are sometimes players.

About 90 percent of all publicly offered muni note issues are sold to dealers through competitive bidding. In the muni note market, even though it is a sector of the money market, the overriding philosophy is that of investment banking—developing a constituency that follows the securities being bid on and getting these securities sold. Thus a muni note dealer, in bidding on and positioning securities, is more interested in what the muni note market is likely to do than in market rates in general. He wants, for example, to know how many highly taxable investors are currently in the market.

Large issuers of muni notes will normally advertise upcoming issues in *The Daily Bond Buyer* or elsewhere to get as many bids as possible. Smaller issues, in contrast, may send notices of sale to only four or five friends. As one dealer noted, "You have to hustle to find out what's there. It's not like a bill auction where the whole world is invited."

---

[6] In the spring of 1975 New York City's notes were rated MIG 1 by Moody's even after the market would no longer accept new issues of its debt securities.

How dealers bid on an issue depends on the size of the issue. On a big issue, $400 million or more, the dealers will form syndicates, and there may be no more than two bids. In contrast, on a $10 to $20 million issue, individual dealers feel they can handle that size alone, and there may be 10 or 15 bids.

The smaller an issue, the more difficult it is for a professional note dealer to know whether he will be able to buy the notes in a truly competitive situation. There is always the possibility that a bank will step in and make a particularly attractive offer because the issue fits its investment needs. Also a local bank may put in a low bid because of a prearranged arbitrage. As one dealer noted, "At times we will bid for 20 or 30 million for a good West Coast credit. We perceive the market for a double-A county credit to be 6.25, so we bid 6.40 to offer at 6.25. Then we find that some local bank has bid 5.98. We ask what the hell is he doing, since PNs in that maturity are trading at 6.15. Then we find out that the county needs the money for only 3 weeks out of a 30-week borrowing period, which leaves 27 weeks for the bank and the county to work an arbitrage based on their effective tax rates."

When dealers form a selling syndicate to bid on and distribute an issue, they usually work on an undivided account basis. Some syndicate members might take $30 million, others less. Each assumes responsibility for the profit or loss on its share. In addition, even if a member sells its share, it is responsible, along with the other syndicate members, for any balance of the issue that remains unsold. In the muni note market, the emphasis is on distribution, getting the securities in and shoving them out. Thus, a dealer will be open with other dealers about his position, and if he has been successful in buying a big issue, he may offer a selling concession to other dealers to get them to work on distributing these securities.

What sort of spread dealers try for when they bid on a new issue depends on the credit of the issuer. On top credits the dealer may work for only an 05 or and 04, while on a lesser credit he might want 3/8 of a point or more. If a dealer offers other dealers a selling concession, this will normally run one third to half of his gross spread.

A note dealer bidding on a new issue cannot strictly speaking presell, but he will solicit interest and take orders, many of which fall through because he misses the deal. In a muni note deal, an investor who puts in a presale order gets his paper with almost no underwriting spread. For example, a dealer that bids for and gets some notes at 8.53 might have taken some presale orders at 8.50. In filling these, the dealer makes only an 03. On a 100 million deal, the dealer might have sold 30 million on a presale basis. If things go well, he will sell another 30 million at the 8.40 level. His real opportunity to make money occurs if the deal starts to heat up; notes start leaving the market, and the dealer is able to mark up the balance of his holdings dramatically.

An early buyer of notes can get a very good deal, but he must take some risk. He might find that no one will buy the rest of the issue and that consequently it will trade down in the market.

In the muni note market, the whole distribution of a 100 million issue might be to only five customers. Thus syndicates of the size required in the muni bond market are not needed; the typical muni bond syndicate comprises a few big shops and some small ones, whereas the typical note syndicate is just a few big guys.

About 10% of all publicly offered muni notes are sold to dealers on a negotiated basis. On a negotiated deal, there is usually much more spread than there is on an issue sold through competitive bidding. Typically note deals done on a negotiated basis are for lesser credits—Michigan, Minnesota, NYC—or, in the case of NYS, on issues where sheer size is a problem; New York State sells 3½ billion notes at a crack. Dealers that buy muni issues on a negotiated basis need on those deals a spread wide enough so they can pay commissions to their registered reps to sell some or all of these issues to individuals in small pieces.

When-issued trading

There is normally a one-week gap between the time notes are awarded to the successful bidder and the time they are issued. The exception is PN notes on which there is a one-month delay. During that time the new issue trades on a *when-issued* (*wi*) basis.

Dealer financing

From a tax point of view, a bank's assets and liabilities are treated as being totally commingled. Thus a bank dealer may carry muni notes tax exempt, and so long as the bank has taxable income, financing its position in muni notes will yield the bank a positive carry under all money market conditions.

A nonbank dealer, in contrast, has to acquire specific liabilities to finance tax-free notes, and when it does, it loses under current tax laws the benefit of the tax exemption on the coupon. Thus nonbank dealers can finance tax-exempt notes only at a negative spread. To get around this problem, nonbank dealers have two options. One is simply to sell their position to a bank for purposes of carry. Under such an arrangement, the nonbank dealer sells his securities to a bank at par and then buys them back from the bank, again at par, as he sells them. A second option is for a nonbank dealer to open a joint account on a trading basis with a bank. Under this arrangement, the bank carries the securities and gets the benefit of positive carry. The bank also assumes underwriting responsibility, and the bank and the nonbank dealer split the underwriting profit or loss.

THE SECONDARY MARKET

There is an active secondary market in muni notes, but it differs in flavor and character from secondary markets in other money market instruments.

Every dealer in muni notes will make a market to customers in anything they have sold him, and dealers do some secondary trading to satisfy customer needs. Investors, however, work their muni note portfolios less hard than they do their taxable portfolios; they buy tax exempts for yield and taxables for trading. One deterrent to trading muni notes is taxes. An investor who, when interest rates decline, sells munis at a gain and replaces them with a lower coupon trades a future stream of tax-exempt income for a current taxable gain, which amounts to giving money to the IRS. Dealers generate a certain amount of secondary market trading by investors when they distribute new issues; they track their customers' holdings and might, to get a new 9-month state note sold, encourage customers to swap out of an old 8-month note for some yield pickup.

The inside or interdealer market in muni notes is active when dealers are long securities. The job of the muni note dealer is distribution, and he is successful to the extent that he pushes one issue after another out to retail. It is when such distribution fails on one or several issues and a lot of securities are backed up on the street that trading between dealers really comes alive, with every dealer trying to get back his bid.

Muni note dealers do not usually quote runs to each other except occasionally in a few actively traded issues. They deal with each other more on a "can do" basis. A dealer will call another to ask for a bid on a particular issue, and the other dealer will tell him what side of the market he's on. In muni notes, dealers are not, as in governments, secretive about their positions. They usually advertise them in the hope that other dealers will work on them.

In the interdealer market, quotes are always good for $1 million, but trades as large as $200 million are done, and $50 million trades are common. Spreads are narrow and may approach those in the bill market when big blocks of high-quality paper trade.

A dealer in muni notes *cannot* short an outstanding issue because in doing so he would be creating new tax-free interest, something that only states and municipalities are permitted to do. A dealer can short municipal issues while they are trading on a "when, as, and if issued" basis, but that is risky. The issues are so distinctive and discrete that the substitution and swapping capabilities that are present in corporates and governments do not exist. If the dealer can't find the actual securities to cover his short, he faces a huge legal problem. Because of this disincentive, almost no one shorts munis even during wi trading.

The fact that muni dealers do not go short means that the dealers are always either a little long or a lot long in the market. Thus the muni note market never achieves the kind of bullish technical position that sometimes occurs in governments: There are a lot of shorts around and a dealer can just feed securities into the market.

The brokers

Since every other sector of the money market is brokered, one would expect to find brokers in the muni note market. They are there and growing in number; whereas four years ago there was only one broker in the market, today there are three highly competitive brokers of muni notes.

One difference between brokers in the muni market and brokers of other money market instruments is that, in the muni note market, interdealer trading in and consequently brokering of big blocks—anything from $5 million on up—occurs primarily in issues that are being distributed or that are at least still relatively fresh.

The brokers do big volume—their real bread and butter business—in PNs and in whatever the big non-project note of the moment is. In March, April, and May, it is NYS notes—massive amounts of them. In the fall there are lots of Pennsylvania notes in the market. Muni note brokers charge an 01 on long notes. A round lot in the market is $5 million, but brokers will do an occasional trade for a smaller amount as an accommodation.

Price volatility

Interest income on municipal securities is tax exempt, but capital gains and losses on such securities are treated for tax purposes in the same way as on taxable securities. Because of this asymmetry in tax treatment, when interest rates move, municipals are more volatile in price than are taxables.

To see why, suppose that PNs with a 6-month maturity are issued at 4% and 6-month bills at 8%. Later interest rates rise, and the bills issued at 8% fall sufficient in price to yield 9%. The PNs issued at 4% also fall in price, and as they do, investors in them acquire short-term taxable capital gains. Assuming that investors' average marginal tax rate is 50 percent, this means that the PNs have to rise on a *percentage basis* twice as fast in yield as (fall faster in price than) the bills to continue to offer investors an equivalent taxable yield equal to half the yield on the bills.[7] Specifically, if Treasuries went to 9%, the PNs in our example would

---

[7] In our example the yield on Treasuries goes from 8 to 9%; a 12.5% increase in yield. The PNs rise in yield from 4 to 5%, a 25% increase in yield.

have to trade at 5%; that would give investors an aftertax yield equal to the 4% coupon plus 50% of the 1% return that accrues in the form of a capital gain—a total aftertax rate of 4.5%, which equals just half the 9% rate at which taxable Treasuries are trading. Should interest rates now reverse the trend and start to fall, the muni notes would rise in price faster than the taxable bills, again for tax reasons.

Dealer's bid on a new issue. The high price volatility of tax exempts affects at times the way a dealer will bid on a new issue. When dealers bid competitively on a note issue, the issue is awarded to the bidder offering the lowest net interest cost—coupon interest paid minus any premium received by the borrower. Because of the high price volatility of tax exempts, dealers want to ensure that, if the market slips back during the distribution period, they will still have a full-coupon security to sell. Consequently in a weak market, a dealer, instead of bidding, say, par and an 8% coupon on an issue, may bid an 8¼% coupon plus premium. If the market then backs up, the dealer will have a security that he can sell at par; alternatively, if rates stay flat, the dealer will pass part or all of the premium on to retail.

A leading indicator

In a bull market developments in the muni market can at times be a precursor of things to happen. As conditions ease and money starts piling up at the banks, banks often react by buying notes before bills. On occasion this has caused the note market to take off while the bill market just sat there, and notes ended up trading on a tax-equivalent basis through bills. In a bear market, in contrast, because notes have a reputation for being less liquid than bills, investors often sell their notes first. Thus the note market may lead the bill market down.

Chapter 20

Money market funds, an attractive alternative for the institutional and the small portfolio manager

A MUTUAL FUND is a device through which investors pool funds to invest in a diversified portfolio of securities. The investor who puts money into a mutual fund gets shares in return and becomes in effect a part owner of the fund. Professional guidance is provided by an outside management company, which charges the fund a fee equal to some small percentage of the fund's total assets. The majority of mutual funds, including those best known to investors, invest almost exclusively in common stocks. Some of these funds have growth and long-term capital gains as their primary objective; others seek high and consistent dividend income. There are also mutual funds that invest in bonds to obtain a high and consistent yield at minimum risk.

In the mid-1970s when money market rates soared above time deposit rates, the stage was set for the birth of a new breed of mutual funds—funds that were able to offer investors high return plus high liquidity by investing in high-yield, short-term debt securities. Mutual funds of this sort, known as *money market funds* (or, more simply, *money funds*) first appeared in 1974; their number grew between 1974 and 1978 from zero to 40 and then from 40 to 450 between 1978 and late 1982.

RAISON D'ÊTRE

Money market funds were initially designed to meet the needs of the small investor, for whom investing in money market securities is awkward for several reasons. Minimum denominations are high. Buying securities and rolling them over involves more work than some people care to bother with, and having a bank or broker take over that job used to at least involve high transaction costs. Also, for some instruments, yields on small denominations are lower than those on large denominations. Finally, the investor with limited funds can't reduce risk by diversifying: by buying a mix of different money market securities.

None of these difficulties exists for the money market funds, which pool the resources of many investors. Because these funds handle large sums of money, high minimum denominations pose no problem. Transaction costs in terms of both money and time spent per dollar invested are minuscule. Finally, money market funds are able to buy a wide range of securities, thereby reducing credit risk to a negligible level.

HOW THEY WORK

Forgetting technicalities and legal niceties, a money market fund resembles a special bank (one that would be illegal in the United States[1]). This special bank accepts demand deposits only, pays daily interest on these deposits, invests all its deposits in money market instruments, holds no reserves, and keeps only a very small profit margin for itself. For the investor, the only significant differences between banking at such a special institution and putting money in a money fund are that (1) deposits in a money fund are *not* federally insured as are bank deposits, and (2) there are minimum-denomination requirements to meet on initial deposits and on certain types of withdrawals.

Investing in a fund

Money funds do not accept deposits; they sell shares—typically $1 buys one share, but at some funds share size is larger. All funds calculate interest daily on outstanding shares and credit interest to the investor's account periodically, usually at the end of the month. Interest credited to an investor's account buys him more shares. Money funds do not issue share certificates. Instead, they send out periodic statements showing deposits, withdrawals, and interest credited to the investor's account.

---

[1] It would be illegal, not because it would be unsound, but because U.S. banks are prohibited from paying market rates of interest on ordinary demand deposit accounts and because all depository institutions are required to hold reserves at the Fed.

Initially some money market funds were load funds; that is, some of the money invested went to pay a commission to the broker who sold the fund. Today, however, no-load funds are the rule, which makes sense, since money market funds are used by many investors much as a checking account—a place to hold temporary liquidity; and deposits and withdrawals are therefore frequent.

Withdrawing funds

A depositor may withdraw funds from a money fund anytime on demand and without penalty. Typically withdrawals can be made by requesting a fund to send the investor a check or to wire out funds from his account at the fund to an account at a commercial bank. A third method of withdrawing funds is by writing a check. Most money funds have set up an arrangement with a commercial bank under which the investor is supplied with checks and can make withdrawals and payments simply by drawing a check against that bank. Generally the check must be for some minimum amount—$500 or $1,000. When the check is presented to the bank against which it is drawn, that bank covers it by redeeming the required number of shares in the investor's money fund account. (With this sort of fund, "shares" differ little from interest-bearing demand deposits.)

Where the money goes

Since money invested in a money fund is available to the investor on demand, a money fund must be prepared for large and unpredictable withdrawals (redemptions of shares for cash). To do so, all funds hold a portfolio of highly liquid money market instruments. In late 1982 the average current maturity of securities in the portfolios of the 10 largest funds ran from 24 to 76 days (Table 20–1).

Generally money funds can meet the cash requirements generated by redemptions through the inflow of funds from new investors plus payments on maturity securities. However, if these sources prove inadequate, a fund can generate additional cash by selling assets in its portfolio. Since money funds hold large amounts of short-maturity securities, the risk of capital loss on such sales due to adverse movements in market price is small.

Money funds seek to offer the investor not only liquidity and high return, but *safety of principal*. The typical fund is restricted, as noted in its prospectus, from doing any of the following: investing in stocks, convertible securities, and real estate; buying on the margin; effecting short sales; trading in commodities; acting as an underwriter of securities;

TABLE 20-1
Money funds with assets over $1 billion, November 1, 1982

Net assets ($ billions)	Fund	Investment results				Portfolio holdings (%)								
		For period ended 10/27/82		12-mo. YTD as of 9/82	Avg. mat. (days)	U.S.		Repos	CDs	Banker's accept	Comm'l paper	Euro$, CDs, TDs	Yankee$, CDs, BAs	Non-prime
		7-Day	30-Day			Treas.	Other							
U.S. Treasury														
2.3	Capital Preservation	6.7	6.8	12.3	26	100	—	—	—	—	—	—	—	—
1.0	Dreyfus M.M. Instrmts Gov't	9.2	9.8	13.1	76	60	—	40M	—	—	—	—	—	—
1.8	GMA Gov't Securities	6.3	7.4	13.5	44	91	—	9M	—	—	—	—	—	—
2.8	Merrill Lynch Gov't	7.9	8.3	13.1	45	99	—	1M	—	—	—	—	—	—
U.S. government and agencies														
4.6	AARP U.S. Gov't M.M.T.	8.9	9.2	12.9	43	22	39	39M	—	—	—	—	—	—
1.4	First Variable Rate	8.8	9.0	13.7	34b	9	11	80M	—	—	—	—	—	—
1.2	Fund/Gov't Investors	8.2	8.4	13.1	46	56	22	22M	—	—	—	—	—	—
1.2	Shearson Gov't & Agencies	8.8	8.9	12.8	41	34	34	32M	—	—	—	—	—	—
Domestic prime														
1.5	Alliance Capital Reserves	8.8	9.0	13.8	24	13	—	8M	28	21	30	—	—	—
1.6	Current Interest M.M.F.	9.4	9.9	13.9	39	23	—	—	21	22	54	ˎ	—	—
1.2	Active Assets M.T. (Dean Witter)	9.8	10.1	14.3	48	12	3	—	46	—	39	—	—	—
9.6	Inter Capital Liq Assets (Dean Witter)	10.0	10.4	14.3	49	15	6	—	40	3	36	—	—	—
3.8	Fidelity Daily Income	9.8	10.1	14.4	33	—	—	—	57	20	23	—	—	—

1.2	Franklin Money Fund	9.3	10.2	13.9	26	—	—	3	6	82	9	—	—	—
5.1	Liquid Capital Income	9.4	9.8	13.8	22	1	3	5	32	7	52a	—	—	—
15.9	CMA Money Fund, Merrill Lynch	6.3	9.1	14.4	51	46	—	5	27	7	14	—	—	1
22.6	Ready Assets Trust, Merrill Lynch	6.4	9.1	14.4	50	41	—	6	22	7	23	—	—	1
6.6	Paine Webber Cashfund	9.4	9.7	14.1	28	10	5	—	33	7	45	—	—	—
1.2	Scudder Cash Investment Trust	9.3	9.6	13.7	32	17	—	—	58	11	14	—	—	—
1.2	Vanguard M.M.T. Prime	9.6	9.9	14.2	34	—	—	—	57	22	21	—	—	—
	Domestic prime and Euros													
7.0	Cash Reserve Management	8.4	10.0	14.1	34	9	1	—	11	6	64	9	—	—
1.0	DBL Cash Fund M.M. Portfolio	9.6	10.0	14.4	32	1	—	—	26	21	37	15	—	—
5.3	Daily Cash Accumulation	9.2	9.4	14.2	25	9	6	1	13	2	68a	2	—	—
11.5	Dreyfus Liquid Assets	10.1	10.6	14.6	48	2	—	—	14	5	14	65	—	—
1.5	Webster Cash Reserve (Kidder Peabody)	9.5	9.8	14.1	31	—	—	6	38	15	32	9	—	—
3.9	Money Mart Assets (Kidder Peabody)	9.6	9.7	14.3	28	—	—	—	54	1	37	8	—	—
2.0	National Liquid Reserve	9.9	10.2	14.2	41	1	—	—	35	16	31	17	—	—
1.6	Oppenheimer M.M.F. Inc.	9.0	9.6	14.1	28	4	10	3	1	1	73	8	—	—
3.1	Reserve-Primary	10.2	10.6	14.0	31	—	—	1	11	16	—	72	—	—
6.5	Shearson Daily Dividend, Inc	9.6	10.0	14.2	55	28	2	—	21	8	—	41	—	—
	Domestic prime and Euros and Yan-kees													
4.8	Cash Equivalent Fund	10.2	10.8	14.7	37	—	—	—	—	—	39	25	17	19
2.0	Delaware Cash Reserve	9.9	10.1	14.5	33	—	—	—	21	10	38	23	8	—
4.2	Fidelity Cash Reserve	9.9	10.3	14.3	37	—	—	—	13	—	9	31	47	—
1.3	IDS Cash Management	9.9	14.2	14.1	47	—	—	—	28	35	27	2	8	—
4.2	Kemper Money Market	10.3	11.0	14.8	39	—	—	—	—	—	37a	28	16	19
3.4	T. Rowe Price Prime Reserve	9.9	9.9	14.3	43	—	—	—	15	10	37	12	15	11

Source: Donoghue's "Money Fund Report," Holliston, Mass.

and placing more than a small percentage of total assets in the securities of any one issuer.

The bailiwick of the market funds is the money market. As a group, they place almost all the funds invested with them in short-term governments and agencies, negotiable CDs, BAs, RPs, and commercial paper. There are, however, differences in practice. A few conservative funds stick to governments and agencies. The more aggressive hold a wider range of money market instruments, including Yankee and Euro paper (see Tables 20–1 and 20–2).

TABLE 20–2
Money market fund assets in June 1982
($ billions)

Demand deposits and currency		−.3
Time deposits		45.0
Security repurchase agreements		16.8
Foreign deposits		22.2
Credit market instruments		114.1
U.S. government securities	35.7	
Open-market paper	78.4	
Miscellaneous		4.1
Total assets		201.9

Source: Board of Governors of the Federal Reserve, Flow of Funds Division.

Accounting procedures

When the money funds industry was new, different people with different ideas and sometimes different objectives came to the SEC with their proposals for setting up a money market mutual fund; one would say, "We are going to account this way for capital gains and losses," and another would say, "We are going to account that way," and so on. Since every proposal looked reasonable, the upshot was that the SEC responded with an OK in each case. Thus was born a new class of institutions, with assets destined to rise from zero to $280 billion over eight years and each firm comprising it using one of four different accounting methods.

Most money funds mark their portfolios to market daily, a sound practice but one that raises the question of how capital gains and losses, realized and unrealized, should be treated—as net income, as a change in net asset value, or what. Some mark-to-market funds that wanted a steady income stream choose to reflect any realized or unrealized capital gains or losses as changes in the net asset value of their shares. Other funds that wanted to maintain a constant net asset value choose to include realized and unrealized gains and losses in their daily dividends. Still other funds that wanted a constant net asset value, for example, because they sold their fund to bank trust departments, municipal bodies, and other institutions that could assume no risk of capital loss, took the straight-line-accrual approach in accounting. Such funds make it a practice to hold money market instruments in which they invest to maturity, they do not mark their portfolios to market daily, and the interest they credit each day to investors equals the average yield on all securities in the fund's portfolio.

A fourth approach, which seems to be the direction in which the industry is headed, is to run what is called a *penny rounded* fund. Such a fund sets net asset value at $1 initially. It then marks its portfolio to market and reflects capital gains or losses in the net asset value of its shares. However, these funds round their net asset value to the nearest penny, i.e., to the second decimal place; this means that their net asset value could deviate from $1 only if a tremendous change occurred in market values. On a yield basis, penny rounded funds are almost equivalent to the amortized-cost funds.

While each of the four accounting schemes sketched above seems reasonable and can be defended as achieving some desirable objective, the existence of differences in the way money funds report net income can and does on some days distort by hundreds of basis points comparisons of current yield among different funds.

To minimize distortions caused by accounting differences, an investor comparing several funds should look at what is called in the industry a *hypothetical:* If $1,000 were put in each fund and left there for one month, what rate of return would each fund have yielded the investor. The Arthur Lipper Service quotes the yields paid by different money funds on such a basis.

Ponzi and Sali

Most money market funds mark their portfolios to market daily to reflect any appreciation or depreciation that has occurred in the value of their assets due to fluctuations in interest rates. Some funds reflect such appreciation or depreciation in the value of their assets through minor changes in their share values. Others reflect it by including changes in asset values in the interest return they credit to shareholders' accounts.

A few money market funds make it a practice to hold money market instruments they have acquired to maturity. They do not mark their portfolios to market daily, and the interest credited each day to the investors in such funds equals the average yield on all securities in the fund's portfolio. A few individuals on the street and at the SEC have voiced concern that such straight-line-accrual funds could operate like a Ponzi scheme—Ponzi, in honor of Charles Ponzi, a Boston swindler who ran a con game in which early investors were paid off with funds supplied by later investors, leaving nothing for the last investors getting out.

How does Charles Ponzi enter the picture with respect to straight-line-accrual funds? Suppose short-term interest rates were to rise sharply; then the market value of the securities in the fund's portfolio would be temporarily depressed. Suppose also that a large number of investors simultaneously redeemed their fund shares for cash. It is conceivable that such a fund would be forced to sell off some of its securities at a loss and that the actual *market* value of the securities backing its remaining outstanding shares would fall below its fixed share value. In that case, if redemptions continued, the fund would run out of money before all shares were redeemed.

This eventuality, while theoretically possible, has a small probability in practice. For it to happen, interest rates would have to rise very sharply *and* rapidly; and *all* the money invested in the fund would have to be *hot* (very sensitive to interest rates), an improbable constellation of conditions.

Nevertheless, the SEC, after considering the question for two years, ruled that it would not allow amortized cost valuation for debt instruments with a current maturity of more than 60 days because such valuation does not reflect the "fair value of the underlying portfolio."

The SEC's ruling was challenged by a number of funds, in particular, funds serving clients such as bank trust departments and local government bodies that were unwilling or unable to invest funds in an instrument to which even a small market risk attached. In response to this challenge, the SEC exempted from its ruling funds which agreed to limit their sales to institutions and to require an initial minimum investment of $50,000. The exempted funds also agreed to limit the average maturity of their portfolios to no more than 120 days, to buy no securities with a current maturity of more than 1 year, and to severely restrict turnover in their portfolios.

Ironically the only money fund that ever came close to experiencing difficulties of the sort envisioned by those who feared a Ponzi-type scenario was an institutional fund administered by that most respected of dealers, Salomon Brothers, and advised by First of Chicago.

Most money coming into money funds, especially from small investors, is *hot* (interest rate sensitive) on the way in but *cold* on the way out; when the rates money funds can pay soar, money pours in, whereas when the rates they can pay fall, money is slow to move out. Investors who put money into a money fund for rate reasons end up keeping their money there, even when money market rates fall, because they like the convenience the funds offer.

In the summer of 1980, Sali's fund, Institutional Liquid Assets (ILA), extended maturities on the incorrect view that money market rates were going to stay put or decline. Instead rates rose sharply, so sharply that in September the fund's institutional clients started withdrawing large sums from ILA and putting that money either into other funds that had stayed short and consequently could pay more than ILA could or into high-yielding money market instruments. To fund these withdrawals, ILA had to sell assets. To prevent the sale at depressed prices of its relatively long-term assets from causing a decline in the net asset value of ILA shares, a rescue package was required: First of Chicago returned $1 million of previously paid advisory fees to ILA, and Sali completed the package by buying $228.5 million of governments from ILA at roughly $700,000 above their market value.

The whole episode, which is unlikely to ever be repeated, has several touches of irony. First the fund that had to be rescued had the most impeccable administrator and advisor imaginable. Second, had the fund catered to small investors, it would probably not have been penalized by large withdrawals for mistakenly extending maturities; doctors, lawyers, and Indian chiefs do not make it a daily practice to compare yields on money funds with yields on money market instruments. Big institutional investors, however, do.

The moral, if any, of this story is that the people in the money fund game who most need to act with care to protect themselves are not unsophisticated individuals who make deposits in general purpose money funds but managers of institutional funds whose clientele is likely to be well laced with market sharpies.

GROWTH OVER TIME

Starting from a zero base in 1974, money funds have grown phenomenally (Figure 20–1). In particular, from the last quarter of 1980 on, their total assets literally shot up in response to the historically high interest rates that prevailed in the money market until the fall of 1982.

From their inception money funds have provided competition to banks and thrifts, since people who put money in such funds clearly think of themselves as making a deposit and in particular view such deposits as an alternative to deposits at a bank or thrift. By November 1982 the total deposits at money funds were within a few billion of total demand deposits!

Competition from banks and thrifts

The rapidly growing money funds, by providing competition to banks and thrifts, have spurred the pace of rate deregulation at these institutions (see Chapter 6). Banks and thrifts, watching money funds pay on deposits rates that they were forbidden by regulations to match, asked

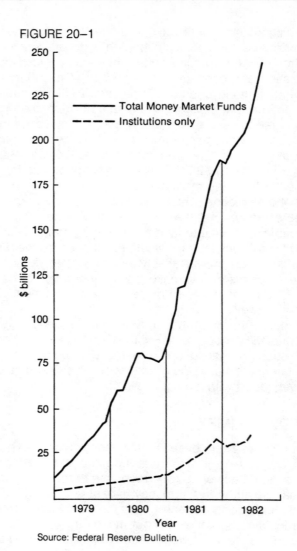

FIGURE 20–1

Source: Federal Reserve Bulletin.

for and got, first state by state and then nationwide in 1978, the right to offer interest-bearing (at the passbook savings rate) checking accounts, called NOW accounts, and to offer a confusing array of savings certificates paying even higher rates for deposits of longer maturity; unfortunately the longer the maturity of the deposit and the higher the rate paid on it, the greater was the potential penalty for early withdrawal. Banks and thrifts lacked any reasonably liquid, high-yielding account that they could offer depositers.

Finally in 1978, in response to pressure from banks and thrifts, these institutions were empowered to offer 6-month money market certificates (MMCs) on minimum deposits of $10,000; the rate banks and thrifts could pay on MMCs was tied to but held below the 6-month bill rate. MMCs, though popular, were too little too late. They were illiquid, had a large minimum denomination, and paid a low yield compared to those paid by money market instruments. As a result—to the despair of banks and thrifts—money funds continued to grow by outsided leaps and bounds.

Passage in 1980 of the Depository Institutions Deregulation and Monetary Control Act was supposed to bring about over a long (6-year) transition period the complete deregulation of rates paid by banks and thrifts. The most telling remark about the long run ever made was that by Lord Keynes: "In the long run we are all dead."

Events moved at a pace that made it impossible for banks, thrifts, and regulators to twiddle around for 6 years dickering about new accounts and tinkering with the terms of old ones. With the passage in September 1982 of the Garn-St. Germain bill, the banks and thrifts got (see Chapter 6) something close to rate deregulation in one fell swoop. This bill stated that banks and thrifts were to be immediately empowered to offer accounts on terms truly competitive with money funds.

After several months of debate, the Depository Institutions Deregulation Committee (DIDC) finally agreed to permit banks and thrifts to offer *money market deposit accounts* with a minimum balance of $2,500 and with provision for six transactions (three by check) per month. On these new accounts, depository institutions could pay any rate they choose. (Table 20–3). Then in January 1983 the DIDC shocked banks and thrifts by permitting them to offer *super NOW accounts:* $2,500-minimum-balance accounts with unlimited checking privileges. On such NOW accounts, depository institutions were permitted to pay any rate they choose—and also to impose any service changes they choose.

The new accounts that banks and thrifts may now offer do not give even individuals the flexibility that a money fund does. In particular an individual can run the balance in his money fund account practically down to zero and still get the full rate paid by the fund, whereas the rate paid on an account at a depository institution drops to the passbook rate if the balance in the account falls below $2,500.

The one and only big attraction, especially to small, unsophisticated investors, that banks and thrifts can offer and money funds cannot is federal insurance on deposits up to $100,000. Banks and thrifts hoped that this advantage would enable them to—in the words of one bank ad—"put money funds out to pasture." To ensure that depositors took note of the new bank and thrift accounts and that they transferred money out of money funds into these accounts, banks and thrifts offered eye-

TABLE 20–3
The new bank and thrift accounts

	Money market deposit account	Super NOW account
Interest rate ceiling	None	None
Minimum balance	$2,500	$2,500
Transactions per month	Six (only three by check)	Unlimited
Maximum length of rate guarantee	One month	One month
Dollar limit on transactions	Set by institution	Set by institution
Interest paid below $2,500	Passbook rate	Passbook rate
Eligibility	All depositors	Individuals only
Limitations on frequency of withdrawal (automatic teller machine, messenger or in person)	None	None
Restrictions on sweep arrangements	None from other accounts. Sweeps to other accounts limited to six.	None

Source: "Donoghue's Money Letter," January 1983, Holliston, Mass.

opening rates, ranging from 10% up to 25%, on funds deposited in a new money market deposit account. Fortunately, or unfortunately for banks and thrifts, the DIDC hamstrung their ability to engage in an all out rate war with money funds by limiting to one month the time for which banks and thrifts could guarantee the high rates they initially advertised on their new accounts.

Just how much money banks and thrifts will be able to bid back from money funds remains to be seen. By combining high rates, liquidity, and federal insurance all into one package, they have managed to convince a lot of holders of lower-rate bank and thrift accounts to switch to the new higher-rate accounts; this did nothing but raise the cost of money to banks and thrifts. About 40% of all money held in money fund accounts is held in accounts by brokers' clients, who will find little value in the new instrument. Another 40% is invested by institutions to whom money market deposit accounts will be unattractive and to whom super NOW accounts will be unavailable. That leaves only 10% of the money in money funds under the control of small investors; it is this money that will really be up for grabs by banks and thrifts.

In the weeks immediately succeeding introduction in mid-December 1982 of money market deposit accounts, money funds lost $4 to $5 billion a week in deposits. No one knew how much of this drop in money fund deposits was due to the transfer of money out of money funds into the new bank and thrift accounts, to a fall off in the rates money funds were paying, to a simultaneous boom in the stock market, or to the paying by depositors of year-end expenses and tax bills.

CMA quacks like a duck

While banks and thrifts were developing new accounts to compete with money funds, money funds, for their part, were not standing still. They were developing innovative new products of their own. Merrill Lynch has long offered customers both its highly successful, general purpose Ready Asset Trust (RAT) Fund and various other more specialized money funds.

Most brokers offer their clients an in-house money fund or some other money fund in which clients may park investment proceeds, funds temporarily withdrawn from the market, or new funds awaiting investment in stocks and bonds. Merrill came up with the brilliant idea that, if some fancy bells and whistles were added by a broker, such an account would generate a big number of large, new accounts. The name Merrill gave to its new account, introduced in 1979, was *Cash Management Account* (*CMA*); the bells and whistles on this account, which requires a minimum deposit of $20,000 in cash or securities, are (1) a CMA checking account (with checks cleared through Bank One of Georgia) that pays interest at money market rates, (2) a weekly sweep of monies coming from a client's brokerage account into his CMA account, (3) and a free Visa card with a line of credit equal to the full amount by which any securities the client has deposited with Merrill could be margined. In lending to customers using stocks and other securities as collateral, Merrill is doing nothing banks have not and could not have done for years. Banks just never thought of making the procedure of borrowing against such collateral so easy and automatic. In November 1982, Merrill's CMA account ranked as the second largest money fund with $15.9 billion in assets. It was surpassed in size only by Merrill's Ready Assets Trust Fund (Table 20-1).

The phenomenal success of Merrill's CMA account has led Shearson and other brokers to seek to imitate it. None has done so with Merrill's panache and success.

In getting CMA off the ground, Merrill had to figure out how to sidestep the SEC, the Fed, and other regulators; it did this by structuring its CMA account so that, in operating it, Merrill technically did nothing incorrect on the turf where it was regulated and it took no step on the turf (banking) where it was unauthorized to tread.

State regulators raised more fuss than federal regulators over the new CMA account. John Olin, Oregon's superintendent of banks, observed that CMA looked like a duck, walked like a duck, and quacked like a duck, and that, since his job was to regulate ducks, he was going to make rules for this new one.

The duck quacks back

While Merrill was seeking with considerable success to quack like a duck, banks were making some very innovative—for them—steps to quack like Merrill and other brokers. Citibank's Walter Wriston ruefully said at a meeting of bankers several years ago that his dream bank already existed: "Don Regan runs it and it's called Merrill Lynch, Pierce, Fenner & Smith."

To compete with wide-service, one-stop-shopping brokers, banks have in recent years attempted to offer brokerage service on the limited terms regulators permit. In this direction the bank that has gone the farthest is Citibank; it offers an Asset Network Account with features quite similar to those of Merrill's CMA account.

If the current trend continues of brokers trying to offer banking services and of banks trying to offer brokerage services, soon the big league hunters of money will all have such similar quacks, walks, and looks that regulators will be hard put to distinguish banks from nonbank financial institutions.[2]

An interesting question that may arise several years down the road is who is to regulate SUPER QUACK: banking authorities, the SEC, or who? The SEC has already shown in negotiating with the CFTC that it knows how to defend its own turf and to wrestle for itself more turf.[3]

Tax-exempt money funds

There are general purpose money funds for individuals and money funds for institutions only that invest in a wide range of good quality money market paper, and there are funds, both for individuals and for institutions only, that restrict their investments to governments or government-guaranteed paper. Like a deli that sells sandwiches, the money fund industry has funds that meet the needs and tastes of just about every investor.

The one exception, until 1980, was the investor who wanted tax-exempt income. By 1980 rates were so high that the idea of offering a tax-exempt money fund that would limit its investments to short-term, top-

---

[2] For a complete description of the CMA account and of the response of Citi and other institutions to it, see "Merrill Lynch Quacks Like a Bank," *Fortune,* October 20, 1980, pp. 134–40, and "Rival Managers for Your Money," *Fortune,* January 24, 1983, pp. 107–10.

[3] See pp. 473–75.

quality muni paper seemed extremely appealing. The hitch, however, was that there was little such paper around. To rephrase that great economist, Say: demand creates its own supply. Every anxious to seize any opportunity to raise funds more cheaply, municipals issuers, with help from some creative dealers, quickly invented the 7-day demand note, a new muni security especially designed for sale to tax-exempt money funds.[4] At the same time, municipal borrowers, as noted in Chapter 19, also began to sell municipal commercial paper for the first time.[5]

Thanks to these innovations, the tax-exempt money funds were able to raise their assets from zero in 1980 to nearly $13 billion in late 1982 (Figure 20–2). These funds appear immune to competition from bank

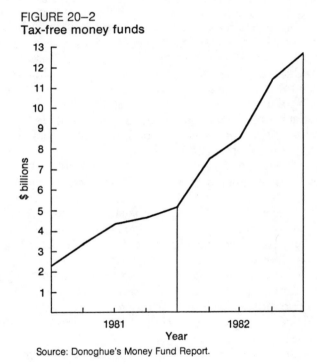

FIGURE 20–2
Tax-free money funds

Source: Donoghue's Money Fund Report.

and thrifts since they offer the investor income exempt from federal taxation, something that the DIDC has not yet managed to figure how bank and thrifts can do.

---

[4] See pp. 651–52.
[5] See pp. 629–30.

USEFULNESS TO THE PORTFOLIO MANAGER

Although money market funds were initially designed to offer individual investors a way to invest indirectly in money market securities, they can also be extremely useful to a corporation or other institution running a small short-term portfolio because the small portfolio manager labors under several disadvantages.

First, since minimum denominations are high in many sectors of the money market (the marketability of a negotiable CD suffers if its face value is less than $1 million), it is difficult for a person managing $10 million or less to diversify adequately; he has only limited ability to reduce credit risk by holding a mix of names and to reduce market risk by investing in different types and maturities of instruments.

Also, the net yield earned on a small portfolio is reduced much more by transactions costs than is the net yield earned on a large portfolio. If a bank imposes a $25 fee on an overnight repo, that fee will, on a $250,000 repo, reduce a gross yield of 8% to 4.35%. Moreover, if the portfolio manager must, in addition, pay a fee to wire his money into and out of the borrowing bank, his net yield will be still lower.

Another problem for the small portfolio manager is that he will inevitably end up buying and selling securities at rates that are less favorable than those big investors can obtain by buying in round-lot amounts from dealers. The problem is particularly acute for the portfolio manager who directs his investments to regional banks rather than to the national money market. An old example of a game still played is an Ohio bank that, at a time when top Chicago banks were paying 4.6% for 1-month CD money, was offering local corporations 4% for 1-month money and 4.2% if they ran their money through a Euro time deposit in the Caribbean.

Still another problem with a small portfolio is that it typically suffers from unprofessional management. The reason is that the gains to be had from managing a small portfolio—for example, by following the market and making the sort of maturity choices described in Chapter 10—are so small in absolute terms that hiring a skilled portfolio manager would not be cost justified.

Because it is difficult to manage small short-term balances effectively, it would make sense for many institutions holding money of this sort to invest it in an institutions-only money fund instead of investing it directly in money market instruments.

The money fund charges for its expenses, which typically amount to ½ of 1%, plus a management fee that runs another 50 basis points or so. These charges, however, are likely to be largely or fully offset by the fact that the fund, because it is professionally managing a big pool of short-term funds, can earn a significantly higher *gross* return than can the small portfolio manager.

There are other advantages to be gleaned by an institution that uses a money fund. Because history suggests that outflows of money from such a fund will be largely offset by inflows, a money fund can extend further out on the yield curve with less risk than a small portfolio manager could. As a result, a corporation investing in a money fund may be able to get a 90-day or longer rate on 30-day, 15-day, or even overnight money, with no market risk. This aspect of a money fund is particularly important to a corporation that has difficulty predicting cash flows that, if it did not invest in a money fund, would consequently feel constrained to roll overnight repo or to invest in very short-dated commercial paper to minimize market risk.

An institution investing in a money fund may also find that its balances with the fund can be used in part as an interest-bearing substitute for checking account balances it formerly maintained. Most money funds will permit investors to write large checks directly against a zero-balance checking account maintained at a bank associated with the fund. An institution that writes checks against a money fund saves an amount equal to the charges the bank would have imposed for clearing these checks. It also continues automatically to earn interest on its balance with the fund until the checks it has written clear, which often takes several days. Taking advantage of float can significantly increase the yield earned on balances invested short term in a money fund. This is particularly true if the money withdrawn from the fund by writing checks is wired into the fund, so that float operates on only one end of the transaction, the one that increases yield to the investor. Still another advantage of writing checks against a money fund is that a firm which does so need not track daily when these checks clear as it would have to if it wrote checks against a bank account that it was attempting to keep at the minimum level its bank required to compensate for services provided.

Low institutional usage

Despite the fact that a firm with small short-term balances to manage could often do better using a money fund that invests directly in money market instruments, business usage of money funds is still small. There are several reasons. First, many corporations think of mutual funds as a vehicle for individuals who can't invest efficiently, which supposedly a corporate treasurer can do. Second, there is the ego problem. The person who is in the best position to perceive the benefits of switching to a money fund is the portfolio manager, who, if he advises such a switch, will eliminate part or all of his own job. Finally, there is the familiar friend, unmeasured opportunity cost. The typical small firm doesn't track the return it earns on its portfolio and then ask: What cost if any did we incur in terms of foregone earnings by doing it ourselves instead of using a money fund?

Perhaps one way to drive home the point of how many more firms and other institutions should be using a money fund rather than investing on their own is to quote a portfolio manager who has tracked his own costs: "If you want to run any money in-house, it is going to cost you $100 to $125,000 just to play the game; that is what it costs you to see the cards. Obviously you have a lot of leverage on that. The same person who can do $10 million can do multiples of that at no additional fixed cost." Assuming that a good portfolio manager can add 100 basis points of yield, which is the amount a money fund takes off in fees, in-house management will not begin to pay unless an institution has $12.5 million to manage. That sum sounds like a lot, but it is far from enough to make active trading of the portfolio worthwhile. To make real money trading, a portfolio manager must deal in $5 million blocks. This means that he needs to control at least $100 million of funds if he is going to be conservative and not put more than 5% of his assets in one name.

Institutions investing money for many

For many institutions, who do or should consider using money funds, convenience and cost savings are important considerations. In the early 1970s, many banks set up *short-term investment funds* (*STIFS*) in their trust departments to invest in a pool cash held short-term for one reason or another in accounts they managed. Such banks often found that they could not afford the software and hardware to do the necessary accounting, to track the earnings on and the money flows into and out of separate accounts. Also, they could not recoup these costs with a fee because they were already charging an overall fee for discretionary management of the funds they held in trust.

To get around this problem (prior to 1977 when W. T. Grant got into trouble), many turned to master notes. As noted in Chapter 18, these provide a stable source of funds to note issuers and provide at no cost to the lender, bank trust departments and others, subaccounting that precisely fits their needs.

The withdrawal of W. T. Grant from the master note program and its later bankruptcy focused attention on the fact that trust account funds invested in a master note—no matter how good the name of the issuer—were exposed to undue credit risk because of the resulting concentration on a single or on several names. Money funds provide trust departments, pension funds, and others running funds for many with the convenience of subaccounting *plus* the comfort of knowing that they are satisfying the prudent man rule for diversification of risk. Currently money funds are replacing many master notes in bank trust departments; they are also being used more widely by others who have similar investment needs.

Money fund yields: A yardstick

In Chapter 10 we stressed the importance of consistently monitoring the yield earned on a portfolio and of comparing that yield with some yardstick. For a small portfolio manager, the natural yardstick is the yield offered by money funds because such funds have the same investment objectives he has: preservation of capital, high liquidity, and high return, in that order.

To make the yield comparison, the portfolio manager should first determine what *net* yield he is earning on the funds he invests, when all transactions costs and all internal costs—part or all of his own salary, clerical costs, and an appropriate amount of overhead—are subtracted from the gross dollars earned on the portfolio. This net yield should then be compared with the net yield offered by money funds.

Also, the opportunity for a firm with an account at a money fund to use that account as a partial substitute for holding demand deposit balances should be taken into account. Money funds offer the business firm a chance to get paid for *having* a checking account instead of *paying* for it; and this opportunity to increase return should be taken into account in the profitability calculation.

The firm that finds it can do better by investing in a money fund than by investing on its own should adopt the philosophy: If you can't beat them, join them.

IMPORTANCE IN THE MARKET

Money funds have grown rapidly from zero outstandings in 1974 to a current level of well in excess of $200 billion. As noted in earlier chapters, money funds have become the dominant buyer of short paper in the bill market, the CD market, and other areas of the money market. The development of new, tax-exempt money funds has also led to the creation of new types of short-term, tax-exempt paper.

What long-run impact the introduction of new money market deposit accounts at banks will have on the growth of money funds remains to be seen. For reasons noted, it is primarily the small individual investor to whom federal deposit insurance is likely to have most appeal. However, such individuals have for years had the option—little used—of getting an implied federal guarantee on money fund deposits by investing in any one of a number of funds that limits its investments to governments or to governments and government-guaranteed paper.

Glossary

Common money market and bond market terms

Accretion (of a discount):   In portfolio accounting, a straight-line accumulation of capital gains on discount bonds in anticipation of receipt of par at maturity.

Accrued interest: Interest due from issue or from the last coupon date to the present on an interest-bearing security. The buyer of the security pays the quoted dollar price plus accrued interest.

Active: A market in which there is much trading.

Actuals: The cash commodity as opposed to the futures contract.

ACUs: *Asian currency units.* An expression for Eurodollars deposited in Far East centers.

Add-on rate: A specific rate of interest to be paid. Stands in contrast to the rate on a discount security, such as a Treasury bill, that pays *no* interest.

Aftertax real rate of return: Money aftertax rate of return minus the inflation rate.

Agencies: Federal agency securities. See also **Agency bank.**

Agency bank: A form of organization commonly used by foreign banks to enter the U.S. market. An agency bank cannot accept deposits or extend loans in its own name; it acts as an agent for the parent bank. Term often used on the street to refer both to foreign bank agencies and branches.

Agent: A firm that executes orders for or otherwise acts on behalf of another (the principal) and is subject to its control and authority. The agent may receive a fee or commission.

691

All-in cost: Total costs, explicit and other. Example: The all-in cost to a bank of CD money is the explicit rate of interest it pays on that deposit *plus* the FDIC premium it must pay on the deposit *plus* the hidden cost it incurs because it must hold some portion of that deposit in a non-interest-bearing reserve account at the Fed.

All or none (AOM): Requirement that none of an order be executed unless all of it can be executed at the specified price.

Amortize: In portfolio accounting, periodic charges made against interest income on premium bonds in anticipation of receipt of the call price at call or of par value at maturity.

Arbitrage: Strictly defined, buying something where it is cheap and selling it where it is dear; e.g., a bank buys 3-month CD money in the U.S. market and sells 3-month money at a higher rate in the Eurodollar market. In the money market, often refers: (1) to a situation in which a trader buys one security and sells a similar security in the expectation that the spread in yields between the two instruments will narrow or widen to his profit, (2) to a swap between two similar issues based on an anticipated change in yield spreads, and (3) to situations where a higher return (or lower cost) can be achieved in the money market for one currency by utilizing another currency and swapping it on a fully hedged basis through the foreign exchange market.

Asked: The price at which securities are offered.

Away: A trade, quote, or market that does not originate with the dealer in question, e.g., "the bid is 98–10 away (from me)."

Back contracts: Futures contracts farthest from expiration.

Back up: (1) When yields rise and prices fall, the market is said to back up. (2) When an investor swaps out of one security into another of shorter current maturity (e.g., out of a 2-year note into an 18-month note), he is said to back up.

Back discount rate: Yield basis on which short-term, non-interest-bearing money market securities are quoted. A rate quoted on a discount basis understands bond equivalent yield. That must be calculated when comparing return against coupon securities.

Bank line: Line of credit granted by a bank to a customer.

Bank wire: A computer message system linking major banks. It is used not for effecting payments, but as a mechanism to advise the receiving bank of some action that has occurred, e.g., the payment by a customer of funds into that bank's account.

Bankers' acceptance (BA): A draft or bill of exchange accepted by a bank or trust company. The accepting institution guarantees payment of the bill.

BANs: Bond anticipation notes are issued by states and municipalities to obtain interim financing for projects that will eventually be funded long term through the sale of a bond issue.

Basis: (1) Number of days in the coupon period. (2) In *commodities* jargon, basis is the spread between a futures price and some other price. A money market participant would talk about *spread* rather than basis.

Basis point: One one hundredth of 1%.

Basis price: Price expressed in terms of yield to maturity or annual rate of return.

Bear market: A declining market or a period of pessimism when declines in the market are anticipated. (A way to remember: "Bear down.")

Bearer security: A security the owner of which is not registered on the books of the issuer. A bearer security is payable to the holder.

Best-efforts basis: Securities dealers do not underwrite a new issue, but sell it on the basis of what can be sold. In the money market, this usually refers to a firm order to buy or sell a given amount of securities or currency at the best price that can be found over a given period of time; it can also refer to a flexible amount (up to a limit) at a given rate.

Bid: The price offered for securities.

Blind broker: A broker who acts as principal and does not give up names to either side of a brokered trade. Blind brokering of securities is common, whereas blind brokering of Fed funds and Euro time deposits would be infeasible.

Block: A large amount of securities, normally much more than what constitutes a round lot in the market in question.

Book: A banker, especially a Eurobanker, will refer to his bank's assets and liabilities as its "book." If the average maturity of the liabilities is less than that of the assets, the bank is running a **short** and **open** book.

Book-entry securities: The Treasury and federal agencies are moving to a book-entry system in which securities are not represented by engraved pieces of paper but are maintained in computerized records at the Fed in the names of member banks, which, in turn, keep records of the securities they own as well as those they are holding for customers. In the case of other securities for which there is a book-entry system, engraved securities do exist somewhere in quite a few cases. These securities do not move from holder to holder but are usually kept in a central clearinghouse or by another agent.

Book value: The value at which a debt security is shown on the holder's balance sheet. Book value is often acquisition cost ± amortization/accretion, which may differ markedly from market value. It can be further defined as "tax book," "accreted book," or "amortized book" value.

Bridge financing: Interim financing of one sort or another.

British clearers: The large clearing banks that dominate deposit taking and short-term lending in the domestic sterling market in Great Britain.

Broken date: See **Cock date.**

Broker: A broker brings buyers and sellers together for a commission paid by the initiator of the transaction or by both sides; he does not position. In the money market, brokers are active in markets in which banks buy and sell money and in interdealer markets.

Bull market: A period of optimism when increases in market prices are anticipated. (A way to remember: "Bull ahead.")

Bullet loan: A bank term loan that calls for no amortization. The term is commonly used in the Euromarket.

Buy a spread: Buy a near futures contract and sell a far one.

Buy-back: Another term for a repurchase agreement.

Calendar: List of new bond issues scheduled to come to market soon.

Call: An option that gives the holder the right to buy the underlying security at a specified price during a fixed time period.

Call money: Interest-bearing bank deposits that can be withdrawn on 24-hours notice. Many Eurodeposits take the form of call money.

Callable bond: A bond that the issuer has the right to redeem prior to maturity by paying some specified call price.

Canadian agencies: Agency banks established by Canadian banks in the United States.

Carry: The interest cost of financing securities held. (See also **Negative** and **Positive carry.**)

Cash commodity or security: The actual commodity or security as opposed to futures contracts for it.

Cash management bill: Very short-maturity bills that the Treasury occasionally sells because its cash balances are down and it needs money for a few days.

Cash market: Traditionally, this term has been used to denote the market in which commodities were traded, for immediate delivery, against cash. Since the inception of futures markets for T bills and other debt securities, a distinction has been made between the cash markets in which these securities trade for immediate delivery and the futures markets in which they trade for future delivery.

Cash price: Price quotation in the cash market.

Cash settlement: In the money market, a transaction is said to be made for cash settlement if the securities purchased are delivered against payment in Fed funds on the same day the trade is made.

CBOE: Chicago Board Options Exchange.

CBT: Chicago Board of Trade, a futures exchange.

Certificate of deposit (CD):   A time deposit with a specific maturity evidenced by a certificate. Large-denomination CDs are typically negotiable.

CHIPS: The New York Clearing House's computerized Clearing House Interbank Payments System. Most Euro transactions are cleared and settled through CHIPS rather than over the Fed wire.

Circle: Underwriters, actual or potential as the case may be, often seek out and "circle" retail interest in a new issue before final pricing. The customer circled has basically made a commitment to purchase the note or bond *or* to purchase it if it comes at an agreed-upon price. In the latter case, if the price is other than that stipulated, the customer supposedly has first offer at the actual price.

Clear: A trade carried out by the seller delivering securities and the buyer delivering funds in proper form. A trade that does not clear is said to fail.

Cock date: In the Euromarket, an off-the-run period; e.g., 28 days. Also referred to as a broken date. A cock date contrasts with a fixed date, which is 30, 60, 90, etc., days hence.

Commercial paper: An unsecured promissory note with a fixed maturity of no more than 270 days. Commercial paper is normally sold at a discount from face value.

Committed facility: A legal commitment undertaken by a bank to lend to a customer.

Competitive bid: (1) Bid tendered in a Treasury action for a specific amount of securities at a specific yield or price. (2) Issuers, municipal and public utilities, often sell new issues by asking for competitive bids from one or more syndicates.

Confirmation: A memorandum to the other side of a trade describing all relevant data.

Consortium banks: A merchant banking subsidiary set up by several banks that may or may not be of the same nationality. Consortium banks are common in the Euromarket and are active in loan syndication.

Convertible bond: A bond containing a provision that permits conversion to the issuer's common stock at some fixed exchange ratio.

Corporate bond equivalent: See **Equivalent bond yield.**

Corporate taxable equivalent: Rate of return required on a par bond to produce the same aftertax yield to maturity that the premium or discount bond quoted would.

Country risk: See **Sovereign risk.**

Coupon: (1) The annual rate of interest on the bond's face value that a bond's issuer promises to pay the bondholder. (2) A certificate attached to a bond evidencing interest due on a payment date.

Cover: Eliminating a short position by buying the securities shorted.

Covered call write: Selling calls against securities owned by the call seller.

Covered interest arbitrage: Investing dollars in an instrument denominated in a foreign currency and hedging the resulting foreign exchange risk by selling the proceeds of the investment forward for dollars.

Credit risk: The risk that an issuer of debt securities or a borrower may default on his obligations, or that payment may not be made on sale of a negotiable instrument. (See **Overnight delivery risk.**)

Cross hedge: Hedging a risk in a cash market security by buying or selling a futures contract for a similar but not identical instrument.

CRTs: Abbreviation for the cathode-ray tubes used to display market quotes.

Current coupon: A bond selling at or close to par; that is, a bond with a coupon close to the yield currently offered on new bonds of similar maturity and credit risk.

Current issue: In Treasury bills and notes, the most recently auctioned issue. Trading is more active in current issues than in off-the-run issues.

Current maturity: Current time to maturity on an outstanding note, bond, or other money market instrument; for example, a 5-year note 1 year after issue has a current maturity of 4 years.

Current yield: Coupon payments on a security as a percentage of the security's market price. In many instances the price should be *gross* of accrued interest, particularly on instruments where no coupon is left to be paid until maturity.

Cushion bonds: High-coupon bonds that sell at only a moderate premium because they are callable at a price below that at which a comparable noncallable bond would sell. Cushion bonds offer considerable downside protection in a falling market.

Daylight overdraft: Being overdrawn (OD) in a deposit account during some of a day's business hours. Foreign banks typically run big daylight overdrafts with their U.S. correspondent bank. A daylight overdraft exposes the institution that extends it to a credit risk.

Day trading: Intraday trading in securities for profit as opposed to investing for profit.

Dealer: A dealer, as opposed to a broker, acts as a principal in all transactions, buying and selling for his own account.

Dealer loan: Overnight, collateralized loan made to a dealer financing his position by borrowing from a money market bank.

Debenture: A bond secured only by the general credit of the issuer.

Debt leverage: The amplification in the return earned on equity funds when an investment is financed partly with borrowed money.

Debt securities: IOUs created through loan-type transactions—commercial paper, bank CDs, bills, bonds, and other instruments.

Default: Failure to make timely payment of interest or principal on a debt security or to otherwise comply with the provisions of a bond indenture.

Delivery month: A month in which a futures contract expires and delivery may be taken or made.

Demand line of credit: A bank line of credit that enables a customer to borrow on a daily or an on-demand basis.

Direct paper: Commercial paper sold directly by the issuer to investors.

Direct placement: Selling a new issue not by offering it for sale publicly, but by placing it with one or several institutional investors.

Discount basis: See **Bank discount rate.**

Discount bond: A bond selling below par.

Discount house: British institution that uses call and overnight money obtained from banks to invest in and trade money market instruments.

Discount paper: See **Discount securities.**

Discount rate: The rate of interest charged by the Fed to member banks that borrow at the discount window. The discount rate is an add-on rate.

Discount securities: Non-interest-bearing money market instruments that are issued at a discount and redeemed at maturity for full face value; e.g., U.S. Treasury bills.

Discount window: Facility provided by the Fed enabling member banks to borrow reserves against collateral in the form of governments or other acceptable paper.

Disintermediation: The investing of funds that would normally have been placed with a bank or other financial intermediary directly into debt securities issued by ultimate borrowers; e.g., into bills or bonds.

Distributed: After a Treasury auction, there will be many new issues in dealers' hands. As those securities are sold to retail, the issue is said to be distributed.

Diversification: Dividing investment funds among a variety of securities offering independent returns.

DM: Deutsche (German) marks.

Documented discount notes: Commercial paper backed by normal bank lines plus a letter of credit from a bank stating that it will pay off the paper at maturity if the borrower does not. Such paper is also referred to as **LOC** (letter of credit) **paper.**

Dollar bonds: Municipal revenue bonds for which quotes are given in dollar prices. Not to be confused with "U.S. Dollar" bonds, a common term of reference in the Euro bond market.

Dollar price of a bond: Percentage of face value at which a bond is quoted.

Don't know (DK, DKed): "Don't know the trade"—a street expression used whenever one party lacks knowledge of a trade or receives conflicting instructions from the other party (for example, with respect to payment).

Due bill: An instrument evidencing the obligation of a seller to delivery securities sold to the buyer. Occasionally used in the bill market.

Dutch auction: Auction in which the lowest price necessary to sell the entire offering becomes the price at which all securities offered are sold. This technique has been used in Treasury auctions.

Edge Act corporation: A subsidiary of a U.S. bank set up to carry out international banking business. Most such "subs" are located within the United States.

Either/or facility: An agreement permitting a bank customer to borrow either domestic dollars from the bank's head office or Eurodollars from one of its foreign branches.

Either-way market: In the interbank Eurodollar deposit market, an either-way market is one in which the bid and asked rates are identical.

Elbow: The elbow in the yield curve is the maturity area considered to provide the most attractive short-term investment; e.g., the maturity range in which to initiate a ride along the yield curve.

Eligible bankers' acceptances: In the BA market an acceptance may be referred to as eligible because it is acceptable by the Fed as collateral at the discount window and/or because the accepting bank can sell it without incurring a reserve requirement.

Equivalent bond yield: Annual yield on a short-term, non–interest-bearing security calculated so as to be comparable to yields quoted on coupon securities.

Equivalent taxable yield: The yield on a taxable security that would leave the investor with the same aftertax return he would earn by holding a tax-exempt municipal; for example, for an investor taxed at a 50 percent marginal rate, equivalent taxable yield on a muni note issued at 3 percent would be 6 percent.

Euro bonds: Bonds issued in Europe outside the confines of any national capital market. A Euro bond may or may not be denominated in the currency of the issuer.

Euro CDs: CDs issued by a U.S. bank branch or foreign bank located outside the United States. Almost all Euro CDs are issued in London.

Euro Feds: Eurodollars transmitted over the Fed wire instead of through CHIPS. Normally Euro Feds move from a foreign branch of one U.S. bank to foreign branch of another U.S. bank; e.g., from Citi Nassau to Morgan London. Foreign banks use CHIPS, not the Fed wire, to pay and receive Euros because they may not run daylight overdrafts at the Fed.

Euro lines: Lines of credit granted by banks (foreign or foreign branches of U.S. banks) for Eurocurrencies.

Eurocurrency deposits: Deposits made in a bank or bank branch that is not located in the country in whose currency the deposit is denominated. Dollars deposited in a London bank are Eurodollars; German marks deposited there are Euromarks.

Eurodollars: U.S. dollars deposited in a U.S. bank branch or a foreign bank located outside the United States.

Excess reserves: Balances held by a bank at the Fed in excess of those required.

Exchange rate: The price at which one currency trades for another.

Exempt securities: Instruments exempt from the registration requirements of the Securities Act of 1933 or the margin requirements of the Securities and Exchange Act of 1934. Such securities include governments, agencies, municipal securities, commercial paper, and private placements.

Exercise: To invoke the right to buy or sell granted under terms of a listed options contract.

Exercise price: The price at which an option holder may buy or sell the underlying security. Also called the striking price.

Extension swap: Extending maturity through a swap, e.g., selling a 2-year note and buying one with a slightly longer current maturity.

Fail: A trade is said to fail if on settlement date either the seller fails to deliver securities in proper form or the buyer fails to deliver funds in proper form.

Fed funds: See **Federal funds.**

Fed wire: A computer system linking member banks to the Fed, used for making interbank payments of Fed funds and for making deliveries of and payments for Treasury and agency securities.

Federal credit agencies: Agencies of the federal government set up to supply credit to various classes of institutions and individuals; e.g., S&Ls, small business firms, students, farmers, farm cooperatives, and exporters.

Federal Deposit Insurance Corporation (FDIC): A federal institution that insures bank deposits, currently up to $100,000 per deposit.

Federal Financing Bank: A federal institution that lends to a wide array of federal credit agencies funds it obtains by borrowing from the U.S. Treasury.

Federal funds: (1) Non-interest-bearing deposits held by member banks at the Federal Reserve. (2) Used to denote "immediately available" funds in the clearing sense.

Federal funds rate: The rate of interest at which Fed funds are traded. This rate is currently pegged by the Federal Reserve through open-market operations.

Federal Home Loan Banks (FHLB): The institutions that regulate and lend to savings and loan associations. The Federal Home Loan Banks play a role analogous to that played by the Federal Reserve Banks vis-à-vis member commercial banks.

Figuring the tail: Calculating the yield at which a future money market instrument (one available some period hence) is purchased when that future security is created by buying an existing instrument and financing the initial portion of life with a term RP.

Firm: Refers to an order to buy or sell that can be executed without confirmation for some fixed period.

Fixed dates: In the Euromarket the standard periods for which Euros are traded (one month out to a year) are referred to as the fixed dates.

Fixed-dollar security: A nonnegotiable debt security that can be redeemed at some fixed price or according to some schedule of fixed values (e.g., bank deposits and government savings bonds).

Fixed-rate loan: A loan on which the rate paid by the borrower is fixed for the life of the loan.

Flat trades: (1) A bond in default trades flat; that is, the price quoted covers both principal and unpaid, accrued interest. (2) Any security that trades without accrued interest or at a price that includes accrued interest is said to trade flat.

Flex repo: A repo for a variable (usually declining) sum done for some period, often several years.

Float: The difference between the credits given by the Fed to banks' reserve accounts on checks being cleared through the Fed and the debits made to banks' reserve accounts on the same checks. Float is always positive, because in the clearing of a check, the credit sometimes precedes the debit. Float adds to the money supply.

Floating-rate note: A note that pays an interest rate tied to current money market rates. The holder may have the right to demand redemption at par on specified dates.

Floating supply: The amount of securities believed to be available for immediate purchase, that is, in the hands of dealers and investors wanting to sell.

Flower bonds: Government bonds that are acceptable at par in payment of federal estate taxes when owned by the decedent at the time of death.

Footings: A British expression for the bottom line of an institution's balance sheet; total assets equal total liabilities plus net worth.

Foreign bond: A bond issued by a nondomestic borrower in the domestic capital market.

Foreign exchange rate: The price at which one currency trades for another.

Foreign exchange risk: The risk that a long or short position in a foreign currency might, due to an adverse movement in the relevant exchange rate, have to be closed out at a loss. The long or short position may arise out of a financial or commercial transaction.

Forward Fed funds: Fed funds traded for future delivery.

Forward forward contract: In Eurocurrencies, a contract under which a deposit of fixed maturity is agreed to at a fixed price for future delivery.

Forward market: A market in which participants agree to trade some commodity, security, or foreign exchange at a fixed price at some future date.

Forward rate: The rate at which forward transactions in some specific maturity are being made; e.g., the dollar price at which DM can be bought for delivery three months hence.

Free reserves: Excess reserves minus member bank borrowings at the Fed.

Full-coupon bond: A bond with a coupon equal to the going market rate and consequently selling at or near par.

Futures market: A market in which contracts for future delivery of a commodity or a security are bought and sold.

Gap: Mismatch between the maturities of a bank's assets and liabilities.

Gapping: Mismatching the maturities of a bank's assets and liabilities, usually by borrowing short and lending long.

General obligation bonds: Municipal securities secured by the issuer's pledge of its full faith, credit, and taxing power.

Give up: The loss in yield that occurs when a block of bonds is swapped for another block of lower-coupon bonds. Can also be referred to as "aftertax give up" when the implications of the profit (loss) on taxes are considered.

Glass-Steagall Act: A 1933 act in which Congress forbade commercial banks to own, underwrite, or deal in corporate stock and corporate bonds.

Go-around: When the Fed offers to buy securities, to sell securities, to do repo, or to do reverses, it solicits competitive bids or offers, as the case may be, from all primary dealers. This procedure is known as a go-around.

Good delivery: A delivery in which everything—endorsement, any necessary attached legal papers, etc.—is in order.

Good funds: A market expression for immediately available money; i.e., Fed funds.

Good trader: A Treasury coupon issue that can readily be bought and sold in size. If a trader can short $10 or $20 million of an issue and sleep at night, that issue is said to be a good trader.

Governments: Negotiable U.S. Treasury securities.

Gross spread: The difference between the price that the issuer receives for its securities and the price that investors pay for them. This spread equals the selling concession plus the management and underwriting fees.

Haircut: Margin in an RP transaction; that is, the difference between the actual market value measured at the bid side of the market and the value used in an RP agreement.

Handle: The whole-dollar price of a bid or offer is referred to as the *handle*. For example, if a security is quoted 101-10 bid and 101-11 offered, 101 is the handle. Traders are assumed to know the handle, so a trader would quote that market to another by saying he was at 10-11. (The 10 and 11 refer to 32nds.)

Hedge: To reduce risk, (1) by taking a position in futures equal and opposite to an existing or anticipated cash position, or (2) by shorting a security similar to one in which a long position has been established.

Hit: A dealer who agrees to sell at the bid price quoted by another dealer is said to *hit* that bid.

IBFs (International Banking Facilities):   Shell branches that U.S. banks in a number of states may form at head office to do limited types of Eurobusiness.

IMM: International Monetary Market, a futures exchange.

In the box: This means that a dealer has a wire receipt for securities indicating that effective delivery on them has been made. This jargon is a holdover from the time when Treasuries took the form of physical securities and were stored in a rack.

Indenture of a bond: A legal statement spelling out the obligations of the bond issuer and the rights of the bondholder.

In-the-money option: An option selling at a price such that it has intrinsic value.

Interest rate exposure: Risk of gain or loss to which an institution is exposed due to possible changes in interest rate levels.

Investment banker: A firm that engages in the origination, underwriting, and distribution of new issues.

Joint account: An agreement between two or more firms to share risk and financing responsibility in purchasing or underwriting securities.

Junk bonds: High-risk bonds that have low credit ratings or are in default.

Leverage: See **Debt leverage.**

Leveraged lease: The lessor provides only a minor portion of the cost of the leased equipment, borrowing the rest from another lender.

LIBOR: The London Interbank Offered Rate on Eurodollar deposits traded between banks. There is a different LIBOR rate for each deposit maturity. Different banks may quote slightly different LIBOR rates because they use different reference banks.

LIFFE: London International Financial Futures Exchange.

Lifting a leg: Closing out one side of a long-short arbitrage before the other is closed.

Line of credit: An arrangement by which a bank agrees to lend to the line holder during some specified period any amount up to the full amount of the line.

Liquidity: A liquid asset is one that can be converted easily and rapidly into cash without a substantial loss of value. In the money market, a security is said to be liquid if the spread between bid and asked prices is narrow and reasonable size can be done at those quotes.

Liquidity diversification: Investing in a variety of maturities to reduce the price risk to which holding long bonds exposes the investor.

Liquidity risk: In banking, risk that monies needed to fund assets may not be available in sufficient quantities at some future date. Implies an imbalance in committed maturities of assets and liabilities.

Locked market: A market is said to be locked if the bid price equals the asked price. This can occur, for example, if the market is brokered and brokerage is paid by one side only, the initiator of the transaction.

Lockup CDs: CDs that are issued with the tacit understanding that the buyer will not trade the certificate. Quite often, the issuing bank will insist that it keep the certificate to ensure that the understanding is honored by the buyer.

Long: (1) Owning a debt security, stock, or other asset. (2) Owning more than one has contracted to deliver.

Long bonds: Bonds with a long current maturity.

Long coupons: (1) Bonds or notes with a long current maturity. (2) A bond on which one of the coupon periods, usually the first, is longer than the others or than standard.

Long hedge: *Purchase* of a *futures* contract to lock in the yield at which an anticipated cash inflow can be invested.

Make a market: A dealer is said to make a market when he quotes bid and offered prices at which he stands ready to buy and sell.

Margin: (1) In an RP or a reverse repurchase transaction, the amount by which the market value of the securities collateralizing the transaction exceeds the amount lent. (2) In futures markets, money buyers and seller must put up to assure performance on the contracts. (3) In options, similar meaning as in futures for sellers of put and call options.

Marginal tax rate: The tax rate that would have to be paid on any additional dollars of taxable income earned.

Market value: The price at which a security is trading and could presumably be purchased or sold.

Marketability: A negotiable security is said to have good marketability if there is an active secondary market in which it can easily be resold.

Match fund: A bank is said to match fund a loan or other asset when it does so by buying (taking) a deposit of the same maturity. The term is commonly used in the Euromarket.

Matched book: If the distribution of the maturities of a bank's liabilities equals that of its assets, it is said to be running a *matched book*. The term is commonly used in the Euromarket.

Merchant bank: A British term for a bank that specializes not in lending out its own funds, but in providing various financial services, such as accepting bills arising out of trade, underwriting new issues, and providing advice on acquisitions, mergers, foreign exchange, portfolio management, etc.

Mismatch: A mismatch between the interest rate maturities of a bank's assets and liabilities. See also **Gap** and **Unmatched book.**

Money market: The market in which short-term debt instruments (bills, commercial paper, bankers' acceptances, etc.) are issued and traded.

Money market (center) bank: A bank that is one of the nation's largest and consequently plays an active and important role in every sector of the money market.

Money Market Certificates (MMCs):   Six-month certificates of deposit with a minimum denomination of $10,000 on which banks and thrifts may pay a maximum rate tied to the rate at which the U.S. Treasury has most recently auctioned six-month bills.

Money market fund: Mutual fund that invests solely in money market instruments.

Money rate of return: Annual return as a percentage of asset value.

Money supply definitions used by the Fed in January 1983:
M-1:   Currency in circulation plus demand deposits plus other checkable deposits including NOW accounts.
M-2:   M-1 plus money market deposit accounts plus overnight RPs and money market funds and savings and small (less than $100,000) time deposits at all depository institutions plus overnight RPs at banks plus overnight Euros held by nonbank U.S. depositors in the Caribbean branches of U.S. banks plus balances at money funds (excluding institutions-only funds).
M-3:   M-2 plus large (over $100,000) time deposits at all depository institutions, term RPs at banks and S&Ls plus balances at institutions-only money funds.

L: M-3 plus other liquid assets such as term Eurodollars held by nonbank U.S. residents, bankers' acceptances, commercial paper, Treasury bills and other liquid governments, and U.S. savings bonds.

Mortgage bond: Bond secured by a lien on property, equipment, or other real assets.

Multicurrency clause: Such a clause on a Euro loan permits the borrower to switch from one currency to another on a rollover date.

Municipal (muni) notes: Short-term notes issued by municipalities in anticipation of tax receipts, proceeds from a bond issue, or other revenues.

Municipals: Securities issued by state and local governments and their agencies.

Naked option position: An unhedged sale of a put or call option.

Naked position: An unhedged long or short position.

Nearby contract: Futures contracts nearest to expiration.

Negative carry: The net cost incurred when the cost of carry exceeds the yield on the securities being financed.

Negotiable certificate of deposit: A large-denomination (generally $1 million) CD that can be sold but cannot be cashed in before maturity.

Negotiated sale: Situation in which the terms of an offering are determined by negotiation between the issuer and the underwriter rather than through competitive bidding by underwriting groups.

New-issues market: The market in which a new issue of securities is first sold to investors.

New money: In a Treasury refunding, the amount by which the par value of the securities offered exceeds that of those maturity.

NOB: Note-bonds spread in futures contracts.

Noncompetitive bid: In a Treasury auction, bidding for a specific amount of securities at the price, whatever it may turn out to be, equal to the average price of the accepted competitive bids.

Note: Coupon issues with a relatively short original maturity are often called *notes*. Muni notes, however, have maturities ranging from a month to a year and pay interest only at maturity. Treasury notes are coupon securities that have an original maturity of up to 10 years.

NOW (Negotiable order of withdrawal) accounts: These amount to checking accounts on which depository institutions (banks and thrifts) may pay a rate of interest subject to federal rate lids.

OCC: Options Clearing Corporation, the issuer of all listed options trading on national options exchanges.

Odd lot: Less than a round lot.

Off-the-run issue: In Treasuries and agencies, an issue that is not included in dealer or broker runs. With bills and notes, normally only current issues are quoted.

Offer: Price asked by a seller of securities.

One-man picture: The price quoted is said to be a one-man picture if both the bid and ask come from the same source.

One-sided (one-way) market: A market in which only one side, the bid or the asked, is quoted or firm.

Open book: See **Unmatched book.**

Open repo: A repo with no definite term. The agreement is made on a day-to-day basis and either the borrower or the lender may choose to terminate. The rate paid is higher than on overnight repo and is subject to adjustment if rates move.

Opportunity cost: The cost of pursuing one course of action measured in terms of the foregone return offered by the most attractive alternative.

Option: (1) **Call option:** A contract sold for a price that gives the holder the right to buy from the writer of the option, over a specified period, a specified amount of securities at a specified price. (2) **Put option:** A contract sold for a price that gives the holder the right to sell to the writer of the contract, over a specified period, specified amount of securities at a specified price.

Original maturity: Maturity at issue. For example, a 5-year note has an original maturity at issue of 5 years; 1 year later, it has a current maturity of 4 years.

Out-of-the-money option: An option selling at a price such that it has no intrinsic value.

Over-the-counter (OTC) market: Market created by dealer trading as opposed to the auction market prevailing on organized exchanges.

Overnight delivery risk: A risk brought about because differences in time zones between settlement centers require that payment or delivery on one side of a transaction be made without knowing until the next day whether funds have been received in account on the other side. Particularly apparent where delivery takes place in Europe for payment in dollars in New York.

Paper: Money market instruments, commercial paper, and other.

Paper gain (loss):   Unrealized capital gain (loss) on securities held in portfolio, based on a comparison of current market price and original cost.

Par: (1) Price of 100%. (2) The principal amount at which the issuer of a debt security contracts to redeem that security at maturity, *face value.*

Par bond: A bond selling at par.

Pass-through: A mortgage-backed security on which payment of interest and principal on the underlying mortgages are passed through to the security holder by an agent.

Paydown: In a Treasury refunding, the amount by which the par value of the securities maturing exceeds that of those sold.

Pay-up: (1) The loss of cash resulting from a swap into higher-price bonds. (2) The need (or willingness) of a bank or other borrower to pay a higher rate to get funds.

Pickup: The gain in yield that occurs when a block of bonds is swapped for another block of higher-coupon bonds.

Picture: The bid and asked prices quoted by a broker for a given security.

Placement: A bank depositing Eurodollars with (selling Eurodollars to) another bank is often said to be making a placement.

Plus: Dealers in governments normally quote bids and offers in 32nds. To quote a bid or offer in 64ths, they use pluses; for example, a dealer who bids 4+ is bidding the handle plus $\frac{1}{32}$ + $\frac{1}{64}$, which equals the handle plus $\frac{9}{64}$.

PNs: Project notes are issued by municipalities to finance federally sponsored programs in urban renewal and housing. They are guaranteed by the U.S. Department of Housing and Urban Development.

Point: (1) 100 basis points = 1%. (2) One percent of the face value of a note or bond. (3) In the foreign exchange market, the lowest level at which the currency is priced. Example: "One point" is the difference between sterling prices of $1.8080 and $1.8081.

Portfolio: Collection of securities held by an investor.

Position: (1) To go long or short in a security. (2) The amount of securities owned (long position) or owed (short position).

Positive carry: The net gain earned when the cost of carry is less than the yield on the securities being financed.

Premium: (1) The amount by which the price at which an issue is trading exceeds the issue's par value. (2) The amount that must be paid in excess of par to call or refund an issue before maturity. (3) In money market parlance, the fact that a particular bank's CDs trade at a rate higher than others of its class, or that a bank has to pay up to acquire funds.

Premium bond: Bond selling above par.

Prepayment: A payment made ahead of the scheduled payment date.

Presold issue: An issue that is sold out before the coupon announcement.

Price risk: The risk that a debt security's price may change due to a rise or fall in the going level of interest rates.

Prime rate: The rate at which banks lend to their best (prime) customers. The all-in cost of a bank loan to a prime credit equals the prime rate plus the cost of holding compensating balances.

Principal: (1) The face amount or par value of a debt security. (2) One who acts as a dealer buying and selling for his own account.

Private placement: An issue that is offered to a single or a few investors as opposed to being publicly offered. Private placements do not have to be registered with the SEC.

Prospectus: A detailed statement prepared by an issuer and filed with the SEC prior to the sale of a new issue. The prospectus gives detailed information on the issue and on the issuer's condition and prospects.

Put: An option that gives the holder the right to sell the underlying security at a specified price during a fixed time period.

RANs (Revenue anticipation notes): These are issued by states and municipalities to finance current expenditures in anticipation of the future receipt of nontax revenues.

Rate risk: In banking, the risk that profits may decline or losses occur because a rise in interest rates forces up the cost of funding fixed-rate loans or other fixed-rate assets.

Ratings: An evaluation given by Moody's, Standard & Poor's, Fitch, or other rating services of a security's credit worthiness.

Real market: The bid and offer prices at which a dealer could do size. Quotes in the brokers market may reflect not the real market, but pictures painted by dealers playing trading games.

"Red" futures contract month: A futures contract in a month more than 12 months away; e.g., in November, the Dec (pronounced Dees) bond contract would mature one month later, the red Dec contract 13 months later.

Red herring: A preliminary prospectus containing all the information required by the Securities and Exchange Commission except the offering price and coupon of a new issue.

Refunding: Redemption of securities by funds raised through the sale of a new issue.

Registered bond: A bond whose owner is registered with the issuer.

Regular way settlement: In the money and bond markets, the regular basis on which some security trades are settled is that delivery of the securities purchased is made against payment in Fed funds on the day following the transaction.

Regulation D: Fed regulation that required member banks to hold reserves against their net borrowings from foreign offices of other banks over a 7-day averaging period. Reg D has been merged with Reg M. Reg D has also required member banks to hold reserves against Eurodollars lent by their foreign branches to domestic corporations for domestic purposes.

Regulation Q: Fed regulation imposing lids on the rates that banks may pay on savings and time deposits. Currently, time deposits with a denomination of $100,000 or more are exempt from Reg Q.

Reinvestment rate: (1) The rate at which an investor assumes interest payments made on a debt security can be reinvested over the life of that security. (2) Also, the rate at which funds from a maturity or sale of a security can be reinvested. Often used in comparison to *give up* yield.

Relative value: The attractiveness—measured in terms of risk, liquidity, and return—of one instrument relative to another, or for a given instrument, of one maturity relative to another.

Reopen an issue: The Treasury, when it wants to sell additional securities, will occasionally sell more of an existing issue (reopen it) rather than offer a new issue.

Repo: See **Repurchase agreement.**

Repurchase agreement (RP or repo):   A holder of securities sells these securities to an investor with an agreement to repurchase them at a fixed price on a fixed date. The security "buyer" in effect lends the "seller" money for the period of the agreement, and the terms of the agreement are structured to compensate him for this. Dealers use RP extensively to finance their positions. Exception: When the Fed is said to be doing RP, it is lending money, that is, increasing bank reserves.

Reserve requirements: The percentages of different types of deposits that member banks are required to hold on deposit at the Fed.

Retail: Individual and institutional customers as opposed to dealers and brokers.

Revenue bond: A municipal bond secured by revenue from tolls, user charges, or rents derived from the facility financed.

Reverse: See **Reverse repurchase agreement.**

Reverse repurchase agreement: Most typically, a repurchase agreement initiated by the lender of funds. Reverses are used by dealers to borrow securities they have shorted. Exception: When the Fed is said to be doing reverses, it is borrowing money, that is; absorbing reserves.

Revolver: See **Revolving line of credit.**

Revolving line of credit: A bank line of credit on which the customer pays a commitment fee and can take down and repay funds according to his needs. Normally the line involves a firm commitment from the bank for a period of several years.

Risk: Degree of uncertainty of return on an asset.

Roll over: Reinvest funds received from a maturing security in a new issue of the same or a similar security.

Rollover: Most term loans in the Euromarket are made on a rollover basis, which means that the loan is periodically repriced at an agreed spread over the appropriate, currently prevailing LIBOR rate.

Round lot: In the money market, round lot refers to the minimum amount for which dealers' quotes are good. This may range from $100,000 to $5 million, depending on the size and liquidity of the issue traded.

RP: See **Repurchase agreement.**

Run: A run consists of a series of bid and asked quotes for different securities or maturities. Dealers give to and ask for runs from each other.

S&L: See **Savings and loan association.**

Safekeep: For a fee, banks will safekeep (i.e., hold in their vault, clip coupons on, and present for payment at maturity) bonds and money market instruments.

Sale repurchase agreement: See **Repurchase agreement.**

Savings and loan association: Federal- or state-chartered institution that accepts savings deposits and invests the bulk of the funds thus received in mortgages.

Savings deposit: Interest-bearing deposit at a savings institution that has no specific maturity.

Scale: A bank that offers to pay different rates of interest on CDs of varying maturities is said to "post a scale." Commercial paper issuers also post scales.

Scalper: A speculator who actively trades a futures contract in the hope of making small profits off transitory upticks and downticks in price.

Seasoned issue: An issue that has been well distributed and trades well in the secondary market.

Secondary market: The market in which previously issued securities are traded.

Sector: Refers to a group of securities that are similar with respect to maturity, type, rating, and/or coupon.

Securities and Exchange Commission (SEC): Agency created by Congress to protect investors in securities transactions by administering securities legislation.

Sell a spread: Sell a nearby futures contract and buy a far one.

Serial bonds: A bond issue in which maturities are staggered over a number of years.

Settle: See **Clear.**

Settlement date: The date on which trade is cleared by delivery of securities against funds. The settlement data may be the trade date or a later date.

Shell branch: A foreign branch—usually in a tax haven—which engages in Eurocurrency business but is run out of a head office.

Shop: In street jargon, a money market or bond dealership.

Shopping: Seeking to obtain the best bid or offer available by calling a number of dealers and/or brokers.

Sort: A market participant assumes a short position by selling as security he does not own. The seller makes delivery by borrowing the security sold or reversing it in.

Short bonds: Bonds with a short current maturity.

Short book: See **Unmatched book.**

Short coupons: Bonds or notes with a short current maturity.

Short the Board: Sell GNMA or T bond futures on the CBT.

Short hedge: *Sale* of a *futures* contract to hedge, for example, a position in cash securities or an anticipated borrowing need.

Short sale: The sale of securities not owned by the seller in the expectation that the price of these securities will fall or as part of an arbitrage. A short sale must eventually be covered by a purchase of the securities sold.

Sinking fund: Indentures on corporate issues often require that the issuer make annual payments to a sinking fund, the proceeds of which are used to retire randomly selected bonds in the issue.

Size: Large in size, as in "size offering" or "in there for size." What constitutes size varies with the sector of the market.

Skip-day settlement: The trade is settled one business day beyond what is normal.

Sovereign risk: The special risks, if any, that attach to a security (or deposit or loan) because the borrower's country of residence differs from that of the investor's. Also referred to as **Country risk.**

Specific issues market: The market in which dealers reverse in securities they want to short.

Spectail: A dealer that does business with retail but concentrates more on acquiring and financing its own speculative position.

Spot market: Market for immediate as opposed to future delivery. In the spot market for foreign exchange, settlement is two business days ahead.

Spot rate: The price prevailing in the spot market.

Spread: (1) Difference between bid and asked prices on a security. (2) Difference between yields on or prices of two securities of differing sorts or differing maturities. (3) In underwriting, difference between price realized by the issuer and price paid by the investor. (4) Difference between two prices or two rates. What a commodities trader would refer to as the *basis*.

Spreading: In the futures market, buying one futures contract and selling a nearby one to profit from an anticipated narrowing or widening of the spread over time.

Stop-out price: The lowest price (highest yield) accepted by the Treasury in an auction of a new issue.

Striking price: See **Exercise price.**

Subject: Refers to a bid or offer that cannot be executed without confirmation from the customer.

Subordinated debenture: The claims of holders of this issue rank after those of holders of various other unsecured debts incurred by the issuer.

Sub right: Right of substitution—to change collateral—on a repo.

Swap: (1) In securities, selling one issue and buying another. (2) In foreign exchange, buying a currency spot and simultaneously selling it forward.

Swap rate: In the foreign exchange market, the difference between the spot and forward rates at which a currency is traded.

Swing line: See **Demand line of credit.**

Swissy: Market jargon for Swiss francs.

Switch: British English for a swap; that is, buying a currency spot and selling it forward.

TABs (tax anticipation bills): Special bills that the Treasury occasionally issues. They mature on corporate quarterly income tax dates and can be used at face value by corporations to pay their tax liabilities.

Tail: (1) The difference between the average price in Treasury auctions and the stop-out price. (2) A *future* money market instrument (one available some period hence) created by buying an existing instrument and financing the initial portion of its life with term RP.

Take: (1) A dealer or customer who agrees to buy at another dealer's offered price is said to take that offer. (2) Eurobankers speak of taking deposits rather than buying money.

Take-out: (1) A cash surplus generated by the sale of one block of securities and the purchase of another, e.g., selling a block of bonds at 99 and buying another block at 95. (2) A bid made to a seller of a security that is designed (and generally agreed) to take him out of the market.

Taking a view: A London expression for forming an opinion as to where interest rates are going and acting on it.

TANs: Tax anticipation notes issued by states or municipalities to finance current operations in anticipation of future tax receipts.

Technical condition of a market: Demand and supply factors affecting price, in particular the net position—long or short—of dealers.

Technicals: (1) Supply and demand factors influencing the cash market. (2) Value or shape of technical indicators.

TED: A spread trade: T bill futures to CD futures.

Tenor: Maturity.

Term bonds: A bond issue in which all bonds mature at the same time

Term Fed funds: Fed funds sold for a period of time longer than overnight.

Term loan: Loan extended by a bank for more than the normal 90-day period. A term loan might run five years or more.

Term RP (repo): Rp borrowings for a period longer than overnight, may be 30, 60, or even 90 days.

Thin market: A market in which trading volume is low and in which consequently bid and asked quotes are wide and the liquidity of the instrument traded is low.

Tick: Minimum price movement on a futures contract.

Tight market: A tight market, as opposed to a thin market, is one in which volume is large, trading is active and highly competitive, and spreads between bid and ask prices are narrow.

Time deposit: Interest-bearing deposit at a savings institution that has a specific maturity.

Tom next: In the interbank market in Eurodollar deposits and the foreign exchange market, the value (delivery) date on a Tom next transaction is the next business day. (Refers to "tomorrow next.")

Trade date: The date on which a transaction is initiated. The settlement date may be the trade date or a later date.

Trade on top of: Trade at a narrow or no spread in basis points to some other instrument.

Trading paper: CDs purchased by accounts that are likely to resell them. The term is commonly used in the Euromarket.

Treasurer's check: A check issued by a bank to make a payment. Treasurer's checks outstanding are counted as part of a bank's reservable deposits and as part of the money supply.

Treasury bill: A non-interest-bearing discount security issued by the U.S. Treasury to finance the national debt. Most bills are issued to mature in 3 months, 6 months, or 1 year.

TT&L account: Treasury tax and loan account at a bank.

Turnaround: Securities bought and sold for settlement on the same day.

Turnaround time: The time available or needed to effect a turnaround.

Two-sided market: A market in which both bid and asked prices, good for the standard unit of trading, are quoted.

Two-way market: Market in which both a bid and an asked price are quoted.

Underwriter: A dealer who purchases new issues from the issuer and distributes them to investors. Underwriting is one function of an investment banker.

Unmatched book: If the average maturity of a bank's liabilities is less than that of its assets, it is said to be running an unmatched book. The term is commonly used in the Euromarket. Equivalent expressions are **open book** and **short book.**

Value date: In the market for Eurodollar deposits and foreign exchange, value date refers to the delivery date of funds traded. Normally it is on spot transactions two days after a transaction is agreed upon and the future date in the case of a forward foreign exchange trade.

Variable-price security: A security, such as stocks or bonds, that sells at a fluctuating, market-determined price.

Variable-rate CDs: Short-term CDs that pay interest periodically on *roll* dates; on each roll date the coupon on the CD is adjusted to reflect current market rates.

Variable-rate loan: Loan made at an interest rate that fluctuates with the prime.

Visible supply: New muni bond issues scheduled to come to market within the next 30 days.

When-issued trades: Typically there is a lag between the time a new bond is announced and sold and the time it is actually issued. During this interval, the security trades, **wi,** "when, as, and if issued."

Wi: When, as, and if issued. See **When-issued trades.**

Wi wi: T bills trade on a wi basis between the day they are announced and the day they are settled. Late Tuesday and on Wednesday, two bills will trade wi, the bill just auctioned and the bill just announced. The latter used to be called the wi wi bill. However, now it is common for dealers to speak of the just auctioned bill as the 3-month bill and of the newly announced bill as the wi bill. This change in jargon resulted from a change in the way interdealer brokers of bills list bills on their screens. Cantor Fitz still lists a new bill as the wi bill until it is settled.

Without: If 70 were bid in the market and there was no offer, the quote would be "70 bid without." The expression *without* indicates a one-way market.

Write: To sell an option.

Yankee bond: A foreign bond issued in the U.S. market, payable in dollars, and registered with the SEC.

Yankee CD: A CD issued in the domestic market (typically in New York) by a branch of a foreign bank.

Yield curve: A graph showing, for securities that all expose the investor to the same credit risk, the relationship at a given point in time between yield and current maturity. Yield curves are typically drawn using yields on governments of various maturities.

Yield to maturity: The rate of return yielded by a debt security held to maturity when both interest payments and the investor's capital gain or loss on the security are taken into account.

Index

Conversion Table
Discount Rate to Equivalent Money Market Yield (Interest on a 360-Day Basis)

Discount rate	Equivalent money market yield					
	1 mo.	2 mo.	3 mo.	6 mo.	9 mo.	1 yr.
5%	5.02	5.04	5.06	5.13	5.20	5.26
5 1/8	5.15	5.17	5.19	5.26	5.33	5.40
5 1/4	5.27	5.30	5.32	5.39	5.47	5.54
5 3/8	5.40	5.42	5.45	5.52	5.60	5.68
5 1/2	5.53	5.55	5.58	5.66	5.74	5.82
5 5/8	5.65	5.68	5.71	5.79	5.87	5.96
5 3/4	5.78	5.81	5.83	5.92	6.01	6.10
5 7/8	5.90	5.93	5.96	6.05	6.15	6.24
6	6.03	6.06	6.09	6.19	6.28	6.38
6 1/8	6.16	6.19	6.22	6.32	6.42	6.52
6 1/4	6.28	6.32	6.35	6.45	6.56	6.67
6 3/8	6.41	6.44	6.48	6.58	6.70	6.81
6 1/2	6.54	6.57	6.61	6.72	6.83	6.95
6 5/8	6.66	6.70	6.74	6.85	6.97	7.10
6 3/4	6.79	6.83	6.87	6.99	7.11	7.24
6 7/8	6.91	6.95	7.00	7.12	7.25	7.38
7	7.04	7.08	7.12	7.25	7.39	7.53
7 1/8	7.17	7.21	7.25	7.39	7.53	7.67
7 1/4	7.29	7.34	7.38	7.52	7.67	7.70
7 3/8	7.42	7.47	7.51	7.66	7.81	7.96
7 1/2	7.55	7.59	7.64	7.79	7.95	8.11
7 5/8	7.67	7.72	7.77	7.93	8.09	8.25
7 3/4	7.80	7.85	7.90	8.06	8.23	8.40
7 7/8	7.93	7.98	8.03	8.20	8.37	8.55
8	8.05	8.11	8.16	8.33	8.51	8.70
8 1/8	8.18	8.24	8.29	8.47	8.65	8.84
8 1/4	8.31	8.37	8.42	8.60	8.79	8.99
8 3/8	8.43	8.49	8.55	8.74	8.94	9.14
8 1/2	8.56	8.62	8.68	8.88	9.08	9.29
8 5/8	8.69	8.75	8.82	9.01	9.22	9.44
8 3/4	8.81	8.88	8.95	9.15	9.36	9.59
8 7/8	8.94	9.01	9.08	9.29	9.51	9.74
9	9.07	9.14	9.21	9.42	9.65	9.89
9 1/8	9.19	9.27	9.34	9.56	9.80	10.04
9 1/4	9.32	9.39	9.47	9.70	9.94	10.19
9 3/8	9.45	9.52	9.60	9.84	10.08	10.34
9 1/2	9.58	9.65	9.73	9.97	10.23	10.50
9 5/8	9.70	9.78	9.86	10.11	10.37	10.65
9 3/4	9.83	9.91	9.99	10.25	10.52	10.80
9 7/8	9.96	10.04	10.12	10.39	10.66	10.96
10	10.08	10.17	10.26	10.53	10.81	11.11
10 1/8	10.21	10.30	10.39	10.66	10.96	11.27
10 1/4	10.34	10.43	10.52	10.80	11.10	11.42
10 3/8	10.46	10.56	10.65	10.94	11.25	11.58
10 1/2	10.59	10.69	10.78	11.08	11.40	11.73
10 5/8	10.72	10.82	10.91	11.19	11.54	11.89
10 3/4	10.85	10.95	11.05	11.36	11.69	12.04
10 7/8	10.97	11.08	11.18	11.50	11.84	12.20
11	11.10	11.21	11.31	11.64	11.99	12.36
11 1/8	11.23	11.34	11.44	11.78	12.14	12.52
11 1/4	11.36	11.46	11.58	11.92	12.29	12.68
11 3/8	11.48	11.59	11.71	12.06	12.44	12.83
11 1/2	11.61	11.72	11.84	12.20	12.59	12.99
11 5/8	11.74	11.88	11.97	12.34	12.74	13.15
11 3/4	11.87	11.98	12.11	12.48	12.89	13.31
11 7/8	11.99	12.11	12.24	12.62	13.04	13.48